Multistate Bar Exam
Outlines

Civil Procedure
Constitutional Law
Contracts & Sales
Criminal Law
Criminal Procedure
Evidence
Real Property
Torts

Final Review Outlines

ISBN 978-1-949634-56-3

Civil Procedure

CIVIL PROCEDURE

Table of Contents

CIVIL PROCEDURE

Statutory citations within this outline are to Chapter 28 of the U.S. Code (e.g., "§ 1332") and the Federal Rules of Civil Procedure ("Rule" or "Rules"), unless otherwise noted.

I.   SUBJECT MATTER JURISDICTION

A.   IN GENERAL

1.   Overview

The term "subject matter jurisdiction" refers to a court's competence to hear and determine cases of the general class and subject to which the proceedings in question belong. The five most common congressional grants of subject matter jurisdiction are (i) federal question jurisdiction, (ii) diversity jurisdiction, (iii) supplemental jurisdiction, (iv) removal jurisdiction, and (v) legislative jurisdiction.

2.   Presumption

A federal court must presume an absence of jurisdiction until it determines that the matter falls within its rightful jurisdiction. The burden is on the party seeking to invoke the court's jurisdiction.

3.   Waiver

Subject matter jurisdiction cannot be waived or agreed to by the parties, unlike personal jurisdiction (discussed in § II. Personal Jurisdiction, *infra*).

4.   Objection to Jurisdiction

An objection to subject matter jurisdiction can be presented by any party at any stage of a proceeding, including on appeal, or may be raised by the court. If, however, the issue of subject matter jurisdiction was not contested, then a judgment ordinarily may not be challenged collaterally on that basis.

5.   Abstention

In general, a federal court with subject matter jurisdiction is required to adjudicate the controversy despite the pendency of a similar action in a state court. A federal court may abstain from hearing a case or stay the matter pending the outcome of the state court action under the following limited circumstances:

i)   Resolution of a state law issue by the state court would eliminate the need for the federal court to decide a federal constitutional issue, *R.R. Comm'n of Texas v. Pullman Co.*, 312 U.S. 496 (1941);

ii)   Avoidance of federal involvement with a complex state regulatory scheme or matter of great importance to the state, *Burford v. Sun Oil Co.*, 319 U.S. 315 (1943); *Louisiana Power & Light Co. v. City of Thibodaux*, 360 U.S. 25 (1959);

iii)   The state action involves punishment of an individual for criminal activity or for contempt of court, or the imposition of a civil fine, and the federal court is asked to enjoin such activity, *Younger v. Harris*, 401 U.S. 37 (1971); and

iv)   Parallel proceedings that go beyond mere waste of judicial resources, such as when there is a federal policy of unitary adjudication of the issues, *Colorado River Water Conservation Dist. v. United States*, 424 U.S. 800 (1976).

There are limited circumstances when federal intervention is appropriate. If a plaintiff can demonstrate unusual circumstances calling for federal equitable relief, significant and dire irreparable injury, or prosecutorial bad faith, then a federal court may intercede.

6. Transfer to Another Federal Court

A federal court that lacks jurisdiction must, if in the interest of justice, transfer the action to another federal court in which the action could have been brought at the time it was filed. The action is treated as if it was filed in the transferee court on the date upon which it was actually filed in the transferor court. 28 U.S.C. § 1631.

B. FEDERAL QUESTION JURISDICTION

1. Basis

Article III, Section 2 of the U.S. Constitution provides that federal judicial power shall extend to all cases "arising under this Constitution, the Laws of the United States, and Treaties made, or which shall be made, under their Authority." This constitutional provision authorizes Congress to give federal courts such jurisdiction. Today, the congressional grant of federal question jurisdiction is codified at 28 U.S.C. § 1331, which provides, "The district courts shall have original jurisdiction of all civil actions arising under the Constitution, laws, or treaties of the United States."

2. Concurrent Versus Exclusive Jurisdiction

State and federal courts have concurrent jurisdiction of federal question claims, except when Congress expressly provides that the jurisdiction of the federal courts is exclusive, as it has with cases under the Securities and Exchange Act of 1934, patent trademark, and copyright cases, and bankruptcy proceedings. *See Charles Dowd Box Co. v. Courtney*, 368 U.S. 502, 507 (1962) ("nothing in the concept of our federal system prevents state courts from enforcing rights created by federal law").

3. Scope

There is no uniform, bright-line standard for determining whether an action arises under the Constitution, laws, or treaties of the United States. In general, if the cause of action in question is expressly created by federal law, and federal law provides the underlying right, then federal question jurisdiction will exist. If a right is created by federal law, and a cause of action may fairly be implied and was intended by Congress, then federal jurisdiction is likely to be found. If the cause of action is neither expressly nor implicitly created by federal law, then federal jurisdiction over a state law claim will lie if a federal issue is: (1) necessarily raised, (2) actually disputed, (3) substantial, and (4) capable of resolution in federal court without disrupting the federal-state balance approved by Congress. *Gunn v. Minton*, 568 U.S. 251, 258 (2013).

Federal law includes the U.S. Constitution, federal statutes, federal administrative regulations, and U.S. treaties. State laws incorporating standards of federal law are not considered laws of the United States for the purposes of § 1331. *See Merrell Dow Pharmaceuticals, Inc. v. Thompson*, 478 U.S. 804 (1986). *Merrell Dow* held that when a substantive federal statute (e.g., the Federal Food, Drug, and Cosmetic Act) does not provide a federal remedy, then an alleged violation of that statute as an element of a state law complaint does not automatically establish § 1331 jurisdiction. Rather, federal courts have discretion to determine whether a federal issue or interest is important enough in a specific case to justify the exercise of jurisdiction.

4. Well-Pleaded Complaint

Generally, federal question jurisdiction exists only when the federal law issue is presented in the plaintiff's complaint. *E.g., Caterpillar, Inc. v. Williams*, 482 U.S. 386 (1987).

a. Consider only elements of the claim, not anticipated defenses

While the federal question must appear on the face of the complaint, the determination of jurisdiction must be made by considering only the necessary elements of the plaintiff's cause of action (i.e., a "well-pleaded" complaint). It is not sufficient to establish jurisdiction that the complaint alleges an anticipated federal law defense. *Louisville & Nashville R.R. v. Mottley*, 211 U.S. 149 (1908).

b. Do not consider answers and counterclaims

Answers and counterclaims are not considered in determining the existence of federal question jurisdiction. *In The Holmes Group, Inc. v. Vornado Air Circulation Systems, Inc.*, 535 U.S. 826 (2002).

c. Declaratory judgment action

Actions for declaratory relief anticipate some future action or infringement of rights and seek a declaratory judgment to resolve uncertainty and to avoid the possibility of a future lawsuit. Most states have enacted statutes permitting their courts to issue declaratory judgments. In an action for declaratory relief in which the complaint asserts a defense to an anticipated future action or infringement of rights, the character of the threatened action, and not of the defense, determines whether there is federal-question jurisdiction. *Pub. Serv. Com. v. Wycoff Co.*, 344 U.S. 237 (1952).

d. Original and removal jurisdiction

The well-pleaded complaint rule applies both to the original jurisdiction of the federal court and to removal jurisdiction (discussed in § I.E. Removal Jurisdiction, *infra*).

5. No Amount-in-Controversy or Diversity Requirements

Unlike federal diversity jurisdiction, federal question jurisdiction has no amount-in-controversy requirement and no diversity-between-parties requirement.

C. DIVERSITY JURISDICTION

1. Basis

Article III, Section 2 of the U.S. Constitution permits Congress to extend federal judicial power to controversies "between citizens of different states ... and between a state or the citizens thereof, and foreign states, citizens or subjects." Under § 1332, Congress gave the U.S. district courts jurisdiction over actions when:

i) The parties to an action are:

   a) Citizens of different states;

   b) Citizens of a state and citizens or subjects of a foreign state;

   c) Citizens of different states and citizens or subjects of a foreign state are additional parties; or

   d) A foreign state as plaintiff and citizens of a state or different states; and

ii) The amount in controversy in the action exceeds $75,000.

In general, when these requirements are met, a federal court may exercise jurisdiction over the action, regardless of the legal subject of the controversy. This is known as "diversity-of-citizenship jurisdiction" or, more commonly, "diversity jurisdiction."

a. State law exclusions

Two areas of state law are generally excluded from diversity jurisdiction: probate matters (probate of a will or administration of an estate) and domestic-relations actions (divorce, alimony, custody disputes). Note, though, that these exceptions apply only to cases that are primarily probate or marital disputes.

b. Suit against a foreign state

Under the Foreign Sovereign Immunities Act (FSIA), a suit may not be brought in federal or state court against a foreign state, including a political subdivision or agency or instrumentality of a foreign state, unless an exception applies. Among the exceptions are engaging in a commercial activity, committing a tort in the United States, or seizing property in violation of international law. § 1602–1611.

2. Complete Diversity

a. Rule of complete diversity

Diversity jurisdiction requires complete diversity between opposing parties in a case. There is no diversity of citizenship if any plaintiff in the case is a citizen of the same state as any defendant in the case or if any plaintiff and any defendant are aliens (i.e., citizens or subjects of a foreign country). *Strawbridge v. Curtiss*, 7 U.S. (3 Cranch) 267 (1806). Two plaintiffs in a case may be from the same state without destroying diversity, as long as no plaintiff is from the same state as any defendant in the case.

> Note that under § 1332(e), the term "state" includes the District of Columbia, Puerto Rico, and the U.S. territories.

b. Exceptions

1) Interpleader

Under 28 U.S.C. § 1335, the Federal Interpleader Act, the holder of property that is claimed by two or more persons may deposit the property with a court to determine ownership. Under the Act, there need be only two adverse claimants of diverse citizenship to establish federal jurisdiction. (*See* § VI.C.1. Federal Interpleader Rule, *infra*, for a discussion of federal rule interpleader, which requires complete diversity).

2) Class actions greater than $5,000,000

For certain class actions in which the amount at issue totals more than $5,000,000, diversity will be met if any member of the plaintiff class is diverse with any defendant. § 1332(d)(2)(A).

3) Multiparty, Multiforum Trial Jurisdiction Act of 2002

Under § 1369(a), for a civil action that "arises from a single accident, where at least 75 natural persons have died in the accident at a discrete location," only one plaintiff need be of diverse citizenship from one defendant for a federal court to have diversity jurisdiction, if:

i) A defendant resides in a state and a substantial part of the accident took place in another state or other location, regardless of whether that defendant is also a resident of the state where a substantial part of the accident took place;

ii) Any two defendants reside in different states, regardless of whether such defendants are also residents of the same state or states; or

iii) Substantial parts of the accident took place in different states.

Even if those requirements are met, however, under § 1369(b), the district court must abstain from hearing the case if:

i) The substantial majority of all plaintiffs are citizens of a single state of which the primary defendants are also citizens; and

ii) The claims asserted will be governed primarily by the laws of that state.

The Act also provides:

i) That anyone involved in the accident is permitted to intervene as a plaintiff; and

ii) Nationwide service of process.

c. **"Realignment"**

In evaluating whether true diversity exists, courts will look beyond the face of the pleadings to determine the "ultimate interests." If necessary, they will "arrange the parties according to their sides in the dispute." Thus, courts will not allow, for example, a party that is actually aligned with the plaintiff to be named as a defendant in order to present a false diversity. *City of Dawson v. Columbia Ave. Sav. Fund, Safe Deposit, Title, & Trust Co.*, 197 U.S. 178 (1905).

d. **Date of determination of diversity**

Diversity is determined at the time the case is filed. *Janzen v. Goos*, 302 F.2d 421 (8th Cir. 1962). There is no requirement that diversity exist at the time the cause of action arose. A change in citizenship after the filing of the case will not affect diversity jurisdiction that was in existence at the time of the filing. In addition, a change in the parties as a result of substitution or intervention will not affect diversity jurisdiction.

3. **Citizenship of Parties**

a. **Individuals**

To be a citizen of a state for the purposes of § 1332, an individual must be a citizen of the United States and a domiciliary of the state.

1) **Domicile**

In general, an individual is a domiciliary of the state in which she is present and intends to reside for an indefinite period. *Janzen v. Goos*, 302 F.2d 421 (8th Cir. 1962).

a) **Only one domicile**

An individual can have only one domicile at a time. The presumption is that a place of domicile continues until it is definitively changed, i.e., when a person:

i) Establishes presence in the new place; and

ii) Manifests intent to remain there for an indefinite period.

Consequently, a compulsory change of residence, such as for incarceration or military purposes, will not result in a change in domicile. Similarly, an intent to move without actual relocation to another state will not result in a change in domicile.

b) When determined

Domicile is determined at the time the action is commenced. Once subject matter jurisdiction has been established, it will not be affected by a party's change of domicile.

c) Factors considered

Some factors used in determining domicile include whether a party exercises civil and political rights (e.g., registration to vote), pays taxes, owns real and personal property, and is employed in the state.

2) Aliens

Diversity jurisdiction based on alienage exists when there are one or more citizens or subjects of a foreign country (i.e., aliens) on one side of the lawsuit and one or more citizens of a state on the other. There is no diversity jurisdiction in an action by one foreign citizen or subject against another, nor is there jurisdiction when an action is between a citizen of a state and an alien admitted into the United States for permanent residence who is domiciled in the same state as the citizen. § 1332(a)(2).

3) Stateless persons

Diversity jurisdiction does not exist if a party is an alien who is present in the United States and is not a citizen or subject of a foreign country, or if a party is a U.S. citizen whose domicile is a foreign country. Such persons are neither citizens of the United States nor citizens or subjects of a foreign country for the purposes of diversity jurisdiction.

4) Minors, incompetents, decedents, and trusts

The legal representative of a minor, an incompetent, or an estate of a decedent will be deemed a citizen of the same state as that minor, incompetent, or decedent. § 1332(c)(2). As to trusts, the old rule was that they were deemed to be a citizen of the same state as the trustee. *See Navarro Savings Ass'n v. Lee*, 446 U.S. 458 (1980). However, this rule has been placed in doubt by *Carden v. Arkoma Assocs.*, 494 U.S. 185 (1990), which held that the citizenship of unincorporated associations is determined by the citizenship of all of its members. At least one lower federal court has recently applied the *Carden* holding to trusts, holding that *Carden* requires that diversity be destroyed if, in a suit against a trust, any beneficiary of the trust is a citizen of the same state as a plaintiff. *See Bergeron ex rel. Ridgewood Elec. Power Trust V v. Ridgewood Elec. Power Trust V*, 2007 U.S. Dist. LEXIS 48555 (D. Mass., Jul. 5, 2007).

An unemancipated minor is generally deemed a citizen of the state in which his parents are domiciled. If a minor's parents are not citizens of the same state, then the child will generally be deemed a citizen of the state of the parent who has custody.

5) Class actions

Diversity in a class action brought pursuant to Rule 23 will generally be determined by the citizenship of the named members of the class bringing the lawsuit. (*See* § VI.E. Class Actions, *infra*, for a discussion of class actions under Rule 23.)

For certain class actions, however, when the amount at issue totals more than $5,000,000, diversity will be met if any member of the plaintiff class is diverse with any defendant. § 1332(d)(2)(A). (*See* § I.C.5.c. Aggregation of claims, *below*.)

b. Business entities

1) Corporations

A corporation may be a party to a diversity action. Under § 1332(c), for the purposes of diversity jurisdiction, "a corporation shall be deemed to be a citizen of every State and foreign state by which it has been incorporated and of the State or foreign state where it has its principal place of business." Thus, corporations, unlike individuals, may be citizens of more than one state for diversity purposes, and diversity jurisdiction will be destroyed if any opposing party is a citizen of any of the states in which the corporation has citizenship.

A pleader does not have the option of alleging that a corporation's citizenship is either its state of incorporation or the state where the principal place of business is located; both states must be listed in the pleading.

a) Incorporation

A corporation's state of incorporation is the state in which the corporate entity is legally established. Every corporation has at least one state of incorporation, and some have multiple states of incorporation. If a corporation is incorporated in more than one state or foreign country, then it is considered a citizen of each state and foreign country in which it is incorporated.

b) Principal place of business

Determining where a corporation maintains its principal place of business is a question of fact more complicated than determining where a corporation is incorporated. A recent Supreme Court decision did away with looking toward where the corporation's actual physical operations were located. Instead, the Court held that "principal place of business" refers to the "nerve center" of the corporation. *Hertz Corp. v. Friend*, 559 U.S. 77 (2010). The nerve center is generally the location from which the high-level officers direct, control, and coordinate the activities of the corporation. Typically, the nerve center is the corporate headquarters.

Unlike with incorporation, which may involve multiple states, a corporation's principal place of business is in only one state or foreign country.

c) Foreign corporations

A foreign corporation will be deemed a citizen of the country in which it is incorporated. In addition, if the foreign corporation also has its principal place of business in the United States, then it will have citizenship in the state where the principal place of business is located.

d) Date of determination

The corporation's citizenship at the time the action is commenced determines jurisdiction.

e) Liability insurers

Under § 1332(c), a special rule applies when a plaintiff allegedly injured by an insured party brings a direct action against the liability insurer. To avoid automatic federal subject matter jurisdiction in cases in which the liability insurer is incorporated or has its principal place of business in a different state from that where the plaintiff is a citizen, § 1332(c) makes the insurer a citizen of the state or foreign country in which its insured is a citizen, in addition to the other states or foreign countries where it has citizenship.

2) Partnerships and other unincorporated associations

a) Generally

An unincorporated association, such as a partnership, is considered a citizen of each state in which each of its members is domiciled. Thus, it is possible that a partnership could be a citizen of all 50 states, if it had partners domiciled in every state. This rule holds for both general and limited partnerships; a limited partnership will therefore be a citizen of every state in which its general and limited partners are domiciled. *Carden v. Arkoma Assocs.*, 494 U.S. 185 (1990).

b) Exception

An unincorporated association may be treated as a class when "it appears that the representative parties will fairly and adequately protect the interests of the association and its members." In that case, the citizenship of the representative parties controls for purposes of diversity jurisdiction. This exception may not be used merely to create diversity jurisdiction, nor may it be used if the association has the capacity under state law to sue or be sued as an entity. Rule 23.2.

4. Amount in Controversy

a. Rule

The amount in controversy must exceed the sum or value of $75,000, exclusive of interest, costs, and collateral effects of a judgment. Although interests and costs are excluded from the amount in controversy, attorney's fees may be made part of the amount in controversy if the fees are recoverable by contract or statute. Punitive damages, as well, may be permitted to be made part of the amount in controversy. The amount in controversy is determined at the time the action is commenced in federal court, or, if the action has been removed to federal court, at the time of the removal. The party seeking to invoke federal court jurisdiction must allege that the action satisfies the amount-in-controversy requirement.

In the case of injunctive relief, when it is difficult to assess a dollar amount, the court determines both the value of the plaintiff's harm if an injunction is not imposed and the defendant's cost of complying with an injunction. If the amount of either exceeds $75,000, then the amount-in-controversy requirement is satisfied. § 1332(a).

> **EXAM NOTE:** Remember that the amount in controversy must **exceed** $75,000; a claim for exactly $75,000 fails.

b. Standard of proof

1) Generally

In general, a plaintiff's good-faith assertion in the complaint that the action satisfies the amount-in-controversy requirement is sufficient, unless it appears to be a legal certainty that the plaintiff cannot recover the amount alleged. *St. Paul Mercury Indem. Co. v. Red Cab Co.*, 303 U.S. 283 (1938).

If an alleged amount in controversy is challenged, then the burden is on the party asserting jurisdiction merely to show that it is not a legal certainty that the claim involves less than the statutory amount.

2) Reduction of a claim after filing

If events after the action has been filed reduce the amount in controversy below the statutory minimum, then jurisdiction will not be lost, as long as the original claim was made in good faith. Additionally, if the plaintiff eventually recovers an amount that is less than the statutory jurisdictional amount, then that fact will not render the verdict subject to challenge on appeal for lack of jurisdiction.

c. Aggregation of claims

1) By a single plaintiff against a single defendant

If the action involves only one plaintiff and one defendant, then the total value of the plaintiff's diversity claims is calculated to determine the amount in controversy.

2) By multiple plaintiffs

If the action involves multiple plaintiffs, then the value of their claims may be aggregated only if the multiple plaintiffs are enforcing a single title or right in which they have a common or undivided interest.

If multiple plaintiffs, each having separate and distinct claims, unite for convenience or economy in a single suit, then each plaintiff's aggregate claims are judged separately in determining whether the amount-in-controversy requirement has been met. If the aggregate claims of at least one plaintiff separately meet the amount-in-controversy requirement, then the court has diversity jurisdiction over that plaintiff's claims, provided the diversity-of-citizenship requirement is met. The court may also have supplemental jurisdiction over the claims of any other plaintiff, even though that plaintiff's claims do not meet the amount-in-controversy requirement (*see* I.D.3. Diversity Jurisdiction Cases, *below*).

3) By a single plaintiff against multiple defendants

The value of a single plaintiff's claims against each defendant may not be aggregated if the claims are separate and distinct. If the defendants are jointly liable to the plaintiff, then aggregation to meet the amount-in-controversy requirement is permissible.

4) Class actions

In general, if any member of the putative class does not have a claim that meets the statutory jurisdictional amount, then the amount-in-controversy requirement will not be met. *Snyder v. Harris*, 394 U.S. 332 (1969); *Zahn v. International Paper*, 414 U.S. 291 (1973).

Note, though, that the Class Action Fairness Act of 2005 amended § 1332(d) to permit aggregation of claims in certain class actions. (See § VI.E.1.e., Class Actions under the Class Action Fairness Act of 2005, *infra.*)

Additionally, when at least one representative plaintiff in a putative class action has a claim that meets the statutory jurisdictional amount, other persons with claims that do not meet the jurisdictional amount can be made part of the class under the doctrine of supplemental jurisdiction. *Exxon Mobil Corp. v. Allapattah Servs., Inc.*, 545 U.S. 546 (2005). (*See* § I.D. Supplemental Jurisdiction, *infra.*)

d. Counterclaims

A counterclaim by a defendant against a plaintiff is not counted for the purposes of determining whether the plaintiff has met the statutory jurisdictional amount. Under some circumstances, though, the counterclaim itself will need to meet the statutory jurisdictional amount in order to be considered by the court.

1) Compulsory counterclaims

A compulsory counterclaim, which is generally a claim arising out of the same transaction or occurrence as the plaintiff's claim, does not have to meet the statutory jurisdictional amount requirement to be considered by the court. *See* Rule 13(a). The court will have supplemental jurisdiction over the compulsory counterclaim. (*See* § I.D. Supplemental Jurisdiction, *infra.*)

To determine whether counterclaims or cross-claims **arise out of the same "transaction or occurrence,"** courts consider whether (i) the issues of fact and law in the claims are essentially the same; (ii) the same evidence would support or refute the claims; (iii) there is a logical relationship between the claims; and (iv) res judicata would bar a subsequent suit on either claim. The most frequently considered factor is whether there is a logical relationship between the claims, but any one of them can support a conclusion that the claims arise from the same "transaction or occurrence."

2) Permissive counterclaims

A permissive counterclaim, which is a claim arising out of a transaction that is unrelated to the plaintiff's claim (*see* Rule 13(b)), has to meet the statutory jurisdictional amount requirement.

3) Removal based on counterclaim

a) Plaintiff

A plaintiff is not allowed to remove a case to federal court, even if the defendant is diverse and has counterclaimed for more than the federal statutory jurisdictional amount. Removal is allowed only by defendants. (*See* § I.E. Removal Jurisdiction, *infra.*)

b) Defendant—permissive counterclaim

When a diverse defendant makes a permissive counterclaim under state law for more than the federal statutory jurisdictional amount, and the plaintiff's claim is for less than the federal statutory jurisdictional amount, the defendant is not permitted to remove the case to federal court.

c) Defendant—compulsory counterclaim

When a diverse defendant makes a compulsory counterclaim under state law for more than the federal statutory jurisdictional amount, and the plaintiff's claim is for less than the federal statutory jurisdictional amount, courts are split on allowing removal by the defendant. Most courts, though, do not allow the defendant to remove the case to federal court.

4. Devices to Create or Destroy Diversity

Federal jurisdiction is prohibited if a party uses improper or collusive devices to invoke such jurisdiction. § 1359.

a. Assignment of claims

When there is a legitimate assignment of a claim, the assignee becomes the real party in interest, and its citizenship, as opposed to the assignor's citizenship, will be determinative. For example, when an insurance company pays an insured party for damages caused by a third party and sues the third party in a subrogation action, the company's citizenship, and not the insured party's citizenship, controls for diversity purposes.

If the assignment is being effected to manufacture or create diversity jurisdiction collusively, however, under § 1359, diversity jurisdiction will not exist. *See, e.g., Kramer v. Caribbean Mills, Inc.*, 394 U.S. 823 (1969) (assignment to a nominal party having no real interest in the claim was collusive).

b. Failure to name indispensable parties

The parties may not manufacture diversity jurisdiction by failing to join a nondiverse indispensable party. (*See* § VI.A.2. Compulsory Joinder, *infra*, regarding the standards for compulsory joinder under Rule 19.)

c. Voluntary change of state citizenship

A party may voluntarily change state citizenship after the accrual of a cause of action, but before the commencement of a lawsuit, and therefore establish or defeat diversity jurisdiction.

A party's motive for changing citizenship is irrelevant, but the change of state citizenship must be genuine to be recognized. In determining whether a party's change of state citizenship is genuine, a court may consider whether the party changed her domicile specifically to create or destroy diversity, but as long as the party intends to stay in the new state indefinitely, this motive will not invalidate the change in domicile. *Compare Williamson v. Osenton*, 232 U.S. 619, 625 (1914) (finding that a wife separated from her husband could establish her own domicile in a new state and maintain an action based on diversity jurisdiction) *with Morris v. Gilmer*, 129 U.S. 315, 328–29 (1889) (finding that the plaintiff did not change his domicile, because he moved there only to create diversity and did not intend to remain in the new state indefinitely).

d. Substitution versus replacement of parties

Sometimes there is a need to exchange parties to a lawsuit. Two processes are in place to do so depending on the circumstances. Rule 25 allows for the **substitution** of a party due to death or incompetence. In this case, the substituted party does not have to satisfy the diversity requirement. The original party's citizenship remains intact and controlling.

A similar doctrine exists when a party must be replaced, such as when the wrong party is named in the complaint. **Replacement** in such instance is possible as long as the replaced party satisfies the diversity requirement.

Notice the subtle distinction between substitution and replacement. Substitution calls for the substituted party to step into the shoes of the original party, whereas replacement removes one party to the lawsuit for another party.

D. SUPPLEMENTAL JURISDICTION

1. In General

A district court with jurisdiction over a claim may exercise "supplemental jurisdiction" over additional claims over which the court would not independently have subject matter jurisdiction (usually state law claims against a nondiverse defendant) but that are so related to the original claim that the additional claims form part of the same case or controversy under Article III of the U.S. Constitution. § 1367(a). In judging whether the claims are related, the test is whether they arise out of a **"common nucleus of operative fact"** such that all claims should be tried together in a single judicial proceeding. *United Mine Workers v. Gibbs*, 383 U.S. 715 (1966).

2. Federal Question Jurisdiction Cases

When the district court's subject matter jurisdiction for a claim is based on the existence of a federal question, additional claims against the same party can be heard by the court through the exercise of supplemental jurisdiction if the common-nucleus-of-operative-fact test is met.

Example 1: Plaintiff sues Defendant, her corporate employer, in federal court under Title VII for sex discrimination and retaliation, matters over which the court has federal question jurisdiction. Plaintiff then seeks to sue Defendant for assault and battery under state law, a claim that arises under the same operative facts that applied to her Title VII claim. The federal court has discretion to exercise supplemental jurisdiction over the assault and battery claim.

Similarly, a district court may have supplemental jurisdiction over claims that involve the joinder or intervention of additional parties over which the court would not otherwise have jurisdiction if the claims involving the additional parties satisfy the common-nucleus-of-operative-fact test. Such jurisdiction is also referred to as "pendent-party jurisdiction."

Example 2: Plaintiff sues Defendant 1, her corporate employer, in federal court under Title VII for sex discrimination and retaliation, matters over which the court has federal question jurisdiction. Plaintiff then seeks to sue Defendant 2, her direct supervisor, for assault and battery, a claim that arises under the same operative facts that applied to her Title VII claim against the corporate employer. The federal court could exercise supplemental jurisdiction over the assault and battery claim against the supervisor.

Dismissal of a federal claim on the merits does not preclude a federal court from exercising pendent-party jurisdiction over the state claim.

3. Diversity Jurisdiction Cases

When a district court has diversity jurisdiction over a claim, the common-nucleus-of-operative-facts rule also applies to determine whether the court can exercise supplemental jurisdiction over an additional claim.

a. Permissive joinder

Although the additional claim is not required to satisfy the amount-in-controversy requirement for purposes of supplemental jurisdiction, when the additional claim is asserted by a **plaintiff** seeking to join the action under Rule 20 (permissive joinder), the addition of that party cannot result in a violation of the requirement for complete diversity of citizenship.

Example 1: Plaintiff 1, a citizen of Pennsylvania, brings a negligence action in federal court for $500,000 against Defendant, a citizen of New York, based on an automobile accident. Plaintiff 2, also a citizen of Pennsylvania and a passenger in Plaintiff 1's car at the time of the accident, seeks to join Plaintiff 1's action by filing a negligence claim against Defendant for $30,000. While diversity jurisdiction does not exist for Plaintiff 2's claim because it does not satisfy the $75,000 amount-in-controversy requirement, the court can exercise supplemental jurisdiction over that claim because it meets the common-nucleus-of-operative-facts test.

Example 2: Assume for this example the same facts as those in Example 1 except that Plaintiff 2 is a citizen of New York. The federal court cannot exercise supplemental jurisdiction over Plaintiff 2's claim because the presence of Plaintiff 2 would defeat the requirement for complete diversity.

EXAM NOTE: Remember that supplemental jurisdiction does not apply to **defendants** sought to be joined under the permissive joinder rule in a case based exclusively on diversity jurisdiction in which exercising jurisdiction would destroy diversity. Thus, if the claims are made solely on the basis of diversity jurisdiction, then there must be complete diversity between the plaintiffs and the joined defendants, and the claims against each defendant must satisfy the amount-in-controversy requirement.

b. **Counterclaims**

A counterclaim may be asserted by a defendant against a plaintiff without satisfying the jurisdictional amount when the counterclaim is compulsory. A permissive counterclaim does not qualify for supplementary jurisdiction and therefore must satisfy the jurisdictional amount and the rule of complete diversity.

c. **Cross-claims**

A cross-claim may be asserted by a defendant against another defendant or by a plaintiff against another plaintiff if the cross-claim arises out of the same transaction or occurrence as the initial claim, without regard to the amount in controversy or the citizenship of the parties to the cross-claim as long as the court has subject matter jurisdiction.

d. **Precluded claims in diversity cases**

Under § 1367(b), in actions in which the original jurisdiction of the federal court is based solely on diversity jurisdiction, supplemental jurisdiction is precluded for:

i) Claims by existing plaintiffs (but not defendants) against persons made parties under one of the following Federal Rules of Civil Procedure: Rule 14 (impleader), Rule 19 (compulsory joinder), Rule 20 (permissive joinder), or Rule 24 (intervention);

ii) Claims by persons to be joined as plaintiffs pursuant to Rule 19; and

iii) Claims by persons seeking to intervene as plaintiffs pursuant to Rule 24, when the exercise of supplemental jurisdiction over such claims would be inconsistent with the requirements for diversity jurisdiction under 28 U.S.C. § 1332.

Example 1: Plaintiff, a citizen of Iowa, sues Defendant, a Nebraska corporation, in federal court under diversity jurisdiction for the wrongful death of Plaintiff's husband. Defendant then impleads Contractor, a citizen of Iowa, under Rule 14, alleging that if Defendant is liable to Plaintiff, then Contractor must indemnify Defendant for any liability to Plaintiff. If Plaintiff then asserts a claim directly against Contractor, because they are both citizens of the same state (Iowa), supplemental jurisdiction in federal court will not apply to the claim, as it would be inconsistent with the requirements for diversity jurisdiction pursuant to § 1367(b). Note that Defendant's claim against Contractor would fall within the federal court's supplemental jurisdiction, as it is derived from the same operative facts being considered by the court under the claim over which it has original jurisdiction and is not precluded by § 1367(b).

Example 2: Plaintiff, a citizen of Arkansas, sues Defendant 1 and Defendant 2, both citizens of Oklahoma, in federal court on the basis of diversity jurisdiction, alleging negligence. Defendant 1 seeks to assert a cross-claim for negligence, under the same operative facts, pursuant to Rule 13(g), against Defendant 2. Although there would be no original jurisdiction in federal court for the cross-claim, because Defendant 1 and Defendant 2 are citizens of the same state (Oklahoma) (*see* § I.C.2. Complete Diversity, *supra*), the federal court could exercise supplemental jurisdiction over the cross-claim, as it is derived from the same operative facts being considered by the court under the claim over which it has original jurisdiction, and it is not excluded under § 1367(b).

4. Discretionary Rejection of Supplemental Jurisdiction

Under § 1367(c), a district court has discretion to decline to exercise supplemental jurisdiction over a claim that would otherwise qualify for supplemental jurisdiction in each of the following circumstances:

i) The supplemental claim raises a novel or complex issue of state law;

ii) The supplemental claim substantially predominates over the claims within original federal jurisdiction;

iii) All of the claims within the court's original jurisdiction have been dismissed; or

iv) In exceptional circumstances, if there are other compelling reasons for declining jurisdiction.

E. REMOVAL JURISDICTION

1. Basis

Any civil action commenced in a state court that is within the original jurisdiction of a U.S. district court may generally be removed by the defendant to the district court for the district and division in which the state court action is pending. § 1441(a).

Generally, the right of removal is a right of the defendant only and is not available to a plaintiff defending a counterclaim that could have originally been brought in federal court. Note that removal jurisdiction is not a substitute for either federal question or diversity jurisdiction, but it is simply a mechanism by which defendants in a state action over which a federal court otherwise has subject matter jurisdiction can get the action into federal court.

a. Removal to another district or division within the same state

The removal statute specifically requires the case to be removed to the district court for the **district and division** in which the state court action is pending. Consequently, a case that is removed to a district court that is within the state but outside the district or division of the original state court is subject to a motion to remand. *Addison v. N.C. Dep't of Crime & Pub. Safety*, 851 F. Supp. 214 (M.D.N.C. 1994). However, since this requirement has been characterized as procedural rather than jurisdictional, some courts have transferred the case to the proper federal court instead of remanding it to the state court. *E.g., Butler v. N.C. DOT*, 154 F. Supp. 3d 252 (M.D.N.C. 2016).

2. Determination

In general, the right of removal is determined by the pleadings filed as of the time of the filing of the petition of removal. In diversity cases, however, diversity must exist at the time of filing the original action as well as at the time the notice of removal is filed, unless the plaintiff dismisses a party who would have destroyed diversity jurisdiction. In other words, removal is permitted when a party who prevents diversity jurisdiction is dismissed from an action. The federal court to which the action is removed is not precluded from hearing and determining any claim in the action because the state court from which the action was removed did not have jurisdiction over that claim. § 1441(f).

3. Other Removal Statutes

In addition to the general rule regarding removal, other statutes authorize removal in specific cases, including:

i) Suits against the United States, any federal agency, or federal officers for acts under color of office (§ 1442);

ii) Suits against federal employees for injuries caused from their operation of a motor vehicle within the scope of their employment (§ 2679(d));

iii) Actions in which any party asserts a claim for relief based on a federal statute relating to patents, plant variety protection, or copyrights (§ 1454); and

iii) Actions involving international banking (12 U.S.C. § 632).

In addition, certain statutes prohibit removal for otherwise removable actions, including:

i) Actions arising under the Federal Employers' Liability Act (FELA) and under the Jones Act against a railroad or its receivers or trustees (§ 1445(a));

ii) Actions against carriers for delay, loss, or damage in shipments, when the amount in controversy does not exceed $10,000 (§ 1445(b));

iii) Actions arising under the workers' compensation laws of the state in which the action is brought (§ 1445(c)); and

iv) Actions arising under § 40302 of the Violence Against Women Act of 1994.

4. Limitation on Removal in Diversity Cases

If removal is sought solely based on diversity jurisdiction, then the claim may be removed only if no defendant is a citizen of the state in which the action was filed. § 1441(b). There is no similar requirement for removal based on federal question jurisdiction.

Example: If a Texas corporation sues Illinois defendants in Illinois state court, then the Illinois defendants are not permitted to remove the action to federal court based on diversity jurisdiction.

5. Removal of Separate and Independent Claims in a Federal Question Jurisdiction Case

If removal is sought on the basis of federal question jurisdiction, and the federal question claims in the state action are joined with claims that are not independently removable, then the entire case may be removed. The district court must then sever and remand to the state court any claims in which state law predominates. § 1441(c).

6. **Procedure**

a. **Notice of removal**

1) **Generally**

Under 28 U.S.C. § 1446, a defendant who wants to remove a state court action to federal district court generally must file a notice of removal with the district court within 30 days after receipt by or service on that defendant of the initial pleading or summons. The notice must be:

i) Signed pursuant to Rule 11 (*see* § V.I. Rule 11, *infra*) and contain a short and plain statement of the grounds for removal;

ii) Filed in the district court for the district and division in which the state action is pending; and

iii) Accompanied by copies of all process, pleadings, and orders served on the defendants seeking removal.

If the case stated by the initial pleading is not removable, a notice of removal may be filed within 30 days after receipt by the defendant, through service or otherwise, of a copy of an amended pleading, motion, order or other paper from which it may first be ascertained that the case is one which is or has become removable. § 1446(b).

In general, all defendants who have been properly joined and served are required to join in or consent to the removal. If the defendants are served at different times and a later-served defendant files a notice of removal, then any earlier-served defendant may join in the removal even though that defendant did not previously initiate or consent to removal. § 1446(b). In cases of removal based on federal question jurisdiction, only those defendants against whom the federal claim is asserted must join in or consent to the removal. § 1441(c)(2). In addition, a class action based on the Class Action Fairness Act of 2005 (CAFA) may be removed by any defendant without the consent of all defendants. § 1453(b).

2) **Removal based on diversity**

A matter cannot be removed based on diversity of citizenship more than one year after the action is commenced. This one-year rule does not apply, however, if the district court finds that the plaintiff has acted in bad faith (such as by deliberately failing to disclose the actual amount in controversy) to prevent a defendant from removing the action. § 1446(c).

If removal is based on diversity and the plaintiff (i) seeks nonmonetary relief, (ii) is not required under state law to demand a specific sum, or (iii) is permitted by state law to recover more than the amount demanded, then the notice of removal may assert that the amount in controversy exceeds $75,000, and the district court will have jurisdiction if it finds, by a preponderance of the evidence, that the amount does exceed $75,000. A defendant's notice of removal need include only a plausible allegation that the amount in controversy exceeds $75,000; it does not need to contain evidentiary submissions. *Dart Cherokee Basin Operating Co. v. Owens*, 574 U.S. 81 (2014).

b. **Additional requirements**

Promptly after the notice of removal is filed with the district court, the defendants must give written notice of the filing to all adverse parties and file a copy of the notice of removal with the clerk of the state court from which the action is sought to be removed. § 1446(d).

Once a copy of the removal notice is filed with the state court, the removal acts as a stay of the state court proceedings. The state court is not allowed to take any further action with regard to the case and can be enjoined by the federal court if it does take any action.

c. Procedure in district court following removal

Once the action is removed, procedure follows the Federal Rules of Civil Procedure. New pleadings are not required unless the court orders otherwise. Rule 81(c)(2). Pleadings filed before removal can be amended pursuant to the federal rules.

The district court may issue all necessary orders and processes to bring before it all proper parties, regardless of whether those parties had been served by process issued by the state court. § 1447(a). If the action was removed before each defendant had been served with process, or if service of process was defective, then service of process can be completed or new process issued in the same manner as in cases originally filed in district court. § 1448.

State court orders issued before removal to district court remain in effect but are subject to district court modification when necessary. § 1450.

d. Procedure for a demand for a jury trial

Once the action is removed to federal court, the removing party, if seeking a jury trial, must file the demand within 14 days of filing for removal or risk losing the right. Similarly, the non-removing party also has 14 days to file, but the countdown begins after service of notice of removal. In both cases, if the demand is not filed in a timely fashion, then the right to a jury trial is waived.

There is an exception to this rule: when a party, prior to removal, exercised his right to a jury trial, no need exists to make the same demand after removal.

7. Remand

a. For lack of subject matter jurisdiction

If at any time before final judgment it appears that the district court lacks subject matter jurisdiction, then the case must be remanded to the state court from which it came. § 1447(c).

For the purposes of § 1447(c) and (d), however, when a case is remanded to a state court because the federal district court declines to exercise supplemental jurisdiction, the remand is not based on a lack of subject matter jurisdiction. *Carlsbad Tech., Inc. v. HIF Bio, Inc.*, 556 U.S. 635 (2009).

b. For other reasons

A party must make any motion to remand the case on the basis of any defect other than lack of subject matter jurisdiction within 30 days after the filing of the notice of removal. § 1447(c).

c. Burden of proof

If the propriety of the removal is challenged, then the burden of establishing proper removal is on the party who removed the case.

d. Costs and attorney's fees

The district court's order remanding the case may require payment of costs, including attorney's fees, incurred as a result of the removal. § 1447(c). The Supreme Court has held that, absent unusual circumstances, federal courts may award attorney's fees under § 1447(c) only when the removing party lacked an objectively reasonable basis for seeking removal. *Martin v. Franklin Capital Corp.*, 546 U.S. 132 (2005).

e. Procedure

A certified copy of the remand order must be mailed by the district court clerk to the clerk of the state court. The state court may thereafter proceed with the case. § 1447(c).

f. Not generally appealable

A remand order is generally not reviewable on appeal or otherwise, with the following exceptions:

i) There is statutory exception for an order remanding a civil rights case removed pursuant to § 1443; or

ii) A remand order is also appealable in a class action, if the application for review is made to the court of appeals not more than 10 days after the entry of the order.

§§ 1447(d), 1453(c)(1).

g. Discretion to remand when the proposed joinder would destroy diversity jurisdiction

Under § 1447(e), if, after removal, the plaintiff seeks to join a defendant who would destroy the federal court's diversity jurisdiction, then the court has discretion to deny the joinder and proceed with the action in federal court, or to permit the joinder and remand the action to state court.

F. LEGISLATIVE JURISDICTION

In addition to the types of jurisdiction listed previously, there are federal courts created by Congress with jurisdiction over specific types of cases. Briefly, these include:

i) **The United States Claims Court** (formerly "the Court of Claims"), with original jurisdiction over actions brought against the United States or its officers, or concerning federal property;

ii) **The United States Court of Appeals for the Federal Circuit**, with appellate jurisdiction over claims against the federal government or its officers, etc.;

iii) **The United States Court of International Trade**, with nationwide jurisdiction over civil actions arising out of United States customs and international trade laws;

iv) **The United States Tax Court**, with jurisdiction over taxpayer challenges to Internal Revenue Service (IRS) deficiency determinations; and

v) **The United States Bankruptcy Court**, with jurisdiction over bankruptcy matters.

There is no amount-in-controversy requirement in the previously listed cases, unless an action is brought against a party other than the United States under the Consumer Product Safety Act.

II. PERSONAL JURISDICTION

A. IN GENERAL

In addition to having subject matter jurisdiction, a court must be able to exercise judicial power over the persons or property involved in the cases or controversies before it. This authority is broadly referred to as "personal jurisdiction" and is governed by state statutes regarding jurisdiction and the due process requirements of the U.S. Constitution.

1. Types

There are three general types of personal jurisdiction: (i) in personam jurisdiction, (ii) in rem jurisdiction, and (iii) quasi-in-rem jurisdiction.

2. Effect of State Jurisdictional Statutes on Personal Jurisdiction in Federal Court

Under Rule 4(k)(1)(A), the service of a summons in a federal action establishes personal jurisdiction over a defendant "who is subject to the jurisdiction of a court of general jurisdiction in the state where the district court is located." A federal court must generally determine personal jurisdiction as if it were a court of the state in which it is situated. Thus, a federal court will look to state jurisdictional statutes (*see* § II.B.2.d. Long-arm statutes, *infra*) to determine if it has personal jurisdiction over the parties before it.

a. Alternative sources of personal jurisdiction

1) Nationwide personal jurisdiction

While a federal court generally is not vested with nationwide personal jurisdiction, *Omni Capital Int'l, Ltd. v. Rudolf Wolff & Co.*, 484 U.S. 97 (1987), a federal court does have national personal jurisdiction when authorized by federal statute, such as for federal statutory interpleader actions (*see* § VI.C.2.b. In personam jurisdiction, *infra*). Rule 4(k)(1)(C).

2) "Bulge provision"

Under Rule 4(k)(1)(B), the so-called "bulge provision," a federal court has personal jurisdiction over a party who is served within a U.S. judicial district and not more than 100 miles from where the summons is issued, even if state law would otherwise not permit such service. *See Mississippi Publ'g Corp. v. Murphree*, 326 U.S. 438 (1946); *Robertson v. R.R. Labor Bd.*, 268 U.S. 619 (1925). This special rule applies to only two types of parties: a third-party defendant who is joined under Rule 14 (*see* § VI.D.4.d. In personam jurisdiction, *infra*) and a required party who is joined under Rule 19 (*see* § VI.A.2.c. In personam jurisdiction, *infra*).

3) Rule 4(k)(2)

Three conditions must be present for a federal court to have personal jurisdiction over a defendant under Rule 4(k)(2):

   i)   The plaintiff's claims must be based on federal law;

   ii) No state court can exercise personal jurisdiction over the defendant;

   iii) The exercise of jurisdiction must be consistent with the U.S. Constitution and laws (i.e., the defendant must have "minimum contacts" with the United States).

This provision is generally used for non-U.S. residents who have contacts with the Unites States generally, but not with any one state in particular.

3. Due Process Requirements for Personal Jurisdiction

The Due Process Clause also limits a court's exercise of personal jurisdiction over a defendant. A court may not exercise personal jurisdiction over a defendant unless the defendant has "minimum contacts" with the state in which the court sits (the forum state), and the exercise of jurisdiction would be fair and reasonable. A court is also required to notify a party of the commencement of an action in which his interests are at stake and provide an opportunity for the party to be heard.

4. Consent or Waiver

Unlike with subject matter jurisdiction, a party may consent to personal jurisdiction. The consent may be express, implied, or made by a voluntary appearance.

An objection to a court's exercise of jurisdiction over persons and things may also be waived by a party. Under Rule 12(b), the defenses of lack of personal jurisdiction over the person, insufficiency of process, and insufficiency of service of process must be asserted in a responsive pleading or by motion before a responsive pleading is submitted. A failure to object in accordance with Rule 12 waives the objection. Rule 12(h).

B. IN PERSONAM JURISDICTION

1. In General

In personam jurisdiction is the power that a court has over an individual party. It is required whenever a judgment is sought that would impose an obligation on a defendant personally. When such personal jurisdiction exists, the court has the authority to issue a judgment against the party personally, which can be satisfied by seizure of all the party's assets. Such a judgment is entitled to full faith and credit in other states (*see* § IX.C. Full Faith and Credit, *infra*).

2. Bases for In Personam Jurisdiction

a. Voluntary presence

If a defendant is voluntarily present in the forum state and is served with process while there, then the court has personal jurisdiction over the defendant. *Burnham v. Superior Court of California*, 495 U.S. 604 (1990). However, most courts today have two exceptions to this rule. If a plaintiff fraudulently brings a defendant into the state for the purpose of serving process on him, then the service will most likely be invalid. A defendant is also immune if he is merely passing through the state to attend other judiciary proceedings.

b. Domicile

If authorized by statute, a court can have jurisdiction over a person who is domiciled in the state in which the court is located, even if the person is temporarily absent from that state. Domicile is established when a person with capacity resides in a state and intends to make that state his home. The same rules of domicile discussed in § I.C.3. Citizenship of Parties, *supra*, are applicable here. Statutory authorization can be enacted retroactively to apply to a cause of action arising before the enactment of the statute. *McGee v. Int'l Life Ins. Co.*, 355 U.S. 220 (1957). Note that the United States has authority to subpoena a citizen of the United States living abroad to appear in court to testify.

c. Consent

Personal jurisdiction can be established by a party's consent. Under Rule 12(b), the defense of lack of personal jurisdiction must be asserted in a responsive pleading or by motion before a responsive pleading is submitted. The failure to timely object to a court's assertion of personal jurisdiction waives the objection. Rule 12(h).

1) Plaintiffs

Plaintiffs consent to personal jurisdiction by filing the lawsuit.

2) Defendants

a) Express consent

A defendant may agree in advance by contract to submit to the jurisdiction of the court if a lawsuit is brought by the plaintiff. Such contractual consent is not effective if the court determines that the contract was a contract of adhesion. A defendant may also stipulate to personal jurisdiction once an action is brought. *Petrowski v. Hawkeye-Security Ins. Co.*, 350 U.S. 495 (1956). Consent is given when a person authorizes an agent to accept service of process. Usually, a state requires nonresidents doing business in a heavily regulated industry to appoint an agent.

b) Implied consent

A defendant may be deemed to have consented through conduct, such as filing a counterclaim or driving a vehicle within a state.

c) Voluntary appearance

Traditionally, voluntary appearance of the defendant in court automatically subjected the defendant to personal jurisdiction, unless he was present with the express purpose of objecting to personal jurisdiction. This was called a "special appearance" and was distinguished from a "general appearance" to litigate the merits of the case (which waives an objection to personal jurisdiction).

The federal courts and many state courts have abolished this distinction and no longer require a "special appearance" to allow a defendant to object to personal jurisdiction; it can be done by motion or in the answer. Under the federal rule, the objection is waived if the personal jurisdiction objection is not raised in the first of (i) a Rule 12 motion, if raised before the answer, or (ii) the answer itself. Fed. R. Civ. P. 12(h)(1).

d. Long-arm statutes

Most states have enacted statutes that authorize personal jurisdiction over nonresidents who engage in some activity in the state or cause some action to occur within the state. In many states, the long-arm statute either directly authorizes or has been interpreted as authorizing jurisdiction to the extent permissible under the Due Process Clause. Thus, a federal court in those states need only determine whether the exercise of personal jurisdiction comports with due process. In some states, the long-arm statute confers jurisdiction only over specific activities undertaken in the state (e.g., owning property, committing a tort, or entering into a contract to supply goods or services in the state). In these states, the federal court must first determine whether the statutory requirements have been met, before determining whether the exercise of personal jurisdiction comports with the Due Process Clause.

e. Attachment

Under "attachment" jurisdiction (a type of quasi-in-rem jurisdiction, *see* § II.C.2. Quasi-In-Rem Jurisdiction, *infra*), historically, a plaintiff asserting a personal claim against a defendant could use attachment of property owned by the defendant and located in the forum state as a device to obtain jurisdiction and, if successful, satisfaction of the claim, at least to the extent of the value of the property attached. However, since *Shaffer v. Heitner*, 433 U.S. 186 (1977), there must be minimum contacts between the defendant and the forum state in order to establish jurisdiction. If the claim is not related to the ownership of the attached property, mere ownership of the attached property is generally not sufficient to satisfy the minimum contacts test. If there are such contacts, then the court generally has in personam jurisdiction over the defendant, and attachment jurisdiction is unnecessary.

3. Due Process Requirements

In general, due process requirements are satisfied if the nonresident defendant has sufficient minimum contacts with the forum state such that the maintenance of the action does not offend traditional notions of fair play and substantial justice. *International Shoe Co. v. State of Washington*, 326 U.S. 310 (1945).

> **EXAM NOTE:** When analyzing a personal jurisdiction question, the focus is on (i) the contacts that the defendant has or had with the forum state and (ii) whether the assertion of jurisdiction by the court would comport with fair play and substantial justice. Personal jurisdiction will depend on the facts of each case.

a. Minimum contacts

1) Required by *Shaffer*

While before *Shaffer* it was possible to gain jurisdiction over a person merely based on the presence within the state of that person's property, since *Shaffer*, such an attempt to gain in personam jurisdiction has been subject to the *International Shoe* requirement of minimum contacts.

Note that *Shaffer* expressly excluded actions to enforce previous judgments by such remedies as attachment, garnishment, and sequestration from the requirement of minimum contacts with the defendant. *See Shaffer v. Heitner*, 433 U.S. at 210.

2) Purposeful availment

To warrant the assertion of in personam jurisdiction, a defendant's contacts with the forum state must be purposeful and substantial, such that the defendant should reasonably anticipate (foresee) being taken to court there. Foreseeability depends on whether a defendant recognizes or anticipates that by running his business, he risks being party to a suit in a particular state. *World-Wide Volkswagen Corp. v. Woodson*, 444 U.S. 286 (1980). This is the "purposeful availment" requirement.

There are situations, however, in which it is difficult to discern whether purposeful availment is present. Such is the case when a product is put into the stream of commerce, not by the manufacturer, but by a person who purchased the product from the manufacturer and incorporated it in the person's own product, which is then put into the stream of commerce. The question remains, did the manufacturer avail himself of the benefits and laws of the jurisdiction in which the product containing the manufacturer's product is used? The Court has not been able to reach a cohesive answer. In *Asahi*, while four justices found sufficiency with the mere knowledge that the product being sold would end up in the forum state, four other justices believed that the manufacturer needed to take an additional step to have availed itself of the forum. *Asahi Metal Industry Co. v. Superior Court of California*, 480 U.S. 102 (1987). (Note: In that case, a majority of the justices concluded that, even assuming the manufacturer's conduct constituted purposeful availment, it violated the notions of fair play and substantial justice for the manufacturer in question, a foreign corporation, to be subject to the jurisdiction of the forum court (*see* b. Fair play and substantial justice, *below*).)

3) Specific and general jurisdiction

The scope of the contacts necessary for the assertion of personal jurisdiction depends on the relationship that the cause of action has with the forum state.

When a cause of action arises out of or closely relates to a defendant's contact with the forum state, jurisdiction may be warranted over that action even if that contact is the defendant's only contact with the forum state. This type of jurisdiction is often referred to as "specific personal jurisdiction." For specific personal jurisdiction to exist, there must be "'an affiliation between the forum and the underlying controversy,' principally, activity or an occurrence that takes place in the forum State and is therefore subject to the State's regulation." *Goodyear Dunlop Tires Operations, S.A. v. Brown*, 564 U.S. 915, 919 (2011).

On the other hand, "general personal jurisdiction" requires that a defendant be domiciled in the state or have continuous and systematic contacts with the forum state. General jurisdiction confers personal jurisdiction even when the cause of action has no relationship with the defendant's contacts with the state. *Helicopteros Nacionales de Colombia, S.A. v. Hall*, 466 U.S. 408 (1984).

4) Imputed contacts

Under some circumstances, the contacts of one defendant with the forum state may be imputed to another defendant for the purposes of determining jurisdiction.

a) To employer

Contacts by a nonresident employer's agents or employees are generally imputed to the employer when the agent or employee is acting within the scope of the agency or employment. An out-of-state corporation, though, is generally not subject to personal jurisdiction solely because of contacts in the state by an independent contractor.

b) To partnership

Each partner is generally an agent of the partnership for the purpose of its business. Accordingly, a partner's activities on behalf of the partnership can confer personal jurisdiction over the partnership entity. Such contacts, though, may not necessarily establish personal jurisdiction over that partner or the other partners of the partnership in their individual capacities.

c) To parent corporation

An out-of-state corporation's contacts with the forum state will not automatically establish jurisdiction over a wholly owned subsidiary of the corporation, and contacts by a wholly owned subsidiary will not automatically confer jurisdiction over a corporate parent. *Cannon Mfg. Co. v. Cudahy Packing Co.*, 267 U.S. 333 (1925). If, however, the subsidiary is the corporate parent's alter ego or is specifically acting as the corporate parent's agent, then its contacts may be imputed to the corporate parent. *Id.*

b. Fair play and substantial justice

Once minimum contacts are established, a court must still examine the facts to determine if maintenance of the action would "offend traditional notions of fair play and substantial justice." *International Shoe, supra.*

Courts consider a variety of factors when making this determination, including:

i) The interest of the forum state in adjudicating the matter;

ii) The burden on the defendant of appearing in the case;

iii) The interest of the judicial system in the efficient resolution of controversies; and

iv) The shared interests of the states in promoting common social policies.

4. In Personam Jurisdiction Over Corporations

a. Resident corporations

For the purposes of in personam jurisdiction, a corporation is a resident corporation only if it is incorporated in the forum state. Any action may be brought against a corporation that is incorporated in the forum state. If the corporation is not incorporated in the state, then, for the purposes of in personam jurisdiction, it will constitute a foreign corporation.

b. Foreign corporations

The rules of minimum contacts and substantial fairness apply to a foreign corporation. To determine whether the corporation is subject to a state's general jurisdiction, the proper inquiry is whether a corporation's affiliations with the forum state are so "continuous and systematic" as to render the corporation essentially "at home" in the forum state. *Daimler AG v. Bauman*, 571 U.S. 117 (2014). A corporate defendant is always at home in the state of the corporation's place of incorporation and the state of its principal place of business. In exceptional cases, a corporate defendant's operations in another forum may be so substantial and of such a nature as to render the corporation at home in that state as well. *Compare BNSF Ry. v. Tyrrell*, 137 S. Ct. 1549 (2017) (foreign railroad company's ownership of over 2,000 miles of track and employment of over 2,000 persons in a state not sufficient to render corporation at home when about 94% of the track it owned and more than 95% of its workforce were out-of-state) *with Perkins v. Benguet Consol. Mining Co.*, 342 U.S. 437 (1952) (a foreign mining company that relocated its management activities (e.g., directors' meetings, business correspondence, banking, stock transfers, payment of salaries, purchasing of machinery) during World War II to a state was at home in that state).

5. Internet Websites

It is generally accepted that merely having a website does not subject a defendant to process everywhere that the site can be viewed. Most courts have followed the approach of *Zippo Mfg. Co. v. Zippo Dot Com, Inc.*, 952 F. Supp. 1119 (W.D. Pa. 1997), which bases jurisdiction over a nonresident's website on the degree of interactivity between the website and the forum. The court set forth a sliding scale approach with regard to the interactivity of websites, ranging from passive sites to those that are integral to the defendant's business.

Merely making a website accessible to the public and posting information is generally considered passive on the sliding scale and should not result in personal jurisdiction. Websites that are integral to a defendant's business, however, are on the other end of the sliding scale. When a website's purpose is to assist in conducting direct business transactions, courts are more likely to find minimum contacts with a state and assert personal jurisdiction.

Example: In the *Zippo* case, the defendant was a nonresident corporation that operated an integral website that had commercial contacts with more than 3,000 Pennsylvania residents and Internet service providers. The court found a high level of interactivity with Pennsylvania and determined that there was personal jurisdiction over the defendant in Pennsylvania.

Courts are struggling with how to draw the lines for sites that are interactive but that do not involve significant commercial activity. The law in this area continues to evolve.

6. **Suits Based on a Contract**

   a. **The contract can be relevant to establishing minimum contacts**

   Although the fact that one party to a contract is a resident of the forum state will not, by itself, confer personal jurisdiction over the nonresident party to the contract, the existence of the contract can be a significant factor in determining that minimum contacts exist, such that the exercise of personal jurisdiction over the nonresident is appropriate. *Burger King v. Rudzewicz*, 471 U.S. 462 (1985).

   b. **Choice-of-law provision**

   If the contract contains a choice-of-law provision indicating that the forum state's law is to be used in any action with regard to the contract, then this will be a significant factor in finding jurisdiction, as it establishes that the nonresident purposefully availed herself of the benefits of the forum's laws.

   c. **Contracts of adhesion or procured by fraud**

   If the contract is adhesive or was procured through fraud, then personal jurisdiction based on the contract is not appropriate.

C. **JURISDICTION OVER THINGS**

Historically, jurisdiction over property has been divided into in rem jurisdiction and quasi-in-rem jurisdiction.

1. **In Rem Jurisdiction**

   a. **Defined**

   In rem jurisdiction is the authority of a court to determine issues concerning rights in property, either real or personal. The court generally determines title to the property, and such determination is conclusive as against all potential claimants. Often, no parties are named, and the case is known by the name of the property at issue. Examples of in rem proceedings include forfeiture and eminent domain actions initiated by the government as well as quiet-title actions, usually initiated by a private party. In an in rem action, the court can extinguish interests in the property of persons who are outside of the forum or who are unknown.

b. Due process

While in rem proceedings are commenced against property, they must still satisfy due process requirements for personal jurisdiction because they affect the rights of individuals in the property. In general, for in rem jurisdiction to exist, the property at issue must be present within the forum state. *Shaffer v. Heitner*, 433 U.S. 186 (1977). In rem jurisdiction can be challenged if the property is fraudulently brought into the state.

Due process is met if the notice is "reasonably calculated, under all the circumstances, to apprise interested parties of the pendency of the action and afford them an opportunity to present their objections." *Mullane v. Central Hanover Bank & Trust Co.*, 339 U.S. 306 (1950). It is not sufficient to simply post the notice on the property or publish the notice in a newspaper as to persons who are known to have an interest in the property and whose whereabouts are reasonably ascertainable. *Walker v. City of Hutchison*, 352 U.S. 112 (1956). In addition, any absent defendant who does not personally receive notice may set aside the judgment at any time within one year of the final judgment. 28 U.S.C. § 1655.

2. Quasi-In-Rem Jurisdiction

a. Defined

While a judgment in rem determines the interests of all persons in particular property, a quasi-in-rem judgment determines only the interests of the parties to the action regarding property located in the forum state. Traditionally, the judgment was not personally binding on the defendant, could not be sued upon in any other court, and could not be enforced by seizing any of the defendant's property other than the property at issue in the quasi-in-rem action.

b. Due process

In a quasi-in-rem action, as with in rem and in personam actions, the defendant whose property is subject to the judgment generally must have sufficient minimum contacts with the forum state to justify the exercise of personal jurisdiction over the matter. *Shaffer v. Heitner*, 433 U.S. 186 (1977). As a consequence, a quasi-in-rem action either can be pursued as an in personam action due to satisfaction of the minimum contacts test or cannot be brought due to lack of personal jurisdiction over the defendant. When the action directly relates to property rights, such as the foreclosure of a mortgage or other lien, the minimum contacts requirement is satisfied because of the relationship between the claim and the property. Provided the owner of the property is given proper notice and an opportunity to be heard, the judgment is personally binding on the defendant. If the defendant chooses not to appear, the judgment of a federal district court is confined to the property that is the subject of the action. 28 U.S.C. § 1655.

When the underlying action does not relate to property rights, but the property instead serves only as the relief sought, such as in a breach of contract action in which the contract does not involve the in-state property, the minimum contacts requirement likely is not satisfied, and the court lacks personal jurisdiction to adjudicate the matter.

c. Federal court's jurisdiction

In an action to determine ownership of real or personal property (e.g., removal of a cloud on the title to the property) or to enforce a lien against real or personal property when the property is located within the district, the federal district court has personal jurisdiction over the claimants to the property. 28 U.S.C. § 1655; Rule 4(n)(1). In other in rem or quasi-in-rem actions, jurisdiction can be obtained by a federal district court under the circumstances and in the manner provided by the law of the state in which the federal district court is located, but only if the federal district court, despite the existence of sufficient minimum contacts, cannot acquire personal jurisdiction over the defendant by service of process under the federal rule (Rule 4). As a consequence, quasi-in-rem jurisdiction is generally limited to exigent circumstances, such as when the defendant is a fugitive or the property is in imminent danger of disappearing. Rule 4(n)(2).

D. NOTICE AND OPPORTUNITY TO BE HEARD

Due process requires that deprivation of property by adjudication be preceded by notice and an opportunity for a hearing appropriate to the nature of the case. *Mullane v. Central Hanover Bank & Trust Co.*, 339 U.S. 306 (1950).

1. Notice

a. Due process

Due process is met if the notice is "reasonably calculated, under all the circumstances, to apprise interested parties of the pendency of the action and afford them an opportunity to present their objections." *Mullane, supra.*

b. Form

If the identity and address of an interested party are known or obtainable through reasonable efforts, then notice through in-person delivery, registered mail, return receipt requested, or some other means likely to notify the particular individual is required. *Mennonite Bd. of Missions v. Adams*, 462 U.S. 791 (1983). If the plaintiff knows that the defendant did not receive notice, then the plaintiff cannot proceed unless there are no other reasonable methods to notify the defendant. *Jones v. Flowers*, 547 U.S. 220 (2006).

If the identity or address of an interested party is not obtainable through reasonable efforts, then other means, such as publication of notice in newspapers, may be satisfactory. The constitutional test is, generally, what is **reasonable under the circumstances**. The standards are less strict for in rem and quasi-in-rem cases than for in personam cases. When there are multiple defendants, each defendant must be served, but the manner of service will depend on whether their identities and addresses are known or unknown.

In situations in which an agent is appointed, either by contract or by statute, the defendant will not be subject to personal jurisdiction if the agent did not advise the defendant of service of process. This rule does not apply when the defendant selects his own agent.

c. Court rules

Satisfying due process is not the only standard for the sufficiency of notice. Both state and federal courts have procedural rules that dictate the form and service of process. While a particular form of notice may meet due process standards, it must also meet the specific procedural requirements that govern in the court where the action is to be heard. Certified mail, for example, meets due process standards, but not every court system permits it to be used.

2. Opportunity to Be Heard

In addition to requiring notice of the claim being made, due process requires that a defendant be given an opportunity to be heard whenever there is a state-sponsored interference with a defendant's property interest. The state must be an active participant in the interference for due process to apply.

E. DEFENSES TO JURISDICTIONAL CLAIMS

1. Special Appearance

A special appearance is a procedure by which a defendant appears before a court for the specific purpose of challenging personal jurisdiction. The defendant is generally not considered to have consented to jurisdiction by making the special appearance, as long as personal jurisdiction is contested in the defendant's initial pleading. If anything going to the merits of the case is raised in the pleadings, then the defendant will likely be found to have made a general appearance in the case and waived any objection with regard to personal jurisdiction.

Under the Federal Rules of Civil Procedure, special appearances have been abolished, but a party may make a motion to dismiss the claim for lack of personal jurisdiction under Rule 12(b)(2) without becoming subject to jurisdiction on that basis.

2. Effect of a Denial of Objection to Personal Jurisdiction

If the court overrules a defendant's objection to personal jurisdiction, most states permit the defendant to defend the case on the merits and still preserve the objection to personal jurisdiction as an issue for appeal.

3. Collateral Attack

Article IV, Section 1 of the U.S. Constitution, the Full Faith and Credit Clause, ensures that judicial decisions rendered by the courts in one state are recognized and honored in every other state (*see* § IX.C. Full Faith and Credit, *infra*). Such decisions, however, are recognized only to the extent that a valid judgment was rendered by a court that had jurisdiction over the parties, and the parties received proper notice of the action and a reasonable opportunity to be heard.

For example, if a default judgment has been entered against a defendant in an action in one state, and the plaintiff sues to enforce the judgment in another state, then the defendant may collaterally attack the judgment on the basis of lack of personal jurisdiction. If, however, the defendant had both notice and an opportunity to be heard, then a collateral attack on the judgment is not permitted under the doctrine of res judicata (*see* § IX.D. Claim Preclusion (Res Judicata), *infra*). *Baldwin v. Iowa State Traveling Men's Ass'n*, 283 U.S. 522 (1931).

4. Immunity

Most states provide immunity from service of process to nonresidents who enter the state for the purposes of attending a trial or deposition as a witness, party, or attorney. The theory behind such immunity is that it promotes full and active participation in the judicial system.

The federal courts also generally provide immunity from federal suit under the same circumstances.

III. VENUE

A. IN GENERAL

Venue concerns which court among the courts having personal and subject matter jurisdiction is the proper forum for hearing the matter. For cases in federal court, the issue is determining the proper geographic district (e.g., Central District of California) in which a trial should occur. Each state has at least one federal judicial district, with a few states having as many as four. Venue requirements are statutory and are intended to ensure the parties a fair and convenient forum for litigating their dispute.

B. LOCAL AND TRANSITORY ACTIONS

The common law created a distinction between local and transitory actions for the purposes of venue. In general, local actions involve title to property and must be brought in a court where the property is located. Transitory actions involve a cause of action based on events that could have taken place anywhere. Many state venue statutes continue to apply this distinction; however, in federal court, venue is determined without regard to whether the action is local or transitory in nature. § 1391(a)(2).

C. GENERAL VENUE RULE

In general, venue in a federal civil action is proper in only one of the following judicial districts:

i) A judicial district in which any defendant resides, if all defendants reside in the same state in which the district is located; or

ii) A judicial district in which a "substantial part of the events or omissions" on which the claim is based occurred, or where a "substantial part of the property" that is the subject of the action is located.

If there is otherwise no judicial district in which the action may be brought, then the "fall back" alternative is that venue is proper in a judicial district in which any defendant is subject to personal jurisdiction with respect to such action. § 1391(b).

1. Residence

a. Natural person

For venue purposes, a natural person, including an alien lawfully admitted for permanent residence into the United States, is deemed to reside in the judicial district where that person is domiciled. § 1391(c)(1).

b. Business entities

A defendant that is an entity with the capacity to sue and be sued, regardless of whether incorporated, is deemed to reside in any judicial district in which the entity is subject to personal jurisdiction with respect to the civil action in question. § 1391(c)(2). In a state that contains multiple judicial districts and in which a defendant corporation is subject to personal jurisdiction at the time the action is commenced, the corporation "shall be deemed to reside in any district in that State within which its contacts would be sufficient to subject it to personal jurisdiction if that district were a separate State." If there is no such district, then the corporation is deemed to reside in the district with which it has the most significant contacts. § 1391(d).

Example: A corporation is incorporated in Delaware, has its principal place of business in Colorado, and maintains a regional sales office in Orlando, Florida (U.S. Middle District Court in Florida), but it conducts no activities anywhere else in Florida. The corporation is sued for breach of a contract executed in the Orlando office and performed in Orlando. For federal venue purposes, the corporation resides in the District of Delaware, the District of Colorado, and the Middle District of Florida. Note that, for federal venue purposes, this corporation is not a resident of any other judicial district in Florida.

If the entity is a plaintiff, then it is deemed to reside only in the judicial district in which it maintains its principal place of business. § 1391(c)(2).

> **EXAM NOTE:** Keep in mind that, with respect to partnerships and unincorporated associations, the "entity" approach is taken only for venue purposes. It does not apply for the purposes of determining diversity jurisdiction, when a partnership or unincorporated association is considered a citizen of each state in which each of its partners or members is domiciled.

c. Nonresident of the United States

A defendant who is not a resident of the United States may be sued in any judicial district, but the joinder of such a defendant is disregarded when determining proper venue with respect to other defendants. § 1391(c)(3).

2. Objection to Improper Venue

An objection to improper venue, unlike an objection regarding subject matter jurisdiction, may be waived by the parties, and it is automatically waived if not asserted in a timely manner by a defendant, i.e., raised in a pre-answer motion to dismiss under Rule 12(b)(3) or in the first responsive pleading, if a motion under Rule 12(b)(3) is not filed. Rule 12(h)(1); § 1406(b).

D. SPECIAL VENUE PROVISIONS

There are special rules for venue in certain types of cases.

1. Case Against a Federal Official

An action against an officer or employee of the United States or its agencies acting in an official capacity or under color of legal authority may be commenced in a judicial district in which:

i)   A defendant in the action resides;

ii) A substantial part of the events or omissions giving rise to the claim occurred, or a substantial part of the property that is the subject of the action is situated; or

iii) The plaintiff resides, if no real property is involved in the action.

§ 1391(e). A suit against a private individual for money damages does not fall within this venue provision merely because the individual is an employee of the federal government; the provision applies only to suits that are essentially against the federal government. *Stafford v. Briggs*, 444 U.S. 527 (1980).

2. Case Brought Under the Federal Tort Claims Act

Venue in a case brought under the Federal Tort Claims Act is proper either in the judicial district where the plaintiff resides or in the judicial district where the act or omission occurred. § 1402(b).

3. Case Against a Foreign State

In a case against a foreign state, including a political subdivision, agency, or instrumentality, venue is proper in any judicial district in which a substantial part of the events or omissions giving rise to the claim occurred, or a substantial part of property that is the subject of the action is situated. If the case is against a foreign state or its political subdivision, venue is also proper in the U.S. District Court for the District of Columbia. § 1391(f).

4. Multiparty, Multiforum Litigation

In a case in which the jurisdiction of the court is based on the multiparty, multiforum provision (e.g., at least 75 natural persons died in an accident at a discrete location), venue is proper in any judicial district in which any defendant resides or in which a substantial part of the accident giving rise to the action took place. § 1391(g).

5.   Case Removed From State Court

In a case that is removed from state court, venue is proper in the federal district court in the district where the state action was pending. It is immaterial that venue would not have been proper under the general venue rule if the action had been brought initially in that district. § 1441(a); *Polizzi v. Cowles Magazines, Inc.*, 345 U.S. 663 (1953).

E.   CHANGE OF VENUE

1.   Change of Venue When the Original Venue Is Proper

"[F]or the convenience of parties and witnesses, in the interest of justice, a district court may transfer any civil action to any other district or division where it might have been brought or to any district or division to which all parties have consented." This transfer may be ordered upon motion of a party, including the plaintiff, or by the court on its own initiative, but it is available only when the jurisdiction and venue of the court considering the issue are proper. The burden of proof with regard to the motion rests on the party seeking the transfer. § 1404(a).

> **EXAM TIP:** Section 1404(a) is essentially a codification of the common-law doctrine of *forum non conveniens* for a subset of cases, allowing transfer from one proper federal forum to a more appropriate federal forum instead of requiring dismissal.

a.   Diversity cases

In a diversity case, if the court transfers the case, then the district court to which the case is transferred must apply the law that would have been applied in the district court that transferred the case. *Ferens v. John Deere Co.*, 494 U.S. 516 (1990).

b.   Federal question cases

In a federal question case transferred to a district court in another appellate circuit, the district court to which the case is transferred must apply the federal law as interpreted by its federal Court of Appeals and not as interpreted by the federal Court of Appeals in which the district court that transferred the matter is located.

c.   Forum selection clause

When transfer is sought on the basis of a forum selection clause in a contract, the clause is accorded respect. Even though the clause itself does not render other forums legally improper, most circuit courts treat forum selection clauses as prima facie valid, to be set aside only upon a strong showing that transfer to the selected court would be unreasonable and unjust or that the clause was invalid for reasons such as fraud or overreaching. *M/S Bremen v. Zapata Off-Shore Co.*, 407 U.S. 1 (1972). Furthermore, in *Atlantic Marine Construction Co. v. United States District Court*, 571 U.S. 49 (2013), the Supreme Court held that a forum selection clause should be given "controlling weight in all but the most exceptional cases." A few circuit courts, however, following *Stewart Organization Inc. v. Ricoh Corp.*, 487 U.S. 22 (1988), treat the clause as a significant, but not determinative, factor.

When venue is transferred between federal courts based on a valid forum selection clause, the transferee court must apply the law, including the choice-of-law rules, of the state in which it is located. The transferee court should not apply the law of the transferor court because the parties have contractually waived their right to the application of that law by agreeing to be subject to the laws of the transferee venue. *Atlantic Marine Construction Co. v. United States District Court*, 571 U.S. 49 (2013).

> **EXAM TIP:** Remember that the enforcement of a forum selection clause may require a different remedy depending on the forum specified by the clause. If the clause specifies a federal forum, it may be enforced by a motion to transfer under §1404(a). If the clause specifies arbitration or a state or foreign forum, then §1404(a) will not apply, and the common-law doctrine of *forum non conveniens* may instead require the action to be dismissed.

2. Change of Venue When the Original Venue Is Improper

If venue in a case is improper, then the district court must dismiss the case, or "if it be in the interest of justice," transfer the case to any district or division in which the case could have been brought. If no timely objection is made to venue, then nothing prevents the district court from maintaining jurisdiction over the case. § 1406.

a. Diversity cases

In diversity cases transferred for improper venue, the district court to which the case is transferred applies the choice-of-law rules of the state in which it is located, as opposed to the state law of the district court that transferred the case.

b. Federal question cases

In federal question cases transferred for improper venue, the district court to which the case is transferred applies the interpretation of federal law by its Court of Appeals.

c. No personal jurisdiction

Even if the court lacks personal jurisdiction over the defendant, the court is not barred from transferring a case to a different venue. *Goldlawr, Inc. v. Heiman*, 369 U.S. 463 (1962).

3. Transfer to Another Division in the Same District

On motion or by stipulation of all parties, a case may be transferred to a different division within a judicial district at the discretion of the court. § 1404(b).

F. FORUM NON CONVENIENS

This common-law doctrine traditionally allows a court to dismiss an action—even if personal jurisdiction and venue are otherwise proper—if the court finds that the forum would be too inconvenient for parties and witnesses, and that another, more convenient, venue is available.

The doctrine of *forum non conveniens* has been codified and relaxed with respect to transfers between federal district courts (*see* § III.E.1. Change of Venue When the Original Venue Is Proper, *supra*), now allowing the remedy of transfer as opposed to outright dismissal. Consequently, this doctrine as a common-law rule is now used by a federal district court primarily when the forum that is deemed most appropriate for the action is a state or foreign court, since the federal statute does not apply in such a circumstance.

In determining whether the common-law doctrine of *forum non conveniens* applies, some of the factors that are generally considered include (i) the availability of an alternative forum; (ii) the law that will apply; and (iii) the location of the parties, witnesses, and evidence. To convince a court to invoke the doctrine of *forum non conveniens*, the defendant ordinarily bears a heavy burden to displace the plaintiff's chosen forum. However, a forum-selection clause designating a state or foreign forum modifies the conventional rule for *forum non conveniens* by shifting the burden to the plaintiff to show why the court should disregard the forum-selection clause. *Atlantic Marine Construction Co. v. United States District Court*, 571 U.S. 49 (2013).

IV. CHOICE OF LAW: THE *ERIE* DOCTRINE

A. IN GENERAL

When an action is commenced in U.S. district court, the court must determine the substantive law and rules of procedure that will govern the action.

1. Federal Question Claim

If the action is a federal question claim, then federal substantive and procedural law will control, as well as federal common law.

2. Federal Diversity Claim

a. Substantive law

In a diversity action, the district court is required to apply the substantive law of the state in which the district court is located, if there is no federal law on point. *Erie R.R. Co. v. Tompkins*, 304 U.S. 64 (1938).

b. Procedure

1) Applicable federal law

With regard to procedure in a diversity action, however, if a procedural issue is addressed by a valid federal law (e.g., a statute or Federal Rule of Evidence), then the federal law will be applied, even if a state rule or statute is in conflict. *Hanna v. Plumer*, 380 U.S. 460 (1965).

2) No applicable federal law

If no federal law applies, then the general rule is that the district court must follow state law with regard to substance, but it can choose to ignore state law with regard to procedure under certain circumstances.

B. SUBSTANCE VERSUS PROCEDURE

1. Analytical Approach

It is sometimes difficult to determine if an issue involves substance or procedure for the purposes of applying the *Erie* doctrine. The following general approach is often used:

i) The district court will start by determining whether there is a **conflict between state and federal law** with respect to the issue before the court. If no conflict exists, then the analysis does not need to proceed any further because the court can apply state and federal law harmoniously to the issue.

ii) If, however, the applicable state and federal laws do conflict, then the district court must ask whether a **valid federal statute** or **Federal Rule** covers the disputed issue. *Hanna, supra*.

a) If there is a **valid federal statute or rule of procedure** on point, then the district court must **apply federal law** rather than state law. Before applying a **Federal Rule** (rather than a federal statute) that is on point, the court must determine whether the rule is valid under the Rules Enabling Act. Specifically, the court must ask whether the Federal Rule abridges, enlarges, or modifies any substantive right. 28 U.S.C. § 2072. If it does not, then the

Federal Rule must be applied. If the Federal Rule can be considered to abridge, enlarge, or modify a substantive right, then the court must determine whether the Federal Rule only incidentally affects a litigant's substantive rights. A Federal Rule that only incidentally affects substantive rights is valid under the Rules Enabling Act and will be applied by the court. *Burlington N.R. Co. v. Woods*, 480 U.S. 1 (1987).

b) If no federal statute or rule is on point, then the court must determine whether federal common law, rather than state law, should be applied. In making this determination with respect to federal common law, the district court will ask **whether the failure to apply state law will lead to different outcomes** in state and federal court. *Guar. Trust Co. v. York*, 326 U.S. 99 (1945).

1) If the answer is no, then the district court will generally apply federal common law, rather than state law.

2) If the answer is yes, then the court will apply state law, unless affirmative countervailing federal interests are at stake that warrant application of federal law. *See* § IV.C. Federal Common Law, *infra.*

c) The court may also choose to examine the issue by weighing the interests of the state and federal judiciaries and applying the law whose policy is of greater importance. *Byrd v. Blue Ridge Rural Elec. Co-op, Inc.*, 356 U.S. 525 (1958).

1) If the state has a greater interest in having its rule applied, then the court will apply state law.

2) Otherwise, the court will apply federal law.

d) Finally, to prevent forum shopping (selecting a court based upon where the plaintiff believes he will receive a favorable outcome), the court will follow state law if selecting state law would prevent overcrowding of the federal court system. *Hanna, supra.*

2. Substantive Law

Examples of specific areas of law that have been held to be substantive rather than procedural include the following.

a. Elements of a claim or defense

The elements of a claim or defense in contract or tort, for example, are considered substantive and are generally controlled by state law in a federal diversity action.

b. Statutes of limitations and tolling provisions

The Supreme Court has indicated that state statutes of limitations and the rules for tolling state statutes of limitations are substantive in nature and are thus applicable in diversity. *Guar. Trust Co. v. York*, 326 U.S. 99 (1945).

c. Burden of proof

The specification of the applicable standards of proof is considered a substantive matter, and the law of the forum state will govern in a diversity case. *Bank of Am. Nat'l Trust & Sav. Ass'n v. Parnell*, 352 U.S. 29 (1956).

3. Procedural Law

Examples of specific areas of law that have been determined to be procedural, rather than substantive, include the following.

a. Judge-jury allocation

If there is a jury in a diversity case on a state-law claim, then the jury, rather than a judge, will decide all factual issues in the case, regardless of whether state law would provide otherwise. *Byrd v. Blue Ridge Rural Elec. Co-op., Inc.*, 356 U.S. 525 (1958).

b. Assessment of attorney's fees

In a diversity case on a state-law claim, the federal court may properly use its inherent power to assess attorney's fees as a sanction for a defendant's bad-faith conduct during the litigation, even if the law of the forum state provides that attorney's fees may not be awarded to a successful party. *Chambers v. NASCO, Inc.*, 501 U.S. 32 (1991).

c. Equitable versus legal

Federal law usually governs whether an issue is legal or equitable. *Simler v. Conner*, 372 U.S. 221 (1963).

C. FEDERAL COMMON LAW

When it is appropriate under the *Erie* doctrine to apply federal law (e.g., a federal question claim or a procedural issue in diversity case), the court may look to federal statutes, constitutional provisions, and federal common law as a source of the law. Federal common law is created when there is no applicable federal statute or constitutional provision. The court therefore must resort to source materials of the common law. It is important to note that there is no **general** federal common law, and the general areas to which federal common law is applicable will be limited.

1. Federal Question Cases

Traditionally, federal courts have determined that federal interests warrant the application of federal common law in the following instances:

i) Admiralty cases;

ii) Cases in which the United States is a party;

iii) Cases involving interstate disputes;

iv) Cases implicating relations with foreign countries;

v) Cases in which the government acts in a proprietary role (e.g., enters into contracts, issues commercial paper, and oversees regulatory programs); and

vi) When Congress has left a gap in a statutory scheme.

2. Diversity Cases

The Supreme Court has also recognized the application of federal common law when a "uniquely federal interest" is at stake and a significant conflict exists between that interest and the operation of state law. *See, e.g., Boyle v. United Technologies Corp.*, 487 U.S. 500 (1988) (a federal defense contractor could assert a defense recognized under federal common law to a state products liability action brought under diversity jurisdiction because the unique interests of the U.S. government in contracting for the procurement of military equipment were directly affected and a significant conflict existed with state law); *Clearfield Trust Co. v. United States*, 318 U.S. 363 (1943) (federal common law governed the federal government's liability for a check issued by the United States that was later stolen and cashed, because it was important to have a uniform standard for determining liability on such commercial paper).

3. State Court Cases

Federal common law may also apply in state court without running afoul of *Erie*. If state jurisdiction is concurrent with federal question jurisdiction (*see* § I.B.2. Concurrent Versus Exclusive Jurisdiction) and federal common law would have applied in federal court, then it will also apply in state court. *See Semtek Int'l Inc. v. Lockheed Martin Corp.*, 531 U.S. 497 (2001).

D. DETERMINING APPLICABLE STATE LAW

Under *Erie*, a U.S. district court with diversity jurisdiction must apply the substantive law of the state in which it is located.

Example: The U.S. District Court of Delaware will generally apply Delaware substantive law to the diversity actions over which it sits.

1. Highest State Court's Rulings on Substantive Law Control

In determining a state's substantive law, the U.S. district court will be bound by the rulings of the state's highest court.

2. Highest State Court Not Yet Ruled

If the state's highest court has not spoken on an issue, however, the federal court must try to determine how the state's highest court would rule on the issue, if it did consider it. To make this determination, the federal court will generally look to any lower state-court decisions that have considered the issue and will follow a lower court's view, unless it believes that the highest state court would not follow it. If no state court has considered the issue, then the federal court will have to determine how it believes the highest court in the state would rule if it looked at the issue today. Some states have procedures that allow the federal district court to certify a question of substantive law to the state supreme court for clarification.

3. Highest Court Rules After the Federal Suit Is Complete

If, after the U.S. district court action has been completed, the state's highest court rules on an issue in a way that is different from the way the district court predicted, then a federal appeals court is bound by the state court's ruling. *Vandenbark v. Owens-Illinois Glass Co.*, 311 U.S. 538 (1941).

4. Conflict of Laws

In diversity actions, a U.S. district court is bound by the conflict-of-laws rules of the state in which the district court is located, but only to the extent that the state's rules are valid under the Full Faith and Credit and Due Process Clauses of the U.S. Constitution. *See Allstate Ins. Co. v. Hague*, 449 U.S. 302 (1981), *Klaxon v. Stentor Elec. Mfg. Co.*, 313 U.S. 487 (1941).

State conflict-of-laws rules frequently determine whether to apply the law of the forum state or the law of a foreign jurisdiction by considering whether the law to be applied is substantive or procedural. States apply their own procedural laws and sometimes apply the substantive law of a foreign jurisdiction. Although the substance-procedure distinction arises in federal-state choice-of-law conflicts under *Erie*, it is not the same substance-procedure distinction that arises in state-state choice-of-law conflicts under *Klaxon*.

Questions about the following issues are generally considered procedural and controlled by the law of the forum state:

i) The proper court in which to bring an action;

ii) The form of the action to be brought;

iii) The sufficiency of the pleadings;

iv) The effect of splitting a cause of action;

v) The proper or necessary parties to an action;

vi) Whether a counterclaim may be brought;

vii) Venue;

viii) The rules of discovery;

ix) The right to a jury trial;

x) Service of process;

xi) The burden of proof;

xii) Trial procedure; and

xiii) The methods of enforcing a judgment.

5. When Venue Is Transferred

If the venue of an action is transferred under § 1404, then the court to which the action is transferred must apply the law of the state of the transferor court, including that state's rules regarding conflict of laws. If the transfer is made pursuant to § 1406(a), however, then the court to which the case is transferred applies the conflict-of-laws rules of the state in which it is located.

V. PLEADINGS

A. COMMENCEMENT OF PROCEEDINGS

1. Manner

Under Rule 3, a civil action is commenced by filing a complaint with the court clerk. For the purposes of a federal diversity action, state law will apply to decide when the action commenced for the purposes of the statute of limitations. *Walker v. Armco Steel Corp.*, 446 U.S. 740 (1980). Thus, if state law provides that an action is commenced by service of process on a defendant, then the state rule will control for the purposes of diversity jurisdiction.

2. Time Computation

a. General rule

Rule 6 sets out guidelines for computing time limits that apply throughout the Federal Rules of Civil Procedure, unless otherwise provided. Under Rule 6(a)(1), whenever a time period is stated in days, the period excludes the day of the event that triggers the period, but it includes **every day** following, **including intervening Saturdays, Sundays, and legal holidays**. If the last day of the period is a Saturday, Sunday, or legal holiday, then the period is extended to include the next non-weekend or non-holiday day. Rule 6(a)(1).

b. Motions, hearings, and affidavits

Under Rule 6(c), a written motion and notice of a hearing must be served at least 14 days prior to the hearing, unless (i) the motion can be heard ex parte, (ii) the Rules provide for it, or (iii) the court orders otherwise. An opposing affidavit must be served at least seven days before the hearing, unless otherwise ordered.

c. Additional time for responses after certain kinds of service

Under Rule 6(d), when a party may or must act within a specified time after being served and service is made under Rule 5(b) by mail, leaving with the clerk, or other means consented to, **three days are added** to the prescribed time period. Rule 5(b) governs service of papers filed after the original complaint, including written motions, discovery, and other pleadings.

B. SERVICE OF PROCESS

Rule 4 sets forth the procedure for service of process in a federal action, detailing the form, content, method of issuance, methods of service, and time of service of a summons and complaint. In the absence of service of process (or waiver of service by the defendant), a court ordinarily may not exercise power over a party named as a defendant in a complaint. *Murphy Bros., Inc. v. Michetti Pipe Stringing, Inc.*, 526 U.S. 344 (1999).

1. Who Must Serve

Under Rule 4(c), the plaintiff is responsible for serving the summons and complaint upon the defendant. Service may be made by any nonparty who is at least 18 years old.

2. Time Limit for Service

Unless service is made in a foreign country, the plaintiff must serve the summons and complaint within 90 days after filing the complaint. If, however, the plaintiff shows "good cause" why service was not timely made, then the court must extend the time for service for an appropriate period. If no such showing is made, then the court, on motion or on its own after notice to the plaintiff, must dismiss the action without prejudice against that defendant or order that service be made within a specified time. Rule 4(m).

3. Methods of Service

Rule 4 establishes different procedures for service of process depending on whether the defendant is an individual or a corporation, a governmental entity or subdivision, and domestic or foreign.

a. Service on individuals

1) In the United States

Service generally may be made by:

i) Personally serving the summons and complaint on the defendant;

ii) Leaving the summons and complaint at the defendant's usual place of abode with a person of suitable age and discretion who resides there; or

iii) Delivering the summons and complaint to an agent appointed by the defendant or otherwise authorized by law to receive service.

In addition, service may be made by following state law for serving a summons in an action brought in courts of general jurisdiction in the state where the district court is located or where service is made. Rule 4(e)(1).

2) Outside the United States

Pursuant to Rule 4(f), service may be effected in any manner, internationally agreed upon, that is reasonably calculated to give notice. If no international agreement exists, or if an international agreement permits service by other means, then service on any competent individual outside the United States may be effected by any method permitted by the law of the foreign country; or, unless the foreign country's law prohibits it, by personal service of the summons and the complaint to the individual or by using any form of mail that the clerk addresses and sends to the individual and that requires a signed receipt; or by any other means not prohibited by international agreement, as ordered by the court.

b. Service on corporations and associations

1) Inside the United States

Service on a corporation or an unincorporated association (e.g., a partnership) in the United States may be effected by delivering the summons and complaint to an officer, managing agent, general agent, or agent appointed or authorized by law to receive process. Rule 4(h).

If the agent is one authorized by statute, and the statute so requires, then the plaintiff must also mail a copy of the summons and complaint to the defendant. Rule 4(h)(1)(B).

In addition, service may be made by following state law for serving a summons in an action brought in courts of general jurisdiction in the state where the district court is located or where service is made. Rule 4(h)(1)(A).

2) Outside the United States

Service on corporations and associations outside the United States may be made using any methods available for service on an individual outside the United States, except personal delivery under Rule 4(f)(2)(c)(i).

c. Service on the U.S. government and its agencies and officers

1) Service on the U.S. government

Under Rule 4(i)(1), to serve the United States, a party must:

i) Deliver a copy of the summons and complaint to the U.S. attorney (or a designee) for the district where the action is brought, or send a copy by registered or certified mail to the civil-process clerk at the U.S. attorney's office;

ii) Send a copy by registered or certified mail to the U.S. Attorney General; and

iii) If the action challenges an order of a nonparty agency or officer of the United States, send a copy by registered or certified mail to the agency or officer.

2) Service on a U.S. agency, officer, or employee sued in an official capacity

Under Rule 4(i)(2), to serve a U.S. agency, officer, or employee sued in an official capacity, a party must serve the United States and also send a copy of the summons and complaint by registered or certified mail to the agency, officer, or employee.

3) Service on a U.S. officer or employee sued individually

Under Rule 4(i)(3), to serve a U.S. officer or employee in an individual capacity for an act or omission occurring in connection with duties performed on behalf of the United States, a party must serve the United States and also serve the officer or employee under the normal rules for serving an individual.

4. Waiver of Service

Pursuant to Rule 4(d), a competent individual, corporation, or association that is subject to service has a duty to avoid unnecessary expenses of serving the summons by waiving service. The plaintiff may notify such a defendant that an action has been commenced and request that the defendant waive service of the summons. This request is not available if the defendant is a government entity or a minor, or if the defendant is incompetent.

a. Request for waiver

A plaintiff's notice and request for waiver of service must be in writing and be addressed to the individual defendant, or, for a corporation, to an officer, managing or general agent, or any other agent authorized by appointment or by law to receive service of process.

It must be accompanied by a copy of the complaint, two copies of a waiver form, and a prepaid means for returning the form, and it must give the defendant a reasonable time of at least 30 days after the request was sent (or at least 60 days if sent to a foreign defendant) to return the waiver. Rule 4(d)(1).

b. The effect of a waiver

Under Rule 4(d)(3), if a defendant timely returns a waiver of service before being served with process, then the defendant does not have to serve an answer to the complaint until 60 days after the request was sent, or 90 days after it was sent to a defendant outside the United States. This is an incentive to waive service, because the normal time period in which an answer must be served is 21 days after service of process. Rule 12(a)(1)(A).

Rule 4(d)(5) specifically provides that waiver of service does not waive any objection to personal jurisdiction or to venue.

If the defendant agrees to waive service, then the date on which the plaintiff files the waiver form with the court will be deemed the date of service. Rule 4(d)(4). However, the defendant must still answer the complaint within 60 (or 90, if foreign) days from the date on which the notice was sent.

c. Failure to waive service

Under Rule 4(d)(2), if a defendant located within the United States fails, without good cause, to sign and return a waiver requested by a plaintiff located within the United States, then the court must impose on the defendant the expenses that are incurred in making service and the reasonable expenses, including attorney's fees, of any motion required to collect such service expenses.

5. Proof of Service

Under Rule 4(l)(1), if formal service is not waived, then the process server must submit proof of service to the court. Generally, this will be by an affidavit of the process server. Failure to make proof of service does not affect the validity of the service.

C. INJUNCTIONS

Rule 65 permits an injunction, which is a form of equitable relief mandating that a defendant perform a specified act or prohibiting a defendant from performing a specified act. An injunction is considered an extraordinary remedy, only to be granted in limited circumstances. *See Weinberger v. Romero-Barcelo*, 456 U.S. 305 (1982). Every order granting injunctive relief must state the reasons for its issuance, specifically state its terms, and specify the acts that the defendant is restrained from performing or required to perform. Additionally, to protect the adverse party against harm in the event of an erroneous grant of preliminary relief, the rule expresses a preference that the moving party post an injunction bond. Rule 65(c), (d).

There are two types of injunctions: mandatory and prohibitory. The determining factor is the type of conduct that is affected by the injunction, if granted.

A mandatory injunction, which is a specific relief, requires a person to engage in an affirmative act that typically changes the status quo. *Yu Juan v. City of New York, et al.*, 181 Fed. Appx. 38 (2d Cir. 2006). When the injunction is directed at providing mandatory relief, as opposed to preserving the status quo, the moving party's burden is particularly heavy. *United States v. Spectro Foods Corp*, 544 F.2d 1175, 1181 (3d Cir. 1976).

A prohibitory injunction, which is a form of preventive relief, restrains or prohibits a party from engaging in a specified behavior.

1. Temporary Restraining Order

A temporary restraining order (TRO) preserves the status quo of the parties until there is an opportunity to hold a full hearing on the application for a preliminary injunction. This interlocutory injunction may remain in effect only a limited number of days, to be set by the court, and no longer than 14 days unless good cause exists or the adversary consents. Rule 65(b)(2). TROs are not generally immediately appealable, unless they have the effect of an injunction, as when the court extends the length of the TRO beyond the time limit specified in the rules.

a. When notice is not required

Pursuant to Rule 65(b)(1), a TRO may issue without notice to the adverse party if:

    i) The moving party can establish, under written oath, that immediate and irreparable injury will result prior to hearing the adverse party's opposition; and

    ii) The movant's attorney certifies in writing any efforts made to give notice and the reason why notice should not be required.

b. Contents

In addition to being filed with the clerk, the TRO must state the following:

    i) The date and time issued;

    ii) The irreparable harm suffered by the plaintiff; and

    iii) The reasoning behind the ex parte issuance.

Rule 65(b)(2).

c. Motion to dissolve

If the TRO is issued without notice, the adverse party may appear and move to dissolve or modify the TRO, but must give the party who obtained the TRO two days' notice unless a shorter time is set by the court. Rule 65(b)(4).

2. Preliminary Injunction

A preliminary injunction is a form of relief issued prior to a full hearing on the merits, but only upon notice to the defendant and a hearing on whether the injunction should issue. Should an expedited decision on the merits be appropriate, a court may order a trial on the merits to be consolidated with the preliminary injunction hearing. Rule 65(a). A plaintiff seeking a preliminary injunction must establish that:

i) He is likely to succeed on the merits;

ii) He is likely to suffer irreparable harm in the absence of relief;

iii) The balance of equities is in his favor; and

iv) The injunction is in the best interests of the public.

Winter v. Natural Resources Defense Council, Inc., 555 U.S. 7 (2008).

3. Permanent Injunction

A permanent injunction is a determination on the merits. Once issued, it continues until dissolved by the court, but any affected person may move for modification or dissolution. The standard for a permanent injunction is essentially the same as for a preliminary injunction except that the plaintiff must show actual success on the merits. *See eBay Inc. v. MercExchange, L.L.C.*, 547 U.S. 388 (2006).

4. Limitations

When a conflict of jurisdiction occurs between state and federal courts, the federal court cannot use an injunction to prohibit pending state-court proceedings unless expressly authorized by statute. Neither can a federal court grant an injunction against the collection of state taxes. In criminal law, state criminal proceedings that have not yet been instituted cannot be enjoined unless to do so would prevent irreparable harm, and appellate remedies would be inadequate to provide relief.

D. COMPLAINT

1. Required Elements

a. In general

The complaint is the initial pleading in an action filed by the plaintiff and serves as notice to the opposing party. Under Rule 8(a), a complaint (or any pleading in which a claim is made) must include:

i) A short and plain statement of the grounds that establish the court's subject matter jurisdiction;

ii) A short and plain statement of the claim establishing entitlement to relief; and

iii) A demand for judgment for the relief sought by the pleader.

b. Subject matter jurisdiction

A complaint in federal court must contain an allegation of the subject matter jurisdiction of the court, unless the court already has jurisdiction and the claim needs no new jurisdictional support.

c. Statement of the claim

Rule 8(a)(2) requires only "a short and plain statement of the claim showing that the pleader is entitled to relief" to "give the defendant fair notice of what [the] plaintiff's claim is and the grounds upon which it rests." *Conley v. Gibson*, 355 U.S. 41, 47 (1957). Detailed factual allegations are not required, but a party must plead facts sufficient to show that the claim has substantive plausibility. A claimant may not merely recite the elements of a cause of action with broad, conclusory statements. *Ashcroft v. Iqbal*, 556 U.S. 662 (2009), *Bell Atlantic Corp. v. Twombly*, 550 U.S. 544 (2007). A complaint should not be dismissed for an imperfect statement of the legal theory. *Johnson v. City of Shelby*, 574 U.S. 10 (2014) (failure to cite to federal statute as legal basis for complaint not grounds for dismissal) (*see* E.2. Motion to Dismiss for Failure to State a Claim Upon Which Relief Can Be Granted, *infra*).

d. Demand for relief

The demand for judgment for the relief sought may include relief in the alternative or different types of relief (e.g., monetary damages, equitable relief, or a declaratory judgment). The demand in a contested case does not limit the nature or scope of relief that the trial court may grant. The plaintiff is entitled to whatever relief is appropriate to the claims alleged in the complaint and proved at trial. Rule 54(c). A plaintiff's complaint may include relief in the alternative or different types of relief (e.g., monetary damages, equitable relief, or a declaratory judgment).

2. Time for Filing and Service

A complaint will generally be filed before service on the defendant(s), which must then generally occur within 90 days of filing. Rule 4(m). For time limits, *see* § V.B.2. Time Limit for Service, *supra*.

3. Special Matters

Rule 9 sets forth certain special rules with regard to pleading, which apply not just in the context of a complaint, but to any pleading. In certain circumstances (described as follows), a party is required to plead with greater detail than under the general rules. Federal courts have no power to require more specific pleading, beyond following the rules set forth in the Federal Rules of Civil Procedure or by statute. *See Swierkiewicz v. Sorema N.A.*, 534 U.S. 506 (2002).

a. Capacity

Under Rule 9(a), except when required to show that the court has jurisdiction, a pleading need not allege a party's capacity to sue or be sued. To challenge a party's capacity, an opposing party must make a specific denial and state any supporting facts that are peculiarly within the party's knowledge.

b. Fraud or mistake

Under Rule 9(b), a party alleging fraud or mistake must state with particularity the circumstances constituting fraud or mistake.

Malice, intent, knowledge, and other conditions of a person's mind, however, may be alleged generally.

c. Conditions precedent

Under Rule 9(c), in pleading conditions precedent in a contract action, a party may allege generally that all conditions precedent have occurred or been performed. When denying that a condition precedent has occurred or been performed, however, the party must do so with particularity.

d. Official document or act

Under Rule 9(d), in pleading an official document or official act, it is sufficient to allege that the document was legally issued or that the act was legally done.

e. Judgment

Under Rule 9(e), in pleading a judgment or decision of a domestic or foreign court, a judicial or quasi-judicial tribunal, or a board or an officer, it is sufficient to plead the judgment or decision without showing any jurisdiction to render it.

f. Special damages

Under Rule 9(g), when an item of special damage is claimed, it must be specifically stated. Special damages are damages that do not normally or necessarily flow from an event.

g. Time and place

When relevant and material, facts regarding time and place must be specified in detail.

E. MOTIONS AGAINST THE COMPLAINT

Under Rule 12, within 21 days of service of process, a defendant must respond to a complaint either by an answer or by a pre-answer motion, or she must seek additional time to answer. If a defendant does not take one of these steps, then she risks a default.

1. Rule 12(b) Motion to Dismiss

a. Basis

Prior to filing an answer, a defendant may file a motion under Rule 12(b), raising any or all of the following defenses:

   i)   Lack of subject matter jurisdiction;

   ii) Lack of personal jurisdiction;

   iii) Improper venue;

   iv) Insufficient process;

   v)   Insufficient service of process;

   vi) Failure to state a claim upon which relief can be granted; and

   vii) Failure to join a necessary or indispensable party under Rule 19.

Such motions generally seek dismissal of the claim. For the defenses of insufficient process and service of process, though, it is common to make a motion to quash the service of process or the process itself.

b. Timing

1) Lack of subject matter jurisdiction defense

The defense of lack of subject matter jurisdiction may be raised at any time, even on appeal. Rule 12(h)(3).

2) Lack of personal jurisdiction, improper venue, insufficient process, and insufficient service of process defenses

The defenses of lack of personal jurisdiction, improper venue, insufficient process, and insufficient service of process must be raised in a pre-answer motion or, if no pre-answer motion is made, in the answer or within the time for amending the answer as of right (*see* V.H.1.a. By right, *infra*), or the defenses will be waived. Rule 12(h)(1). Although Rule 12(b) states that a motion asserting one of these defenses must be made before pleading if a responsive pleading is allowed, courts have concluded, based on the waiver provision in Rule 12(h)(1), that a motion to dismiss based on one of these defenses may be filed after an answer is filed if the answer pleads one of these defenses. *Royal Globe Ins. Co. v. Logicon, Inc.*, 487 F. Supp. 1245 (N.D. Ill. 1980)(lack of personal jurisdiction defense).

Under the "omnibus motion" rule, when a party makes a pre-answer motion raising one of these defenses but omitting the others, the party may not make another pre-answer motion raising one of the omitted defenses that was available to the party when the earlier motion was filed. The party is deemed to have waived the excluded defenses. Rule 12(g)(2), (h)(1)(A).

3) Defenses of failure to state a claim upon which relief can be granted and failure to join a necessary or indispensable party

The defenses of failure to state a claim upon which relief can be granted and failure to join a necessary or indispensable party under Rule 19 may be raised in any pleading, in a motion for judgment on the pleadings, or at trial. Rule 12(h)(2).

2. Motion to Dismiss for Failure to State a Claim Upon Which Relief Can Be Granted

a. Rule 12(b)(6)

Under Rule 12(b)(6), a claim for relief can be dismissed if it either fails to assert a legal theory of recovery that is cognizable at law or fails to allege facts sufficient to support a cognizable claim. In deciding a motion under Rule 12(b)(6), courts treat all well-pleaded facts of the complaint as true, resolve all doubts and inferences in the plaintiff's favor, and view the pleading in the light most favorable to the plaintiff.

b. More than speculation

The facts alleged in the complaint must "raise a right to relief above the speculative level ... on the assumption that all the allegations in the complaint are true (even if doubtful in fact)." *Bell Atl. Corp. v. Twombly*, 550 U.S. 544, 545 (2007). The complaint must state enough facts to raise a reasonable expectation that discovery will reveal evidence of the necessary element.

c. What the court may consider

In ruling on a motion to dismiss under Rule 12(b)(6), the court may consider only the allegations in the complaint, any exhibits attached to the complaint, and any matters subject to judicial notice. If a matter outside the pleadings, such as an affidavit, is presented to the court and is not excluded by the court in its review, then the motion must be treated as a motion for summary judgment under Rule 56, and all parties must be given an opportunity to present all material information for the court's consideration. Rule 12(d).

Note that a court also can consider other matters with regard to a motion to dismiss under other Rule 12(b) defenses. *E.g., Thompson v. Chrysler Motors Corp.*, 755 F.2d 1162 (5th Cir. 1985) (court in determining motion to dismiss for lack of personal jurisdiction can consider not only affidavits but also evidence obtained by discovery methods, such as depositions and interrogatories).

d. Two-step analysis

The U.S. Supreme Court has established a two-step analysis for adjudicating a motion to dismiss under Rule 12(b)(6). First, the court must identify and reject legal conclusions unsupported by factual allegations. This includes mere conclusory statements and assertions devoid of facts. For example, a complaint that alleges that a defendant caused an injury, without explanation as to how it occurred, does not meet the requirements of Rule 8(a) and, as a result, cannot survive a Rule 12(b)(6) motion. Second, the court should assume the truth or veracity of well-pleaded factual allegations and should include a "context specific" analysis that "draw[s] on [the Court's] judicial experience and common sense" to determine whether the allegations "plausibly give rise to an entitlement of relief." *Ashcroft v. Iqbal*, 556 U.S. 662 (2009).

e. Outcome

1) Motion granted

If the claim is dismissed, then the plaintiff may generally amend the pleading and continue the action. If the plaintiff does not wish to do so, then a judgment will be entered, and the plaintiff can appeal.

2) Motion denied

If the defendant's motion to dismiss is denied, then the defendant may either answer the claim or allow a default judgment to be entered and then appeal.

3. Motion for Judgment on the Pleadings

a. In general

After the pleadings are closed, a party may move for judgment on the pleadings pursuant to Rule 12(c). A motion for judgment on the pleadings allows a court to dispose of a case when the material facts are not in dispute and a judgment on the merits can be achieved based on the content of the pleadings. Motions under Rule 12(c) are not often used because of the availability of motions under Rule 12(b)(6) and motions for summary judgment under Rule 56.

b. Timing

A motion under Rule 12(c) must be made after an answer is filed.

c. Standard

The standard for a motion under Rule 12(c) is generally the same as that for a motion under Rule 12(b)(6). Likewise, if matters outside the pleadings are presented to the court and the court does not exclude them, then the motion is to be treated as a motion for summary judgment under Rule 56.

4. Motion for a More Definite Statement

a. Vague and ambiguous

If a pleading is so vague or ambiguous that a party cannot reasonably draft a required responsive pleading, then the responding party may move for a more definite statement. The motion must specify the defects in the pleading, as well as the details sought by the party making the motion. Rule 12(e).

b. Standard

Courts are generally reluctant to grant a motion for a more definite statement, because discovery is available to get more information about an issue. The standard for granting such a motion is whether the pleading provides enough information for the responding party to draft a responsive pleading and commence discovery. A motion for a more definite statement may be appropriate when the pleader fails to allege facts required to be specifically pleaded, such as allegations of fraud or mistake under Rule 9(b).

c. Timing

The party must make a motion for a more definite statement before filing a responsive pleading. The court may strike a party's pleading if the party fails to respond to a court order granting this motion within 14 days of the notice of the order. Rule 12(e).

5. Motion to Strike

a. Rule 12(f)

Under Rule 12(f), if a pleading contains any insufficient defense, or redundant, immaterial, impertinent, or scandalous material, then the court, upon motion or upon its own initiative, may order that such defense or material be stricken. Defenses that tend to complicate litigation significantly or that are insufficient at law may be stricken to avoid unnecessary time and money in litigating invalid and spurious issues. *See Anchor Hocking Corp. v. Jacksonville Elec. Auth.*, 419 F. Supp. 992. (M.D. Fla. 1976); *SEC v. Gulf & Western Indus., Inc.*, 502 F. Supp. 343 (D.D.C. 1980).

b. Timing

When a responsive pleading is permitted, the responding party must move to strike prior to responding to such a pleading. When no responsive pleading is permitted, the party must make a motion to strike within 21 days after service of the pleading.

6. Amending a Motion

Although not specifically provided for in the Rules, courts have generally allowed a party to amend a motion to dismiss to raise an omitted ground if the party acts promptly and before the court rules on the original motion. The courts reason that "an amendment made just a few days following the motion is consistent with the spirit of Rule 12(h) and neither prejudices the plaintiff nor burdens the court." *Friedman v. World Transportation, Inc.*, 636 F. Supp. 685 (N.D. Ill. 1986).

F. ANSWER

An answer is a pleading by the defendant that responds to a plaintiff's complaint. A plaintiff would also file an answer if responding to a defendant's counterclaim.

1. Admissions or Denials

The answer must admit or deny the allegations of the plaintiff's complaint. Rule 8(b). If the defendant is without knowledge or information sufficient to form a belief as to the truth or falsity of an allegation, then the defendant must say so in the answer. This response has the effect of a denial, pursuant to Rule 8(b). Before pleading lack of sufficient knowledge, however, the defendant must make a reasonable investigation into whether the information exists and how difficult it would be to ascertain.

a. Specific denial

A specific denial is a denial of a particular paragraph or allegation in the complaint or other claim for relief (e.g., counterclaim, cross-claim, etc.). A party can respond to each paragraph of the complaint by either denying the allegation in the paragraph, admitting it, pleading insufficient knowledge to either admit or deny it, or admitting part of the allegation and either denying or pleading insufficient knowledge as to the rest.

b. General denial

Alternatively, a party can make a general denial, stating that he denies every allegation of the complaint. This may only be done, however, if the party, in good faith, intends to controvert all of the allegations.

A party could also make a qualified general denial, stating that he denies every allegation in the complaint, except certain specified allegations.

c. Effect of a failure to deny

An allegation, other than one relating to the amount of damages, will be deemed admitted if a responsive pleading is required and the allegation is not denied.

2. Affirmative Defenses

The answer must state any avoidance or affirmative defense that the defendant (or responding party) has, or that defense is deemed waived.

Rule 8(c) lists some such affirmative defenses:

i) Accord and satisfaction;

ii) Arbitration and award;

iii) Assumption of risk;

iv) Contributory negligence;

v) Duress;

vi) Estoppel;

vii) Failure of consideration;

viii) Fraud;

ix) Illegality;

x) Injury by a fellow servant;

xi) Laches;

xii) License;

xiii) Payment;

xiv) Release;

xv) Res judicata;

xvi) Statute of Frauds;

xvii) Statute of limitations; and

xviii) Waiver.

This list is nonexclusive; thus, if there are other affirmative defenses that the party has in addition to those listed previously (e.g., novation, qualified immunity), even if they are inconsistent, then they must be raised in the answer as well. A party may raise alternative defenses, even if they are inconsistent. Rule 8(d).

3. Counterclaims

If a defendant has a claim against the plaintiff, then the defendant may state it as a counterclaim in the answer to the complaint. Under certain circumstances, a counterclaim will be compulsory (*see* § VI.D.2. Counterclaims, *infra*) under Rule 13; it must be pleaded or it will be precluded in any future litigation. A party may state separate claims as well as defenses, regardless of consistency. Rule 8(d).

4. Time and Procedure for Serving an Answer to a Complaint

a. Service under Rule 5

Service of a pleading filed after the original complaint, including answers, is governed by Rule 5 unless the court orders otherwise because there are numerous defendants. Rule 5(a). If a party is represented by an attorney, service under this rule must be made on the attorney unless the court orders service on the party. Rule 5(b)(1).

Service under Rule 5 may generally be accomplished by:

- i) Leaving the pleading:
    - a) At the person's office with a clerk or someone in charge or, if no one is in charge, in a conspicuous place in the office; or
    - b) If the person has no office or the office is closed, at the person's dwelling or usual place of abode with someone of suitable age and discretion who resides there;
- ii) Mailing it to the person's last known address;
- iii) Leaving it with the court clerk if the person has no known address;
- iv) Sending it to a registered user by filing it with the court's electronic-filing system or sending it by other electronic means that the person consented to in writing; or
- v) Delivering it by any other means that the person consented to in writing.

b. No motion made under Rule 12

If no motion is made under Rule 12, then under Rule 12(a)(1)(A)(i), a defendant must serve an answer within 21 days after being served with the summons and complaint.

If the defendant has timely waived service under Rule 4(d), then she must serve the answer within 60 days after the request for a waiver was sent, or within 90 days after it was sent to her outside any judicial district of the United States. Rule 12(a)(1)(A)(ii).

c. Motion made under Rule 12

When a motion is made under Rule 12, a defendant will not have to file an answer while the motion is pending. If the court denies or postpones disposition of the motion until a trial on the merits, then the answer must be served within 14 days after notice of the court's action. Rule 12(a)(4)(A). If the court grants a motion for a more definite statement under Rule 12(e), then the answer must be served within 14 days after service of the more definite statement.

G. REPLY

1. Defined

A reply is a response by the plaintiff to a defendant's answer. It can also be a response by a defendant to a plaintiff's counterclaim answer, a third-party answer, or a cross-claim answer.

2. Court Order

A reply is made only when the court orders it. Rule 7(a)(7).

3. Timing

In general, a party must serve a reply to an answer within 21 days after being served with an order to reply, unless the order specifies a different time. Rule 12(a)(1)(C).

H. AMENDMENTS AND SUPPLEMENTAL PLEADINGS

Rule 15 provides the rules with regard to when and how pleadings can be amended or supplemented.

1. Amendments

a. By right

Under Rule 15(a), a party may amend a pleading once as of right within 21 days if no responsive pleading is required, or, if a responsive pleading is required, within 21 days of service of the responsive pleading or within 21 days of being served with a motion under Rule 12(b), whichever is earlier. Thus, a plaintiff may amend his complaint even after being served with an answer (up to 21 days), but he is also limited to 21 days to amend after being served with a Rule 12(b) motion. A party may amend a pleading during and after a trial if doing so will conform to the evidence and as long as the opposing party had an opportunity to prepare. Due process is required for the amended pleading.

b. By leave of the court

The court should freely give leave to amend a pleading when justice so requires. Rule 15(a)(2). Generally, a court will first determine if the proposed amendment to the pleading would be futile because it would immediately be subject to dismissal under Rule 12(b)(6). If it would not, the amendment will generally be permitted unless it would result in undue prejudice to the opposing party. However, when the court has issued an order regarding the trial plan after a final pretrial conference, which may include the issues for trial, the court may modify that order only to prevent manifest injustice. Rule 16(e).

c. Effect

An amended pleading supersedes the prior pleading.

d. Relation back

1) New claim

Under Rule 15(c)(1), an amendment to a pleading will relate back to the date of the original pleading when the amendment asserts a claim or defense that arose out of the conduct, transaction, or occurrence set out, or attempted to be set out, in the original pleading. This may be important for the purposes of complying with the applicable statute of limitations. An amendment will also relate back to the date of the original pleading if the law that provides the applicable statute of limitations allows relation back.

2) New party

Under Rule 15(c)(1)(C), if the amendment changes the party or the naming of the party against whom a claim is asserted, then it will relate back to the date of the original pleading if:

   i)   It asserts a claim or defense that arose out of the conduct, transaction, or occurrence set out, or attempted to be set out, in the original pleading;

   ii)   Within 90 days after the filing of the original complaint, the party to be brought in by amendment receives notice of the action such that he will not be prejudiced in defending on the merits; and

   iii)   The party to be brought in by amendment knew or should have known that the action would have been brought against him, but for a mistake concerning the proper party's identity.

The proper focus when applying the third element is on the defendant's knowledge, rather than on information in the plaintiff's possession. Although the latter may be relevant, it is not dispositive. *Krupski v. Costa Croceiere*, 560 U.S. 538 (2010).

e. Time to respond to an amended pleading

Unless the court orders otherwise, a party must respond to an amended pleading within the later of 14 days after service of the amended pleading or within the time remaining for response to the original pleading. Rule 15(a)(3).

2. Supplemental Pleadings

A court has discretion under Rule 15(d) to permit supplemental pleadings that describe events occurring after the filing of an earlier pleading. The court may permit supplementation even though the original pleading is defective in stating a claim or defense. The court may also order that the opposing party respond to the supplemental pleading within a specified time. A supplemental pleading does not supersede an original pleading.

I.   RULE 11

Rule 11 establishes the standards that attorneys and individual parties must meet when filing pleadings, motions, or other papers. It also provides for sanctions against parties, attorneys, and law firms for violations of the rule.

1.   Signature

Under Rule 11(a), every pleading, written motion, and other paper filed with the court must be signed by at least one attorney of record, or by a party personally if unrepresented. The paper must state the signer's physical address, e-mail address, and telephone number. The court must strike an unsigned paper unless the omission is promptly corrected after being called to the attention of the attorney or party.

While Rule 11 requires the signature of an attorney of record, or a party if unrepresented, on every pleading, written motion, or other paper filed with the court, this rule does not require that the signature be verified (i.e., sworn to).

2. Certification to the Court

Under Rule 11(b), by presenting to the court a pleading, written motion, or other paper, an attorney or unrepresented party certifies that to the best of her knowledge, information, and belief, formed after an inquiry reasonable under the circumstances:

i) The paper is not being presented for any improper purpose, such as to harass, cause unnecessary delay, or needlessly increase the cost of litigation;

ii) The claims, defenses, and other legal contentions are warranted by existing law or by a nonfrivolous argument for extending, modifying, or reversing existing law or for establishing new law;

iii) The factual contentions have evidentiary support or, if specifically so identified, will likely have evidentiary support after a reasonable opportunity for further investigation or discovery; and

iv) The denials of factual contentions are warranted on the evidence or, if specifically so identified, are reasonably based on belief or a lack of information.

"Presenting" a pleading under Rule 11 includes "signing, filing, submitting, or later advocating" a position presented in the pleading.

3. Sanctions

a. In general

Under certain circumstances, after notice and a reasonable opportunity to respond, the court may, in its discretion, impose sanctions on attorneys, law firms, and parties for violations of Rule 11. Absent exceptional circumstances, a law firm must be held jointly responsible for a violation committed by its partner, associate, or employee. Rule 11(c)(1). Pursuant to Rule 11(c)(4), sanctions "must be limited to what suffices to deter repetition of the conduct or comparable conduct by others similarly situated."

b. How initiated

Sanctions can be initiated either by motion or by the court on its own initiative.

1) Motion

A motion for sanctions must be made separately from any other motion and must describe the specific conduct alleged to violate Rule 11. The motion must first be served on the opposing party under Rule 5. The opposing party must then be given 21 days to withdraw or correct the challenged pleading. If this 21-day "safe harbor" period passes, and the opposing party fails to correct the pleading, the party seeking sanctions may file the motion with the court. Rule 11(c)(2).

2) Sua sponte

On its own initiative, the court may order an attorney, a law firm, or a party to show cause why conduct specifically described in the order has not violated Rule 11.

c. Types of sanctions

Sanctions may include:

i) Nonmonetary directives;

ii) An order to pay a penalty into court; or

iii) If imposed on motion and warranted for effective deterrence, an order directing payment to the movant for part or the entirety of reasonable attorney's fees and other expenses directly resulting from the violation.

d. Procedure

The court cannot impose a monetary sanction on its own, unless it issued an order to show cause before the claims were voluntarily dismissed or settled by or against the party who is, or whose attorneys are, to be sanctioned.

The court also is not permitted to impose a monetary sanction against a represented party for violating the requirement that the claims, defenses, and other legal contentions of the paper be warranted by existing law or by a nonfrivolous argument for extending, modifying, or reversing existing law or for establishing new law.

An order imposing a sanction under Rule 11 must describe the sanctioned conduct and explain the basis for the sanction. Rule 11(c)(6).

VI. MULTIPLE PARTIES AND CLAIMS

A. JOINDER OF PARTIES

The Federal Rules of Civil Procedure provide for joining parties to existing litigation, generally for reasons of efficiency and economy. Joinder may be permissive (pursuant to Rule 20) or compulsory (pursuant to Rule 19).

1. Permissive Joinder

Rule 20 sets forth the circumstances in which a plaintiff may join other plaintiffs in an action or in which defendants may be joined in the same action.

a. Plaintiffs

Pursuant to Rule 20(a)(1), persons may join in one action as plaintiffs if:

i) They assert any right to relief jointly, severally, or in the alternative with respect to or arising out of the same transaction, occurrence, or series of transactions or occurrences; and

ii) Any question of law or fact common to all plaintiffs will arise in the action.

b. Defendants

Pursuant to Rule 20(a)(2), persons may be joined in one action as defendants if:

i) Any right to relief is asserted against them jointly, severally, or in the alternative with respect to or arising out of the same transaction, occurrence, or series of transactions or occurrences; and

ii) A question of law or fact common to all defendants will arise in the action.

c. Extent of relief

The same relief need not be demanded among the joined plaintiffs or against the joined defendants. Rule 20(a)(3).

d. Protective measures

To avoid unfairness or hardship to any party, the court may order separate trials on any claims joined or may make any other order to prevent delay or undue expense to any party. Rule 20(b).

e. Jurisdiction and venue

1) Subject matter jurisdiction

A plaintiff or defendant sought to be joined must also meet the requirements of federal subject matter jurisdiction.

a) Supplemental jurisdiction

i) Joinder of defendants

Under 28 U.S.C. § 1367(b), supplemental jurisdiction does not apply to defendants sought to be joined under the permissive joinder rule in a case based exclusively on diversity jurisdiction in which exercising jurisdiction would destroy diversity. Thus, if the claims are made solely on the basis of diversity jurisdiction, then there must be complete diversity between the plaintiffs and the defendants, and each claim must exceed the jurisdictional amount in controversy of $75,000.

> **Example:** While driving his car, Plaintiff, a citizen of Arizona, is hit by a truck operated by Defendant 1, a citizen of New Mexico. Plaintiff is thrown from his car and is further injured by a car driven by Defendant 2, a citizen of Nevada. Plaintiff brings a negligence suit for $100,000 against Defendant 1 in federal court based on diversity jurisdiction. Plaintiff then joins Defendant 2 under Rule 20, suing for $25,000. Under § 1367(b), there is no supplemental jurisdiction against Defendant 2 and no diversity jurisdiction against Defendant 2 because the statutory jurisdictional amount is not met.

ii) Joinder of plaintiffs

If multiple plaintiffs, however, join together under Rule 20, then supplemental jurisdiction can exist for a claim that does not meet the statutory jurisdictional amount, provided the parties still meet the requirement of complete diversity. *Exxon Mobil Corp. v. Allapattah Servs., Inc.*, 545 U.S. 546 (2005).

> **Example:** Plaintiff 1 and Plaintiff 2, who are citizens of California, join together under Rule 20 as plaintiffs against Defendant, a citizen of Oregon, in a diversity suit for negligence. The claims arise out of the same occurrence or transaction. Plaintiff 1 claims $200,000 and Plaintiff 2 claims $25,000. There is supplemental jurisdiction over Plaintiff 2's claim even though the claim does not meet the statutory jurisdictional amount. If Plaintiff 2 was a citizen of Oregon, however, there would not be complete diversity, and Plaintiff 2 would have to be dropped from the federal case.

2) In personam jurisdiction

If a defendant is joined pursuant to Rule 20, then the court must have in personam jurisdiction over the defendant in order for joinder to be proper.

3) Venue

Joinder under Rule 20 also is subject to any applicable venue requirements.

2. **Compulsory Joinder**

Rule 19 specifies circumstances in which additional parties must be joined. Note that the requirements of jurisdiction (both subject matter and personal) and venue must still be met in order for compulsory joinder to occur. Under certain circumstances, if compulsory joinder cannot occur because of jurisdictional or venue issues, Rule 19(b) may require the action to be dismissed from federal court.

a. **Necessary parties**

Under Rule 19(a), a person who is subject to service of process and whose joinder will not deprive the court of subject matter jurisdiction or destroy venue must be joined as a party if:

i) Complete relief cannot be provided to existing parties in the absence of that person; or

ii) Disposition in the absence of that person may impair the person's ability to protect his interest; or

iii) The absence of that person would leave existing parties subject to a substantial risk of multiple or inconsistent obligations.

A necessary party is therefore a person whose participation in the lawsuit is **necessary for a just adjudication**. The Supreme Court has specifically held that tortfeasors facing joint and several liability are **not** parties who must be joined under Rule 19. *Temple v. Synthes Corp.*, 498 U.S. 5 (1990).

b. **Subject matter jurisdiction**

A plaintiff or defendant to be joined under Rule 19 must meet the requirements of federal subject matter jurisdiction. Thus, if the exclusive basis for the court's subject matter jurisdiction is diversity jurisdiction, and a party sought to be joined would destroy diversity, joinder is not permitted.

Note that under 28 U.S.C. § 1367(b), supplemental jurisdiction does not apply to the claims of a party sought to be joined under Rule 19 in a case based exclusively on diversity jurisdiction if the exercise of jurisdiction would be inconsistent with the diversity requirements.

c. **In personam jurisdiction**

There must be personal jurisdiction over the required party. A required party may be served within 100 miles from where the summons was issued, even if the service is outside of the state and beyond its long-arm statute jurisdiction. Rule 4(k)(1)(B).

d. **Venue**

If a joined party objects to venue and the joinder would make venue improper, the court must dismiss that party.

e. **Indispensable parties: when joinder is not feasible**

Under Rule 19(b), if a necessary party cannot be joined because of jurisdictional or venue concerns, then the court must determine whether, in equity and good conscience, the action should proceed among the existing parties or be dismissed. Among the factors for the court to consider are:

i) The extent to which a judgment rendered in the person's absence might prejudice that person or the existing parties;

ii) The extent to which any prejudice could be reduced or avoided by protective provisions in the judgment, shaping the relief, or other measures;

iii) Whether a judgment rendered in the person's absence would be adequate; and

iv) Whether the plaintiff would have an adequate remedy if the action were dismissed for nonjoinder.

When the court dismisses an action because of the inability to join a necessary party, the party is said to be "indispensable."

B. INTERVENTION

Rule 24 governs the circumstances under which a nonparty may join in a lawsuit. In some circumstances, the nonparty may intervene as of right. In other circumstances, the nonparty must have the permission of the court. Note that in either case, a motion to intervene must be timely.

1. Intervention as of Right

Under Rule 24(a)(1), a nonparty has the right to intervene in an action when a federal statute confers the right, and the nonparty timely moves to intervene. Additionally, under Rule 24(a)(2), upon a timely motion, a nonparty has the right to intervene when:

i) The nonparty has an interest in the property or transaction that is the subject matter of the action;

ii) The disposition of the action may, as a practical matter, impair the nonparty's interest; and

iii) The nonparty's interest is not adequately represented by existing parties.

The criteria for intervention as of right under Rule 24(a)(2) are similar to the criteria for compulsory joinder under Rule 19(a).

The burden of proof is on the person seeking to intervene.

2. Permissive Intervention

Under Rule 24(b), the court may allow intervention, upon timely motion, when either:

i) The movant has a conditional right to intervene under a federal statute; or

ii) The movant's claim or defense and the original action share a common question of law or fact.

In exercising its discretion, the court must consider whether the intervention will unduly delay or prejudice the adjudication of the rights of the original parties.

3. Timeliness

The decision of whether the nonparty timely moved to intervene is in the discretion of the trial court, considering factors such as:

i) The length of time the movant knew or reasonably should have known that its interest was threatened before moving to intervene;

ii) The prejudice to existing parties if intervention is permitted; and

iii) The prejudice to the movant if intervention is denied.

4. Subject Matter Jurisdiction

A claim of an intervenor must be supported by its own jurisdictional basis.

Pursuant to § 1367(b), supplemental jurisdiction does not apply to the claims of a person seeking to intervene under Rule 24 (either as of right or permissively) in a case based exclusively on diversity jurisdiction if the exercise of jurisdiction would be inconsistent with the requirements of diversity jurisdiction.

Example: X, a citizen of Ohio, sues Y, a citizen of Michigan, in federal court under diversity jurisdiction. Z, a citizen of Michigan, seeks to intervene (as of right or permissively) pursuant to Rule 24. Z cannot intervene because she would destroy diversity jurisdiction in the action. If Z were a citizen of any state other than Michigan, then she could intervene, provided the requirements for intervention under Rule 24 were established.

C. INTERPLEADER

Interpleader allows a person holding property (traditionally known as the "stakeholder") to force all potential claimants to the property into a single lawsuit to determine who has a right to the property.

1. Federal Interpleader Rule

a. Basis

Under Rule 22, persons with claims that may expose a plaintiff to double or multiple liability may be joined as defendants and required to interplead. Such joinder is proper even though the claims of the claimants, or the titles on which their claims depend, lack a common origin or are adverse and independent rather than identical, or even though the plaintiff denies liability in whole or in part to any or all of the claimants. A defendant who is exposed to similar liability may seek interpleader through a cross-claim or counterclaim. Rule 22(a).

The primary standard for determining the propriety of an interpleader action under Rule 22 is whether the party bringing the action legitimately fears multiple claims against the property.

b. Subject matter jurisdiction

Rule 22 does not create subject matter jurisdiction in interpleader actions. Rather, the court must already have jurisdiction over all parties. Thus, a plaintiff will need federal question jurisdiction or, for diversity jurisdiction, the citizenship of the party bringing the action must be completely diverse from that of the claimants, and the statutory amount in controversy must be met. While the stakeholder needs to be diverse from the claimants, the claimants need not be diverse among themselves.

c. In personam jurisdiction

An interpleader action is an action against the claimants, so the general requirements of in personam jurisdiction in federal court must be met.

d. Venue

Federal venue requirements must also be met in interpleader actions under Rule 22.

2. Federal Statutory Interpleader

There are some key differences in the requirements for federal statutory interpleader pursuant to § 1335.

a. Subject matter jurisdiction

For statutory interpleader, diversity jurisdiction is met if any two adverse claimants are citizens of different states. With regard to the amount in controversy in a statutory interpleader action, the property at issue must merely exceed $500 in value, not meet the $75,000 threshold required for regular diversity matters.

b. In personam jurisdiction

Statutory interpleader provides for nationwide personal jurisdiction and service of process and permits the federal court to enjoin other federal and state proceedings that may affect the property that is subject to dispute. § 2361.

c. Venue

Venue is proper in any federal judicial district where one of the claimants resides. § 1397.

d. Deposit

For statutory interpleader, unlike for federal rule interpleader, the stakeholder is required to either deposit with the court the property at issue or post a bond in an appropriate amount.

D. JOINDER OF CLAIMS

1. Permissive Joinder

a. In general

Pursuant to Rule 18(a), a party who can assert a claim, counterclaim, cross-claim, or third-party claim (i.e., a qualifying claim that clearly can be brought under the Federal Rules) may join with it as many independent or alternative claims of whatever nature as the party may have against an opposing party.

> Rule 18 permits joinder of claims, but it does not compel it. However, res judicata (claim preclusion) concerns will often require joinder. (*See* § IX.D. Claim Preclusion (Res Judicata), *infra*.)

b. Joinder of contingent claims

Pursuant to Rule 18(b), a party may join two claims even though one of them is contingent on the disposition of the other.

> **Example:** A plaintiff may assert both a claim for monetary damages and a claim to set aside a conveyance that was fraudulent as a result of the defendant's transfer of assets to try to frustrate enforcement of the claim for monetary damages.

c. Subject matter jurisdiction

To join a claim under Rule 18, the court must have subject matter jurisdiction over it.

If subject matter jurisdiction is based on diversity jurisdiction, then a party may aggregate all diversity claims against an opposing party to satisfy the statutory jurisdictional amount-in-controversy requirement.

If the original claim is based on federal question jurisdiction, then a nonfederal claim may be joined only if diversity jurisdiction exists or if the two claims are part of the same case or controversy as the federal claim such that supplemental jurisdiction applies.

d. Venue

The venue requirements for federal court must be satisfied in order to join a claim under Rule 18.

2. Counterclaims

A counterclaim is a claim for relief made against an opposing party after an original claim has been made. A counterclaim may be asserted in the answer to the complaint and the reply to a counterclaim. Rule 13 governs the requirements for bringing a counterclaim.

A party must serve an answer to a counterclaim (or cross-claim) within 21 days of service. Rule 12(a)(1)(B).

a. Compulsory

1) In general

A pleading is required to state as a counterclaim any claim that, at the time of service, the pleader has against an opposing party if the claim arises out of the same transaction or occurrence that is the subject matter of the opposing party's claim and does not require adding another party over whom the court cannot acquire jurisdiction. Rule 13(a)(1).

However, the pleader is not required to make the claim if, at the time the action was commenced, the claim was the subject of another pending action, or if the opposing party's action is in rem or quasi in rem and the party does not assert any other counterclaim in that action. Rule 13(a)(2).

2) Failure to state a compulsory counterclaim

A party who fails to assert a compulsory counterclaim waives the right to sue on the claim and is generally precluded from ever suing on the claim in federal court.

3) Subject matter jurisdiction

A federal court must have subject matter jurisdiction over the counterclaim. By definition, though, a compulsory counterclaim arises out of the same transaction or occurrence as does the original claim before the court. Thus, a compulsory counterclaim (unlike a permissive counterclaim) will likely fall under the supplemental jurisdiction of the federal court and not need independent subject matter jurisdiction from the original claim.

b. Permissive

1) In general

Under Rule 13(b), a pleading may state as a counterclaim against an opposing party any claim that is not compulsory. Thus, a party has discretion as to whether to raise the counterclaim in the action before the court or in a separate action.

2) Subject matter jurisdiction

A permissive counterclaim does not necessarily fall within the supplemental jurisdiction of the federal court, as it does not arise out of the same transaction or occurrence as the original claim. Thus, a permissive counterclaim must on its own meet the requirements for federal subject matter jurisdiction (either diversity or federal question).

c. By third parties

A third-party defendant may file a counterclaim against either an original defendant or an original plaintiff. Whether a third-party defendant's counterclaim is classified as compulsory or permissive is governed by the requirements of Rule 13(a)–(b).

Pursuant to Rule 13(h), new parties to a counterclaim may be joined as long as they meet the requirements for joinder under Rule 20. New parties must be joined if they are indispensable parties under Rule 19.

3. Cross-Claims

a. In general

A cross-claim is a claim made against a coparty, as when one defendant makes a claim against another defendant.

Under Rule 13(g), a pleading may state as a cross-claim any claim by one party against a coparty that arises out of the same transaction or occurrence that is the subject matter of the original action or of a counterclaim, or if the claim relates to any property that is the subject matter of the original action. The cross-claim may include a claim that the coparty is liable to the cross-claimant for all or part of a claim asserted in the action against the cross-claimant.

b. Cross-claim not mandatory

A party is never required to assert a cross-claim against a coparty. Pursuant to Rule 13(h), new parties to a cross-claim may be joined as long as they meet the requirements for joinder under Rule 20. New parties must be joined if they meet the requirements for joinder under Rule 19.

c. Subject matter jurisdiction

A cross-claim must fall within the subject matter jurisdiction of the federal court. This requirement is generally not a problem because, by definition, a cross-claim must arise out of the same transaction or occurrence as the subject matter of the original action or of a counterclaim or it must relate to the property at issue, and therefore it would fall under the court's supplemental jurisdiction.

d. In personam jurisdiction and venue

Because the parties are already before the court, personal jurisdiction is satisfied. Additionally, if venue was proper over the original claim, then a party cannot object to venue with regard to the cross-claim.

4. Third-Party Claims (Impleader)

a. In general

Rule 14 sets out the rules governing impleader (third-party claims). These are claims that are made by a defending party against a nonparty for all or part of the defending party's liability on an original claim. The plaintiff may also assert related claims against the impleaded party. In both cases, the impleaded claim must relate to the original claim against the defending party. The court may sever any third-party claim if justice demands it.

b. Procedure

A defending party—including a plaintiff against whom a counterclaim has been asserted—may assert a third-party claim at any time after the complaint is filed. The defending party, referred to for impleader purposes as the "third-party plaintiff," must serve a summons and third-party complaint on the nonparty (third-party defendant). The third-party plaintiff must obtain the court's permission if he files more than 14 days after service of his original answer. Rule 14(a)(1). There are some states, however, that do not permit a defendant to implead his own insurance company unless the company has denied coverage.

The third-party defendant may (and in some cases must) assert defenses, counterclaims, and cross-claims against any of the parties as appropriate under the Rules and may also implead another nonparty who is or may be liable to the third-party defendant for the claim on which he was impleaded. Rule 14(a)(2).

c. Subject matter jurisdiction

A third-party claim must fall within the federal court's subject matter jurisdiction. Because, by definition, a third-party claim will be closely related to the original claim, the court generally will have supplemental jurisdiction over the matter. If the original claims are based exclusively on diversity jurisdiction, however, under § 1367(b), supplemental jurisdiction will not apply to claims by the plaintiff against a third-party defendant brought in under Rule 14. Such claims need to meet diversity or federal question jurisdiction requirements on their own.

d. In personam jurisdiction

There must be personal jurisdiction over the third-party defendant for impleader to apply. Third parties joined by impleader may be served within 100 miles of where the summons was issued, even if the service is outside of the state and beyond its long-arm statute jurisdiction. Rule 4(k)(1)(B).

E. CLASS ACTIONS

In a class action, the court authorizes a single person or a small group of people to represent the interests of a larger group. Rule 23 and the Class Action Fairness Act of 2005 govern class actions.

1. Prerequisites

a. Basic requirements

Rule 23(a) establishes four requirements for representative members of a class to sue or be sued on behalf of all members of the class:

i) The class must be so numerous that joinder of all members is impracticable (**numerosity**);

ii) There must be questions of law or fact that are common to the class (**commonality**);

iii) The claims or defenses of the representatives must be typical of the class (**typicality**); and

iv) The representatives must fairly and adequately protect the interests of the class (**adequacy**).

b. Three types

In addition to the requirements of Rule 23(a), before a class action can be certified, it must fit within one of the three situations specified in Rule 23(b).

1) Risk of prejudice

Under Rule 23(b)(1), the class is maintainable if the prosecution of separate actions would create the risk that the class opponent would become subject to incompatible standards of conduct resulting from inconsistent adjudications, or if prosecution of the claims through separate actions would, as a practical matter, impair the interests of the class members.

2) Final equitable relief

Under Rule 23(b)(2), a class seeking final injunctive or declaratory relief may be certified if the class shares a general claim against the opposing party. An additional claim for monetary damages may not be sought, at least when the monetary relief is not incidental to the injunctive or declaratory relief. Moreover, a claim for individualized monetary relief is not available because a claim under Rule 23(b)(2) is available only when a single, indivisible remedy would provide relief to each class member. *Wal-Mart Stores, Inc. v. Dukes*, 564 U.S. 338 (2011) (a claim for backpay due to alleged gender discrimination could not be certified in an action seeking injunction and declaratory relief for such discrimination).

3) Common legal or factual questions

Under Rule 23(b)(3), a class can be certified if questions of law or fact that are common to the class members predominate over any questions affecting only individual members, and a class action is the superior method for bringing about a fair and efficient adjudication of the controversy. In making this determination, the court must consider, among other things:

  i) The class members' interests in individually controlling the prosecution or defense of separate actions;

  ii) The extent and nature of any litigation concerning the controversy already begun by or against class members;

  iii) The desirability or undesirability of concentrating the litigation of the claims in the particular forum; and

  iv) The likely difficulties in managing a class action.

The class representatives need not establish that success on a common question of law is likely in order for the class to be certified. *Amgen Inc. v. Conn. Ret. Plans & Tr. Funds*, 568 U.S. 455 (2013).

c. Subject matter jurisdiction

A class action must also satisfy federal subject matter jurisdiction requirements. A class action can invoke federal question jurisdiction or diversity jurisdiction.

1) Diversity jurisdiction

If diversity jurisdiction is invoked in a class action, then diversity of citizenship will be satisfied if the class representatives are diverse from the party or parties opposing the claim.

When at least one representative plaintiff of a putative class action has a claim that meets the statutory jurisdictional amount (generally it must exceed $75,000), other persons with claims that do not meet the jurisdictional amount can be made part of the class under the doctrine of supplemental jurisdiction. *Exxon Mobil Corp. v. Allapattah Servs., Inc.*, 545 U.S. 546 (2005).

d. Venue

When the class action involves a defendant class, venue is determined on the basis of the residences of the representative parties, not the residences of all the class members.

e. Class actions under the Class Action Fairness Act of 2005

The Class Action Fairness Act of 2005 (CAFA) made it easier to satisfy federal subject matter jurisdiction for certain large class actions. Subject matter jurisdiction will be met if:

i) The class action involves at least 100 members;

ii) The primary defendants are not states, state officials, or other government entities against whom the district court may be foreclosed from ordering relief;

iii) The action does not involve certain securities-related cases, or litigation concerning the internal affairs or governance of a corporation;

iv) The amount in controversy exceeds the sum or value of $5,000,000, exclusive of interest and costs; and

v) Minimum diversity exists. Minimum diversity is satisfied when any member of a class of plaintiffs is a citizen of a state different from any defendant.

1) Removals and exclusions

Under CAFA, any defendant can remove the case to federal court. If the class action claim is based only on federal securities law or corporate governance, then there is no federal jurisdiction under CAFA. This exclusion also applies to primary defendants who are government entities.

2) Protections

The benefit to filing under CAFA is the various protections afforded to the class members. The court will generally protect members against loss in consumer class actions, ensure that the settlement is fair to the members, and ensure that the settlement is equally distributed. It will also notify federal and state officials of the proposed settlement. If no notice is given, then the class member may choose not to be bound by the agreement.

3) Limitations on jurisdiction

The court is required to repudiate jurisdiction when the primary injuries were incurred in the state in which the action was filed, when more than two-thirds of the proposed plaintiffs are citizens of the state in which the case was filed, and when significant relief is sought from a defendant who is a citizen of the state in which the case was filed.

If between one-third and two-thirds of the proposed plaintiffs and the primary defendants are citizens of the state in which the case was filed, then the court is given discretion to decline jurisdiction.

2. Approval of the Court

Pursuant to Rule 23(c), at an early practicable time after a person sues or is sued as a class representative, the court must determine by order whether to certify the action as a class action. The class must meet all the previously listed requirements to be certified. If a class is certified, then the court's order must define the class and the class's claims, issues, or defenses and must appoint counsel for the class. A party may seek an appeal to the certification even though the certification is not a final judgment.

3. Notice of the Class Action

Notice of the class action is required only for class actions under Rule 23(b)(3). The notice must be the best notice that is practicable under the circumstances, including individual notice to all members who can be identified through reasonable effort. The notice must clearly and concisely state in plain, easily understood language:

   i) The nature of the action;

   ii) The definition of the class;

   iii) The class claims, issues, or defenses;

   iv) That a class member may enter an appearance through an attorney if the member so desires;

   v) That the court will exclude from the class any member who requests exclusion;

   vi) The time and manner for requesting exclusion; and

   vii) The binding effect of a class judgment on members.

Rule 23(c)(2)(B). Generally, the cost of notifying the class member is borne by the plaintiff, even in cases in which the plaintiff is likely to succeed. *Eisen v. Carlisle & Jacquelin*, 417 U.S. 156 (1974).

For class actions under Rule 23(b)(1) and (b)(2), notice of the action is at the court's discretion. The court may order that appropriate notice be given to the members of the class, which often can take the form of publication notice. Rule 23(c)(2)(A).

4. Settlement or Dismissal

Under Rule 23(e), the claims, issues, or defenses of the certified class may be voluntarily settled, compromised, or dismissed only with the approval of the court.

a. Notice

When a proposal for settlement or dismissal is made to the court, the court must direct notice in a reasonable manner to all class members who would be bound by the proposal.

b. Standard for approval

If the proposal would bind class members, then the court may approve it only after a hearing and on finding that it is fair, reasonable, and adequate. The parties seeking approval must file a statement identifying any collateral agreements made in connection with the proposal.

c. Objection by class members

Any class member may object to the proposal if it requires court approval. An objection may be withdrawn only with the court's approval. Rule 23(e)(5). Once the named representative class members reach a settlement that is approved over the objections of a class member who was not a named representative, the objecting class member's interests diverge from those of the class representatives, and the class member who objects may appeal the court's approval of a settlement. *Devlin v. Scardelletti*, 536 U.S. 1 (2002); *Marino v. Ortiz*, 484 U.S. 301 (1988).

d. Second opt-out opportunity

If a class action was certified under Rule 23(b)(3), the court may refuse to approve of the settlement unless class members are given a second opportunity to "opt out" of the litigation and proceed on their own. Rule 23(e)(4). A class member who fails to opt out is bound by the settlement.

5. Judgment

In general, a valid judgment binds all members of the class. In a class action certified under Rule 23(b)(3), a valid judgment does not bind those class members who opted out of the lawsuit; a class member who does not opt out, however, is bound by the judgment, even when that class member did not have minimum contacts with the forum state. *Phillips Petroleum Co. v. Shutts*, 472 U.S. 797 (1985).

F. SHAREHOLDER DERIVATIVE SUITS

A shareholder may bring a derivative action on behalf of the corporation to enforce a right of the corporation that the corporation has failed to enforce. While not generally subject to the Rules with regard to a class action, the shareholder must represent the shareholders of the corporation fairly and adequately. The shareholder is bound to plead with particularity that he made a demand on the directors, and, if state law requires, also made a demand on the shareholders, or if a demand is not made, he must state why. He must also assert his status as a shareholder at the time the transaction occurred or that he subsequently gained this status by operation of law (e.g., by inheritance). Finally, he must allege that the action is not a collusive effort to impart jurisdiction on the court. Rule 23.1.

VII. PRETRIAL PROCEDURE AND DISCOVERY

A. MANDATORY DISCLOSURES

Rule 26(a) requires the parties, three times prior to trial, to make certain disclosures: (i) initial disclosures, (ii) disclosures of expert testimony 90 days before trial, and (iii) pretrial disclosures 30 days before trial. These disclosures are mandatory and must be made even if an opposing party does not ask for such information. Unless otherwise ordered by the court, the disclosures must be in writing, signed, and served.

1. Initial Disclosures

a. In general

Under Rule 26(a)(1), unless otherwise agreed by stipulation or ordered by the court, each party must provide to the other parties:

i) The name and, if known, address and telephone number of each individual likely to have discoverable information, along with the subjects of that information that the disclosing party may use to support its claims or defenses, unless the use would be solely for purposes of impeachment;

ii) A copy, or a description by category and location, of all documents, electronically stored information, and tangible things that the disclosing party has in its possession, custody, or control and may use to support its claims or defenses, unless the use would be solely for impeachment;

iii) A computation of each category of damages claimed by the disclosing party, who must also make available for inspection and copying the documents or other evidentiary material on which each computation is based, including materials bearing on the nature and extent of injury, unless privileged or protected from disclosure; and

iv) For inspection and copying, any insurance agreement under which an insurance business may be liable to satisfy all or part of a possible judgment in the action or to indemnify or reimburse for payments made to satisfy the judgment.

Pursuant to Rule 26(a)(1)(E), a party must make its initial disclosures based on the information that is then reasonably available to it. A party is not excused from making its disclosures because it has not fully investigated the case, because it challenges the sufficiency of another party's disclosures, or because another party has not made its disclosures.

b. Exceptions

Rule 26(a)(1)(B) excludes nine categories of proceedings from the initial disclosure requirements:

i) Actions for review on an administrative record;

ii) Forfeiture actions in rem arising from a federal statute;

iii) Petitions for habeas corpus or any other proceeding to challenge a criminal conviction or sentence;

iv) Actions brought without an attorney by a person in the custody of the United States, a state, or a state subdivision;

v) Actions to enforce or quash an administrative summons or subpoena;

vi) Actions by the United States to recover benefit payments;

vii) Actions by the United States to collect on a student loan guaranteed by the United States;

viii) Proceedings that are ancillary to proceedings in another court; and

ix) Actions to enforce an arbitration award.

c. Time for initial disclosures

A party must make the initial disclosures required by Rule 26(a)(1) at or within 14 days after the parties' Rule 26(f) conference (*see* § VII.C. Discovery Conference, *infra*), unless a different time is set by stipulation or court order.

2. Disclosure of Expert Testimony

a. In general

Rule 26(a)(2) requires parties to disclose the identities of persons who may testify as expert witnesses and to produce an expert report for each such witness. The expert report must be prepared and signed by the expert and contain:

i) A complete statement of and basis for all opinions to be expressed;

ii) The facts or data considered by the expert in forming the opinions;

iii) Any exhibits used as support for or as a summary of the opinions;

iv) The qualifications of the expert;

v) A listing of all publications authored by the expert in the past 10 years;

vi) The expert's compensation; and

vii) A list of all other cases in which the expert has testified at trial or deposition in the past four years.

b. Time to disclose expert testimony

A party must make these disclosures at the times and in the sequence that the court orders, but absent a stipulation or court order, the disclosures must be made at least 90 days before the date set for trial or for the case to be ready for trial. If the evidence is intended solely to contradict or rebut the opposing party's expert evidence on the same subject matter, then disclosure must be made within 30 days after the other party's disclosure. Rule 26(a)(2)(D).

c. Supplementing the disclosure

The parties must supplement these disclosures when required under Rule 26(e). (*See* § VII.B.7. Supplementation, *infra*.) For an expert whose report must be disclosed, the party's duty to supplement extends both to information included in the report and to information given during the expert's deposition. Any additions or changes to this information must be disclosed by the time that the party's pretrial disclosures under Rule 26(a)(3) are due.

3. Pretrial Disclosures

a. In general

Pursuant to Rule 26(a)(3)(A), in addition to the initial and expert disclosures, the parties must make certain disclosures regarding evidence that they may present at trial other than for impeachment purposes. They must file with the court:

i) The name and, if not previously provided, the address and telephone number of each witness, separately identifying those the party expects to present and those it may call if the need arises;

ii) The designation of those witnesses whose testimony the party expects to present by deposition and, if not taken stenographically, a transcript of the pertinent parts of the deposition; and

iii) An identification of each document or other exhibit, including summaries of other evidence, separately identifying those items the party expects to offer and those it may offer if the need arises.

b. Time for pretrial disclosures

Under Rule 26(a)(3)(B), unless the court orders otherwise, these disclosures must be made at least 30 days before trial.

c. Objections

Within 14 days after the disclosures are made, unless the court sets a different time, a party may serve and promptly file objections to the use of the depositions at trial and to the admissibility of disclosed documents and exhibits. If an objection is not made at this point, then it will be waived, unless excused by the court for good cause or unless the objection relates to relevancy, prejudice, or confusion pursuant to Rules 402 and 403 of the Federal Rules of Evidence. Rule 26(a)(3)(B).

B. DISCOVERY SCOPE AND LIMITS

In addition to obtaining information under the mandatory disclosure rules, parties may use a variety of discovery methods set forth in Rules 27–36 and discussed as follows. Rule 26 sets forth rules establishing the scope and limitations of such discovery.

1. **Scope**

   a. **In general**

   Under Rule 26(b)(1), discovery is generally permitted with regard to any non-privileged matter relevant to any party's claim or defense in the action and proportional to the needs of the case, considering the importance of the issues at stake in the action, the amount in controversy, the parties' relative access to relevant information, the parties' resources, the importance of the discovery in resolving the issue, and whether the burden or expense of the proposed discovery outweighs its likely benefit.

   b. **Relevance**

   Information within the scope of discovery need not be admissible in evidence to be discoverable. The test is whether the information sought is relevant to any party's claim or defense.

   c. **Privilege**

   Privileged information is not discoverable. In federal question cases, privileges are determined under federal common law, pursuant to Rule 501 of the Federal Rules of Evidence. In diversity or supplemental claims in which a state's substantive laws apply, that state's law determines whether a privilege applies.

2. **Limitations on Discovery**

   a. **Timing**

   In general, a party may not seek discovery until after the discovery conference pursuant to Rule 26(f). A party may seek discovery before the discovery conference if it is ordered by the court, stipulated by the parties, or authorized by a specific rule, or if the proceeding is exempt from initial disclosures. Rule 26(d).

   b. **Required limitations**

   On motion or on its own, the court is required to limit the frequency or extent of discovery otherwise allowed by the rules if it determines that:

   i) The discovery sought is unreasonably cumulative or can be obtained from some other source that is more convenient or less expensive;

   ii) The party seeking discovery has had ample opportunity to obtain the information by discovery in the action; or

   iii) The proposed discovery is outside the scope permitted by Rule 26(b)(1) (not relevant and proportional).

   When discovery is challenged, the court must weigh the party's interests in seeking discovery against the privacy interests of the party resisting discovery. *Eckstein Marine Serv., Inc. v. M/V Basin Pride*, 168 F.R.D. 38 (W.D. La. 1996). For example, discovery with respect to personnel records may be limited due to privacy concerns. *Gehring v. Case Corp.*, 43 F.3d 340 (7th Cir. 1994).

   c. **Discretion to alter limits**

   The court may alter the limits in the rules as to the number of depositions, interrogatories, or requests for admission, or on the length of oral depositions.

   d. **Limitations on electronically stored information**

   A party is not required to provide discovery of electronically stored information from sources that the party identifies as not reasonably accessible because of undue burden or cost. If challenged, the party will have the burden to show the undue burden and cost. Even if undue burden and cost is shown, the court may still order such discovery if the requesting party shows good cause. Rule 26(b)(2)(B). Moreover, the requesting party may specify the form in which the documents should be produced.

3. Trial Preparation Materials

Rule 26(b)(3) provides limited protection for otherwise discoverable trial preparation materials or attorneys' work product. In general, a party may not discover documents and tangible things that are prepared in anticipation of litigation or for trial by or for another party or its representative.

Such materials will be subject to discovery, however, if the party shows that it has substantial need for the materials to prepare its case and cannot, without undue hardship, obtain a substantial equivalent by other means. If the court orders discovery of trial preparation materials, Rule 26(b)(3)(B) requires the court to protect against disclosure of the mental impressions, conclusions, opinions, or legal theories of a party's attorney or other representative concerning the litigation.

4. Experts

Under Rule 26(b)(4)(A), a party is entitled to depose any expert witness of an opposing party whose opinions may be presented at trial. Rule 26(b)(3) protects drafts of any expert report or disclosure required under Rule 26(a)(2). *See* § VII.A.2. Disclosure of Expert Testimony, *supra*. Any communications between the party's attorney and an expert witness who is required to provide a report are also protected, except to the extent that the communications (i) relate to the expert's compensation, (ii) identify facts or data that the party's attorney provided and that the expert considered in forming his opinion, or (iii) identify assumptions that the party's attorney provided and the expert relied upon.

If the expert was retained or specially employed by another party in anticipation of litigation or to prepare for trial but is not expected to be called as a witness, then discovery is permitted only on a showing of exceptional circumstances under which it is impracticable for the party to obtain facts or opinions on the same subject by other means. Rule 26(b)(4)(D).

A report of an examining physician who is not expected to testify, however, can be obtained as provided under Rule 35(b).

5. Claims of Privilege

Under Rule 26(b)(5)(A), whenever a party withholds information on the basis of a privilege, such as the attorney-work-product privilege, the party must expressly state the claim of privilege and describe the materials or communications not produced in a manner that will enable other parties to assess the applicability of the privilege or protection.

6. Signature Requirement and Certification

Each initial or pretrial disclosure, as well as each discovery request, response, or objection, must be signed by at least one attorney of record, or by the party personally if unrepresented. By signing, the attorney or party certifies that to the best of the person's knowledge, information, and belief formed after a reasonable inquiry:

i) With respect to a disclosure, it is complete and correct as of the time it is made; and

ii) With respect to a discovery request, response, or objection, it is:

a) Consistent with the rules and warranted by existing law or by a nonfrivolous argument for extending, modifying, or reversing existing law, or for establishing new law;

b) Not interposed for any improper purpose, such as to harass, cause unnecessary delay, or needlessly increase the cost of litigation; and

c) Neither unreasonable nor unduly burdensome or expensive, considering the needs of the case, prior discovery in the case, the amount in controversy, and the importance of the issues at stake in the action.

If a certification violates this rule without substantial justification, the court, on motion or on its own, must impose an appropriate sanction on the signer, the party on whose behalf the signer was acting, or both. The sanction may include an order to pay the reasonable expenses, including attorney's fees, caused by the violation. Rule 26(g).

7. Protective Orders

Under Rule 26(c), the court may, for good cause, enter orders to protect parties and other persons from annoyance, embarrassment, oppression, or undue burden or expense resulting from discovery. For example, a party may seek a court order limiting the time and manner of conducting a physical examination, and a nonparty who is served with a subpoena to attend a deposition may, by filing a motion to quash the subpoena, seek a court order to that effect.

8. Supplementation

Pursuant to Rule 26(e)(1)(A), if a party who has made a required disclosure or responded to an interrogatory, a request for production, or a request for admission learns that the disclosure or response is materially incomplete or incorrect, then the party is required to supplement or correct the disclosure or response in a timely manner.

There is no duty to supplement or correct if such information has otherwise been made known to the other parties in discovery or in writing.

As to an expert whose report must be disclosed under Rule 26(a)(2)(B), the party's duty to supplement extends both to information included in the expert's report and to information given during the expert's deposition. Rule 26(e)(2).

C. DISCOVERY CONFERENCE

1. Rule 26(f)

Under Rule 26(f), except in a proceeding exempted from the initial-disclosure rules or if the court orders otherwise, the parties must confer as soon as is practicable, and in any event at least 21 days before a scheduling conference is to be held or a scheduling order is due under Rule 16(b) (*see* § VII.G. Pretrial Conferences, *infra*) to:

i) Consider the nature and basis of their claims and defenses and the possibilities for promptly settling or resolving the case;

ii) Make or arrange for the automatic disclosures required by Rule 26(a)(1);

iii) Discuss any issues about preserving discoverable information; and

iv) Develop a proposed discovery plan.

The attorneys of record and all unrepresented parties who have appeared in the case are jointly responsible for arranging the conference, for attempting in good faith to agree on the proposed discovery plan, and for submitting to the court within 14 days after the conference a written report outlining the plan.

The discovery plan must state:

i) The parties' views and proposals on the discovery that may be needed in the case;

ii) The schedule for such discovery;

iii) Any modifications and limits to the scope of the parties' required disclosures and discovery;

iv) Any issues about electronically stored information or privilege; and

v) Any scheduling or protective order that should be entered by the court.

The discovery plan must also indicate when the initial automatic disclosures were or are to be made. The various other discovery devices are not employed until the scope and schedule of discovery are set in this initial conference.

In addition, the court may decide to hold a pretrial conference if it believes that such a conference will foster a settlement and expedite the trial. An order must be entered after the pretrial conference is held.

2. Failure to Participate in the Framing of the Discovery Plan

Pursuant to Rule 37(f), if a party or her attorney fails to participate in good faith in the development and submission of a proposed discovery plan as required by Rule 26(f), then the court may, after providing an opportunity for a hearing, order the party or attorney to pay the reasonable expenses, including attorney's fees, incurred as a result of such failure.

D. DISCOVERY DEVICES

1. Depositions

Depositions are widely used and can take two forms: (i) oral depositions, which are common to almost all litigation in federal court, and (ii) written depositions, which are rarely used.

a. Oral depositions

1) When an oral deposition may be taken

Under Rule 30, a party may take the deposition of any party or nonparty witness at any time after the discovery conference pursuant to Rule 26(f).

Without leave of the court, the plaintiffs, the defendants, and the third-party defendants, each as a group, are limited to 10 depositions by oral or written examination.

Unless the parties agree to the deposition, leave of the court must be obtained to:

i) Exceed the 10-deposition limitation;

ii) Depose a witness a second time; or

iii) Depose a person before the discovery conference under Rule 26(f).

2) Notice of deposition

A party who seeks an oral deposition of a person must give reasonable written notice to every other party, stating the time and place of the deposition and, if known, the deponent's name and address.

Notice of deposition is all that is needed to compel attendance by any party, even a party who is beyond the reach of the court's subpoena power. To compel attendance by a nonparty, a subpoena must be served. Rule 30(b).

3) Deposing a corporation, partnership, association, or government entity

When deposing a corporation, partnership, association, or government entity, Rule 30(b)(6) states that the notice must describe with reasonable particularity the areas of inquiry, and it must state that the named entity has the duty to designate a representative with respect to the designated areas of inquiry. The named entity must then designate one or more officers, directors, managing agents, or other persons who consent to testify on the entity's behalf with regard to those areas.

4) Conducting an oral deposition

A deposition must be conducted before an officer who is appointed or designated under Rule 28 to administer oaths and take testimony, unless the parties agree otherwise.

By stipulation of the parties or by court order, a deposition may be taken by telephonic or other remote electronic means.

 i) Examination of the deponent may proceed as permitted at trial under the Federal Rules of Evidence, except that cross-examination is not limited to matters raised on direct examination. Rule 30(c).

 ii) The deponent is to be placed under oath, and the testimony is to be recorded either by stenographic or electronic means. Rule 30(b).

 iii) Any objections are to be made on the record, but the examination still proceeds. The testimony is taken subject to any objection. Rule 30(c)(2).

 iv) A person may instruct the deponent not to answer only when necessary to preserve a privilege, to enforce a limitation ordered by the court, or to present a motion to terminate or limit the examination. Rule 30(c)(2).

Under Rule 30(d)(1), a deposition is limited to one day of seven hours, unless the parties agree otherwise or the court orders otherwise. The court must allow additional time if needed to fairly examine the deponent, or if the deposition is impeded or delayed by a deponent, another person, or any other circumstance.

5) Motion to terminate or limit an oral deposition

At any time during an oral deposition, the deponent or a party may move to terminate or limit such deposition on the ground that it is being conducted in bad faith or in a manner that unreasonably annoys, embarrasses, or oppresses the deponent or party. Rule 30(d)(3)(A).

6) Failure to attend a deposition

Pursuant to Rule 30(g), if a party given notice to attend a deposition attends expecting such deposition, and the noticing party fails to attend or proceed with the deposition, then the noticing party is subject to a court order requiring payment of reasonable expenses to the other party.

b. Written depositions

Pursuant to Rule 31, depositions may be taken by providing written questions to the deponent. The same rules regarding leave of the court and deposing an organization that apply to oral depositions apply to written ones. They are as follows:

    i) To take a written deposition, the deposing party must serve the questions and a notice, identifying the deponent and the officer before whom the deposition will be taken, to all other parties. Rule 31(a)(3).

    ii) The other parties may then serve cross-questions, redirect questions, and re-cross questions on all other parties. Rule 31(a)(5).

    iii) The deposing party serves the notice and all questions on the officer designated in the notice. Rule 31(b).

    iv) The officer asks the written questions of the deponent and records the deponent's oral responses stenographically or by electronic means. *Id.*

c. Irregularities in depositions

Certain errors and irregularities in depositions are waived if not objected to in a timely manner. There must be a written objection promptly served on the party giving notice when there are irregularities with the notice and its service. A seasonable objection must be made if there are errors in the manner of taking the deposition, while a motion to suppress is required when there are errors related to the signing, certification, and transmittal of depositions. Finally, in noting errors as to the form of the written questions, the party submitting the questions should receive notice within five days after service of the last questions authorized.

2. Interrogatories

a. Availability

Pursuant to Rule 33(a), any party may serve no more than 25 written interrogatories on any other party. Interrogatories may not be used on nonparty witnesses.

b. Scope

Pursuant to Rule 33(a)(2), interrogatories may relate to any matters permitted to be inquired into under Rule 26(b)(1) (i.e., non-privileged matters relevant to any party's claim or defense and proportional to the needs of the case). An interrogatory is not objectionable merely because it asks for an opinion or contention that relates to fact or the application of law to fact, but the court may order that the interrogatory need not be answered until designated discovery is complete, or until a pretrial conference or some other time.

c. Answers and objections

Under Rule 33(b)(1), the interrogatories must be answered by the party to whom they are directed or, if that party is a corporation, partnership, association, or government entity, by any officer or agent, who must furnish the information available to the party.

Each interrogatory must be answered fully and separately under oath, unless the responding party objects to the interrogatory. The grounds for objecting to an interrogatory must be stated with specificity. Any ground not stated in a timely objection is deemed waived, unless the court, for good cause, excuses the failure. Rule 33(b)(2), (3).

The responding party must serve its answers and any objections within 30 days after being served with the interrogatories. The court may order, or the parties may stipulate to, a shorter or longer time. Rule 33(b)(4).

The person who makes the answers must sign them, and the attorney who objects must sign any objections. Rule 33(b)(5).

d. Option to produce business records

Under Rule 33(d), if the answer to an interrogatory may be ascertained from the business records (including electronically stored information) or summation of the business records of the responding party, and the burden of deriving the answers is substantially the same for the party serving the interrogatories as for the responding party, then the responding party may answer the interrogatory by specifying the records from which the answer may be derived and providing the party who served the interrogatories with an opportunity to examine and copy such records.

3. Requests to Produce Documents and Inspect Land

a. In general

Under Rule 34(a)(1), a party may serve on any other party a request to produce and to permit the requesting party or its representative to inspect, copy, test, or sample any of the following items in the responding party's possession, custody, or control:

   i) Any designated documents or electronically stored information (including writings, drawings, graphs, charts, photographs, sound recordings, images, and other data or data compilations) stored in any medium from which information can be obtained either directly or, if necessary, after translation by the responding party into a reasonably usable form; or

   ii) Any designated tangible things.

A party may also serve a request to enter onto another party's land to inspect, measure, survey, photograph, test, or sample the property or a designated object or operation on the property, if relevant to the action. Rule 34(a)(2).

Although these requests may be directed only to other parties, nonparties may be compelled to produce documents and other things or submit to an inspection pursuant to a subpoena served under Rule 45. Rule 34(c).

b. Contents of the request

Pursuant to Rule 34(b)(1), the request:

   i) Must describe with reasonable particularity each item or category of items to be inspected;

   ii) Must specify a reasonable time, place, and manner for the inspection and for performing the related acts; and

   iii) May specify the form or forms in which electronically stored information is to be produced.

c. Responses and objections

The party to whom the request is directed must respond in writing within 30 days after being served or within 30 days after the parties' first Rule 26(f) conference, if the request was served prior to that conference, unless a shorter or longer time is stipulated by the parties or ordered by the court. If a party fails to respond to a document request or to allow inspection, or objects to a request, then the requesting party may move to compel under Rule 37(a). Rule 34(b)(2)(A). The responding party may state that it will produce copies of documents or electronically stored information instead of permitting inspection. The production must be completed no later than the time for inspection specified in the request or another reasonable time specified in the response. Rule 34(b)(2)(B).

With regard to electronically stored information, if a request does not specify a form for its production, then a party must produce it in a form or forms in which it is ordinarily maintained or in a reasonably usable form or forms. A party need not produce the same electronically stored information in more than one form. Rule 34(b)(2)(E).

4. Physical and Mental Exams

a. In general

Under Rule 35(a), if the mental or physical condition (including blood group) of a party or a person in the legal custody or control of a party is in controversy, then the court may order such person to submit to a physical or mental examination by a "suitably licensed or certified examiner."

b. Procedure

Such an order may be made only upon motion, for good cause shown, and the person to be examined and all parties must be given prior notice specifying the time, place, conditions, and scope of the examination and the identity of the examiner. Rule 35(a)(2).

A "suitably licensed or certified examiner" need not be a physician and can include others licensed to report on physical or mental conditions, including dentists or psychologists.

c. The examiner's report

On request by the party or person examined, the party who requested the examination must provide a copy of the examiner's written report, including results of all tests, diagnoses, and conclusions, as well as any reports of earlier examinations of the same condition. If the examiner refuses to make a report, then the examiner's testimony may be excluded at trial. Rule 35(b).

d. Other examinations

After delivery of the examiner's report, a party who was examined must provide the party who moved for the examination, on request, a report of all other previous or subsequent examinations of the same condition in that party's custody or control. Rule 35(b)(3).

If the party who was examined obtains the report of the examination or conducts a deposition of the examiner, then the party waives any privilege it may have regarding the testimony of any other person who has examined or thereafter examines the party with respect to the same condition. Rule 35(b)(4).

5. Requests for Admission

a. In general

Under Rule 36, a party may serve upon any other party a written request for the admission of any relevant, non-privileged matters discoverable under Rule 26. The requested matters may relate to statements or opinions of fact or to the application of law to fact, including the genuineness of any documents described in the request. Rule 36(a)(1). Each matter for which an admission is requested must be set forth separately. A request to admit the genuineness of a document must be accompanied by a copy of the document unless it is, or has been, otherwise furnished or made available for inspection and copying. Rule 36(a)(2).

b. Responses and objections

A matter will be admitted unless, within 30 days after being served, the party to whom the request is directed serves on the requesting party a written answer or objection addressed to the matter and signed by the party or her attorney. Rule 36(a)(3).

If a matter is not admitted, then the answer must specifically deny it or state in detail why the answering party cannot truthfully admit or deny it. A denial must fairly respond to the substance of the matter, and when good faith requires that a party qualify an answer or deny only a part of a matter, the answer must specify the part admitted and qualify or deny the rest. Rule 36(a)(4).

An answering party may assert lack of knowledge or information as a reason for failing to admit or deny only if the party states that he has made a reasonable inquiry and that the information he knows or can readily obtain is not sufficient to enable him to admit or deny. *Id.*

c. Effect of an admission

A matter admitted under Rule 36 is conclusively established unless the court, on motion, permits the admission to be withdrawn or amended. The court may permit such withdrawal or amendment if (i) doing so would promote the presentation of the merits of the action, and (ii) the court finds that it would not prejudice the requesting party in maintaining or defending the action on the merits. Rule 36(b).

An admission under Rule 36 is an admission only in the pending action and cannot be used against the party in any other proceeding. *Id.*

E. USE OF DISCOVERY AT TRIAL

Information gathered through the use of discovery devices is not automatically admissible as evidence at trial. To be admissible, the information must comply with the evidentiary rules.

1. Use of Depositions

a. At trial

Depositions may be used by a party to impeach the testimony of the deponent as a witness or for any other purpose permitted by the Federal Rules of Evidence. Rule 32(a)(2). Pursuant to Rule 32(a)(3), an adverse party may use for any purpose the deposition of a party or a person who, when deposed, was the party's officer, director, managing agent, or designated deponent.

In addition, a party may use for any purpose the deposition of a witness, whether or not a party, if the court finds that:

  i) The witness is dead;

  ii) The witness is more than 100 miles from the trial or is outside the United States, unless it appears that the witness's absence was procured by the party offering the deposition;

  iii) The witness cannot attend or testify because of age, illness, infirmity, or imprisonment;

iv) The party offering the deposition could not procure the witness's attendance by subpoena; or

v) On motion and notice, exceptional circumstances make it desirable in the interest of justice to permit the deposition to be used.

Rule 32(a)(4). If admissible, a deposition may generally be offered against any party who was present or represented at the deposition or had reasonable notice of it.

b. Depositions taken in an earlier action involving the same matter and parties

A deposition lawfully taken and, if required, filed in any federal- or state-court action may be used in a later action involving the same subject matter between the same parties, or their representatives or successors in interest, to the same extent as if taken in the later action. Rule 32(a)(8).

c. Objections to the admissibility of depositions

Pursuant to Rule 32(b), an objection to the admission of any deposition testimony that would be inadmissible if the witness were present and testifying may generally be made at the time the deposition is offered at a hearing or trial.

2. Answers to Interrogatories

Under Rule 33(c), an answer to an interrogatory may be used to the extent allowed by Federal Rule of Evidence 801(d)(2), whereby a party's answer will generally constitute a party admission. An interrogatory answer could, however, constitute hearsay if offered against another party.

F. ENFORCEMENT

1. Motion to Compel

a. In general

If a party fails to make the automatic disclosures required by Rule 26(a) or fails to respond to discovery that has been properly served, then the party seeking the information may move to compel such disclosure or discovery. An evasive or incomplete disclosure, answer, or response is treated as a failure to disclose, answer, or respond. Rule 37(a).

b. Procedure

A motion to compel must be served on all parties and be accompanied by a certificate that the movant has in good faith conferred or attempted to confer with the opposing party in an effort to obtain the disclosure or secure the information or material without court action. Rule 37(a)(1).

If the subject of the motion to compel is a party, then the motion must be filed with the court in which the action is pending. If the subject of the motion is a nonparty who was subpoenaed under Rule 45, then the motion must be filed in the court that issued the subpoena. Rule 37(a)(2).

c. Fees and expenses

1) If the motion is granted

A successful movant is entitled to recover her reasonable expenses incurred in connection with the motion, including reasonable attorney's fees. The court may order the opposing party, his attorney who advised the refusal of disclosure or discovery, or both to pay the expenses. Rule 37(a)(5)(A).

Expenses cannot be awarded if:

i)   The movant failed to make a good-faith effort to secure the information before filing the motion;

ii) The opposing party demonstrates that his nondisclosure, response, or objection was substantially justified; or

iii) Other circumstances render an award of expenses unjust.

2) If the motion is denied

If the motion to compel is denied and the court determines that the motion was made without substantial justification, then the court must, after providing an opportunity to be heard, require the movant, the attorney filing the motion, or both to pay the party or deponent who opposed the motion her reasonable expenses incurred in opposing the motion, including attorney's fees. Rule 37(a)(5)(B).

3) If the motion is granted in part and denied in part

If the motion is granted in part and denied in part, then the court may apportion fees in its discretion, after providing an opportunity for the parties to be heard. Rule 37(a)(5)(C).

2. Sanctions

a. Failure to comply with a court order

If a party fails to obey a court order regarding discovery, then the court may impose any of the following sanctions pursuant to Rule 37(b)(2):

i)   Directing that the matters addressed in the order or other facts be taken as established for the purposes of the action;

ii)   Prohibiting the disobedient party from supporting or opposing designated claims or defenses, or from introducing designated matters in evidence;

iii) Striking pleadings in whole or in part;

iv)   Staying further proceedings until the order is obeyed;

v)   Dismissing the action in whole or in part;

vi)   Rendering a default judgment against the disobedient party; and

vii) Treating as contempt of court the failure to obey any order, except an order to submit to a physical or mental examination.

The list of sanctions in Rule 37(b)(2) is not exhaustive. The court may order any sanction that is "just." Instead of, or in addition to, such sanctions, the court may also require the disobedient party, his attorney, or both to pay the movant's reasonable expenses, including attorney's fees incurred as a result of the failure to comply, except when the failure was substantially justified or imposition of fees would be unjust. Rule 37(b)(2)(C).

b. Failure to make automatic disclosures

Under Rule 37(c)(1), if a party fails to make or supplement its automatic disclosures as required by Rules 26(a) and (e), then the party will not be permitted to use the documents or witnesses that were not disclosed unless the nondisclosure was substantially justified or was harmless.

This rule applies to the use of such evidence at trial and for motions and hearings, but it does not apply to the use of such evidence for impeachment purposes, because Rule 26(a) does not require disclosure of impeachment evidence or witnesses.

c. **Failure to admit under Rule 36**

Pursuant to Rule 37(c)(2), when a party fails to admit a matter requested under Rule 36 and another party proves the matter to be true at trial, the party proving the matter can move for the award of reasonable expenses, including reasonable attorney's fees, incurred in proving the matter.

d. **Failure of a party to attend her own deposition, serve answers to interrogatories, or respond to a request for inspection**

Under Rule 37(d)(1)(A)(i), if a party fails to appear at her own deposition after being properly notified, then the court may impose sanctions. A failure to appear will not be excused on the ground that the discovery sought was objectionable, unless the party failing to act has a pending motion for a protective order.

The court may also impose sanctions if a party fails to answer or object to properly served interrogatories under Rule 33 or fails to serve a written response to a properly served request for the production of documents or other things under Rule 34. Rule 37(d)(1)(A)(ii). A party moving for sanctions under such circumstances must certify that she conferred with or attempted to confer with the opposing party in good faith in an effort to obtain a response without court action. Rule 37(d)(1)(B).

e. **Electronically stored information**

If electronically stored information that should have been preserved in the anticipation or conduct of litigation is lost because a party failed to take reasonable steps to preserve it, and it cannot be restored or replaced through additional discovery, then the court: (i) upon finding prejudice to another party, may order measures no greater than necessary to cure the prejudice, or (ii) upon finding that the party acted with the intent to deprive another party of the information, may presume the lost information was unfavorable to the party, instruct the jury that it may or must presume the information was unfavorable, or dismiss the action or enter a default judgment. Rule 37(e).

f. **"Abuse of discretion" review standard**

Sanctions are subject to review under the "abuse of discretion" standard. Generally, the harshest sanctions—dismissal of the action and entry of a default judgment—are reserved for misconduct that is serious, repeated, contumacious, extreme, or inexcusable. Usually, a court should impose lesser sanctions before meting out more severe ones. *See Bachier-Ortiz v. Colon-Mendoza*, 331 F.3d 193 (1st Cir. 2003).

G. PRETRIAL CONFERENCES

Under Rule 16(a), the court may direct counsel and unrepresented parties to appear for pretrial conferences for such purposes as expediting disposition of the action, effective case management, and facilitating settlement. The court may require that a party or its representative be present or reasonably available by telephone or by more sophisticated electronic means to consider possible settlement. If counsel or a party fails to appear, fails to participate in good faith, or fails to obey a pretrial conference order, then the court may generally impose the same sanctions as those permitted for failure of a party to comply with a discovery order, including contempt of court or dismissal of an action (*see* § VII.F.2. Sanctions, *supra*). Dismissal of an action is a severe sanction, and generally it is appropriate only when a party's conduct is serious, repeated, extreme, and otherwise inexcusable.

H. ADJUDICATION WITHOUT TRIAL

1. Dismissal

Rule 41 sets forth the procedure for obtaining dismissal of a complaint, counterclaim, cross-claim, or third-party claim. Dismissal can be voluntary or involuntary under the rule.

a. Voluntary

1) By filing notice or by stipulation of the parties

Pursuant to Rule 41(a)(1)(A), a plaintiff may dismiss an action without leave of the court by filing a notice of dismissal at any time before the opposing party serves either an answer or a motion for summary judgment or by filing a stipulation of dismissal signed by all parties who have appeared in the action.

Unless otherwise stated in the notice or stipulation, the voluntary dismissal will be without prejudice. If, however, a plaintiff had dismissed a prior action, whether a state or federal action, based on the same claim, then the dismissal is with prejudice. This is referred to as the "two-dismissal" rule. Rule 41(a)(1)(B).

2) By motion and court order

Except as provided previously, an action may be dismissed at the plaintiff's request only by court order, on terms that the court considers proper. Rule 41(a)(2).

A voluntary dismissal by court order is without prejudice unless the order states otherwise. However, when a plaintiff moves for dismissal without prejudice under Rule 41(a)(2), the decision to dismiss with or without prejudice is left to the discretion of the court, and voluntary dismissal without prejudice is not a matter of right. *See Mobil Oil Corp. v. Advanced Envtl. Recycling Techs., Inc.*, 203 F.R.D. 156 (D. Del. 2001); *Jaskot v. Brown*, 167 F.R.D. 372 (S.D.N.Y. 1996).

The purpose of Rule 41(a)(2) is primarily to prevent voluntary dismissals that unfairly affect the defendant. *See Mobil Oil Corp. v. Advanced Envtl. Recycling Techs., Inc.*, 203 F.R.D. 156 (D. Del. 2001); *see also Chess v. Nieport*, 386 F. Supp. 312 (E.D. Cal. 1974). If voluntary dismissal under Rule 41(a)(2) would unfairly affect the defendant, then the court may respond to a Rule 41(a)(2) motion to dismiss with an order dismissing the action with prejudice. However, if the court intends to do so, it must provide the plaintiff with notice of its intention and an opportunity to respond or withdraw the motion. *Mich. Surgery Inv., LLC v. Arman*, 627 F.3d 572 (6th Cir. 2010); *Jaramillo v. Burkhart*, 59 F.3d 78 (8th Cir. 1995); *Andes v. Versant Corp.*, 788 F.2d 1033 (4th Cir. 1986).

The court may consider any relevant factors in determining whether the requested voluntary dismissal by court order would prejudice the defendant. These factors may include: (i) the defendant's efforts and funds expended toward preparing for trial, (ii) the plaintiff's undue delay or lack of diligence in prosecuting or moving to dismiss the action, (iii) the plaintiff's explanation for needing to dismiss, (iv) any duplicative expenses involved in a likely second suit, (v) whether dismissal is sought to avoid an adverse determination on the merits or to correct a failure to pursue the case in a timely fashion, (vi) whether dismissal will result in the loss of beneficial discovery rulings on behalf of the defendant, and (vii) whether the claim appears to be vexatious, frivolous, groundless, or brought in bad faith. If the dismissal by an order of the court under Rule 41(a)(2) is with prejudice, then the dismissal operates as an adjudication on the merits.

The "two-dismissal" rule is not generally implicated when the first dismissal is by an order of the court under Rule 41(a)(2) because a dismissal obtained under Rule 41(a)(2) does not pose the same danger of abuse or harassment as does a unilateral Rule 41(a)(1) dismissal by the plaintiff's notice, and because the court has discretion to determine whether a Rule 41(a)(2) dismissal will be with or without prejudice or conditions. *ASX Inv. Corp. v. Newton*, 183 F.3d 1265 (11th Cir. 1999); *see In re Estate of Migliaccio*, 436 F. Supp. 2d 1095 (C.D. Cal. 2006). However, when a plaintiff has a history of vexatiously delaying the adjudication of dispositive issues by interposing meritless motions or voluntary dismissals of the same claims, courts often find that a voluntary dismissal would unfairly affect the defendant and choose to dismiss the case with prejudice to prevent continued vexatious litigation and impermissible forum-shopping. *See, e.g., Russell-Brown v. Jerry*, 270 F.R.D. 654 (N.D. Fla. 2010).

3) Counterclaim, cross-claim, or third-party claim

A voluntary dismissal of a counterclaim, cross-claim, or third-party claim must be made before a responsive pleading is served or, if there is no responsive pleading, before evidence is introduced at a hearing or trial.

b. Involuntary

Under Rule 41(b), if the plaintiff fails to prosecute or to comply with the Rules or a court order, then a defendant may move to dismiss the action or any claim against him.

Unless the court's dismissal order specifies otherwise, a dismissal under Rule 41(b) is with prejudice and operates as an adjudication on the merits. A dismissal based on a lack of jurisdiction, improper venue, or failure to join an indispensable party under Rule 19, however, does not operate as an adjudication on the merits.

2. Default and Default Judgment

a. Standard

When a party has failed to plead or otherwise defend an action and that failure is shown by affidavit or otherwise, the court clerk must enter the party's default. Rule 55(a). Once a default is entered against a party, the plaintiff may seek a default judgment. If the party against whom a default judgment is sought has appeared personally or by a representative, that party or its representative must be served with written notice of the application at least seven days before the hearing. If the relief sought is a sum certain or an amount that can be made certain by computation, the default judgment can generally be entered by the court clerk on the plaintiff's request accompanied by an affidavit showing the amount due. Otherwise, the plaintiff must apply to the court for a default judgment. Rule 55(b). Defaults and default judgments, however, are considered drastic remedies and are strongly disfavored by the courts. *See, e.g., Hughes v. Holland*, 320 F.2d 781 (D.C. Cir. 1963).

b. Setting aside a default

An entry of default may be set aside for good cause. Rule 55(c). Courts have interpreted this standard broadly. The three factors the courts generally consider are: (i) whether the defendant's failure to act was willful, (ii) whether setting the default aside would prejudice the plaintiff, and (iii) whether the defendant has presented a meritorious claim. *See Lacy v. Sitel Corp.*, 227 F.3d 290, 292 (5th Cir. 2000), *Berthelsen v. Kane*, 907 F.2d 617, 620 (6th Cir. 1990). If a final default judgment has been entered, the general rule for relief from a judgment governs (*see* IX.A.2. Rule 60(b): Relief From a Judgment or Order, *infra*).

3. Summary Judgment

a. Standard

Under Rule 56, a motion for summary judgment is applicable to all civil actions and must be granted if the pleadings, the discovery and disclosure materials on file, and any affidavits show that there is no genuine dispute as to any material fact and that the movant is entitled to judgment as a matter of law. A genuine issue of material fact exists when a reasonable jury could return a verdict in favor of the nonmoving party. *Anderson v. Liberty Lobby, Inc.*, 477 U.S. 242 (1986). In ruling on a motion for summary judgment, the court must construe all evidence in the light most favorable to the nonmoving party and resolve all doubts in favor of the nonmoving party.

b. Burden of proof

The movant has the burden of persuasion on a motion for summary judgment. Once the movant makes a prima facie showing that summary judgment is appropriate, the burden shifts to the opposing party to set forth specific evidence showing the existence of a genuine issue of fact for trial. *Celotex Corp. v. Catrett*, 477 U.S. 317 (1986). "When opposing parties tell two different stories, one of which is blatantly contradicted by the record, so that no reasonable jury could believe it, a court should not adopt that version of the facts for purposes of ruling on a motion for summary judgment." *Scott v. Harris*, 550 U.S. 372, 380 (2007).

c. Evidence

In deciding a motion for summary judgment, the court must consider the materials cited by the parties—affidavits, documents, electronically stored information, pleadings, deposition transcripts, interrogatory answers, admissions, and stipulations filed by the party—even if they are not presented in a form that is admissible at trial, as long as the facts contained in the submissions are admissible at trial. *Stinnett v. Iron Works Gym/Executive Health Spa, Inc.*, 301 F.3d 610, 613 (7th Cir. 2002). The court is not limited to these materials, however; it may also consider other materials in the record. Supporting and opposing affidavits must be made on personal knowledge, must set out facts that would be admissible in evidence, and must establish the affiant's competency to testify on the matters stated. An unsworn declaration, under penalty of perjury, will have the same force and effect as an affidavit if it meets the previously listed requirements and is signed and dated by the person setting out the facts, and if it states, "I declare (or certify, verify, or state) under penalty of perjury that the foregoing is true and correct. Executed on (date). (Signature)." 28 U.S.C.S. § 1746.

d. Response by the opposing party

If a motion for summary judgment is properly made and supported, an opposing party may not rely merely on allegations or denials in her own pleading, but she must set out specific facts showing a genuine dispute for trial. Although there is no explicit requirement in Rule 56 that discovery be complete before summary judgment is entered, granting summary judgment is generally improper unless the nonmovant is given a sufficient opportunity to obtain discovery. *See White's Landing Fisheries v. Buchholzer*, 29 F.3d 229 (6th Cir. 1994); *Weir v. Anaconda Co.*, 773 F.2d 1073 (10th Cir. 1985). If the opposing party shows by affidavit or declaration that, for specified reasons, she cannot present facts essential to oppose the motion, then the court may, in its discretion: (i) defer considering the motion or deny it, (ii) allow time to obtain affidavits or declarations or to conduct discovery, or (iii) issue any other appropriate order. Rule 56(d). If the opposing party does not so respond, then summary judgment, if appropriate, will be entered against that party. Rule 56(e).

e. Partial summary judgment

Pursuant to Rule 56(g), if the court does not grant all the relief requested by the motion, then it may enter an order stating any material fact—including an item of damages or other relief—that is not genuinely in dispute and treating the fact as established in the case.

f. Time for making the motion

Unless a different time is set by local rule, under Rule 56(b), a party may file a motion for summary judgment at any time until 30 days after the close of all discovery.

g. Appeal

In general, an order denying summary judgment is not subject to immediate appeal. A grant of full summary judgment is a final disposition on the merits and is subject to appeal.

However, if a party fails to properly support an assertion of fact or fails to properly address another party's assertion of fact as required by Rule 56(c), then the court may (i) give an opportunity to properly support or address the fact, (ii) consider the fact undisputed for the purposes of the motion, (iii) grant summary judgment if the motion and supporting materials show that the movant is entitled to it, or (iv) issue any other appropriate order. Rule 56(e).

4. Declaratory Judgment

A declaratory judgment is a ruling in which the court tells the parties to a dispute what their rights, responsibilities, or obligations are, without awarding damages or ordering the parties to do (or refrain from doing) anything. Parties generally seek a declaratory judgment to resolve uncertainty and to avoid the possibility of a future lawsuit. Under the federal Declaratory Judgment Act, 28 U.S.C. § 2201, a federal court may award declaratory relief in actions within the court's original jurisdiction, with the exception of certain actions concerning taxes, bankruptcy, free trade, or drug patents. Most states have enacted statutes permitting their courts to issue declaratory judgments.

VIII. TRIAL PROCEDURE

A. JURY TRIAL

1. Right to a Jury Trial

Rule 38 provides that the right of trial by jury as declared by the Seventh Amendment to the U.S. Constitution, or as provided by a federal statute, is preserved to the parties inviolate. In general, an action at law (e.g., an action for damages) is tried on demand to a jury, but an action in equity (e.g., an action for injunction) is not. If a new cause of action that was unknown at common law is created, then the court must look to the remedy sought and allow a jury if the relief sought is legal rather than equitable.

a. Legal and equitable claims—trial order

The right to trial by jury is evaluated for each claim. If an action involves both legal and equitable claims, then the jury normally determines the legal claims first, and the court then determines the equitable claims, but the court is bound by the jury's findings on the legal claims. *Beacon Theatres, Inc. v. Westover*, 359 U.S. 500 (1959).

b. Diversity cases

With regard to state-law claims in diversity actions, federal law generally determines whether there is a right to a jury trial and whether an issue is legal or equitable. *Simler v. Conner*, 372 U.S. 221 (1963). However, federal courts apply state law when taking into account a motion for a new trial based on excessiveness of the verdict. *Gasperini v. Center for Humanities*, 518 U.S. 415 (1996).

2. Jury Demand and Waiver

Under Rule 38(b), any party may make a demand for a trial by jury. The demand must be in writing. It may be filed separately or made in a pleading. It must be served within 14 days after service of the last pleading directed to the issue that is sought to be tried by a jury. A party waives a jury trial unless her demand is properly served and filed.

a. Issues

A party may specify the issues for which it is demanding a jury trial. Otherwise, a jury trial demand is treated as requesting a jury trial with respect to all issues triable by a jury. If a party requests a jury trial for only some issues triable by a jury, then any other party may serve a jury trial demand on any or all remaining issues that are triable by a jury. This party must file its demand within 14 days of being served with the earlier jury trial demand or any shorter time set by the court. Rule 38(c).

b. Withdrawal

A party may withdraw a jury trial demand with the consent of the other parties. Rule 38(d).

c. Removal of a case from state court

If a case is removed from state court, a party who has made a jury trial demand in accordance with state law need not renew the demand. If state law does not require a party to make a jury trial demand, then a party need not make one after removal unless the court orders the parties to do so. A party may request that the court make such an order, and the court must comply. If all necessary pleadings have been filed prior to removal, a party entitled to a jury trial under Rule 38 may make a jury trial demand within 14 days after filing a notice of removal or within 14 days of being served with such a notice filed by another party. Rule 81(c)(3).

3. Jury Size

Under Rule 48(a), a jury must initially have at least six and no more than 12 members. Having been selected, a juror must participate in the verdict unless dismissed for good cause. There is no provision in the federal rules for the selection of alternate jurors, as is the practice in some states.

4. Jury Selection

a. Voir dire

Under Rule 47(a), the court may permit the parties or their attorneys to examine prospective jurors or may do so itself. If the court examines the jurors, then it must permit the parties or their attorneys to make any further inquiry it considers proper, or it must itself ask any of their additional questions that it considers proper.

b. Challenges to jurors

1) Peremptory challenges

In a civil case, as in a criminal case, peremptory challenges may not be made for racial or gender-based reasons. *Edmonson v. Leesville Concrete Co.*, 500 U.S. 614 (1991); *J.E.B. v. Alabama*, 511 U.S. 127 (1994). (*See* MBE Criminal Procedure outline § V.A.3.b.5. Peremptory Challenges, regarding the rules for contesting a discriminatory use of a peremptory challenge.) Rule 47(b) requires the court to allow the number of peremptory challenges provided by 28 U.S.C. § 1870, which is three for each party in civil cases. Several defendants or several plaintiffs may be considered as a single party for the purposes of making such challenges, or the court may allow additional peremptory challenges and permit them to be exercised separately or jointly.

2) Challenges for cause

Each party is entitled to an unlimited number of challenges for cause, such as bias or a personal relationship with a litigant. The court rules on such challenges. 28 U.S.C. § 1870.

5. Jury Instructions

If the jury is to render a general verdict, it is the judge's duty to instruct the jury on the law that governs the verdict. If the jury is to render specific written findings of fact, it is the judge's duty to give the jury sufficient instructions and explanations. Rule 49(a)(2),(b)(1); Notes of Advisory Committee on 2003 amendments to Rule 51.

a. Party's right to request specific instructions

Under Rule 51, a party has the right to request that the court give specific instructions to the jury regarding its verdict.

1) Timing of a request

At the close of evidence, a party may file and furnish to every other party proposed jury instructions. The court may require that the party do this at an earlier reasonable time, including prior to trial, but even after the close of evidence, a party has the right to file requests for instructions on issues that could not reasonably have been anticipated at that earlier time. In addition, the court may permit a party to file an untimely request. Rule 51(a).

b. Court's proposed instructions

Prior to final arguments, the court must inform the parties of any instructions it proposes to give to the jury with regard to its verdict. The court must also inform the parties of its proposed action on the parties' requests for jury instructions. Rule 51(b).

c. Party's objection to the court's proposed instructions

The court must provide the parties with an opportunity to object to its proposed instructions on the record and out of the jury's hearing before the instructions and arguments are delivered. Rule 51(b)(2). If the court fails to do this, a party's objection is timely if it is made promptly after learning that an instruction has been or will be given or a request has been refused. Rule 51(c)(2). The party's objection must be made on the record and specifically state the instruction or request objected to and the grounds for the objection. Rule 51(c)(1).

d. Timing of instructions

The court may instruct a jury regarding its verdict at any time before the jury is discharged. Consequently, the court may instruct the jury before as well as after the lawyers' closing arguments. The court may, when the need arises (e.g., in response to questions submitted to the court by the jury), again instruct the jury after the jury has retired for deliberation. Rule 51(b)(1).

e. Appeal

Unless a party timely and properly objects on the record to an erroneous instruction given or proposed to be given by the court or to the court's failure to give an instruction timely requested by a party, the party generally cannot raise the matter on appeal. A plain error with regard to the jury instructions that affects substantial rights may nevertheless be addressed by an appellate court. Rule 51(d).

6. Juror's Duties

A juror is required to listen to the evidence presented in court and weigh that evidence fairly when reaching a verdict. Jurors should not consider other matters not formally admitted into evidence (e.g., investigate the scene of an accident on their own). Jurors should not discuss the facts of the case with a nonjuror.

7. Excusing a Juror

The court may excuse a juror for good cause not only prior to the submission of the case to the jury, but also during jury deliberations. Rule 47(c). Sickness, family emergency, or juror misconduct can constitute good cause for excusing a juror, but refusal of a juror to agree with other members of the jury does not. Notes of Advisory Committee on 1991 amendments to Rule 47.

8. Jury Verdicts

A verdict is a formal decision rendered by a jury at the conclusion of a trial.

a. Unanimity requirement

The jury verdict must be unanimous unless the parties stipulate otherwise. Rule 48(b).

b. Number of jurors

The verdict must be returned by a jury of at least six members unless the parties stipulate otherwise. Rule 48(b).

c. Form of verdict

There are three types of permissible verdicts. Rule 49. The type used is subject to the discretion of the court. *Flanigan v. Burlington Northern, Inc.*, 632 F.2d 880 (8th Cir. 1980), *cert. den.* 450 U.S. 921 (1981).

1) Special

A special verdict is a written finding made by the jury on each issue of ultimate fact. The court submits written questions to the jury correlating to each ultimate fact of the case and asks the jury to make a finding on each fact (e.g., "Was the defendant negligent?"). The court may specifically direct the jury's response to a question (e.g., "Yes or No") or may permit the jury to respond with a brief answer (e.g., the percentage of a defendant's fault in a negligence action). The judge then determines the legal consequences of those findings. Rule 49(a)(1). Even in a case based on diversity jurisdiction, the court is not bound by a state law that requires the use of a special verdict. Notes of Advisory Committee on Rule 49.

a) Waiver

A party waives the right to a jury trial on any issue of fact raised by the pleadings or evidence but not submitted to the jury, unless, before the jury retires, the party demands submission of the issue to the jury. Otherwise, the court may make a finding on that issue. When the court does not do so, it is deemed to have made a finding consistent with its judgment on the special verdict. Rule 49(a)(3).

2) General

A general verdict is typically a decision by the jury as to the prevailing party and, if the plaintiff is the prevailing party, the amount of damages. It is the usual form of a jury verdict in a civil case.

3) General with special interrogatories

This type of verdict couples a general verdict with a special verdict. It is used to ensure that the jury independently considered the material facts of the case in arriving at its verdict. If the answers to the interrogatories are consistent with each other but not with the general verdict, then the court may: (i) approve a judgment that is consistent with the answers, notwithstanding the general verdict, (ii) direct the jury to reconsider its answers and verdict, or (iii) order a new trial. In cases of inconsistency between the answers, the court cannot enter a judgment, but must either direct the jury to reconsider its answers or order a new trial. Rule 49(b).

4) Verdicts in error

When, prior to the dismissal of the jury, a party believes that the jury has returned an erroneous verdict that can be corrected, the party must raise this issue with the court. If the court believes that the jury did not properly follow its instructions, then the court may set aside the verdict and ask the jury to reconsider the issue. Alternatively, the court may order a new trial.

d. Polling

After the jury returns a verdict and before the jury is dismissed, the court must poll the jurors individually if a party requests; the court may also do so on its own initiative. If there is a lack of unanimity or assent by the number of jurors to which the parties stipulated, the court may order the jury to continue deliberations, or it may order a new trial. Rule 48(c).

9. Juror Misconduct

Misconduct can occur when a juror conceals facts relating to his qualifications or gives false testimony during voir dire. To obtain a new trial, a party must not only demonstrate that the juror failed to answer honestly a material question on voir dire, but also show that a proper response would have provided a valid basis for a challenge for cause. *McDonough Power Equip. v. Greenwood*, 464 U.S. 548 (1984).

If the juror violates the confidentiality of deliberations, is improperly influenced by nonjurors, or takes it upon himself to investigate facts outside of those presented at trial, then the court may dismiss the juror or, if necessary, order a new trial. Note that, while generally a juror may not impeach her own verdict, she may testify on the question of whether extraneous prejudicial information was improperly brought to the jury's attention or whether any outside influence was improperly brought to bear on a juror. Fed. R. Evid. 606(b).

B. TRIAL BY THE COURT

A case will be tried by the court without a jury if no right to a jury trial exists (or if such right has been waived). The court is the finder of fact; it must find the facts specially and state its conclusions of law separately. The findings and conclusions may be stated on the record after the close of evidence or may appear in an opinion or a memorandum of decision filed by the court. The court is not required to state findings or conclusions when ruling on a motion under Rule 12 (motions against the complaint) or Rule 56 (summary judgment) or, unless the rules provide otherwise, on any other motion. Rule 52(a).

C. CONSOLIDATION ACTIONS AND SEPARATE TRIALS

If actions before the court involve a common question of fact or law, the court may join for hearing or trial any or all matters at issue in the actions, consolidate the actions, or issue any other orders to avoid unnecessary cost or delay. Rule 42(a). Conversely, a court may order a separate trial of one or more issues, claims (including cross-claims, counterclaims, and third-party claims) for convenience, to avoid prejudice, or to expedite and economize. When doing so, the court must preserve any federal right to a jury trial. Rule 42(b).

D. PREJUDGMENT ATTACHMENT

At the commencement and through the course of an action, a plaintiff may file a motion for prejudgment attachment as allowed by the state where the court is located. A prejudgment attachment provides for seizing a person or property to secure satisfaction of a potential judgment. Federal statute governs the extent to which the state statute may be applied, and remedies include arrest, attachment, garnishment, replevin, sequestration, and other equivalent remedies.

In addition to filing the motion, the plaintiff must give the defendant notice and an opportunity to be heard by preparing a writ of attachment in addition to a summons and complaint. A court will grant a prejudgment attachment only if the plaintiff shows that there is a likelihood of success of recovering an amount equal to the amount being sought to attach. Rule 64.

E. JUDGMENT AS A MATTER OF LAW

Rule 50 provides procedural requirements for challenging the sufficiency of the evidence in a civil jury trial. The rule establishes two separate but related stages for such challenges. Prior to submission of the case to the jury, a party may file a motion for judgment as a matter of law under Rule 50(a). This is also called a "motion for a directed verdict." After the verdict and entry of judgment, a party may renew their motion for judgment as a matter of law pursuant to Rule 50(b). This renewed motion may also be referred to as a "motion for judgment notwithstanding the verdict."

1. **Motion for Judgment as a Matter of Law ("Directed Verdict")**

    Under Rule 50(a), once a party has been fully heard on an issue at a jury trial, the court may grant a motion for judgment as a matter of law resolving the issue against a party if the court finds that there is insufficient evidence for a jury reasonably to find for that party. The court may also grant such a motion against the party on any claim or defense that is dependent on a favorable finding on that issue.

    a. **Standard**

        The court must view the evidence in the light most favorable to the opposing party and draw all reasonable inferences from the evidence in favor of the opposing party. It may not consider the credibility of witnesses or evaluate the weight of the evidence, and it must disregard all evidence favorable to the moving party that the jury is not required to believe. *Reeves v. Sanderson Plumbing Prods., Inc.,* 530 U.S. 133 (2000). If reasonable persons can draw different inferences, then the issue is for the jury to decide, and the motion cannot be granted.

    b. **Procedure and timing**

        A motion for judgment as a matter of law may be made at any time before the case is submitted to the jury. The motion must specify the judgment sought and the law and facts that entitle the movant to the judgment.

    c. **Judgment on partial findings**

        In a nonjury trial, a defendant, instead of making a motion for a judgment as a matter of law, can move for a judgment on partial findings if the plaintiff has failed to prove his case. Rule 52(c).

2. **Renewed Motion for Judgment as a Matter of Law (JNOV)**

    Under Rule 50(b), if the court does not grant a motion for judgment as a matter of law, then the court is considered to have submitted the action to the jury subject to the court's later deciding the legal questions raised by the motion. The movant may file a renewed motion for judgment as a matter of law no later than 28 days after the entry of judgment. If the motion addresses a jury issue not decided by a verdict, then the renewed motion must be filed no later than 28 days after the jury was discharged.

    A post-verdict motion under Rule 50(b) is only a renewal of the earlier motion made at the close of the evidence, and it can be granted only on grounds advanced in the pre-verdict motion. Therefore, filing a motion under Rule 50(a) for a judgment as a matter of law before the case is submitted to the jury is a requirement for consideration of a renewed motion for judgment as a matter of law under Rule 50(b). If a party fails to move for a judgment as a matter of law before the case goes to the jury, then an appellate court will not review whether a district court erred in refusing to grant the party's renewed motion for judgment as a matter of law. *See, e.g., Catlett v. Local 7370 of United Paper Workers Int'l Union,* 69 F.3d 254 (8th Cir. 1995); *Firestone Tire & Rubber Co. v. Pearson,* 769 F.2d 1471 (10th Cir. 1985).

    In ruling on the renewed motion, the court may: (i) allow judgment on the verdict if the jury returned a verdict, (ii) order a new trial, or (iii) direct the entry of judgment as a matter of law. The same standards apply to the entry of the renewed motion as applied to the initial motion.

Under Rule 50(c), if the renewed motion for judgment as a matter of law is granted and the party had alternatively moved for a new trial, the court must also determine whether the motion for a new trial should be granted if the judgment is reversed or vacated on appeal.

F. JUDGMENT

A judgment is a decree or order by a court that resolves the parties' rights and demands for relief in a manner that permits it to be appealed (*see* IX.B. Appeals, *infra*). Rule 54(a).

1. Agreement With Pleadings

In general, a judgment should grant a party the relief to which the party is entitled, even if the party has not demanded such relief in its pleadings. However, a default judgment must not differ in kind or exceed in amount what is demanded in the pleadings. Rule 54(c).

2. Costs

Unless a federal statute, rule, or court order provides otherwise, the prevailing party is allowed court costs, other than attorney's fees, without needing to file a motion. The court clerk may tax costs on 14 days' notice. A party may challenge the clerk's action by serving a motion within seven days. Rule 54(d)(1). By serving on an opposing party an offer to allow judgment on specified terms at least 14 days prior to the date set for trial, a defending party may limit such costs to the costs then accrued if the opposing party does not accept the offer and the judgment is less favorable to the opposing party than the offer. A similar offer may be made once a party is determined to be liable but damages have not been determined. Evidence of an unaccepted offer is not admissible except in a proceeding to determine costs. Rule 68.

3. Attorney's fees

Unless a statute or court order provides otherwise, a claim for attorney's fees that is not required by law to be proved at trial as an element of damages must be made by a motion filed within 14 days after entry of judgment. Unless the court orders otherwise, this motion does not extend the time for filing an appeal. Rule 54(d)(2).

G. MOTION TO AMEND OR MAKE ADDITIONAL FINDINGS

In a nonjury trial, a party may make a motion for the court to amend its findings or to make additional findings. This motion must be made within 28 days of the entry of judgment and may be combined with a new trial motion. Rule 52(b).

On appeal, a court's finding of facts can be set aside only if clearly erroneous. The reviewing court must give due regard to the trial court's opportunity to judge the witnesses' credibility. Rule 52(a)(6).

H. MOTION TO ALTER OR AMEND A JUDGMENT

A party may make a motion for the court to alter or amend a judgment. This motion must be made within 28 days of the entry of the judgment. Rule 59(e).

I. MOTION FOR A NEW TRIAL

1. Grounds

Under Rule 59(a), the court may, on motion by a party or on its own, grant a new trial on all issues or with respect to only certain issues or parties. Rule 59 does not specifically list the grounds that will justify a new trial, but in practice, the overarching theme is that the court may grant a new trial to prevent a miscarriage of justice. Some of the reasons that have been held to justify a new trial include:

i)   Error at trial that renders the judgment unfair;

ii) Newly discovered evidence that existed at the time of the trial was excusably overlooked and would likely have altered the outcome of the trial;

iii) Prejudicial misconduct of counsel, a party, the judge, or a juror;

iv) A verdict that is against the clear weight of the evidence;

v)   A verdict that is based on false evidence; or

vi) A verdict that is excessive or inadequate.

In general, whether a new trial is warranted rests within the sound discretion of the trial court. *Montgomery Ward & Co. v. Duncan*, 311 U.S. 243 (1940). Under Rule 61, the court must disregard all errors and defects that do not affect any party's substantial rights. This is the "harmless error" rule.

After giving the parties notice and an opportunity to be heard, the court may grant a timely motion for a new trial for a reason not stated in a party's motion. The court must specify the reasons in its order.

2.   Remittitur

If the court determines that a verdict was excessive, then it may offer a reduction of the verdict, known as a remittitur, and grant a new trial on the condition that the remittitur is not accepted. *See Hetzel v. Prince William County.*, 523 U.S. 208 (1998). If the court determines that the verdict was inadequate, then it only has the option of ordering a new trial. An additur (enhanced judgment) is not permitted.

3.   Timing

Pursuant to Rule 59(b), a motion for a new trial must be filed no later than 28 days after the entry of judgment.

When the motion is based on affidavits, those affidavits must be filed with the motion. The opposing party then has 14 days after being served to file opposing affidavits. The court may permit reply affidavits. Rule 59(c).

IX.   POST-TRIAL PROCEDURE

A.   ALTERATION OF OR RELIEF FROM JUDGMENT

1.   Rule 60(a): Correction of a Judgment

Rule 60(a) allows a court to correct a clerical or other mistake resulting from oversight or omission whenever one is found in a judgment, order, or other part of the record. Rule 60(a). An example of such a mistake would be when a court meant to enter a judgment for the plaintiff for $100,000, and it appeared in the written judgment as "$10,000." The court may make such a correction on motion by a party or on its own initiative, with or without notice. However, once an appeal from the judgment or order has been docketed in the appellate court, such a correction can be made only with leave of the appellate court. *Id.*

2.   Rule 60(b): Relief From a Judgment or Order

Rule 60(b) allows a court to relieve a party from a final judgment or order for a motion filed:

i)   Within a reasonable time, and **no later than one year following the entry of the judgment or order** for:

   a) Mistake, inadvertence, surprise, or excusable neglect;

b) Newly discovered evidence that could not have been earlier discovered with reasonable diligence; or

c) Fraud (intrinsic or extrinsic), misrepresentation, or misconduct by an opposing party; or

ii) Within a reasonable time, with no definite limiting period, on the grounds that: a judgment is void; a judgment has been satisfied, released, or discharged; a judgment was based on a judgment that was reversed or vacated; applying the judgment prospectively is no longer equitable; or for any other reason that justifies relief.

In sum, Rule 60(b) allows a court to exercise its equitable jurisdiction to relieve a party from a judgment in any case in which enforcing the judgment would work injustice, and the party seeking relief or its counsel was not guilty of misconduct or gross negligence. If a motion for relief is made, but the court lacks the authority to rule because of the pendency of an appeal, then the court may (i) defer, (ii) deny the motion, or (iii) state that it would grant the motion upon remand. Rule 62.1.

The court may provide any relief that it believes to be appropriate based on the evidence, and it is not limited to the relief requested in the pleadings.

3. Other Remedies

Despite the limitations otherwise imposed by Rule 60, a court may nevertheless:

i) Entertain an independent action to relieve a party from an order, judgment, or proceeding;

ii) Grant relief to a defendant who was not personally notified of the action (28 USC § 1655); or

iii) Set aside a judgment for fraud on the court.

Rule 60(d). Fraud on the court is fraud that is "limited to fraud which seriously affects the integrity of the normal process of adjudication." *Kupferman v. Consol. Research & Mfg. Corp.*, 459 F.2d 1072, 1078 (2d Cir. 1972). "[O]nly the most egregious misconduct, such as bribery of a judge or members of a jury, or the fabrication of evidence by a party in which an attorney is implicated, will constitute a fraud on the court." *Rozier v. Ford Motor Co.*, 573 F.2d 1332, 1338 (5th Cir. 1978).

B. APPEALS

The notice of appeal required in a civil case must generally be filed with the district clerk within **30 days** after the judgment or order being appealed is entered. If one of the parties is the United States, a federal agency, or a federal officer or employee sued in an official capacity or sued in an individual capacity for conduct occurring in connection with the duties performed on behalf of the United States, then the period is extended to 60 days. If a party timely files one or more of the following motions, the 30-day period does not start for any party until the entry of the order disposing of the last remaining motion:

i) A renewed motion for judgment (*see* § VIII.E.2. Renewed Motion for Judgment as a Matter of Law (JNOV), *supra*);

ii) A motion to amend or make additional factual findings (*see* § VIII.G. Motion to Amend or Make Additional Findings, *supra*), whether or not granting the motion would alter the judgment;

iii) A motion to alter or amend the judgment (*see* § VIII.H. Motion to Alter or Amend a Judgment, *supra*);

iv) A motion for a new trial (*see* § VIII.I., Motion for a New Trial, *supra*);

v) A motion for alteration or relief from judgment under Rule 60 (*see* § IX.A. Alteration or Relief from Judgment, *above*), if the motion is filed no later than 28 days after the judgment is entered; or

vi) A motion for attorney's fees (*see* § VIII.F.3. Attorney's fees, *supra*), if the court orders that the motion will extend the time to appeal.

Fed. Rules App. Proc., Rule 4.

1. Final Judgment Rule

Under 28 U.S.C. § 1291, the federal courts of appeals have jurisdiction over appeals of the final judgments of the district courts. A final judgment is a decision by the court on the merits that leaves nothing for the court to do but execute the judgment. *Catlin v. United States*, 324 U.S. 229(1945). Judicial economy alone is insufficient grounds to expand a court's jurisdiction to include non-final judgments. Parties must demonstrate that review of the non-final judgment together with the appealable order will assist the court in reviewing the appealable order. *Swint v. Chambers County Comm'n.*, 514 U.S. 35 (1995).

Pursuant to Rule 54(b), if more than one claim is presented in a case, or if there are multiple parties, then the district court may direct entry of a final judgment as to one or more issues or parties, but only if the court "expressly determines that there is no just reason for delay." This modifies the rule's default position that any order or other decision, however designated, that adjudicates fewer than all of the claims or the rights and liabilities of fewer than all of the parties will not end the action as to any of the claims or parties, and it may be revised at any time before the entry of a judgment adjudicating all of the claims and all of the parties' rights and liabilities.

2. Appeal of Interlocutory Orders

Although most interlocutory orders, such as the denial of a summary judgment motion, a motion to dismiss, or the granting of a new trial motion, are not immediately appealable, 28 U.S.C. § 1292(a) makes certain equitable orders reviewable immediately as a matter of right, including:

i) An order granting, modifying, refusing, or dissolving an injunction;

ii) An order appointing or refusing to appoint a receiver; and

iii) A decree determining the rights and liabilities of the parties to admiralty cases in which appeals from final decrees are allowed.

In addition, under 28 U.S.C. § 1292(b), if a district court certifies (i) that an order involves a controlling question of law as to which there is substantial ground for difference of opinion, and (ii) that an immediate appeal from the order may materially advance the ultimate termination of the litigation, then a court of appeals has discretion to permit an appeal to be taken from such order. In such a case, however, the application must be made within 10 days after the entry of the order, rather than the 30-day period that applies to an appeal of other interlocutory orders that are immediately appealable as of right.

3. Collateral-Order Doctrine

Under the so-called **collateral-order doctrine**, a court of appeals has discretion to hear and rule on a district court order if it: "1) conclusively determines the disputed question, 2) resolves an important issue that is completely separate from the merits of the action, and 3) is effectively unreviewable on appeal from a final judgment."

Mohawk Indus., Inc. v. Carpenter, 558 U.S. 100, 105 (2009) (holding that a disclosure order whose enforcement would allegedly violate attorney-client privilege did not qualify for review under the collateral-order doctrine). For example, an order imposing on the defendant 90 percent of the cost of notifying members of a class was appealable under this doctrine. *Eisen v. Carlisle & Jacquelin*, 417 U.S. 156 (1974).

4. Mandamus Review

Under a writ of mandamus, an appellate court can immediately review an order of a lower court that is an abuse of judicial authority. In addition to establishing the existence of an error of law, the petitioner must establish that there is no other adequate means of obtaining the desired relief and that the right to such relief is clear and indisputable. *Compare Kerr v. U.S. Dist. Court*, 426 U.S. 394 (1976) (mandamus inappropriate to vacate a lower court's discovery orders) *with Dairy Queen, Inc. v. Wood*, 369 U.S. 469 (1962) (mandamus appropriate when a trial court denied the right to a jury trial on a legal issue).

5. Class Action Certification

A court of appeals has the discretion to permit an appeal from a district court order granting or denying class action certification. The petition for permission to appeal must be filed with the circuit clerk within 14 days after the order is entered. If the appeal is permitted, it does not stay proceedings in the district court unless the district court or the court of appeals so orders. Rule 23(f).

6. Standards of Review

The standard of review focuses on the degree to which an appellate court defers to a decision by the trial court or jury. It is a procedural matter that is governed by federal law, even in an action based on diversity jurisdiction.

a. Review of a trial court's factual findings—clearly erroneous

A trial court's findings of fact, including a master's findings that have been adopted by the court, may not be set aside unless "**clearly erroneous.**" The appellate court must give due regard to the trial court's opportunity to judge the witnesses' credibility. Rule 52(a). A finding is clearly erroneous when, although there is evidence to support it, the appellate court, based on the entirety of the evidence, is left with the definite and firm conviction that a mistake has been committed. *United States v. U.S. Gypsum Co.*, 333 U.S. 364 (1948). A party may challenge the sufficiency of the evidence supporting such findings on appeal even though the party took no action in the trial court with regard to them. Rule 52(a)(5).

b. Review of legal rulings—de novo

In general, appellate review of legal rulings is **de novo**. While an appellate court relies on the record created in a trial court and does not entertain the admission of additional evidence, the appellate court reviews the evidence and law without deference to the trial court's legal rulings. Thus, the appellate court may reach its own independent conclusions as to the applicable law.

c. Review of discretionary rulings—abuse of discretion

A trial court's rulings on discretionary matters, such as the admissibility of evidence, sanctions for violation of discovery rules, or the granting or denial of a motion to transfer venue or to sever actions, are generally subject to review under the **abuse of discretion** standard. *GE v. Joiner*, 522 U.S. 136 (1997).

d. Review of a jury verdict

In determining whether to set aside a jury verdict, it is not sufficient that the verdict is against the weight of the evidence. *Lavender v. Kurn*, 327 U.S. 645 (1946). Some appellate courts refuse to set aside a jury verdict if there is substantial evidence supporting the verdict. Other courts require only sufficient evidence to sustain a jury verdict. Still others uphold a jury verdict unless there is no evidence to support the verdict. However, to preserve for appeal a challenge to the sufficiency of the evidence supporting a jury verdict, a party must properly renew a motion for directed verdict with a motion for judgment notwithstanding the verdict under Rule 50(b) or must raise a motion for a new trial under Rule 59. If a party fails to do so, there is no basis for review of the challenge to the overall sufficiency of the evidence in a court of appeals, and appellate review will instead be limited to any specific claims of error that were properly preserved. *Unitherm Food Sys. v. Swift-Eckrich, Inc.*, 546 U.S. 394 (2006).

C. FULL FAITH AND CREDIT

1. State to State

Article IV, Section 1 of the U.S. Constitution provides that "Full Faith and Credit shall be given in each State to the public Acts, Records, and judicial Proceedings of every other State." The clause is invoked primarily to enforce the judgment of one state court in another state.

If a valid judgment is rendered by a court that has jurisdiction over the parties, and the parties receive proper notice of the action and a reasonable opportunity to be heard, then the Full Faith and Credit Clause requires that the judgment receive the same effect in other states as in the state where it was rendered. Thus, a party who obtains a judgment in one state may petition the court in another state to enforce the judgment. In general, the issues are not re-litigated, and the court in the state in which enforcement is sought must honor the judgment of the other state's court.

The same principle applies to challenges based on an alleged lack of personal or subject matter jurisdiction; a party against whom enforcement is sought may collaterally challenge the original state judgment based on lack of personal jurisdiction or subject matter jurisdiction **only** if the jurisdictional issues were not litigated or waived in the original action. *Durfee v. Duke*, 375 U.S. 106 (1963).

The requirement of full faith and credit extends to the preclusive effects of the original state-court judgment. Thus, if the original state-court judgment would bar a subsequent action in the original state, then it acts to bar a subsequent action in any other state. This is the case even if the subsequent action would otherwise be permitted in that state. (*See* § IX.D. Claim Preclusion (Res Judicata), and § IX.E. Issue Preclusion (Collateral Estoppel) *infra*, for a discussion of preclusion generally.)

2. Federal to State

Under 28 U.S.C. § 1738, federal courts must also give full faith and credit to state-court judgments. The same rules as discussed previously for states apply with respect to a federal court.

3. State to Federal in Diversity Cases

Federal law determines the effects under the rules of res judicata of a judgment of a federal court. Restatement (Second) of Judgments, § 87. However, federal common law requires that the claim-preclusive effect of a judgment by a federal court sitting in diversity must be governed by the law of claim preclusion of the federal court's forum state. *Semtek Int'l Inc. v. Lockheed Martin Corp.*, 531 U.S. 497 (2001).

D. CLAIM PRECLUSION (RES JUDICATA)

1. In General

The doctrine of claim preclusion (res judicata) provides that a final judgment on the merits of an action precludes a party from successive litigation of an identical **claim** in a subsequent action. *New Hampshire v. Maine*, 532 U.S. 742, 748 (2001).

2. Requirements

a. Valid final judgment on the merits

1) Valid

The judgment must be valid, generally requiring that the court had both personal and subject matter jurisdiction, and the defendant had proper notice and an opportunity to be heard. However, when a defendant participates in an action and litigates or could have litigated the existence of jurisdiction, a judgment may be given preclusive effect even though, after the judgment has become final, it is ascertained that the court lacked jurisdiction.

2) Final

The judgment must also be final, meaning that there is nothing further for the court to do but order entry of judgment.

3) On the merits

The decision must have been made in consideration of the merits of the claim or defense, rather than on technical grounds. A claim or defense does not actually need to have been raised in the earlier action to be barred in the later action. If the claim or defense could have been raised in the earlier action, it will be precluded in the later action. A judgment on the merits includes judgment entered after a full trial, summary judgment, judgment as a matter of law, and default judgment when the court has subject matter jurisdiction and personal jurisdiction over the parties.

4) Voluntary dismissal without prejudice

A voluntary dismissal "without prejudice" expressly reserves the right to sue again on the same claim in the same court as long as the statute of limitations has not expired. Unless the notice of dismissal states otherwise, a voluntary dismissal will be "without prejudice." Rule 41(a)(1)(B).

5) Voluntary dismissal with prejudice

A voluntary dismissal "with prejudice" is treated as a judgment on the merits and will have a preclusive effect in the court that issued the order of dismissal. A dismissal on the merits under Rule 41(b) will bar a plaintiff from refiling the claim only in the same federal court, not in state court. *Semtek, supra.*

6) Involuntary dismissal

Unless otherwise provided by the order of dismissal, an involuntary dismissal on non-jurisdictional grounds will constitute an adjudication on the merits. Rule 41(b). While such an involuntary dismissal bars refiling of the claim in the same federal court, it does not preclude refiling of the claim in state court. *Semtek, supra.*

7) Dismissal for lack of jurisdiction

Under Rule 41(b), a dismissal on jurisdictional grounds, or for lack of venue or failure to join a party under Rule 19, is without prejudice because a court that has no jurisdiction cannot adjudicate a matter on the merits.

8) Diversity jurisdiction

If a federal court with diversity jurisdiction over an action issues a judgment, then federal common law provides that a state court must give such judgment the same claim-preclusion effect that the judgment would have been given by the courts of the state where the federal court was located. *Semtek, supra.*

9) Family law decisions

A divorce decree must generally be given a preclusive effect as long as the court had jurisdiction, which usually requires only a long-term connection of the plaintiff-spouse with the forum state rather than in personam jurisdiction over the defendant-spouse. However, a decision involving property rights, including alimony or child custody, is not entitled to a preclusive effect unless the court had in personam jurisdiction over the defendant-spouse. *Estin v. Estin*, 334 U.S. 541 (1948).

b. Sufficiently identical claims

The original and subsequently brought claims must be sufficiently identical to be barred under claim preclusion. Federal courts apply a transactional approach under which they bar a subsequent claim with respect to all or any part of the transaction, or series of connected transactions, out of which the original claim arose. If a plaintiff sues on less than all claims arising from a transaction, then the unraised claims merge with the judgment if the plaintiff wins, and they are barred if the plaintiff loses.

Factors that are considered in determining what constitutes a transaction or series of transactions include:

  i) Whether the facts are related in time, space, origin, or motivation;

  ii) Whether the facts form a convenient trial unit; and

  iii) Whether treating the facts as a unit conforms to the parties' expectations.

c. Sufficiently identical parties

For claim preclusion to apply, the claimant and the defendant must be the same (and in the same roles) in both the original action and the subsequently filed action. Note that claim preclusion is limited to the parties (or their privies). Thus, a similar action by a different party is generally not precluded.

E. ISSUE PRECLUSION (COLLATERAL ESTOPPEL)

1. In General

The doctrine of issue preclusion, often called "collateral estoppel," precludes the re-litigation of issues of fact or law that have already been necessarily determined in an earlier adjudication.

2. Nonparty Preclusion

Unlike claim preclusion, issue preclusion does not require strict mutuality of parties; it requires only that the party against whom the issue is to be precluded was a party to the original action. Thus, "offensive" use of collateral estoppel is permitted.

Trial courts have "broad discretion" to determine whether offensive collateral estoppel should be applied. If a plaintiff could easily have joined in the earlier action or if offensive estoppel is found to be unfair to a defendant, then a trial judge should not allow it. *Parklane Hosiery Co. v. Shore*, 439 U.S. 322 (1979).

There are six exceptions to the general rule against nonparty preclusion:

i) A party who agreed to be bound by a judgment;

ii) Certain types of "substantial legal relationships" between the party and the nonparty, such as a bailor-bailee relationship;

iii) A nonparty who was "adequately represented by someone with the same interests," as is found in class action suits or suits by trustees;

iv) A nonparty who "assumes control" over the case;

v) A party who attempts to re-litigate by using a proxy; or

vi) Special statutory schemes that prohibit successive litigation and are consistent with due process.

Taylor v. Sturgell, 553 U.S. 880 (2008).

3. Requirements

a. Same issue

The issue sought to be precluded must be the same as that involved in the prior action. The facts relevant to the particular issue and the applicable law must be identical in order for issue preclusion to apply. *Comm'r of Internal Revenue v. Sunnen*, 333 U.S. 591 (1948).

b. Actually litigated

The issue must have been actually litigated in the prior action in order for issue preclusion to apply. *Stoll v. Gottlieb*, 305 U.S. 165 (1938) (issue preclusion applies to findings of jurisdiction that are fully litigated).

c. Final, valid judgment

The issue must have been determined by a valid and binding final judgment. Generally, this requires that the first determination of the issue was within the authority of the court that decided it, and that the determination was made in a final decision on the merits.

d. Essential to the judgment

The determination of the issue must have been essential to the prior judgment. Generally, an issue that constitutes a necessary component of the decision reached will be considered essential to the judgment.

4. Equitable Issues

Issues decided under a court's equitable power, such as a bankruptcy court's avoidance of preferential transfers, can be precluded from re-litigation just as legal issues can, if all the requirements for collateral estoppel are met. *See Katchen v. Landy*, 382 U.S. 323 (1966).

5. Criminal Prosecution

Issues determined in a criminal prosecution in favor of the prosecution are generally preclusive in a civil action against the defendant based on the same conduct as in the criminal prosecution. Restatement (Second) of Judgments § 85. Issues determined in a criminal prosecution in favor of the defendant are not preclusive in a civil action against the defendant based on the same conduct as in the criminal prosecution because the plaintiff in the civil action was not a party to the criminal prosecution.

Constitutional Law

CONSTITUTIONAL LAW

Table of Contents

CONSTITUTIONAL LAW

PART ONE: POWERS OF THE FEDERAL GOVERNMENT

I. JUDICIAL POWER

A. SOURCE AND SCOPE

1. Source—Article III

Article III, Section 1 of the United States Constitution provides that "[t]he judicial power of the United States shall be vested in one Supreme Court and in such inferior courts as the Congress may from time to time ordain and establish."

Federal courts are generally created by the United States Congress under the constitutional power described in Article III. As noted above, Article III requires the establishment of a Supreme Court and permits the Congress to create other federal courts and place limitations on their jurisdiction. Although many specialized courts are created under the authority granted in Article I, greater power is vested in Article III courts because they are independent of Congress, the President, and the political process.

2. Scope

Article III, Section 2 delineates the jurisdiction of federal courts as limited to **cases or controversies**:

i) Arising under the Constitution, laws, and treaties of the United States;

ii) Affecting foreign countries' ambassadors, public ministers, and consuls;

iii) Involving admiralty and maritime jurisdiction;

iv) When the United States is a party;

v) Between two or more states, or between a state and citizens of another state;

vi) Between citizens of different states or between citizens of the same state claiming lands under grants of different states; or

vii) Between a state, or its citizens, and foreign states, citizens, or subjects.

a. Judicial review of congressional and executive actions

The judiciary has the power—although it is not enumerated in the text of the Constitution—to review an act of another branch of the federal government and to declare that act unconstitutional, *Marbury v. Madison*, 5 U.S. 137 (1803), as well as the constitutionality of a decision by a state's highest court, *Martin v. Hunter's Lessee*, 1 Wheat. 304 (1816). The central ideas of *Marbury v. Madison* are that (i) the Constitution is paramount law, and (ii) the Supreme Court has the final say in interpreting the Constitution.

b. Judicial review of state actions

The federal judiciary has the power, under the Supremacy Clause (Article VI, Section 2), to review state actions (e.g., court decisions, state statutes, executive orders) to ensure conformity with the Constitution, laws, and treaties of the United States. *Fletcher v. Peck*, 10 U.S. 87 (1810).

3. Limitations—Eleventh Amendment

The Eleventh Amendment is a jurisdictional bar that prohibits the citizens of one state from suing another state in federal court. It immunizes the state from suits in federal court for money damages or equitable relief when the state is a defendant in an action brought by a citizen of another state or a foreign country. In addition, the Eleventh Amendment bars suits in federal court against state officials for violating **state** law. *Pennhurst State School & Hospital v. Halderman*, 465 U.S.89 (1984).

The Supreme Court has expanded the amendment's reach to also preclude citizens from suing their own state in federal court. *Hans v. Louisiana*, 134 U.S. 1 (1890).

Note that the Supreme Court has also barred federal-law actions brought against a state government without the state's consent in its own courts as a violation of **sovereign immunity.** *Alden v. Maine*, 527 U.S. 706 (1999). Similarly, states retain their sovereign immunity from private suits brought in the courts of other states. *Franchise Tax Bd. Of Cal. v. Hyatt*, 587 U.S. ___, 139 S. Ct. 1485 (2019) (overruling *Nevada v. Hall*, 440 U.S. 410 (1979)).

a. Exceptions

There are, however, a few notable exceptions to the application of the Eleventh Amendment.

1) Consent

A state may consent to suit by waiving its Eleventh Amendment protection. *Lapides v. Board of Regents of Univ. System of Ga.*, 535 U.S. 613 (2002) (state removal of case to federal court constituted a waiver).

2) Injunctive relief

When a state official, rather than the state itself, is named as the defendant in an action brought in federal court, the state official may be enjoined from enforcing a state law that violates federal law or may be compelled to act in accord with federal law despite state law to the contrary. *Ex parte Young*, 209 U.S. 123 (1908), *Edelman v. Jordan*, 415 U.S. 651 (1974).

Note: A state also cannot invoke its sovereign immunity to prevent a lawsuit by a state agency seeking to enforce a federal right against a state official. *Virginia Office for Prot. & Advocacy v. Stewart*, 563 U.S. 247 (2011).

3) Damages to be paid by an individual

An action for damages against a state officer is not prohibited, as long as the officer himself (rather than the state treasury) will have to pay. Such is the case when an officer acts outside the law; the action is against the officer as an individual and not in his representative capacity.

4) Prospective damages

As long as the effect of a lawsuit is not to impose retroactive damages on a state officer to be paid from the state treasury, a federal court may hear an action against a state officer, even if the action will force a state to pay money to comply with a court order.

5) Congressional authorization

Congress may abrogate state immunity from liability if it is clearly acting to enforce rights created by the remedial provisions of the Thirteenth, Fourteenth, and Fifteenth Amendments (i.e., the Civil War Amendments), and does so expressly. *Fitzpatrick v. Bitzer*, 427 U.S. 445 (1976). Congress generally may not abrogate state immunity by exercising its powers under Article I (e.g., Commerce Clause powers). *Seminole Tribe of Florida v. Florida*, 517 U.S. 44 (1996).

b. Not barred by the Eleventh Amendment

1) Actions against local governments

The Eleventh Amendment applies only to states and state agencies. Local governments (e.g., counties, cities) are not immune from suit.

2) Actions by the United States government or other state governments not barred

The Eleventh Amendment has no application when the plaintiff is the United States or another state.

3) Bankruptcy proceedings

The Eleventh Amendment does not bar the actions of a Bankruptcy Court that impacts state finances. *Central Cmty. Coll. v. Katz*, 546 U.S. 356 (2006).

B. JURISDICTION OF THE SUPREME COURT

1. Original

Article III, Section 2 gives the Supreme Court "original jurisdiction" (i.e., the case may be filed first in the Supreme Court) over "all cases affecting ambassadors, other public ministers and consuls and those in which a State shall be a party." Congress may not expand or limit this jurisdiction. *Marbury v. Madison*, 5 U.S. 137 (1803). It may, however, grant concurrent original jurisdiction to lower federal courts, which it has for all cases except those between states. 28. U.S.C. § 1251.

2. Appellate

Article III, Section 2 also provides that "in all other cases before mentioned, the Supreme Court shall have appellate jurisdiction...with such exceptions, and under such regulations as the Congress shall make."

a. Means

There are two means of establishing appellate jurisdiction in the Supreme Court: certiorari (discretionary review) and direct appeal.

1) Certiorari

Almost all cases now come to the Supreme Court by way of a petition for a writ of certiorari, i.e., discretionary review. The Court takes jurisdiction only if at least four Justices vote to accept the case (the "rule of four").

2) Direct appeal

The Supreme Court **must** hear by direct appeal only a small number of cases—those that come from a decision on injunctive relief issued by a special three-judge district court panel. 28 U.S.C. § 1253. Although these panels (and appeals) were once fairly common, they are now limited to cases brought under a few specific statutes (e.g., the Voting Rights Act).

b. Limitations

Congress has some power to limit the Supreme Court's appellate jurisdiction by statute. *Ex parte McCardle*, 74 U.S. 506 (1868). There are constraints on this power, because to deny all Supreme Court jurisdiction over certain types of cases would undermine the constitutional system of checks and balances. *Boumediene v. Bush*, 553 U.S. 723 (2008) (Congress and President cannot remove Supreme Court's authority to say "what the law is" (quoting *Marbury v. Madison*, 5 U.S. 137 (1803))).

> Note that most federal cases are filed in district court and appealed, if at all, to the courts of appeals. The jurisdiction of the federal courts is set, within the framework of Article III, by statute. For example, Congress requires the amount in controversy necessary for federal jurisdiction over a case between citizens of different states to exceed $75,000. 28 U.S.C. § 1332.

c. Adequate and independent state grounds

A final state-court judgment that rests on adequate and independent state grounds may not be reviewed by the U.S. Supreme Court (or it would be an advisory opinion). The state-law grounds must fully resolve the matter (i.e., be adequate) and must not incorporate a federal standard by reference (i.e., be independent). If a state court chooses to rely on federal precedents, the court can avoid federal review by making a plain statement in its judgment or opinion that the federal cases are being used only for the purpose of guidance and did not compel the court's judgment. When it is not clear whether the state court's decision rests on state or federal law, the Supreme Court may hear the case, decide the federal issue, and remand to the state court for resolution of any question of state law. *Michigan v. Long*, 463 U.S. 1032 (1983).

C. JUDICIAL REVIEW IN OPERATION

Standing, timing (mootness or ripeness), and other issues of justiciability may dictate whether a case may be heard by a federal court.

1. Standing

Article III, Section 2 restricts federal judicial power to "cases" and "controversies." A federal court cannot decide a case unless the plaintiff has standing—a concrete interest in the outcome—to bring it. Congress cannot statutorily eliminate the constitutional standing requirement simply by allowing citizen suits, *Lujan v. Defenders of Wildlife*, 504 U.S. 555 (1992), but it can create new interests, the injury to which may establish standing, *Massachusetts v. EPA*, 549 U.S. 497 (2007).

a. General rule

To have standing, a plaintiff bears the burden of establishing three elements:

   i) **Injury in fact**;

   ii) **Causation** (the injury must be caused by the defendant's violation of a constitutional or other federal right); and

   iii) **Redressability** (the relief requested must prevent or redress the injury).

See, e.g., Lujan v. Defenders of Wildlife, 504 U.S. 555 (1992); *Valley Forge Christian College v. Americans United for Separation of Church and State, Inc.*, 454 U.S. 464 (1982).

In addition to the Article III requirements, the federal judiciary has also established a "prudential standing" requirement, i.e., that a plaintiff is a proper party to invoke a judicial resolution of the dispute. *Bender v. Williamsport Area School District*, 475 U.S. 534 (1986). Meeting this requirement depends in large part on whether the plaintiff's grievance comes within the "zone of interests" protected or regulated by the constitutional guarantee or statute under consideration. *Bennett v. Spear*, 520 U.S. 154 (1997); *Thompson v. N.Am. Stainless, LP*, 562 U.S. 170 (2011).

> **EXAM NOTE:** When answering questions about standing, eliminate answer choices involving only the substance of the claim and focus on whether the plaintiff is legally qualified to press a claim, regardless of merit.

1) Injury in fact

The injury must be both **concrete** and **particularized.**

a) Individualized injury

When a plaintiff has been directly injured "it does not matter how many people" were also injured; when "a harm is concrete, though widely shared," there is standing. *Massachusetts v. EPA*, 549 U.S. 497 (2007). However, even though an injury may satisfy the injury-in-fact standard, the court may refuse to adjudicate a claim by the application of the principles of prudence. Under this prudential-standing principle, an injury that is shared by all or a large class of citizens (i.e., a generalized grievance) is not sufficiently individualized to give the plaintiff standing. *Warth v. Seldin*, 422 U.S. 490 (1975).

b) Type of injury

The injury need not be physical or economic. *United States v. SCRAP*, 412 U.S. 669 (1973). While a generalized harm to the environment does not confer standing, a harm that affects recreational "or even mere esthetic interests" is sufficient. *See Summers v. Earth Island Inst.*, 555 U.S. 488 (2009).

c) Future injury

While the threat of future injury can suffice, it cannot be merely hypothetical or conjectural, but must be actual and imminent. When a future injury is alleged, damages cannot be obtained, but an injunction can be sought.

2) Causation

The plaintiff must show that the injury was fairly traceable to the challenged action—that is, that the defendant's conduct caused the injury. *Warth v. Seldin*, 422 U.S. 490 (1975).

3) Redressability

It must be likely (as opposed to speculative) that a favorable court decision will redress a discrete injury suffered by the plaintiff.

b. Taxpayer status

Usually, a taxpayer does not have standing to file a federal lawsuit simply because the taxpayer believes that the government has allocated funds in an improper way. However, a taxpayer does have standing to litigate whether, or how much, she owes on her tax bill. See *United States v.* Windsor, 570 U.S. 744 (2013) (litigating disallowance of estate tax exemption for surviving same-sex spouse under the Defense of Marriage Act.)

> **EXAM NOTE:** The standing of taxpayers is frequently tested on the MBE. A taxpayer has standing when the taxpayer challenges governmental expenditures as violating the Establishment Clause.

1) Governmental conduct

The conduct of the federal government, or of any state government, is too far removed from individual taxpayer returns for any injury to the taxpayer to be traced to the use of tax revenues. *DaimlerChrysler Corp. v. Cuno*, 547 U.S. 332 (2006). Long-standing precedent, however, suggests that a municipal taxpayer does have standing to sue a municipal government in federal court. *Crampton v. Zabriskie*, 101 U.S. 601 (1879).

2) Exception—Establishment Clause challenge

There is an exception for a taxpayer suit challenging a **specific legislative appropriation** made under the taxing and spending powers for violation of the Establishment Clause. *Flast v. Cohen*, 392 U.S. 83 (1968) (congressional grant to religious schools). This exception does not apply to the transfer of property to a religious organization by Congress under the Property Power, *Valley Forge Christian College v. Americans United for Separation of Church and State*, 454 U.S. 464 (1982), nor to expenditures made by the President to religious organizations from monies appropriated by Congress to the President's general discretionary fund, *Hein v. Freedom From Religion Foundation*, 551 U.S. 587 (2007), nor to a tax credit for contributions to student tuition organizations that provide scholarships to students attending private schools, including religious schools. *Ariz. Christian Sch. Tuition Org. v. Winn*, 563 U.S. 125 (2011).

c. Third-party standing

A litigant generally has no standing to bring a lawsuit based on legal claims of a third party. There are a few notable exceptions to this rule, however:

i) If the third parties would experience difficulty or are **unable to assert their own rights,** such as a Caucasian defendant raising equal protection and due process objections to discrimination against African-American people in the selection of grand juries, *Campbell v. Louisiana*, 523 U.S. 392 (1998);

ii) If there is a **special relationship between the plaintiff and the third parties,** such as an employer asserting the rights of its employees, a doctor asserting the rights of his patients in challenging an abortion ruling, *Singleton v. Wulff*, 428 U.S. 106 (1976), or a private school asserting its students' rights to attend despite a statute requiring attendance at public schools, *Pierce v. Society of Sisters*, 268 U.S. 510 (1925); and

iii) If a plaintiff suffers an injury, and **the injury adversely affects the plaintiff's relationship with a third party,** the plaintiff may assert the third-party's rights. *Craig v. Boren*, 429 U.S. 190 (1976).

The rule that a litigant has no standing to bring a lawsuit on behalf of a third party is based on prudential or discretionary considerations. The federal courts may refuse to hear any case on **prudential-standing** grounds. *Elk Grove Unified School Dist. v. Newdow*, 542 U.S. 1 (2004).

1) Organizational standing

An organization may bring an action when it has suffered an injury. In addition, an organization may bring an action on behalf of its members (even if the organization has not suffered an injury itself) if:

  i)   Its members would have standing to sue in their own right; and

  ii) The interests at stake are germane to the organization's purpose.

Hunt v. Washington State Apple Adver. Comm'n., 432 U.S. 333 (1977). When damages are sought, generally neither the claim asserted nor the relief requested can require the participation of individual members in the lawsuit. But note that the damages limitation is not constitutionally mandated and can be waived by Congress. *United Food & Commer. Workers Union Local 751 v. Brown Group*, 517 U.S. 544 (1996).

2) Parental standing

Generally, a parent has standing to bring an action on behalf of the parent's minor child. However, after a divorce, the right to bring such an action may be limited to only one of the child's parents. Moreover, when the right to bring such an action is based on family-law rights that are in dispute, the federal courts should not entertain an action if prosecution of the lawsuit may have an adverse effect on the child. *Elk Grove Unified School District v. Newdow*, 542 U.S. 1 (2004) (noncustodial parent with joint legal custody could not challenge school policy on behalf of his daughter when the custodial parent opposed the action).

d. Assignee standing

An assignee of a claim has standing to enforce the rights of an assignor, even when the assignee is contractually obligated to return any litigation proceeds to the assignor (e.g., an assignee for collection), provided the assignment was made for ordinary business purposes and in good faith. *Sprint Commc'ns Co., L.P. v. APCC Servs., Inc.*, 554 U.S. 269 (2008).

e. Citizenship standing

Citizens do not have standing to assert a claim to enforce a constitutional provision merely because they are citizens, although a citizen may bring an action against the government to compel adherence to a specific federal statute. Even in such a case, the plaintiff must have directly suffered an injury in fact.

f. Standing to assert a Tenth Amendment violation

A party has standing to challenge the constitutionality of a federal statute on the grounds that it exceeds Congress's enumerated powers and intrudes upon the powers reserved to the states by the Tenth Amendment. *Bond v. United States*, 564 U.S. 211 (2011) (defendant prosecuted for violation of federal statute).

g. Legislator's standing

Generally, a legislator who voted against a bill does not have standing to challenge the resulting statute. *Coleman v. Miller*, 307 U.S. 433 (1939) (state legislators lacked standing); *Raines v. Byrd*, 521 U.S. 811, 823 (1997) (members of Congress lacked standing).

h. Section 1983 claims

42 U.S.C. 1983 ("section 1983") provides that any person acting under color of state law who deprives any citizen of the United States (or any other person within the United States) of any rights, privileges, or immunities secured by the Constitution and laws can be held personally liable for the deprivation. Section 1983 does not provide any substantive rights. Instead, it provides a method to enforce the substantive rights granted by the Constitution and other federal laws.

1) Proper defendants

Individual government employees at any level of government may be sued under section 1983 in their individual capacities for damages, declaratory or injunctive relief. *Hafer v. Melo*, 502 U.S. 25 (1991); *City of Oklahoma City v. Tuttle*, 471 U.S. 808 (1985); *Bivens v. Six Unknown Named Agents of the Federal Bureau of Narcotics*, 403 U.S. 388 (1971). This is permitted because a suit against a government employee in his individual capacity does not represent a suit against the government entity. *Kentucky v. Graham*, 473 U.S. 159 (1985). Municipalities and local governments are also considered "persons" subject to suit pursuant to section 1983 for damages and prospective relief. *Monell v. Dept. of Social Services of New York*, 436 U.S. 658 (1978).

2) Color of state law

To use section 1983 as a remedy for the deprivation of a federally secured right, a plaintiff must show that the alleged deprivation was committed by a person acting **under color of state law**. The traditional definition of acting under the color of state law requires the defendant to have exercised power "possessed by virtue of state law and made possible only because the wrongdoer is clothed with the authority of state law." *West v. Atkins*, 487 U.S. 42, 49 (1988)(quoting *United States v. Classic*, 313 U.S. 299, 326 (1941)). Purely private conduct is not within the reach of the statute, but a private actor may be found to have acted under color of state law under certain circumstances.

> **EXAM NOTE:** The "color of state law" requirement is functionally identical to the "state action" prerequisite to trigger constitutional liability. *Lugar v. Edmondson Oil Co.*, 457 U.S. 922 (1982); *see* X. "State Action," *infra*.

2. Timeliness

An action that is brought too soon ("unripe") or too late ("moot") will not be heard.

a. Ripeness

"Ripeness" refers to the readiness of a case for litigation. A federal court will not consider a claim before it has fully developed; to do so would be premature, and any potential injury would be speculative.

For a case to be "ripe" for litigation, the plaintiff must have experienced a **real injury** (or imminent threat thereof). Hence, if an ambiguous law has a long history of non-enforcement, a case challenging that law may lack ripeness. *See Poe v. Ullman*, 367 U.S. 497 (1961).

b. Mootness

A case has become moot if further legal proceedings would have no effect; that is, if there is no longer a controversy. A **live controversy** must exist **at each**

stage of review, not merely when the complaint is filed, in order for a case to be viable at that stage.

> **Example:** The classic example of mootness is the case of *DeFunis v. Odegaard,* 416 U.S. 312 (1974). The plaintiff was a student who had been denied admission to law school and had then been provisionally admitted while the case was pending. Because the student was scheduled to graduate within a few months at the time the decision was rendered, and there was no action that the law school could take to prevent it, the Court determined that a decision on its part would have no effect on the student's rights. Therefore, the case was dismissed as moot.

1) Exception—capable of repetition, yet evading review

A case will not be dismissed as moot if there is a reasonable expectation that the same complaining party will be subjected to the same action again ("capable of repetition") but that the action will not last long enough to work its way through the judicial system ("yet evading review"). *Turner v. Rogers,* 564 U.S. 431 (2011).

> **Example:** The most cited example of this exception is *Roe v. Wade,* 410 U.S. 113 (1973), when the state argued that the case was moot because the plaintiff, who was challenging a Texas statute forbidding abortion, was no longer pregnant by the time the case reached the Supreme Court. Because of the relatively short human gestation period (compared to a lawsuit), abortion litigation was readily capable of being repeated, but also likely to evade review, and the case was not dismissed as moot.

2) Exception—voluntary cessation

A court will not dismiss as moot a case in which the defendant voluntarily ceases its illegal or wrongful action once litigation has commenced. The court must be assured that "there is no reasonable expectation that the wrong will be repeated." *United States v. W.T. Grant Co.,* 345 U.S. 629 (1953).

3) Exception—class actions

If the named plaintiff's claim in a certified class action is resolved and becomes moot, that fact does not render the entire class action moot. *United States Parole Comm'n. v. Geraghty,* 445 U.S. 388 (1980).

3. Justiciability—Further Issues

Federal courts may invoke a variety of other reasons not to decide a case.

a. Advisory opinions

Federal courts may not render advisory opinions on the basis of an abstract or a hypothetical dispute. An actual case or controversy must exist.

> **EXAM NOTE:** Fact patterns involving a request for declaratory judgment are likely testing advisory opinion prohibition.

b. Declaratory judgments

The courts are not prohibited from issuing declaratory judgments, however, that determine the legal effect of proposed conduct without awarding damages or injunctive relief. The challenged action must pose a real and immediate danger to a party's interests for there to be an actual dispute (as opposed to a hypothetical one).

c. Political questions

A federal court will not rule on a matter in controversy if the matter is a political question to be resolved by one or both of the other two branches of government. *Baker v. Carr*, 369 U.S. 186 (1962).

A political question not subject to judicial review arises when:

i) The Constitution has assigned decision making on this subject to a different branch of the government; or

ii) The matter is inherently not one that the judiciary can decide.

Example: Details of Congress's impeachment procedures (constitutionally assigned to a branch other than the judiciary) and the President's conduct of foreign affairs (not within judicial competence) are examples of political questions.

Compare: The political question doctrine does not bar courts from adjudicating the constitutionality of a federal statute directing that an American child born in Jerusalem is entitled to have Israel listed as her place of birth in her U.S. passport. The Court held that the Constitution did not commit the issue to another branch of government and resolving the case would involve examining "textual, structural, and historical evidence" concerning statutory and constitutional provisions, something within judicial competence. *Zivotofsky ex rel. Zivotofsky v. Clinton*, 566 U.S. 189 (2012).

4. Abstention

A federal court may abstain from deciding a claim when strong state interests are at stake.

a. *Pullman* doctrine

A court may refrain from ruling on a federal constitutional claim that depends on resolving an unsettled issue of state law best left to the state courts. *Railroad Comm'n of Texas v. Pullman*, 312 U.S. 496 (1941).

b. *Younger* abstention

A court will not enjoin a pending state criminal case in the absence of bad faith, harassment, or a patently invalid state statute. *Younger v. Harris*, 401 U.S. 37 (1971). Abstention also may be appropriate with regard to a civil enforcement proceeding or a civil proceeding involving an order uniquely in furtherance of the state courts' ability to perform their judicial functions, such as a civil contempt order. *Sprint Commc'ns, Inc. v. Jacobs*, 571 U.S. 69 (2013).

II. THE POWERS OF CONGRESS

Just as the federal courts are courts of limited jurisdiction, the powers of Congress are not plenary or exclusive. As the Tenth Amendment makes clear, the federal government may exercise only those powers specifically enumerated by the Constitution; it is state governments and the people, not the national government, that retain any powers not mentioned in the federal charter. Any action by the federal government must be supported by a source of power originating in the Constitution. Article I, Section 1 vests all legislative powers of the federal government in Congress.

EXAM NOTE: Congress may amend or repeal existing law and direct that the change be applied in all related *pending* actions, i.e., those in which a final judgment has not been entered. If a bar exam question involves application of new legislation, pay attention to the status of any case to which it is to be applied.

EXAM NOTE: Congress has no general police power to legislate for the health, safety, welfare, or morals of citizens. The validity of a federal statute on the bar exam may not be justified based on "federal police power."

A. COMMERCE

Article I, Section 8, Clause 3 of the Constitution, known as the Commerce Clause, empowers Congress "[t]o regulate Commerce with foreign Nations, and among the several States, and with the Indian Tribes." The term "commerce" has been defined to include essentially all activity—including transportation, traffic, or transmission of gas, electricity, radio, TV, mail, and telegraph—involving or affecting two or more states.

1. Interstate Commerce

a. Power to regulate

Congress has the power to regulate (i) the **channels** (highways, waterways, airways, etc.) and (ii) the **instrumentalities** (cars, trucks, ships, airplanes, etc.) of interstate commerce, as well as (iii) any activity that **substantially affects** interstate commerce, provided that the regulation does not infringe upon any other constitutional right. *United States v. Lopez*, 514 U.S. 549 (1995).

b. Construed broadly

The Supreme Court has upheld acts of Congress seeking to prohibit or restrict the entry of persons, products, and services into the stream of interstate commerce, as well as acts regulating the interstate movement of kidnap victims, stolen vehicles, and telephone transmissions. However, the Commerce Clause does not give Congress the power to mandate that individuals not engaged in commercial activities engage in commerce. *Nat'l Fed'n of Indep. Bus. v. Sebelius (The Patient Protection and Affordable Care Cases)*, 567 U.S. 519 (2012) (requiring individuals not engaged in commercial activities to buy unwanted health insurance could not be sustained as a regulation of interstate commerce).

2. "Substantial Economic Effect"

Congress has the power to regulate any activity, intra- or interstate, that in and of itself or in combination with other activities has a "substantial economic effect upon" or "effect on movement in" interstate commerce.

a. Aggregation

With respect to an intrastate activity that does not have a direct economic impact on interstate commerce, such as growing crops for personal consumption, as long as there is a **rational basis** for concluding that the "total incidence" of the activity in the aggregate substantially affects interstate commerce, Congress may regulate even a minute amount of that total. *Gonzales v. Raich*, 545 U.S. 1 (2005) (prohibition on personal cultivation and use of medical marijuana upheld due to effect on overall interstate trade). The practical effect of this rule is that with regard to economic activity, a substantial economic effect is presumed.

Example: The Supreme Court upheld congressional restriction of wheat production, even when applied to a farmer growing only 23 acres of wheat, primarily for personal use. The rationale behind the decision was that if every small farmer were allowed to grow an unrestricted amount of wheat, the combined effect could have an impact on supply and demand in the interstate market. *Wickard v. Filburn*, 317 U.S. 111 (1942).

3. Non-Economic Activity

Congress's power under the Commerce Clause to regulate **intrastate** activity that is not obviously economic (so-called "non-economic" activity) is limited to some degree by principles of federalism, at least when the regulation involves an area of traditional state concern. The non-economic activity must have a substantial economic effect on interstate commerce. *Nat'l Fed'n of Indep. Bus. v. Sebelius (The Patient Protection and Affordable Care Cases)*, 567 U.S. 519 (2012) (requiring individuals not engaged in commercial activities to buy unwanted health insurance could not be sustained as a regulation of interstate commerce); *United States v. Morrison*, 529 U.S. 598 (2000) (federal civil remedy for victims of gender-motivated violence held invalid); *United States v. Lopez*, 514 U.S. 549 (1995) (federal statute regulating possession of a firearm within 1,000 feet of a public school struck down).

B. TAXATION AND SPENDING

Article I, Section 8 provides: "Congress shall have power to lay and collect taxes, duties, imposts and excises, to pay the debts and provide for the common defense and general welfare of the United States; but all duties, imposts and excises shall be uniform throughout the United States."

> **EXAM NOTE:** If you see the terms "appropriation bill" or "authorization bill" on the exam, the power to spend is likely a consideration.

1. Taxing Power

A tax by Congress will generally be upheld if it has a **reasonable relationship to revenue production**.

> **Example:** The Affordable Health Act's individual mandate, requiring individuals to buy health insurance or pay a penalty, merely imposed a tax on those who failed to buy insurance and therefore could be sustained under the taxing power. *Nat'l Fed'n of Indep. Bus. v. Sebelius (The Patient Protection and Affordable Care Cases)*, 567 U.S. 519 (2012).

a. Any purpose

Of the three branches of the federal government, Article I, Section 8 of the Constitution gives Congress the plenary (i.e., exclusive) power to raise revenue through the imposition of taxes. The government has no burden to prove that the tax is necessary to any compelling governmental interest. Instead, the General Welfare Clause has been interpreted as permitting Congress to exercise its power to tax for any public purpose. (Note: This clause has been interpreted as having the same effect on the spending power, as discussed at § II.B.2. Spending, *infra*.)

> While the General Welfare Clause gives Congress broad power in exercising its spending and taxing powers, it does not give Congress the specific power to legislate for the public welfare in general. Such "police power" is reserved for the states.

b. Indirect tax—uniformity

The requirement that indirect federal taxes (i.e., duties, sales taxes, and import & excise taxes) must be uniform throughout the United States has been interpreted to mean **geographical** uniformity only; the product or activity at issue must be identically taxed in every state in which it is found. Differences in state law do not destroy this uniformity. *Fernandez v. Wiener*, 326 U.S. 340 (1945) (federal estate tax on "community property" valid despite variation in state laws regarding marital property).

c. **Direct tax—apportionment**

Article I, Section 2 provides that "[r]epresentatives and direct taxes shall be apportioned among the several states," and Article I, Section 9 provides that "no...direct tax shall be laid, unless in proportion to the Census...." A direct tax (one imposed directly on property or persons, such as an ad valorem property tax) would therefore have to be apportioned evenly among the states. The difficulty of ensuring this outcome explains Congress's reluctance to enact such taxes—or perhaps the Supreme Court's reluctance to find that federal taxes are "direct." The Sixteenth Amendment gave Congress the power to lay and collect **income tax** without apportionment among the states.

d. **Export tax prohibition**

Goods exported to foreign countries may not be taxed by Congress. Article I, Section 9. Under this Export Taxation Clause, a tax or duty that falls on goods during the course of exportation or on services or activities closely related to the export process is prohibited. *United States v. International Business Machines Corp.*, 517 U.S. 843 (1996) (tax on insurance premiums paid to foreign insurers of goods being exported).

e. **Origination Clause**

Article I, Section 7, Clause 1 provides that "All Bills for raising Revenue shall originate in the House of Representatives; but the Senate may propose or concur with Amendments as on other Bills." Known as the Origination Clause, this provision is limited to "bills that levy taxes in the strict sense of the word, and are not bills for other purposes which may incidentally create revenue." *United States v. Munoz-Flores*, 495 U.S. 385, 397 (1990), citing *Twin City Bank v. Nebeker*, 167 U.S. 196, 202 (1897).

2. **Spending Power**

The spending power has been interpreted very broadly. Congress has the power to **spend for the "general welfare"**—i.e., any public purpose—not just to pursue its other enumerated powers. *U.S. v. Butler*, 297 U.S. 1 (1936). For example, Congress can provide for the public funding of presidential nominating conventions as well as election campaigns. *Buckley v. Valeo*, 424 U.S. 1 (1976). Although there are areas in which Congress cannot directly regulate, it can use its spending power to accomplish such regulation indirectly by conditioning federal funding. *See South Dakota v. Dole*, 483 U.S. 203 (1987) (statute upheld withholding federal highway funds from states unless they barred the sale of alcoholic beverages to individuals under the age of 21).

Congress cannot, however, impose unconstitutional conditions, such as requiring distribution of the Ten Commandments to patients as a condition of Medicaid funding. *See id.*, 210-211; *Steward Machine Co. v. Davis*, 301 U.S. 548, 590 (1937); *Nat'l Fed'n of Indep. Bus. v. Sebelius (The Patient Protection and Affordable Care Cases)*, 567 U.S. 519 (2012). Moreover, to be enforceable, conditions must be set out unambiguously. *Arlington Cent. Sch. Dist. Bd. of Educ. v. Murphy*, 548 U.S. 291 (2006) (parents who prevailed against local school board for violation of Individuals with Disabilities Education Act could not recover expert fees from local school board under a provision providing for recovery of costs).

C.   WAR AND DEFENSE POWERS

Article I, Section 8 gives Congress the power to declare war, raise and support armies, provide and maintain a navy, make rules for governing and regulating the land and naval forces, and provide for the organizing of a militia.

1.   Providing for the National Defense

The authority granted to Congress under the war power is very broad. Congress may take whatever action it deems necessary to provide for the national defense in both wartime and peacetime. The Court has upheld the military draft and selective service; wage, price, and rent control of the civilian economy during wartime (and even during the post-war period); and the exclusion of civilians from restricted areas.

2.   Courts and Tribunals

Congress has the power to establish military courts and tribunals under Article I, Section 8, Clause 14 and the Necessary and Proper Clause. These courts may try enemy soldiers, enemy civilians, and current members of the U.S. armed forces, but they do not have jurisdiction over U.S. civilians. U.S. citizens captured and held as "enemy combatants" are entitled, as a matter of due process, to contest the factual basis of their detention before a neutral decision maker. *Hamdi v. Rumsfeld*, 542 U.S. 507 (2004). Under the Suspension Clause of Article I, Section 9, Clause 2, all persons held in a territory over which the United States has sovereign control are entitled to habeas corpus (or similar) review of the basis for their detention, unless the privilege of seeking habeas corpus has been suspended. *Boumediene v. Bush*, 553 U.S. 723, (2008).

Because military tribunals are not Article III courts, not all constitutional protections apply (such as the right to a jury trial or grand jury indictment).

3.   National Guard

National Guard units are under the dual control of the federal and state governments. Under the Militia Clauses (Art. I, Sec. 8, Cl. 15, 16), Congress has the power to authorize the President to call National Guard units to execute federal laws, suppress insurrections, and repel invasions. This constitutional authority extends to use of National Guard units in domestic situations and non-emergency circumstances, and is not subject the approval or veto of the governor of a state. *Perpich v. Dep't of Def.*, 496 U.S. 334 (1990). (Note: By statute, Congress has restricted the exercise of this constitutional authority. 10 U.S.C. §§ 331-335; 18 U.S.C. § 1385.)

D.   INVESTIGATORY POWER

Congress does not have an express power to investigate, but the Necessary and Proper Clause allows Congress broad authority to conduct investigations incident to its power to legislate. *McGrain v. Daugherty*, 273 U.S. 135 (1927).

1.   Scope

The investigatory power may extend to any matter within a "legitimate legislative sphere." According to the Speech and Debate Clause of Article I, Section 6, members of Congress cannot be questioned in regard to activities such as speech or debate taking place during a session in either House of Congress in relation to the business before it. This provides an absolute immunity from judicial interference. *Eastland v. Unites States Servicemen's Fund*, 421 U.S. 491 (1975).

2. Enforcement and Witness's Rights

A subpoenaed witness who fails to appear before Congress or refuses to answer questions may be cited for contempt. The witness is entitled to certain rights, including procedural due process (e.g., presence of counsel) and the privilege against self-incrimination.

E. PROPERTY POWER

The Federal Property Clause of Article IV, Section 3 gives Congress the "power to dispose of and make all needful rules and regulations respecting the territory or other property belonging to the United States." There is no express limit on Congress's power to **dispose** of property owned by the United States. Under the Fifth Amendment, however, Congress may only **take** private property for public use (eminent domain) with just compensation and in order to effectuate an enumerated power.

F. POSTAL POWER

Congress has the exclusive power "to establish post offices and post roads" under Article I, Section 8, Clause 7. Congress may impose reasonable restrictions on the use of the mail (such as prohibiting obscene or fraudulent material to be mailed), but the postal power may not be used to abridge any right guaranteed by the Constitution (e.g., the First Amendment).

G. POWER OVER ALIENS AND CITIZENSHIP

1. Aliens

Congress has plenary power over aliens. *Fiallo v. Bell*, 430 U.S. 787 (1977). Aliens have no right to enter the United States and may be refused entry for reasons such as their political beliefs. *Kleindienst v. Mandel*, 408 U.S. 753 (1972). However, this power is subject to the constraints of the Fifth Amendment Due Process Clause for an alien within the United States. *Zadvydas v. Davis*, 533 U.S. 678 (2001). An alien may generally be removed from the United States, but only after notice and a removal hearing. 8 U.S.C. §§ 1229, 1229a.

2. Naturalization

Congress has exclusive authority over naturalization. Article I, Section 8, Clause 4 allows Congress to "establish a uniform rule of naturalization."

Example: Children born abroad whose parents are U.S. citizens are not automatically entitled to U.S. citizenship. Congress can grant citizenship conditioned on the child's return to the U.S. within a specified timeframe or for a specified duration. *Rogers v. Bellei*, 401 U.S. 815 (1971).

However, the right of national citizenship in the Fourteenth Amendment prevents Congress from taking away the citizenship of any citizen without her consent, unless that citizenship was obtained by fraud or in bad faith. *Afroyim v. Rusk*, 387 U.S. 253 (1967) (federal statute that stripped citizenship for voting in a foreign election struck down); *Costello v. United States*, 365 U.S. 265 (1961) (citizen's willful failure to accurately state his occupation on a naturalization application resulted in loss of citizenship).

H. OTHER ARTICLE I POWERS

Congress has power over **bankruptcies, maritime matters, coining of money,** fixing of **weights and measures,** and **patents and copyrights.**

1. Power Over the District of Columbia

Article I, Section 8, Clause 17 provides that Congress has the power to "exercise exclusive Legislation in all Cases whatsoever, over such District (not exceeding ten Miles square) as may, by Cession of particular States, and the acceptance of Congress, become the Seat of the Government of the United States." Under this provision, which is known as the "Enclave Clause," Congress has supreme authority over Washington, D.C., and may legislate freely with regard to D.C. law.

2. Elections Clause

Article I, Section 4 of the Constitution provides: "The times, places and manner of holding elections for Senators and Representatives shall be prescribed by each state legislature, but Congress may...make or alter such regulations." The Elections Clause explicitly empowers Congress to override state laws concerning federal elections.

3. Necessary and Proper Clause

Congress is given the power to enact any legislation necessary and proper to execute any authority granted to any branch of the federal government. *McCulloch v. Maryland*, 17 U.S. 316 (1819). The Necessary and Proper Clause is not an independent source of power, but it permits Congress's otherwise designated authority to be exercised fully. This clause permits Congress to enact legislation to execute a treaty. *Missouri v. Holland*, 252 U.S. 416, 432 (1920).

> **EXAM NOTE:** Because the Necessary and Proper Clause is not an independent source of power, it is not a correct answer choice by itself unless it carries into effect other enumerated powers.

I. POWER TO ENFORCE THE THIRTEENTH, FOURTEENTH, AND FIFTEENTH AMENDMENTS (CIVIL WAR AMENDMENTS)

Each of the Thirteenth, Fourteenth, and Fifteenth Amendments contains a provision that authorizes Congress to pass "appropriate legislation" to enforce the civil rights guaranteed by those amendments.

1. Thirteenth Amendment—Ban on Slavery

Congress has the power to adopt legislation rationally related to eliminating racial discrimination, as it is among the "badges or incidents" of slavery. *Jones v. Alfred H. Mayer Co.*, 392 U.S. 409 (1968). This power has been broadly interpreted to allow Congress to regulate both private and government action, including racial discrimination by private housing sellers, private schools, and private employers. (This is the only amendment that authorizes Congress to regulate purely private conduct.) This clause also gives Congress the power to eliminate involuntary servitude.

2. Fourteenth Amendment—Equal Protection and Due Process

The Fourteenth Amendment, Section 5 Enabling Clause permits Congress to pass legislation to enforce the equal protection and due process rights guaranteed by the amendment, but not to expand those rights or create new ones. Under the separation of powers doctrine, the job of defining such rights falls to the Supreme Court. In enforcing such rights, there must be a **"congruence and proportionality"** between the injury to be prevented or remedied and the means adopted to achieve that end. *City of Boerne v. Flores*, 521 U.S. 507 (1997) (Religious Freedom Restoration Act held invalid for failure to show widespread religious discrimination and for disproportion to any purported remedial goal). Congress may override state government action that infringes upon Fourteenth Amendment rights, but it may not under this amendment regulate wholly private conduct. In the exercise of Fourteenth Amendment powers,

Congress can override the Eleventh Amendment immunity of states. *Fitzpatrick v. Bitzer*, 427 U.S. 445 (1976).

3. Fifteenth Amendment—Voting

The Fifteenth Amendment prohibits both the state and federal governments from denying any citizen the right to vote on the basis of race, color, or previous condition of servitude. The courts have interpreted the right to vote to include the right to have that vote meaningfully counted. In enacting provisions based on the Fifteenth Amendment, Congress cannot treat states differently and thereby impinge on their "equal sovereignty" unless the different treatment is rationally justified by current circumstances. *Shelby Cty. v. Holder*, 570 U.S. 2 (2013).

J. QUALIFICATIONS OF MEMBERS

The qualifications for members of Congress are set forth in Article I and cannot be altered by Congress or the states. *United States Term Limits, Inc. v. Thornton*, 514 U.S. 779 (1995) (state-mandated term limits for federal representatives invalid); *Powell v. McCormack*, 395 U.S. 486 (1969) (House of Representatives could not refuse to seat a scandal-plagued member who satisfied constitutional criteria for service).

III. THE POWERS OF THE PRESIDENT

Article II, Section 1 grants the "executive power" to the President. The extent the President's executive power has been interpreted broadly by the Supreme Court, and includes the power to enforce federal law and manage the executive branch. *See Nixon v. Fitzgerald*, 457 U.S. 731 (1982). Although the Supreme Court has emphasized that the President has no power to make laws, the President's enforcement power includes the exercise of prosecutorial discretion. *Davis v. U.S.*, 512 U.S. 452 (1994). Presidents may also exercise control over agencies by issuing executive orders. Generally speaking, the President's authority is broader in the area of foreign affairs than in domestic matters.

A. DOMESTIC POWER

1. Pardon Power for Federal Offenses

Article II, Section 2 provides the President with the power to "grant reprieves and pardons for offenses against the United States, except in cases of impeachment." This power applies only to federal cases; the President may not grant pardons for state crimes. The pardon or reprieve may be granted at any time after commission of the offense. *Ex parte Garland*, 71 U.S. (4 Wall.) 333, 380 (1867). The pardon or reprieve may be made subject to conditions and may take or encompass various lesser acts, such as remission of fines, penalties, and forfeitures or commutation of sentences. *Ex parte William Wells*, 59 U.S. (18 How.) 307 (1856). The power may be exercised with respect to groups of people as well as individuals. James Carter, Executive Order 11967, issued Jan. 21, 1977 (amnesty for Vietnam War draft dodgers).

2. Veto Power

Once passed by both houses of Congress, a bill must be presented to the President. Upon presentment, the President has 10 days to act on the proposed legislation. If the President signs the bill, it becomes law. Article I, Section 7 also gives the President the power to veto any bill presented to him. The President may also veto the bill by sending it back, with objections, to the house in which it originated. Congress may override the veto and enact the bill into law by a two-thirds vote in each house.

A third option is that the President does nothing at all. If Congress is still in session at the end of the 10-day period, the bill becomes law without the President's signature. If Congress has adjourned during that time, however, the bill does not become law, because the President could not have returned it to its originating house. The President's failure to act on a bill in this situation is known as the "pocket veto" and cannot be overridden.

The President may not exercise a "line item" veto, refusing part of a bill and approving the rest, because it violates the Presentment Clause. *Clinton v. City of New York*, 524 U.S. 417 (1998).

3. Appointment and Removal of Officials

a. Appointment

Article II, Section 2 authorizes the President, **with the advice and consent of the Senate,** to appoint all "officers of the United States," including ambassadors and Justices of the Supreme Court. Congress may, however, delegate the appointment of "inferior" officials to the President alone (i.e., without Senate approval), the heads of executive departments, or the courts. "Inferior" officials are those supervised by Senate-confirmed appointees. Congress may not itself appoint members of a body with administrative or enforcement powers; such persons are "officers of the United States" and must be appointed by the President. *Buckley v. Valeo*, 424 U.S. 1 (1976) (makeup of the Federal Election Commission invalidated because a majority of its members were to be appointed by the President Pro Tem of the Senate and the Speaker of the House; the FEC's tasks were executive in nature, therefore, Congress had no right to appoint such federal officers).

b. Removal

The Constitution says nothing about the President's power to remove executive officers, but it is generally accepted that the President may remove any executive appointee without cause (and without Senate approval). Congress may not shield appointees from removal by the President by imposing a multi-tiered system in which persons at each level may be removed from office only for good cause. *Free Enterprise Fund v. Public Company Accounting Oversight Bd.*, 561 U.S. 477 (2010) (holding 15 U.S.C.S. §§ 7211(e)(6) and 7217(d)(3) unconstitutional and invalid because the multilevel protection from removal of members of the Public Company Accounting Oversight Board was contrary to Article II's vesting of the executive power in the President and contravened the Constitution's separation of powers).

Federal judges, however, are protected under Article III, Section 1, which provides that they may "hold their offices during good behavior"; they may be removed only by impeachment.

4. Authority as Chief Executive

The scope of the President's power to issue executive orders and to govern domestic affairs is extensive but not clearly delineated. The best-known exposition holds that the President's authority varies with the degree of congressional authorization of the action. Thus, when the President acts:

i) With the express or implied authorization of Congress, presidential authority is at its highest, and the action is strongly presumed to be valid;

ii) When Congress has not spoken, presidential authority is diminished, and the action is invalid if it interferes with the operations or power of another branch of government; and

iii) When Congress has spoken to the contrary, presidential authority is "at its lowest ebb," and the action is likely invalid.

Youngstown Sheet & Tube Co. v. Sawyer, 343 U.S. 579, 72 S. Ct. 863 (1952).; *See Hamdan v. Rumsfeld*, 548 U.S. 557 (2006) (military commission (i.e., tribunal) had no jurisdiction to proceed because the executive order authorizing the commission exceeded congressional limitations placed on the President to convene commissions).

5. Duty to Faithfully Execute Laws

Article II, Section 3 imposes on the President the duty to "take care that the laws be faithfully executed." Known as the "Take Care Clause," this section ensures that the President will enforce laws, despite disagreeing with them.

B. FOREIGN AFFAIRS

1. Commander in Chief

Although the President is the commander in chief of the military, only Congress may formally declare war. The President may take military action without a declaration of war in the case of actual hostilities against the United States. Congress may in turn limit the President's military activities through exercise of its military appropriation (i.e., funding) power. The questions of whether and to what extent the President may deploy troops overseas without congressional approval is unsettled; presidents routinely do so, and Congress routinely asserts its authority to approve the deployment. The courts have generally left the question to the political branches.

2. Treaties

Pursuant to the Treaty Clause (Art. II, Sec. 2. Cl. 2), the President has the exclusive power to negotiate treaties, although a treaty may only be ratified with the concurrence of two-thirds of the Senate.

a. Effect of a treaty

The Constitution is superior to a treaty, and any conflict is resolved in favor of the Constitution. *Reid v. Covert*, 354 U.S. 1 (1957). A treaty has the same authority as an act of Congress; should the two conflict, the one most recently adopted controls. A non-self-executing treaty (one that requires legislation in order to implement its provisions) does not have the same force of law as an act of Congress until legislation is passed effectuating the treaty. In the absence of implementing legislation by Congress, the President does not have the authority to make a non-self-executing treaty binding on the states. *Medellin v. Texas*, 552 U.S. 491 (2008); *Youngstown Sheet & Tube v. Sawyer*, 343 U.S. 579 (1952) (Jackson, J., conc.). A ratified treaty takes precedence over any inconsistent state law. *Missouri v. Holland*, 252 U.S. 416 (1920).

3. Executive Agreements

The President has the power to enter into executive agreements with foreign nations (e.g., reciprocal trade agreements) that do not require the approval of two-thirds of the Senate. Although not expressly provided for in the Constitution, executive agreements may be made, without congressional authorization, pursuant to the President's authority over foreign affairs.

Conflicting federal statutes and treaties take precedence over executive agreements, but executive agreements take precedence over conflicting state laws.

4. International Affairs

The President represents and acts for the United States in day-to-day international affairs. In addition to appointing and receiving ambassadors, the President has the exclusive power to recognize a foreign government. *Zivotofsky v. Kerry*, 576 U.S. ___, 135 S. Ct. 2076 (2015).

IV. FEDERAL INTERBRANCH RELATIONSHIPS

The separation of powers doctrine, which is inherent in the structure of the Constitution, ensures that the executive, legislative, and judicial branches of government remain separate and distinct in order to provide a system of checks and balances.

A. CONGRESSIONAL LIMITS ON THE EXECUTIVE

1. Impeachment

Article II, Section 4 states: "The President, Vice President and all civil officers of the United States shall be removed from office on impeachment for, and conviction of, treason, bribery, or other high crimes and misdemeanors." The House of Representatives determines what constitutes "high crimes and misdemeanors" and **may impeach (i.e., bring charges) by a majority vote.** The Senate tries the impeached official, and **a two-thirds vote is necessary for conviction.**

2. Appropriation

If Congress explicitly mandates an allocation, distribution, or expenditure of funds, the President has no power to impound those funds (e.g., refuse to spend them or delay the spending). The President is permitted to exercise discretion if the authorizing legislation so provides. *Train v. New York*, 420 U.S. 35 (1975);_*Kendall v. United States*, 37 U.S. 524 (1838).

> **EXAM NOTE:** Separation of powers questions often center on the President trying to impound funds appropriated by Congress. Remember that if Congress fails to mandate that the funds are to be allocated, distributed, or spent, then impoundment is not a separation of powers violation.

3. Legislative Veto

It is unconstitutional for Congress to attempt a "legislative veto" of an executive action—that is, to retain direct control over the actions of an executive agency, rather than going through the proper channels of passing a bill.

> **Example:** In *INS v. Chadha*, 462 U.S. 919 (1983), a provision of law permitted either house of Congress to overturn a decision by the Attorney General granting an alien relief from deportation. The Supreme Court held such a one-house congressional "veto" of a matter delegated to the executive to be unconstitutional as violating the carefully wrought legislative procedures set forth in Article I, which require passage of legislation by both Houses of Congress (i.e., bicameralism) and sending to the President pursuant to the Presentment Clauses for his approval or return. Thus, the Court made clear that a two-house legislative veto would be equally unconstitutional.

B. DELEGATION OF LEGISLATIVE POWER

Because Congress is vested by Article I with "all legislative powers," it may not delegate that power to any other branch of government. This principle is known as the "nondelegation doctrine." However, delegation of some of Congress's authority to the executive branch has consistently been held constitutional, so long as Congress specifies an "intelligible principle" to guide the delegate. *Whitman v. Am. Trucking Ass'ns, Inc.*, 531 U.S. 457 (2001).

> **Example:** The IRS has been given the power to collect taxes that are assessed under the Internal Revenue Code. Although Congress has determined the amount to be taxed, it has delegated to the IRS the power to determine how such taxes are to be collected.

Almost any legislative delegation passes the "intelligible standards" requirement, so even broadly phrased standards have been upheld.

Examples: A delegation of authority to an executive agency to regulate broadcast licenses to the extent that "public interest, convenience, and necessity require" has been upheld. *Nat'l Broad. Co. v. United States*, 319 U.S. 190 (1943). Similarly, an administrative agency could set "just and reasonable" rates for natural gas sold in interstate commerce. *FPC v. Hope Natural Gas Co.*, 320 U.S. 591 (1944).

Certain powers, however, are nondelegable, such as the power of impeachment and the power to declare war.

> **EXAM NOTE:** Because there is almost no limitation on the ability of Congress to delegate to the executive and judiciary branches, an answer choice on the MBE indicating that Congress has "exceeded its power to delegate" is almost always incorrect.

C. JUDICIAL LIMITATION OF CONGRESSIONAL POWER

Under the doctrine of separation of powers, Congress may not reinstate the right to bring a legal action after the judgment in the action has become final.

Example: An action brought in federal court under federal question jurisdiction was dismissed with prejudice because it was not timely filed. A statute that revived the plaintiff's right to bring the action was struck down as a violation of the separation of powers doctrine. *Plaut v. Spendthrift Farm, Inc.*, 514 U.S. 211 (1995).

Similarly, Congress cannot prescribe rules of decision to the federal courts in cases pending before it. *United States v. Klein*, 80 U.S. 128 (1872). However, when Congress changes the law underlying a judgment awarding ongoing relief, that relief is no longer enforceable to the extent it is inconsistent with the new law. *Miller v. French*, 530 U.S. 327 (2000).

D. IMMUNITIES AND PRIVILEGES

1. Judicial

A judge is absolutely immune from civil liability for damages resulting from her judicial acts, including grave procedural errors and acts done maliciously or in excess of authority unless there is a clear absence of all jurisdiction. *Butz v. Economou*, 438 U.S. 478 (1987); *Stump v. Sparkman*, 435 U.S. 349 (1978). The judge is not immune, however, to lawsuits regarding nonjudicial activities, such as hiring and firing court employees. *Forrester v. White*, 484 U.S. 219 (1988).

Prosecutors are subject to similar immunity rules. *Imbler v. Pachtman*, 424 U.S. 409 (1976). Court officers who perform ministerial duties, such as court reporters, are entitled only to qualified, not absolute, immunity. *Antoine v. Byers & Anderson*, 508 U.S. 429 (1993).

2. Legislative

The Speech or Debate Clause of Article I, Section 6 protects members of Congress from civil and criminal liability for statements and conduct made **in the regular course of the legislative process,** including a speech given on the floor of Congress, committee hearings, and reports. The activities of congressional aides are also protected if a legislator performing the same acts would be immune. *Gravel v. United States*, 408 U.S. 606 (1972).

State legislators: The Speech or Debate Clause does not apply to state legislators, but under the principles of federalism, state legislators are immune from liability for actions within the sphere of legitimate legislative activity (*see* § VI.B.1.b.2, State legislators, *infra*).

This protection does not foreclose prosecution for a crime, including the taking of bribes, when the crime does not require proof of legislative acts or inquiring into the motive behind those acts. *United States v. Brewster*, 408 U.S. 501 (1972). This protection also does not apply to speeches made outside Congress, or the "re-publication" (i.e., repeating) of a defamatory statement originally made in Congress. *Hutchinson v. Proxmire*, 443 U.S. 111 (1979).

3. Executive

a. Executive privilege

Executive privilege is a privilege with respect to the disclosure of confidential information by the executive branch to the judiciary or Congress. This privilege and the more narrow presidential privilege, which applies to communications made in the performance of a president's responsibilities to shape policies and make decisions, have been recognized by the Supreme Court. The presidential privilege survives an individual president's tenure, but this privilege is not absolute. *Cheney v. United States*, 542 U.S. 367 (2004); *United States v. Nixon*, 418 U.S. 683 (1974).

1) Criminal trial

Presidential communications must be made available in a criminal case if the prosecution demonstrates a need for the information. A judge may examine the communications in camera to determine whether the communications fall within the privilege. *United States v. Nixon, supra*.

2) Civil proceedings

An executive branch decision to withhold production of information in civil proceedings will be given greater deference than in a criminal trial because the need for information is "weightier" in the latter case. In a civil case, the court may be required to consider the issue of separation of powers without first requiring the executive branch to assert executive privilege. *Cheney v. United States Dist. Court, supra*.

3) Historical preservation

Congress can require the preservation of presidential papers and tape recordings. *Nixon v. Adm'r of Gen. Servs.*, 433 U.S. 425 (1977).

4) State secrets

Claims of privilege based on national security are generally accorded enhanced deference. *United States v. Reynolds*, 345 U.S. 1 (1953) (recognizing a "state secrets" privilege). *But see In re NSA Telcoms. Records Litig.*, 564 F. Supp. 2d 1109 (2008) (the "state secrets" privilege was a common-law privilege that could be limited by congressional action).

b. Executive immunity

1) Official duties

The President may not be sued for civil damages with regard to any acts performed as part of the President's **official responsibilities.** *Nixon v. Fitzgerald*, 457 U.S. 731 (1982). The President has no immunity, however, from a civil action based on conduct alleged to have occurred **before the President took office** or completely unrelated to carrying out his job.

Moreover, the President may be subject to such a suit even while in office. *Clinton v. Jones*, 520 U.S. 681 (1997).

a) Presidential advisor

A senior presidential advisor (e.g., cabinet member) is not automatically entitled to enjoy derivatively the protection of absolute executive immunity. Although the Supreme Court has stated that such an advisor may be entitled to such protection when performing special functions that are vital to national security or foreign policy, the Court has also held that an Attorney General did not qualify for absolute immunity with respect to the authorization of a warrantless wiretap for national security purposes. The burden for establishing such immunity rests with the advisor. *Harlow v. Fitzgerald*, 457 U.S. 800 (1982); *Mitchell v. Forsyth*, 472 U.S. 511 (1985).

b) Federal officials

A federal official, in performing a discretionary (as opposed to ministerial) act, is entitled to qualified immunity from liability for civil damages when the official's conduct does not violate clearly established statutory and constitutional rights of which a reasonable person would have known. This is an objective standard; a plaintiff's bare allegations of malice are insufficient to overcome this immunity. *Harlow v. Fitzgerald*, 457 U.S. 800 (1982).

Example: The Attorney General, in authorizing a warrantless wiretap for national security purposes, while not entitled to absolute immunity, was entitled to qualified immunity. The unconstitutionality of this authorization was not clearly established at the time of the authorization. *Mitchell v. Forsyth*, 472 U.S. 511 (1985).

PART TWO: THE FEDERAL SYSTEM

V. FEDERAL AND STATE POWERS

The federal system, under which the federal and state governments each have exclusive authority over some areas, yet share authority over other areas, is one of the Constitution's basic checks on governmental power.

A. EXCLUSIVE FEDERAL POWERS

The Constitution explicitly provides for some powers of the federal government to be exclusive, such as the powers to coin money or enter into treaties. Article I, Sec. 10. Other powers are by their nature exclusively federal, such as the power to declare war and the power over citizenship; a state's attempt to exercise authority in these areas would essentially subvert the power of the federal government.

B. EXCLUSIVE STATE POWERS

The Tenth Amendment provides that all powers not assigned by the Constitution to the federal government are reserved to the states, or to the people. In theory, this gives the states expansive, exclusive power. In practice, however, given the broad interpretation of the Commerce Clause and the spending power, the federal government has very broad authority, making state power rarely exclusive.

C. CONCURRENT FEDERAL AND STATE LAWS—SUPREMACY CLAUSE

It is possible (and common) for the federal and state governments to legislate in the same area. When this happens, the Supremacy Clause (Article VI, paragraph 2) provides that federal law supersedes conflicting state law (*see* § VIII. Federal Preemption of State Law, *infra*).

VI. INTERGOVERNMENTAL IMMUNITIES

A. FEDERAL IMMUNITY

1. Regulation by the States

The states have no power to regulate the federal government—for example, by imposing state wage-and-hour laws on local federal offices—unless Congress permits the state regulation or unless the state regulation is not inconsistent with existing federal policy.

2. Taxation by the States

The federal government and its instrumentalities (such as a national bank chartered by the federal government) are immune from taxation by the states. *McCulloch v. Maryland*, 17 U.S. 316 (1819). States may, however, impose generally applicable indirect taxes so long as they do not unreasonably burden the federal government (e.g., state income taxes on federal employees). Note that imposing state sales tax on purchases made by the federal government is often unreasonably burdensome and, therefore, unconstitutional. *Panhandle Oil Co. v. Mississippi*, 277 U.S. 218 (1928).

B. STATE IMMUNITY

1. Federal Regulation

The federal government has virtually unlimited power to regulate the states.

a. Congressional action

As long as Congress is exercising one of its enumerated powers, Congress generally may regulate the states. For example, a federal minimum wage and overtime statute enacted under the commerce power can be applied to state employees. *Garcia v. San Antonio Metropolitan Transit Authority*, 469 U.S. 528 (1985). Similarly, Congress can prohibit the disclosure by state officials of personal information obtained from driver's license applications because such information constitutes an article of commerce that is being sold in interstate commerce. *Reno v. Condon*, 528 U.S. 141 (2000).

If Congress determines that a state is violating a person's civil liberties, it can place limits on that state's activities by using the power of the Fourteenth and Fifteenth Amendments. *See Oregon v. Mitchell*, 400 U.S. 112 (1970).

1) "Commandeering" limitation

Congress cannot "commandeer" state legislatures by commanding them to enact specific legislation or enforce a federal regulatory program, and it may not circumvent that restriction by conscripting a state executive officer directly. *Printz v. United States*, 521 U.S. 898 (1997); *New York v. United States*, 505 U.S. 144 (1992). There is no distinction between compelling a state to enact legislation and prohibiting a state from enacting new laws—in either case Congress is precluded from issuing direct orders to state legislatures. *Murphy v. National Collegiate Athletic Assn*, 584 U.S. ___ (2018) (act preventing states from legalizing sports betting violated anti-commandeering limitation). However, through the use of the taxing and spending powers, Congress may encourage state action that it cannot directly compel.

2) "Coercion" limitation

While, as noted, Congress, through the use of its taxing and spending powers, can encourage states to act in ways in which it cannot directly compel, Congressional encouragement may not exceed the point at which "pressure turns into compulsion." *Steward Machine Co. v. Davis,* 301 U.S. 548, 590 (1937); *Nat'l Fed'n of Indep. Bus. v. Sebelius (The Patient Protection and Affordable Care Cases),* 567 U.S. 519 (2012).

b. Judicial action

1) Remedying constitutional violations

The federal judiciary has broad equitable powers in fashioning a remedy for a constitutional violation. For example, while a court may not directly impose a tax in order to fund a racial-discrimination remedy, it may order a local government with taxing authority to levy such a tax, and it may do so despite a state statutory limitation that would otherwise prevent such action. *Missouri v. Jenkins,* 495 U.S. 33 (1990).

2) State legislators

State legislators are absolutely immune from suit for damages and for declaratory and injunctive relief for actions within the sphere of legitimate legislative activity. *Supreme Court of Virginia v. Consumers Union of U.S., Inc.,* 446 U.S. 719 (1980); *Tenney v. Brandhove,* 341 U.S. 367 (1951).

2. Federal Taxation

Pursuant to the Supremacy Clause of Article VI, the federal government may tax a state; the Tenth Amendment does not protect a state from all federal taxation. *New York v. United States,* 326 U.S. 572 (1946) (excise tax impose on sale of mineral water could be imposed on mineral water from state-owned property); *South Carolina v. United States,* 199 U.S. 437 (1905) (federal licensing tax imposed on sellers of alcohol could be imposed on sellers who were agents of the state even when the tax was paid by the state). However, states have partial immunity from direct federal taxation that would unduly interfere with the performance of the states' "sovereign functions of government." Therefore, the federal government generally may not impose significant taxes directly on states for property used for or income received from the state's performance of basic governmental functions (e.g., public schools, state parks, etc.). *See New York v. United States,* 326 U.S. 572 (1946).

A tax on a payment made by a state to private person that is not directly imposed on the state is constitutional, even though the tax may have a substantial adverse impact on the state. *Id.,* (federal income tax on interest received by holders of state bonds); *Helvering v. Gerhardt,* 304 U.S. 405 (1938) (federal income tax on salaries of state employees).

3. Litigation Involving the United States and Its Officers

In suits between a state and the United States, the United States must consent before the state can file suit against it; conversely, the United States does not need to obtain consent from a state to file suit against that state. As between states, no consent is needed for one state to file suit against another state.

Suits against federal officers are limited, and generally prohibited, because such suits are considered to be brought against the United States if payment of the award will be made from the public treasury. However, if the federal officer acted outside the scope of his professional capacity, then a suit may be instituted against the officer individually.

Under 42 U.S.C. § 1983, a damage claim can be brought against a state official personally for violation of constitutional rights. The Supreme Court has recognized that a similar claim can be brought against federal officials. *Bivens v. Six Unknown Named Agents of Fed. Bureau of Narcotics*, 403 U.S. 388 (1971).

VII. STATE REGULATION AND TAXATION OF COMMERCE

The Constitution contemplates a system of regulation of commerce and taxation that includes both the federal and state governments.

A. THE DORMANT COMMERCE CLAUSE

The Dormant Commerce Clause (sometimes referred to as the Negative Commerce Clause) is a doctrine that limits the power of states to legislate in ways that impact interstate commerce. The Commerce Clause (Article I, Section 8, Clause 3) reserves to Congress the power "[t]o regulate commerce with foreign nations, and among the several states, and with the Indian tribes"; as a corollary, individual states are limited in their ability to legislate on such matters.

1. General Rule

If Congress has not enacted legislation in a particular area of interstate commerce, then the states are free to regulate, so long as the state or local action does not:

i) **Discriminate** against out-of-state commerce;

ii) **Unduly burden** interstate commerce; or

iii) Regulate **extraterritorial** (wholly out-of-state) activity.

Note: Unlike the Comity Clause of Article IV, Section 2, the Dormant Commerce Clause does not exclude corporations and aliens from its protection against state or local action. *See* XIV.A.1. "Prohibits State Discrimination Against Nonresidents," *infra*.

2. Discrimination Against Out-of-State Commerce

A state or local regulation discriminates against out-of-state commerce if it protects local economic interests at the expense of out-of-state competitors. *See City of Philadelphia v. New Jersey*, 437 U.S. 617 (1978) (state statute prohibiting importation of out-of-state garbage discriminated in favor of local trash collectors); *Dean Milk Co. v. City of Madison*, 340 U.S. 349 (1959) (state law discriminated against out-of-state milk suppliers by requiring all milk sold in the city to be processed and bottled locally).

a. Necessary to important state interest

If a state or local regulation, on its face or in practice, is discriminatory, then the regulation may be upheld if the state or local government can establish that:

i) An important local interest is being served; and

ii) No other nondiscriminatory means are available to achieve that purpose.

Hunt v. Wash. State Apple Adver. Comm'n, 432 U.S. 333 (1977). Discriminatory regulation has rarely been upheld. In a few instances, a discriminatory state or local regulation that furthers an important, non-economic state interest, like health and safety, has not been struck down. *Maine v. Taylor*, 477 U.S. 131 (1986) (upheld a prohibition against importation into the state of out-of-state live baitfish that may pose contamination hazards to local waters).

1) Burden exclusively on out-of-state businesses

The mere fact that the entire burden of a state's regulation falls on out-of-state businesses is not sufficient to constitute discrimination against interstate commerce. The Dormant Commerce Clause "protects the interstate market, not particular interstate firms, from prohibitive or burdensome regulations." *Id.* pp. 127-128. *Exxon Corp. v. Governor of Maryland*, 437 U.S. 117 (1978) (ban on refiner-owned service stations by state in which no refiners were located upheld).

b. Market-participant exception

A state may behave in a discriminatory fashion if it is acting as a market participant (buyer or seller), as opposed to a market regulator. If the state is a market participant, it may favor local commerce or discriminate against nonresident commerce as could any private business. *E.g., Reeves, Inc. v. Stake*, 447 U.S. 429 (1980) (state-owned cement plant may, in times of shortage, sell only to in-state buyers).

Be aware that the market-participant exception does not apply to challenges pursuant to the Privileges and Immunities Clause of Article IV. *See United Bldg. & Constr. Trades Council v. Camden*, 465 U.S. 208 (1984). Therefore, when a state acting as a market participant has discriminated against out-of-staters with regard to the privileges and immunities it accords its own citizens, there still must be a sufficient justification for the discrimination to avoid a violation of the Privileges and Immunities Clause of Article IV.

c. Traditional government function exception

State and local regulations may favor state and local **government** entities, though not local **private** entities, when those entities are performing a traditional governmental function, such as waste disposal. For example, an ordinance may require all trash haulers to deliver to a local **public** waste-treatment facility, but **not** to a local **private** facility. *Compare United Haulers Ass'n, Inc. v. Oneida-Herkimer Solid Waste Mgmt. Auth.*, 550 U.S. 330 (2007) (public facility), *with C & A Carbone, Inc. v. Town of Clarkstown*, 511 U.S. 383 (1994) (private facility). Similarly, a state may discriminate against out-of-state interests when raising money to fund state and local government projects. *Dep't of Revenue of Kentucky v. Davis*, 553 U.S. 328 (2008) (upholding state income tax exemption for income earned on state and local bonds, but not out-of-state bonds).

d. Subsidy exception

A state may favor its own citizens when providing for subsidy. For example, a state may offer in-state residents a lower tuition rate to attend a state college or university than out-of-state residents. *Vlandis v. Kline*, 412 U.S. 441 (1973).

e. Exception—congressionally permitted discrimination

Because Congress has exclusive authority over interstate commerce, it may explicitly permit states to act in ways that would otherwise violate the Dormant Commerce Clause. *Prudential Ins. Co. v. Benjamin*, 328 U.S. 408 (1946) (state tax only on out-of-state insurance companies upheld when Congress had enacted a law permitting states to regulate insurance in any manner consistent with federal statutes). It must be unmistakably clear that Congress intended to permit the otherwise impermissible state regulation; Congress must expressly allow or "affirmatively contemplate" such state legislation. The fact that the state policy appears to be consistent with federal policy or that the state policy furthers the goals that Congress had in mind is insufficient. *South–Central Timber Dev., Inc. v. Wunnicke*, 467 U.S. 82, 90 (1984).

3. Undue Burden on Interstate Commerce

A state regulation that is not discriminatory may still be struck down as unconstitutional if it imposes an undue burden on interstate commerce. The courts will balance, case by case, the objective and purpose of the state law against the burden on interstate commerce and evaluate whether there are less restrictive alternatives. If the benefits of the state law are grossly outweighed by the burdens on interstate commerce, then even nondiscriminatory regulation may be struck down. *Pike v. Bruce Church, Inc.*, 397 U.S. 137 (1970). This balancing test is not a cost-benefit analysis or a form of close scrutiny of state economic regulation. *United Haulers Ass'n v. Oneida-Herkimer Solid Waste Mgmt. Auth.*, 550 U.S. 330 (2007).

4. "Extraterritoriality"

States may not regulate conduct that occurs wholly beyond their borders. Thus, Connecticut could not require that beer sold in Connecticut not be priced higher than beer sold in any of the four neighboring states, because the Connecticut regime had the practical effect of regulating beer prices in those states. *Healy v. Beer Inst., Inc.*, 491 U.S. 324 (1989). There may be an exception for the regulation of the internal affairs of corporations. *CTS Corp. v. Dynamics Corp.*, 481 U.S. 69 (1987).

B. STATE TAXATION OF COMMERCE

1. Interstate Commerce

Much as with regulation, the states may tax interstate commerce only if Congress has not already acted in the particular area and if the tax does not discriminate against or unduly burden interstate commerce.

a. *Complete Auto* Test

The Supreme Court applies a four-part test to determine whether a state tax on interstate commerce comports with the Commerce Clause. *Complete Auto Transit, Inc. v. Brady*, 430 U.S. 274 (1977).

1) Substantial nexus

There must be a **substantial nexus** between the activity being taxed and the taxing state. A substantial nexus requires significant (i.e., more than minimum) contacts with, or substantial activity within, the taxing state. A physical presence within the state is not required. *South Dakota v. Wayfair, Inc.*, 585 U.S. ___ (2018).

2) Fair apportionment

The tax must be fairly apportioned according to a rational formula (e.g., taxing only the state's portion of the company's business), such that interstate commerce does not pay total taxes greater than local commerce by virtue of having to pay tax in more than one state. The burden is on the taxpaying business to prove unfair apportionment.

3) Nondiscrimination

The tax may not provide a direct commercial advantage to local businesses over their interstate competitors (unless Congress specifically authorizes such a tax). A tax that is neutral on its face still may be unconstitutional if its effect is to favor local commerce. *West Lynn Creamery Inc. v. Healy*, 512 U.S. 186 (1994) (tax affecting all milk dealers, the revenue from which went to a fund used to subsidize in-state dairy farmers, violated the Commerce Clause). In addition, the denial of tax exemption to a state entity unless the entity operates primarily for the benefit of state residents may be unconstitutional. *Camps Newfound/Owatonna v. Town of Harrison*, 520 U.S. 564 (1997).

4) Fair relationship to services provided

The tax must be fairly related to the services provided by the taxing state. *Evansville-Vanderburg Airport Auth. Dist. v. Delta Airlines, Inc.*, 405 U.S. 707 (1972) (tax on airline passengers was related to benefits the passengers received from the state airport facilities).

b. Violation of other constitutional provisions

A state tax may violate more than just the Commerce Clause.

i) A tax that discriminates against nonresident individuals—for example, an income tax that exempts local residents—may violate the **Comity Clause** of Article IV. *Austin v. New Hampshire*, 420 U.S. 656 (1975).

ii) A discriminatory tax on out-of-state businesses, even if authorized by Congress and therefore allowed under the Commerce Clause, may still violate the **Equal Protection Clause** of the Fourteenth Amendment, if there is no rational basis to support it. *Metropolitan Life Ins. Co. v. Ward*, 470 U.S. 869 (1985).

iii) An income-based tax imposed on nonresidents that taxes income earned outside the state's borders may violate the Due Process Clause of the Fourteenth Amendment. *ASARCO Inc. v. Idaho Tax Comm'n*, 458 U.S. 307 (1982).

c. Types of taxes

1) Ad valorem property tax

An ad valorem tax is based on the value of real or personal property and is often assessed at a particular time (e.g., tax day). Such taxes, which may be imposed on the full value of the property, are generally valid, but a state may **not** levy ad valorem taxes on **goods in the course of transit** (from the time the goods are delivered to an interstate carrier or begin their interstate journey until they reach their destination). *Standard Oil Co. v. Peck*, 342 U.S. 382 (1952). However, once the goods are stopped for a business purpose (i.e., obtain a "taxable situs"), they may be taxed.

A state may tax the "instrumentalities of commerce" (airplanes, railroad cars, etc.), provided that:

i) The instrumentality has a **taxable situs** within—or **sufficient contacts** with—the taxing state (i.e., it receives benefits or protection from the state); and

ii) The tax is **fairly apportioned** to the amount of time the instrumentality is in the state.

2) Sales tax

A sales tax imposed on the seller of goods is valid as long as the sale takes place within the state. Sales tax generally does not discriminate against interstate commerce as long as there is a substantial nexus between the taxpayer and the state, and the tax is properly apportioned.

> It is no longer required that the seller have a physical presence in the state. State sales taxes apply to any sellers (including online retailers) who engage in a significant quantity of business within the state. *South Dakota v. Wayfair, Inc., supra.*

3) Use tax

A use tax on goods purchased out of state but used within the taxing state is valid so long as the use tax rate is not higher than the sales tax rate on the same item. Even though a use tax does, on its face, seem to discriminate against out-of-state purchases, the rationale for its validity is that such a tax equalizes the tax on in-state and out-of-state goods. *Henneford v. Silas Mason Co., Inc.,* 300 U.S. 577 (1937).

4) "Doing business" taxes

Taxes levied against companies for the privilege of doing business in a state (made up of privilege, license, franchise, or occupation taxes) are valid as long as they pass the *Complete Auto* test (see B.1.a. "*Complete Auto* Test," above). Such a tax may be measured by a flat annual fee or by a graduated rate proportional to the amount of revenue derived from the taxing state. The burden of showing that a tax is unfairly apportioned is on the taxpayer.

2. Foreign Commerce

The Import-Export Clause of Article I, Section 10 prohibits the states, without the consent of Congress, from imposing any tax on any imported or exported goods, or on any commercial activity connected with imported goods, except what is absolutely necessary for executing its inspection laws. *Brown v. Maryland,* 25 U.S. 419 (1827).

In addition, the Commerce Clause vests in Congress the power to regulate international commerce in which the United States is involved. In addition to meeting the same requirements as a tax on interstate commerce (*see* VII.B.1.a. "*Complete Auto* Test," *supra*), a state tax on foreign commerce must not (i) create a substantial risk of *international* multiple taxation or (ii) prevent the federal government from "speaking with one voice" regarding international trade or foreign affairs issues. *Barclays Bank PLC v. Franchise Tax Board,* 512 U.S. 298 (1994).

C. ALCOHOLIC BEVERAGE REGULATION

The Twenty-First Amendment repealed prohibition and specifically gave states the authority to prohibit the transportation or importation of alcoholic beverages into the state for delivery or use within the state. However, this authority is narrowly confined. State regulations concerning alcoholic beverages are subject to the restrictions of the Dormant Commerce Clause, *Granholm v. Heald,* 544 U.S. 460 (2005), as well as the protections of the First and Fourteenth Amendments. *44 Liquormart, Inc. v. Rhode Island,* 517 U.S. 484 (1996) (Free Speech Clause); *Larkin v. Grendel's Den, Inc.,* 459 U.S. 116 (1982) (Establishment Clause); *Craig v. Boren,* 429 U.S. 190 (1976) (Equal Protection Clause).

In addition, this amendment does not prevent Congress from exercising control over economic transactions that involve alcoholic beverages under the Commerce Clause or its spending power. *324 Liquor Corp. v. Duffy,* 479 U.S. 335 (1987) (Commerce Clause); *South Dakota v. Dole, supra* (spending power).

VIII. FEDERAL PREEMPTION OF STATE LAW

The Supremacy Clause of Article VI, Section 2 provides that the "Constitution, and the laws of the United States" are the "supreme law of the land." Any state constitutional provision or law that directly or indirectly conflicts with a federal law, including federal regulations, is void under this clause. However, the Supreme Court has frequently stated that there is a presumption against preemption, especially in areas in which states have traditionally exercised police power. *Wyeth v. Levine*, 555 U.S. 555 (2009) (health and safety).

A. EXPRESS PREEMPTION

Federal law **expressly** preempts state law in cases in which the Constitution makes the federal power exclusive (such as the powers to coin money or declare war) or when Congress has enacted legislation that explicitly prohibits state regulation in the same area (e.g., the Federal Cigarette Labeling and Advertising Act forbids state laws that regulate either cigarette labels or the "advertising or promotion" of labeled cigarettes "based on smoking and health," 15 U.S.C. § 1334).

1. Narrow Construction

An express federal preemption must be narrowly construed. *Altria Group, Inc. v. Good*, 555 U.S. 70 (2008) (Federal Cigarette Labeling and Advertising Act did not preempt a suit based on a state's general deceptive-practices statute because such a statute was not based on smoking and health).

Example: The National Bank Act prohibited states to "exercise visitorial powers with respect to national banks, such as conducting examinations, inspecting or requiring the production of books or records," but it was not clear from the Act's language whether it completely prohibited the state from exercising enforcement powers when state law is violated. The Court concluded that the Act's structure and purpose differentiate between the sovereign's "visitorial powers" and its power to enforce the law. While the state could not issue administrative subpoenas to banks, it could file suit to punish violations of state banking laws. *Cuomo v. Clearing House Ass'n*, 557 U.S. 519 (2009).

2. Savings Clause

Federal law may also contain "savings clauses" that explicitly preserve or allow state laws that regulate in the same area, e.g., 33 U.S.C. § 1365 (The Clean Water Act preserves "any right which any person (or class of persons) may have under any statute or common law.").

B. IMPLIED PREEMPTION

1. When Applicable

Federal preemption is **implied** when any of the following circumstances exist:

i) Congress intended for federal law to **occupy the field** (*e.g., Hines v. Davidowitz*, 312 U.S. 52 (1941) (new federal law requiring registration of all aliens preempted preexisting state law requiring registration of aliens within the state));

Intent to occupy a field can be inferred from a framework of regulation so pervasive that Congress left no room for states to supplement it or when there is a federal interest so dominant that the federal system will be assumed to preclude enforcement of state laws on the same subject. *Rice v. Santa Fe Elevator Corp.*, 331 U.S. 218, (1947). When Congress occupies an entire field, even complementary state regulation is impermissible. Field preemption reflects a congressional decision to foreclose any state regulation in the area, even if it is parallel to federal standards. *Arizona v. U.S.*, 567 U.S. 387 (2012) (even if state may make violation of federal law a crime in some instances, it cannot do so in a field, like alien registration, that has been occupied by federal law).

ii) The state law **directly conflicts** with the federal law by, for example, requiring conduct that is forbidden by the federal law or making it impossible (or nearly so) to comply with both, *e.g., Rose v. Arkansas State Police*, 479 U.S. 1 (1986) (federal law providing that federal death benefits for state law-enforcement officers be in addition to other state benefits preempted contrary state law requiring that other benefits be reduced by the amount of death benefits); or

Example 1: Under 42 U.S.C. § 1983, all persons who violate federal rights while acting under color of state law may be sued for damages. A state law shielding state corrections officers from liability under § 1983 by excluding claims brought against them from being heard in state court violated the Supremacy Clause. *Haywood v. Drown*, 556 U.S. 729 (2009).

Example 2: Although a federal statute provides for preemption of state tort claims with regard to medical devices approved by the Federal Drug Administration, 21 U.S.C. § 360(k), there is no express preemption with regard to prescription drugs. However, a state-imposed duty on generic drug manufacturers to warn users of dangers through labeling was preempted by an FDA rule that required the label on generic drugs to match the label of the corresponding brand name drug. The court found that it was impossible for the generic drug manufacturers to comply with both federal regulations and state law. *PLIVA, Inc. v. Mensing*, 564 U.S. 604 (2011).

Compare: The manufacturer of a brand-name drug failed to establish preemption of a state-law duty to warn when the manufacturer was permitted under FDA regulations to change the drug label and then request FDA approval for the change. *Wyeth v. Levine, supra*.

iii) The state law **indirectly conflicts** with federal law by creating an obstacle to or frustrating the accomplishment of that law's purpose, e.g., *Perez v. Campbell*, 402 U.S. 637 (1971) (state law suspending licenses of all drivers with unpaid accident judgments frustrates the purpose of federal bankruptcy laws to provide a fresh start).

The existence of a valid purpose for a state law does not prevent federal preemption. *Id.*

2. Absence of Preemption

If federal law does not preempt state law, a state is free to enact legislation regarding the same issue. *Colorado Anti-Discrimination Comm'n. v. Continental Air Lines, Inc.*, 372 U.S. 714 (1963) (state statute prohibiting racial discrimination valid despite the existence of identical federal law). If there has not been federal preemption in a given area, a state is free to set more stringent standards than those imposed by the federal government. In addition, a state may recognize individual rights that exceed those granted by the federal constitution or federal statutes. *Pruneyard Shopping Ctr. v. Robbins*, 447 U.S. 74 (1980) (California's constitutional grant of greater free speech rights than the federal constitution confers upheld).

> **EXAM NOTE:** Under the Supremacy Clause, federal law sets a **floor** below which state law generally cannot go, but it does **not** set a **ceiling** beyond which state law cannot go.

IX. RELATIONS AMONG STATES

A. INTERSTATE COMPACTS

An interstate compact is an agreement, similar to a treaty or a contract, between two or more states. Article I, Section 10, Clause 3 (the "Interstate Compact Clause") allows states to enter into such agreements only with the consent of Congress. However, the only agreements that qualify as "compacts" requiring the consent of Congress are those that either affect a power delegated to the federal government or alter the political balance within the federal system.

B. FULL FAITH AND CREDIT

The Full Faith and Credit Clause of Article IV, Section 1 provides that "[f]ull faith and credit shall be given in each state to the public acts, records, and judicial proceedings of every other state."

1. Judgments

Full faith and credit requires that out-of-state **judgments** be given in-state effect. *Baker v. General Motors Corp.*, 522 U.S. 222 (1998). However, to be given full faith and credit, a decision must meet three requirements:

 i) The court that rendered the judgment must have had **jurisdiction** over the parties and the subject matter;

 ii) The judgment must have been **on the merits** rather than on a procedural issue; and

 iii) The judgment must be **final**.

2. Laws (Public Acts)

The Full Faith and Credit Clause is "less demanding" with respect to choice of law and the application of the laws of other states (i.e., which state's law should apply in a situation when either might). *Id.* However, the Constitution prohibits state courts of general jurisdiction from refusing to hear a case solely because the suit is brought under a federal law, and a state may not discriminate against rights arising under federal laws. *McKnett v. St. Louis & S. F. R. Co.*, 292 U.S. 230 (1934).

PART THREE: INDIVIDUAL RIGHTS

> **EXAM NOTE:** Approximately half of the Constitutional Law questions on the MBE will cover Individual Rights— that is, everything from here to the end of the outline.

X. STATE ACTION

The Constitution generally protects against wrongful conduct by the government, not private parties (with the exception of the Thirteenth Amendment's prohibition against slavery, which applies to private and government action). In other words, state action is a necessary prerequisite to triggering constitutional protections. A private person's conduct must constitute state action in order for these protections to apply. For example, state action may exist in cases of private parties carrying out traditional governmental functions or significant state involvement in the activities.

A. TRADITIONAL GOVERNMENTAL FUNCTION

State action is found when a private person carries on activities that are **traditionally performed exclusively by the state,** such as running primary elections or governing a "company town." *Terry v. Adams,* 345 U.S. 461 (1953); *Marsh v. Alabama,* 326 U.S. 501 (1946). By contrast, a shopping center that is open to the public does not thereby assume or exercise municipal functions, and therefore is not treated as a state actor. *Hudgens v.*

NLRB, 424 U.S. 507 (1976) (shopping mall not required to permit picketing on its private sidewalks). Similarly, merely providing a product or service that the government **could** offer is not sufficient to make the provider a state actor. *Flagg Brothers v. Brooks*, 436 U.S. 149 (1978) (statutorily sanctioned but not compelled sale of goods by bailee not state action). However, the use of peremptory challenges, even by private litigants, constitutes state action because the selection of jurors is a traditional state function and because the judge (i.e., the government) plays a significant role in the process. *Edmonson v. Leesville Concrete*, 500 U.S. 614 (1992).

B. SIGNIFICANT STATE INVOLVEMENT

State action may exist if there are sufficient mutual contacts between the conduct of a private party and the government to find that the government is so pervasively entwined with the private entity that constitutional standards should apply to the private actor. *Brentwood Acad. v. Tenn. Secondary Sch. Ath. Ass'n*, 531 U.S. 288 (2001) (athletic association was a federal actor because the association was pervasively entwined with government policies and was managed and controlled by government officials in their government capacity). State action also exists if the actions of a private party and the government are so intertwined that a mutual benefit results, such as if the parties are involved in a joint venture. *Lugar v. Edmondson Oil Co.*, 457 U.S. 922 (1982) (state action was present when a clerk and sheriff acted together with a private citizen to obtain attachment against a property of the debtor). Similarly, when the government creates a corporation by special law for the furtherance of governmental objectives and retains permanent authority to appoint a majority of the directors of that corporation, the corporation is part of the government for the purposes of the First Amendment even if the enabling statute explicitly states that the corporation is a private entity. *Lebron v. Nat'l R.R. Passenger Corp.*, 513 U.S. 374 (1995).

The Supreme Court has not laid out a test to determine what constitutes significant state involvement, but some general guidelines exist. Mere licensing or regulation of a private party does not constitute state action; the state must **act affirmatively** to facilitate, encourage, or authorize the activity. *Moose Lodge No. 107 v. Irvis*, 407 U.S. 163 (1972). Even when the state explicitly prohibits behavior that violates a person's civil rights, state action may exist if it appears the state has sanctioned the violative act.

States are constitutionally forbidden from facilitating or authorizing discrimination, but they are not required to make discrimination illegal.

C. INSIGNIFICANT STATE INVOLVEMENT

Businesses that the government substantially regulates or to which the government grants a monopoly, such as utility companies, do not exercise state action. Further exclusions include nursing homes that accept Medicaid, schools that receive government funds but are operated by a private corporation, and congressional grants of a corporate charter.

XI. PROCEDURAL DUE PROCESS

The Due Process Clause of the **Fifth Amendment,** which applies against the **federal government,** provides that "[n]o person shall be ... deprived of life, liberty, or property, without due process of law."

The Due Process Clause of the **Fourteenth Amendment,** which applies against the **states,** provides that "no state shall make or enforce any law which shall ... deprive any person of life, liberty, or property, without due process of the law."

A. DUE PROCESS GENERALLY

These clauses operate at a number of levels to protect the rights of individuals and other "persons"—e.g., corporations—against the government. At the most basic level, each clause ensures that the federal and state governments must follow certain procedures before depriving any person of "life, liberty, or property." These safeguards, like notice and a hearing, are the cornerstone of **procedural due process.**

At another level, the Fourteenth Amendment, through its guarantee of rights respecting life, liberty, and property, has been interpreted to make **most provisions of the Bill of Rights** (which by its terms applies to the federal government) **applicable against the states as well.** That is, the Fourteenth Amendment Due Process Clause **incorporates** the protections of the First, Second, Fourth and Eighth Amendments, as well as most of the protections of the Fifth and Sixth Amendments. (However, the Fifth Amendment right to grand jury indictment and the Sixth Amendment right to a unanimous jury verdict in a criminal trial are not incorporated.) The Seventh Amendment right to a jury in civil trials has been held not applicable to the states.

Finally, both Due Process Clauses contain a "substantive" component that guarantees certain fundamental rights to all persons. This **substantive due process** acts as something of a catchall for rights not explicitly set forth elsewhere in the Constitution.

B. PROCEDURAL DUE PROCESS APPLIED

1. General Principles

The concept of "fundamental fairness" is at the heart of the right to procedural due process. It includes an individual's right to be **notified** of charges or proceedings against him and the opportunity to be **heard** at those proceedings. When one's liberty or property interests are adversely affected by governmental action, two questions are asked:

i) Is the threatened interest a **protected** one?

ii) If so, **what process** is due?

> Note that procedural due process only applies in quasi-judicial or adjudicatory settings, and not with respect to the adoption of general legislation. *See Minnesota State Bd. for Cmty. Colls. V. Knight,* 465 US 271 (1984).

a. Neutral decision maker

Due process entitles a person to a fair decision maker. A judge must recuse herself when she has a direct, personal, substantial, pecuniary interest in a case (i.e., actual bias) or there is a serious objective risk of actual bias. In the latter instance, proof of actual bias is not required, and subjective impartiality is not sufficient to justify a refusal to recuse. *Caperton v. A. T. Massey Coal Co.,* 556 U.S. 868 (2009).

> **Example:** An attorney running for a judgeship on the state supreme court had received a $3 million contribution that had a significant and disproportionate influence on the electoral outcome. The contribution exceeded the sum total of all other contributions the attorney had received and exceeded by 50% the combined amount spent by the attorney's and his opponent's campaigns. The contribution was made by the president of a company that had received an adverse $50 million verdict in a lower court of the state prior to the election. It was foreseeable that the judgment would be appealed to the state supreme court at the time that the contribution was made. Consequently, the Due Process Clause required the judge who had received the contribution to recuse himself. *Caperton v. A. T. Massey Coal Co., supra.*

b. Intentional conduct

Due process addresses injury that results from an intentional governmental act. Mere negligent conduct by a government employee does not trigger a due process right. *Daniels v. Williams*, 474 U.S. 327 (1986) (prisoner's injury due to correction officer's negligence was not a deprivation of liberty).

2. Protected Interests

a. Liberty

An impingement on liberty is generally construed to mean **significant** governmental restraint on one's **physical freedom,** exercise of **fundamental rights** (i.e., those guaranteed by the Constitution), or **freedom of choice or action.**

Examples of loss of liberty include commitment to a mental institution, parole revocation, and loss of parental rights. Injury to reputation alone is not a deprivation of liberty, unless the injury is so great that the individual has lost **significant employment or associational rights.**

b. Property

A cognizable property interest involves more than an abstract need or desire; there must be a "legitimate claim of entitlement" by virtue of statute, employment contract, or custom. *Board of Regents v. Roth*, 408 U.S. 564, 577 (1972) (non-tenured professor with a one-year contract had no liberty or property interest in being rehired).

The rights to government-issued licenses and continued welfare and disability benefits are legitimate property interests. For example, although a patient may have a legitimate property interest in the continued receipt of medical benefits to pay for the patient's stay in a qualified nursing home, there is no legitimate property interest in the patient's continued residence in the nursing home of the patient's choice. As a result, a patient is not entitled to a hearing before the government disqualifies a nursing home from participating in a public benefits program. *O'Bannon v. Town Court Nursing Ctr.*, 447 U.S. 773 (1980).

1) Public employment

There is a legitimate property interest in continued public employment only if there is an employment contract or a clear understanding that the employee may be fired only for cause. *Arnett v. Kennedy*, 416 U.S. 134 (1974). An "at will" governmental employee has no right to continued employment. *Bishop v. Wood*, 426 U.S. 341 (1976). If, however, the government gives the "at will" public employee assurances of continual employment or dismissal for only specified reasons, then there must be a fair procedure to protect the employee's interests if the government seeks to discharge the employee from his position. Such entitlement to procedural due process can also result from statutory law, formal contract terms, or the actions of a supervisory person with authority to establish terms of employment.

Note, though, that even those employees who lack any entitlement to continued employment cannot be discharged for reasons that in and of themselves violate the Constitution. Thus, an "at-will" governmental employee cannot be fired for having engaged in speech protected by the First Amendment. *Board of Regents v. Roth*, 408 U.S. 564 (1972). Similarly, discharge of an "at-will" governmental employee because of the employee's political views or affiliations would violate the employee's right to freedom of expression and association, unless it can be demonstrated that effective performance of the employee's job requires certain political views or affiliations. *Branti v. Finkel,* 445 U.S. 507 (1980). To be entitled to a hearing, however, the employee must make a prima facie claim that she is being discharged for reasons that violate specific constitutional guarantees. *Mt. Healthy City School Dist. Bd. of Educ. v. Doyle,* 429 U.S. 274 (1977). A dismissal will be upheld if the government can prove that the employee would have been discharged in any event for reasons unrelated to any constitutionally protected activities.

2) Public education

There is a property right to a public education. *Goss v. Lopez,* 419 U.S. 565 (1975). Although such a right is not specifically recognized by the Constitution, all states recognize the right to a public education. *See, e.g., Serrano v. Priest,* 487 P.2d 1241 (Cal. 1971); Tex. Const. art. VII. § 1. However, the Supreme Court has never determined whether a student at a public institution of higher learning has a property (or liberty) interest in her education there. *Board of Curators of University of Missouri v. Horowitz,* 435 U.S. 78 (1978) (Supreme Court assumed without deciding that a medical student had a liberty or property interest; federal appellate court had found that the student had a liberty interest); *See Regents of University of Michigan v. Ewing,* 474 U.S. 214 (1985) (Supreme Court assumed without deciding that a medical student had a liberty or property interest; federal appellate court had found that the student had a property interest).

3. Notice and Hearing

If an individual's protected interest is threatened by governmental action, the next step is to determine what type of process is due. The Court considers three factors in determining the amount of process that is due:

i)   The **private interest** affected by the governmental action;

ii) The risk of erroneous deprivation of that interest using current procedures and the probable **value of additional or substitute safeguards**; and

iii) The **government's interest**, including the function involved and the **burden (fiscal and administrative cost)** of providing the additional process.

Mathews v. Eldridge, 424 U.S. 319 (1976). The greater the importance of the threatened interest, the greater the likelihood that the Court will require extensive procedural safeguards prior to the termination of the interest.

Generally, the person whose interest is being deprived is entitled to **notice** of the government's action by an unbiased decision maker and an **opportunity to be heard,** although the hearing need not necessarily occur before the termination of the interest.

Example: While the state must give notice and hold a hearing prior to terminating **welfare benefits,** in cases of terminating **disability benefits or public employment,** the state must give prior notice, but only a post-termination evidentiary hearing is required. *Goldberg v. Kelly,* 397 U.S. 254 (1970), *Mathews v. Eldridge, supra.*

When determining what procedures are required, while the government can create a liberty or property interest, the Constitution as interpreted by the Court, not the legislature, determines the minimum procedures required for the deprivation of that interest. *Cleveland Bd. of Educ. v. Loudermill*, 470 U.S. 532 (1985).

a. Enemy combatants

United States citizens held as enemy combatants are entitled to meaningful opportunity to dispute the facts of their detention by a neutral decision maker, albeit the opportunity is adapted to reduce burdens on executive authority brought on by an ongoing military conflict. *Boumediene v. Bush*, 553 U.S. 723, (2008).

b. Parental status

Different burdens of proof are applied to termination of parental rights and paternity actions. Because termination of parental rights deprives parents of a fundamental right, the state must use clear and convincing evidence to support allegations of neglect. *Santosky v. Kramer*, 455 U.S. 745 (1982).

When a mother or child is initiating a paternity suit, due process requires proof by only a preponderance of evidence. *Rivera v. Michigan*, 483 U.S. 574 (1987). In a paternity action initiated by the state, the state must pay for the necessary blood work used in determining paternity. *Little v. Streater*, 452 U.S. 1 (1981).

c. Forfeitures

Forfeiture is an involuntary relinquishment of property that the government alleges is connected to criminal activity. Generally, the government is required to provide the owner with notice and a hearing prior to seizure of real property. *United States v. James Daniel Good Real Property*, 510 U.S. 43 (1993). However, the government does not need to provide notice prior to the seizure of personal property. *Calero-Toledo v. Pearson Yacht Leasing Co.*, 416 U.S. 663 (1974).

d. Public employees

A public employee who may be discharged only for cause has a property interest in his job and therefore is entitled to **notice** of termination and a **pre-termination opportunity to respond.** A formal hearing is not required, as long as there is pre-termination notice, an opportunity to respond to the decision maker, and a **post-termination evidentiary hearing.** *Cleveland Bd. of Educ. v. Loudermill, supra.* If there is a significant reason for immediately removing a "for-cause" employee from the job, a prompt post-suspension hearing with reinstatement and back pay if the employee prevails constitutes sufficient due process. *Gilbert v. Homar*, 520 U.S. 924 (1997).

e. Public education

1) Academic dismissal

A student is not entitled to a hearing regarding dismissal from a public institution of higher learning. *Board of Curators of University of Missouri v. Horowitz, supra* (medical school student was fully informed respondent of the faculty's dissatisfaction with her clinical progress and the danger that this posed to timely graduation and continued enrollment); *See also Regents of University of Michigan v. Ewing, supra* (challenge to dismissal of medical student on substantive due process grounds rejected; court refused to override academic decision unless it is such a substantial departure from accepted academic norms as to demonstrate that the person or committee responsible did not actually exercise professional judgment).

2) Disciplinary suspension

When a student is suspended from public school for disciplinary reasons, due process requires that the student be given oral or written notice of the charges against him and, if he denies them, an explanation of the evidence the authorities have and an opportunity to present his side of the story. *Goss v. Lopez, supra*, at 581. However, a student whose presence poses a continuing danger to persons or property or an ongoing threat of disrupting the academic process may be immediately removed from school and the necessary notice and rudimentary hearing can follow as soon as practicable. *Id., at 582-3.*

3) Corporal punishment

While state-sanctioned disciplinary corporal punishment by a public-school authority that results in the restraint of the student and the infliction of appreciable physical pain implicates the student's liberty interests, the student is not entitled to notice or a hearing. If the punishment is excessive, the student could seek damages in a civil action. *Ingraham v. Wright*, 430 U.S. 651 (1977).

f. Government benefits

The state must give notice and hold a hearing *prior to* terminating **welfare benefits**. In cases of terminating **disability benefits,** the state must give prior notice, but only a *post-termination* evidentiary hearing is required. *Goldberg v. Kelly*, 397 U.S. 254 (1970), *Mathews v. Eldridge, supra.*

4. Court Access—Indigents

a. Court fees

The government cannot deny an indigent person access to the court system because of his inability to pay the required court fees, if such imposition of fees acts to deny a fundamental right to the indigent. Due process requires such fees to be waived. Conversely, if the matter does not involve a fundamental right, no waiver is required.

b. Right to counsel

While the Sixth Amendment provides that an indigent defendant has a constitutional right to have counsel appointed in any criminal case, including a non-summary criminal contempt proceeding in which the defendant is sentenced to incarceration (*United States v. Dixon*, 509 U.S. 688 (1993)), there is no similar due process right to have counsel appointed when an indigent defendant is held in contempt in a civil proceeding and incarcerated, but procedures must be in place to ensure a fundamentally fair determination of any critical incarceration-related question (e.g., defendant's ability to comply with order for which the defendant is held in contempt). *Turner v. Rogers*, 564 U.S. 431 (2011) (defendant held in contempt for violation of child support order; the plaintiff, who was the custodial parent seeking enforcement of the child support order, was also not represented by counsel).

XII. SUBSTANTIVE DUE PROCESS

The guarantee of substantive due process is based upon the idea that laws should be reasonable and not arbitrary.

A.   STANDARD OF REVIEW

The standard of review in substantive due process cases is generally twofold: a governmental action that infringes upon a **fundamental right** is generally subject to **strict scrutiny.** If the interest infringed upon is not fundamental, then there need be only a **rational basis** for the regulation.

1.   Strict Scrutiny

a. Test

The law must be the **least restrictive** means to achieve a **compelling** governmental interest.

1) Least restrictive means

For the law to be the least restrictive means to achieve the government's interest, there cannot be a way to achieve the same interest that is less restrictive of the right at issue. A law will not fail simply because there are other methods of achieving the goal that are equally or more restrictive.

Under strict scrutiny, the law should be neither over-inclusive (reaching more people or conduct than is necessary) nor under-inclusive (not reaching all of the people or conduct intended).

2) Compelling interest

Although there is no precise definition of what is "compelling," it is generally understood to be something that is necessary or crucial, such as national security or preserving public health or safety.

3) Strict in theory, fatal in fact

The strict scrutiny standard is very difficult to meet. The great majority of laws reviewed under strict scrutiny are struck down.

b. Burden of proof

The burden is on the government to prove that the law is necessary to achieve a compelling governmental interest.

c. Applicability

The strict scrutiny test is generally applied if a **fundamental right** is involved.

2.   Rational Basis

a. Test

A law meets the rational basis standard of review if it is **rationally related** to a **legitimate** state interest. This is a test of minimal scrutiny and generally results in the law being upheld.

b. Burden of proof

Laws are presumed valid under this standard, so the burden is on the challenger to overcome this presumption by establishing that the law is **arbitrary or irrational.**

In court, the government's stated interest in enacting the law need not be one that it offered when the law was passed. Any legitimate reason will suffice.

This factor distinguishes rational basis review from strict scrutiny, when the government must defend the interest that it stated at the outset.

c. Applicability

The rational basis standard is used in all cases to which strict scrutiny or intermediate scrutiny does not apply. *Heller v. Doe*, 509 U.S. 312 (1993). In practice, most legislation related to lifestyle, taxation, zoning, and punitive damages is reviewed under this standard.

Although punitive damages do not violate due process, excessive damages may. The court considers whether the defendant had fair notice of the possible magnitude before it will bar a punitive-damages award.

The government cannot presume facts about an individual that will deprive that individual of certain benefits or rights. By doing so, the government creates an arbitrary classification that may violate due process as well as equal protection.

1) Retroactive legislation

The retroactive application of a statute does not in and of itself violate substantive due process. Consequently, a law that is applied retroactively must merely meet the rational basis test. *United States v. Carlton*, 512 U.S. 26 (1994) (retroactive application of estate tax law that resulted in denial of a deduction upheld). Similar treatment applies to a statutory change that is remedial in nature (i.e., affects a remedy but does not create or abolish a right). *Chase Securities Corp. v. Donaldson*, 325 U.S. 304 (1945) (lengthening of statute of limitations that permitted an otherwise time-barred lawsuit to be maintained upheld). Note, however, that the extension of a criminal statute of limitations may violate the prohibition on an ex post facto law (*see* § XVI.B. Ex Post Facto Laws, *infra*).

B. FUNDAMENTAL RIGHTS

Some rights are so deeply rooted in our nation's tradition and history that they are considered fundamental. These rights include: (i) the right to travel; (ii) the right to vote; and (iii) the right to privacy (including marriage, sexual relations, abortion, child rearing, and the right of related persons to live together). Under **strict scrutiny,** a law interfering with the fundamental rights of travel and privacy will generally be upheld only if it is **necessary** to achieve a **compelling governmental interest.** With regard to the fundamental right to vote, the level of scrutiny can depend on the degree to which this right is restricted.

Government infringement upon **nonfundamental rights**—those related to social or economic interests such as business, taxation, lifestyle, or zoning—requires only a **rational relationship** between the law and a **legitimate governmental interest.**

> **EXAM NOTE:** If, on a question, a fundamental right is being infringed upon for all persons, the issue is likely one of substantive due process. If the right is being denied to only a particular class of persons, then equal protection is in play.

1. Travel

a. Interstate

There is a fundamental right to travel from state to state. *Shapiro v. Thompson*, 394 U.S. 618 (1969). This includes the right to enter one state and leave another, to be treated as a welcome visitor, and, for those who wish to become permanent residents, the right to be treated equally to native-born citizens with respect to state benefits. *Saenz v. Roe*, 526 U.S. 489 (1999) (state statute denying full welfare benefits to people who had not resided in the state for one year struck down; state's interests in discouraging fraud and establishing an objective residency test were not compelling).

Reasonable residency restrictions or waiting periods may be imposed on the receipt of some government benefits. *See, e.g., Vlandis v. Kline*, 412 U.S. 441 (1973) (declining to strike down a state statute requiring one year of residence before qualifying for in-state tuition). However, durational residence requirements that impinge on the right of interstate travel by denying newcomers "basic necessities of life" are only permitted if the state can establish that they are necessary to serve a compelling state interest. In order to justify such a durational residency requirement, the state must do more than show that the policy saves money. *Mem'l Hosp. v. Maricopa Cty.*, 415 U.S. 250 (1974) (holding that a residency requirement of one year as a condition to an indigent's receiving medical care at the county's expense impermissibly burdened the right of interstate travel because fiscal savings were an insufficient state interest to uphold the requirement). Once a person qualifies as a resident, she must be treated equally. *Zobel v. Williams*, 457 U.S. 55 (1982) (division of state royalties from minerals and oil based on length of state residency unconstitutional).

b. International

Although there is a right to travel internationally, it is not a fundamental right invoking strict scrutiny. Hence, the U.S. government may limit travel to certain countries as long as it has a rational basis for doing so. *Regan v. Wald*, 468 U.S. 222 (1984).

2. Voting and Ballot Access

a. Right to vote

Under the Twenty-Sixth Amendment, the right to vote is fundamental to all U.S. citizens who are 18 years of age or older. This right applies to all federal, state, and local elections, including primary elections. Despite being a fundamental right, strict scrutiny does not apply to all laws that restrict this right. The level of scrutiny to which a governmental restriction of this right is subject depends on the degree to which the restriction affects the exercise of this right; the more significant the impact, the greater the degree of scrutiny. *Burdick v. Takushi*, 504 U.S. 428 (1992); *Crawford v. Marion County Election Bd.*, 553 U.S. 181 (2008).

1) Residency

A restriction on the right to participate in the political process of a governmental unit imposed upon those who reside within its borders is typically upheld as justified on a rational basis; nonresidents generally may be prohibited from voting. *Holt Civic Club v. City of Tuscaloosa*, 439 U.S. 60 (1978) (citizens who lived outside city boundaries could be denied the right to vote in city elections, even though they were subject to business licensing fees imposed by the city).

A person must be given the opportunity to prove residency before being denied the right to vote because of lack of residency. *Carrington v. Rash*, 380 U.S. 89 (1965).

a) Length of residency

A person may be required to be a resident of a governmental unit (e.g., state, city) for a short period prior to an election in order to vote in that election. *Marston v. Lewis*, 410 U.S. 679 (1973) (50-day period upheld); *Dunn v. Blumstein*, 405 U.S. 330 (1972) (three-month and one-year periods struck down).

b) Presidential elections

Congress can supersede state residency requirements with respect to presidential elections. *Oregon v. Mitchell*, 400 U.S. 112 (1970).

2) Property ownership

Generally, property ownership is not a valid ground upon which to restrict the right to vote. *Kramer v. Union Free School District No. 15*, 395 U.S. 621 (1969) (restriction of the right to vote on school board members to property owners or parents of school-age children struck down). A limited exception exists for elections involving special-purpose entities, such as a water-storage district. *Ball v. James*, 451 U.S. 355 (1981).

3) Poll tax

Payment of a fee in order to vote (i.e., a poll tax) in an election for federal office is prohibited by the Twenty-Fourth Amendment. More broadly, the imposition of a poll tax in order to vote in any election violates the Equal Protection Clause, as a poll tax is unrelated to voter qualifications. *Harper v. Virginia Bd. of Elections*, 383 U.S. 663 (1966).

4) Voter ID

A state may require that a citizen who votes in person present a government-issued photo ID. With regard to this neutral, nondiscriminatory requirement, the Supreme Court declined to apply a strict scrutiny standard. *Crawford v. Marion County Election Bd.*, *supra*.

5) Felon

Pursuant to Section 2 of the Fourteenth Amendment, a state may prohibit a felon from voting, even one who has unconditionally been released from prison. *Richardson v. Ramirez*, 418 U.S. 24 (1974).

6) Write-in voting

A person's right to vote does not extend to the right to vote for any possible candidate. A state may ban all write-in candidates in both primary and general elections, at least when the state provides reasonable means by which a candidate can get on the ballot. *Burdick v. Takushi*, 504 U.S. 428 (1992) (state's legitimate interests, such as preventing unrestrained factionalism, outweighed the limited burdens placed on the right to vote by the ban).

b. Public office and ballot access

There is no fundamental right to hold office through election or appointment, but all persons do have a constitutional right to be considered for office without the burden of invidious discrimination. *Turner v. Fouche*, 396 U.S. 346 (1970).

1) Property ownership

The ownership of property cannot be made a condition of holding public office. *Turner v. Fouche*, *supra* (appointment to local school board).

2) Filing fee

A candidate for elected public office generally may be required to pay a reasonable filing fee, but an exorbitant filing fee, such as one that imposes the entire cost of the election on the candidates, is unconstitutional. Moreover, alternative provisions must be made for a candidate who is unable to pay the fee. *Lubin v. Parish*, 415 U.S. 709 (1974); *Bullock v. Carter*, 405 U.S. 134 (1972).

3) Public support requirements

An independent candidate for elected public office can be required to obtain the signatures of voters on a petition in order to appear on the ballot, but such a requirement cannot deny independent candidates ballot access. *Jenness v. Fortson*, 403 U.S. 431 (1971) (state requirement that an independent candidate obtain five percent of the number of registered voters at the last general election for the office in question upheld). State election laws imposing undue burdens on placing new or small parties on the state ballots must serve a compelling state interest in the regulation of a subject within the state's constitutional power. *Williams v. Rhodes*, 393 U.S. 23 (1968) (state election scheme that effectively prohibited independent candidacies in such a way as to exclude virtually all but the two major parties struck down). Unless the requirement imposes such undue burdens on minority groups, a state can deny a candidate access to the general-election ballot if the candidate failed to receive a sufficient number of votes in the primary election. *Munro v. Socialist Workers Party*, 479 U.S. 189 (1986) (minor party senatorial candidate who failed to receive one percent of the votes cast in primary election not entitled to appear on the general ballot).

4) Write-in candidates

A state may ban all write-in candidates in both primary and general elections, at least when the state provides other reasonable means by which a candidate can get on the ballot. *Burdick v. Takushi, supra.*

5) Candidate for other office

A state may prohibit a state office holder from becoming a candidate for another state office; the office holder must resign his current office in order to run for another office. *Clements v. Fashing*, 457 U.S. 957 (1982).

6) Replacement of elected official

A state may permit a political party to name a replacement for an elected public official from that party who dies or resigns while in office. *Rodriguez v. Popular Democratic Party*, 457 U.S. 1 (1982). The governor must call an election to fill a vacant congressional seat. Article I, Section 2 (House member); Seventeenth Amendment (Senator). (Note: The Seventeenth Amendment permits the state legislature to authorize the governor to appoint a temporary replacement senator.)

3. Privacy

Though it has not found that a generalized right to privacy is contained in the Constitution, the Supreme Court has recognized guaranteed "zones of privacy" under the Constitution. *See Roe v. Wade*, 410 U.S. 113 (1973). Various privacy rights have been deemed fundamental.

a. Marriage

The right to marry is fundamental. *Obergefell v. Hodges*, 576 U.S. ___, 135 S. Ct. 2584 (2015) (same-sex couples); *Loving v. Virginia*, 388 U.S. 1 (1967) (interracial couples); *Turner v. Safley*, 482 U. S. 78 (1987) (prisoners); *Zablocki v. Redhail*, 434 U.S. 374 (1978) (fathers delinquent in child-support payments).

b. Contraception

Married persons have the right to use contraceptives, *Griswold v. Connecticut*, 381 U.S. 479 (1965), as do unmarried persons, *Eisenstadt v. Baird*, 405 U.S. 438 (1972). A state may not limit the sale of contraceptives to dispensation only by pharmacists or only to individuals older than age 16. *Carey v. Population Services International*, 431 U.S. 678 (1977).

c. Intimate sexual behavior

There is no legitimate state interest in making it a crime for fully consenting adults to engage in private sexual conduct—including homosexual conduct—that is not commercial in nature. *Lawrence v. Texas*, 539 U.S. 558 (2003).

d. Abortion

The landmark case of *Roe v. Wade*, 410 U.S. 113 (1973), established the principle that a woman has a fundamental right to an abortion. The Court acknowledged that this privacy right must be considered along with the state's compelling interests in protecting both the health of the pregnant woman and the potential life of the fetus. The resulting rule allowed for varying degrees of state restriction based on the trimester of the pregnancy. The decades since *Roe* have resulted in numerous, often conflicting, judicial opinions on the subject. The current standard is the "undue burden" test, the meaning of which depends on whether the fetus is viable (likely to survive outside the womb).

1) Pre-viability

An undue burden exists when the purpose or effect of a state law places **substantial obstacles** in the way of a woman's right to seek an abortion before the fetus attains viability. *Planned Parenthood of Southeastern Pennsylvania v. Casey*, 505 U.S. 833 (1992).

The following requirements have been held **not** to impose an undue burden:

i)   A requirement that only a licensed physician may perform an abortion;

ii) A requirement that the physician must provide the woman with truthful information about the nature of the abortion procedure, the associated health risks, and the probable gestational age of the fetus;

iii) A requirement that a woman must wait 24 hours after giving informed consent before the abortion is performed;

iv) A requirement that a minor obtain her parents' consent, or if consent is not required, provide the parents with notice of the abortion. However, this consent requirement has been found to be an undue burden unless, at least for mature minors, the consent requirement can be judicially bypassed. *Planned Parenthood Association of Kansas City Missouri Inc. v. Ashcroft*, 462 U.S. 476 (1983).

v)   A ban on a particular uncommon abortion technique, *Gonzales v. Carhart*, 550 U.S. 124 (2007). The Court found that the State may use its regulatory power to bar certain procedures and substitute others if it has a rational basis to act and it does not impose an undue burden.

An undue burden has been found when a state requires a woman to notify her husband before having an abortion, even when the requirement provides exceptions to the rule. *Planned Parenthood v. Casey*, 505 U.S. 833, 887 (1992) (spousal notification imposed an undue burden, even when the requirement could be bypassed with the woman's signed statement certifying that a statutory exception applied).

2) Post-viability

Once the fetus reaches viability, the state may regulate, and even prohibit, abortion, as long as there is an exception to preserve the health or life of the mother. In other words, at the point of viability, the state's interest in protecting fetal life may supersede a woman's right to choose; because the state's interest in protecting fetal life cannot supersede its interest in protecting a woman's health, however, there must be an exception for the woman's health.

3) Government funding

There is no constitutional right to have the government provide indigent women with funding for an abortion or for medical care related to an abortion, even if the government does provide indigent funding for medical care at childbirth. *Maher v. Roe*, 432 U.S. 464 (1977). Furthermore, a state may prohibit all use of public facilities and public employees in performing abortions. *Webster v. Reproductive Health Services*, 492 U.S. 490 (1989).

e. Parental rights

The fundamental parental right to make decisions regarding the care, custody, and control of one's children includes the right to privately educate one's child outside the public school system subject to reasonable educational standards imposed by the state, *Pierce v. Society of Sisters*, 268 U.S. 510 (1925), *Wisconsin v. Yoder*, 406 U.S. 205 (1972), and to limit visitation of grandparents, *Troxel v. Granville*, 530 U.S. 57 (2000).

f. Family relations

Related persons, including extended family members, have a fundamental right to live together in a single household. *Moore v. City of East Cleveland*, 431 U.S. 494 (1977).

g. Obscene material

There is a fundamental right to possess obscene material in the privacy of one's home, *Stanley v. Georgia*, 394 U.S. 557 (1969), with the exception of child pornography, *Osborne v. Ohio*, 495 U.S. 103 (1990). The state, however, may severely restrict the sale, purchase, receipt, transport, and distribution of obscene material. *Paris Adult Theater v. Slaton*, 413 U.S. 49 (1973).

h. Right to refuse medical treatment

It is an established liberty interest that a person may not be forced to undergo unwanted medical procedures, including lifesaving measures, but the Court has not ruled on whether this right is "fundamental." *Cruzan v. Missouri Department of Health*, 497 U.S. 261 (1990).

There is no fundamental right to commit suicide; therefore, the state may ban the assistance of suicide. *Washington v. Glucksberg*, 521 U.S. 702 (1997). The Court distinguished this decision from *Cruzan* by stating that forced medication is a battery, and there is a long tradition of protecting the decision to refuse unwanted medical treatment.

i. Right to avoid disclosure of personal medical information

Numerous courts include personal medical information within a "zone of privacy." *See, e.g., Doe v. Attorney General of the United States*, 941 F.2d 780 (9th Cir. 1991), *United States v. Westinghouse Electric Corp.*, 638 F.2d 570 (3rd Cir. 1980). Though the right to protect personal, confidential information is not absolute, courts weigh it against competing interests, employing a balancing test that generally includes consideration of the government's need for access to the information and the adequacy of safeguards, as well as the type and substance of the requested records and the potential for harm in non-consensual disclosure. *See C.N. v. Ridgewood Board of Education*, 430 F.3d 159, 178 (3rd Cir.2005).

4. The Second Amendment

The Second Amendment guarantees **an individual's right to possess a firearm** unconnected with service in a militia and to use that firearm for traditionally lawful purposes, such as self-defense within the home. *District of Columbia v. Heller*, 554 U.S. 570 (2008) (ban on handgun possession in the home violates Second Amendment). As mentioned previously, the Second Amendment is applicable to the states through the Fourteenth Amendment. *McDonald v. Chicago*, 561 U.S. 3025 (2010).

Like most rights, the Second Amendment right to bear arms is not unlimited. Examples of lawful regulations include imposing conditions and qualifications on the commercial sale of arms, as well as prohibitions on (i) concealed weapons, (ii) possession of firearms by felons and the mentally ill, and (iii) carrying guns in schools, government buildings, and other sensitive places are presumed to be legitimate. *District of Columbia v. Heller, supra.*

XIII. EQUAL PROTECTION

A. GENERAL CONSIDERATIONS

1. Constitutional Basis

a. State action

The Equal Protection Clause of the Fourteenth Amendment provides that "no state shall ... deny to any person within its jurisdiction the equal protection of the laws." This clause applies only to states and localities.

b. Federal action

Although there is no federal equal protection clause, the Supreme Court has held that the Fifth Amendment Due Process Clause includes the rights guaranteed by the Equal Protection Clause, thereby making discrimination by the federal government subject to review under the same standards as discrimination by the states. *Bolling v. Sharpe*, 347 U.S. 497 (1954).

2. Standards of Review

When reviewing government action under equal-protection theories, the Court applies one of three levels of review, depending on the classification of persons or the type of right concerned.

a. Strict scrutiny

1) Test

The law must be the **least restrictive** means to achieve a **compelling** governmental interest.

2) Burden of proof

The burden is on the government to prove that the law is necessary. Because the strict scrutiny test is a very difficult one to pass, the government rarely meets its burden, and most laws subjected to this standard of review are struck down.

3) Applicability

The strict scrutiny test is applied if a **fundamental right** or a **suspect classification** is involved. The suspect classifications are race, ethnicity, national origin, and, if the classification is by state law, alienage. (*See* § XIII.B., *infra,* for a complete discussion of suspect classifications.)

b. Intermediate scrutiny

1) Test

To be constitutional, the law must be **substantially related** to an **important** governmental interest.

2) Burden of proof

Although the Court has not clearly stated the rule, the burden appears generally to be on the government to prove that the law in question passes intermediate scrutiny. As with strict scrutiny (and unlike rational basis review), the government must defend the interest(s) it stated when the law was enacted, not just some conceivable legitimate interest.

3) Applicability

Intermediate scrutiny is used when a classification is based on **gender** or status as a **nonmarital child** (legitimacy). Note that in gender cases there must be an "exceedingly persuasive justification" for the classification, which may bring the standard in such cases closer to strict scrutiny. *See United States v. Virginia*, 518 U.S. 515 (1996).

c. Rational basis

1) Test

A law passes the rational basis standard of review if it is **rationally related** to a **legitimate** governmental interest. This is a test of minimal scrutiny. It is not required that there is actually a link between the means selected and a legitimate objective. However, the legislature must *reasonably believe* there is a link.

2) Burden of proof

Laws are presumed valid under this standard, so the burden is on the challenger to overcome this presumption by establishing that the law is **arbitrary or irrational.**

3) Applicability

The rational basis standard is used in all cases in which one of the higher standards (intermediate or strict scrutiny) does not apply. Thus, rational basis review applies to laws drawing distinctions based on age, wealth, weight, or most other classifications, as well as to any distinctions drawn for business or economic reasons.

The Court generally gives extreme deference to the legislature's right to define its objectives. In order to determine the legislature's purpose, the Court will look at the statute and the preamble. If the legislative purpose is not clear from the statute, the Court may consider any conceivable purpose that may have motivated the legislature. *U.S. Railroad Retirement Bd. v. Fritz*, 449 U.S. 166 (1980).

Some classifications, although nominally subject to rational basis review, in practice receive heightened scrutiny. *See e.g., Romer v. Evans*, 517 U.S. 620 (1996) (sexual orientation); *Cleburne v. Cleburne Living Center, Inc.*, 473 U.S. 432 (1985) (developmental disability). When the government has acted out of animus toward or fear of a particular group, that action—even if not involving a suspect or a quasi-suspect classification—will be searchingly reviewed and may be struck down even under a rational basis test. *See e.g., United States v. Windsor*, 570 U.S. 744 (2013) (Defense of Marriage Act and same-sex marriage).

3. Proving Discrimination

To trigger strict or intermediate scrutiny, there must be **discriminatory intent** on the part of the government. The fact that legislation has a disparate effect on people of different races, genders, etc., without intent, is insufficient. Discriminatory intent can be shown facially, as applied, or when there is a discriminatory motive.

a. Facial discrimination

A law that, by its very language, creates distinctions between classes of persons is discriminatory on its face.

Example: An ordinance states that only males will be considered for a city's training academy for firefighters.

b. Discriminatory application

A law that appears neutral on its face may be applied in a discriminatory fashion. If the challenger can prove that a discriminatory purpose was used when applying the law, then the law will be invalidated.

Example: A city's ordinance concerning the police academy says nothing about gender, but in practice only men are considered for admission.

c. Discriminatory motive

A law that is neutral on its face and in its application may still result in a disparate impact. By itself, however, a disparate impact is not sufficient to trigger strict or intermediate scrutiny; proof of discriminatory motive or intent is required to show a violation of the Equal Protection Clause. *Arlington Heights v. Metropolitan Hous. Dev. Corp.*, 429 U.S. 252 (1977).

Example: A city's paramedic training school is theoretically open to both men and women, but the entrance test includes a height requirement that disproportionately excludes women for the purpose of discriminating against women.

B. SUSPECT CLASSIFICATIONS

Laws that categorize based on race, ethnicity, national origin, or (in some cases) alienage are considered suspect and therefore require closer judicial examination. Such laws are subject to strict scrutiny and are invalid unless they are **necessary** to achieve a **compelling** governmental interest.

1. **Race, Ethnicity, and National Origin**

Laws or regulations that intentionally disadvantage on the basis of race, ethnicity, or national origin have almost always been struck down for failing to advance a compelling state interest. One exception was *Korematsu v. United States*, 323 U.S. 214 (1944), in which the internment of Japanese-Americans during World War II was upheld in the name of national security.

a. **School integration**

Because discrimination must be intentional in order to violate the Constitution, only intentional (de jure) segregation in schools violates the Equal Protection Clause. *Keyes v. Sch. Dist. No. 1*, 413 U.S. 189 (1973). Moreover, a court cannot impose a remedy that involves multiple school districts unless there is evidence of intentional segregation in each district. *Milliken v. Bradley*, 418 U.S. 717 (1974); *Missouri v. Jenkins*, 515 U.S. 70 (1995) (state not compelled to create magnet schools in order to attract students from outside the district).

If a school board does not take steps to eliminate intentional racial segregation of schools, a court can order the district to implement measures, such as busing, to remedy the discrimination. Court-ordered busing is temporary, however, and must be terminated once the "vestiges of past discrimination" have been eliminated. *Bd. of Educ. v. Dowell*, 498 U.S. 237 (1991).

b. **Affirmative action**

Programs that favor racial or ethnic minorities are also subject to strict scrutiny. *Adarand Constructors, Inc. v. Pena*, 515 U.S. 200 (1995) (overruling application of the intermediate standard to federal discrimination).

1) **Past discrimination by government**

For a governmental affirmative action program based on race to survive, the relevant governmental entity must show more than a history of societal discrimination. The government—whether federal, state, or local—must itself be guilty of specific past discrimination against the group it is seeking to favor, and the remedy must be narrowly tailored to end that discrimination and eliminate its effects. In other words, the elimination of past discrimination in a particular governmental institution is a compelling state interest; attempting to remedy general societal injustice through affirmative action is not.

2) **Diversity in public universities and colleges**

Race may be used as a "plus factor" (i.e., one of a range of factors to consider) in determining whether a student should be admitted to a public college or university, as there is a compelling interest in obtaining the educational benefits of a diverse student body. The use of racial quotas or of race as a determinative criterion, however, violates equal protection and is unconstitutional. *Grutter v. Bollinger*, 539 U.S. 306 (2003); *Gratz v. Bollinger*, 539 U.S. 244 (2003); *Regents of University of California v. Bakke*, 438 U.S. 265 (1978). Race may not be considered unless the admissions process used to achieve a diverse student body can withstand strict scrutiny. Strict scrutiny here requires the university to clearly demonstrate that its purpose or interest is both constitutionally permissible and substantial, and that its use of the classification is **necessary** to the accomplishment of its purpose. *Fisher v. Univ. of Texas*, 570 U.S. 297 (2013). Further, a university must regularly evaluate available data and "tailor its approach in light of changing circumstances, ensuring that race plays no greater role than is necessary to meet its compelling interest." *Fisher v. Univ. of Texas*, 579 U.S. ___, 136 S. Ct. 2198 (2016).

State laws that commit policy determinations regarding racial preferences to the voters (e.g., ballot issues) do not violate equal protection. Courts may not disempower the voters from choosing whether race-based preferences should be adopted, continued, or ended. The privilege to enact laws is a basic exercise of voters' democratic power. The constitutional validity of the choices made is a separate question. *Schuette v. Coalition to Defend Affirmative Action*, 572 U.S. 291 (2014) (upholding amendment to Michigan's constitution prohibiting state universities from considering race as part of the admission process).

3) Diversity in public elementary and high schools

A school district may not assign students to schools on the basis of race unless it is necessary to accomplish a compelling interest—e.g., remedy past discrimination. However, a district may use facially race-neutral criteria that may have the same effect, such as strategic site selection for new schools or the redrawing of attendance zones. *Parents Involved in Community Schools v. Seattle School Dist. No. 1*, 551 U.S. 701 (2007).

The Equal Protection Clause applies only to governmental action, so private persons generally are not restricted by it (*see* X. State Action, *supra*). Discrimination by private persons in various areas, such as employment, housing, and public accommodations, is nonetheless regulated by federal statute pursuant to Congress's power under the enabling clauses of the Thirteenth and Fourteenth Amendments and the Commerce Clause, as well as in most states by statute.

c. Racial gerrymandering

Race may not be the predominant factor in determining the boundary lines of legislative districts (*see* § XIII.E.2.a., Racial discrimination, *infra*).

2. Alienage

Classifications based on status as a lawful resident of the United States (as opposed to a citizen) are subject to a variety of different standards, depending on the level of government and the nature of the classification.

a. Federal classification

Because Congress has plenary power over aliens under Article I, a federal alienage classification is likely valid unless it is **arbitrary** and **unreasonable.**

Example: Medicare regulations may require a five-year residency period for eligibility despite thereby excluding many lawful resident aliens. *Matthews v. Diaz*, 426 U.S. 67 (1976).

b. State classifications

1) Generally struck down

The Court will generally apply the strict scrutiny test and strike down state laws that discriminate against aliens, such as laws prohibiting aliens from owning land, obtaining commercial fishing licenses, or being eligible for welfare benefits or civil service jobs.

2) Exception—participation in government functions

A growing exception exists, however, for state laws that restrict or prohibit an alien's **participation in government functions.** Such laws need only have a **rational relationship** to a legitimate state interest. Laws prohibiting aliens from voting, serving on a jury, or being hired as police officers, probation officers, or public-school teachers have been upheld as preventing aliens from having a direct effect on the functioning of the government.

> **EXAM NOTE:** When determining whether a position or license from which aliens are excluded falls under the government function or political function exception, consider whether the position or license would allow the alien to "participate directly in the formulation, execution, or review of broad public policy" or would allow the alien to exercise "broad discretion."

c. Undocumented aliens

Undocumented aliens are not a suspect class, but the states may not deny primary or secondary public education benefits to undocumented aliens. *Plyler v. Doe*, 457 U.S. 202 (1982).

C. QUASI-SUSPECT CLASSIFICATIONS

1. Gender

Discrimination based on gender is "quasi-suspect" and subject to **intermediate scrutiny,** which is less stringent than strict scrutiny but tougher than the rational basis test. Just as with suspect classifications and fundamental rights, there must be **discriminatory intent** by the government to trigger intermediate scrutiny; disparate impact is not enough. Under intermediate scrutiny, the burden is on the state to show that a statute or regulation that treats the sexes differently is **substantially related** to an **important** governmental interest. This test applies whether the classification is invidious or benign, and it is now applied rather stringently, requiring the government to show that an "exceedingly persuasive justification" exists for the distinction, and that separate facilities (such as separate sports team facilities as state universities) are "substantially equivalent." *United States v. Virginia*, 518 U.S. 515 (1996).

a. Discrimination against women

Intentional discrimination through gender classification will generally be struck down under the intermediate scrutiny standard. For example, a state law giving preference to men over women to be administrators of decedents' estates was invalid. *Reed v. Reed*, 404 U.S. 71 (1971) (ease in determining who should serve as administrator is not an important interest). *See also United States v. Virginia*, 518 U.S. 515 (1996) (Virginia Military Institute could not exclude women from admission to public college based on overbroad generalizations about the physical capabilities and preferred educational methods of males and females).

b. Discrimination against men

Intentional discrimination against males is generally struck down for violating equal protection. However, there have been some instances of discrimination against men being upheld because of the important governmental interest:

  i) Draft registration of males, but not females, *Rostker v. Goldberg*, 453 U.S. 57 (1981) (interest of preparing combat troops); and

ii) A statutory rape law that held only men criminally liable for such conduct, *Michael M. v. Sonoma County Superior Court*, 450 U.S. 464 (1981) (interest in preventing teenage pregnancy).

c. Affirmative action (benign discrimination)

The Court has upheld affirmative action regulations granting beneficial treatment to women over men (such as tax exemptions, increased social security benefits, and increased protection from mandatory armed forces discharge) because providing a remedy for past gender-based discrimination is an important governmental interest. *See Califano v. Webster*, 430 U.S. 313 (1977); *Schlesinger v. Ballard*, 419 U.S. 498 (1975).

2. Legitimacy

Classifications on the basis of status as a nonmarital child (i.e., those that distinguish between "legitimate" and "illegitimate" children) are subject to **intermediate scrutiny**—they must be **substantially related** to an **important** governmental interest. The Court will closely examine the purpose behind the distinction, and it will not uphold legislation designed to punish the offspring of a nonmarital relationship. To that end, states may not prohibit children of unmarried parents from receiving welfare benefits, *New Jersey Welfare Rights Org. v. Cahill*, 411 U.S. 619 (1973), workers' compensation benefits upon the death of a parent, *Weber v. Aetna Cas. and Sur. Co.*, 406 U.S. 164 (1972), or an inheritance from an intestate father, *Trimble v. Gordon*, 430 U.S. 762 (1977). In addition, a state cannot require a paternity action brought on behalf of an illegitimate child to be commenced within a limited time after birth in order to secure child support, while not imposing a similar time limit on a legitimate child seeking child support from a parent. *Clark v. Jeter*, 486 U.S. 456 (1988).

D. NONSUSPECT CLASSIFICATIONS

1. Age

Age discrimination in violation of the Age Discrimination in Employment Act of 1967 does not provoke heightened scrutiny; laws and other governmental actions classifying on the basis of age are reviewed under the **rational basis** standard. *See, e.g., Massachusetts Bd. of Ret. v. Murgia*, 427 U.S. 307 (1976) (police officers may be forced to retire at age 50, even if they are as physically fit as younger officers).

2. Poverty

Most statutes and regulations that classify on the basis of wealth (i.e., discriminate against the poor) are subject only to **rational basis** scrutiny and will be upheld. There is an exception for cases in which governmental action prohibits the poor from exercising a fundamental right because of a government-imposed fee; strict scrutiny will usually apply in those situations. For example, the availability of appeal in a criminal case cannot hinge on ability to pay for a trial transcript. *Griffin v. Illinois*, 351 U.S. 12 (1956). Also, poll taxes are unconstitutional because wealth is unrelated to a citizen's ability to vote intelligently. *Harper v. Virginia Bd. of Elections*, 383 U.S. 663 (1966).

3. Sexual Orientation

There is currently a division among the federal courts as to the standard of scrutiny that is applicable to discrimination on the basis of sexual orientation. The Supreme Court has struck down bans on same-sex marriage as violations of a fundamental right on both Due Process and Equal Protection grounds, but it has not resolved the issue of whether discrimination based on sexual orientation is subject to heightened scrutiny.

The government, however, cannot impose a burden upon or deny a benefit to a group of persons solely based on animosity toward the class that it affects. *Romer v. Evans*, 517 U.S. 620 (1996). Among the rights, benefits, and responsibilities of marriage to which same-sex partners must have access are birth and death certificates, which give married partners a form of legal recognition that is not available to unmarried partners. *Pavan v. Smith*, 582 U.S. ___, 137 S. Ct. 2075 (2017), citing *Obergefell v. Hodges*, 576 U.S. ___, 135 S. Ct. 2584 (2016).

E. FUNDAMENTAL RIGHTS UNIQUE TO EQUAL PROTECTION

The fundamental rights guaranteed by substantive due process are often protected by equal protection principles as well. Thus, impingement of the right to vote, to travel, or to marry may trigger an inquiry under either the Due Process Clause or the Equal Protection Clause. However, certain rights and principles are particular to equal protection.

> **EXAM NOTE:** The right to **travel** and the right to **vote** are the most frequently tested fundamental rights in the area of **equal protection**. (Often, both the Due Process Clause and the Equal Protection Clause will apply. Equal protection predominates if the question emphasizes denial of a right to a particular group, and it does not apply if the denial of the right is universal.)

1. One Person, One Vote

The principle of "one person, one vote" holds that one person's vote must be essentially equal to any other person's vote. To that end, when the government establishes voting districts for the election of representatives, the number of persons in each district must be approximately equal. *Reynolds v. Sims*, 377 U.S. 533 (1964). Voter approval of a redistricting plan will not justify a violation of the "one person, one vote" rule. *Lucas v. Colorado General Assembly*, 377 U.S. 713 (1964).

a. Congressional districts

When states establish districts for congressional elections, they must achieve nearly precise mathematical equality between the districts. This restriction is imposed on the states by Article I, Section 2, which requires members of the House to be chosen by "the People of the several States." An unexplained deviation of less than one percent may invalidate the statewide congressional district plan. Variations may be justified by the state on the basis of consistently applied, legitimate state objectives, such as respecting municipal political subdivision boundaries, creating geographic compact districts, and avoiding contests between incumbent representatives. In addition, variations based on anticipated population shifts may be acceptable when such shifts can be predicted with a high degree of accuracy, and population trends are thoroughly documented. *Kirkpatrick v. Preisler*, 394 U.S. 526 (1969) (variation in population of slightly less than six percent violated the "one person, one vote" rule); *Karcher v. Daggett*, 462 U.S. 725 (1983) (variation of slightly less than 0.7 percent violated the "one person, one vote" rule).

1) Congressional apportionment of House members

Congress, in apportioning members of the House among the states pursuant to Article I, Section 2, is not held to the "mathematical equality" standard. The method adopted by Congress is entitled to judicial deference and is assumed to be in good faith. *Dept. of Commerce v. Montana*, 503 U.S. 442 (1992) (Montana's loss of a congressional seat upheld, even though retention of the seat would have placed Montana closer to the ideal population size for a congressional district).

b. State and local districts

The size of electoral districts may vary much more in the case of state and local elections, as long as the variance is not unjustifiably large. A variation of less than 10% is rebuttably presumed to be a minor deviation that does not constitute a prima facie case for discrimination. *Cox v. Larios*, 300 F. Supp. 2d 1320 (N.D. Ga.), *aff'd*, 542 U.S. 947 (2004); *Brown v. Thompson*, 462 U.S. 835 (1983). When the maximum variation is 10% or greater, the state must show that the deviation from equality between the districts is reasonable and designed to promote a legitimate state interest. *Mahan v. Howell*, 410 U.S. 315 (1973) (maximum difference of 16% in size of population between state legislative districts permitted when the state respected the boundaries of political subdivisions).

1) Bodies performing governmental functions

The "one person, one vote" rule applies to local elections of entities that perform governmental functions, even when the functions are specialized rather than general in nature. *Hadley v. Junior College Dist.*, 397 U.S. 50 (1970) (election of trustees to junior college district).

2) Relevant population

In addition to requiring relative equality with respect to the weight of a person's vote, the Equal Protection Clause subjects the restriction of voting of a particular class of persons to strict scrutiny, which generally results in the invalidation of the law. *Kramer v. Union Free School District No. 15*, 395 U.S. 621 (1969) (state law that restricted voting in school board election to property owners and parents with school-aged children struck down). The restriction of voting to a class of persons (e.g., landowners) and the allocation of voting weight on a basis other than personhood (e.g., the amount of land owned) has been upheld only with regard to water-district elections. *Ball v. James*, 451 U.S. 355 (1981); *See Hadley v. Junior College Dist., supra* (determination of districts for junior college trustees based on school age population violated "one person, one vote" rule).

A state may draw its legislative districts on the basis of total population rather than eligible or registered voters. *Evenwel v. Abbott*, 578 U.S. ___, 136 S. Ct. 1120 (2016).

c. At-large elections

While an election in which members of a governmental unit (e.g., county council members) are elected by all voters within that unit (i.e., an at-large election) does not violate the one-person, one-vote rule, it may conflict with another constitutional provision, such as the Equal Protection Clause. *Rogers v. Lodge*, 458 U.S. 613 (1982) (use of countywide system to elect county board unconstitutionally diluted the voting power of African-American citizens).

Note: Federal law bans at-large elections for congressional representatives in states that have more than one House member (i.e., the single-member district rule). 2 U.S.C.S. § 2c.

2. Gerrymandering

a. Racial discrimination

1) Vote dilution

When a state draws election districts for the purpose of scattering a racial or ethnic minority among several districts in order to prevent the minority from exercising its voting strength, the state's action is a violation of the Equal Protection Clause. *Gomillion v. Lightfoot*, 364 U.S. 339 (1960) (redrawing city boundaries to exclude African-American voters unconstitutional); *Rogers v. Lodge, supra.*

2) Majority-minority districts

Under the Equal Protection Clause, election districts for public office may not be drawn using race as the predominant factor in determining the boundary lines, unless the district plan can survive strict scrutiny. This restriction applies even when the district is drawn to favor historically disenfranchised groups. The state can use traditional factors—such as compactness, contiguity, or honoring political subdivisions—as the bases for the district, and it may only consider race if it does not predominate over other considerations. *Miller v. Johnson*, 515 U.S. 900 (1995). To be narrowly tailored within the strict scrutiny standard, the legislature must have a "strong basis in evidence" in support of the race-based choice that it has made. Note that the legislature need not show that its action was **actually necessary** to avoid a statutory violation, only that the legislature had **good reasons to believe** its use of race was needed. *Bethune-Hill v. Virginia State Bd. Of Elections*, 580 U.S. ___, 137 S. Ct. 788 (2017), *Alabama Legislative Black Caucus, et al. v. Alabama et al.*, 575 U.S. ___, 135 S. Ct. 1257 (2015).

A district's bizarre shape can be used as evidence that race was a predominating factor, but such a shape is not necessary for a finding of racial gerrymandering. *Shaw v. Reno*, 509 U.S. 630 (1993).

a) Voting Rights Act

The Voting Rights Act (42 U.S.C. § 1973 et seq.) requires racial gerrymandering to ensure minority success in elections by creating majority-minority districts (i.e., affirmative gerrymandering). Until recently, the Act required federal pre-clearance for changes in voting rules, including redistricting, for specific southern states and a few other local governmental units. However, the formula used as a basis for subjecting jurisdictions to preclearance has been declared unconstitutional because it no longer reflects current conditions; therefore, it can no longer be used. *Shelby County v. Holder,* 570 U.S. 529 (2013). Receiving federal pre-clearance for a redistricting plan does not ensure that plan will avoid conflicting with the Equal Protection Clause. *Miller v. Johnson*, 515 U.S. 900 (1995).

The Voting Rights Act does not require a jurisdiction to maintain a particular numerical minority percentage. Instead, it requires the jurisdiction to maintain a minority's ability to elect a preferred candidate of choice. *Alabama Legislative Black Caucus, et al. v. Alabama et al.*, 575 U.S. ___, 135 S. Ct. 1257 (2015).

b. Political discrimination

Partisan political gerrymandering may violate the Equal Protection Clause if the challenger can show "both intentional discrimination against an identifiable political group and an actual discriminatory effect on that group." *Davis v. Bandemer*, 478 U.S. 109, 127 (1986). However, lack of comprehensive and neutral principles for drawing electoral boundaries as well as the absence of rules to confine judicial intervention prevents the Court from adjudicating political gerrymandering claims. *Rucho v. Common Cause*, 588 U.S. ___, 139 S. Ct. 2484 (2019).

XIV. PRIVILEGES AND IMMUNITIES CLAUSES

A. ARTICLE IV

Article IV, Section 2, known as the Comity Clause, provides that "the citizens of each state shall be entitled to all privileges and immunities of citizens in the several states."

1. Prohibits State Discrimination Against Nonresidents

The Comity Clause, in essence, prohibits one state from discriminating against the citizens of another state. In this context, the term "citizen" does not include corporations or aliens.

2. Rights Protected

Nonresident citizens are protected against discrimination with respect to fundamental rights or essential activities. Examples include the pursuit of employment, transfer of property, and access to state courts.

> **Example:** Discrimination against out-of-state residents in setting the fee for a **commercial** activity, such as a commercial shrimping license, violates the Privileges and Immunities Clause of Article IV, but similar discrimination for a **recreational** activity, such as a recreational hunting license, does not, if there is a rational basis for the fee differential. *Compare Toomer v. Witsell*, 334 U.S. 385 (1948) (fee for out-of-state commercial shrimper that was 100 times greater than the fee for an in-state shrimper unconstitutional), *with Baldwin v. Fish & Game Comm'n*, 436 U.S. 371 (1978) (fee for out-of-state resident to hunt elk that was 25 times greater than the fee for an in-state hunter constitutional).

> Note that discrimination against an out-of-state resident with regard to access to a state's natural resources may violate the Dormant Commerce Clause. *New England Power Co. v. New Hampshire*, 455 U.S. 331 (1982) (prohibition on sale of hydroelectric power outside the state unconstitutional).

3. Exception—Substantial Justification

Discrimination against out-of-state citizens may be valid if the state can show a substantial reason for the difference in treatment. A substantial reason exists if:

i)   The nonresidents either cause or are a part of the problem that the state is attempting to solve; and

ii) There are no less-restrictive means to solve the problem.

> **Example:** Discrimination against nonresidents with respect to the use of scarce water resources was upheld when the purpose was to preserve natural state-owned resources. *Sporhase v. Nebraska*, 458 U.S. 941 (1982).

> **EXAM NOTE:** Although the Privileges and Immunities Clause of Article IV and the Commerce Clause are not coextensive, they tend to mutually support each other; thus, consider both when analyzing a bar exam question.

B. FOURTEENTH AMENDMENT—NATIONAL CITIZENSHIP

The Fourteenth Amendment provides that "[n]o state shall make or enforce any law which shall abridge the privileges or immunities of citizens of the United States." This clause protects citizens (not corporations or aliens) from infringement by the states upon the privileges or immunities of **national** citizenship.

The privileges or immunities of national citizenship include the right to travel interstate, to petition Congress for redress of grievances, to vote for national offices, to enter public lands, to be protected while in the custody of U.S. marshals, and to peaceably assemble. *Twining v. New Jersey*, 211 U.S. 78 (1908). The guarantees of the Bill of Rights, however, are not privileges or immunities of national citizenship within the context of the Fourteenth Amendment. *Slaughterhouse Cases*, 83 U.S. 36 (1873). Therefore, those rights are protected from state action only by the Due Process Clause and the Equal Protection Clause.

This provision is seldom successfully invoked; under the limiting interpretation of the *Slaughterhouse Cases,* the rights that the clause provides are redundant to rights provided elsewhere in the Constitution. Although the Supreme Court has since relied on the clause to underscore the right to move freely among states, *Saenz v. Roe*, 526 U.S. 489 (1999) (invalidating a duration requirement for welfare benefits), there has been no subsequent expansion of use; the Fourteenth Amendment's Privileges or Immunities Clause applies, in practice, only to the right to travel.

XV. TAKINGS CLAUSE

The power of the government to take private property for public purposes is known as **"eminent domain."** The Takings Clause of the Fifth Amendment acts as a check on this power; it provides that private property may not "be taken for public use, without just compensation." The Fourteenth Amendment Due Process Clause makes the Takings Clause applicable to the states.

A. PROPERTY INTEREST

For a person to challenge a governmental action as an unconstitutional taking, the person must have a property interest. When a person does not have an interest in the property that the government takes, the Takings Clause does not apply.

> **Example:** An organization of homeowners challenged a beach restoration project undertaken by a state agency and local governments. The homeowners objected to the creation of land beyond the mean high water line, which represented the boundary of the homeowners' property, because this infringed upon their right as owners of property along a shore to receive accretions and because they lost the right to control public access to the shoreline. However, because, under state law, the newly created land belonged to the state, and the homeowners did not enjoy property rights with respect to this land, there was no taking of their property rights. *Stop the Beach Renourishment, Inc. v. Fla. Dep't of Envtl. Prot.*, 560 U.S. 702 (2010). (Note: A plurality of the Supreme Court justices also found that the Takings Clause applies to a judicial taking.)

1. Types of Property

Property that may be subject to the protection of the Takings Clause includes not only land and other real property, but also tangible personal property as well as intangible property, such as contract and patent rights and trade secrets. *Ruckelshaus v. Monsanto Co.*, 467 U.S. 986 (1984); *Lynch v. United States*, 292 U.S. 571 (1934); *James v. Campbell*, 104 U.S. 356 (1882).

2. Types of Interests

In addition to the transfer of a fee simple interest in property, a taking may involve an easement, leasehold interest, or a lien. *Nollan v. California Coastal Commission*, 483 U.S. 825 (1987); *Armstrong v. United States*, 364 U.S. 40 (1960); *United States v. General Motors*, 323 U.S. 373 (1945). A taking may involve the rights of a property owner, such as the right to control access to the property. *Kaiser Aetna v. United States*, 444 U.S. 164 (1980) (federal government's imposition of public-access servitude on a waterway created on private property constituted a taking).

B. TYPES OF TAKING

1. Seizure of Property

The classic application of the Takings Clause is the seizure of private property for governmental use, such as acquiring privately held land in order to construct a courthouse or other government building. In such a case, the property owner's primary challenge to the seizure is whether he has received just compensation (*see* § XV.C., Just Compensation, *infra*).

a. Public-use challenge

A government may seize private property not only for its own direct use but also to transfer the property to another private party. Although such a seizure is subject to challenge as not being made for a public use, the taking need merely be **"rationally related** to a **conceivable public purpose."** *Hawaii Hous. Auth. v. Midkiff*, 467 U.S. 229 (1984). This is a highly deferential standard, and the burden is on the person challenging the taking to prove a lack of legitimate interest or rational basis. In addition to traditional health, safety, and welfare justifications, economic redevelopment goals constitute a sufficient public purpose to justify the seizure. *Kelo v. City of New London*, 545 U.S. 469 (2005). Moreover, a government-mandated transfer of property from one private party directly to another (e.g., from lessor to lessee) may nevertheless be for a public use. *Hawaii Housing Authority v. Midkiff*, 467 U.S. 229 (1984).

2. Damage to or Destruction of Property

A destruction of property or property rights by the federal, state, or local government can also result in a taking. The destruction need not directly benefit the government. The Takings Clause is not limited to possessory interests in property; instead, it can extend to takings of non-possessory property rights, such as easements or liens. *Armstrong v. United States*, 364 U.S. 40 (1960).

Example: A federal statute that prevented the transfer by devise or descent of fractional shares of an interest in tribal land upon the death of the owner and instead provided for such interest to escheat to the tribe constituted an unconstitutional taking when there was no provision for compensation of the owner. *Hodel v. Irving*, 481 U.S. 704 (1987).

Similarly, physical damage to property or interference with a property owner's rights by governmental action can result in a taking.

Example: County ownership of an airport that resulted in an invasion of the airspace of nearby property owners by planes taking off and landing at the airport constituted a taking. *Griggs v. Allegheny County*, 369 U.S. 84 (1962).

Note: A statute that requires an owner of property rights to take action in order to preserve an unused right does not result in a taking if the owner fails to take such action. *Texaco, Inc. v. Short*, 454 U.S. 516 (1982).

a. Exception—public peril

The governmental destruction of private property in response to a public peril does not trigger the right to compensation.

Example: The owners of infected cedar trees located near apple orchards were not entitled to compensation when the cedar trees were destroyed pursuant to a state statute in order to prevent the spread of the infection to the orchards. *Miller v. Schoene*, 276 U.S. 272 (1928).

3. Re-characterization of Property

The Takings Clause prevents a government from re-characterizing private property as public property.

Example: Interest on the purchase price of an insolvent corporation placed by the buyer in an account with the court as part of an interpleader action involving the corporation's creditors was private property. A state court's interpretation of a statutory provision that the interest was public money constituted a taking. *Webb's Fabulous Pharmacies, Inc. v. Beckwith*, 449 U.S. 155 (1980).

4. Regulatory Taking

Generally, a governmental regulation that adversely affects a person's property interest is not a taking, but it is possible for a regulation to rise to the level of a taking.

In determining whether a regulation creates a taking, the following factors are considered:

i) The economic impact of the regulation on the property owner;

ii) The extent to which the regulation interferes with the owner's reasonable, investment-backed expectations regarding use of the property; and

iii) The character of the regulation, including the degree to which it will benefit society, how the regulation distributes the burdens and benefits among property owners, and whether the regulation violates any of the owner's essential attributes of property ownership, such as the right to exclude others from the property.

Penn Central Transportation Co. v. City of New York, 438 U.S. 104 (1978).

a. Public-use challenge

In the context of a regulation, a state or local government can act under its police power for the purposes of health, safety, and welfare. In addition, a public purpose can encompass aesthetic and environmental concerns. Moreover, it is generally inappropriate for a court to examine whether a regulation substantially advances a legitimate governmental interest. (Note, however, that an arbitrary or irrational regulation may constitute a due-process violation.) *Lingle v. Chevron U.S.A. Inc.*, 544 U.S. 528 (2005).

b. Per se takings

In two instances, a regulation clearly results in a taking.

1) Physical occupation

A taking has occurred when the governmental regulation results in a **permanent physical occupation** of the property by the government or a third party.

Example: A law requiring a landlord to permit a cable company to install equipment on the landlord's property that would remain indefinitely constituted a taking, even though the installation had only a minimal economic impact on the landlord. *Loretto v. Teleprompter Manhattan CATV Corp.*, 458 U.S. 419 (1982).

2) No economically viable use

When a regulation results in a **permanent total loss of the property's economic value,** a taking has occurred. *Lucas v. South Carolina Coastal*

Council, 505 U.S. 1003 (1992) (zoning ordinance precluding owner of coastal property from erecting any permanent structure on the land was a taking); *Tahoe-Sierra Preservation Council, Inc. v. Tahoe Regional Planning Agency*, 535 U.S. 302 (2002) (32-month building moratorium was not a taking).

> **Adverse economic impact:** A regulation that results in a dramatic decline in the value of the regulated property does not necessarily constitute a taking.

c. Post-adoption acquisition

A person who acquires property rights after the adoption of a regulation that affects those rights may nevertheless challenge the regulation as an unconstitutional taking. *Palazzolo v. Rhode Island.*, 533 U.S. 606 (2001).

5. Exaction as a Taking

A local government may exact promises from a developer, such as setting aside a portion of the land being developed for a park in exchange for issuing the necessary construction permits. Such exactions do not violate the Takings Clause if there is:

i) An **essential nexus** between legitimate state interests and the conditions imposed on the property owner (i.e., the conditions substantially advance legitimate state interest); and

ii) A **rough proportionality** between the burden imposed by the conditions on property owner and the impact of the proposed development.

Nollan v. California Coastal Commission, 483 U.S. 825 (1987) (state-required grant of an easement across beachfront property as a condition on the issuance of a building permit was a taking due to lack of essential nexus); *Dolan v. City of Tigard*, 512 U.S. 374 (1994) (state-required dedication of land to the city for use as a greenway and pedestrian/bicycle pathway in exchange for permit to expand a store and parking lot was a taking due to lack of rough proportionality).

In determining whether there is rough proportionality between the burden and the impact, the government must make an individualized determination that the conditions are related both in nature and extent to the impact.

The government's conditions must satisfy the requirements of *Nollan* and *Dolan* even when the government denies the permit and even when its demand is for money rather than property rights. *Koontz v. St. Johns River Water Mgmt. Dist.*, 570 U.S. 595 (2013).

These requirements are limited to exactions; they do not apply to regulatory takings. *Lingle v. Chevron U.S.A. Inc., supra* (rent cap was not an exaction taking, but instead was a valid regulation under the Takings Clause).

C. JUST COMPENSATION

The phrase "just compensation" has been interpreted to mean **fair market value,** which is the reasonable value of the property at the time of the taking. This value is measured in terms of the loss to the owner, not the benefit to the government.

1. Worthless Property

Property that is worthless to the owner but has value to the government may be taken without compensation.

> **Example:** Clients whose funds were held by lawyers and deposited in a trust account pursuant to state law to be paid to an entity in order to provide legal services for the poor were not entitled to compensation because each client's funds would not

separately have earned interest. *Brown v. Legal Foundation of Washington*, 538 U.S. 216 (2003).

2. Only Portion Taken

When only a portion of an owner's property is taken, the owner may also receive compensation for any diminution in value of the remaining portion that is attributable to the taking but must reduce any compensation by the value of any special and direct benefits (e.g., a highway access) conferred on the remaining portion.

3. Return of Property

When governmental action constitutes a taking, the government cannot escape all liability by returning the property to its owner, but instead must pay the owner compensation for the period that the government possessed the property. *First English Evangelical Church v. County of Los Angeles*, 482 U.S. 304 (1987).

D. MANNER OF TAKING

Typically, when a property owner objects to the seizure of his property by the government, the government will institute condemnation proceedings, and the property owner can raise the Takings Clause as a defense to this action. When the governmental action that allegedly constitutes a taking is a statute, regulation, or ordinance, the property owner may institute a suit seeking an injunction or a declaratory judgment; this type of legal action is sometimes referred to as an inverse condemnation.

XVI. PROHIBITED LEGISLATION

A. BILLS OF ATTAINDER

A bill of attainder is a **legislative** act that declares a person or group of persons guilty of some crime and punishes them without a trial. Article I, Sections 9 and 10 forbid the federal government and the states, respectively, from enacting such "legislative trials." It applies only to criminal or penal measures.

Barring particular individuals from government employment qualifies as punishment under the prohibition against bills of attainder. *United States v. Lovett*, 328 U.S. 303 (1946).

B. EX POST FACTO LAWS

The constitutional prohibition on an "ex post facto" law is confined to a retroactive change to a **criminal or penal** law. A law that is civil in purpose is treated as a criminal law only if its punitive effect clearly overrides its civil purpose. *Smith v. Doe*, 538 U.S. 84 (2003).

Under Article I, Sections 9 and 10, a **federal or state** statute will be struck down as being ex post facto if it:

i) **Criminalizes** an act that was not a crime when it was originally committed;

ii) Authorizes, after an act was committed, the imposition of a **more severe penalty** on that act;

iii) **Deprives the defendant of a defense** available at the time the act was committed; or

iv) **Decreases the prosecution's burden of proof** required for a conviction to a level below that which was required when the alleged offense was committed.

Collins v. Youngblood, 497 U.S. 37 (1990).

Example: A change in the relevant statute of limitations that resulted in the revival of a prosecution for an act of sexual abuse for which the statute of limitations had expired violates the prohibition on ex post facto laws; the change retroactively withdrew a complete defense to the crime after it had vested. *Stogner v. California*, 539 U.S. 607 (2003).

Compare: The retroactive application of state law that required registration of convicted sex offenders and child kidnappers, and public notification of information about the convicts, including name, current address, and place of employment did not constitute an ex post facto law. The law was a nonpunitive regulatory scheme enacted for the protection of the public. *Smith v. Doe, supra.*

C. **OBLIGATION OF CONTRACTS**

Article I, Section 10 (i.e., the "contracts clause"), prohibits the states from passing any law "impairing the obligation of contracts." This prohibition applies only to **state legislation**— not state-court decisions and not federal legislation—that **retroactively** impairs contractual rights. It does not apply to contracts not yet entered into.

1. **Private Contracts**

   State legislation that **substantially** impairs a contract between private parties is invalid, unless the government can demonstrate that the interference was **reasonable** and **necessary** to serve an **important** governmental interest. *Allied Structural Steel Co. v. Spannaus*, 438 U.S. 234 (1978); *Energy Reserves Group, Inc. v. Kansas Power and Light Co.*, 459 U.S. 400 (1983). Substantial impairment generally requires that the state legislation destroy most or all of a party's rights under a preexisting contract. *See Home Bldg. and Loan Ass'n v. Blaisdell*, 290 U.S. 398 (1934); *Keystone Bituminous Coal Ass'n v. DeBenedictus*, 480 U.S. 470 (1987).

2. **Public Contracts**

   Impairment by the state of a **public contract** (one to which the state or local government is a party) is subject to essentially the same "reasonable and necessary" test as private contracts, but with a somewhat stricter application. The state must show that its important interest cannot be served by a less-restrictive alternative and that the impairment it seeks is necessary because of unforeseeable circumstances. *U.S. Trust Co. v. New Jersey*, 413 U.S. 1 (1977).

   Note that there is no substantial impairment if the state reserved—by statute, law, or in the contract itself—the right to revoke, alter, or amend.

XVII. **FREEDOM OF RELIGION**

The First Amendment provides that "Congress shall make no law respecting an establishment of religion, or prohibiting the free exercise thereof." Both the Establishment Clause and the Free Exercise Clause have been incorporated into the Due Process Clause of the Fourteenth Amendment and are therefore applicable to the states.

A. **ESTABLISHMENT**

When a governmental program shows preference to one religion over another, or to religion over nonreligion, strict scrutiny applies. *Bd. of Educ. v. Grumet*, 512 U.S. 687 (1994) (creation of special school district to benefit members of one religion invalid); *Larkin v. Grendel's Den, Inc.*, 459 U.S. 116 (1982) (delegating or sharing ability to make discretionary decisions, like zoning decisions, to a religious institution invalid).

1. **Standard of Review**

   Not every governmental action that impacts religion is unconstitutional. To determine whether a particular program violates the Establishment Clause, the Court has most often applied the three-part test developed in *Lemon v. Kurtzman*, 403 U.S. 602 (1971).

A governmental action that benefits religion is valid if:

i)   It has a **secular purpose**;

ii) Its principal or primary effect **neither advances nor inhibits** religion; and

iii) It does not result in **excessive government entanglement** with religion.

Though still applied, the Lemon test has often been modified or set aside in the Supreme Court's more recent Establishment Clause cases. *See, e.g., Am. Legion v. Am. Humanist Ass'n*, 588 U.S. ___, 139 S. Ct. 2067 (2019) (presumption of constitutionality for longstanding monuments, symbols, and practices); *Good News Club v. Milford Central School*, 533 U.S. 98 (2001) (permitting Christian organization to use public school cafeteria for after-school meetings did not violate Establishment Clause); *Bd. of Educ. v. Grumet*, 512 U.S. 687 (1994) (creation of school district to serve distinctive religious population violated Establishment Clause).

2. Financial Aid

a. Aid to religious institutions

Governmental financial assistance to religious institutions is permitted if the aid is secular in nature, used only for secular purposes, and, when the aid is distributed among secular and religious institutions, the distribution criteria must be religiously neutral. *Mitchell v. Helms*, 530 U.S. 793 (2000) (elementary and secondary school); *Tilton v. Richardson*, 403 U.S. 672 (1971) (college); *Bradfield v. Roberts*, 175 U.S. 291 (1899) (hospital). Aid in the form of secular textbooks, computers, standardized tests, bus transportation, school lunches, and sign language interpreters for deaf students has been upheld. While parochial elementary and secondary schools were at one time considered to be so pervasively sectarian that direct aid to them was not permitted, that is no longer the case. *Mitchell v. Helms, supra*. In applying the *Lemon* test, the third element (no excessive governmental entanglement) is not a separate requirement, but instead is one factor to be considered in ascertaining whether the second element (no advancement or inhibition of religion) has been met. *Agostini v. Felton*, 521 U.S. 203, 233 (1997).

b. Tax exemptions for religious organizations

Property-tax exemptions for religious institutions have been held valid as being equivalent to exemptions given to other charitable organizations and therefore neither advancing nor inhibiting religion. *Walz v. Tax Comm'n*, 397 U.S. 664 (1970). Tax exemptions that are available only for religious activities or organizations, however, violate the Establishment Clause as an endorsement of religion. *Texas Monthly v. Bullock*, 489 U.S. 1 (1989).

c. Tax deductions and aid for parochial school expenses

Tax deductions given to reimburse tuition expenses only for parents of students in religious schools are invalid. If such a deduction is available to *all* parents for actual educational expenses of attending any public or private school (including parochial schools), it is valid. *Mueller v. Allen*, 463 U.S. 388 (1983).

In addition, giving parents tuition vouchers to assist them in paying religious-school tuition does not violate the Establishment Clause if the choice of whether to use the vouchers for religious or non-religious private school tuition lies with the parents. *Zelman v. Simmons-Harris*, 536 U.S. 639 (2002). However, states may deny state funds to a student pursuing a religious career without violating the Free Exercise Clause of the federal constitution. *Locke v. Davey*, 540 U.S. 712 (2004) (denial of state scholarship funds to a student seeking a career in religious instruction did not violate the Free Exercise Clause because the state was free to choose not to fund a distinct category of instruction in order to avoid the establishment of religion).

3. Public School Activities

Generally, officially sponsored religious activities in public schools or at public school events violate the Establishment Clause. The following practices have been held invalid as clearly promoting religion:

i) **Prayer** and **Bible reading,** *Engel v. Vitale,* 370 U.S. 421 (1962);

ii) A designated period of silence during the school day for **"meditation or voluntary prayer"** lacking any secular purpose, *Wallace v. Jaffree,* 472 U.S. 38 (1985); *but see Brown v. Gilmore,* 258 F.3d 265 (4th Cir. 2001) (divided court holding that short periods of mandatory silence did not necessarily implicate the establishment of religion, and that moment-of-silence requirements with dual legitimate purposes (i.e., a secular purpose along with a purpose to accommodate free exercise of religion) satisfy the first *Lemon* prong and may still pass the *Lemon* test);

iii) **Nondenominational (i.e., nonsectarian) prayer** at school events, *Lee v. Weisman,* 505 U.S. 577 (1992) (prayer led by a cleric at a graduation ceremony); *Santa Fe Indep. Sch. Dist. v. Doe,* 530 U.S. 290 (2000) (school policy of student-led prayer at high school football games); *but see Town of Greece v. Galloway,* 572 U.S. 565 (2014) (prayer before sessions of town council did not violate Establishment Clause due to tradition of such prayers and lack of coercion with regard to participation by nonbelievers);

iv) Posting the **Ten Commandments** on public-school classroom walls, *Stone v. Graham,* 449 U.S. 39 (1980); and

v) **Prohibiting the teaching of Darwinism** (i.e., human biological evolution), or mandating that such teaching be accompanied by instruction regarding "creation science," *Edward v. Aguillard,* 482 U.S. 578 (1987); *Epperson v. Arkansas,* 393 U.S. 97 (1968).

4. Access to Public Facilities by Religious Groups

If a public school allows student groups or organizations to use its facilities when classes are not in session, allowing a religious organization to use those facilities does not violate the Establishment Clause. Furthermore, to prohibit such a group from using those facilities because religious topics would be discussed would violate the First Amendment guarantee of free speech. *Good News Club v. Milford Central School,* 533 U.S. 98 (2001); *Widmar v. Vincent,* 454 U.S. 263 (1981). The Court has often responded to public educational institutions' Establishment Clause concerns by focusing on the free speech rights of religious students. *E.g., Rosenberger v. Univ. of Virginia,* 515 U.S. 819 (1995) (state university could not refuse to pay for printing of religious student newspaper on Establishment Clause grounds when it funded nonreligious papers).

5. Religious Displays

a. Ten Commandments

A display of the Ten Commandments on public property is an impermissible violation of the Establishment Clause if the display has a **"predominantly religious purpose."** *McCreary County v. ACLU,* 545 U.S. 844 (2005) (Ten Commandments posted in courthouse impermissible). If the display also communicates a secular moral message, or its context conveys a historical and social meaning, it may be upheld. *Van Orden v. Perry*, 545 U.S. 677 (2005) (Ten Commandments monument on the state capitol grounds displaying 17 monuments and 21 historical markers commemorating the state's "people, ideals, and events that compose its identity" was permitted because the "Ten Commandments have an undeniable historical meaning" in addition to their "religious significance." Because of the unique historical message, which is separate from any religious message, installing the Ten Commandments in a public park did not violate the Establishment Clause). This is a highly context-dependent, case-specific inquiry.

b. Holiday displays

Government holiday displays will generally be upheld unless a reasonable observer would conclude that the display is an **endorsement** of religion. The context of the display is key—a nativity scene in a courthouse under a banner reading "*Gloria in Excelsis Deo*" was struck down as endorsing religion, but a nearby outdoor display of a Christmas tree, Chanukah menorah, and other seasonal symbols was upheld as mere recognition that Christmas and Chanukah are both parts of a highly secularized winter holiday season. *County of Allegheny v. ACLU*, 492 U.S. 573 (1989).

B. FREE EXERCISE

The Free Exercise Clause of the First Amendment has been construed to include two freedoms: the freedom to believe and the freedom to act. The degree of protection that individuals are afforded from governmental interference in religion depends on whether religious belief or conduct is involved.

1. Religious Belief

The freedom to believe in any religion or none at all is absolutely protected and cannot be restricted by law. The government may not deny benefits or impose burdens based on religious belief, *Cantwell v. Connecticut*, 310 U.S. 296 (1940); it may not require affirmation of a belief, *West Virginia State Bd. of Educ. v. Barnette*, 319 U.S. 624 (1943); and it may not determine the reasonableness of a belief, although it may determine the sincerity of the person asserting that belief, *United States v. Ballard*, 322 U.S. 78 (1944). When there is a property dispute between two religious groups, a court may not decide questions of religious doctrine, but may apply religiously neutral principles of law to resolve the dispute. *Jones v. Wolf*, 443 U.S. 595 (1979).

2. Religious Conduct

Religious conduct, on the other hand, is not absolutely protected. Generally, only state laws that **intentionally target** religious conduct are subject to strict scrutiny. Neutral laws of general applicability that have an impact on religious conduct are subject only to the rational basis test.

a. Targeting religious conduct

Strict scrutiny applies when the government purposely targets conduct because it is religious or displays religious beliefs. *Church of the Lukumi Babalu Aye, Inc. v. City of Hialeah*, 508 U.S. 520 (1993) (city ordinance banning all ritual sacrifice of animals not for the purpose of food consumption struck down as targeting the Santeria religion). A state law that is designed to suppress activity because it is religiously motivated is valid only if it is necessary to achieve a compelling governmental interest.

Other laws that have been struck down as violating the Free Exercise Clause include compulsory school attendance for the Amish, *Wisconsin v. Yoder*, 406 U.S.

205 (1972), and denial of unemployment benefits to one whose faith prevented her from taking a job that required her to work on the Sabbath, *Sherbert v. Verner*, 374 U.S. 398 (1963).

b. Generally applicable laws

Neutral state laws of general applicability that have the incidental effect of interfering with one's ability to engage in religious practices are subject only to the rational basis test. *Employment Div. v. Smith*, 494 U.S. 872 (1990) (criminalization of peyote that did not contain an exception for use in Native American religious rituals upheld, as the ban was not motivated by any desire to burden religious conduct).

Example: A parent's right to pray over a child who has contracted meningitis, rather than seeking medical assistance, may be limited by state child-neglect and manslaughter laws. Parents do not have the right to endanger the lives of their children on the grounds of freedom of religion. *See Prince v. Massachusetts*, 321 U.S. 158 (1944).

c. Access to benefits

Strict scrutiny applies when the government purposely denies a religious entity access to an otherwise available public benefit purely on account of its religious status. The avoidance of entanglement of church and state is not a sufficient governmental interest to justify this denial. *Trinity Lutheran Church of Columbia, Inc. v. Comer*, 582 U.S. ___, 137 S. Ct. 2012 (2017) (church-run preschool could not be denied, solely on the basis of its religious status, a state grant to resurface playground); *but see Locke v. Davey*, *supra* (state not required to fund degree in devotional theology as part of a state scholarship program).

d. Religious Freedom Restoration Act

Under the Religious Freedom Restoration Act, which is applicable only to the federal government, not to the states, even neutral laws of general applicability are subject to strict scrutiny if they substantially burden the free exercise of religion.

C. MINISTERIAL EXCEPTION TO DISCRIMINATION LAWS

Religious institutions can rely on a "ministerial exception" to federal and state employment discrimination laws in their decision to hire or fire a minister. The purpose of the ministerial exception, which is based on both the Establishment and Free Exercise Clauses of the First Amendment, is not merely to safeguard a church's decision to discharge a minister when it is made for a religious reason but also to ensure that the authority to select and control who will serve as a minister to the church's faithful, a strictly ecclesiastical matter, is solely the church's decision. The exception operates as an affirmative defense to an otherwise cognizable claim, but not as a jurisdictional bar. *Hosanna-Tabor Evangelical Lutheran Church and School v. E.E.O.C.*, 565 U.S. 171 (2012) (employee whose responsibilities included religious instruction was "minister" within scope of ministerial exception, and as such, church and school could not be held liable in E.E.O.C.'s discrimination enforcement action on her behalf).

XVIII. FREEDOM OF EXPRESSION AND ASSOCIATION

In addition to its religion clauses, the First Amendment provides that "Congress shall make no laws...abridging the freedom of speech, or of the press; or the right of the people to peaceably assemble, and to petition the Government for a redress of grievances." These aspects of the First Amendment are applicable to the states via the Fourteenth Amendment.

Freedom of expression is not absolute. While governmental regulation of the content of speech is severely constrained, governmental regulation of the time, place, and manner of speech is subject to less restriction.

A. REGULATION OF SPEECH

1. Expressive Conduct

Protected speech can include not only written, oral, and visual communication, but also activities such as picketing and leafleting. Expressive conduct (or symbolic speech) may also be protected as speech, but it is subject to a lesser degree of protection. Governmental regulation of expressive conduct is upheld if:

i) The regulation is **within the government's power** to enact (e.g., through a local government's police power);

ii) The regulation furthers an **important governmental interest**;

iii) The governmental interest is **unrelated to the suppression of ideas**; and

iv) The burden on speech is **no greater than necessary.**

United States v. O'Brien, 391 U.S. 367 (1968) (prohibition against burning draft cards upheld as furthering the important governmental interest in a smoothly functioning draft system).

An example of permissible regulation of expressive conduct includes upholding a ban on public nudity, such as nude dancing in adult entertainment venues, pursuant to the important governmental interest in preventing the "harmful secondary effects" of adult entertainment on neighborhoods, which is unrelated to the suppression of expression. *City of Erie v. Pap's A.M.*, 529 U.S. 277 (2000).

Examples of impermissible regulation of expressive conduct include:

i) A ban against students wearing black armbands to protest the war in Vietnam, because the government's only interest in banning the conduct was prohibiting communication, *Tinker v. Des Moines Indep. Cmty. Sch. Dist.*, 393 U.S. 503 (1969);

ii) A federal prohibition against burning the American flag because the law was intended to suppress messages of disapproval of governmental policy, rather than any conduct-related consequences of the burning of a flag, *United States v. Eichman*, 496 U.S. 310 (1990); and

iii) An ordinance prohibiting leafleting that results in littering on public streets, because the governmental interest in clean streets is insufficient justification, and such a ban on distribution is not narrowly tailored to protect the communication of information and opinion. *Schneider v. State of New Jersey Town of Irvington*, 308 U.S. 147 (1939).

The act of signing a petition constitutes expressive conduct. Public disclosure of the petition, and, thereby, the names of the individuals who signed the petition does not violate the First Amendment because such disclosure is substantially related to the important interest of preserving the integrity of the electoral process. *Doe v. Reed*, 561 U.S. 186 (2010).

2. Overbreadth

A law that burdens a substantial amount of speech or other conduct constitutionally protected by the First Amendment is **"overbroad"** and therefore void. A statute's overbreadth must be substantial both in an absolute sense and relative to the statute's plainly legitimate reach. The mere fact that some impermissible applications of a statute can be conceived of is not sufficient to render a statute overbroad. *United States v. Williams*, 553 U.S. 285 (2008). This doctrine does not apply to commercial speech. *Hoffman Estates v. The Flipside, Hoffman Estates, Inc.*, 455 U.S. 489 (1982).

In order to prevent a **"chilling effect"** on protected speech (i.e., frightening people into not speaking for fear of prosecution), overbroad statutes may be challenged as **"facially invalid"** even by those who are validly regulated on behalf of those who are not. *Broadrick v. Okla.*, 413 U.S. 601 (1973). The challenger of a law bears the burden of establishing that substantial overbreadth exists. *N.Y. State Club Ass'n v. City of N.Y.*, 487 U.S. 1 (1988).

3. Vagueness

A statute is **"void for vagueness"** if it fails to provide a person of ordinary intelligence with fair notice of what is prohibited. *United States v. Williams, supra.*

As with overbreadth, vagueness is impermissible for fear that constitutionally protected speech will be "chilled." In addition, the "void for vagueness" doctrine is grounded in the due process requirement of notice. Under due process principles, laws that regulate persons or entities must give fair notice of conduct that is forbidden or required. *FCC v. Fox Television Stations, Inc.*, 567 U.S. 239 (2012), Statutes that tie criminal culpability to conduct that involves subjective judgments without providing statutory definitions, narrow context, or settled legal meanings have been struck down for vagueness. *Reno v. ACLU*, 521 U.S. 844 (1997) (indecent speech); *Coates v. Cincinnati*, 402 U.S. 611 (1971) (annoying conduct).

4. Prior Restraints

A prior restraint is a regulation of speech that occurs in advance of its expression (e.g., publication or utterance). Prior restraints are generally presumed to be unconstitutional, with limited exceptions. *Bantam Books, Inc. v. Sullivan*, 372 U.S. 58 (1963). These rare exceptions require at a minimum that:

i)   There is a **particular harm** to be avoided (like publication of troop movements); and

ii) Certain **procedural safeguards** are provided to the speaker. Examples of such safeguards include:

   a) The standards must be narrowly drawn, reasonable, and definite, *Butterworth v. Smith*, 494 U.S. 624 (1990);

   b) The censoring body must promptly seek an injunction, *Teitel Films v. Cusack*, 390 U.S. 139 (1968); and

   c) There must be a prompt and final judicial determination of the validity of the restraint, *National Socialist Party v. Village of Skokie*, 432 U.S. 43 (1977).

The **burden is on the government** to prove that the material to be censored is not protected speech. *Freedman v. Maryland*, 380 U.S. 51 (1965).

Prior restraints have been rejected even when national security was at issue, *New York Times v. United States*, 403 U.S. 713 (1971) (Pentagon Papers), and even when press coverage threatened the fairness of a trial, *Nebraska Press Ass'n v. Stewart*, 427 U.S. 539 (1976) (prior restraint must be the only way to accomplish a goal).

5. Unfettered Discretion

A law or regulation that permits a governmental official to restrict speech (e.g., requires an official to issue a permit before a rally can be held) must provide definite standards as to how to apply the law in order to prevent governmental officials from having unfettered discretion over its application. Such a law or regulation must be related to an important governmental interest and contain the procedural safeguards mentioned above. A statute that gives officials unfettered discretion is void on its face; speakers need not apply for a permit and may not be punished for violating the licensing statute. *Lovell v. City of Griffin*, 303 U.S. 444 (1938).

6. Freedom Not to Speak

The First Amendment protects not only freedom of speech, but also the freedom not to speak. One such example is a child's right not to recite the Pledge of Allegiance. *West Virginia State Board of Education v. Barnette*, 319 U.S. 624 (1943). Similarly, the private organizers of a parade cannot be compelled by the government to include in the parade a group that espouses a message with which the organizers disagree. *Hurley v. Irish-American Gay, Lesbian & Bisexual Group of Boston*, 515 U.S. 557 (1995). Nor can the government mandate as a condition of federal funding that recipients explicitly agree with the government's policy to oppose prostitution and sex trafficking. *Agency for International Development v. Alliance for Open Society*, 570 U.S. 205 (2013). However, a state can compel a private entity (e.g., a shopping mall) to permit individuals to exercise their own free-speech rights when the private entity is open to the public and the message is not likely to be attributable to the private entity. *Pruneyard Shopping Center v. Robins*, 447 U.S. 74 (1980). A state may also require professional fundraisers to file certain public financial disclosures about fundraising activities in order to allow donors to make informed charitable contributions and to prevent fraud. *Schaumberg v. Citizens for a Better Env't*, 444 U.S. 620 (1980); *Sec'y of Md. v. Joseph H. Munson Co.*, 467 U.S. 947 (1984).

a. Compelled financial support

Although one can be compelled to join or financially support a group with respect to one's employment, one cannot be forced to fund political speech by that group. *Abood v. Detroit Bd. of Educ.*, 431 U.S. 209 (1977) (teacher required to pay union dues); *Keller v. State Bar of California*, 496 U.S. 1 (1990) (lawyer required to join a bar association). A student, however, can be required to pay a university activity fee even though the fee may support groups that espouse messages with which the student disagrees, at least when the fee is allocated in accord with a viewpoint-neutral scheme. *Board of Regents v. Southworth*, 529 U.S. 217 (2000).

7. Government Speech

When the government itself speaks, it is not constrained by the Free Speech Clause of the First Amendment. Therefore, government speech (public service announcements, agricultural marketing campaigns, etc.) need not be viewpoint-neutral. *Johanns v. Livestock Mkt'ing Ass'n*, 544 U.S. 550 (2005). This Government Speech Doctrine, however, is subject to the requirements of the Establishment Clause (*See* § XVII.A., *supra*).

a. Monuments on public property

The display of a monument on public property, even if the monument has been donated by a private person, constitutes government speech. *Pleasant Grove City v. Summum*, 555 U.S. 460 (2009) (government installed a Ten Commandments monument donated by a private person in a public park; the Court held that governmental entities may exercise "selectivity" in choosing a monument being offered by a private donor).

b. Specialty license plates

Specialty license plates, even if designed by private individuals, are government speech and, as such, the state may refuse proposed designs based on the content of those designs. *Walker v. Tex. Div., Sons of Confederate Veterans*, 576 U.S. ___, 135 S. Ct. 2239 (2015) (rejection of proposed Texas license plate featuring Confederate battle flag).

c. Funding of private messages

The government may fund private messages. However, it must generally do so on a viewpoint-neutral basis. *Rosenberger v. Rector and Visitors of the University of Virginia*, 515 U.S. 819 (1995). The exception to this is when the government decides to fund artists; the decision of which artist to fund is necessarily based on the content of the artist's work. *National Endowment for the Arts v. Finley*, 524 U.S. 569 (1998).

d. Speech by government employees

When a government employee contends that her rights under the Free Speech Clause of the First Amendment have been violated by her employer, the employee must show that she was speaking as a citizen on a matter of public concern. *Borough of Duryea v. Guarnieri*, 564 U.S. 379 (2011). When a government employee is speaking pursuant to her official duties, the employee is generally not speaking as a citizen and the Free Speech Clause does not protect the employee from employer discipline. *Garcetti v. Ceballos*, 547 U.S. 410 (2006). In determining whether a government employee is speaking pursuant to her official duties, the critical question is whether the speech at issue is itself ordinarily within the scope of an employee's duties, not whether it merely concerns those duties. *Lane v. Franks*, 573 U.S. 228 (2014).

When an employee is speaking as a citizen on a matter of public concern, the First Amendment interest of the employee must be balanced against the interest of the state, as an employer, in effective and efficient management of its internal affairs. *Pickering v. Bd. of Educ.*, 391 U.S. 563 (1968); *Connick v. Myers*, 461 U.S. 138 (1983); *Borough of Duryea v. Guarnieri, supra*. This approach also applies to a government employee who petitions the government for redress of a wrong pursuant to the Petition Clause of the First Amendment. *Id.*

8. Campaign Related Speech

a. Political campaign contributions

Statutes limiting campaign contributions are subject to intermediate scrutiny: they must be "closely drawn" to correspond with a sufficiently important interest. *McConnell v. Federal Election Commission*, 540 U.S. 93 (2003); *Randall v. Sorrell*, 548 U.S. 230 (2006). The government's failure to assist a party in exercising a fundamental right does not infringe upon that right and therefore is not subject to strict scrutiny. *Ysursa v. Pocatello Education Association*, 555 U.S. 353 (2009) (state's decision to limit public employer payroll deductions for a union's political purposes did not abridge the union's right to speech).

1) Contributions to candidates

The government may limit contributions to individual candidates because excessive contributions to candidates create a danger of corruption and the appearance of corruption. *Buckley v. Valeo*, 424 U.S. 1 (1976). However, because aggregate limits on the amount a donor may contribute to candidates for federal office, political parties, and political action committees restrict participation in the political process and do little to further the prevention of "quid pro quo" corruption or the appearance of such corruption in campaign financing, they are invalid under the First Amendment. *McCutcheon v. Federal Election Commission*, 572 U.S. 185 (2014). Limits on campaign contributions to candidates for state office ranging from $275 to $1,000 have been upheld. *Nixon v. Shrink Missouri Gov't PAC*, 528 U.S. 377 (2000). However, the government cannot set differential contribution limits that penalize a candidate who finances his own campaign. *Davis v. Federal Election Commission*, 554 U.S. 724 (2008).

2) Contributions to political parties

The government may limit contributions to a political party that are used to expressly advocate for the election or defeat of a particular candidate (also known as "hard money") as well as contributions that are used for other purposes, such as promoting the party itself (also known as "soft money"). *McConnell v. Federal Election Commission, supra*. In addition, the government may require a political party to disclose contributors and recipients unless the party can show that such disclosure would cause harm to the party. *Brown v. Socialist Workers '74 Campaign Committee*, 454 U.S. 112 (1982).

3) Contributions to political action committees (PACs)

The government may limit contributions to a political action committee (PAC). *California Medical Assn. v. FEC*, 453 U.S. 182 (1981).

b. Political campaign expenditures

In contrast to campaign contributions, restrictions on expenditures by individuals and entities (including corporations and unions) on communications during an election campaign regarding a candidate are subject to strict scrutiny. So long as the source of the funding is disclosed, there is no legal limit to the amount that corporations and unions may spend on "electioneering communications." *Citizens United v. Federal Election Comm'n*, 558 U.S. 310 (2010). In addition, expenditures by a candidate on her own behalf cannot be limited. *Buckley v. Valeo, supra; Davis v. Federal Election Commission, supra*.

c. Political speakers

In addition to individuals, corporations (both nonprofit and for-profit) enjoy First Amendment protection with regard to political speech. *Citizens United, supra*. Similarly, a candidate for a judgeship has a First Amendment right to express his views on disputed legal or political issues. *Republican Party of Minnesota v. White*, 536 U.S. 765 (2002). A state law banning judicial candidates from personally soliciting campaign funds, however, does not necessarily violate the First Amendment. *Williams-Yulee v. The Florida Bar*, 575 U.S. ___, 135 S. Ct. 1656 (2015).

B. REGULATION OF TIME, PLACE, AND MANNER OF EXPRESSION

The government's ability to regulate speech varies with the forum in which the speech takes place.

1. **Public Forum**

   A **"public forum"** may be **traditional** or **designated.** Traditional public forums are those that are historically associated with expression, such as sidewalks, streets, and parks. A designated (or limited) public forum is one that has not historically been used for speech-related activities, but which the government has opened for such use, such as civic auditoriums, publicly owned theaters, or school classrooms that the public is allowed to use afterhours. The practical difference between the two is that the government can change a designated forum to a nonpublic forum, but it cannot do the same with a traditional forum.

   In either type of public forum, the government may impose reasonable restrictions on the time, place, or manner of protected speech, provided the restrictions:

   i) Are **content-neutral** as to both subject matter and viewpoint (i.e., it is not necessary to hear what is said in order to apply the regulation);

   ii) Are **narrowly tailored** to serve a **significant governmental interest**; and

   iii) Leave open ample **alternative channels for communication** of the information.

   Ward v. Rock Against Racism, 491 U.S. 781 (1989). However, additional restrictions, such as an absolute prohibition of a particular type of expression, will be upheld only if narrowly drawn to accomplish a compelling governmental interest, i.e., only if they satisfy strict scrutiny. *United States v. Grace,* 461 U.S. 171 (1983); *see, e.g., United States v. Kokinda*, 497 U.S. 720 (1990) (considering a ban on all solicitation in a public forum). Restrictions that are not content-neutral are also subject to **strict scrutiny** (*see* § XVIII.C., Regulation of Content, *infra*).

   a. **Residential areas**

      There is no right to focus picketing on a particular single residence. However, a person may solicit charitable funds in a residential area. Door-to-door solicitation does not require a permit, as long as the solicitation is for noncommercial or nonfundraising purposes. *Cantwell v. Conn.*, 310 U.S. 296, 306 (1940).

   b. **Injunctions**

      The test for the constitutionality of injunctions in public forums depends on whether the injunction is content-neutral or content-based. If an injunction is **content-neutral**, then the test is whether it burdens **no more speech than is necessary** to achieve an **important** governmental interest. On the other hand, if the injunction is **content-based,** it must be **necessary** for the government to achieve a **compelling** governmental interest.

   c. **Public schools**

      When a public school, as a designated (limited) public forum, permits the public to use its facilities, it cannot discriminate against organizations based on its beliefs. *Lamb's Chapel v. Center Moriches Union Free School District*, 508 U.S. 384 (1993) (religious organizations); *Widmar v. Vincent*, 454 U.S. 263 (1981); *Healy v. James*, 408 U.S. 169 (1972) (political organization). Similarly, a public school may provide funding and other benefits (e.g., free use of facilities) to student groups, but it must do so on a viewpoint-neutral basis.

      Example 1: A university that provided funds to various student publications could not withhold funds from a student religious publication on the grounds that the publication espoused religion. *Rosenberger v. Rector and Visitors of the University of Virginia*, 515 U.S. 819 (1995).

Example 2: A public university law school could adopt an "all comers policy" with which student organizations must comply in order to receive school funding and other benefits. Under the policy, a student organization had to admit any student as a member and permit any student to hold office in the organization. Because the policy was viewpoint-neutral, its application to a religious organization was constitutional. *Christian Legal Soc'y Chapter of Univ. of California, Hastings Coll. of Law v. Martinez*, 561 U.S. 661 (2010).

2. Nonpublic Forum

A nonpublic forum is essentially all public property that is not a traditional or designated public forum. Examples include government offices, schools, jails, military bases, and polling places. Sidewalks on postal service property and airport terminals are also considered nonpublic forums. The government may regulate speech-related activities in nonpublic forums as long as the regulation is (i) **viewpoint-neutral** and (ii) **reasonably related to a legitimate governmental interest.**

Note that a governmental fundraising campaign is a nonpublic forum for the expression of speech. The decision to exclude some charities (but not others) cannot be made because the government disagrees with a particular organization's political views; such a decision must be ideologically neutral. *Cornelius v. NAACP Legal Def. and Educ. Fund, Inc.*, 473 U.S. 788 (1985).

a. Viewpoint-neutral

The regulation need not be content-neutral, but it must be viewpoint-neutral. In other words, the government may prohibit speech on certain issues altogether, but it may not allow only one side of an issue to be presented. For example, while a restriction on all public speeches in airports related to firearms regulation would likely be upheld, a restriction only on pro-NRA speeches would not.

Contrast this with restrictions on speech in a public forum, which must be both content- and viewpoint-neutral.

b. Reasonable

The restriction on speech-related activities in nonpublic forums must only be rationally related to a legitimate governmental interest. For example, a city may sell commercial advertising space inside city buses but refuse to sell such space for political advertising in order to avoid the appearance of favoritism and imposition on a captive audience. *Lehman v. City of Shaker Heights*, 418 U.S. 298 (1974).

3. Personal Property

Governmental regulation of speech on a person's own private property will rarely be upheld, particularly content-based regulations. While the government has some limited powers to regulate speech on private property, outright bans on certain types of speech, such as signs in a person's yard or window, are impermissible. *City of Ladue v. Gilleo*, 512 U.S. 43 (1994) (statute banning all residential signs in order to fight "visual clutter" was found unconstitutional).

C. REGULATION OF CONTENT

Any governmental regulation of speech that is **content-based on its face** will only be upheld if the regulation is necessary to achieve a compelling governmental interest and is narrowly tailored to meet that interest (i.e., the **strict scrutiny** test). *Reed v. Town of Gilbert*, 576 U.S. ___, 135 S. Ct. 2218 (2015). However, even regulations that are not content-based on their face may still be content-based in application or in intent, and these laws, too, will generally be subject to strict scrutiny. *Brown v. Entm't Merchs. Ass'n*, 564 U.S 786 (2011) (state law that prohibited the sale of violent video games to minors is an unconstitutional content restriction on speech); *Simon & Schuster, Inc. v. Members of the New York State Crime Victims Board*, 502 U.S. 105 (1991). The government must identify an actual problem, and the regulation of speech must be necessary to solve that problem. This standard is incredibly stringent and is not often met. *U.S. v. Playboy Entm't Group, Inc.*, 529 U.S. 803 (2000).

However, the government may restrict speech on the basis of content if the speech falls into one of the following historic and traditional categories: obscenity, subversive speech, fighting words, defamation, or commercial speech. *U.S. v. Alvarez*, 567 U.S. 709 (2012). States are not free to create new categories of content-based restrictions without persuasive evidence that such restrictions have a long-standing history of proscription. *Brown v. Entm't Merchs. Ass'n, supra*.

1. **Obscenity and Child Pornography**

    Neither obscene speech nor child pornography is protected by the First Amendment Free Speech Clause. *Roth v. United States*, 354 U.S. 476 (1957).

    a. **Obscenity test**

        To be considered obscene, speech must meet each part of a three-prong test developed in *Miller v. California*, 413 U.S. 15 (1973). Under the *Miller* test, the **average person,** applying **contemporary community standards,** must find that the material, **taken as a whole**:

        i)   Appeals to the **"prurient interest"**;

        ii) Depicts sexual conduct in a **patently offensive** way; and

        iii) **Lacks serious literary, artistic, political, or scientific value.**

        > **EXAM NOTE:** *Standards Distinguished* – The first two prongs of this test use a contemporary **community** standard, which may be national but is generally considered to be local or statewide. A **national** standard must be applied, however, to the third prong of the test—determining the value of the work—because the work may merit constitutional protection despite local views to the contrary. *Pope v. Illinois*, 481 U.S. 497 (1987). With regard to the third prong, the judge, not the jury, determines whether this standard has been met.

        Courts have recently begun to distinguish legally obscene speech from pornography. Merely establishing that speech constitutes pornography is generally insufficient to establish that the speech is obscene. Therefore, content-based restrictions on pornography are generally subject to strict scrutiny. *United States v. Playboy Entm't Grp. Inc.*, 529 U.S. 803 (2000).

        Either an appellate court or a jury can assess whether the material is obscene. Evidence of similar material on newsstands is not automatically admissible, nor is expert testimony required to make such a determination.

    b. **Prohibited activities**

        The sale, distribution, and exhibition of obscene material may be prohibited. *Stanley v. Georgia*, 394 U.S. 557 (1969). However, the right to privacy generally precludes criminalization of possession of obscenity in one's own home. *Stanley v. Georgia, supra*.

c. Land-use restrictions

Narrowly drawn zoning ordinances may be used to restrict the location of certain adult entertainment businesses (e.g., adult theaters, adult bookstores, strip clubs) if the purpose of the regulation is to reduce the impact on the neighborhood of such establishments, but they may not be used to ban such establishments entirely. It does not matter that such establishments may be found in adjoining jurisdictions. *Los Angeles v. Alameda Books*, 535 U.S. 425 (2002); *City of Renton v. Playtime Theatres, Inc.*, 475 U.S. 41 (1986).

d. Minors

Material that appeals to the prurient interests of minors may be regulated as to minors, even if it would not be considered obscene to an adult audience. *Ginsberg v. New York*, 390 U.S. 629 (1968). The government may not, however, block adults' access to indecent materials in order to prevent them from reaching children. *Reno v. ACLU*, 521 U.S. 844 (1997).

e. Child pornography

The First Amendment also does not protect child pornography, which is sexually explicit visual portrayals that feature children. Because of the state's compelling interest in protecting minor children from exploitation, the sale, distribution, and even private possession of child pornography may be prohibited, even if the material would not be obscene if it involved adults. *Osborne v. Ohio*, 495 U.S. 103 (1990); *New York v. Ferber*, 458 U.S. 747 (1982).

Simulated child pornography (i.e., pornography using young-looking adults or computer-generated images) may not be banned as child pornography. *Ashcroft v. Free Speech Coalition*, 535 U.S. 234 (2002). However, offers to sell or buy simulated child pornography that contain actual depictions of children even though the sexually explicit features are simulated may be criminalized when the material is presented as actual child pornography. *United States v. Williams*, 553 U.S. 285 (2008).

f. Violence

Violence is not included in the definition of obscenity that may be constitutionally regulated. *Brown v. Entm't Merchs. Ass'n, supra*; *Winters v. New York*, 333 U.S. 507 (1948).

2. Incitement to Violence

A state may forbid speech that advocates the use of force or unlawful action if:

i) The speech is **directed to inciting or producing imminent lawless action**; and

ii) It is **likely to incite or produce such action** (i.e., creates a clear and present danger).

Brandenburg v. Ohio, 395 U.S. 444 (1969).

Advocacy requires the use of language reasonably and ordinarily calculated to incite persons to such action. *Yates v. United States*, 354 U.S. 298 (1957). The abstract expression of ideas, including the teaching of the moral propriety or even moral necessity for a resort to force and violence, is not the same as the actual incitement of violence. There must be substantial evidence of a strong and pervasive call to violence. *Noto v. United States*, 367 U.S. 290 (1960).

3. Fighting Words

A speaker may be criminally punished for using "fighting words," which are words that **by their very nature** are likely to incite an immediate breach of the peace. *Chaplinsky v. New Hampshire*, 315 U.S. 568 (1942). Words that are simply annoying or offensive are not fighting words; there must be a genuine likelihood of imminent violence by a hostile audience. *Cohen v. California*, 403 U.S. 15 (1971).

> **EXAM NOTE:** Attempts to forbid fighting words almost always fail as vague, overbroad, or otherwise constitutionally infirm.

Statutes designed to punish only fighting words that express certain viewpoints are unconstitutional. *R.A.V. v. City of St. Paul*, 505 U.S. 377 (1992) (the Court struck down an ordinance that applied only to fighting words that insulted or provoked on the basis of race, religion, or gender).

However, actual threats of violence are outside the protection of the First Amendment, given the need to protect individuals from (i) the fear of violence, (ii) the disruption that fear engenders, and (iii) the possibility that the threatened violence will occur. *R.A.V. v. City of St. Paul*, 505 at 388.

4. Defamation

Limits on punishment for defamatory speech may apply in cases in which the plaintiff is a public official or public figure, or when a defamatory statement involves a matter of public concern. In addition to the elements of a prima facie case of defamation, the plaintiff must in these cases prove both **fault** and the **falsity** of the statement.

a. Public figure or official

A public figure is someone who is known to the general public and includes any person who has voluntarily injected herself into the public eye. The plaintiff must prove that the defendant acted with **actual malice,** i.e., knowledge of the statement's falsity or reckless disregard for whether it was true or false. *New York Times v. Sullivan*, 376 U.S. 254 (1964). Scientists who publish in scientific journals, criminals, and spouses of wealthy persons are not considered public figures.

b. Public concern

If the plaintiff is a private figure but the defamatory statement involves a matter of public concern, then the standard is lower, but the plaintiff still must establish negligence with respect to the falsity of the statement. *Gertz v. Robert Welch, Inc.*, 418 U.S. 323 (1974).

[See the Themis Torts outline for a full discussion of defamation actions.]

5. Commercial Speech

Commercial speech—advertising and similarly economically oriented expression—is entitled to an intermediate level of First Amendment protection. Restrictions on commercial speech are reviewed under a **four-part test**:

i) The commercial speech must **concern lawful activity** and be **neither false nor misleading** (fraudulent speech or speech which proposes an illegal transaction may be prohibited);

ii) The asserted governmental interest must be **substantial**;

iii) The regulation must **directly advance** the asserted interest; and

iv) The regulation must be **narrowly tailored** to serve that interest. In this context, narrowly tailored does not mean the least restrictive means available; rather, there must be a **"reasonable fit"** between the government's ends and the means chosen to accomplish those ends. *Board of Trustees of State University of New York v. Fox*, 492 U.S. 469 (1989).

Central Hudson Gas & Elec. v. Pub. Svc. Comm'n, 447 U.S. 557 (1980). Under this test, the Court has struck down laws prohibiting truthful advertising of legal abortions, contraceptives, drug prices, alcohol prices, and attorneys' fees and regulation of billboards on the basis of aesthetic value and safety.

Example: A Massachusetts regulation that prohibited tobacco billboards within 1,000 feet of a school was struck down because the means—effectively barring most outdoor tobacco advertising in urban areas—were not narrowly tailored to the ends of protecting children. *Lorillard Tobacco Co. v. Reilly*, 533 U.S. 525 (2001).

Note that solicitation of funds for charitable purposes, however, is recognized as a form of protected speech. *See Village of Schaumburg v. Citizens for a Better Env't*, 444 U.S. 620 (1980). However, fraudulent charitable solicitations, such as false or misleading representations designed to deceive donor as to how donations will be used, are not protected. *Ill. ex rel. Madigan v. Telemarketing Assocs.*, 538 U.S. 600, (2003). Additionally, because there is a strong government interest in preventing fraud and allowing donors to make informed choices about their charitable contributions, the government may require professional fundraisers to file certain public financial disclosures about fundraising activities. *Village of Schaumberg v. Citizens for a Better Env't, supra*; *Sec'y of Md. v. Joseph H. Munson Co.*, 467 U.S. 947 (1984).

D.   **REGULATION OF THE MEDIA**

Although the First Amendment specifically mentions freedom of the press, the media has no greater First Amendment rights than the general public.

1.   **General Considerations**

The press has the right to publish information about matters of public concern, and the viewers have a right to receive it. This right may be restricted only by a regulation that is narrowly tailored to further a compelling governmental interest (i.e., strict scrutiny applies).

a.   **Gag orders**

A gag order is a judicial order prohibiting the press from publishing information about court proceedings. Such orders are subject to prior-restraint analysis. Gag orders are almost always struck down because they are rarely the least restrictive means of protecting the defendant's right to a fair trial. The trial judge has other alternatives available, such as change of venue, postponement of the trial, careful voir dire, or restricting the statements of lawyers and witnesses. *Nebraska Press Ass'n v. Stuart*, 427 U.S. 539 (1972).

b.   **Attending trials**

The public and the press both have the right to attend criminal trials, but this right is not absolute. It may be outweighed if the trial judge finds an **overriding** interest that cannot be accommodated by less restrictive means. The Supreme Court has not determined whether this right also applies to civil trials. However, the Supreme Court has held that the defendant's right to a public trial extended to voir dire, and the trial court must consider reasonable alternatives to closing the voir dire to the public in addressing the trial court's concerns. *Presley v. Georgia*, 558 U.S. 209 (2010).

c. **No constitutional privilege to protect sources**

A journalist has no First Amendment right to refuse to testify before a grand jury regarding the content and source of information relevant to the criminal inquiry. *Branzburg v. Hayes*, 408 U.S. 665 (1972).

d. **Illegally obtained and private information**

The First Amendment shields the media from liability for publishing information that was obtained illegally by a third party as long as the information involves a matter of public concern and the publisher neither obtained it unlawfully nor knows who did. *Bartnicki v. Vopper*, 532 U.S. 514 (2001).

Similarly, the First Amendment shields the media from liability for publication of a lawfully obtained private fact, e.g., the identity of a rape victim, so long as the news story involves a matter of public concern. *See Florida Star v. BJF*, 491 U.S. 524 (1989); *Cox Broadcasting v. Cohn*, 420 U.S. 469 (1975).

e. **First Amendment conflict with state right of publicity**

Some states recognize a right of publicity—the right of a person to control the commercial use of his or her identity. The right is an intellectual property right derived under state law, the infringement of which creates a cause of action for the tort of unfair competition. In *Zacchini v. Scripps-Howard Broad. Co.*, 433 U.S. 562 (1977), the Supreme Court considered a conflict between the First Amendment and a person's state-law right of publicity. A news program had televised a videotape of a daredevil's entire 15-second performance at a local fair when he was shot out of a cannon. The lower court held that the First Amendment protected the telecast from a tort suit regarding the right of publicity. The Supreme Court reversed, holding that the First and Fourteenth Amendments do not immunize the news media from civil liability when they broadcast a performer's entire act without his consent, and the Constitution does not prevent a state from requiring broadcasters to compensate performers. Note that a state government may pass a law shielding the press from liability for broadcasting performers' acts.

f. **No immunity from laws of general applicability**

As mentioned previously, the press has no greater First Amendment rights than does the general public, i.e., there is no special privilege allowing the press to invade the rights of others. As such, members of the press are not immune from the application of generally applicable laws, even if the application of such laws has a negative incidental effect on the ability to gather and report the news. *Cohen v. Cowles Media Co.*, 501 U.S. 663 (1991).

> **Example:** A reporter who trespasses on another's property while investigating a story is not shielded from liability by the First Amendment.

2. **Broadcast**

Because the broadcast spectrum is a limited resource, radio and television broadcasters are said to have a greater responsibility to the public, and they therefore can be more closely regulated than print and other media. Broadcasters may be sanctioned, therefore, for airing "patently offensive sexual and excretory speech," even if such speech does not qualify as obscene under the *Miller* test, in the interest of protecting children likely to be listening. *FCC v. Pacifica Found.*, 438 U.S. 726 (1978).

3. Cable Television

The First Amendment protection provided to cable television falls somewhere between the extensive protection given to print media and the more limited protection for broadcasting. As such, a law requiring cable operators to carry local television stations is subject to intermediate scrutiny. *Turner Broad. Sys., Inc. v. FCC*, 512 U.S. 622 (1994).

Content-based regulations of cable broadcasts are subject to **strict scrutiny,** however. *United States v. Playboy Entm't. Group, Inc.*, 529 U.S. 803 (2000).

4. Internet

Because the Internet is not composed of scarce frequencies as are the broadcast media, and because of the reduced risk of an unexpected invasion of privacy over the Internet, any regulation of Internet content is subject to strict scrutiny. *Reno v. ACLU*, 521 U.S. 844 (1997).

E. REGULATION OF ASSOCIATION

Freedom of association protects the right to form or participate in any group, gathering, club, or organization virtually without restriction, although the right is not absolute. An infringement upon this right may be justified by a compelling state interest. *See, e.g., Board of Dirs. of Rotary Int'l v. Rotary Club of Duarte*, 481 U.S. 537 (1987) (discrimination against women was not in furtherance of or necessary for any of the expressive activity undertaken by the organization); *but see Boy Scouts of America v. Dale*, 530 U.S. 640 (2000) (requiring the Boy Scouts to accept leaders who acted in a manner contrary to Boy Scout principles would unduly intrude upon the Boy Scouts' expressive associational rights).

1. Public Employment

An individual generally cannot be denied public employment based simply upon membership in a political organization. *Keyishian v. Board of Regents*, 385 U.S. 589 (1967).

a. Test

A person may only be punished or deprived of public employment based on political association if that individual:

i) Is an active member of a **subversive organization**;

ii) Has **knowledge** of the organization's illegal activity; and

iii) Has a **specific intent** to further those illegal objectives.

Scales v. United States, 367 U.S. 203 (1961) (conviction based on active, knowing, and purposive membership in an organization advocating the violent overthrow of the government upheld).

b. Loyalty oaths

Public employees may be required to take loyalty oaths promising that they will support the Constitution and oppose the forceful, violent, or otherwise illegal or unconstitutional overthrow of the government. *Connell v. Higgenbotham*, 403 U.S. 207 (1971). However, oaths that forbid or require action in terms so vague that a person of common intelligence must guess at the oath's meaning and differ as to its application are often found to be so vague or overbroad as to deprive an individual of liberty or property without due process. *E.g., Cramp v. Board of Public Instruction*, 368 U.S. 278 (1961) (striking down as vague a statute requiring public employees to swear that they have not and will not lend "aid, support, advice, counsel, or influence to the Communist Party"); *Shelton v. Tucker*, 364 U.S. 479 (1960) (striking down as overbroad a statute requiring teachers to file an affidavit listing every organization to which they have belonged or regularly contributed during the past five years).

2. Bar Membership

Although the state can inquire into the character of a candidate for bar admission, such admission cannot be denied on the basis of political association unless the candidate knowingly belongs to a subversive organization with specific intent to further its illegal ends. *Schware v. Board of Bar Exam'rs*, 353 U.S. 232 (1957). The state may, however, deny bar membership to a candidate who refuses to answer questions about political affiliations if that refusal obstructs the investigation of the candidate's qualifications. *Konigsberg v. State Bar of California*, 366 U.S. 36 (1961).

3. Elections and Political Parties

a. Voters in primary elections

A state cannot require a local political party to select presidential electors in an open primary (i.e., a primary in which any voter, including members of another party, may vote) when the national party prohibits nonparty members from voting. *Democratic Party v. LaFolette*, 450 U.S. 107 (1981). A state can require a semi-closed primary system, in which only registered party members and independents can vote in the party's primary, even if the party wants to permit anyone to vote. *Clingman v. Beaver*, 544 U.S. 581 (2005). On the other hand, a state may not prohibit a political party from allowing independents to vote in its primary. *Tashjian v. Republican Party of Connecticut*, 479 U.S. 208 (1986).

1) Blanket primary

A state may adopt a blanket primary system (i.e., a primary in which all voters regardless of party affiliation or lack thereof vote) that is nonpartisan. Under a nonpartisan primary system, the voters choose candidates for the general election without regard for their party affiliation. A nonpartisan blanket primary system in which a candidate identifies his own party preference or his status as an independent and that identification appears on the ballot has withstood a facial challenge, despite assertions that this self-designation violates the party's First Amendment rights as compelled speech and forced association. *Washington State Grange v. Washington State Republican Party*, 552 U.S. 442 (2008). By contrast, a partisan blanket primary system in which a party's nominees are chosen violates the party's First Amendment rights of free speech and association. *Cal. Democratic Party v. Jones*, 530 U.S. 567 (2000).

b. Ballot access to general election

A state may refuse to grant a political party's candidate access to the general-election ballot unless the party demonstrates public support through voter signatures on a petition, voter registrations, or previous electoral success. *Timmons v. Twin Cities Area New Party*, 520 U.S. 351 (1997); *Munro v. Socialist Workers Party*, 479 U.S. 189 (1986).

c. Fusion candidate

A state may prohibit a fusion candidate (i.e., a candidate who is nominated by more than one political party) from appearing on the general-election ballot as a candidate of multiple parties. This limitation on the associational rights of political parties is justified by the state's interests in ballot integrity and political stability. *Timmons v. Twin Cities Area New Party*, 520 U.S. 351 (1997).

d. Replacement candidate

When a state gives a political party the right to select an interim replacement for an elected state official who was a member of that party, the party may select the replacement through an election at which only party members may vote. *Rodriguez v. Popular Democratic Party*, 457 U.S. 1 (1982).

4. Criminal Penalty

A statute that purports to criminally punish mere membership in an association violates the First and Fourteenth Amendments. *Brandenburg v. Ohio*, 395 U.S. 444 (1969). Instead, such membership may only be criminalized if (i) the group is actively engaged in unlawful activity, or is engaging in advocacy that passes the *Brandenburg* "clear and present" danger test (i.e., speech directed to inciting or producing imminent lawless action that is likely to incite or produce such action); and (ii) the defendant knows of and specifically intends to further the group's illegal activity. *See, e.g., Whitney v. California*, 274 U.S. 357 (1927).

Contracts & Sales

CONTRACTS & SALES

Table of Contents

CONTRACTS & SALES

I. FORMATION OF CONTRACTS

A contract is a legally enforceable agreement. A legally enforceable contract is created through the process of mutual assent (i.e., offer and acceptance) and consideration, provided no valid defense to contract exists.

A. MUTUAL ASSENT

Mutual assent occurs upon acceptance of a valid offer to contract.

1. Objective Theory of Contracts

In contract law, intent is determined by the "objective theory" of contracts and not by the subjective intent or belief of a party. The objective theory is key to determining whether an offer or acceptance is valid.

Whether a party intends to enter into a contract is judged by outward objective facts, as interpreted by a reasonable person. The intent of a party is what a reasonable person in the position of the other party would believe as a result of that party's objective manifestation of intent. Thus, when the other party knew or should have known that the party lacked the intent to enter into a contract, a contract is not formed, whereas the party's mere subjective lack of intent is not sufficient to prevent the formation of a contract.

When words express the intent of the parties, the contract is an express contract. When conduct indicates assent or agreement, the agreement is considered implied in fact.

Example: Without paying, B joins a tour group that is walking through a downtown area learning about landmark buildings. The tour guide can charge B the fee for the tour because B's conduct of joining the group implied agreement with the contract.

2. Offer and Acceptance

a. Offer

An offer is an objective manifestation of a willingness by the offeror to enter into an agreement that creates the power of acceptance in the offeree. In other words, it is a communication that gives power to the recipient to conclude a contract by acceptance.

1) Intent

A statement is an offer only if the person to whom it is communicated could **reasonably interpret** it as an offer. It must express the **present intent** of a person to be legally bound to a contract. As noted above, the primary test of whether a communication is an offer is based on the objective theory of contracts; i.e., whether an individual receiving the communication would believe that he could enter into an enforceable deal by satisfying the condition.

2) Knowledge by the offeree

The offeree must have knowledge of the offer in order to have the power to accept the offer.

3) Terms

For a contract to exist, the terms of the contract must be certain and definite, or the contract fails for indefiniteness.

a) Essential terms

Under common law, all essential terms (i.e., the parties, subject matter, price, and quantity) must be covered in the agreement. The UCC allows for a more liberal contract formation. Under the UCC, a contract is formed if both parties intend to contract and there is a reasonably certain basis for giving a remedy. The only essential term is quantity, and as long as the parties intend to create a contract, the UCC "fills the gap" if other terms are missing, such as the time or place for delivery, or even the price for the goods. Requirements or output contracts satisfy UCC contract formation requirements even without naming specific quantities because the UCC implies good faith as a contract term.

b) Duration term

In most ongoing contracts, if a duration term is not specified in the agreement, courts will imply that the contract will last for a reasonable period of time.

i) Employment contracts

If an employment contract does not state duration, there is a rebuttable presumption that the employment is "at will." In an employment-at-will relationship, either party can terminate the relationship at any time, without the termination being considered a breach of the contract (unless the termination is against public policy, such as when an employee is discharged for filing a discrimination claim).

If an employment contract provides for "permanent employment," most courts hold that, in the absence of a proven contrary intention, the employment is "at will," because the duration term in the contract is considered too vague. If the offer promises "lifetime employment," some courts hold that the agreement is for at-will employment, while others take the term literally.

Many employment agreements overcome the default rule of employment at will by express terms of the contract, by rules published by the employer (such as those in an employee handbook), or by implication (by usage or conduct).

> **EXAM NOTE:** When presented with a question involving an employment agreement that is *not* at will, use a traditional breach-of-contract analysis.

c) Missing terms

A contract may still be formed when a term is missing, if it appears that the parties intended to create a contract. The court may supply the missing term because there is a presumption that the parties intended to include a reasonable term.

The UCC "fills the gap" for missing terms other than subject matter and quantity, such as the time (reasonable) or place for delivery (the seller's place of business), the time of payment (when the buyer is to receive the goods), the assortment of goods (reasonable choice of the buyer), and even the price for the goods. If the contract omits a price or if the parties agree to set the price in the future and then fail to agree, the UCC supplies a reasonable price at the time of delivery. UCC § 2-305. The contract must have an objective standard for the court to reference. UCC § 2-305.

d) Vague terms

When the terms of the contract are vague, the same presumption cannot be made, because the parties have manifested an intent that cannot be determined because of the vagueness of the terms.

4) Language

The offer must contain words of promise, undertaking, or commitment (as distinguished from words that merely indicate intention to sell or interest in buying). The offer must also be targeted to a number of people who could actually accept.

If a return promise is requested, then the contract is a **bilateral** contract. If an act is requested, then the contract is a **unilateral** contract. (*See* § I.A.2.c.1. Bilateral versus unilateral offer, *below.*)

5) Invitation to deal

Offers must be distinguished from invitations to deal.

> Compare, for example, the question, "what is your lowest price?" with the response to that question, "we can quote you $5 per gross for immediate acceptance." The first question is merely an inquiry, whereas the second statement is an offer. (Note that for the offeree to accept the offer, the offeree must supply the quantity term in order for the contract to meet the definiteness requirement.)

Advertisements generally are considered invitations to receive offers from the public, unless associated with a stated reward. An advertisement that is sufficiently specific and limiting as to who may accept may also qualify as an offer (e.g., "Used car for sale for $5,000. First come, first served.").

> **EXAM NOTE:** Be careful not to mistake a true offer for language that sounds like an offer but is actually just an invitation to receive offers. The more definite the statement (e.g., "I will sell you X for..."), the more likely it is to be an offer.

b. Termination of offers

An offer can be accepted only when it is still outstanding (i.e., before the offer is terminated). Offers can be terminated in the following ways.

1) Lapse of time in offer

If the offer specifies a date on which the offer terminates, then the time fixed by the offer controls. If the offer states that it will terminate after a specified number of days, the time generally starts to run from the time the offer is received, not sent, unless the offer indicates otherwise. If the offeree is aware (or should have been aware) that there is a delay in the transmittal of the offer, the offer expires when it would have expired had there been no delay.

If the offer does not set a time limit for acceptance, the power of acceptance terminates at the end of a reasonable period of time. What is reasonable is a question of fact and depends on a variety of factors, including the nature of the contract, the purpose and course of dealing between the parties, and trade usage. For an offer received by mail, an acceptance that is sent by midnight of the day of receipt generally has been made within a reasonable period of time. Unless otherwise agreed upon, if the parties bargain in person or via telephone, the time for acceptance does not ordinarily extend beyond the end of the conversation. Restatement (Second) of Contracts § 41.

2) Death or mental incapacity

An offer terminates upon the death or mental incapacity of the offeror, even if the offeree does not learn of the offeror's death or mental incapacity until after the offeree has dispatched what he believes is an acceptance. An exception exists for an offer that is an option, which does not terminate upon death or mental incapacity because consideration was paid to keep the offer open during the option period, and the offer is therefore made irrevocable during that period.

Compare accepted offer: If an offer has been accepted, death of the offeror does not automatically terminate the contract. The contract may be enforceable unless there is some reason, such as impracticability, that justifies discharge of the contractual obligation.

3) Destruction or illegality

An offer involving subject matter that is destroyed is terminated. Similarly, an offer that becomes illegal is terminated.

4) Revocation

In general, an offer can be revoked by the offeror at any time prior to acceptance. An offer is revoked when the offeror makes a manifestation of an intention not to enter into the proposed contract. Restatement (Second) of Contracts § 42. A revocation may be made in any reasonable manner and by any reasonable means, and it is not effective until communicated. A revocation sent by mail is not effective until received.

Example: On day 1, A mails an offer to B. On day 2, A mails a revocation to B. If B receives the offer and accepts before receiving the revocation, a contract is formed.

At common law, a written revocation (as well as a written rejection or acceptance) is received when it comes into the possession of the person addressed or the person authorized to receive it on his behalf, or when it is deposited in some place he has authorized for deposit for this or similar communications. Restatement (Second) of Contracts § 68. Under the UCC, a person receives notice when: (i) it comes to that person's attention or (ii) it is duly delivered in a reasonable form at the place of business or where held out as the place for receipt of such communications. Receipt by an organization occurs at the time it is brought to the attention of the individual conducting the transaction or at the time it would have been brought to that individual's attention were due diligence exercised by the organization. UCC § 1-202.

If the offeree acquires reliable information that the offeror has taken definite action inconsistent with the offer, the offer is automatically revoked (i.e., a constructive revocation occurs).The offeror's power to revoke an offer is limited by the following items.

a) Option (promise not to revoke)

An option is an independent promise to keep an offer open for a specified period of time. Such a promise limits the offeror's power to revoke the offer until after the period has expired, while also preserving the offeree's power to accept.

If the option is a promise not to revoke an offer to enter a new contract, the offeree must generally give separate consideration for the option to be enforceable. If the option is within an existing contract, no separate consideration is required.

b) UCC firm offer rule

Under the UCC, an offer to buy or sell goods is irrevocable if:

i) The offeror is a merchant;

ii) There is an assurance that the offer is to remain open; and

iii) The assurance is contained in a signed writing from the offeror.

> No consideration by the offeree is needed to keep the offer open under the UCC firm offer rule. UCC § 2-205.

i) "Merchant" defined

For purposes of this rule, a merchant includes not only a person who regularly deals in the type of goods involved in the transaction or otherwise by his occupation holds himself out as having knowledge or skill peculiar to the practices or goods involved in the transaction, but also any businessperson when the transaction is of a commercial nature. UCC § 2-104(1) cmt. 2.

ii) Time period

If the time period during which the option is to be held open is not stated, a reasonable term is implied. However, irrevocability cannot exceed three months, regardless of whether a time period is stated or implied, unless the offeree gives consideration to validate it beyond the three-month period.

iii) Signed writing

The primary purpose of the signed writing requirement is to ensure that the merchant deliberately makes a current firm offer binding.

Therefore, a full handwritten signature is not always required, such as when merely initialing the relevant clause is appropriate under the circumstances, or when the offeror handwrites on her letterhead that she "confirms" that a firm offer was already made. U.C.C. § 2-205, cmt. 2.

NOTE: A firm offer in a form prepared by the offeree must be **separately signed** by the offeror to protect against inadvertent signing. U.C.C. § 2-205, cmt. 4.

EXAM NOTE: Provisions of the UCC requiring a signed writing may be satisfied by an electronic record and electronic signature. The Uniform Electronic Transactions Act (UETA), adopted in most states, provides that an electronic signature cannot be denied legal effect solely because it is in electronic form.

c) Promissory estoppel (detrimental reliance)

When the offeree reasonably and detrimentally relies on the offeror's promise prior to acceptance, the doctrine of promissory estoppel may make the offer irrevocable. It must have been reasonably foreseeable that such detrimental reliance would occur in order to imply the existence of an option contract. The offeror is liable to the extent necessary to avoid injustice, which may result in holding the offeror to the offer, reimbursement of the costs incurred by the offeree, or restitution of the benefits conferred. (*See* § I.C.4. Promissory Estoppel, *infra.*)

d) Partial performance

If the offer is for a unilateral contract, the offeror cannot revoke the offer once the offeree has begun performance. Once performance has begun, the offeree will have a reasonable amount of time to complete performance but cannot be required to complete the performance. A unilateral contract is not formed until performance is complete. Restatement (Second) of Contracts § 45.

Commencement of performance of a bilateral contract operates as a promise to render complete performance. Restatement (Second) of Contracts § 62.

Whether the contract is unilateral or bilateral, the offeree must have had knowledge of the offer when she began performance.

5) Revocation of general offers

A "general offer" is an offer made to a large number of people, generally through an advertisement. A general offer can be revoked only by notice that is given at least the same level of publicity as the offer. So long as the appropriate level of publicity is met, the revocation will be effective even if a potential offeree does not learn of the revocation and acts in reliance on the offer. Restatement (Second) of Contracts § 46. Note that if a person has actual knowledge of the intent to revoke but did not see the notice, then the revocation will be effective as to such person.

6) Rejection by offeree

An offer is terminated by rejection. In other words, the offeree clearly conveys to the offeror that the offeree no longer intends to accept the offer. A rejection is usually **effective upon receipt**. An offeree cannot accept an offer once it has been terminated.

A counteroffer acts as a rejection of the original offer and creates a new offer. An exception exists for an option holder, who has the right to make counteroffers during the option period without terminating the original offer.

> **EXAM NOTE:** Remember that a **counteroffer** is both a **rejection and a new offer.** Examine the offeree's statement closely. It may be a rejection, but it may also be only an inquiry (e.g., "Is that a 2005 model car?") or merely indecision (e.g., "I'll keep your offer under advisement."); in either case the offer remains open.

7) Revival of offer

A terminated offer may be revived by the offeror. As with any open offer, the revived offer can be accepted by the offeree.

> **Example:** A offers to paint B's house for $500. B rejects the offer. A states that the offer remains open. B can change her mind and accept the revived offer.

c. Acceptance

An acceptance is an objective manifestation by the offeree to be bound by the terms of the offer. Only a party to whom an offer is extended may accept or, if the offer is extended to a class, a party who is a member of the class may accept.

An offeree must know of the offer upon acceptance for it to be valid. In addition, the offeree must communicate the acceptance to the offeror.

1) Bilateral versus unilateral offer

The offeror can detail the manner of proper acceptance.

A **bilateral contract** is one in which a promise by one party is exchanged for a promise by the other. The exchange of promises is enough to render them both enforceable. An offer requiring a promise to accept can be accepted either with a return promise or by starting performance. Commencement of performance of a bilateral contract operates as a promise to render complete performance. Restatement (Second) of Contracts § 62.

A **unilateral contract** is one in which one party promises to do something in return for an act of the other party (e.g., a monetary reward for finding a lost dog). Unlike in a bilateral contract, in a unilateral contract, the offeree's promise to perform is insufficient to constitute acceptance. Acceptance of an offer for a unilateral contract **requires complete performance**. Once performance has begun, the offer is irrevocable for a reasonable period of time to allow for complete performance unless there is a manifestation of a contrary intent. However, the offeree is not bound to complete performance. In addition, while the offeror may terminate the offer before the offeree begins to perform, expenses incurred by the offeree in preparing to perform may be recoverable as reliance damages. Restatement (Second) of Contracts § 45.

> **EXAM NOTE:** The offeree of a unilateral contract can accept only an offer that he is aware of. In other words, if the offeree does not become aware of the offer until after acting, then his acts do not constitute acceptance.

When there is doubt as to whether an offer may be accepted by a promise to perform or by performance, the offeree may accept the offer by either. Restatement (Second) of Contracts § 32.

2) Means of acceptance

The offeror is master of the offer and can dictate the manner and means by which an offer may be accepted. For example, the offeror can require the offeree to accept in writing or to accept by means of a phone call. Unless the offeror specifically requires the offeree to accept in a particular manner or by using a particular means, the offeree can accept in any reasonable manner and by any reasonable means. UCC § 2-206(1)(a). A means of acceptance is reasonable if it was used by the offeror, used customarily in the industry, or used between the parties in prior transactions. Restatement (Second) of Contracts § 65. Even if the acceptance is by unauthorized means, it may be effective if the offeror receives the acceptance while the offer is still open. Restatement (Second) of Contracts § 67.

a) Silence

Generally, silence does not operate as an acceptance of an offer, even if the offer states that silence qualifies as acceptance (or, more likely, implied acceptance), unless:

i) The offeree has reason to believe that the offer could be accepted by silence, and he was silent with the intent to accept the offer by silence; or

ii) Because of previous dealings or patterns of behavior, it is reasonable to believe that the offeree must notify the offeror if the offeree intends not to accept.

b) Shipment of goods

If the buyer requests that the goods be shipped, then the buyer's request will be construed as inviting acceptance by the seller either by a **promise to ship** or by **prompt shipment** of conforming or nonconforming goods.

If the seller ships nonconforming goods, then the shipment is both an acceptance of the offer and a breach of the contract. The seller is then liable for any damage caused to the buyer as a result of the breach.

If, however, the seller "seasonably" notifies the buyer that the nonconforming goods are tendered as an accommodation, then no acceptance has occurred, and no contract is formed. The accommodation is deemed a counteroffer, and the buyer may then either accept (thereby forming a contract) or reject (no contract formed).

3) Mailbox rule

An acceptance that is mailed within the allotted response time is effective **when sent** (not upon receipt), unless the offer provides otherwise. The mailing must be properly addressed and include correct postage.

> **EXAM NOTE:** Keep in mind that the mailbox rule applies only to **acceptance**, and therefore it almost exclusively applies to bilateral contracts (when there is one promise in exchange for another promise), because unilateral contracts require action as acceptance.

a) Rejection following acceptance

If the offeree sends an acceptance and later sends a communication rejecting the offer, then the acceptance will generally control even if the offeror receives the rejection first. If, however, the offeror receives the rejection first and detrimentally relies on the rejection, then the offeree will be estopped from enforcing the contract.

b) Acceptance following rejection

If a communication is sent rejecting the offer, and a later communication is sent accepting the contract, then the mailbox rule will not apply, and the first one to be received by the offeror will prevail. An acceptance or rejection is received when the writing comes into the possession of the offeror or her agent, or when it is deposited in her mailbox. The offeror need not actually read the communication that is received first for it to prevail.

c) Revocations effective upon receipt

Offers revoked by the offeror are effective upon receipt.

d) Options and other irrevocable offers

The mailbox rule does not apply to an option contract, which requires that the acceptance be received by the offeror before the offer expires, or to offers that specify that acceptance must be received by a certain date. Restatement (Second) of Contracts § 63(b) cmt. f.

e) Medium

If the acceptance is via an "instantaneous two-way communication," such as telephone or traceable fax, it is treated as if the parties were in each other's presence. Restatement (Second) of Contracts § 64.

4) Notice

a) Unilateral contract

In a unilateral contract, an offeree is not required to give notice after performance is complete, unless he has reason to know that the offeror would not learn of performance within a reasonable time, or the offer requires notice.

If notice is required but not provided, the offeror's duty is discharged, unless:

i) The offeree exercises reasonable diligence to notify the offeror;

ii) The offeror learns of performance within a reasonable time; or

iii) The offer indicates that notification of acceptance is not required.

Restatement (Second) of Contracts § 54(2).

b) Bilateral contract

An offeree of a bilateral contract must give notice of acceptance. Under the mailbox rule, because acceptance becomes valid when sent, a properly addressed letter sent by the offeree operates as an acceptance when mailed, even though the offeror has not yet received the notice. Under the UCC, notice is required within a reasonable time if acceptance is made by beginning performance and failure to do so will result in a lapse of the offer. UCC § 2-206(2).

d. Effect of additional or different terms

1) Common-law mirror-image rule

The acceptance must mirror the terms of the offer. Any change to the terms of the offer, or the addition of another term not found in the offer, acts as a rejection of the original offer and as a new counteroffer. Mere suggestions or inquiries, including requests for clarification or statements of intent, made in a response by the offeree do not constitute a counteroffer. A conditional acceptance terminates the offer and acts as a new offer from the original offeree.

2) UCC rule—acceptance contains additional or different terms

The UCC does not follow the mirror-image rule. Additional or different terms included in an acceptance of an offer do not automatically constitute a rejection of the original offer. Generally, for a sale of goods, an acceptance that contains additional or different terms with respect to the terms in the offer is nevertheless treated as an acceptance rather than a rejection and a counteroffer. An exception exists when the acceptance is expressly conditioned on assent to the additional or different terms, in which case the acceptance is a counteroffer. UCC § 2-207(1).

Whether the additional or different terms are treated as part of the contract depends on whether the parties are merchants.

a) One or both parties are not merchants

When the contract is for the sale of goods between nonmerchants or between a merchant and a nonmerchant, a definite and seasonable expression of acceptance or written confirmation that is sent within a reasonable time operates as an acceptance of the original offer. This is true even if it states terms that are additional to or different from the offer, unless the acceptance is made expressly conditional on the offeror's consent to the additional or different terms. The additional terms are treated as a proposal for addition to the contract that must be separately accepted by the offeror to become a part of the contract. UCC § 2-207(2).

b) Both parties are merchants—battle of the forms

> **EXAM NOTE:** The MBE has consistently tested the situation in which both parties to the contract are merchants. In this situation, remember that a contract exists **under the terms of the acceptance**, unless (i) the terms materially alter the agreement, (ii) the offer expressly limits the terms, or (iii) the offeror objects to the new terms within a reasonable time after notice of the new terms is received.

When both parties are merchants, the parties often use sales forms that might not be designed for the particular sale in question. As a consequence, the acceptance often contains different and additional terms. In this "battle of the forms" over whose terms will form the basis of the contract, the rules may vary depending on whether the terms are additional terms or different terms.

i) Acceptance includes additional terms

An additional term in the acceptance is **automatically included** in the contract when both parties are merchants, unless:

    i)   The term materially alters the original contract;

    ii) The offer expressly limits acceptance to the terms of the offer; or

    iii) The offeror has already objected to the additional terms, or objects within a reasonable time after notice of them was received.

If any one of these three exceptions is met, the term will not become part of the contract, and the offeror's original terms control. UCC § 2-207(2).

> **"Materially Alter":** A term that results in surprise or hardship if incorporated without the express awareness by the other party materially alters the original contract. Examples of terms found to have materially altered the original contract include a warranty disclaimer, a clause that flies in the face of trade usage with regard to quality, a requirement that complaints be made in an unreasonably short time period, and other terms that surprise or create hardship without express awareness by the other party. Terms that usually **do not** materially alter the contract include fixing reasonable times for bringing a complaint, setting reasonable interest for overdue invoices, and reasonably limiting remedies. UCC § 2-207 cmts. 4,5.

ii) Acceptance includes different terms

The courts in different jurisdictions disagree as to the result when different terms are included in the merchant offeree's acceptance. A few jurisdictions treat different terms the same as additional terms and apply the rule described above. Most, however, apply the **"knock-out" rule**, under which different terms in the offer and acceptance nullify each other and are "knocked out" of the contract. When gaps are created after applying the knock-out rule, the court uses Article 2's gap-filling provisions to patch the holes. (*See* § I.A.2.a.3.c. Missing terms, *above.*)

c) UCC rule—acceptance based on conduct

If the offer and purported acceptance differ to such a degree that there is no contract, but the parties have begun to perform anyway (i.e., demonstrated conduct that recognizes the existence of a contract), then Article 2 provides that there will be a contract, and its terms will consist of those terms on which the writings of the parties agree, together with any supplementary terms filled in by the provisions of the UCC. UCC § 2-207(3).

e. Auction contracts

The UCC has special rules for auction sales.

1) Goods auctioned in lots

If goods in an auction sale are offered in lots, each lot represents a separate sale.

2) Completion of a sale

An auction sale is complete when the auctioneer announces its end, such as by the fall of the auctioneer's hammer or in any other customary way. When a bid is made contemporaneously with the falling of the hammer, the auctioneer may, at her discretion, treat the bid as continuing the bidding process or declare the sale completed at the fall of the hammer.

3) Reserve and no-reserve auctions

In a reserve auction, the auctioneer may withdraw the goods any time before she announces completion of the sale. An auction is with reserve unless specifically announced as a no-reserve auction.

In a no-reserve auction, after the auctioneer calls for bids on the goods, the goods cannot be withdrawn unless no bid is received within a reasonable time.

In either type of auction, a bidder may retract her bid until the auctioneer announces the completion of the sale. A retraction, however, does not revive any earlier bids.

4) When the seller bids

When an auctioneer knowingly accepts a bid by the seller or on her behalf, or procures such a bid to drive up the price of the goods, the winning bidder may avoid the sale or, at her option, take the goods at the price of the last good-faith bid prior to the end of the auction. There are two exceptions to this rule, which are that (i) a seller may bid at a forced sale and (ii) a seller may bid if she specifically gives notice that she reserves the right to bid.

B. CONSIDERATION

If there is a valid offer and acceptance that creates an agreement, the agreement can be legally enforceable if there is consideration.

1. Bargain and Exchange

Valuable consideration is evidenced by a bargained-for change in the legal position between the parties. Most courts conclude that consideration exists if there is a detriment to the promisee, irrespective of the benefit to the promisor. A minority of courts look to either a detriment or a benefit, not requiring both. The Second Restatement asks only whether there was a bargained-for exchange. Restatement (Second) of Contracts § 71.

a. Legal detriment and bargained-for exchange

For the legal detriment to constitute sufficient consideration, it must be bargained for in exchange for the promise. The promise must induce the detriment, and the detriment must induce the promise ("mutuality of consideration").

Consideration can take the form of:

i)   A return promise to do something;

ii) A return promise to refrain from doing something legally permitted;

iii) The actual performance of some act; or

iv) Refraining from doing some act.

b. Gift distinguished

A promise to make a gift does not involve bargained-for consideration and is therefore unenforceable.

A promise by A to give B $1,000 when B turns 21 years old is not enforceable because the act of attaining the age of 21 is not bargained for and is thus not sufficient consideration. There also can be no reliance on the promise (B will turn 21 years of age regardless of A's promise), so promissory estoppel does not apply.

Alternatively, if A offers B $1,000 to quit smoking, it is assumed that A is bargaining for B's act and that B would rely on the promise of the payment when he quit smoking.

> **EXAM NOTE:** The test to distinguish a gift from valid consideration is whether the offeree could have **reasonably believed that the intent of the offeror was to induce the action**. If yes, there is consideration, and the promise is enforceable.

A party's promise to make a gift is enforceable under the doctrine of promissory estoppel if the promisor/donor knows that the promise will induce substantial reliance by the promisee, and the failure to enforce the promise will cause substantial injustice. (*See* § I.C.4. Promissory estoppel, *below.*)

2. Adequacy of Consideration

The basic concept of legal detriment is that there must be something of **substance**, either an act or a promise, which is given in exchange for the promise that is to be enforced. In general, a party cannot challenge a contract on the grounds that the consideration is inadequate. A difference in economic value between the items exchanged is not grounds for finding that a contract did not exist due to inadequate consideration.

a. Subjective value

The benefit to the promisor does not need to have an economic value. Regardless of the objective value of an item, as long as the promisor wants it, the giving of it will constitute adequate consideration.

b. Preexisting-duty rule

1) Common law

At common law, a promise to perform a preexisting legal duty does not qualify as consideration because the promisor is already bound to perform (i.e., there is no legal detriment). Note that if the promisor gives something in addition to what is already owed (however small) or varies the preexisting duty in some way (however slight), most courts find that consideration exists. Restatement (Second) of Contracts § 73.

> **Example 1:** A borrower knows that he owes a lender $1,000 today. The borrower promises to repay the loan if the lender promises to lend the borrower an additional $100. The borrower has not provided consideration for the lender's promise.

> **Example 2:** A borrower knows that he owes a lender $1,000 tomorrow. The borrower offers to pay the lender $900 today if the lender agrees to forego the additional $100. The lender accepts the offer. The borrower has provided the lender with consideration for the lender's promise.

2) Exception for a third party

There is an exception to the preexisting-duty rule when a third party offers a promise contingent upon performance of a contractual obligation by a party. Under the exception, the third party's promise is sufficient consideration. Restatement (Second) of Contracts § 73.

Example: C contracts with P for P to install plumbing in a house being built by C for H. C subsequently becomes insolvent and walks away from the project. H contracts with P and promises to pay P the same amount P would have received from C if P installs the plumbing. P's completion of the job constitutes consideration for the promise by H, even though P was already contractually obligated to C to do the work.

c. Past consideration

Under the common law, something given in the past is typically not adequate consideration because it could not have been bargained for, nor could it have been done in reliance upon a promise.

Example: A is drowning, and B dives in and saves A. Grateful to have been saved, A promises B $500. Under the common-law approach, there is no consideration, and the promise is therefore unenforceable. It is based on a mere moral obligation arising out of past conduct.

There is a modern trend, adopted by the Second Restatement, however, toward enforcing some such promises under material benefit rule (*see* I.C.3. Promise to Pay Benefits Received—Material Benefit Rule, *infra*).

d. Modification

1) Common law

At common law, modification of an existing contract must be supported by consideration. Agreements to modify a contract may still be enforced if:

i) There is a rescission of the existing contract by tearing it up or by some other outward sign, and then the entering into of a new contract, whereby one of the parties must perform more than she was to perform under the original contract;

ii) There are unanticipated difficulties, and one of the parties agrees to compensate the other when the difficulties arise if the modification is fair and equitable in light of those difficulties; or

iii) There are new obligations on both sides.

The modification must rest in circumstances not anticipated as part of the context in which the contract was made but need not have been completely unforeseeable. When such a reason is present, the relative financial strength of the parties, the formality with which the modification is made, the extent to which it is performed or relied on and other circumstances may be relevant.

2) UCC

Unlike under the common law, under Article 2, no consideration is necessary to modify a contract; however, good faith is required. Thus, if one party is attempting to extort a modification, it will be ineffective under the UCC.

Good faith requires honesty in fact and fair dealing in accordance with reasonable commercial standards. UCC § 1-201(20). The definition of "good faith" no longer limits the fair dealing prong of the rule to merchants. The same definition of good faith applies to all parties, both merchants and nonmerchants alike.

EXAM NOTE: The MBE frequently tests the different common-law and UCC rules regarding contract modification. At common law, modifications require consideration; under the UCC, they require only good faith.

Example: If a party demands an increase in price because the other party has no choice but to agree, the courts will invalidate such a bad-faith modification.

a) Installment contracts

Generally, a party benefited by a condition under a contract may orally waive that condition without new consideration. However, in installment contracts, the waiver may be retracted by providing the other party with reasonable notice that strict performance is required. The retraction is allowed unless it would be unjust because of a material change of position by the other party in reliance on the waiver.

e. Accord and satisfaction

1) Accord

Under an accord agreement, a party to a contract agrees to accept a performance from the other party that differs from the performance that was promised in the existing contract, in satisfaction of the other party's existing duty. Restatement (Second) of Contracts § 281.

a) Dispute of a monetary claim

When a party agrees to accept a lesser amount in full satisfaction of its monetary claim, there must be consideration or a consideration substitute for the party's promise to accept the lesser amount. For example, consideration can exist if the other party honestly disputes the claim or agrees to forego an asserted defense (*see* i. Settlement of a legal claim, *below*), or if the payment is of a different type than called for under the original contract (*see* b.1) Common law, *above*). Restatement (Second) of Contracts § 281, cmt. d.

Example 1: On Monday, a contractor completes construction of a garage for a homeowner. Under the terms of the contract, the homeowner owes the contractor $40,000 in cash. The homeowner offers to deliver a sports car worth $35,000 to the contractor on Friday in satisfaction of his contractual obligation. The contractor agrees. The contractor's acceptance of the homeowner's offer creates an accord. Because the homeowner is offering payment in a different form than that called for under the contract (i.e., a car instead of cash), it does not matter that the car is worth less than $40,000.

2) Satisfaction

A "satisfaction" is the performance of the accord agreement; it will discharge both the original contract and the accord contract. However, there is no satisfaction until performance, and the original contract is not discharged until satisfaction is complete. Therefore, if an accord is breached by the party who has promised a different performance, the other party can sue either on the original contract **or** under the accord agreement.

> **Example 2:** Assume the same facts as those in Example 1, except that on Wednesday, the contractor changes his mind and seeks to collect the $40,000 from the homeowner. The contractor cannot enforce the original contract. Although the debt is not yet satisfied, because there was an accord regarding the sports car, the homeowner's obligation under the original contract is suspended until Friday.
>
> **Example 3:** Assume the same facts as those in Example 1, except that on Friday, the homeowner delivers the sports car to the contractor. This constitutes satisfaction. The contractor cannot enforce the contractual obligation of the homeowner to pay $40,000 in cash.
>
> **Example 4:** Assume the same facts as those in Example 1, except that on Friday, the homeowner fails to deliver the sports car to the contractor. At that point, the contractor may seek to enforce the homeowner's original promise to pay $40,000 in cash **or** the homeowner's promise to deliver the sports car to the contractor.
>
> **Note:** Compare accord with a substituted contract, which is a second agreement that immediately discharges the original contract, such that the remedy for breach is limited to the terms of the second contract. Whether an agreement is an accord or a substitute contract turns on how formal the agreement is; the less formal, the more likely it is an accord.

3) Use of a negotiable instrument

If a claim is unliquidated or otherwise subject to dispute, it can be discharged if (i) the person against whom the claim is asserted in good faith tenders a negotiable instrument (e.g., a check) that is accompanied by a conspicuous statement indicating that the instrument was tendered as full satisfaction of the claim (e.g., "Payment in full"), and (ii) the claimant obtains payment of the instrument. The addition of a restriction by the claimant to his indorsement of the check, such as "under protest," does not operate to preserve his right to seek additional compensation. UCC § 3-311(a), (b).

When the claimant is an organization, the discharge is not effective if the instrument is not tendered to a person, place, or office designated by the organization. If no such designation is made, or if the claimant is not an organization, the discharge is not effective if the claimant returns the payment within 90 days. However, regardless of the type of claimant, these exceptions do not apply and the claim is discharged when the claimant, or the claimant's agent who has direct responsibility with respect to the disputed obligation, knew, within a reasonable time before collection was initiated, that the instrument was tendered in full satisfaction of the claim. The burden to establish such knowledge is on party seeking discharge. UCC § 3-311(c).

f. Illusory promises

An illusory promise is one that essentially pledges nothing because it is vague or because the promisor can choose whether to honor it. Such a promise is not legally binding.

> **Example:** B promises, "I will give you $100, at my option." B's promise is an illusory promise.

A promise that is based on the occurrence of a condition within the control of the promisor may be illusory, but courts often find that the promisor has also promised to use her best efforts to bring about the condition. Restatement (Second) of Contracts § 76 cmt. d. Similarly, a promise to purchase goods upon the promisor's satisfaction with the goods is not illusory because the promisor is required to act in good faith. UCC § 1-304.

g. Voidable and unenforceable promises

A promise that is voidable or unenforceable by a rule of law (e.g., infancy) can nevertheless constitute consideration. Restatement (Second) of Contracts § 78.

> **Example:** A car dealer promises to sell a used car to a minor for $5,000. The car dealer may not escape selling the car to the minor for $5,000 on the grounds that, because the minor's promise is voidable, the car dealer did not receive consideration for its promise.

h. Requirements and output contracts

A requirements contract is a contract under which a buyer agrees to buy all that he will require of a product from the other party. An output contract is a contract under which a seller agrees to sell all that she manufactures of a product to the buyer. There is consideration in these agreements because the promisor suffers a legal detriment. The fact that the party may go out of business does not render the promise illusory.

Because a covenant of good faith and fair dealing is implied in all contracts (common law and UCC), any quantities under such a contract may not be unreasonably disproportionate to any stated estimates, or if no estimate is stated, to any normal or otherwise comparable prior requirements or output.

i. Settlement of a legal claim

A promise not to assert or a release of a claim or defense that proves to be invalid does not constitute consideration, unless the claim or defense is in fact doubtful due to uncertainty of facts or law, or the party promising not to assert or releasing the claim or defense believes in good faith that it may be fairly determined to be valid. Restatement (Second) of Contracts § 74(a).

> **Example 1:** A borrower knows that he owes a lender $1,000. The borrower offers to pay the lender $900 in exchange for the lender's promise not to seek the remaining $100. The lender accepts the offer and makes the promise. The borrower pays the lender $900. The lender may nevertheless seek the remaining $100 from the borrower because there was no uncertainty as to the validity of the debt or the amount owed. As such, there was no consideration for the lender's promise.
>
> **Example 2:** Due to an ambiguity in the wording of a contract, an employee contends that she is owed a commission of $500. The employer contends that the employee is owed nothing. The employer promises to pay the employee $250 in exchange for the employee's promise to forego of her claim of $500. The employee's promise constitutes consideration for the employer's promise to pay $250. If the employer fails to pay the employee $250, the employee can enforce the employer's promise.

C. PROMISES BINDING WITHOUT CONSIDERATION

There are a number of circumstances in which a promise will be enforceable despite the fact that it is not supported by consideration.

1. **Promise to Pay a Debt Barred by the Statute of Limitations or Bankruptcy**

A **new promise** to pay a debt after the statute of limitations has run is enforceable without any new consideration. When the new promise is an express promise, most states require that the new promise be in writing and signed by the debtor. In addition, a new promise may be implied when the obligor (i) voluntarily transfers of something of value (e.g., money, negotiable note) to the obligee as interest on, part payment of, or collateral security for the prior debt, (ii) voluntarily acknowledges to the obligor the present existence of the prior indebtedness, or (iii) states to the obligee that the statute of limitations will not be pled as a defense.

A new promise made to pay a debt discharged in bankruptcy is enforceable without any new consideration. While there must an express promise to pay rather than a mere acknowledgment or partial payment of the discharged debt, the new promise need not be in writing.

Because it is the new promise that is enforceable and not the prior debt obligation itself, the amount to which the obligee is entitled may be less than the prior debt obligation.

2. **Promise to Perform a Voidable Duty**

A new promise to perform a duty that is voidable will be enforceable despite the absence of consideration, provided that the new promise does not suffer from an infirmity that would make it, in turn, voidable.

Example: X, who is 15 years old, enters into a contract with Y that is voidable because of X's infancy. Upon reaching the age of majority, X promises to perform the contract. Such promise will be enforceable without any new consideration. Note that if X reaffirmed the promise before reaching the age of majority, such promise would be voidable (because of X's continued infancy).

3. **Promise to Pay Benefits Received—Material Benefit Rule**

Under the material benefit rule, when a party performs an unrequested service for another party that constitutes a material benefit, the modern trend permits the performing party to enforce a promise of payment made by the other party after the service is rendered, even though, at common law, such a promise would be unenforceable due to lack of consideration.

This rule is not enforced when the performing party rendered the services without the expectation of compensation (e.g., as a gift). In addition, the promise is enforced only to the extent necessary to prevent injustice, and it is not enforceable to the extent that the value of the promise is disproportionate to the benefit received, or the promisor has not been unjustly enriched.

Example: P sees D's horse running free and knows that D is out of town. P feeds and houses the horse for two weeks at a cost of $30 while awaiting D's return. When D returns, D thanks P and promises to pay P $50 at the end of the month. At common law, this promise is unenforceable due to lack of consideration. Under the material benefit rule, the promise is not enforceable to the extent that it is disproportionate to the benefit received. Thus, P's promise can be enforced to the extent of $30.

Note that, apart from a contract remedy, the provider of services may also be able to recover under a quasi-contract theory (*see* § I.G.2. Implied-in-Law ("Quasi") Contracts, *infra*).

Requested services distinguished: If one party requests another party to perform a service but does not indicate a price, and the service is performed, this generally creates an "implied-in-fact" contract. The party who performed the requested service is generally entitled to recover the reasonable value of her services in a breach-of-contract action in which the party who enjoyed the benefit of the services refused to pay. An exception applies, however, when the services were rendered without the expectation of payment.

4. **Promissory Estoppel**

Promissory estoppel is referred to as a consideration "substitute." The doctrine of promissory estoppel (detrimental reliance) can be used under certain circumstances to enforce a promise that is not supported by consideration.

a. **Requirements**

A promise is binding if:

   i)   The promisor should reasonably expect it to induce action or forbearance on the part of the promisee or a third person;

   ii) The promise does induce such action or forbearance; and

   iii) Injustice can be avoided only by enforcement of the promise.

Note that, in general, the promisee must actually rely on the promise, and such reliance must have been reasonably foreseeable to the promisor. See below, however, for an exception regarding charitable subscriptions.

The remedy may be limited or adjusted as justice requires. Generally, this results in the award of reliance damages rather than expectation damages.

Example: X, who is very wealthy, knows that her nephew Y is poor but wants to go to college. X promises to pay Y $100,000 when Y gets his diploma. Y then chooses to go to a state college and takes out $50,000 in loans to cover all tuition and expenses. In April of his senior year, Y is told by X that she won't pay anything. Y gets his degree in May and sues X. While there is no consideration for X's promise, the promise is still enforceable under the doctrine of promissory estoppel. X reasonably should have expected that Y would rely on her promise. Y did in fact rely by going to college, and it would seem unjust not to enforce the promise. Note, though, that Y's remedy can be limited "as justice requires." The proper amount would likely be $50,000 (the amount of Y's out-of-pocket expenses in reliance), not the $100,000 that X originally promised.

EXAM NOTE: Always consider whether there is a valid contract before considering promissory estoppel as the correct answer choice.

b. **Exception to the reliance requirement for charitable subscriptions**

Courts often apply the doctrine of promissory estoppel to enforce promises to charitable institutions. In some cases, they presume that the charity detrimentally relied on the promised contribution. A charitable subscription (i.e., a written promise) is enforceable under the doctrine of promissory estoppel without proof that the charity relied on the promise. Restatement (Second) of Contracts § 90(2).

Example: B promises in writing to give a university a $10,000 donation. Under the Second Restatement, the university may enforce the promise under the doctrine of promissory estoppel, even though the university does not establish that it relied to its detriment on B's promise.

c. Construction contracts and promissory estoppel

In the construction industry, it would be unjust to permit a subcontractor to revoke a bid after inducing justifiable and detrimental reliance in the general contractor. Thus, an agreement not to revoke a sub-bid offer can be enforceable under the theory of promissory estoppel.

Because the sub-bid is only an outstanding offer, the **general contractor is not bound** to accept it upon becoming the successful bidder for the general contract. A general contractor can enter into a subcontract with another subcontractor for a lower price.

D. ENFORCEABILITY

A contract may be unenforceable based upon a defense to formation or a defense to enforcement. Proof of the defense may render the contract void or voidable.

1. Void Contracts

A void contract results in the entire transaction being regarded as a nullity, as if no contract existed between the parties.

2. Voidable Contracts

A voidable contract operates as a valid contract, unless and until one of the parties takes steps to avoid it.

3. Unenforceable Contracts

An unenforceable contract is a valid contract that cannot be enforced if one of the parties refuses to carry out its terms.

> **EXAM NOTE:** Remember that a void contract cannot be enforced, but a party may opt to avoid a voidable contract.

E. DEFENSES TO FORMATION

A person who is asserted to be in breach of a contract can defend the action by showing that there was no "meeting of the minds" due to a mistake or misunderstanding, misrepresentation or fraud, undue influence or duress, or the party's own lack of capacity.

1. Mistake

A mistake is a belief that is not in accord with the facts as to a basic assumption on which the contract was made that materially affects performance. Note that the mistake must be with regard to a belief about an **existing fact** and not with regard to something that will happen in the future. Risks with regard to changing facts are governed by the doctrines of impracticability and frustration of purpose.

a. Mutual mistake

Mutual mistake occurs when both parties are mistaken as to an essential element of the contract. In such a situation, the contract may be **voidable** by the adversely affected party upon proof of the following:

   i)   Mistake of fact existing at the time the contract was formed;

   ii) The mistake relates to a basic assumption of the contract;

   iii) The mistake has a material impact on the transaction; and

   iv) The adversely affected party did not assume the risk of the mistake.

Example: Rescission of a contract to sell a cow was granted on grounds of mutual mistake when both parties completed the exchange of the cow on the mistaken understanding that the cow was barren. *Sherwood v. Walker*, 33 N.W. 919 (Mich. 1887).

When reformation of the contract is available to cure a mistake, neither party can avoid the contract.

1) Conscious ignorance

A party may bear the risk of a mistake, however, when she is aware at the time of the contract that she has only limited knowledge of the facts to which the mistake relates, and she accepts her limited knowledge as sufficient. Note that the risk created by conscious ignorance rests on the party being aware of her limited knowledge. Restatement (Second) of Contracts § 154.

2) Mistaken party's negligence

When the mistake is attributable to a party's failure to know or discover facts before entering into the contract, the party may nonetheless assert the defense of mistake, unless the party failed to act in good faith and in accordance with the reasonable standards of fair dealing. The mistaken party's negligence with regard to the mistake is not sufficient to prevent the mistaken party from avoiding the contract. Restatement (Second) of Contracts § 157.

b. Unilateral mistake

When only one of the parties was mistaken as to an essential element of the contract at the time the contract was formed, either party can generally enforce the contract on its terms. However, the mistaken party can void the contract if the elements for a mutual mistake exist and either:

i) The mistake would make enforcement of the contract unconscionable; or

ii) The non-mistaken party caused the mistake, had a duty to disclose or failed to disclose the mistake, or knew or should have known that the other party was mistaken.

For a unilateral mistake to form the basis for rescission, there must be an **absence of serious prejudice to the other party**. Restatement (Second) of Contracts § 154.

c. Reformation for mistake

When a writing fails to express the agreement because of a mistake of both parties, the court may, at the request of a party, reform the writing to express the agreement, except to the extent that rights of third parties who have relied on the document, such as good-faith purchasers for value, will be unfairly affected. Restatement (Second) of Contracts § 155.

Reformation of a writing for mistake is available if:

i) There was a prior agreement (either oral or written) between the parties;

ii) There was an agreement by the parties to put that prior agreement into writing; and

iii) As a result of a mistake, there is a difference between the prior agreement and the writing.

> Note that if one party, without the consent of the other party, intentionally omits a term from the writing that had been agreed upon by the parties, reformation would be available on the grounds of misrepresentation. (*See* § I.E.3.f. Avoidance or reformation for misrepresentation, *infra*.)

2. Misunderstanding

A misunderstanding occurs when both parties believe that they are agreeing to the same material terms, but they in fact agree to different terms. Restatement (Second) of Contracts § 20.

a. Neither party knows or should know of the misunderstanding

If the misunderstanding involves a material term, and neither party knows or has reason to know that there is a misunderstanding, then there is no contract.

b. One party knows or should know of the misunderstanding

If a material term in the offer and acceptance is ambiguous, and only one party knows or has reason to know that the other party has a different understanding of the meaning of the ambiguous term, then there will be a contract formed based on the meaning of the term as understood by the unknowing party.

> While a contract exists, the contract may be voidable on grounds of mistake or misrepresentation due to the conduct of the party with the superior knowledge.

c. Both parties know of the misunderstanding

There is no contract if both parties at the time of contracting knew or had reason to know that a material terms was ambiguous, unless both parties intended the same meaning.

d. Waiver of the misunderstanding

Even if there is a misunderstanding, one party may waive the misunderstanding and choose to enforce the contract according to the other party's understanding.

e. Subjective determination of misunderstanding

In determining the existence of a misunderstanding, it is each party's knowledge or reason to know of the misunderstanding that governs, not what a reasonable person would know. In this regard, the objective theory of contracts does not apply. In addition, in determining what a party knows or has reason to know, the principles regarding conscious ignorance and negligence apply (*see* E.1.a.1) Conscious ignorance, and E.1.a.2) Mistaken party's negligence, *above*).

3. Misrepresentation, Nondisclosure, and Fraud

A misrepresentation is an untrue assertion of fact. In order to constitute a fact, the assertion must be about a present event or past circumstance. An assertion of an opinion, such a belief or judgment as to the quality, value, or authenticity of an item or the occurrence of a future event, is generally not an assertion of a fact. However, an assertion of an opinion may, if reasonable, be interpreted by a party as an assertion that the person knows facts that are not incompatible with the opinion or that the person knows facts sufficient to justify the formation of the opinion.

> Note that the use of an "as is" provision in a contract can shift the risk to a buyer in the absence of unconscionability.

Misrepresentation can be innocent, negligent, or fraudulent.

a. Fraudulent misrepresentation

Fraudulent misrepresentation requires proof of the following:

   i)   The misrepresentation is **fraudulent**;

       a) A false assertion of fact made knowingly, or recklessly **without** knowledge of its truth; and

       b) With intent to mislead the other party;

   ii) The misrepresentation **induced assent** to the contract; and

   iii) The adversely affected party **justifiably relied** on the misrepresentation.

b. Nondisclosure

Affirmative conduct to conceal a fact is equivalent to an assertion that the fact does not exist. In addition, mere nondisclosure of a known fact is tantamount to an assertion that the fact does not exist, if the party not disclosing the fact knows that:

   i)   Disclosure is necessary to prevent a previous assertion from being a misrepresentation or fraudulent or material;

   ii) Disclosure would correct a mistake of the other party as to a basic assumption, and the failure to disclose would constitute lack of good faith and fair dealing;

   iii) Disclosure would correct a mistake of the other party as to the contents or effect of a writing evidencing their agreement; or

   iv) The other party is entitled to know the fact because of a confidential or fiduciary relationship.

c. Effect

1) Fraud in the factum

Fraud in the factum (or fraud in the execution) occurs when the fraudulent misrepresentation prevents a party from knowing the character or essential terms of the transaction. In such a case, no contract is formed, and the apparent contract is **void** (i.e., not enforceable against either party), unless reasonable diligence would have revealed the true terms of the contract.

2) Fraud in the inducement

Fraud in the inducement occurs when a fraudulent misrepresentation is used to induce another to enter into a contract. Such a contract is **voidable** by the adversely affected party if she justifiably relied on the misrepresentation in entering into the agreement.

d. Nonfraudulent misrepresentation

Even if nonfraudulent, a misrepresentation (innocent or negligent) can still render a contract **voidable** by the adversely affected party if:

   i)   The misrepresentation is **material** (i.e., information that would cause a reasonable person to agree or that the person making the misrepresentation knows would cause this particular person to agree);

   ii) The misrepresentation induced assent to the contract; and

   iii) The adversely affected party justifiably relied on the misrepresentation.

e. Effect of party's fault in not knowing or discovering facts

A party's fault in not knowing or discovering facts before entering into the contract does not prevent the party's reliance on the misrepresentation from being justified unless it constitutes a failure to act in good faith and in accordance with the reasonable standards of fair dealing. The party's negligence with regard to learning about the falsity of the misrepresentation is not sufficient to prevent the party from avoiding the contract.

f. Cure of a misrepresentation

If, following a misrepresentation but before the deceived party has avoided the contract, the facts are cured so as to be in accord with the facts that were previously misrepresented, then the contract will no longer be voidable by the deceived party.

g. Avoidance or reformation for misrepresentation

When one party misrepresents the content or legal effect of a writing to another party, the other party may elect to avoid the contract or to reform it to express what had been represented.

4. Undue Influence

A party to a contract who is a victim of undue influence can void the contract. Restatement (Second) of Contracts § 177.

a. Unfair persuasion

Undue influence is the unfair persuasion of a party to assent to a contract. It can occur by virtue of a relationship in which one party is dominant and the other dependent, either due to lack of expertise or experience, or because the dependent person has diminished mental capacity. Such relationships include trustee-beneficiary, lawyer-client, doctor-patient, financial advisor–client, and, in some cases, parent-child.

> **Compare duress and misrepresentation:** Undue influence can provide a party with relief in circumstances in which the behavior of the other party to the contract does not rise to the level of duress or misrepresentation.

The key is whether a party has been able to exercise free and competent judgment or whether the persuasion of the other party has seriously impaired that judgment. Relevant factors can include the fairness of the bargain, the availability of independent advice, and the susceptibility of a party to being persuaded.

> **Caution:** Although a person who is mentally or physically infirm may be more susceptible to persuasion, the mere existence of an infirmity is not grounds for avoiding a contract. Similarly, the existence of a confidential relationship, by itself, is not grounds for avoiding a contract.

b. Confidential relationship—fairness and disclosure

When a confidential relationship between contracting parties is established, the burden of proving that the contract is fair may be placed upon the dominant party. The dominant party to the contract may also be held to a higher standard of disclosure than she would be in a contract between arms-length parties. Restatement (Second) of Contracts § 173.

c. Third-party undue influence

When the undue influence is caused by the person who is not a party to the contract, the victim may void the contract, unless the nonvictim party to the contract gave value or materially relied on the contract while acting in good faith and without reason to know of the undue influence. Restatement (Second) of Contracts § 177(3).

d. Damages

Restitution damages may be available to the party induced to enter a contract because of undue influence.

5. Duress

Duress is an **improper threat** that deprives a party of meaningful choice.

a. Improper threat

Examples of improper threats include threats of a crime, a tort, or criminal prosecution, or the threat of pursuing a civil action (when made in bad faith). In addition, it is improper to threaten to breach a contract if doing so would violate the duty of good faith and fair dealing. Restatement (Second) of Contracts § 176.

1) Threat of criminal prosecution

The threat of criminal prosecution is an improper means by which to induce a person to enter into a contract. It does not matter that the person making the threat honestly believes that the person who would be subject to criminal prosecution is guilty. Nor does it matter that the person threatened with prosecution is in fact guilty of the crime.

2) Threat of civil action

Unlike the threat of criminal prosecution, the threat of a civil action is generally not improper. The lack of success in pursuing a civil action does not make the threat improper unless the civil action is pursued in bad faith.

b. Deprivation of meaningful choice

A person is deprived of meaningful choice only when he does not have a reasonable alternative to succumbing to the threat. Thus, with regard to the threat of a civil action, a person generally has the reasonable alternative of defending against the action. However, if the threat also involves the seizure of property in conjunction with the civil action, or if it causes the person to be unable to fulfill other contractual obligations, then the person may be deprived of a meaningful choice. Restatement (Second) of Contracts § 175.

> **EXAM NOTE:** In assessing the effect of the threat, the test is a subjective one: Did the threat induce the person's assent?

c. Effect on the contract

When a party's agreement to enter into a contract is physically compelled by duress, such as the threat to inflict physical harm, the contract is **void**. In other instances when a party is induced to enter into a contract by duress, such as when the threat is a breach of the duty of good faith and fair dealing, the contract is **voidable**.

When the duress is caused by the person who is not a party to the contract, the victim may void the contract, unless the nonvictim party to the contract gave value or materially relied on the contract while acting in good faith and without reason to know of the undue influence. Restatement (Second) of Contracts § 177(3).

Generally, restitution damages are available to the party induced to enter a contract under duress. Restatement (Second) of Contracts §§ 174, 175.

6. **Capacity to Contract**

Parties to a contract must be competent (i.e., have the legal capacity to be held to contractual duties). Incompetency arises because of infancy, mental illness or defect, guardianship, intoxication, and corporate incapacity.

a. **Infancy**

Infants (in most states, individuals who are under the age of 18) do not have the capacity to contract. When a contract is made by an infant with a person who does not lack capacity, it is **voidable** by the infant but not by the other party. This means that the infant may either disaffirm (void) the contract and avoid any liability under it or choose to hold the other party to the contract. The disaffirmance must be effectuated either before the individual reaches the age of majority or within a reasonable time thereafter. If the contract is not disaffirmed within a reasonable time after the individual reaches the age of majority, then the individual is deemed to have ratified the contract. If the contract is disaffirmed, the individual must restore any benefits received under the contract, if possible. Restatement (Second) of Contracts § 14.

1) **Liability for necessities**

An exception to the infancy rule exists when the contract is based on necessities. When necessities are furnished to the infant, the infant must pay for them, but the recovery by the person furnishing the necessities is limited to the **reasonable value** of the services or goods (not the agreed-upon price). Recovery is under a theory of quasi-contract.

2) **Statutory exceptions**

By statute, an education loan made to a minor student may not be voidable by the student but instead may be fully enforceable by the lender. Similar treatment may also be accorded an insurance contract entered into by a minor.

b. **Mental illness**

If an individual is adjudicated mentally incompetent, a purported contract made by the individual is **void**. On the other hand, if there has been no adjudication, a contract is **voidable** and may be disaffirmed if the individual is unable to:

i) Understand the nature and consequences of the transaction; or

ii) Act in a reasonable manner with regard to the transaction, **and** the other party has reason to know of this fact.

If a contract is made during a lucid period, the contract is fully enforceable, unless the person has been adjudicated incompetent. A mentally incompetent person may be liable for the reasonable value of necessities furnished by another party. Restatement (Second) of Contracts § 15.

c. **Guardianship**

If an individual's property is under guardianship by reason of an adjudication (such as for mental illness or defect, habitual intoxication, narcotics addiction), that individual has no capacity to contract, and a purported contract made by the individual is void. A person under guardianship may be liable for the reasonable value of necessities furnished by another party. Restatement (Second) of Contracts § 13.

d. Intoxication

A contract entered into while intoxicated due to alcohol or drugs is **voidable** by the intoxicated party if that person was unable to understand the nature and consequences of the transaction, and the other party had reason to know of the intoxication. The intoxicated party must act promptly to disaffirm the contract and is required to return any value received, if possible. Generally, the intoxicated party may be liable in quasi-contract for the fair value of the goods or services furnished. Restatement (Second) of Contracts § 16.

F. DEFENSES TO ENFORCEMENT

A party to a contract can assert that the nature of the agreement or the manner in which it was arrived at should prevent its enforcement.

1. Illegality

If the consideration or performance that is to occur under a contract is illegal, then the contract itself is illegal and is unenforceable. If a contract contemplates illegal conduct, it is void. If a contract becomes illegal after it is formed, the duty to perform under the contract is discharged. Note that a contract is "illegal" for contract purposes when it contravenes a statute or a rule of common law; it need not involve activity that results in criminal penalties.

Examples of illegal contracts include contracts that are usurious and contracts for the commission of crime.

a. Effect of illegality

Illegal transactions are not recognized or enforceable, restitution is not awarded for consideration, and no remedy is available for partial performance.

b. Exceptions

1) Ignorance of illegality

When one party is justifiably ignorant of the facts that make the contract illegal, that party may recover if the other party to the contract acted with knowledge of the illegality. Restatement (Second) of Contracts § 180.

2) Lack of illegal purpose

If a contract does not involve illegal consideration or the performance of an act that is illegal, and a party has substantially performed, then that party may recover if she is unaware of the illegal purpose that the other party intends to make of that performance.

Example 1: The maker of an electronic device ships the device to a buyer. The maker is unaware that the buyer intends to export the device in violation of federal law. The maker may recover the price of the device from the buyer even though the buyer had an illegal purpose in acquiring the device.

In addition, the party who has substantially performed can recover even if she knows of the illegal use that the other party intends to make of the performance, unless the performing party acted for the purpose of furthering the illegal use or the use involves grave social harm. A party's purpose of furthering an improper use may be evidenced by additional acts that facilitate that illegal use or by a course of dealing with persons engaged in the illegal conduct. Restatement (Second) of Contracts § 182.

> **Example 2:** The owner of a rifle delivers a rifle to a buyer. The sale of the rifle to this buyer is legal. The buyer tells the owner that he intends to use the rifle over the weekend to hunt deer. The owner knows that deer-hunting season has passed. Other than transferring the rifle to the buyer, the owner takes no action with regard to the buyer's intended use of it. The owner may recover the price of the rifle from the buyer even though the owner knew of the illegal use that the buyer intended to make of the rifle.
>
> **Example 3:** Assume the same facts as those in Example 2, except that the buyer tells the owner that he intends to use the rifle to kill his wife. The owner may not recover the price of the rifle from the buyer because the owner knew both that the buyer intended to put the rifle to illegal use and that the illegal use involved grave social harm.

3) Divisible contracts

If a contract can be easily separated into legal and illegal parts, then recovery may be available on the legal part(s).

4) Licensing violation

When a party fails to comply with a licensing or similar requirement and is prohibited from performing an act, the party may not enforce the contract if the requirement has a regulatory purpose and the public policy for the requirement clearly outweighs the interest in enforcing the promise. Where the purpose of the requirement is only to raise revenue, the requirement does not have a regulatory purpose. In weighing the policy for the requirement against the interest in enforcing the promise, the nature of the interest protected (e.g., health and safety vs. economic) and magnitude of the penalty should be taken into account as well as whether the violation was intentional or inadvertent. Restatement (Second) of Contracts § 181.

5) Availability of restitution

a) Not in pari delicto

When the parties are not equally at fault (not *in pari delicto*), the less guilty party may be able to recover restitutionary damages. Restatement (Second) of Contracts § 198.

b) Withdrawal

A party to an illegal contract who withdraws from the transaction before the improper purpose has been achieved may be entitled to restitution for a performance that the party has rendered when the party has not engaged in serious misconduct. Restatement (Second) of Contracts § 199.

2. Unconscionability

A court may modify or refuse to enforce a contract or part of a contract on the grounds that it is unconscionable.

A contract (or part of a contract) is unconscionable when it is so unfair to one party that no reasonable person in the position of the parties would have agreed to it. The contract or part of the contract at issue must have been offensive at the time it was made. Unconscionability may also be applied to prevent unfair surprise. Restatement (Second) of Contracts § 208.

Factors rendering a contract unconscionable are often categorized as either procedural unconscionability or substantive unconscionability. Procedural unconscionability occurs when a party is induced to enter the contract without a meaningful choice due to deception, compulsion, or significantly unequal bargaining positions. Examples of procedural unconscionability may include boilerplate contract provisions that are inconspicuous, hidden, or difficult for a party to understand, or contracts of adhesion (a take-it-or-leave-it contract) when there is greatly unequal bargaining power between the parties. Substantive unconscionability occurs when the substance of the contract itself is unduly unfair. *See, e.g., Frostifresh Corp. v. Reynoso*, 274 N.Y.S.2d 757 (1966).

The question of whether a contract is unconscionable is a question of law for the court to decide; the issue does not go to the jury.

3. Public Policy

Even if a contract is neither illegal nor unconscionable, it may be unenforceable if it violates a significant public policy, such as a contract in restraint of marriage, a contract for the commission of a tort, or a contract that unreasonably restrains trade. These contracts may be enforceable when exceptions similar to those discussed at § I.F.1.b., Exceptions, are applicable. Restatement (Second) of Contracts §§ 178-196.

> **EXAM NOTE:** When a contract violates a policy that was intended for the benefit of the contracting party seeking relief, the contract may still be enforceable to avoid frustrating the purpose behind the policy.

G. IMPLIED-IN-FACT CONTRACTS AND QUASI-CONTRACTS

1. Implied-in-Fact Contracts

When a person verbally expresses assent to an offer, the resulting agreement is characterized as an express contract. When a person's assent to an offer is inferred solely from the person's conduct, the resulting agreement is typically labeled an "implied-in-fact" contract. To be contractual bound, a person must not only intend the conduct but also know or have reason to know that his conduct may cause the offeror to understand that conduct as assent to the offer.

> **Example:** B joins a tour group that is walking through a downtown area learning about landmark buildings. Although B knows that members of the group have each paid the guide $15, he believes that his presence does not add to the guide's existing duties to the group. The tour guide can charge B the same fee paid by other members of the tour group because B's assent to the payment of the fee can be inferred from his conduct in joining the group.

2. Implied-in-Law ("Quasi") Contracts

When a plaintiff confers a benefit on a defendant and the plaintiff has a reasonable expectation of compensation, allowing the defendant to retain the benefit without compensating the plaintiff would be unjust. In this case, the court can permit the plaintiff to recover the value of the benefit to prevent the unjust enrichment. Although this type of action is often characterized as based on an implied-in-law contract or a quasi-contract, quantum meruit recovery does not depend on the existence of a contract.

A court may allow restitutionary recovery if:

    i)   The plaintiff has conferred a **measurable benefit** on the defendant;

    ii) The plaintiff acted **without gratuitous intent**; and

    iii) It would be unfair to let the defendant retain the benefit because either (i) the defendant had an opportunity to decline the benefit but knowingly accepted it, or (ii) the plaintiff had a reasonable excuse for not giving the defendant such opportunity (e.g., because of an emergency).

For a discussion of the amount that a plaintiff may recover, *see* § VIII.D.1. Restitutionary Recovery, *infra*.

H. WARRANTIES IN SALE-OF-GOODS CONTRACTS

UCC Article 2 allows not only for express warranties, but also for the implied warranties of merchantability and fitness for a particular purpose.

1. Express Warranty

Any promise, affirmation, description, or sample that is part of the basis of the bargain is an express warranty, **unless it is merely the seller's opinion** or commendation of the value of the goods. The use of a sample or model will create a warranty that the goods the buyer is to receive will be like the proffered sample or model. UCC § 2-313.

An express warranty can be made subsequent to the contract for sale. Although this would modify the original agreement, under the UCC, no consideration is needed to make a modification enforceable.

Under Article 2, words or conduct relevant to the creation of an express warranty and words or conduct tending to negate or limit warranty are construed as consistent with each other, but negation or limitation is inoperative to the extent such construction is unreasonable. Thus, disclaimer clauses that grossly conflict with the express warranties, such as "all warranties, express or implied, are disclaimed," are ignored. Note, however, that the parol evidence rule may bar evidence of oral express warranties or disclaimers of such warranties. UCC § 2-316.

2. Implied Warranty of Merchantability

A warranty of merchantability is implied whenever the seller is a **merchant**. To be merchantable, goods must be **fit for their ordinary purpose** and pass without objection in the trade under the contract description. A breach of this warranty must have been present at the time of the sale. UCC § 2-314.

Unless the circumstances indicate otherwise, the warranty can be disclaimed by use of "as is," "with all faults," or similar language that makes plain that there is no implied warranty. The disclaimer may be oral, but it must use the term "merchantability" and must be conspicuous if in writing. UCC § 2-316.

If the buyer, before entering into the contract, has examined the goods or a sample or model as fully as the buyer desires, or has refused to examine the goods, then there is no implied warranty with respect to defects that an examination ought to have revealed to the buyer. UCC § 2-316(3).

3. Implied Warranty of Fitness for a Particular Purpose

A warranty that the goods are fit for a particular purpose is implied whenever the seller has reason to know (from any source, not just from the buyer) that the buyer has a particular use for the goods, and the buyer is relying upon the seller's skill to select the goods. UCC § 2-315.

Note that the seller need not be a merchant for this implied warranty to apply.

An implied warranty of fitness for a particular purpose can be disclaimed by general language (including by the use of "as is"), but the **disclaimer must be in writing and be conspicuous**. UCC § 2-316(2).

II. DISCHARGE

If conditions are excused or satisfied, the parties have an absolute duty to perform, unless that duty is discharged. If some supervening event or change in circumstances arises after the formation of the contract, the duty to perform might be discharged.

A. IMPRACTICABILITY

A party's duty to perform can be dismissed by impracticability. The defense of impracticability is available if:

i) Performance becomes **illegal** after the contract is made;

ii) The specific subject matter of the contract (e.g., the goods) is **destroyed**;

iii) In a personal services contract, the performing party to the contract **dies or becomes incapacitated**; or

iv) Performance becomes **impracticable**.

UCC § 2-615; Restatement (Second) of Contracts §§ 261-264.

If the contract is a contract to perform services that can be delegated, it is not discharged by the death or incapacity of the party who was to perform the services. (Note that the death or incapacity of a person whose existence is required for the performance of a duty can give rise to the defense of impracticability, even though the person is not the performing party, such as the death of one party's child who is to receive lessons from the other party.)

Unforeseen natural disasters, wars, trade and military embargoes, strikes, and local crop failures have all been found sufficient to excuse performance. However, non-extraordinary increases in the cost of performance are not sufficient.

Impossibility: Traditionally, the defense of impossibility was restricted to circumstances wherein performance was objectively impossible, which is now considered too restrictive. Under the modern view, adopted by the Restatement, "impracticability" better expresses the extent of the increased burden that is required.

1. Elements of Impracticability

For the defense of impracticability to be available, the following conditions must also be met:

i) An **unforeseeable event** has occurred;

ii) **Nonoccurrence** of the event was a basic assumption on which the contract was made; and

iii) The **party seeking discharge is not at fault**.

When performance becomes impracticable for a seller of goods, the seller must notify the buyer. Restatement (Second) of Contracts § 261. While the impracticability usually arises after the formation of a contract, a fact that makes a party's performance impractical can exist at the time a contract is made, if the party has no reason to know the fact and the non-existence of the fact is a basic assumption on which the contract is made. Restatement (Second) of Contracts § 266(1).

2. Assumption of the Risk

If a party assumes the risk of an event happening that makes performance impracticable, then the defense of impracticability will not apply.

> Note that impracticability is not available merely when a party has made a bad deal and will have to pay more, even a lot more, than originally contemplated. It requires some totally unexpected occurrence that completely upsets the parties' expectations. Generally, the cost increase must be extreme.

3. Partial Impracticability

When impracticability does not prevent a seller from delivering some of the goods, the goods actually produced must be apportioned among all of the buyers with whom the seller has contracted. The buyer, however, may refuse to accept and may cancel the contract. UCC §§ 2-615(b), 2-616.

4. Failure of a Particular Source of Supply

If the contract provided that a specific source of supply be used, and that source of supply fails, performance is discharged. This is so even when other sources are readily available. Courts will excuse performance when the parties have specifically identified the source in the contract.

5. Failure of Agreed-Upon Method of Transportation

If, by no fault of either party, the agreed-upon delivery facility or method of transportation or payment becomes unavailable or commercially impracticable, delivery or payment by any commercially reasonable method may be tendered and must be accepted.

B. FRUSTRATION OF PURPOSE

The doctrine of frustration of purpose applies when an unexpected event arises that destroy one party's purpose in entering into the contract, even if performance of the contract is not rendered impossible. The frustrated party is entitled to rescind the contract without paying damages. The event that arises must not be the fault of the frustrated party, and its nonoccurrence must have been a basic assumption of the contract. If this is the case, the party's duty to render performance is discharged, unless the language of the agreement or the circumstances otherwise indicate. Restatement (Second) of Contracts § 265.

The occurrence need not be completely unforeseeable to the parties. It must, however, be unexpected and not a realistic prospect. For the doctrine of frustration of purpose to be applicable, the frustration must be so severe that it is not within the assumed risks inherent under the contract. Restatement (Second) of Contracts § 265, comment a.

> **Example:** A contracts with B to rent B's apartment for one day to get a prime view of a marathon run that will occur on that day. A agrees to pay a price that is far more than the typical rental value of the apartment. The marathon run is canceled because of a terrorist threat. A may be excused from performance under the doctrine of frustration of purpose because her essential purpose in renting the apartment has been frustrated, and the event that arose was not her fault and was completely unexpected.

As with the defense of impracticability, the defense of frustration of purpose can arise when a fact that substantially frustrates a party's principal purpose exists at the time a contract is made, if the party has no reason to know the fact and the non-existence of which is a basic assumption on which the contract is made. Restatement (Second) of Contracts § 266(2).

C. RESCISSION BY MUTUAL AGREEMENT

Rescission (or cancellation) of a contract can occur by the mutual agreement of the parties. The surrender of rights under the original contract by each party is consideration for the rescission by mutual agreement.

In cases of third-party beneficiaries, a contract cannot be rescinded by mutual agreement if the rights of the third-party beneficiary have already vested.

D. RELEASE

A release is a writing that manifests intent to discharge another party from an existing duty. For common-law contracts, the release must generally be supported by consideration to discharge the duty.

Under the UCC, however, a claim or right can be discharged in whole or in part without consideration by a written waiver or renunciation signed and delivered by the aggrieved party. No consideration is needed to support the release.

E. DESTRUCTION OR INJURY TO IDENTIFIED GOODS

If a contract calls for the delivery of goods identified at the time the contract is made, and the goods are destroyed by no fault of either party before the risk of loss passes to the buyer, then the contract is avoided. Both parties are discharged; neither party must perform, and neither party has breached. If the goods are damaged but not destroyed, then the contract is avoided, unless the buyer chooses to take the goods at a reduced price without any other claim against the seller. (Note: If the risk of loss has passed to the buyer, then the contract is not avoided, and the seller may demand performance by the buyer (*see* § VIII.F.3. Risk of Loss, *infra*).)

III. THIRD-PARTY BENEFICIARY CONTRACTS

A third-party beneficiary contract results when the parties to a contract intend that the performance by one of the parties is to benefit a third person who is not a party to the contract.

A. CREDITOR AND DONEE BENEFICIARIES

The First Restatement classifies third-party beneficiaries as creditor, donee, or incidental beneficiaries. If performance of a promise would satisfy an actual, supposed, or asserted duty of the promisee to a third party, and the promisee did not intend to make a gift to the third party, then the third party is called a **creditor beneficiary**. A creditor beneficiary has the right to sue either the promisor or the promisee to enforce the contract.

Example 1: A agrees to paint B's house in return for B's promise to pay $500 to C because A owes C $500. C is a creditor beneficiary and can recover the $500 from B.

If the promisee entered the contract for the purpose of conferring a gift on a third party, then the third-party **donee beneficiary** is given the right to sue the promisor.

Example 2: A pays B to build a house for C. C is a donee beneficiary of the contract between A and B.

An incidental beneficiary—a beneficiary who is not a donee or creditor beneficiary—has no rights to enforce the contract.

B. INTENDED AND INCIDENTAL BENEFICIARIES

The Second Restatement abandons the donee beneficiary and creditor beneficiary categories. Instead, a third party can enforce the contract if the third party is an intended beneficiary. Otherwise, the third party is an incidental beneficiary who cannot enforce the contract.

1. **Intended Beneficiary**

   In general, an intended beneficiary is one to whom the promise of the performance will satisfy the obligation of the promisee to pay money to the beneficiary or the circumstances indicate that the promisee intends to give the beneficiary the benefit of the promised performance. In addition, recognition of the right to performance in the beneficiary must effectuate the intent of the parties to the contract. Restatement (Second) of Contracts § 302(1).

   > **Example:** A agrees to paint B's house in return for B's promise to pay $500 to C. C is an intended beneficiary, whether C is A's creditor to whom A owes money or A's child to whom A wishes to make a gift.

   > **Note:** A minority of jurisdictions continue to follow the characterization of the First Restatement that the third-party beneficiary must be either a donee beneficiary or a creditor beneficiary to be able to enforce the contract. Under the Second Restatement, the term "intended beneficiary," while encompassing both a donee beneficiary and a creditor beneficiary, focuses on the intent of the parties to the contract rather than on whether the beneficiary is a donee or creditor of one of the parties. Consequently, a third party to whom the promisee thinks she owes money but does not may be treated as an intended beneficiary even though the third party would not qualify as a creditor beneficiary.

2. **Incidental beneficiary**

   An incidental beneficiary is one who benefits from a contract even though there is no contractual intent to benefit that person. An incidental beneficiary has no rights to enforce the contract. Restatement (Second) of Contracts § 302(2).

   > **Example:** A promises to buy B a car manufactured by C. C is an incidental beneficiary who cannot sue A if A reneges on her promise to buy the car.

   > **EXAM NOTE:** On the exam, if the promise indicates that the promisor will pay the third party directly to relieve the promisee from a debt, then the third party is likely an intended beneficiary. In contrast, if the promisor is to pay the promisee in order that she may pay the third party, then the third party is most likely an incidental beneficiary.

C. **PARTIES WHOM INTENDED BENEFICIARIES CAN SUE**

   Generally, an intended beneficiary of a "gift promise" (i.e., a donee beneficiary) may sue only the promisor because the promisee is not under an obligation to the intended beneficiary. However, if the promisee tells the intended beneficiary about the contract and should reasonably foresee reliance, and the beneficiary does justifiably rely to his detriment, then the intended beneficiary may also sue the promisee.

   An intended beneficiary to whom the promisee owed money (i.e., a creditor beneficiary) or an intended beneficiary to whom the promisee is under a legal obligation, may sue either the promisor to enforce his contractual promise, or the promisee on the underlying obligation, but only one recovery is allowed.

D. **VESTING OF BENEFICIARY'S RIGHTS**

   The rights of an intended beneficiary vest when the beneficiary:

   i) **Materially changes position in justifiable reliance** on the rights created;

   ii) **Manifests assent** to the contract at one party's request; or

   iii) **Files a lawsuit** to enforce the contract.

Once the beneficiary's rights have vested, the original parties to the contract are both bound to perform the contract. Any efforts by the promisor or the promisee to rescind or modify the contract after vesting are void, **unless the third party agrees** to the rescission or modification.

E. PROMISOR'S DEFENSES

The promisor can raise any defense against the third-party beneficiary that the promisor had against the original promisee.

Example 1: A agrees to paint B's house in return for B's promise to pay $5,000 to C, to whom A owes $5,000. A paints half of B's house. B does not pay C. C sues B. B can assert the defense of A's material breach of their contract as a defense against C.

The beneficiary is liable for counterclaims arising from the contract that the promisor can establish against the promisee, but the beneficiary's liability cannot exceed the amount that the promisor owes under the contract.

Example 2: A agrees to paint B's house in return for B's promise to pay $5,000 to C, to whom A owes $5,000. A paints B's house, but fails to paint the trim around several windows. B hires D to paint the trim around those windows for $250. B does not pay C. C can sue B for $5,000, and B can counterclaim $250 against C.

The promisor generally may not assert any defenses that the promisee has against the intended beneficiary.

Example 3: A agrees to paint B's house in return for B's promise to pay $5,000 to C, to whom A owes $5,000. A paints B's house. The statute of limitations expires with regard to A's debt to C. B does not pay C. C can sue B for $5,000. B cannot raise the expiration of the statute of limitations as a defense to C's action.

However, if the promisor's promise is one to assume the promisee's obligation, then the promisor can raise the promisee's defense.

Example 4: In example 3, above, if B's promise is to pay C whatever A owes C, then B can raise the expiration of the statute of limitations as a defense to C's action.

F. PROMISEE'S RIGHTS

When the promisor fails to pay the third-party beneficiary, the promisee, on behalf of the third-party beneficiary, can sue the promisor for specific performance of the promise. In addition, when the promisee has paid a creditor beneficiary pursuant to their agreement, the promisee can directly sue the promisor for reimbursement to the extent of the promise and, if the creditor beneficiary's claim is fully satisfied, by subrogation to the beneficiary's claim against the promisor.

IV. ASSIGNMENT OF RIGHTS AND DELEGATION OF DUTIES

"Assignment" is the transfer of rights under a contract, and "delegation" is the transfer of duties and obligations under a contract.

A. ASSIGNMENT OF RIGHTS

Almost all contract rights can be assigned. Partial assignments are permissible, as is the assignment of future or unearned rights.

1. Limitations on Assignment

An assignment is not allowed, however, if it materially increases the duty or risk of the obligor or materially reduces the obligor's chance of obtaining performance. In addition, a contract provision can render an otherwise allowable assignment void (e.g., "any assignment of rights under this contract is void") and unenforceable by the assignee against the obligor. By contrast, a contract provision that merely prohibits an assignment (e.g., "An assignment of rights under this contract is prohibited"), while giving rise to an action for breach against the assignor, does not operate to prevent the assignor from assigning those rights (the assignor retains the power to make an assignment) nor the assignee from suing the obligor. Unless circumstances indicate the contrary, the prohibition on the assignment of a contract (e.g., "this contract may not be assigned"), does not affect the assignment of contract rights, but only bars the delegation of duties.

NOTE: Courts often narrowly interpret a prohibition provision, such as by finding that such a provision only applies to a specific contractual right, and that the assignment in question thus did not violate the provision.

2. **Requirements**

No formalities are needed for an assignment, but there must be a present intent to transfer the right immediately. No consideration is needed, but the lack of consideration would affect revocability of the assignment.

Distinguish promise of a future payment: A promise by a party to a contract to pay to monies received pursuant to the contract to third party is not an assignment of the party's contractual rights, but a promise of a future payment. As a consequence, the third party is not an assignee of the contract.

3. **Revocability**

a. **Assignment for Consideration**

If an assignment is for consideration, it is **irrevocable**.

b. **Gratuitous Assignment**

If no consideration supports the assignment (a gratuitous assignment), then it will generally be **revocable**, unless the obligor has already performed or promissory estoppel applies. In addition, if the contract right that is being assigned is evidenced by a document that symbolizes the right (e.g., a bankbook, an insurance policy, or a stock certificate), then delivery of the document makes the assignment irrevocable. Also, the delivery of written assignment signed by the assignor to the assignee makes the assignment irrevocable. A gratuitous assignment that is revocable will be automatically revoked upon the death, incapacity, or bankruptcy of the assignor. Restatement (Second) of Contracts § 332.

4. **Rights of the Assignee**

An assignee **takes all of the rights of the assignor as the contract stands at the time of the assignment**, but she takes **subject to any defenses that could be raised against the assignor**. The rights of the assignee are subject to setoff if the transaction giving rise to the setoff occurred prior to the time the obligor was given notice of the assignment. In addition, the rights of the assignee are subject to a setoff that arises out of the same transaction. The assignee is also subject to any modification of the contract made prior to the time the obligor obtained notice of the assignment. Thus, payment by the obligor to the assignor can be raised as a defense, provided the payment was made before the obligor had notice of the assignment.

5. **Rights of the Assignor**

When there is assignment of a party's rights under a contract, and the assignment is not revoked, the assignor cannot enforce the contract.

6. **Subsequent Assignment**

A subsequent assignment of the same right revokes any prior **revocable** assignment. If the first assignment was an **irrevocable** assignment, then the first assignee will have priority over the second assignee, unless the second assignee is a bona fide purchaser for value without notice of the first assignment, in which case the assignee who obtains payment from the obligor or judgment first will have priority. If the second assignee knows about a prior assignment, then he is estopped from asserting a claim over the first assignee even if he would have otherwise prevailed.

B. **DELEGATION OF DUTIES**

Generally, obligations under a contract can be delegated.

1. **When Disallowed**

Delegation is not permitted when a party to the contract has a substantial interest in having the delegating party perform (for example, in a personal services contract involving taste or a special skill), or the delegation is prohibited by the contract. Unless circumstances indicate the contrary, the prohibition on the assignment of a contract (e.g., "this contract may not be assigned"), bars the delegation of duties, even though it does not affect the assignment of rights.

2. **Effect on Delegator**

When obligations are delegated, the **delegator is not released from liability**, and recovery can be had against the delegator if the delegatee does not perform, unless the other party to the contract agrees to release that party and substitute a new one (a novation). Merely consenting to a delegation does not create a novation.

a. **Novation**

A novation is the substitution of a new contract for an old one when the original obligor is released from his promises under the original agreement. A novation may be express or implied after delegation if (i) the original obligor repudiates liability to the original promisee and (ii) the obligee subsequently accepts performance of the original agreement from the delagatee without reserving rights against the obligor.

3. **Effect on Delegatee**

Acceptance by the delegatee of a delegation of contract duties constitutes a promise to perform those duties. That promise is enforceable against the delegatee if the delegatee has received consideration or there is a consideration substitute that makes the promise enforceable.

4. **Effect on Other Party to the Contract**

Any delegation of performance under a contract for the sale of goods may be treated by the other party as creating **reasonable grounds for insecurity**. UCC § 2-210(5). The other party may, without prejudice to his rights against the delegator, demand assurances from the delegatee (UCC § 2-609, *see* §§ VIII.B.2–3. Anticipatory Repudiation under the Common Law and Anticipatory Repudiation under the UCC, *infra*). However, as long as the delegation was permitted, the other party must accept the conforming performance of a delegatee or be in breach of the contract.

If the promise is enforceable by the delegator, such as when the promise is supported by consideration, the other party to the contract is treated as a third-party beneficiary of the delegation and may be able to enforce the delegatee's promise.

5.   Effect of Assignment of Contract

An assignment of a contract that is not limited to contractual rights (e.g., "this contract is assigned to") is typically treated as both an assignment of rights and a delegation of duties.

V.   STATUTE OF FRAUDS

A.   WRITING REQUIRED

Contracts that fall within the Statute of Frauds are **unenforceable** unless evidenced by a **writing**. The writing must:

i)   **Be signed** by the party against whom enforcement is sought; and

ii)   Contain the **essential elements** of the deal.

The writing need not be formal (i.e., receipts or correspondence can serve as memoranda). The essential elements may be in more than one writing if one of the writings references the other(s). The writing need not be delivered to the party trying to enforce the contract. Even if it is lost or destroyed, it still operates to satisfy the Statute of Frauds, and its prior existence can be proved by oral evidence.

> **EXAM NOTE:** Note that a memorandum sufficient to satisfy the Statute of Frauds does not need to be written at the time a promise is made. The memorandum also does not have to be addressed to the promisee to be enforceable by the promisee.

B.   TYPES OF CONTRACTS WITHIN THE STATUTE OF FRAUDS

Most states require that the following five categories of contracts be evidenced by a writing:

Marriage - A contract made upon consideration of marriage;

Suretyship - A contract to answer for the debt or duty of another;

One year - A contract that cannot be performed within one year from its making;

UCC - Under the UCC, a contract for the sale of goods for a price of $500 or more; and

Real property contract - A contract for the sale of an interest in real property.

> **EXAM NOTE:** Statute of Frauds issues are often tested on the MBE. You can remember which types of contracts are governed by the Statute by using the mnemonic **Mr. SOUR** (Marriage, Suretyship, One year, UCC, Real property).

1.   Marriage Provision

Any agreement in consideration of marriage is within the Statute of Frauds, except the promises by each to marry the other (i.e., the marriage contract itself). A prenuptial agreement is the paradigm of an agreement made in consideration of marriage that is subject to the Statute of Frauds. A promise made in consideration of marriage does not become enforceable merely because the marriage has taken place in reliance on it. However, additional part performance or action in reliance may make such a promise enforceable. Restatement (Second) of Contracts § 124.

2.   Suretyship Provision

a.   Rule

Suretyship is a three-party contract, wherein one party (the surety) promises a second party (the obligee) that the surety will be responsible for any debt of a third party (the principal) resulting from the principal's failure to pay as agreed. A suretyship induces the second party to extend credit to the third party. A promise to answer for the debt of another must generally be in writing to be enforceable.

> Note: A contract of an executor (or administrator) of an estate may fall into this category insofar as the executor promises the creditor of the decedent that if the estate does not have the funds to pay the debt, he will assume personal liability for that debt. The statute applies only to debts incurred by the decedent, not to new debts incurred by the estate after his death. Because the executor undertakes to answer for the debt of the decedent, such contracts fall under the suretyship provision.

b. Exceptions

1) Indemnity contracts

An indemnity contract (i.e., a promise to reimburse for monetary loss) does not fall within the Statute of Frauds as a suretyship provision.

2) Main-purpose exception

If the main purpose of the surety in agreeing to pay the debt of the principal is the surety's own economic advantage, rather than the principal's benefit, then the contract does not fall within the Statute of Frauds, and an oral promise by the surety is enforceable.

3. Real Property Contracts

a. Types

A promise to transfer or receive **any interest in real property** is within the Statute of Frauds. The Statute does not apply to the conveyance itself (which is governed by a separate statute), but it does apply to a **contract providing for** the subsequent conveyance of an interest in real property. The Statute of Frauds also applies to a promise to create an interest in real property, the assignment of a right to purchase real property, an option contract for the sale of an interest in real property, and a promise to give a mortgage or other lien as security. Although leases and easements, as property interests, are generally subject to the Statute of Frauds, a lease or easement for one year or less is usually not covered by the Statute. In addition, licenses and assignments of mortgages are typically not within the Statute.

b. Part performance

Even if an oral contract for the transfer of an interest in real property is not enforceable at the time it is made, **subsequent acts** by either party that show the existence of the contract may make it enforceable, even without a memorandum. Such acts include:

  i)   Payment of all or part of the purchase price;

  ii) Possession by the purchaser; or

  iii) Substantial improvement of the property by the purchaser.

Most jurisdictions require at least two of the above three acts to establish sufficient part performance.

c. Full performance

When a party to an oral contract who has promised to convey real property performs, that party can enforce the other party's oral promise unless the promise is itself the transfer of a real property interest.

> **Example:** During a face-to-face conversation, a seller agrees to transfer land to the buyer in exchange for the buyer's promise to pay $50,000 to the seller. The seller tenders the deed to the buyer and the buyer accepts the deed. The seller can enforce the buyer's oral promise to pay $50,000 to the seller.

4. One-Year Provision

Contracts that **cannot** be performed within one year because of the constraints of the terms of the agreement must be in writing. The year starts **the day after** the contract is made. It is the time that the contract is made that is important, not the length of performance.

> The fact that a contract is not completed within one year does not mean that it is voidable under the Statute of Frauds. For the Statute to apply, the **actual terms** of the contract must make it impossible for performance to be completed within one year.

Full performance by either party to the contract will generally take the contract out of the Statute of Frauds. Although part performance would not take the contract out of the Statute of Frauds, restitution would be available to the party who performed.

5. Sale of Goods for $500 or More

> **EXAM NOTE:** The UCC Statute of Frauds requirements and exceptions for goods when the price is at least $500 are frequently tested on the MBE.

a. Sufficiency of the writing

When the price of goods is at least $500, the UCC requires a memorandum of the sale that must:

i) Indicate that a contract has been made;

ii) Identify the parties;

iii) Contain a quantity term; and

iv) Be signed by the party to be charged.

A signature includes any authentication that identifies the party to be charged, such as a letterhead on the memorandum. UCC § 2-201(1), cmt. 1.

> The memorandum needs to be signed only by the party disputing the existence of the contract; it is not necessary for the enforcing party to have signed the writing.

1) Type of writing required

To satisfy the Statute of Frauds, the above terms must be in writing, but that writing need not be an actual contract. It does not even need to be contained on one piece of paper—a series of correspondence between the parties may suffice.

2) Mistake in writing

A mistake in the memorandum or the omission of other terms does not destroy the memorandum's validity. An omitted term can be proved by parol evidence.

However, enforcement is limited to the quantity term actually stated in the memorandum.

> **EXAM NOTE:** Some states have raised the threshold amount from $500 to $5,000. On the exam, assume that the amount is $500, unless stated otherwise.

b. Exceptions—writing not required

1) Specially manufactured goods

No writing is required if (i) the goods are to be specially manufactured for the buyer, (ii) the goods are not suitable for sale to others, and (iii) the seller has made "either a substantial beginning of their manufacture or commitments for their procurement." UCC § 2-201(3)(a).

2) Payment and acceptance by seller

A contract is outside the UCC Statute of Frauds to the extent that payment has been made and accepted. UCC § 2-201(3)(c). When a portion of the purchase price for a single item has been paid, most courts treat the contract as enforceable.

3) Receipt and acceptance by buyer

A contract is outside the UCC Statute of Frauds to the extent that goods are received and accepted. UCC § 2-201(3)(c). Acceptance of a part of a commercial unit is acceptance of the entire unit. UCC § 2-606(2).

4) Failure to respond to a memorandum (when both parties are merchants)

If both parties are merchants and a memorandum sufficient against one party is sent to the other party, who has reason to know its contents, and the receiving party does not object in writing **within 10 days** of receipt of the memorandum, then the contract is enforceable against the receiving party even though he has not signed it. UCC § 2-201(2).

c. Modifications

Under UCC § 2-209(3), the requirements of the Statute of Frauds must be satisfied if the contract as modified is within its provisions. Any of the above exceptions would apply, though, to take a modification out of the Statute of Frauds.

The UCC would also enforce a provision in a contract for the sale of goods that required a modification to be in writing. Thus, even if the contract was for a sale of goods valued at less than $500 or involved one of the exceptions discussed above, if the contract specifically provided that any modification be in writing, then the UCC would enforce that requirement. *See* UCC § 2-209(2). Note that under a common-law contract, a provision requiring a modification to be in writing even though the modification would not otherwise fall within the Statute of Frauds would not be enforceable.

C. GENERAL EXCEPTIONS—PROMISSORY ESTOPPEL

1. Promissory Estoppel

A promise that the promisor should reasonably expect to induce action or forbearance on the part of the promisee or a third person and that does induce the action or forbearance is enforceable notwithstanding the Statute of Frauds if injustice can be avoided only by enforcement of the promise. The remedy may be limited as justice requires. Restatement (Second) of Contracts § 139.

2. Judicial Admission

A promise is enforceable against a party to the extent admitted by the party through discovery admissions or by testimony at trial.

VI. PAROL EVIDENCE RULE

Before signing a written agreement, parties typically negotiate their contract through a series of conversations, phone calls, letters, faxes, e-mails, etc. When the written contract is finally signed, it may or may not include all of the terms of these negotiations, or it may change the terms in some way. The parol evidence rule generally prevents a party to a written contract from presenting extrinsic evidence of a prior or contemporaneous agreement that contradicts the terms of the contract as written. The rule is concerned with whether any of the earlier oral or written terms are part of the parties' contract, even though they are absent from the parties' written agreement.

A. INTEGRATION

The first step is to determine whether the parties' writing is "integrated," meaning that the parties intended it to be their final agreement. The parol evidence rule applies only to a document that is an integration.

If the document is determined not to be an integration (i.e., not to be the final expression of the parties' agreement), such as a preliminary negotiation document or tentative draft agreement, then the parol evidence rule will not apply.

1. Total versus Partial Integration

If the writing is determined to be an integration, then the second step is to decide whether it completely expresses all of the terms of the parties' agreement.

a. Total integration

If the writing completely expresses all of the terms of the parties' agreement, then it is a **total integration**, and the parties cannot introduce any extrinsic evidence (oral or written) of prior or contemporaneous understandings or negotiations.

b. Partial integration

If, on the other hand, the writing sets forth the parties' agreement about some terms, but not all terms, then it is a **partial integration**. The parties are then permitted to introduce supplementary extrinsic evidence (oral or written) of other terms as long as the evidence is **consistent** with the writing, but not if the evidence contradicts the terms of the writing.

2. Intent of the Parties

The intent of the parties determines whether there is total, partial, or no integration.

a. Common-law four-corners rule

Under the common law, a court was permitted to look only to the writing itself (within the "four corners" of the document) for evidence of intent. If the written contract appeared to be detailed, then a court would likely conclude that it was totally integrated. A merger clause is evidence of complete integration, and it usually states: "This contract is the final and complete expression of the parties' agreement and supersedes all prior contracts, agreements, understandings, negotiations, assurances, guarantees, or statements."

b. Second Restatement rule

The Second Restatement adopts a different approach to the parol evidence rule. If, under the circumstances, an extrinsic term of an agreement would "naturally be omitted" from a writing, then that term can be introduced, so long as it does not contradict the writing. Restatement (Second) of Contracts § 213.

c. UCC rule

In contrast to the common law and Second Restatement parol evidence rules, the UCC rule is much more lenient. The UCC essentially presumes that a written contract is only a partial integration and allows any additional consistent terms unless a court concludes that the parties "certainly" would have included the term in the written contract. UCC § 2-202. Because that standard is difficult to establish, parties usually can bring in outside evidence.

B. WHEN THE PAROL EVIDENCE RULE IS INAPPLICABLE

The parol evidence rule does not apply to communications that occur after the execution of the written contract; it applies only to agreements reached before or contemporaneously with the execution of the written contract.

1. Raising a Defense to the Formation of a Contract

The parol evidence rule does not apply when a party is raising a defense to the formation of a contract, such as mistake, misunderstanding, or misrepresentation. Parties may always introduce evidence that would show that no valid contract exists or that the contract is voidable.

2. Establishing a Defense to the Enforcement of the Contract

Similarly, the parol evidence rule does not apply to evidence offered to establish a defense such as mistake, misrepresentation, incompetence, illegality, duress, or lack of consideration. If the evidence would make the contract void or voidable, then the parol evidence rule will not apply.

3. Separate Deal

Even when there is full integration, evidence may be offered if it represents a distinct and separate contract.

4. Condition Precedent

Parol evidence may also be admitted to prove a condition precedent to the existence of the contract.

5. Ambiguity and Interpretation

Evidence may be admitted for the purpose of interpreting or clarifying an ambiguity in the agreement. This can include evidence of trade usage or even local custom to show that a particular word or phrase had a particular meaning. Courts approach interpretation in two ways.

a. Plain-meaning rule

This rule provides that the objective definitions of contract terms control the meaning of the contract, regardless of whether the meaning corresponds with the actual intent of the parties. Sometimes, courts will go outside the document to clarify the ordinary meaning of terms that are ambiguous or overly vague.

b. Context rule

Some states permit courts to use a contextual approach to contract interpretation. Under the context rule, judges determine the contract's meaning by considering all evidence of the facts and circumstances related to the transaction. The goal is to effectuate the parties' actual contract objectives and purposes.

6. Subsequent Agreements

The parol evidence rule does not apply to evidence of agreements between the parties subsequent to execution of the writing.

7. UCC Rule—Trade Usage and Course of Dealing or Performance

Even if the terms of a written contract for the sale of goods appear to be unambiguous, a party may explain or supplement the terms by evidence of trade usage or course of dealings or performance. UCC § 2-202.

If the express contract terms are inconsistent with the course of performance, course of dealing, or trade usage, priority is given as follows: (i) express terms prevail over all others, (ii) course of performance prevails over course of dealing and trade usage, and (iii) course of dealing prevails over trade usage. UCC § 1-303(e).

Note that there are similar standards of preference in interpretation for contracts not governed by the UCC. Restatement (Second) of Contracts § 203.

a. Course of performance

A course of performance is a sequence of conduct that is relevant to understanding an agreement between the parties if: (i) the agreement involves repeated occasions for performance by a party, **and** (ii) the other party accepts performance without objection and with knowledge of the course of performance. UCC § 1-303(a). A course of performance is relevant to show a waiver or modification of any term inconsistent with the course of performance. UCC § 1-303(f).

b. Course of dealing

A course of dealing is a sequence of conduct **concerning previous transactions** between the parties that can reasonably establish a common basis of understanding for interpreting their conduct. UCC § 1-303(b).

c. Trade usage

Trade usage is any **practice or method of dealing** in the particular business or industry that is practiced with such regularity so as to justify an expectation that it will be practiced in the instant case. UCC § 1-303(c).

VII. CONDITIONS AND PERFORMANCE

A "condition" is a future event that must take place before a party's contractual rights or obligations are created, destroyed, or enlarged. By contrast, a "promise" constitutes a party's obligation to act or refrain from acting.

Example: A buyer and seller enter into a contract for the sale of a house if the buyer can obtain a loan. Under the contract, the seller has promised to sell the house to the buyer, and the buyer has correspondingly promised to buy the house. However, both promises are conditioned on the buyer obtaining a loan.

Ambiguity as to whether a statement creates a promise or a condition is usually resolved in favor of a promise over a condition. Restatement (Second) of Contracts § 227.

EXAM NOTE: Remember, the failure of a **condition** relieves a party of the **obligation** to perform; the failure of a party to perform a **promise** constitutes **breach**.

A. TYPES OF CONDITIONS

A condition may be express (clearly stated in the agreement) or implied (presumed based on the nature of a transaction).

1. Express Conditions

Express conditions are expressed in the contract. Words in the contract such as "on the condition that" or "provided that" are typical examples of express conditions. Express conditions must be complied with fully unless excused; substantial performance will not suffice. Arbitration clauses are enforceable, except when a consumer might be waiving an important substantive right. An express condition is enforceable even when the failure to meet the condition results in the denial of compensation.

2. Implied Conditions

Implied conditions that are deemed to be part of the contract because the nature of the agreement suggests that the parties truly intended the condition but failed to expressly include it, are "implied in fact" conditions. These are distinguished from "constructive" or "implied in law" conditions, which are supplied by a court if reasonable under the circumstances. Restatement (Second) of Contracts § 226 cmt. c. The most common types of court-supplied implied conditions are called "constructive conditions of exchange" and arise most frequently in construction and employment contracts. A court will imply that the builder or employee must perform first (at least "substantially") before the other side's performance (the payment of money) becomes due. In addition to good faith, the UCC implies a duty of cooperation on the parties when performance of one party is dependent upon the cooperation of the other party. If a party fails to cooperate, the other party may suspend her own performance without being in breach. UCC § 2-311(3).

> Substantial performance is all that is required to satisfy an implied condition.

B. TIMING OF CONDITIONS

Performance by one or both of the parties may be made expressly conditional in the contract, and the condition may precede the obligation to perform (**condition precedent**) or may excuse the duty to perform after a particular event occurs (**condition subsequent**). A condition subsequent exists only with respect to a duty that is absolute. (Note: Under the Restatement (Second) of Contracts, a condition subsequent is treated as a discharging event rather than as a condition. Restatement (Second) of Contracts §§ 224, 230.)

> **Example 1:** A agrees to hire B if B passes the bar exam. B agrees to work as a clerk for C until B passes the bar exam. B's passing of the bar exam is a condition precedent to being hired by A and a condition subsequent to B's employment with C.

A condition may also be a **concurrent condition** with another condition; each party's duty to perform is conditioned on the other party's duty to perform. Concurrent conditions effectively require each party to perform simultaneously.

> **Example 2:** A agrees to purchase a television from B for $1,000. A's duty to pay B $1,000 and B's duty to give the television to A are concurrent conditions.

1. Burden of Proof

If a defendant's duty is subject to a condition precedent, then the plaintiff has the burden of proving that the condition occurred in order to recover. If the defendant's duty is subject to a condition subsequent, then the defendant must prove the happening of the condition to avoid liability.

C. SATISFACTION OF CONDITIONS

The approach to determine whether a condition is satisfied is usually an objective standard based upon whether a reasonable person would be satisfied. In most contracts, it is easy to conclude that all conditions have been satisfied. In contracts based upon aesthetic taste, however, the occurrence of the condition may be more difficult to determine.

When the aesthetic taste of a party determines whether the other party's performance is satisfactory (e.g., painting a family portrait), satisfaction is determined under a subjective standard. Under this standard, if the party is honestly dissatisfied, even if the dissatisfaction is unreasonable, the condition has not been met. However, the party's dissatisfaction must be in good faith, or a claim of dissatisfaction can be a breach, such as when a party is asserting dissatisfaction merely to avoid its own contractual obligation. There is a preference for the objective standard when the matter subject to a party's satisfaction involves the quality of non-unique goods or workmanship, rather than aesthetic taste. Restatement (Second) of Contracts § 228.

D. PERFORMANCE OF CONTRACTUAL DUTY

1. Order of Performance

When only one party's performance of his contractual duty requires a period of time, that party must complete his performance before the other party is required to perform, unless the language or circumstances indicate otherwise. By contrast, when a party's performance can be rendered at the same time as the other party's performance, each party's performance is conditioned on the other party's performance (known as "the constructive condition of exchange"); consequently, both parties' performances are due simultaneously, unless the language or circumstances indicate otherwise. In such a case, the failure of one party to perform excuses the other party's performance. Restatement (Second) of Contracts § 234.

2. Substantial Performance

When parties expressly agree to a condition precedent (or a concurrent condition), they are generally held strictly to that condition; a party must fully comply with that condition before the other party's performance is due. With an implied or constructive condition precedent (or an implied or constructive concurrent condition), a party who substantially complies with an implied or constructive condition can trigger the obligation of the other party to perform. This is known as the doctrine of "substantial performance." The doctrine of substantial performance does not generally apply to a contract for the sale of goods.

a. Effect on damages

The doctrine of substantial performance permits a party who substantially performs to recover on the contract even though that party has not rendered full performance. In general, the party who substantially performed her contractual obligations can recover the contract price minus any amount that it will cost the other party to obtain the promised full performance. A party who has not substantially performed generally cannot recover damages based on the contract, but she may be able to recover through restitution (*see* VIII.D.1.a Benefit conferred pursuant to a contract, *infra*). The other side to substantial performance is material breach. A party who fails to substantially perform is in material breach.

b. Willful breach

Substantial performance is less likely to be found when a party intentionally furnishes services that are materially different from what he promised. Such a breach is more likely to be treated as a material breach.

c. Delay in performance

A party's delay in performing an obligation suspends the duty that is conditioned on that performance, but it does not necessarily prevent the performance of that duty from constituting substantial performance. Among the factors considered are the degree to which the delay deprives the other party of benefit for which he contracted and the extent to which that party can be compensated for that deprivation. Restatement (Second) of Contracts § 241.

1) Time-is-of-the-essence clause

Although generally the doctrine of substantial performance does not apply when the parties have expressly provided for a specific condition, stock phrases that appear in many contracts do not automatically prevent the application of this doctrine. For example, even though a contract for the sale of land contains the phrase "time is of the essence," a slight delay in performance typically does not give the other party the right to refuse to perform. Restatement (Second) of Contracts § 242.

3. Perfect Tender Under the UCC

Under the UCC, the basic obligations of a seller are to **transfer ownership** of the goods to the buyer and to **tender goods** conforming to the warranty obligations. The UCC requires "perfect tender," and substantial performance will not suffice except for installment contracts or when the parties agree that it applies. The buyer has a **right to inspect** the goods, and once he accepts them, he has an **obligation to pay**. If a buyer rejects goods as nonconforming and time still remains to perform under a contract, the seller has a right to cure and tender conforming goods.

a. Transferring ownership

The UCC implies a warranty of title in all sales contracts, providing that the seller automatically warrants that (i) she is conveying good title, (ii) the transfer is rightful, and (iii) the goods are delivered free from any security interest of which the buyer has no knowledge at the time of the contract. Actual knowledge by the buyer of a security interest on the goods nullifies the warranty of title. UCC § 2-312(1).

The UCC permits disclaimer of the warranty of title, but such disclaimer must be by specific language or a circumstance that gives the buyer reason to know that the seller does not claim rightful title or that the seller is only purporting to sell such rights as the seller or a third person possesses. UCC § 2-312(2).

b. Seller's obligation to tender goods

The seller must tender the goods in accordance with the contract provisions or in accordance with the UCC if the contract is silent on tender. UCC § 2-503.

1) Time of tender

In the absence of a specific contract provision, the goods must be tendered within a reasonable time after the contract is made. UCC § 2-309.

2) Manner of tender

The goods are to be delivered in one delivery, unless otherwise provided in the contract, or the circumstances give either party a right to make or demand delivery in lots (as when a party would clearly have no room to store the goods if they were delivered all at once). UCC § 2-307.

3) Place of tender

Unless otherwise agreed, the place of tender is the seller's place of business (or residence, if the seller has no place of business), unless the goods are identified and the parties know that they are at some other location, in which case that location will be the place of tender. UCC § 2-308.

4) Method of tender

The four methods of tender are as follows.

a) Seller's place of business

If the goods are tendered at the seller's place of business, then the seller must place the goods at the disposition of the buyer and give the buyer notice, if notice is necessary to enable the buyer to take delivery. UCC § 2-503.

b) Shipment contract

If the contract does not specify a place of delivery, it is a shipment contract (often identified by the words "F.O.B. (free on board) seller's place of business"), and the seller must deliver the goods to the carrier, make a proper contract for their shipment, obtain and deliver any document necessary for the buyer to obtain possession of the goods, and give the buyer notice that the goods have been shipped. UCC §§ 2-319(1)(a), 2-504.

c) Destination contract

If the contract is a destination contract (often identified by the words "F.O.B. (free on board) buyer's place of business"), then the seller must deliver the goods to a particular place (specified in the contract) and tender them there by holding the goods at the buyer's disposition and giving the buyer notice. UCC § 2-319(1)(b).

d) Goods in the hands of a bailee

When goods are in the hands of a bailee and are to be transferred without being moved, the seller must obtain a negotiable document of title or acknowledgment from the bailee of the buyer's rights in the goods. However, unless the buyer seasonably objects, the seller can supply the buyer with a nonnegotiable document of title or a written direction to the bailee to deliver the goods to the buyer. UCC § 2-503(4).

A contract that requires the seller to ship goods to the buyer by a third-party carrier is either a shipment contract or a destination contract. When the contract is otherwise silent, a shipment contract is presumed when the contract requires shipment by a third-party carrier. UCC § 2-503 cmt. 5.

5) C.I.F. (cost, insurance, and freight) and C & F (cost and freight)

In a C.I.F. contract, the price includes the cost of the goods, the cost of transporting the goods, and the cost of insuring the goods during shipment. In a C & F contract, the price includes the cost of the goods plus the cost of shipment.

6) F.A.S. contracts

When a contract specifies F.A.S. (free alongside ship), the seller is obligated to deliver the goods **alongside** a designated vessel in a manner that comports with the ordinary course of business of the port of delivery, or at a specified dock.

c. Buyer's obligations

When a conforming tender is made, the buyer is obligated to accept and pay the price under the contract. UCC § 2-507. Rejection amounts to breach of contract.

An agreement that is otherwise sufficiently definite will not be made invalid merely because it omits details regarding the performance to be specified by one of the parties. The UCC implies an obligation of good faith within the parameter of "commercial reasonableness." UCC § 2-311(1).

When a contract fails to specify the assortment of goods, the UCC imposes a duty on the buyer to specify, whereas arrangements relating to shipment are the seller's duty to specify. UCC § 2-311(2).

If the buyer fails to specify the assortment of goods, then the seller can treat the failure as a breach by failure to accept the contracted-for goods only if the buyer's failure materially impacts the seller's performance. UCC § 2-311(3).

1) Noncarrier cases versus carrier cases

Unless otherwise specified in the contract, when goods are shipped by carrier, payment is due from the buyer at the moment the buyer receives the goods. In noncarrier cases, payment is due upon tender of delivery by the seller.

2) Shipment under reservation

A seller who ships by carrier under a contract that does not specify the method or form of payment may send the goods **under reservation**, meaning that the carrier will hold the goods until the buyer pays. This is accomplished by the seller's obtaining a negotiable or nonnegotiable bill of lading.

3) Tender of payment

a) Delivery and tender concurrent conditions of exchange

Unless otherwise agreed, tender of payment is a condition to the seller's duty to tender and complete any delivery.

b) Sufficiency of tender of payment

Tender of payment is sufficient when made by any means or in any manner consistent with the ordinary course of business, unless the seller (i) demands payment in legal tender (i.e., cash) and (ii) gives any extension of time reasonably necessary to procure such legal tender.

c) Payment by check

If payment is made by check, payment is conditional until the check is paid or dishonored.

d. Buyer's right to inspect

A buyer has a right to inspect goods that are tendered, delivered, or identified to the contract for sale, unless the contract provides otherwise.

1) Prior to payment

A buyer's right to inspect is a condition to payment. An inspection may occur at any reasonable time and place and in any reasonable manner, even when the goods are held under reservation. However, the parties can agree that inspection can occur in a particular form, time, or place. If the seller is required or authorized to send the goods to the buyer, then the inspection may be made after their arrival.

2) When not entitled to inspect

Unless otherwise agreed, the buyer is **not** entitled to inspect the goods before payment of the price if the contract (i) provides for delivery "C.O.D." or (ii) is on other terms that, under the applicable course of performance, course of dealing, or trade usage are interpreted to preclude inspection before payment. Similarly, the buyer is not entitled to inspect the goods before payment, unless otherwise agreed, if the contract provides for payment against documents of title, except when such payment is due only after the goods are to become available for inspection.

3) Expenses of inspection

Expenses of inspection must be paid by the buyer, but they may be recovered from the seller if the goods do not conform and are rejected.

4. Divisible or Installment Contracts

a. Common law

A divisible or installment contract is one in which the obligations imposed on the contracting parties can be separated into corresponding pairs of part performances such that each pair constitutes **agreed equivalents**. Recovery is limited to the performance promised for the corresponding portion of the contract that has been performed. Damages may be recoverable for breach of other obligations under other portions of the contract.

b. UCC

Special rules apply to installment contracts for the sale of goods. The most important difference between installment contracts and other contracts is that the perfect-tender rule does not apply; instead, the right to reject is determined by a "substantial conformity" standard. UCC § 2-612.

1) Multiple shipments

Under the UCC, an installment contract is defined as one in which the goods are to be delivered in multiple shipments, and each shipment is to be separately accepted by the buyer. Parties cannot vary or contract out of this definition under the code. Payment by the buyer is due upon each delivery, unless the price cannot be apportioned. UCC § 2-612.

2) Nonconforming segment

If the seller makes a nonconforming tender or tenders nonconforming goods under one segment of an installment contract, the buyer can reject only if the nonconformity:

i) **Substantially impairs the value** of that shipment to the buyer; and

ii) Cannot be **cured**.

If the seller makes adequate assurances that he can cure the nonconformity, then the buyer must accept the shipment. UCC § 2-612(2).

3) Remaining segments

When there is a nonconforming tender or a tender of nonconforming goods under one segment of an installment contract, the buyer may cancel the contract only if the nonconformity **substantially impairs the value** of the entire contract to the buyer.

> **EXAM NOTE:** When presented with nonconforming goods in installment contracts, look for clues in the fact pattern as to whether a nonconformity substantially impairs the value of the entire contract.

5. Implied Duty of Good Faith and Fair Dealing

A duty of good faith and fair dealing is imposed on each party in the performance and enforcement of any contract, whether governed by common law or by the UCC. Restatement (Second) of Contracts § 205; UCC § 1-304. "Good faith" means "honesty in fact and the observance of reasonable commercial standards of fair dealing." UCC § 1-201(20). Note that while this duty is imposed on all contracts, there are situations, such as the modification of a contract, in which the existence of good faith can have a different effect, depending on whether the contract is governed by the common law or by the UCC (*see* I.E.3.b. Modification, *supra*).

The implied duty to deal fairly and in good faith does not apply as such to the formation of a contract. While bad faith in negotiating may have consequences, such as enforcement of a promise made in bad faith under the doctrine of promissory estoppel or the denial of enforcement of a promise made in reliance on a fraudulent assertion, the implied duty to deal fairly and in good faith arises once a contract exists. Restatement (Second) of Contracts § 205, cmt. c.

E. SUSPENSION OR EXCUSE OF CONDITIONS

If a condition is suspended, then the condition is restored upon expiration of the suspension. If the condition is excused, then the party having the benefit of the condition can never raise it as a defense.

1. Waiver

A party whose duty is subject to the condition can waive the condition, either by words or by conduct. The condition may be reinstated if:

i)   The waiving party communicates a retraction of the waiver before the condition is due to occur; and

ii) The other party has not already suffered detrimental reliance.

For contracts subject to the common law only a condition that is not a material part of the agreement may be waived without consideration. For contracts subject to the UCC, while a condition that is a material part of the agreement may be waived in good faith without consideration, the contract as modified may be subject to the Statute of Frauds if the price is $500 or more.

2. Wrongful Interference

The duty of good faith and fair dealing, which is implied in any contract, includes the duty not to hinder the other party's performance and a duty to cooperate, when necessary. In addition, if the party whose duty is subject to the condition wrongfully prevents or interferes with the occurrence of that condition, then, under the doctrine of prevention, the condition is excused and the party wrongfully interfering has an absolute duty to perform. Restatement (Second) of Contracts §§ 225, 245 cmt. a.

3. Election

A party who chooses to continue with a contract after a condition is not met effectively elects to waive that condition as justification for the party's own nonperformance of a contractual duty, although the party may be able to seek damages resulting from the non-occurrence of the condition.

4. Estoppel

A party who indicates that a condition will not be enforced may be estopped from using that condition as a defense if the other party reasonably relied on the party's words or conduct that the condition had been waived.

VIII. BREACH OF CONTRACT AND REMEDIES

A. BREACH OF CONTRACT

Once a duty to perform exists, nonperformance is a breach of contract unless the duty is discharged (by agreement, statute, inability to perform, waiver, etc.).

1. Common Law

Under common law, a material breach of contract (i.e., when the nonbreaching party does not receive the substantial benefit of its bargain) allows the nonbreaching party to withhold any promised performance and to pursue remedies for the breach, including damages. If the breach is minor (i.e., the breaching party has substantially performed), then the nonbreaching party is entitled to any remedies that would apply to the nonmaterial breach. If a minor breach is accompanied by an anticipatory repudiation, then the nonbreaching party may treat the breach as a material breach.

The party who commits a material breach of his contract obligations cannot sue for contract damages but would ordinarily be entitled to the fair value of any benefit conferred on the nonbreaching party.

> **EXAM NOTE:** Keep in mind that if a breach is minor, the nonbreaching party may be able to recover damages, but that party also still must perform under the contract. If the breach is material, the nonbreaching party does not need to perform.

2. UCC

Under the UCC, the seller generally must strictly perform all obligations under the contract or be in breach. The doctrine of material breach applies only in the context of installment contracts or when the parties so provide in their contract.

B. ANTICIPATORY REPUDIATION

1. Anticipatory Repudiation

a. Repudiation of promise

The doctrine of anticipatory repudiation is applicable when a promisor repudiates a promise before the time for performance is due. The repudiation must be **clear and unequivocal** (as opposed to mere insecurity) and may be by conduct or words.

b. Nonbreaching party's options

Repudiation excuses the occurrence of any condition that would otherwise prevent the repudiating party's duty from being absolute. Upon repudiation, the promisee can generally treat the repudiation as a breach and sue the promisor immediately or ignore it and demand performance. If the repudiation is ignored, then continued performance by the promisee must be suspended if the performance would increase the damages of the promisor.

However, when the date of performance has not passed and the promisee has fully performed, the promisee must wait until the promisor's performance is due before filing suit. In this situation, anticipatory breach is inapplicable; the promisee must wait for actual breach before filing suit. Typically, this occurs when the promisor's obligation is the payment of money.

c. Retraction of repudiation

Repudiation may be retracted until such time as the promisee (i) acts in reliance on the repudiation, (ii) signifies acceptance of the repudiation, or (iii) commences an action for breach of contract. Notice of the retraction must be sufficient enough to allow for the performance of the promisee's obligations.

d. Unilateral contracts

The doctrine of anticipatory repudiation **does not apply to a unilateral contract** when the offeror withdraws the offer once the offeree has begun to perform since offeree is not required to complete her performance.

2. Prospective Inability to Perform

A party's expectations of performance may be diminished by an event that occurs after the contract was made.

> **EXAM NOTE:** On the exam, be reluctant to excuse a party from performing solely on the ground that the party does not expect counter-performance to occur.

A party can demand assurance of performance if there are reasonable grounds for insecurity about the other party's ability or willingness to perform. Once such assurances are requested, performance may be suspended until they are provided. Failure to give adequate assurances within a reasonable time can be treated as repudiation. (Under the UCC, the demand must be made in writing and a reasonable time in which to give adequate assurances is limited to 30 days.) UCC § 2-609; Restatement (Second) of Contracts § 251. Even then, the repudiating party can still retract his repudiation until his next performance is due, unless the other party has already materially changed his position or otherwise indicated that he considers the repudiation final. UCC § 2-611.

a. Commercial standards for merchants

Between merchants, the reasonableness of grounds for insecurity and the adequacy of any assurance offered are determined according to commercial standards. Thus, for example, if a supplier writes to a manufacturer demanding assurances of financial solvency, and the manufacturer provides its latest audited financial statements as well as a satisfactory credit report from his banker, then that would likely constitute adequate assurances of his financial status.

b. Effect of acceptance

In an installment contract, the acceptance of any improper delivery or payment does not preclude an aggrieved party from demanding adequate assurance of future performance.

C.   REMEDIES: DAMAGES FOR BREACH OF CONTRACT

Compensatory damages are meant to compensate the nonbreaching party for actual economic losses. The goal of compensatory damages is to put the nonbreaching party in as good a position as performance would have done (i.e., expectation damages), plus consequential and incidental damages, if any, less possible mitigation of damages. Alternatively, the plaintiff might recover liquidated damages, reliance damages, or restitutionary relief.

1.   Expectation Damages

a.   In general

Expectation (benefit-of-the-bargain) damages are intended to put the nonbreaching party in the same position as if the contract had been performed.

Expectation damages must be calculated with reasonable certainty. If expectation damages are too speculative, the plaintiff may instead seek reliance damages (*see* § VIII.D. Restitution and Reliance Recoveries, *below*).

To calculate expectation damages, compare the value of performance without the breach (what was promised) with the value of the performance with the breach (what was received).

Example: B breaches a contract with A to fix A's car for $500. A finds another mechanic, C, to fix A's car for $700, which is the market value of performance. A can recover $200 from B.

1)   Construction contracts

In construction contracts, the general measure of damages for a contractor's failure to begin or to complete the building or other structure is the difference between the contract price and the cost of construction by another builder, plus any progress payments made to the breaching builder and compensation for delay in completion of the construction. The general measure of damages for the owner's failure to pay the contract price, in whole or in part, is the profits that the builder would have earned, plus any costs incurred by the builder, less the amount of any payments made by the owner to the contractor and any materials purchased by the contractor that are used by the contractor on another job.

2)   Sale-of-goods contracts

Damages for failing to deliver goods are measured by the difference between the contract price and the market value of the goods (or the cost of cover). *See* F. Remedies under the UCC, *below*.

3)   Real-estate contracts

Damages for failing to perform a real-estate sales contract also are measured by the difference between the contract price and the market value. In the case of late delivery, damages are measured by the fair market rental value of the property for the time that the buyer was denied possession.

4)   Contract to lend money

The measure of damages for breach of a contract to lend money is the additional cost of obtaining a loan from another lender (e.g., the difference in cost over time between the interest rates of the original loan and the subsequent loan).

5) Formula

The general expectation formula can be computed as follows:

Expectation Damages = loss in value + other loss − cost avoided − loss avoided

"Loss in value" is the difference between the performance that the nonbreaching party should have received under the contract and what was actually received, if anything. These are also referred to as a party's direct damages.

"Other loss" includes consequential and incidental damages, if any.

"Cost avoided" is the additional cost that the nonbreaching party can avoid by rightfully discontinuing performance under the contract as a result of the other party's breach.

"Loss avoided" is the beneficial effect of the breach due to the nonbreaching party's ability to salvage or reallocate resources that otherwise would have been devoted to performing under the contract. Loss avoided is subtracted only if the savings results from the injured party not having to perform rather than from some unrelated event. Restatement (Second) of Contracts § 347.

b. Partial performance

A partially performing party can generally recover for work performed, plus expectation damages for the work not yet performed.

Example 1: B agrees to paint A's house for $500, which covers $400 in supplies and labor and $100 in profit. After B paints half of the house and incurs $200 in costs, A breaches. B can recover the $200 for costs already incurred and the $100 of profit, but not the remaining $200 for costs not yet incurred.

If at the time of a breach the only remaining duties of performance are (i) those of the party in breach and (ii) for the payment of money in installments not related to one another, then breach by nonperformance as to less than the whole, whether or not accompanied or followed by a repudiation, does not give rise to a claim for damages for total breach and is a partial breach of contract only. Restatement (Second) of Contracts § 243(3).

Example 2: A borrows $10,000 from B. The loan is to be paid back in monthly installments with interest over one year. A fails to make the first installment payment and tells B that he will be unable to make the other payments as well. B has a claim for partial breach of the contract but cannot sue for a total breach of the contract. (Note: Lenders circumvent this rule by including in the loan agreement an acceleration clause that causes the entire loan to become due upon the failure by the borrower to timely make an installment payment.)

c. Defective performance

1) Construction contracts

In construction contracts, damages for defective construction are generally measured by the cost of correcting the defect.

2) Sale-of-goods contracts

By contrast, in contracts for the sale of goods, damages for nonconformity with the contract generally are measured by the difference between the value of the goods as warranted and the actual value of the tendered nonconforming goods.

The purpose of both measures is to place the plaintiff in as good a position as if the defendant had performed the contract according to its specifications.

d. Economic waste

In a construction contract, when a breach results in a defective or unfinished construction, if the award of damages based on the cost to fix or complete the construction would result in economic waste, then a court may instead, at its discretion, award damages equal to the diminution in the market price of the property caused by the breach. Economic waste occurs when the cost to fix or complete the construction is clearly disproportional to any economic benefit or utility gained as a result.

> **Example:** Landowner grants Mining Company a five-year license to remove coal from his property. In return for the license, Mining Company agrees to restore the property to its original state at the end of the five-year period. After five years, Mining Company refuses to restore the land. The restoration work would cost $29,000, but, if completed, it would result in only a $300 increase in the property's value. The court may elect to award only $300 in damages, instead of $29,000. *Peevyhouse v. Garland Coal and Mining Co.*, 382 P.2d 109 (Okla. 1962).

If the breach is willful, and only completion of the contract will give the nonbreaching party the benefit of its bargain, then a court may award damages based on the cost to fix or complete the construction even if that award would result in economic waste. Restatement (Second) of Contracts § 248(2), cmt. c.

e. UCC—Breach of warranty damages

The measure of damages for breach of warranty is the difference **at the time and place of acceptance** between the value of the goods accepted and the value they would have had if they had been as warranted, unless special circumstances show proximate damages of a different amount. UCC § 2-714(2). Repair costs often are used to determine this difference in value, but when repairs fail to restore the goods to their value as warranted, a further adjustment is required.

2. Consequential Damages and Foreseeability

At common law, actual damages can be either direct or consequential. Direct damages are the necessary and usual result of the defendant's wrongful act. They are awarded to compensate the plaintiff for the loss, damage, or injury that is conclusively presumed to have been foreseen or contemplated by the breaching party, and are reflected in the difference between the value of the performance that the nonbreaching party should have received under the contract and what was actually received (i.e., "loss of value" calculation for determining expectation damages).

Consequential damages, on the other hand, result naturally from the breach, but need not be the usual result of the breaching party's conduct. Instead, consequential damages need only be a reasonably foreseeable result of the breach in the parties' specific circumstances.

a. Consequential damages

Consequential damages are damages that arise out of special circumstances unique to the parties to the contract, rather than arising necessarily from the transaction itself. Consequential damages still result directly from the breach, but may not be foreseeable to one of the parties unless the special circumstances are known.

b. Foreseeability

Consequential damages must be **reasonably foreseeable** by the breaching party in order to be recoverable. Unforeseeable consequential damages are not recoverable unless the breaching party had some reason to know about the possibility of these unforeseeable consequential damages.

Damages are considered foreseeable if they were the natural and probable consequences of breach, or if they were "in the contemplation of the parties at the time the contract was made," or if they were otherwise foreseeable. *Hadley v. Baxendale*, 156 Eng. Rep. 145 (Ex. Ch. 1854). For example, with regard to a contract to lend money, because it is assumed that a borrower will be able to obtain a substitute bank loan, the borrower's lost profit due to the failure of the lender to make the loan is considered unforeseeable.

c. Causation

Although consequential damages do not arise directly from the breach itself, there must be a **causal link** between the breach and the damages for the damages to be recoverable. A defendant can defend on the ground that the losses that the plaintiff seeks to recover would have occurred even if the defendant had not breached the contract.

d. Reasonable certainty

To recover consequential damages, the damages cannot be speculative. Instead, a plaintiff must prove the dollar amount of the damages with **reasonable certainty**. Courts are hesitant to award damages for lost profits, as they are difficult to prove. When lost profits are considered too speculative, such as with a new venture, courts often limit a party's recovery to reliance damages (i.e., reasonable expenditures made in connection with the contract).

> **EXAM NOTE:** Although courts are hesitant to award damages for lost profits and lost opportunities, such damages are still recoverable for breach-of-contract claims. Beware of questions that conclude in absolute terms that such damages are not recoverable. Such damages are not likely, but they are still possible.

e. UCC—Breach of warranty damages—limitation or exclusion

Although generally consequential damages for breach of warranty may be limited or excluded unless the limitation or exclusion is unconscionable, limitation of consequential damages for injury to the person in the case of consumer goods is prima facie unconscionable. Limitation of damages when the loss is commercial is not. UCC § 2-719(3).

3. Incidental Damages

Incidental damages may be awarded to the nonbreaching party as compensation for commercially reasonable expenses incurred as a result of the other party's breach. In the sale of goods, incidental damages resulting from the seller's breach include expenses reasonably incurred in inspection, receipt, transportation, care, and custody of goods rightfully rejected, any commercially reasonable charges, expenses, or commissions in connection with effecting cover, and any other reasonable expense incident to the delay or other breach. UCC § 2-715(1). Incidental damages to an aggrieved seller include any commercially reasonable charges, expenses, or commissions incurred in stopping delivery, in the transportation, care, and custody of goods after the buyer's breach, in connection with return or resale of the goods, or otherwise resulting from the breach. UCC § 2-710.

4. Liquidated Damages and Penalties

Liquidated damages are damages to be recovered by one party without proof of actual loss in the event the other party breaches the contract.

a. Enforceability

For a liquidated damages clause to be enforceable, the following two-prong test must be met at the time of contracting:

    i) The **amount of liquidated damages was reasonable**, bearing some relation to the damages that might be sustained; and

    ii) **Actual damages were uncertain** in amount and would be difficult to prove.

Some jurisdictions, as well as the UCC and the Second Restatement, add a third prong to this test, and refuse to enforce a clause under which the liquidated damages are disproportionate to the actual damages incurred by a party. A few jurisdictions, as well as the Second Restatement, refuse to enforce a liquidated damages clause if the party does not suffer any damages as a consequence of the breach.

If the liquidated damages clause is unenforceable, recovery is limited to any actual damages that a party can prove.

b. Reasonableness of damages

A liquidated damages clause may not merely serve as a threat to secure performance or as a means to punish nonperformance; otherwise it is unenforceable as a penalty. A liquidated damages clause that fails to take into consideration the gravity of the breach or its relationship to the performance rendered by the breaching party may be found to be unreasonable as may a clause that measures damages in a way that is not linked to the loss suffered by a party (e.g., gross revenue rather than net profits).

The parties' characterization of a provision as a liquidated damages clause rather than a penalty, while entitled to consideration, is not determinative.

5. Punitive Damages

Punitive damages are rarely available in contract actions. Some states allow punitive damages to punish fraud, for violation of a fiduciary duty, for acts of bad faith, or for deterrence. Under the Restatement (Second) of Contracts § 355, punitive damages are not recoverable "unless the conduct constituting the breach is also a tort for which punitive damages [can be recovered]."

6. Nominal Damages

Damages do not need to be alleged in a cause of action for breach. If no damages are alleged or no damages are proved, the plaintiff is still entitled to a judgment for "nominal" damages (e.g., one dollar).

7. Attorney's Fees

Attorney's fees are generally not recoverable by a successful litigant in a contract action unless the parties have agreed otherwise or there is specific law authorizing the recovery of such fees. The UCC does not authorize the recovery of such fees.

8. Mitigating Damages

A party to a contract must avoid or mitigate damages to the extent possible by taking steps that do not involve undue risk, expense, or inconvenience. The nonbreaching party is held to a standard of reasonable conduct in preventing loss. A party under a contract to provide services is generally not required to accept any type of employment, but instead only employment of the same type as the party was contracted to perform.

Although the standard is often phrased as a "duty to mitigate damages," a nonbreaching party's failure to mitigate does not give the breaching party a right to sue the nonbreaching party for such failure; it only reduces the damages that may be recovered by the nonbreaching party. For example, with regard to a sale of goods, a nonbreaching buyer's failure to take reasonable steps to mitigate damages by buying substitute goods (i.e., cover) will prevent a claim for consequential damages but will not deprive the buyer of damages measured by the difference between the contract and market prices. Note that reasonable expenses incurred as a result of efforts to mitigate damages can be recovered, even if the mitigation attempt was unsuccessful.

D. RESTITUTION AND RELIANCE RECOVERIES

Restitution seeks to restore to a party the benefit conferred on the other party, while reliance damages are based on the out-of-pocket expenses incurred by the nonbreaching party. Reliance damages put the party in the same position as if the contract were never formed.

1. Restitutionary Recovery

When a defendant is unjustly enriched by the plaintiff, restitution generally allows the plaintiff to recover on the **benefit conferred** by the plaintiff upon the defendant (rather than on the harm suffered by the plaintiff). Generally, this benefit may be measured by either the reasonable value of the defendant obtaining that benefit from another source or the increase in the defendant's wealth from having received that benefit (e.g., the increase in value of property owned by the defendant). Restatement (Second) of Contracts §§ 370, 371.

a. Benefit conferred pursuant to a contract

1) Recovery by nonbreaching party

Instead of seeking to enforce a contract, a nonbreaching party may seek restitution for any benefit conferred on the breaching party by way of part performance or reliance. Restitution is available whether the breach is by nonperformance or by repudiation, but in the case of nonperformance, restitution is available only if the breach gives rise to a claim for damages for total, not partial, breach. Restatement (Second) of Contracts § 373(1).

> **Example 1:** The owner of a warehouse agrees to sell it to a retailer for $1,000,000. The retailer pays the owner $50,000 as a down payment. The owner then refuses to transfer the warehouse to the retailer. The retailer can seek restitution of the $50,000 down payment.

> **Example 2:** A homeowner enters into a contract with a contractor to build an addition on his home for $50,000. The homeowner makes an initial payment of $10,000. The contractor inadvertently uses lumber not specified in the contract that gives rise to an immaterial breach. The homeowner cannot seek restitution of the $10,000 payment because the breach did not give rise to a claim for total breach. (Note: The homeowner could seek damages for breach of the contract.)

Restitution can result in a recovery for the nonbreaching party in a losing contract, even if recovery exceeds the contract price.

Example 3: A corporation contracts with a landscaper to design and install the landscaping for its new headquarters at a price of $75,000. When the landscaper's work is 90 percent complete, the corporation repudiates the contract. If the landscaper can establish that the fair market value of his work for the corporation is $80,000, then he can seek in restitution to recover $80,000.

However, the nonbreaching party cannot seek restitution if he has performed all of his contractual duties and the only performance that remains due from the other party is the payment of a definite sum of money. Restatement (Second) of Contracts § 373(2).

Example 4: Assume the same facts as those in Example 3, but assume instead that the corporation refuses to pay the landscaper when he completes the work. The landscaper cannot seek restitution, but instead he would be limited to expectation damages of $75,000.

2) Recovery by breaching party

If a plaintiff has not substantially performed and is in breach of the contract, the plaintiff is not permitted to recover under the contract. However, if the defendant has benefited from the plaintiff's performance, the plaintiff can generally recover in restitution for the benefit conferred on the defendant less the defendant's damages for the breach. In general, the breaching party's recovery is limited to a ratable portion of the contract price. Restatement (Second) of Contracts § 374(1).

a) Exceptions

i) Willful breach

Most courts hold that a plaintiff in breach is permitted to recover in restitution only if her breach is not willful. If a party intentionally furnishes services that are materially different from what she promised, then she cannot recover anything in restitution unless the nonbreaching party has accepted or agreed to accept the substitute performance. Restatement (Second) of Contracts § 374 cmt. b.

ii) Liquidated-damages clause

An exception exists if the contract provides for the nonbreaching party to retain the breaching party's performance (e.g., a down payment on the purchase price) as liquidated damages; restitution is not allowed if the liquidated damages are reasonable. Restatement (Second) of Contracts § 374(2).

iii) Sale of goods—payment by the defaulting buyer

For contracts for the sale of goods, a defaulting buyer is entitled to a refund of any payments made on the contract, less either (i) the amount to which the seller is entitled by virtue of an enforceable liquidated-damages provision, or (ii) a penalty of "20 percent of the value of the total performance for which the buyer is obligated under the contract, or $500, whichever is smaller." This amount is subject to an offset for any contract damages that the seller can establish other than those arising under a liquidated damages provision. UCC § 2-718(2),(3).

3) Unenforceable contract

If a contract is unenforceable due to the Statute of Frauds or is voidable due to lack of capacity, mistake, misrepresentation, duress, or undue influence, then a party is entitled to restitution of any benefit conferred on the other party by way of part performance or reliance. Similarly, a party whose duty is discharged or does not arise as a result of impracticability of performance, frustration of purpose, or the nonoccurrence of a condition is entitled to restitution of any benefit conferred on the other party by way of part performance or reliance. Restatement (Second) of Contracts §§ 375–377.

b. Benefit conferred independent of a contract (quasi-contract)

A person who confers a benefit on another in the absence of any contractual relationship, such as a doctor who happens upon an accident and renders emergency medical services to a victim, may be able to recover in restitution to the extent that retention of the benefit would result in unjust enrichment of the recipient. *See* I.G.2. Implied-in-Law ("Quasi") Contracts, *supra*.

2. Reliance Damages

Reliance damages may be recovered if a nonbreaching party incurs expenses in reasonable reliance upon the promise that the other party would perform. Unlike with a restitutionary recovery, with reliance damages, there is no requirement that the defendant benefit from the plaintiff's expenditures.

The injured party can choose to pursue reliance damages instead of expectation damages, but **a party cannot recover both reliance and expectation damages**. Reliance damages are mitigated by any losses that the plaintiff would have sustained if the contract had been performed. In addition, reliance damages generally may not exceed the full contract price. Restatement (Second) of Contracts § 349.

E. SPECIFIC PERFORMANCE

When damages are an inadequate remedy, the nonbreaching party may pursue the equitable remedy of specific performance.

1. Factors Considered

In determining whether the legal remedy is adequate, the court will consider a variety of factors, including the difficulty of proving damages with reasonable certainty, hardship to the defendant, balance of the equities, the wishes and understandings of the parties, practicality of enforcement, and mutuality of the agreement.

> **EXAM NOTE:** Be aware of fact patterns involving land or other unique goods, when damages are more obviously insufficient to put the nonbreaching party in as good a position as he would have been without the breach.

2. Real Property

Contracts involving the transfer of an interest in real property may be enforced by an order of specific performance because every parcel of **real property is considered unique**.

3. UCC

Specific performance may be granted to the buyer when the goods are rare or unique, or in other circumstances, such as for breach of a requirements contract when there is not another convenient supplier. UCC § 2-716.

4. Limitations

Even if the remedy of damages is inadequate, specific performance will not be granted when the court cannot supervise enforcement. Thus, courts rarely grant specific enforcement of contracts for personal services, although they may restrain the breaching party from working for another when the contract contains a noncompete clause (known as the *Lumley* doctrine).

5. Defenses

Equitable defenses, such as laches (prejudicial delay in bringing the action) or unclean hands (when the nonbreaching party is guilty of some wrongdoing in the transaction at issue) may be raised by the breaching party. A party may also seek an injunction against the breaching party to enforce the contract.

F. REMEDIES UNDER THE UCC

The following sections more specifically address the remedies that are available to buyers and sellers under the UCC. These rules are frequently tested on the MBE.

1. Buyer's Remedies

When the seller's time for performance arises, the seller may:

i) Do **nothing** (breach by the seller);

ii) Make a **nonconforming tender** (breach by the seller); or

iii) Make a **conforming tender** (performance by the seller).

a. Failure to tender

Under the UCC, the buyer has several alternative remedies if the seller fails to tender the goods. UCC § 2-711.

1) Cancel the contract

When the contract is an installment contract and the breach goes to the entire contract, the buyer may cancel the contract. UCC § 2-711(1).

2) Recovery of payments

Whether the buyer cancels the contract, the buyer is entitled to recover any payments made to seller for the goods. UCC § 2-711(1).

a) Security interest

On rightful rejection or justifiable revocation of acceptance, a buyer also has a security interest in goods in his possession or control for any payments made on their price and any expenses reasonably incurred in their inspection, receipt, transportation, care and custody and may hold such goods and resell them the same manner as an aggrieved seller would be able to do. UCC § 2-711(3).

3) Damages

The buyer may recover the market price minus the contract price. The market price is the price that existed at the time of the breach at the place where tender was to occur under the contract. When the seller has anticipatorily breached the contract, the market price is measured as of the time that the buyer learned of the breach. Most courts treated this time as the time that the buyer learned of the repudiation. UCC § 2-713.

a) Incidental and consequential damages

A buyer may recover incidental and consequential damages resulting from the seller's breach. Incidental damages are damages that are incidental to the seller's failure to perform, such as the costs of warehousing, transportation, inspection, etc. Consequential damages are any losses resulting from general or particular requirements and needs of which the seller, at the time of contracting, had reason to know and which could not be reasonably prevented by purchasing substitute goods or otherwise. Consequential damages may be limited or excluded unless such limitation or exclusion would be unconscionable. UCC § 2-719(3).

b) Liquidated damages

The buyer can receive damages in the amount provided in a liquidated damages clause, provided the amount is reasonable. UCC § 2-718(1).

4) Cover

Alternatively, the buyer may purchase similar goods elsewhere and recover the replacement price minus the contract price. UCC § 2-712.

5) Specific performance

The buyer may demand specific performance for **unique** goods. In addition, specific performance may be had in other proper circumstances. An inability to cover is strong evidence of such circumstances. The court may grant specific performance on terms and conditions that the court deems just. UCC § 2-716(1).

6) Replevin

a) Payment by the buyer

When the buyer has made at least partial payment for identified goods, the buyer can obtain the undelivered goods from the seller if:

i)   The seller becomes insolvent within 10 days of receiving the first payment from the buyer; or

ii) The goods were for family, personal, or household purposes, and the seller has repudiated or failed to deliver the goods as required by the contract.

To obtain the goods, the buyer must tender any unpaid portion of the price to the seller. UCC § 2-502.

b) Buyer's inability to cover

The buyer can also obtain identified, undelivered goods from the seller if:

i)   The buyer is unable to effect cover;

ii) The circumstances reasonably indicate that reasonable effort to obtain cover will be unavailing; or

iii) The goods have been shipped under reservation, and satisfaction of the security interest in the goods has been made or tendered.

UCC § 2-716(3).

b. **Nonconforming tender**

Under the UCC, if either the tender or the goods is nonconforming, then the buyer has the **right to accept or reject** all of the goods. When the goods are sold in commercial units, the buyer can accept one or more commercial unit(s) and reject the rest. UCC § 2-601.

The buyer has the **right to inspect** the goods before deciding whether to accept or reject. Payment does not constitute acceptance if there is no right of inspection before payment (e.g., C.O.D., C.I.F., or C & F contracts). UCC § 2-513.

1) **Rejection**

a) **Requirements**

A valid rejection requires that the buyer:

i) Give notice to the seller;

ii) Within a reasonable time; and

iii) Before acceptance.

UCC §§ 2-602(1), § 2-607(2). Upon a rightful rejection, the buyer is entitled to a return of any payments made on the goods. UCC § 2-711(3).

b) **Retain possession**

The buyer must retain possession of rejected goods for a reasonable time to allow for the seller to reclaim them. UCC § 2-602(2).

c) **Perishable and nonperishable goods**

In the absence of other instructions from the seller, a merchant buyer may store nonperishable goods at the seller's expense, reship them to the seller, or sell them for the seller's account. If the goods are perishable and the seller has no local agent to whom they can be returned, in the absence of other instructions from the seller, a merchant buyer is required to sell the goods on the seller's behalf. UCC § 2-603.

d) **Remedies**

The same remedies are available to the buyer after a rightful rejection as if no tender was made by the seller, such as a return of any payments made by the buyer on the goods (*see* F.1.a. Failure to tender, *above*). UCC 2-711.

Need for notice: A failure to give notice of the breach to the seller within a reasonable time after the buyer discovers or should have discovered the breach will preclude the buyer from any remedies.

2) **Acceptance**

Under the UCC, the buyer accepts goods by:

i) **Expressly stating** acceptance;

ii) **Using** the goods; or

iii) **Failing to reject** the goods.

UCC § 2-606. Acceptance of the goods precludes rejection of the goods. UCC § 2-607(2).

a) Measure of damages for nonconforming goods

When the buyer accepts goods that are nonconforming, the buyer may recover damages for the resulting loss. When the buyer accepts goods that violate one of the seller's warranties, the buyer may recover damages measured as the difference (at the time and place of acceptance) between the value of the goods as accepted and the value they would have had if they had been as warranted, plus any appropriate consequential and incidental damages. Typically, the amount of such damages is the cost to repair or replace the goods. UCC § 2-714.

b) Notice

To recover damages, the buyer must give notice to the seller of the breach within a reasonable time after the buyer discovers or should have discovered the breach. If such notice is not given, the buyer will be barred from any remedy. UCC § 2-607(3)(a).

c) When the Buyer Resells Goods and is Sued by a Subsequent Buyer

If the buyer resells the goods and is sued for breach of a warranty or other obligation for which the seller would be answerable over the buyer, then the buyer may give the seller written notice of the litigation and that the seller may come in and defend, and that if the seller does not do so, the seller will be bound in any action against him by the buyer with regard to any determination of fact common to the two litigations. If the seller, after seasonable receipt of the notice, does not come in and defend, then the seller will be bound by the litigation. This is referred to as "vouching in." As a practical matter, this procedure would only be used if the buyer is unable to implead the seller because the seller has insufficient contacts with the forum jurisdiction. UCC § 2-607(5).

3) Revocation of acceptance

A buyer may revoke an acceptance of goods if the nonconformity **substantially impairs** their value to the buyer and:

i)   The buyer accepted the goods on the reasonable belief that the seller would cure the nonconformity, but the seller has failed to do so; **or**

ii) The buyer accepted the goods without discovery of the nonconformity, and such acceptance was reasonably induced either by the difficulty of discovering the nonconformity before acceptance or because the seller gave assurances that the goods were conforming.

a) Timing of revocation

The buyer must inform the seller of its decision to revoke within a reasonable time after the nonconformity is discovered or should have been discovered by the buyer.

Note: If the buyer fails to exercise due diligence in discovering a defect, then his notice to the seller is untimely, and revocation will be barred.

Revocation of acceptance must occur before any substantial change in the condition of the goods not caused by the defect. UCC § 2-608.

Note: When a buyer receives nonconforming goods and later causes or allows a substantial change in the goods, the buyer may be prevented from revoking his acceptance despite the original nonconformity.

b) Buyer's rights and duties after revocation

A buyer's rights and duties with respect to the goods for which acceptance is justifiably revoked are the same as those for goods that the buyer properly rejected.

c) Buyer's remedies

A buyer who justifiably revokes acceptance may be entitled not only to a return of purchase price paid but also damages based on the difference between the market price and the contract price or cover. UCC § 2-608, cmt. 1.

4) Withdrawal of refusal to accept

A buyer's original refusal to accept may be withdrawn by a later acceptance if the seller indicates that he is holding the tender open. UCC § 2-601. However, if the buyer attempts to accept after his original rejection caused the seller to arrange for other disposition of the goods, then the buyer is liable for any ensuing damage. The buyer is liable even if the seller chooses to treat his action as acceptance rather than conversion. UCC § 2-601 cmt. 2.

5) Right to cure

The seller has a right to cure a defective tender if:

i) The **time for performance** under the contract has not yet elapsed; or

ii) The seller had **reasonable grounds** to believe that the buyer would accept despite the nonconformity.

The seller must give notice of the intent to cure and make a new tender of conforming goods. If the seller had reasonable grounds to believe that the buyer would accept despite the nonconformity, the tender must be made within a reasonable time. Once cured, the tender is considered proper and valid. UCC § 2-508.

2. Seller's Remedies

a. Right to price

In certain circumstances, a seller may seek to recover the full contract price (or if a price has not been agreed upon, a reasonable price) plus any incidental damages. This remedy is analogous to the remedy of specific performance that the buyer has in limited circumstances.

1) Accepted goods

When a buyer has accepted the goods and fails to pay the price when it becomes due, the seller may sue for the price. UCC § 2-709(1)(a).

2) Goods lost or damaged after risk of loss has passed to the buyer

If the risk of loss has passed to the buyer and the conforming goods then are lost or damaged, the seller may maintain an action for the price of the conforming goods if the buyer fails to pay the price as it becomes due. UCC § 2-709(1)(a).

3) Identified goods

If goods have been identified and the buyer fails to pay the price as it becomes due, the seller may recover the price only if the seller is unable to sell the goods at a reasonable price after a reasonable effort or circumstances indicate that such an effort will not yield a sale. UCC § 2-709(1)(b).

b. Right to reclaim goods

1) Insolvent buyer

When an insolvent buyer receives goods on credit, and the seller learns that the buyer is insolvent, the seller may reclaim the goods, provided a demand is made **within 10 days** after the buyer's receipt of the goods. This 10-day limitation does not apply if the buyer has misrepresented solvency to the seller in writing within three months before delivery. Otherwise, the seller cannot base a right to reclaim goods on the buyer's fraudulent or innocent misrepresentation of solvency or of intent to pay. In addition, this right is subordinate to the rights of a buyer in the ordinary course or other good-faith purchaser, and, if exercised, precludes all other remedies with respect to the reclaimed goods. UCC § 2-702.

Pre-delivery insolvency: As a condition for the seller to reclaim goods from a buyer, the buyer must have received the goods on credit while insolvent. If the buyer becomes insolvent **after** delivery, then the seller may not reclaim the goods.

2) Delivered Goods to a Buyer Who Pays With a Check

If the buyer pays with a check that is subsequently dishonored, then the seller may reclaim the goods following a demand made within a reasonable time. The seller's right to reclaim is subject to the right of a good-faith purchaser. UCC §§ 2-507, 2-511(3).

c. Stoppage of goods in transit

1) Buyer's breach

A seller can stop the goods in transit because of the buyer's breach; goods can be stopped in transit only if shipped in large-sized (e.g., carload, truckload) lots. The seller cannot stop goods in transit once the:

    i)   Buyer has received the goods;

    ii) Carrier or warehouseman has acknowledged the buyer's rights;

    iii) Goods have been reshipped by the carrier; or

    iv) Title has been given to or negotiated with the buyer.

UCC § 2-705(1),(2).

2) Buyer's insolvency

If the buyer becomes insolvent before the delivery of the goods, then the seller can stop goods in transit and refuse delivery except for cash. UCC § 2-705(1).

Compare buyer's breach: When a buyer is insolvent, the seller can stop goods in transit, regardless of the size of the shipment.

d. Wrongful rejection

If the buyer wrongfully rejects, then the seller has three alternative remedies and would also be entitled to incidental damages. UCC § 2-703. (Note: If the buyer wrongfully retains the goods, the seller may be able to pursue a tort action for conversion.)

1) Collect damages

The seller would ordinarily be entitled to the contract price minus the market price at the time and place for tender, together with any incidental damages, less any expenses saved as a result of the buyer's breach. UCC § 2-708(1).

a) Lost profits

In some circumstances, a seller cannot be made whole through resale at the contract price. This is true for volume sellers (those sellers who have an unlimited supply of the goods and who make a profit per item). Although they can resell the goods at the same price as the contract price, they have lost the opportunity to sell them in the first instance when the buyer breached or repudiated. They are, therefore, entitled to those lost profits. To qualify as a "lost volume" seller, the seller needs to show only that it could have supplied both the breaching purchaser and the resale purchaser with the goods. In general, the measure of lost profit would be the list price minus the cost to the dealer or manufacturer. UCC § 2-708(2).

Example: S, a high-volume maker of personal computers, contracts to sell 100 computers to B for $100,000 (the list price). B subsequently repudiates the contract, and S resells the computers to another customer. S can recover its lost profit (the list price of $100,000 minus its manufacturing cost), as well as any incidental damages from B.

b) Liquidated damages

The seller can receive damages in the amount provided in a liquidated damages clause provided the amount is reasonable. UCC § 2-718(1).

2) Resell the goods

If the seller elects to resell and sue for the contract price minus the resale price, then the resale must be (i) only of goods identified in the contract and (ii) commercially reasonable. UCC § 2-706. However, if the seller wishes to resell the goods in a private sale, the seller must first give the buyer reasonable notice of his intent to resell. UCC § 2-706(3).

3) Recover the price

The seller can recover the price after rejection only if the seller is unable to sell the goods at a reasonable price after a reasonable effort or circumstances indicate that such an effort will not yield a sale. UCC § 2-709(1)(b). If not defined in the contract, the price is a reasonable price. UCC § 2-305.

4) Incidental damages

Note that **in addition to** any of the remedies listed above, the seller is entitled to recover incidental damages (including storage and shipping costs). UCC § 2-710.

3. **Risk of Loss**

a. **General rules—non-identified goods, no breach**

Unless the parties otherwise agree, if goods that have not been identified are damaged or destroyed without the fault of either party to the contract, then the risk of loss is generally on the seller until the seller satisfies the contractual delivery obligations. Upon the happening of that event, the risk of loss shifts to the buyer. UCC § 2-509.

1) **Goods to be shipped by a third-party carrier**

If the contract requires or authorizes the seller to ship the goods by carrier, the event necessary to shift the risk of loss is dependent upon whether the contract is a "shipment" or "destination" contract. UCC § 2-509(1).

a) **Shipment contract**

If the contract is a shipment contract (often identified by the words "F.O.B. (free on board) seller's place of business"), then the seller must deliver the goods to the carrier, make a proper contract for their shipment, obtain and deliver any document necessary for the buyer to obtain possession of the goods, and give the buyer notice that the goods have been shipped.

b) **Destination contract**

If the contract is a destination contract (often identified by the words "F.O.B. buyer's place of business"), then the seller must deliver the goods to a particular place (specified in the contract) and tender them there by holding the goods at the buyer's disposition and giving the buyer notice.

Example: B orders a computer from S that is identical to a display model shown on the floor of S's store. The contract specifies that the computer is to be tendered by S at B's place of residence. In transit, the computer is destroyed by the shipping company through no fault of S. S bears the risk of loss.

2) **Goods held by a bailee**

When goods that are held by a bailee are to be transferred without being moved, the risk of loss generally passes to the buyer on the buyer's receipt of a negotiable document of title covering the goods or on acknowledgment by the bailee of the buyer's right to possession of the goods. UCC § 2-509(2).

3) **All other cases**

Unless the parties agree otherwise, in other cases (e.g., the buyer picks up the goods from the seller or the seller delivers the goods to the buyer), risk of loss passes to the buyer upon the taking of physical possession if the seller is a merchant; otherwise, risk passes on tender of delivery. UCC § 2-509(3).

b. **Effect of a breach of contract on risk of loss**

1) **Seller's breach**

If the seller delivers nonconforming goods, the risk of loss remains on the seller until the buyer accepts or there is a cure. If the buyer rightfully revokes acceptance, the risk of loss shifts back to the seller to the extent of any lack of insurance coverage by the buyer. UCC § 2-510(1,2).

2) Buyer's breach

If the **buyer repudiates or breaches** after the goods have been identified but before the risk of loss shifts, then the risk of loss is immediately shifted to the buyer to the extent of any lack of insurance coverage by the seller. UCC § 2-510(3).

c. Effect of destruction of or damage to identified goods

If the **contract deals with identified goods** (e.g., a specific painting or specifically identified items of inventory), then the seller is excused if the goods are totally destroyed through no fault of the seller prior to the risk of loss being shifted to the buyer. Neither party is required to perform; neither party has breached. If the specifically identified goods are damaged but not totally destroyed, then the contract is avoided unless the buyer chooses to take the goods at a reduced price without any other claim against the seller. UCC § 2-613.

> **EXAM NOTE:** When approaching risk-of-loss problems, first ask whether the contract sets forth the risk of loss. If it does, the agreement controls. If not, ask whether there is a breach or repudiation by either party. If so, the breaching party usually bears the risk. If not, determine whether the contract is a shipment or destination contract and continue the analysis under UCC § 2-509.

4. Insurable Interest in Goods

a. Seller's insurable interest

The seller of goods retains an insurable interest in the goods as long as the seller retains title to the goods or has a security interest in them. Unless the contract specifies otherwise, the title passes from the seller to the buyer when the seller completes his delivery obligations. At that point, the seller's insurable interest ceases unless the seller retains a security interest in the goods. When the seller alone identifies the goods, the seller may substitute other goods for those identified until default, insolvency, or notification to the buyer that the identification is final. UCC §§ 2-401; 2-501(2).

b. Buyer's insurable interest

The buyer of goods obtains an insurable interest in the goods as soon as the goods are identified in the contract. Identification can be made at any time by the parties' explicit agreement. In the absence of such an agreement, identification occurs when the contract is made if it is for the sale of goods already existing and identified; for future goods, identification occurs when the goods are shipped, marked, or otherwise designated by the seller as the goods to which the contract refers. UCC § 2-501(1).

5. Title and Good-Faith Purchasers

a. Entrusting provisions

The UCC provides that entrustment of goods by the owner to one who sells goods of that kind gives the transferee the power to convey good title to a buyer in the ordinary course. A "buyer in the ordinary course" is one who in good faith and without knowledge of a third party's ownership rights or security interest buys goods from someone selling goods of that kind. UCC § 2-403.

"Entrusting" includes any delivery and acquiescence in possession regardless of any condition expressed between the parties and regardless of whether the procurement of the entrusting or the possessor's disposition of the goods has been larcenous. UCC § 2-403(3).

b. Voidable title

When the true owner of goods sells them to another, but the sale is voidable because of fraud, because of lack of capacity, or because it was a cash sale and the buyer failed to pay or paid with a dishonored check, the buyer may transfer good title to a good-faith purchaser. UCC § 2-403.

6. Statute of Limitations on a Breach of a Sales Contract or Warranty

a. Period of limitations

Under Article 2, an action for breach of any sales contract or warranty must be commenced within **four years** after the cause of action accrues.

b. When a cause of action accrues

In general, a cause of action accrues when the breach occurs, regardless of whether the aggrieved party knows of the breach. A breach of warranty generally accrues when delivery is made. If a warranty expressly extends to the future performance of the goods, the cause of action will accrue when the breach is or should have been discovered by the aggrieved party.

c. Modification of limitations period

By their original agreement, the parties may reduce the four-year limitations period of Article 2 to not less than one year, but they may not extend it.

G. REFORMATION, RESCISSION, AND CANCELLATION

Reformation, rescission, and cancellation are equitable remedies.

1. Reformation

Reformation is the modification of a contract by a court upon petition by a party. The modification is typically based on the failure of the contract to reflect the intent of the parties to the contract.

2. Rescission

Rescission is the unmaking of a contract, whether the contract is oral or written. Rescission leaves the parties to a contract in the same position they would have been · in if the contract had never existed.

3. Cancellation

The UCC characterizes the negation of a contract for the sale of goods as a cancellation. In general, the buyer or seller of goods may cancel the contract of sale upon breach by the other party. Such a remedy does not foreclose the buyer or seller from also pursuing monetary damages. UCC §§ 2-703(f) (seller), 2-711 (buyer).

4. Grounds

As equitable remedies, reformation, rescission, and cancellation require justification for modifying or negating existing legal rights. Generally, defenses that can be raised to the formation or enforcement of a contract can serve as grounds for these remedies (*see* I.E. Defenses to Formation, *supra*). Among the most prominent grounds are mistake, fraud, undue influence, duress, and lack of capacity. These grounds must have occurred prior to or contemporaneously with the execution of the instrument or formation of the contract.

5. Failure of Consideration

Rescission of a contract may be allowed when there has been a failure of consideration, but rescission is not allowed when the failure is only partial and there has been part performance by the defendant. However, substantial failure of consideration can constitute evidence of fraud.

6. Limitations

Reformation, rescission and cancellation are not available if the contract or other instrument concerns property that has been transferred to a bona fide purchaser who is unaware of the conduct (e.g., fraud) that gives rise to a justification for the reformation, rescission, or cancellation. In addition, a party to a contract is generally required to tender any consideration received in order to pursue an action for rescission.

H. DECLARATORY JUDGMENT

If the rights and obligations of the parties under a contract are unclear, and an actual dispute exists between the parties concerning those rights and obligations, then either party may bring a declaratory-judgment action to obtain an adjudication of those rights and duties. Declaratory judgment is not available, however, to resolve moot issues or theoretical problems that have not risen to an actual dispute.

Criminal Law

CRIMINAL LAW

Table of Contents

CRIMINAL LAW

EDITOR'S NOTE

There are three sources of criminal law covered on the Multistate Bar Exam: common law, statutes, and the Model Penal Code (MPC). Crimes created by the court and enforced in absence of an applicable statute are common-law crimes. Most common-law crimes have been replaced by statute at the local, state, and federal level. Knowledge of specific statutes is not required on the MBE, though the statutory "modern trend" or "modern approach" is testable. The MPC is a set of rules created by the American Law Institute as a guideline for legislators to use when drafting state statutes. Many states have adopted portions of the MPC, but no state has adopted the MPC in its entirety.

On the Multistate Bar Exam, applicants are instructed to apply "generally accepted fundamental legal principles, unless otherwise noted." Whether a principle is "generally accepted" might not be well settled, and in that case the fact pattern will indicate what law to apply (e.g., common law). A question might require application of a specific rule (e.g., M'Naghten) or viewpoint (e.g., Model Penal Code), or the fact pattern might include statutory language to apply.

I. GENERAL PRINCIPLES

The elements of a criminal offense include the *mens rea*, or guilty mind; the *actus reus*, the bad or unlawful act; and causation. With the exception of strict liability crimes, which have no *mens rea*, every statute defining a substantive criminal offense proscribes a particular *mens rea* and *actus reus* that must be proved by the prosecution beyond a reasonable doubt for criminal liability to result.

A. *ACTUS REUS*—ACTS AND OMISSIONS

Before there can be a crime, there must be a criminal act (*actus reus*). The criminal act must generally be a voluntary, affirmative act that causes a criminally proscribed result. The act requirement may also be satisfied by an "omission" or failure to act under circumstances imposing a legal duty to act. A bad thought standing alone cannot result in criminal liability.

1. Voluntary Act

The criminal act must be physical and voluntary. Actions during unconsciousness, sleep, or hypnosis are not voluntary. Other acts that are not considered voluntary are reflexive or convulsive acts as well as conduct that is not the product of the actor's determination.

Example: Person A pushes Person B into a bystander, injuring the bystander. Person B cannot be held criminally liable.

If an epileptic knows of the possibility of a seizure and engages in the voluntary act of driving a car, has a seizure while driving, and causes a fatal accident, then the epileptic is criminally responsible.

Example: An epileptic may still be criminally responsible if (i) he knows of the possibility of seizure and (ii) the last act was voluntary.

The best example of when liability is not generally imposed is for acts committed while sleepwalking.

2. Failure to Act When Duty Exists

A legal duty to act and the failure to do so results in criminal liability in these five instances:

i) Imposed by statute (e.g., the obligation to file a tax return);

ii) Contract (e.g., a lifeguard saving a drowning person);

iii) Special relationship (e.g., a parent's duty to her child or the duty to one's spouse);

iv) Detrimental undertaking (e.g., leaving a victim in worse condition after treatment); and

v) Causation (e.g., failing to aid after causing a victim's peril).

The defendant must have knowledge of the facts giving rise to the duty to act and yet fail to act. Additionally, it must be reasonably possible for the defendant to perform the duty.

Contrast absence of a duty: When there is not a duty to act, a defendant is not criminally liable because she fails to help others in trouble. A mere bystander has no duty to act.

B. *MENS REA*—STATE OF MIND

Mens rea is the requirement of a guilty mind or legally proscribed mental state that a defendant must possess to commit a crime. Except for strict liability crimes, a crime is committed when a criminal act (*actus reus*) is coupled with a guilty mind—both the mental and physical elements exist at the same time. Strict liability crimes have no *mens rea* requirement and require only an *actus reus*.

1. Specific Intent Crimes

Specific intent crimes require that the defendant possess **a subjective desire, specific objective, or knowledge to accomplish a prohibited result**. When dealing with specific intent crimes, it is necessary to identify specific intent for two reasons. First, the prosecution must prove the specific intent in order to prosecute the defendant; second, certain defenses (e.g., voluntary intoxication and unreasonable mistake of fact) are applicable only to specific intent crimes.

The specific intent crimes include:

i) **F**irst-degree murder;

ii) **I**nchoate offenses (attempt, solicitation, conspiracy);

iii) **A**ssault with intent to commit a battery; and

iv) **T**heft offenses (larceny, larceny by trick, false pretenses, embezzlement, forgery, burglary, robbery).

EXAM NOTE: A simple way to remember the specific intent crimes is by using the mnemonic "FIAT." Whenever a fact pattern defines the crime as requiring "the intent to...," the crime is a specific intent crime.

2. Malice Crimes

The crimes of common-law murder and arson require malice, **a reckless disregard of a high risk of harm**. Although these two crimes appear to have an "intent" requirement (e.g., intent to kill), malice requires only a criminal act without excuse, justification, or mitigation. Intent can be inferred from the accomplishment of the act.

3. General Intent Crimes

General intent crimes require only the **intent to perform an act** that is unlawful. Examples include battery, rape, kidnapping, and false imprisonment.

Motive is not the same as intent. The motive is the reason or explanation for the crime and is immaterial to the substantive criminal offense.

a. Transferred intent

When a defendant acts with an intent to cause harm to one person or object and that act directly results in harm to another person or object, the defendant can be liable for the harm caused under the doctrine of transferred intent.

Example: D points a gun at A, intending to shoot and kill A, but accidentally shoots and kills B instead. D is guilty of two crimes: the murder of B under the doctrine of transferred intent and the attempted murder of A.

Note that the doctrine of transferred intent applies only to "bad aim" cases and not to cases of mistaken identity.

Example: If D shoots at A and hits A, although mistakenly believing that A is B, the doctrine of transferred intent is unnecessary because D hit the very body he intended to hit; the intent, therefore, does not need to be transferred—D is guilty of shooting A.

Transferred intent, also known as the unintended victim rule, is usually confined to homicide, battery, and arson. Any defenses that the defendant could assert against the intended victim (e.g., self-defense) may also transfer to the unintended victim.

Note that transferred intent does not apply to attempted crimes, only completed crimes.

Example: D shoots at A with the intent to kill him, but D instead shoots B. The shot does not kill B, but merely injures her. D can be convicted of the attempted murder of A and of battery against B, but cannot be convicted of the attempted murder of B.

The Model Penal Code, while not specifically recognizing the doctrine of transferred intent, does recognize liability when purposely, knowingly, recklessly, or negligently causing a particular result is an element of an offense. This element can be established even if the actual result is not within the purpose or contemplation of the defendant, or is not within the risk of which the defendant is aware, so long as the result differs from the intended, contemplated, or probable result only insofar as (i) a different person or different property is harmed or (ii) the contemplated injury or harm would have been more serious or more extensive than the harm actually caused. MPC § 2.03.2(2, 3).

4. Model Penal Code

A crime defined by statute generally states the requisite *mens rea*. The following levels of culpability are based on the Model Penal Code ("MPC"), and could be expressly asked for in an MBE question.

a. Purposely

When a defendant acts "purposely," his conscious objective is to engage in the conduct or to cause a certain result. MPC § 2.02(2)(a).

b. Knowingly or willfully

"Knowingly" or "willfully" requires that the defendant be **aware that his conduct is of the nature required by the crime** or that circumstances required by the crime exist. In other words, the defendant must be aware or know that **the result is practically certain to occur** based on his conduct. MPC § 2.02(2)(b).

c. **Recklessly**

"Recklessly" requires the defendant **to act with a conscious disregard of a substantial and unjustifiable risk** that a material element of a crime exists or will result from his conduct. The risk must constitute a gross deviation from the standard of conduct of a law-abiding person. MPC § 2.02(2)(c). Mere realization of the risk is not enough.

d. **Negligently**

A defendant acts "negligently" when that defendant **should be aware of a substantial and unjustifiable risk** that a material element of a crime exists or will result from his conduct. The risk must constitute a gross deviation from the standard of care of a reasonable person in the same situation. MPC § 2.02(2)(d).

e. **Hierarchy of mental states**

The MPC mental states are ordered from negligence as the lowest degree of fault to purposefully as the highest level of fault. Consequently, if a statute specifies a mental state, proof of a more culpable mental state satisfies the mens rea requirement. For example, if a statutory crime required that an act be undertaken knowingly, establishing that the act was committed purposefully satisfies the mens rea requirement with respect to that act. MPC § 2.02(5).

f. *Mens rea* **not stated**

If the requisite *mens rea* is not stated in a criminal statute, it is established if the defendant acted at least recklessly. If the *mens rea* does not state the culpable mind applicable to all material elements of the crime, then the *mens rea* applicable to one material element is applicable to all material elements, unless a contrary purpose plainly appears. MPC § 2.02(3),(4).

5. **Strict-Liability Crimes**

A strict-liability crime does not require a *mens rea*, rather, proof of the *actus reus* is sufficient for a conviction. Examples of strict-liability crimes include statutory rape; bigamy; regulatory offenses for public welfare; regulation of food, drugs, and firearms; and selling liquor to minors.

a. **Public welfare offense**

A public welfare offense is a strict-liability crime for which no *mens rea* is required. Conduct that is subject to stringent public regulation includes that which could seriously threaten the public's health or safety or is inherently dangerous.

Examples: Typical examples include adulteration of food or drugs, regulation of waste disposal, and selling liquor to minors.

b. **Presumption against strict liability**

Criminal offenses requiring no *mens rea* are generally disfavored. *United States v. United States Gypsum, Co.,* 438 U.S. 422, 438 (1978). Thus, courts have traditionally held that there must be some clear indication of congressional intent, express or implied, to dispense with *mens rea* as an element of the crime. In determining legislative intent, courts will often consider the severity of the associated penalty, finding crimes with relatively light penalties to be strict liability offenses, and those with more severe penalties (such as felony crimes) to have a *mens rea* element. *Staples v. United States*, 511 U.S. 600 (1994).

6. **Vicarious Liability**

Vicarious liability differs from strict liability in that strict-liability crimes require only a personal act on the part of the defendant (*actus reus*); vicarious liability crimes do not require an *actus reus* by the defendant. Instead, vicarious liability imposes criminal liability on the defendant for the *actus reus* of a third party.

a. **Application to strict-liability crimes**

Courts often impose vicarious liability for strict-liability crimes, most commonly when an employer or principal is vicariously liable for the crimes of an employee or agent. However, sometimes it is unclear whether the legislature intended for vicarious liability to apply to a strict-liability offense. When the punishment for a strict-liability crime is light, courts are more likely to find that vicarious liability applies. The modern trend is to limit vicarious liability to regulatory crimes.

Vicarious liability may present due process issues because it can involve criminal liability without a personal act on the part of the defendant. Although imprisonment for a faultless crime may have constitutional due process implications, when the punishment for a crime is merely a fine, the application of vicarious liability is unlikely to constitute a denial of due process.

b. **Application to corporations**

When dealing with corporations, common law held that corporations had no criminal liability because a corporation could not form the necessary *mens rea*. Modern statutes, on the other hand, impose vicarious liability on corporations when the offensive act is performed by an agent of the corporation acting within the scope of his employment or when the act is performed by a high-ranking corporate agent who likely represents corporate policy. Under the MPC, a corporation may be held criminally liable if (i) the corporation fails to discharge a specific duty imposed by law, (ii) the board of directors or a high-ranking agent of the corporation acting within the scope of his employment authorizes or recklessly tolerates the offensive act, or (iii) the legislative purpose statutorily imposes liability on a corporation for a specific act. The individual agent of the corporation who violated the statute may also be held criminally liable, and the corporation's conviction does not preclude conviction of the individual. MPC § 2.07.

7. **Causation**

When mens rea is a requirement of a crime, that mens rea must generally cause the actus res. In addition, the defendant's act must cause the particular result made unlawful by statute.

8. **Mistake as a Defense**

a. **Mistake of fact**

1) **Negation of intent**

Mistake of fact may negate criminal intent but it must be an "honest mistake." The defense applies differently between specific- and general-intent crimes. Mistake of fact is never a defense to a strict-liability crime because strict-liability offenses do not have a *mens rea*.

2) Reasonableness of mistake

a) Specific-intent crimes

A mistake of fact is a defense to a specific-intent crime, even if the mistake is unreasonable.

> **Example:** An athlete takes an expensive gold watch from a table mistakenly thinking that it was her inexpensive black plastic sports watch. Even though the athlete's mistake of fact is unreasonable, the athlete lacks the intent to steal necessary to commit larceny, a specific-intent crime.

b) General-intent and malice crimes

A mistake of fact must be reasonable in order to be a defense to a general-intent or malice crime.

3) MPC approach

Under the Model Penal Code, a mistake or ignorance of fact that negates the required state of mind for a material element of a crime is a defense. MPC § 2.04(1).

b. Mistake of law

Mistake or ignorance of the law generally is not a valid defense, except when:

i) There is reliance on the decision of a court, administrative order, or official interpretation of the law determined to be erroneous after the conduct;

ii) A statute defining a *malum prohibitum* crime (i.e., a crime for engaging in conduct not obviously wrong, such as a failure to obtain a license) was not reasonably made available prior to the conduct; or

iii) An honestly held mistake of law negates the required intent (e.g., specific intent) or mental state (e.g., purposefully) for a material element of the crime. MPC § 2.04(1).

> **Example:** A forcibly takes money from B to settle a debt that B owed to A. A has the mistaken belief that the law allows for self-help in such situations. A's belief negates the specific intent required for the crime of robbery (i.e., the specific intent to gain control over the property of another person).

Incorrect or bad legal advice from an attorney is not itself a valid mistake-of-law defense, but it may negate the required intent or mental state for a material element of the crime.

> Similarly, a mistake of law as to the existence of a defense does not permit a defendant to raise the defense unless one of the exceptions enumerated above applies.

C. JURISDICTION

Criminal jurisdiction addresses the authority of the federal and state governments to create criminal laws and the authority of courts to enforce those laws. (Procedural rules that affect the conduct of a trial, such as the admissibility of a defendant's confession, are discussed in the Themis Criminal Procedure outline.)

1. **Constitutional Limits on Authority**

   a. **State authority**

   State authority to create crimes is based on the states' broad, inherent police power, which is implicitly recognized by the Tenth Amendment.

   b. **Federal authority**

   Federal authority to create crimes is limited. There is no federal common law of crimes; all crimes are statutory. Under the U.S. Constitution, Congress is granted power over only a handful of crimes, including treason and currency counterfeiting.

   c. **State and federal authority**

   Under the Constitution, neither federal nor state governments may criminalize conduct that has already occurred (i.e., an ex post facto law) or impose punishment without a trial (i.e., a bill of attainder). The Due Process Clauses of the Fifth and Fourteenth Amendments prevent both federal and state governments from imposing criminal liability without giving clear warnings as to the conduct prohibited. *Papachristou v. City of Jacksonville*, 405 U.S. 156, 162–63 (1972) (vagrancy ordinance struck down as "void for vagueness").

   Additionally, many jurisdictions are in the process of eliminating multiple convictions against a defendant with more than one offense if those multiple offenses were all part of the same criminal transaction. Some states have statutorily prohibited such convictions, while other states apply the doctrine of merger or double jeopardy to eliminate the multiple convictions.

2. **Territorial Considerations**

   a. **Federal**

   Congress has the power to criminalize conduct occurring over federally owned or controlled territory (national parks or the District of Columbia), conduct by United States nationals abroad, and conduct on ships or airplanes.

   b. **State authority**

   A state has the authority to prosecute a person for a crime committed within the state and for a crime that is only partly committed within the state if an element of the crime is committed within the state. In addition, the following actions may be prosecuted by the state:

   i) Conduct outside the state that constitutes an attempt to commit a crime within the state;

   ii) Conduct outside the state that constitutes a conspiracy to commit an offense within the state when an overt act in furtherance of the conspiracy occurs within the state;

   iii) Conduct within the state to commit attempt, solicitation, or conspiracy of a crime in another jurisdiction when the state and the other jurisdiction recognize the crime; and

   iv) The failure to perform outside the state a duty imposed by the state.

D. **PARTIES TO A CRIME**

Under the modern rule, in most jurisdictions, the parties to a crime can be a principal, an accomplice, and an accessory after the fact.

At common law, the principal was called the principal in the first degree, and an accessory who was actually or constructively present at the scene of the crime was called the principal in the second degree. An accomplice who was not present at the crime scene was called an accessory before the fact or after the fact, depending on when he provided assistance.

1. Principal

A principal is the person whose **acts or omissions are the *actus reus*** of the crime, in other words, the perpetrator of the crime. The principal must be actually or constructively present at the scene of the crime. A principal is constructively present when some instrumentality he left or controlled resulted in the commission of the crime.

If two or more people are directly responsible for the *actus reus*, they are joint principals (i.e., co-principals).

2. Accomplice Liability

An accomplice (i.e., an accessory before the fact or a principal in the second degree) is a person who, with the requisite mens rea, aids or abets a principal prior to or during the commission of the crime.

a. Accomplice's status

Some states draw a distinction between an accessory before the fact and a principal in the second degree based upon presence at the scene of the crime. An accomplice who is physically or constructively present during the commission of the crime is a principal in the second degree. For example, a getaway driver some distance from the scene is deemed constructively present and will be considered a principal in the second degree.

An accomplice who is neither physically nor constructively present during the commission of the crime, but who possesses the requisite intent, for example someone who helped plan the crime or acquired tools or weapons necessary to commit the crime, is an accessory before the fact.

b. Accomplice's mental state

1) Majority rule

Under the majority and MPC rule, a person is an accomplice in the commission of an offense if he acts with the purpose of **promoting or facilitating** the commission of the offense. The accomplice must solicit, aid, agree, or attempt to aid in the planning or commission of the crime, with the intent that the crime actually be committed. Model Penal Code § 2.06(3). Mere knowledge that another person intends to commit a crime is not enough to make a person an accomplice.

2) Minority rule

A minority of states hold a person liable as an accomplice if he **intentionally or knowingly** aids, induces, or causes another person to commit an offense. *See, e.g.*, Ind. Code Ann. § 35-41-2-4. Under the minority rule, any voluntary act that actually assists or encourages the principal in a known criminal aim is sufficient for accomplice liability even if the person does not act with the intent of aiding the commission of the crime.

3) Criminal facilitation

In jurisdictions that have adopted the majority rule, a person encouraging or assisting a criminal who is not guilty of the crime itself as an accomplice may be guilty of a lesser crime, such as criminal facilitation.

4) Reckless or negligence mental state crimes

When the crime committed by the principal only requires the principal to act recklessly or negligently (e.g., involuntary manslaughter), a person may be an accomplice to that crime under the majority rule if the person merely acts recklessly or negligently with regard the principal's commission of the crime, rather than purposefully or intentionally. *See* Model Penal Code § 2.06(4).

c. Accomplice's criminal liability

An accomplice is responsible for the crime to the same extent as the principal. If the principal commits crimes other than the crimes for which the accomplice has provided encouragement or assistance, then the accomplice is liable for the other crimes if the crimes are the natural and probable consequences of the accomplice's conduct.

Example: D encourages E to burn V's house, and E does so. The fire spreads to W's house, and it was foreseeable that it would do so. D is an accomplice to the burning of W's house.

An accomplice may be criminally liable even though she cannot be a principal.

Example: A woman who could not commit rape at common law as a principal could be liable for rape if she aided the male principal (e.g., restraining the victim) in his rape of the victim.

d. Withdrawal

To legally withdraw (and therefore avoid liability for the substantive crime), the accomplice must (i) repudiate prior aid, (ii) do all that is possible to countermand prior assistance, and (iii) do so before the chain of events is in motion and unstoppable.

A mere change of heart, a flight from the crime scene, an arrest by law enforcement, or an uncommunicated decision to withdraw is ineffective. Notification to the legal authorities must be timely and directed toward preventing others from committing the crime.

> **EXAM NOTE:** Be careful not to confuse these rules with the rules regarding withdrawal for inchoate offenses such as solicitation, attempt, and conspiracy. The rules are different.

e. Persons not accomplices

A person who is a member of the class protected by a statute cannot be an accomplice. Similarly, when the crime requires another party, the other party is not, simply by engaging in the criminal act, guilty of the crime as an accomplice. For example, the buyer of drugs is not guilty of the crime of distributing drugs simply by purchasing the drugs (but of course he may be guilty of a different crime).

f. Effect of the principal's status

At common law, the accomplice could be convicted of a crime only if the principal was also previously convicted of the crime. However, a principal in the second degree could be convicted even if the principal in the first degree was not convicted. A small minority of jurisdictions still subscribes to this approach. By statute, however, in most jurisdictions, an accomplice may be convicted of a crime even if the principal is not tried, is not convicted, has been given immunity from prosecution, or is acquitted.

3. Accessory After the Fact

An accessory after the fact is a person who aids or assists a felon in avoiding apprehension or conviction after commission of the felony. An accessory after the fact must know that a felony was committed, act specifically to aid or assist the felon, and give the aid or assistance for the purpose of helping the felon avoid apprehension or conviction. An accessory after the fact is not subject to punishment for the crime committed by the felon, but instead has committed a *separate crime*, frequently labeled "obstruction of justice" or "harboring a fugitive."

a. Failure to report a crime

The mere failure to report a crime is not generally itself a crime. However, a person who gives false information to the police in order to prevent the apprehension of a felon can be an accessory after the fact.

b. Misprision

Misprision is a common-law misdemeanor that punishes a failure to report or the hiding of a known felon.

The defendant must have (i) had full knowledge that the principal committed and completed the felony alleged, (ii) failed to notify the authorities, and (iii) taken an affirmative step to conceal the crime. *U.S. v. Ciambrone*, 750 F.2d 1416, 1417 (1986).

c. Compounding a crime

A person who receives valuable consideration for agreeing not to prosecute a crime may be guilty of compounding a crime.

E. RESPONSIBILITY

1. Insanity

Insanity encompasses mental abnormalities that may affect legal responsibility. It is a legal term rather than a psychiatric term. The four tests for insanity are the *M'Naghten* test, the irresistible-impulse test, the *Durham* rule, and the Model Penal Code test. These tests expressly exclude the "sociopathic" or "psychopathic" criminals who have a tendency to commit antisocial and sometimes violent acts and are incapable of experiencing guilt. A defendant who puts his sanity at issue can be compelled to submit to psychiatric testing after being informed of his Fifth Amendment rights.

a. *M'Naghten* test

Under the *M'Naghten* test, the defendant is not guilty if, because of a defect of reason due to a mental disease, the defendant did not know either (i) the nature and quality of the act or (ii) the wrongfulness of the act.

Without knowing that the act is wrong, a defendant could not have formed the requisite criminal intent. Therefore, it is important to assess whether the defendant's actions would have been criminal if the facts, as he believed them to be, supported his delusions. However, a defendant is not necessarily exculpated simply because he believes his acts to be morally right, although a few states do allow for such a defense. Loss of control because of mental illness is not a defense under this test. This is the "right from wrong" test.

b. Irresistible-impulse test

Under the irresistible-impulse test, the defendant is not guilty if he lacked the capacity for self-control and free choice because mental disease or defect prevented him from being able to conform his conduct to the law. The loss of control need not be sudden. This is an impulse that the defendant cannot resist.

c. *Durham* rule

Under the *Durham* rule, a defendant is not guilty if the unlawful act was the product of the defendant's mental disease or defect and would not have been committed but for the disease or defect. This is the "but-for" test.

d. Model Penal Code test

The Model Penal Code combines the *M'Naghten* and irresistible-impulse tests. The defendant is not guilty if, at the time of the conduct, he, as a result of a mental disease or defect, did not have substantial capacity to appreciate the wrongfulness of the act or to conform his conduct to the law. MPC § 4.01.

e. Burden of proof

In the majority of jurisdictions, the defendant has the burden of proving insanity. The level of proof required in these jurisdictions can be either a preponderance of the evidence or clear and convincing evidence. Other jurisdictions require the defendant to overcome the presumption of sanity by introducing evidence of the defendant's insanity, and then shift the burden of persuasion to the prosecution, which must prove beyond a reasonable doubt that the defendant is sane.

2. Intoxication

Intoxication can be caused by any substance (e.g., alcohol, drugs, or prescription medicine). There are two types of intoxication defenses: voluntary and involuntary.

a. Voluntary intoxication

Voluntary intoxication is the intentional taking of a substance known to be intoxicating; actual intoxication need not be intended.

1) Specific-intent crimes

Voluntary intoxication is a defense to specific-intent crimes if the intoxication prevents the formation of the required intent. For example, intoxication may prevent the formation of the premeditation required for first-degree murder but not second-degree murder.

Under the MPC, voluntary intoxication is a defense to crimes for which a material element requires a mental state that is purposely or knowingly, and the intoxication prevents the formation of that mental state. MPC § 2.08(1),(2).

2) When inapplicable

Voluntary intoxication is not a defense when the intent was formed before intoxication or when the defendant becomes intoxicated for the purpose of establishing the defense of voluntary intoxication. Voluntary intoxication is not a defense to crimes involving malice, recklessness, or negligence, or for strict-liability crimes.

> **Note:** Although common-law murder and arson sound like specific-intent crimes because they require the "intent to kill" or the "intent to burn," they are malice crimes, and the specific-intent defenses (e.g., voluntary intoxication) do not apply.

b. Involuntary intoxication

Involuntary intoxication is a defense when the intoxication serves to negate an element of the crime, including general as well as specific-intent and malice crimes. To be considered involuntary, the intoxicating substance must have been taken:

i) Without knowledge of the intoxicating nature of the substance, including substances taken pursuant to medical advice; or

ii) Under duress.

In addition, although intoxication and insanity are two separate defenses, excessive drinking and drug use may bring on actual insanity. Thus, involuntary intoxication can give rise to an insanity defense if the requirements for that defense are met.

3. Immaturity/Infancy

At common law, a child under the age of seven could not be convicted of a crime. A child at least seven years old but less than 14 years old was rebuttably presumed to be incapable of committing a crime. A child at least 14 years old could be charged with a crime as an adult.

Modern statutes have modified this rule and provide that no child can be convicted of a crime until a certain age is reached, usually between the ages of 11 and 14.

F. TYPES OF CRIMES

There are two basic types of crimes: felonies and misdemeanors. A felony is a crime punishable by death or imprisonment for more than one year; a misdemeanor is a crime punishable by imprisonment for one year or less or by a fine or by both.

II. HOMICIDE

A. DEFINITION

Homicide is the killing of a living human being by another, and includes the offenses of murder and manslaughter. At common law, homicide was divided into three categories: (i) homicide justified by law, (ii) criminal homicide, and (iii) excusable homicide. Criminal homicides were divided into three offenses: murder, voluntary manslaughter, and involuntary manslaughter.

Common-law murder is the unlawful killing of another living human being with malice aforethought. Malice can be shown by any one of the following states of mind: (i) intent to kill, (ii) intent to do serious bodily injury, (iii) reckless indifference to human life (depraved-heart murder), and (iv) intent to commit a felony (felony murder). (*See* § II.B., Types of Homicide, *infra*.) Manslaughter includes two types: voluntary and involuntary. Voluntary manslaughter involves an intentional killing, and involuntary manslaughter is an unintentional killing.

1. Killing a Person

For a homicide to occur, a living human being must die. A body need not be found; death can be established by circumstantial evidence.

A person cannot be killed twice. Shooting a corpse is not homicide, but it can be a crime (e.g., abuse of a corpse).

At common law, a fetus is not a living person.

2. Causation

To prove a homicide, the prosecution must show that the defendant caused the victim's death. The prosecution must prove both actual and proximate causation.

a. Actual cause

If the victim would not have died **but for** the defendant's act, then the defendant's act is the actual cause (i.e., cause-in-fact) of the death. When the defendant sets in motion forces that led to the death of the victim, the defendant is the actual cause of the victim's death.

Example: A mechanical device set up by the defendant kills an individual. The defendant is considered to have caused that individual's death.

1) Substantial factor

Actual causation can be found when there are multiple causes, (i.e., other persons are also responsible for the victim's death) and the defendant's act was a substantial factor in causing the death.

Simultaneous acts by different individuals who are acting independently may each be considered the actual cause of a victim's death, even though the victim would have died in the absence of one of the acts.

Example: Two individuals simultaneously shoot a third individual. Either of the shots would have killed the victim. Each shot is considered the actual cause of the victim's death.

2) Independent cause

A defendant's act will not be deemed the cause of death when a victim is killed by an independent cause before the defendant's act can kill the victim.

Example: A plans to kill B by stabbing him. A approaches B, finding him lying on the bed in a nonresponsive state. A assumes that B is asleep and stabs him multiple times. In reality, however, B had died one hour previously due to a massive heart attack. A's actions did not cause B's death; therefore, there is no homicide (A may be guilty of attempted murder).

3) Victim's preexisting condition

A victim's preexisting condition that contributes to the victim's death does not supplant the defendant's conduct as an actual cause of the victim's death.

Example: A victim has heart condition. The defendant hits the victim with a club intending to kill the victim, but the blow would not have killed the victim if the victim had not had the heart condition. The defendant's actions are nevertheless the actual cause of the victim's death.

4) Mercy killing

Providing a person with the **means** by which that person can commit suicide generally does not make the provider guilty of murder as an accomplice (because suicide is not homicide) but instead guilty of a lesser crime, such as assisting a suicide. Note, however, that consent is not a defense to homicide, so a "mercy killing" (i.e., euthanasia) can be a criminal homicide even if the person was willing to die because of a painful terminal illness.

b. Proximate cause

Proximate cause (i.e., legal cause) exists only when the defendant is deemed legally responsible for a homicide. For the defendant to be legally responsible for a homicide, the death must be foreseeable. A death caused by the defendant's conduct is deemed foreseeable if death is the natural and probable result of the conduct. Actions by a third party (e.g., negligence by the doctor treating the victim), as well as actions by the victim (e.g., suicide to escape the pain that resulted from the injuries inflicted by the defendant), are generally foreseeable. However, actions by third parties will relieve the defendant of liability if they are independent of the defendant's conduct and unforeseeable, or dependent on the defendant's conduct and "abnormal" (i.e., not just unforeseeable, but unusual or extraordinary in hindsight). 2 Wayne R. LaFave, Substantive Criminal Law § 14.5(d), at 453 (2d ed. 2003). Actions by a force of nature that are not within the defendant's control are generally not foreseeable (e.g., a lightning strike that kills a victim the defendant tied to a tree).

An act that accelerates death is a legal cause of that death.

> **EXAM NOTE:** Proximate cause is commonly tested in the context of the felony-murder rule. A frequently applied standard is that the homicide must be a natural and probable consequence of the defendant's actions.

c. Year-and-a-day rule

At common law, the defendant's act was conclusively presumed not to be the proximate cause of the killing if the victim died more than one year and one day after the act was performed. Most states either have abolished this rule or have extended the time period of responsibility.

B. TYPES OF HOMICIDE

1. Murder

Common-law murder is the:

i) Unlawful (i.e., without a legal excuse);

ii) Killing;

iii) Of another human being;

iv) Committed with malice aforethought.

"Malice aforethought" includes the following mental states: intent to kill, intent to inflict serious bodily injury, reckless indifference to an unjustifiably high risk to human life (depraved heart), or intent to commit certain felonies (felony murder).

a. Intent to kill

Conduct accompanied by the intent to kill that is the legal cause of the death of a living person constitutes intent-to-kill murder unless the legal circumstances surrounding the homicide are such that the crime is reduced to voluntary manslaughter. An inference of intent to kill may be made if a deadly weapon was used intentionally in the commission of the crime.

Example: A intends to kill B and, by his conduct of shooting B, kills him.

b. Intent to inflict serious bodily harm

A person who intends to do serious bodily injury or "grievous bodily harm" but actually succeeds in killing is guilty of murder despite the lack of intention to kill.

Example: A intentionally hits B over the head with a baseball bat, intending to hurt B but not kill him, and B later dies from a skull fracture.

Intent to inflict serious bodily harm is an unintentional killing that results in death.

Intent to inflict serious bodily harm can be inferred from the use of a deadly weapon to inflict the bodily injury.

c. Depraved heart

A killing that results from reckless indifference to an unjustifiably high risk to human life is a depraved-heart murder.

Example: A stands on top of a highway overpass and as a joke drops a bowling ball into oncoming traffic, resulting in the death of B, a passing motorist.

Depraved-heart murder is an unintentional killing that results in death. There is a split among jurisdictions as to whether the requisite depravity exists when a defendant is actually unaware of the risk involved in the conduct, but the majority of states and the MPC impose liability only when the defendant actually realizes the danger. (The minority objective standard imposes guilt if a reasonable person would have recognized the danger.) Note that even those states that ordinarily follow a subjective standard allow a conviction if the reason the defendant failed to appreciate the risk was due to voluntary intoxication.

Generally, reckless driving alone will not lead to a charge of depraved-heart murder. Such a charge would be appropriate only if the reckless driving was extreme, such as if it were combined with intoxication or other aggravating factors. *See, e.g., Cook v. Commonwealth*, 129 S.W.3d 351 (Ky. 2004) (an intoxicated defendant driving at an excessive speed); *State v. Woodall*, 744 P.2d 732 (Ariz. Ct. App. 1987) (intoxicated defendant drove almost 70 mph on a 40-mph double curve).

d. Felony murder

Felony murder is an unintended killing proximately caused by and during the commission or attempted commission of an inherently dangerous felony. The felonies traditionally considered inherently dangerous are: **B**urglary, **A**rson, **R**ape, **R**obbery, and **K**idnapping. [Mnemonic: **BARRK**]. (Common-law felonies also include murder, manslaughter, mayhem, and sodomy, but the BARRK crimes are most commonly tested in the context of felony murder; neither murder nor manslaughter can be the basis for a felony-murder charge.) To convict a defendant of felony murder, the prosecution must establish the underlying felony and that the defendant committed that felony. In addition, in most states, any aggravated felony committed with the use of a dangerous weapon is subject to the felony-murder rule. However, such an aggravated felony must be independent of the killing itself to qualify as an underlying felony for felony murder (e.g., aggravated battery cannot be the basis for a felony-murder charge).

Example: X accidentally shoots the owner of a home while committing a burglary. X can be charged with felony murder.

There is no charge of attempted felony murder if the unintended victim does not die. Generally, co-felons (including accessories) are vicariously liable for the death if the death is a foreseeable consequence of the underlying inherently dangerous felony.

If one of two co-felons kills the other during the commission or attempted commission of a dangerous felony, then this act will also constitute felony murder. If the co-felon is killed by a victim or a police officer, though, then the defendant is generally not guilty of felony murder.

Note: The underlying felony will generally "merge" into the crime of felony murder for the purposes of Double Jeopardy. That is, the predicate felony is generally deemed a lesser-included offense of the felony murder. For example, in the majority of jurisdictions, a defendant who kills the proprietor of a store while committing a robbery can be punished only for felony murder; the robbery conviction would "merge" into the felony-murder conviction. A minority of jurisdictions have enacted statutes explicitly allowing cumulative punishment for both the felony murder and the underlying felony; while these statutes have been held to pass constitutional muster, for purposes of the bar exam, you should assume that cumulative punishment violates Double Jeopardy.

1) Defenses to felony murder

One of the following circumstances can constitute a defense to a felony-murder charge:

i)   A valid defense to the underlying felony;

ii) The felony was not distinct from or independent of the killing itself (e.g., aggravated battery);

iii) Death was not a foreseeable result or a natural and probable consequence of the felony (i.e., there was no proximate causation); or

iv) Death occurred after the commission of the felony and the ensuing flight from the scene of the crime.

2) Killing by a felony victim or the police

a) Death of a bystander

When **someone other than a co-felon** is killed by a police officer or dies as a result of resistance by the victim of the felony, the felon's liability for that death will depend on whether an agency theory or proximate-cause theory is applied. Under an agency theory, the felon will not be liable for the death of a bystander caused by a felony victim or police officer because neither person is the felon's agent. Under the proximate-cause theory, liability for the bystander's death may attach to the felon because the death is a direct consequence of the felony.

The same analysis is applicable when a victim of the underlying felony or a police officer is killed by someone who is not one of the felons.

EXAM NOTE: Agency theory is the majority position and should be applied on the MBE unless the question specifically indicates that the jurisdiction is a proximate-cause theory jurisdiction.

b) Death of a co-felon

Under the *Redline* doctrine, a defendant is generally not guilty of felony murder when a victim or a police officer, acting in self-defense or trying to prevent the escape of the defendant or his co-felon, kills the co-felon. Instead, the killing by the victim or the police officer is considered justifiable homicide. *Commonwealth v. Redline*, 137 A.2d 472 (Pa. 1958).

2. Statutory Crimes of Murder

At common law, there were no degrees of murder. Under modern statutory rules, murder is generally divided into two degrees: first-degree and second-degree murder.

> **EXAM NOTE:** Because degrees of murder do not exist at common law, the fact pattern on the MBE must supply a statute if you are to consider degrees of murder.

a. First-degree murder

First-degree murder is generally defined as a deliberate and premeditated murder. First-degree murder, defined in this manner, is a specific-intent crime, which means that specific-intent defenses are available for a defendant (*see* I.B.1. Specific Intent Crimes, *supra*). In addition, felony murder is frequently classified as first-degree murder.

1) Created by statute

Because the specific criteria for first-degree murder are established only by statute, a homicide cannot be first-degree murder without a corresponding statute.

2) Premeditation

The distinguishing element of first-degree murder is premeditation, meaning the defendant reflected on the idea of killing or planned the killing. The amount of time needed for premeditation may be brief, as long as, after forming the intent to kill, the defendant had sufficient time to become fully conscious of the intent and to consider the killing (i.e., had time for reflection). This requirement does not apply to felony murder.

3) During the commission of an inherently dangerous felony

If a murder is committed during the perpetration of an enumerated felony, then it may be first-degree murder. The most commonly enumerated felonies are **B**urglary, **A**rson, **R**ape, **R**obbery, and **K**idnapping. [Mnemonic: **BARRK**].

> **NOTE:** A homicide committed during the commission of an inherently dangerous felony may be treated as first or second-degree murder depending upon the jurisdiction.

4) Heinous murder

A murder resulting from an egregious act, such as ambush (i.e., lying in wait), torture, bombing, terrorism, or poisoning, may be classified as first-degree murder.

b. Second-degree murder

Second-degree murder is a homicide committed with the necessary malicious intent: the intent to kill, the intent to do great bodily injury, or a depraved-heart murder. In addition, a murder that occurs during the commission of a felony other than the felonies that trigger first-degree murder may statutorily be treated as second-degree murder.

> **EXAM NOTE:** Be sure to differentiate between second-degree murder and first-degree murder when answering exam questions. First-degree murder is a specific-intent crime, whereas second-degree murder, like common-law murder, is a malice crime.

3. Voluntary Manslaughter

Voluntary manslaughter is homicide committed with malice aforethought, but also with mitigating circumstances.

a. "Heat of passion"

Murder committed in response to adequate provocation (i.e., in the "heat of passion") is voluntary manslaughter. The "heat of passion" means that the defendant was provoked by a situation that could inflame the passion of a reasonable person to the extent that it could cause that person to momentarily act out of passion rather than reason. The defendant cannot have been set off by something that would not bother most people.

> **EXAM NOTE:** Remember that "heat of passion" is NOT a defense; it merely reduces murder to voluntary manslaughter.

1) Adequate provocation

A serious battery, a threat of deadly force, or discovery of adultery by a spouse constitutes adequate provocation. Usually mere words, such as taunts, do not.

While an intentional killing committed when resisting arrest is generally murder, the intentional killing can be manslaughter if the arrest is unlawful and the defendant acts in the "heat of passion."

2) "Cooling off"

If there was sufficient time between the provocation and the killing for a reasonable person to cool off, then murder is not mitigated to manslaughter. If there was sufficient time to cool off for a reasonable person even though the defendant himself did not regain self-control, the murder is not mitigated to manslaughter.

Second provocation: Even when the defendant has "cooled off," a second encounter with the victim may give rise to another situation in which the defendant acts in the "heat of passion."

3) Causation

There must be a causal connection between provocation, passion, and the fatal act. There will be no mitigation if the intent to kill was formed prior to the provocation.

4) Transferred provocation

When, because of a reasonable mistake of fact, the defendant is in error in identifying her provoker, or accidentally kills the wrong person, she will be guilty of voluntary manslaughter if that would have been her crime had she killed the provoker. If, however, the defendant, in her passion, intentionally kills another person known to her to be an innocent bystander, then there will be no mitigation, and murder, rather than voluntary manslaughter, will apply.

b. Imperfect defense

In many states, murder may be reduced to voluntary manslaughter when the defendant contends that his use of deadly force was necessary in defense of himself or others, but (i) the defendant started the altercation or (ii) the defendant unreasonably (if truly) believed in the necessity of using deadly force.

For a more detailed discussion of imperfect self-defense and self-defense for an initial aggressor, *see* § V.B.1, Self-Defense, *infra*.

4. Involuntary Manslaughter

Involuntary manslaughter is an unintentional homicide committed with criminal negligence (recklessness under the MPC) or while engaged in an unlawful act.

a. Criminal negligence

Criminal negligence is grossly negligent conduct that puts another person at a significant risk of serious bodily injury or death. It requires more than ordinary negligence for tort liability and something less than the extremely reckless conduct required for depraved-heart murder. For example, the failure of a parent, under a duty of care, to provide medical care to a sick minor child constitutes criminal negligence.

Under the Model Penal Code rule, the defendant must have acted recklessly, which is a "gross deviation from the standard of conduct that a law-abiding person would observe in the actor's situation." MPC § 2.02(2)(c). The defendant must have been actually aware of the risk his conduct posed.

b. Unlawful act

The unlawful act may occur in one of two ways:

i) Under the misdemeanor-manslaughter rule, which is a killing committed in the commission of a *malum in se* (wrong in itself) misdemeanor; or

ii) A killing committed in the commission of a felony that is not statutorily treated as first-degree felony murder or second-degree murder.

The term *malum in se* means "wrong in itself," or "inherently evil," and includes crimes such as assault and battery. *Malum prohibitum* refers to wrongs that are merely prohibited (i.e., not inherently immoral or hurtful, but wrong because of a statute), such as a parking violation, smuggling, or failure to obtain a license. A homicide resulting from a wrong that is *malum prohibitum* will constitute involuntary manslaughter only if the unlawful act was willful or constituted criminal negligence.

c. Causation

There must be a causal connection between the unlawful act and the death for involuntary manslaughter to apply.

III. OTHER CRIMES

A. CRIMES AGAINST PROPERTY

1. Larceny

Larceny is the:

i) Trespassory;

ii) Taking and;

iii) Carrying away;

iv) Of the personal property;

v) Of another;

vi) With the intent to permanently deprive that person of the property (i.e., intent to steal).

a. Trespass

The property must be taken without the owner's consent. If the original taking was without consent, yet was not unlawful because there was no intent to steal at the time of the taking, then larceny may be committed at a later time if the intent to steal is later formed. Under the "continuing trespass" rule, the original trespass is deemed to be "continuing" in order for the criminal act to coincide with the criminal intent. The defendant's original taking must have been wrongful (e.g., a taking based on knowledge that the property belonged to another, such as a taking with the intent to borrow and return the property).

b. Taking

The taking (also known as "caption") requirement is satisfied by any trespassory removal of the property from the owner's possession into another's control.

1) Destruction of property in the owner's possession

The destruction of property while it is in the owner's possession (e.g., breaking an object held by the owner) is not a taking.

2) Use of an agent

A taking occurs if the defendant uses an agent, even one who is unaware of the defendant's criminal intent, to remove the property from the owner's possession.

c. Carrying away (asportation)

The carrying away requirement (also known as "asportation") is satisfied by even a slight movement of the property (e.g., inches).

d. Personal property

The property taken must be personal, not real, property. Electricity or gas supplied by a utility constitutes personal property.

1) Intangibles

Intangible property will not suffice; however, documents that represent the rights to intangible property (e.g., stocks, bonds) are treated as personal property.

2) Services

Modern theft statutes usually criminalize obtaining services without paying for them (i.e., the theft of services).

> **EXAM NOTE:** Services taken without paying for the services (e.g., a massage) do not constitute personal property for the purposes of the MBE.

3) Real-property items

The taking of fixtures (i.e., items affixed to real property) or real-property items (e.g., trees, unharvested crops) is not larceny when the defendant's act of severance occurs immediately before the carrying away of the fixture or other real-property items. However, when the real-property items have previously been severed from the land by the owner, they become personal property (e.g., picked apples), and the carrying away of such items can be larceny.

e. Another's property

The property must be in the possession of someone other than the defendant.

> **Contrast with embezzlement:** For embezzlement, the defendant is legally entrusted with the property by the owner, and then the defendant later fraudulently converts the property to his own use. With larceny, the initial taking must be trespassory; there cannot be lawful entrustment by the owner. This is the main difference between the two crimes.

1) Owner of property

The owner of property (i.e., a person who has title to it) can commit larceny when someone other than the owner (e.g., a lessee) is entitled to current possession of the property.

2) Thief

Larceny may even be committed against a thief. The taking of stolen property from a thief can constitute larceny unless the taker has a superior possessory interest in the property (e.g., an owner or a lessee of the property).

3) Joint owners

A joint owner of property who takes possession of the property from a co-owner is not guilty of larceny because the taker has an equal right to possess the property.

4) Constructive possession

"Constructive possession" means legal possession when factual possession does not exist.

> An owner has constructive possession of property when actual possession, but not title, is taken from her by fraud. The crime is called "larceny by trick." *See* § III.A.2, Larceny by Trick, *infra*.

a) Employee's control over employer's property

Low-level employees can only be guilty of larceny whereas high-level employees are typically guilty of embezzlement. An employer generally has constructive possession of property in the hands of a lower-level employee. Such an employee has custody, not possession, of the employer's property. A higher-level employee (e.g., company president) who has greater authority with respect to the employer's property may have possession of, rather than custody of, such property and may be guilty of embezzlement, rather than larceny, for taking the property.

b) Bailee possession

A bailee is guilty of larceny if, with intent to steal, the bailee opens and takes property from closed containers belonging to the bailor. Otherwise, the bailee simply has possession.

5) Abandoned versus lost property

Property that has been abandoned by its owner (i.e., the owner has surrendered all rights to the property) is not subject to larceny. Property that has been lost by its owner can be the subject of larceny if, at the time of the finding, the finder knows the owner or believes that he can locate the owner and the finder possesses the necessary intent to permanently deprive the owner of the property.

6) Mistakenly delivered property

Property that has been mistakenly delivered may be the subject of larceny if the recipient of the property realizes that a mistake has been made at the time of the receipt of the property and the recipient possesses the necessary intent to permanently deprive.

a) Special problems

When a defendant takes legitimate possession of an item, but he discovers another item enclosed in the larger item (the container), the issue arises as to whether the defendant had possession of the enclosed item at the time the defendant legitimately possessed the larger item. If so, there is no larceny because the defendant has not taken the property from another's possession. However, determining whether there is possession is a difficult task. Larceny may depend on whether the parties intended to transfer the container. If the intent is to transfer, then no larceny is committed because the defendant effectively takes immediate possession of both items. A few states hold that the defendant does not take possession of the enclosed property until he discovers it, at which point, if he forms the intent to keep the property, he is guilty of larceny.

f. Intent to permanently deprive

Larceny is a **specific-intent** crime. The intent to permanently deprive the owner of the property must be present at the time of the taking. There is no defense of restoration if the defendant later has a change of heart and restores the property to the rightful owner. The crime is complete at the time of the taking.

Examples: The intent to permanently deprive the owner of the property can occur when the defendant takes property with the intent to claim a reward, the defendant intends to throw away or abandon the property, the defendant intends to sell the property back to the owner, or the defendant intends to pledge or pawn the property without being able to redeem it.

1) Insufficient intent

The necessary specific intent does not exist when the defendant's intent is to:

i)   Borrow property with the ability to return it;

ii) Pay for merchandise that she has the means to buy; or

iii) Take money as repayment of a debt.

a) Intent to borrow

If the defendant intends only to borrow the property with the ability to do so, then larceny does not occur because there is no intent to permanently deprive the owner of the property (e.g., borrowing a car to run an errand).

If property is taken with the intent to return the property and is accidently damaged or destroyed, larceny has not occurred.

Example: D takes A's car to run an errand. On the way back to A's house, D is in a car accident, and A's car is totaled. D is not guilty of larceny.

b) Intent to pay

A defendant's intent to pay for property is not sufficient to prevent larceny when the property is not offered for sale.

c) Repayment of debt

If a defendant takes property with the honest belief that she is entitled to the property as repayment of a debt (i.e., a claim of right), then the taking does not constitute larceny. (Note, however, that a claim of right cannot serve as a justification for robbery in most states.)

d) Rewards

A defendant intending to return property in expectation of claiming a reward has not committed larceny, unless his intent is to return the property only upon receiving the reward.

2) Sufficient intent

There is sufficient intent if the defendant intends to create a substantial risk of loss of the property or if the defendant intends to sell the goods back to the owner.

3) Time for measuring intent

The intent to permanently deprive is generally measured at the time of the taking. The continuing-trespass rule may apply to stretch the time at which intent is measured. *See* § III.A.1.a, Trespass, *supra*.

2. Larceny by Trick

Larceny by trick is

i) Larceny

ii) Accomplished by fraud or deceit

iii) That results in the conversion of the property of another.

Larceny by trick requires that the defendant fraudulently induce the victim to deliver possession of, but not title to, the property to the defendant.

a. False representation of material present or past fact

The representation (whether oral, written, or by actions) must be false in fact and be of a material past or present fact. A prediction about a future event, a false promise, or an opinion, such as sales talk or puffing, is not sufficient.

b. Reliance by the victim

The victim must rely upon the false representation, and that reliance must cause the victim to give possession to the defendant. This standard is subjective, not objective.

c. Conversion of property

Unlike larceny, larceny by trick requires that the property be converted. Property is converted when the defendant, in a manner so serious as to deprive the victim of the use of the property, deprives the victim of possession of the property or interferes with the property. The deprivation must be substantial enough to justify a court to order the defendant to pay the full fair market value of the property.

Contrast with false pretenses: Under larceny by trick, the defendant obtains possession. Under false pretenses, the defendant obtains title. *See* § III.A.5, False Pretenses, *infra*.

3. Forgery

Forgery is the:

   i)   Making;

   ii) Of a false writing;

   iii) With apparent legal significance; and

   iv) With the intent to defraud (i.e., make wrongful use of the forged document).

a. Making

Making includes creating, altering, or fraudulently inducing another to sign a document when that person is unaware of the significance of the document. The defendant need not use the document; the crime is complete upon the "making" of the document. When property is acquired by use of the forged document, the defendant may also be guilty of another crime, such as false pretenses (*see* § III.A.5, False Pretenses, *infra*).

b. False writing

The writing itself must be false, instead of merely including false information in an otherwise genuine document. (Note: Signing another person's name on a check or other commercial paper makes the check itself false.) When there is an alteration, the alteration must be material.

c. Apparent legal significance

A document has legal significance if it has value beyond its own existence. A contract, deed, will, or check has value beyond the document itself; a painting does not.

d. Intent to defraud

The defendant must intend to make wrongful use of the writing, (e.g., cashing a check with a forged drawer's signature). There must be intent to defraud, even if no one actually is defrauded.

4. Embezzlement

Embezzlement is the:

   i)   Fraudulent;

ii) Conversion;

iii) Of the property;

iv) Of another;

v) By a person who is in lawful possession of the property.

a. Conversion

Conversion is the inappropriate use of property, held pursuant to a trust agreement, which causes a serious interference with the owner's rights to the property. Interference with the owner's rights to the property can be caused by selling the property, damaging it, or unreasonably withholding possession. The defendant need not personally benefit from the conversion. No movement or carrying away of the property is required. If it is unclear whether there was a conversion of the property, then the victim must demand a return of the property, and the embezzler must refuse to return the property before a claim for embezzlement can be made.

b. Intent to defraud

The defendant must intend to defraud the owner of the property. If the defendant intends to return the exact property that is converted and has the ability to do so at the time that the intent is formed, then the defendant lacks the intent to defraud the property owner. If the defendant intends to return similar property or the cash equivalent of the value of the property, then the defendant has the intent necessary to commit embezzlement. A conversion pursuant to a claim of right also is not embezzlement.

c. Type of property

Property that is subject to larceny is also subject to embezzlement. In some states, real property, as well as personal property, may be embezzled.

d. Another's property

The property embezzled must belong to another. The inability to fulfill a contractual obligation (e.g., pay back a loan) is not embezzlement.

e. Lawful possession

The embezzler must be in lawful possession of the property at the time that the intent to defraud occurs, although some states limit embezzlement to property entrusted to the embezzler.

5. False Pretenses

False pretenses (also called "obtaining property by false pretenses" or "larceny by false pretenses") is:

i) Obtaining title to the property;

ii) Of another person;

iii) Through the reliance of that person;

iv) On a known false representation of a material past or present fact; and

v) The representation is made with the intent to defraud.

a. Title must pass

Title to the property must pass from the victim to the defendant. Title can be obtained without possession of the property, but mere possession does not constitute false pretenses. If the defendant subjectively believes that he owns the property in question, he will not be guilty of false pretenses.

Contrast larceny by trick: Mere possession of the property without legal title by a defendant can be sufficient for larceny by trick.

b. Type of property

Generally, property that may be subject to larceny is also subject to false pretenses.

c. False factual representation

The representation must be false and must be of a material past or present fact. A prediction about a future event, a false promise, or an opinion, such as sales talk or puffing, is not sufficient. The representation may be made orally, in writing, or by actions (e.g., resetting a car's odometer). Silence does not constitute a representation, even when the defendant is aware of the owner's misunderstanding, unless the defendant caused the misunderstanding or the defendant has a fiduciary obligation to the victim.

d. Reliance by the victim

The victim must rely upon the false representation, and that reliance must cause the victim to pass title to the defendant. This standard is subjective, not objective.

e. Intent to defraud

The defendant must know that the representation is false and specifically intend to defraud. Most courts find that a defendant acts knowingly and has knowledge of a particular fact when he is aware of a high probability of the fact's existence and deliberately avoids learning the truth. A few states require actual knowledge of a particular fact.

A defendant has the intent to defraud required to establish false pretenses when she intends that the person to whom the false representation is made will rely upon it.

6. Robbery

Robbery is:

i) Larceny;

ii) From the person or presence of the victim;

iii) By force or intimidation.

a. Elements of larceny

All of the elements of larceny are necessary for robbery. Larceny is the (i) trespassory, (ii) taking and carrying away, (iii) of the personal property of another, (iv) with the intent to steal (*see* III.A.1. Larceny, *supra*).

b. From the person or presence

The property taken must be on the victim's person or within the victim's reach or control (i.e., in the presence of the victim). For example, if a victim is restrained by the defendant within the victim's home prior to the seizure of the property, items taken from the entire house can be treated as "from the victim's presence."

c. By force or intimidation

The taking of the property must be accomplished by force or intimidation. The force or intimidation must occur before the taking, simultaneously with the taking, or immediately following the taking to retain the stolen property or to effect an escape.

1) Force

The force used by the defendant must be more than the amount necessary to effectuate taking and carrying away the property.

When a pickpocket takes the victim's property without the victim's knowledge, the taking does not constitute robbery unless the victim notices the taking and resists. Similarly, most state courts that have considered the issue have said that purse-snatching is not robbery unless additional circumstances transform the larceny into a robbery. Such circumstances are present when the victim notices the taking and resists, or when the victim is intimidated, knocked down, struck, or injured by greater force than is required to carry away the property.

> **EXAM NOTE:** The MBE often tests the degree of force necessary for robbery. Remember that slight force is sufficient. Common law required that the force must be manifested immediately before or at the same time as the taking, while the modern trend in many jurisdictions is that the force may be immediately following the taking (e.g., during escape).

2) Intimidation

The threat must be of immediate serious physical injury to the victim, a close family member, or other person present. A threat to damage or destroy property, other than the victim's home, is probably not sufficient.

d. Merger

Larceny, assault, and battery all merge into robbery or attempted robbery.

> **EXAM NOTE:** Merger of these crimes is often tested on the MBE by asking, "which is the highest crime D can be convicted of?"

7. Extortion

a. Common law

At common law, extortion was the unlawful taking of money by a government officer.

b. Modern approach

Most jurisdictions have enacted statutes that more broadly define extortion as the taking of money or property from another by threat. In most jurisdictions, it is the making of threats (rather than the obtaining of the property) that is the essence of the crime. In a minority of jurisdictions, however, the accused must actually obtain the property to be guilty.

Extortion differs from robbery in two respects:

i) The threats need not be of immediate harm, nor need they be of a physical nature (e.g., threatening future exposure of the victim's marital infidelity); and

ii) The property intended to be taken need not be on the victim or in his presence.

8. Burglary

Common-law burglary is the:

i) Breaking and;

ii) Entering;

iii) Of the dwelling;

iv) Of another;

v) At nighttime;

vi) With the specific intent to commit a felony therein.

a. Breaking

Breaking is accomplished by using force to create an opening into a dwelling, such as by shattering a window or kicking in a door. The force used may be slight, such as opening an unlocked door or window.

Note: It is not a breaking to enter a dwelling through an open door or window, unless the opening must be enlarged to allow the entry.

1) Breaking without use of force

If entry is obtained by fraud or threat, then there is a breaking. If the defendant had consent by the owner to enter, then no breaking occurs unless the consent was obtained by fraud, or the defendant exceeded the scope of such consent.

2) Breaking within dwelling

If entry is gained with consent, a breaking can still occur if the defendant breaks into a part of the dwelling structure, such as by opening a closet door or wall safe. The mere opening of an object within the dwelling, such as a desk drawer, trunk, or box, does not constitute a breaking.

3) Use of force to exit—no breaking

The use of force to exit a dwelling does not constitute a breaking.

Most states now require only that the defendant enter the premises; a breaking is not required. The common law requires a breaking.

b. Entering

Entering occurs when any portion of the defendant's body (e.g., a hand through a broken windowpane) or an instrument used by the defendant to gain entry (e.g., a rock thrown through a window) crosses into the dwelling without permission through the opening created by the breaking.

Breaking and entering need not happen at the same time.

c. Dwelling of another

A dwelling is a structure regularly occupied for habitation. It need not be occupied at the time of the breaking, but it must not be abandoned.

All states have statutes that expand the type of structure to include non-dwellings, such as businesses, buildings, or cars, and surrounding areas, such as yards.

The dwelling must be that of another person. A person cannot burglarize his own dwelling, but the owner of a dwelling who has transferred the possessory interest to another (e.g., a tenant) can be guilty of burglary.

d. Nighttime

Nighttime occurs during the period of darkness between sunset and sunrise. It is not considered nighttime if there is sufficient natural daylight to see the burglar's face.

The common law required that the breaking and entering occur during nighttime. Only a very few states require that all forms of burglary be committed at night, although many states impose more severe penalties on nighttime burglaries.

e. Specific intent to commit a felony

At the time of the breaking and entering, the defendant must have the intent to commit a felony (e.g., larceny, robbery, rape, murder) inside the dwelling.

A defendant who fails to commit the underlying felony may nevertheless be guilty of burglary as well as attempt to commit the underlying felony. If the underlying felony is completed, it does **not** merge with the burglary.

Many states have broadened the scope of the crimes intended to be committed to include misdemeanor thefts.

9. Arson

Arson is the:

i) Malicious;

ii) Burning;

iii) Of the dwelling;

iv) Of another.

a. Malice

Malice does not require ill will. The defendant is not required to intend to burn the dwelling of another; it is sufficient that the defendant performs an act with reckless disregard that creates a substantial risk of such burning.

b. Burning

The damage to the dwelling must be caused by fire. Smoke damage alone is insufficient. In addition, the damage must affect the structure of the building; mere scorching (i.e., discoloration due to heat) of the walls and burning of the contents of the dwelling are insufficient. When the dwelling is constructed of wood, there must be at least a charring of the wood (i.e., damage to the wood itself).

c. Another's dwelling

Ownership is not required. The test is whether a person has the right to possession or occupancy of the dwelling. Many states have expanded arson to include the burning of one's own dwelling. At common law, however, the burning of one's own dwelling (house burning) that was located near other houses or in a city was only a misdemeanor, and burning one's own building for insurance fraud was not considered arson.

Most states have expanded arson to include the burning of buildings other than dwellings, but burning the contents of a building alone does not constitute arson.

EXAM NOTE: The MBE has not always been consistent with regard to the definition of arson in its questions. Some questions in the past have included the burning of non-dwellings or of the defendant's own dwelling as arson, without indicating a statutory definition. If a situation looks like "arson" from a common-sense point of view, it generally will be considered arson on the MBE.

10. Possession Offenses

Possession of a prohibited object (e.g., drug paraphernalia, burglar's tools) or a substance (e.g., illegal narcotics) is unlawful if the defendant exercises control over such object or substance. The defendant is not required to be aware that possession of the object is illegal. Dominion and control must exist for a period long enough to have provided the defendant with an opportunity to cease such dominion and control.

11. Receiving Stolen Property

Receiving stolen property is a statutory crime that requires:

i) Receiving control of stolen property;

ii) Knowledge that the property is stolen; and

iii) Intent to permanently deprive the owner of the property.

a. Receiving control of stolen property

Knowledge that the property is stolen must coincide with the act of receiving the property. The property must have been stolen (e.g., unlawfully obtained through larceny, embezzlement, false pretense) at the time it is received. Only control, not possession, is necessary.

a. Knowledge that property is stolen

Knowledge that the property is stolen must coincide with the act of receiving the property. (Note that some jurisdictions characterize the crime as "possession of stolen property," which does not require that knowledge that the property is stolen coincide with the receipt of the property.)

Traditionally, the defendant must have actual subjective knowledge that the property has been stolen. Under the modern view, the defendant's knowledge can be inferred from facts that would alert a reasonable person to unlawful acquisition of the property.

12. Legislative Changes to Theft Crimes

There are several changes made to the common-law property offenses under the MPC and through states' criminal codes. Larceny, false pretenses, embezzlement, and receipt of stolen goods are treated as a single statutory crime of theft. The definition of property has been expanded to cover intangibles, services, and documents. In addition, the defendant need only have unauthorized control over the property.

B. CRIMES AGAINST THE PERSON

1. Battery

Battery is the:

i)   Unlawful;

ii) Application of force;

iii) To another person;

iv) That causes bodily harm to that person or constitutes an offensive touching.

a. Unlawful

"Unlawful" means that the force is applied without legal excuse. Excessive use of force by a police officer during an arrest is unlawful.

b. Application of force

The touching, however slight, must result in bodily harm (e.g., a bruise) or an offensive touching (e.g., an unwanted kiss). The force can be applied by a third party acting under the defendant's direction or by an object controlled by the defendant (e.g., a brick thrown by the defendant).

c. To the person of another

The application of force to an object near, carried by, or attached to the victim constitutes a battery if the victim suffers bodily harm or an offensive touching.

Example: A battery occurs if a defendant kicks a cane used by a victim for support, causing the victim to fall and injure herself.

d. Requisite intent

Battery is a general-intent crime that includes not only intentional conduct but also criminal negligence (i.e., conduct that carries a high degree of risk to others).

e. Consent defense

Although consent is generally not a defense to a crime, consent may be a defense to a battery. Consent may be explicit (e.g., a signed authorization for surgery) or implicit (e.g., participation in an athletic event).

f. Aggravated battery

Battery may carry a greater penalty, by statute, when serious bodily injury is inflicted or bodily injury is caused by the use of a deadly weapon.

2. Assault

Assault is:

i)   An attempt to commit a battery; or

ii) Intentionally placing another in apprehension of imminent bodily harm.

Battery Distinguished: The defendant **must** cause bodily injury or actually touch the victim (or something attached to his person) for a battery to occur. An assault can occur if the defendant does not touch the victim.

a. Attempted battery

The defendant must take a substantial step toward the commission of a battery. Like all attempt crimes, the defendant must have the specific intent to commit a battery.

b. Fear of harm

The "fear of harm" type of assault (also called "apprehension assault") is a general-intent crime—the defendant must intend to cause bodily harm or apprehension of such harm. The victim's apprehension must be reasonable. Unlike attempted battery, because actual apprehension is necessary, the victim's lack of awareness of the threat of harm is a defense to this type of assault.

c. Consent defense

As is the case with battery, consent may be a defense to assault.

d. Aggravated assault

Assault may carry a greater penalty, by statute, when a deadly weapon is used.

3. Mayhem

Mayhem is a common-law felony battery that causes the dismemberment or permanent disfigurement of a person. It is the equivalent of modern statutory aggravated battery.

4. Kidnapping

Kidnapping is the:

  i) Unlawful;

  ii) Confinement of a person;

  iii) Against that person's will;

  iv) Coupled with either:

    a) The movement; or

    b) The hiding of that person.

Note: There is no requirement for a ransom demand in order to establish kidnapping.

a. Unlawful

The unlawful requirement excludes legally sanctioned actions, such as the imprisonment of a felon by the state after his conviction.

b. Confinement

The victim's freedom of movement must be significantly restricted. It is not enough that the victim is prevented from taking a path or entering an area; the victim must be prevented from leaving an area or compelled to go to a place the victim does not want to go.

c. Against the victim's will

The confinement must be accomplished by force, threats, or fraud.

Consent of the victim to the confinement is a defense if given by a person with the capacity to consent. A child cannot consent to being taken out of the control of a parent or guardian.

d. Movement

The victim need only be moved a short distance (e.g., forced from the driver's seat into the trunk of a car). If the kidnapping occurs incident to another crime (e.g., robbery), then the movement must be more than is necessary for the commission of that crime in order for a defendant to be liable for both kidnapping and the separate offense.

e. Hidden location

Instead of movement, the victim may be concealed for a substantial period of time at a hidden location.

f. Enhanced punishment

A kidnapping that results in bodily injury, interferes with a governmental function, or is done for the purpose of collecting a ransom may be subject to enhanced punishment, by statute.

5. False Imprisonment

False imprisonment is the:

i) Unlawful;

ii) Confinement of a person;

iii) Without consent.

a. Unlawful

The confinement is unlawful unless it is consented to or specifically authorized by law.

b. Confinement

Confinement may be effected by forcing a person to go where he does not want to or by preventing him from going where he does want so long as no alternative routes are available to him. This may be done by actual force, threat of force, or a show of force.

c. Consent

To be effective, consent must be given freely, and the one consenting must have the capacity to do so.

C. RAPE AND OTHER SEX CRIMES

1. Rape

Rape is:

i) Unlawful;

ii) Sexual intercourse;

iii) With a female;

iv) Against her will by force or threat of immediate force.

Most modern statutes are gender-neutral and have replaced the force requirement with lack of consent.

a. Unlawful—exclusion of husband

At common law, a husband could not rape his wife. Most states have either abolished this restriction or removed the immunity if the husband and wife have separated or filed for divorce.

b. Sexual intercourse

Actual penetration, however slight, is required; emission is not.

c. With a female

Traditionally, the victim of rape could only be a woman. Most states recognize homosexual rape as a crime labeled "sexual assault" rather than rape. Most states also have defined rape in a gender-neutral manner; under such statutes, a woman could be the perpetrator of a rape.

d. Without consent

When a woman consents to sexual intercourse, rape has not occurred. Consent does not exist if intercourse is procured by force or threat of harm, or when the female is unable to consent due to a drug-induced stupor or unconsciousness.

1) Threat of harm

Consent is ineffective if a woman consents to sexual intercourse because of a threat of harm, although the harm threatened must be imminent and must involve bodily harm. Economic duress is not sufficient.

2) Fraud

Fraud rarely negates consent. Consent obtained by fraud regarding the nature of the act itself—fraud in factum (e.g., the defendant convinces the victim that the act is not intercourse but part of a medical exam)—is not a valid defense. Consent obtained by fraud in the inducement (e.g., a promise of marriage in exchange for sex) is a valid defense.

3) Resistance of the victim

Resistance of the victim is not required, but it can be evidence of the victim's lack of consent.

e. Intent

Rape is a general-intent crime requiring only the intent to commit intercourse without the consent of the female. Intent is negated if a defendant reasonably believes that the victim's lack of resistance indicates consent.

2. Statutory Rape

Statutory rape is sexual intercourse with a person under the age of consent. It is a strict-liability crime with respect to the age of the victim. Consent by the underage victim is not a defense. A defendant's reasonable mistake of fact concerning the victim's age is not a defense.

3. Adultery and Fornication

Adultery and fornication are considered misdemeanor offenses in some states. Adultery involves sexual intercourse or cohabitation with a person who is not a spouse. Fornication is open and notorious cohabitation or sexual intercourse between unmarried persons.

4. Crimes Against Nature

There are two crimes under this category: sodomy and bestiality. Both are considered common-law felonies. However, in light of *Lawrence v. Texas*, 539 U.S. 558 (2003), it is most improbable that a defendant could be successfully prosecuted for the crime of sodomy. Because the majority in *Lawrence* held that intimate consensual sexual conduct was part of the liberty protected by the Fourteenth Amendment, *Lawrence* effectually invalidated similar laws that purport to criminalize sodomy. Bestiality (sexual intercourse with an animal by a human) continues to survive.

5. Incest

In most jurisdictions, incest is marriage or sexual acts between persons that are too closely related. However, there is no uniformity in classifying the degree of relationship. While some states restrict incest to blood relatives, many other states extend the felony to non-blood relatives as well.

6. Bigamy

A strict-liability offense (with respect to marital status), bigamy is the act of marrying someone while still legally married to someone else. Common law considered a defendant guilty even when the defendant incorrectly believed that an alleged divorce was valid or that his spouse was dead.

7. Seduction

Seduction occurs when a man induces a woman to have sexual intercourse with him on the false promise of marriage. Subsequent marriage may be a defense in some jurisdictions.

D. PERJURY AND BRIBERY

1. Perjury

Perjury involves the willful act of falsely promising to tell the truth, either verbally or in writing, about material matters that affect the outcome of a case. A witness cannot be prosecuted for making two contradictory statements if they are made during the same proceeding and the witness admits, prior to the end of the proceeding, that one of the statements is false. All witnesses are absolutely immune from civil liability based on their alleged perjured testimony in litigation brought under the Civil Rights Act, 42 U.S.C. § 1983.

2. Subornation of Perjury

At common law, subornation of perjury was a separate offense committed when one persuaded or induced another to commit perjury. Some states have eliminated subornation of perjury from the perjury statute.

3. Bribery

Under common law, bribery was a misdemeanor involving the corrupt payment of something of value for the purpose of influencing the action of an official in the discharge of his public or legal duties. Under modern law, bribery can be a felony and may extend to persons who are not public officials. Mutuality is not required. Further, the offering or taking of a bribe may constitute a felony as well. In some jurisdictions, failure to report a bribe constitutes a misdemeanor.

IV.   INCHOATE CRIMES

The term "inchoate" literally means "unripened." With an inchoate offense, the intended crime need not be committed for a defendant to be guilty. The inchoate offenses are solicitation, conspiracy, and attempt. Inchoate offenses are specific-intent crimes.

A.   MERGER

Traditionally, under the doctrine of merger, if a person's conduct constitutes both a felony and a misdemeanor, then the misdemeanor merges into the felony, and the person can be convicted of the felony but not the misdemeanor. However, if the crimes are of the same degree, i.e., all felonies or all misdemeanors, then there is no merger of the crimes.

Modern law does not subscribe to the doctrine of merger based on the felony-misdemeanor distinction, but does apply this doctrine with respect to solicitation and attempt and the solicited or completed crime. A defendant may be tried, but not punished, for solicitation and the completed crime or for attempt and the completed crime. Solicitation and attempt are said to "merge" into the completed crime.

Contrast conspiracy: Unlike a solicitation and attempt conviction, a conviction for conspiracy does **not** merge into a conviction for the completed crime.

Under the MPC, a defendant may be concurrently prosecuted, but not punished, for more than one inchoate offense (i.e., solicitation, conspiracy, and attempt) based on conduct designed to culminate in the commission of the same crime. MPC 5.05(3). At common law, conspiracy and attempt do not merge.

Note: The Double Jeopardy Clause generally prohibits a defendant from being convicted of both a crime and a lesser-included offense (i.e., an offense all the elements of which are also elements of the more-significant crime), such as robbery and larceny. Many jurisdictions characterize this prohibition as a "merger" of the lesser-included offense into the greater. For further discussion of double jeopardy, please refer to the Themis Criminal Procedure outline.

B.   SOLICITATION

Solicitation is the:

i)   Enticing, encouraging, requesting, or commanding of another person;

ii)   To commit a crime;

iii) With the intent that the other person commits the crime.

1.   Encouragement

The encouragement may take the form of enticement, incitement, request, or command. The crime is completed upon the encouragement. The other person need not agree to commit the crime.

2.   Relationship to Other Crimes

If the other person does agree, then the solicitor and the person solicited may also become co-conspirators.

3.   Defenses to Solicitation

a.   Renunciation

At common law, renunciation was no defense to solicitation. Under the Model Penal Code, voluntary renunciation may be a defense, provided the defendant thwarts the commission of the solicited crime. MPC § 5.02(3).

b. Factual impossibility

Factual impossibility is not a defense to solicitation. If a solicitor is part of a group that was meant to be exempted by the statute, then the solicitor cannot be guilty of solicitation (e.g., a minor female soliciting sex cannot be guilty of statutory rape).

C. CONSPIRACY

Conspiracy is:

i) An agreement;

ii) Between two or more persons;

iii) To accomplish an unlawful purpose;

iv) With the intent to accomplish that purpose.

The majority rule and federal law, as well as the MPC, now require the commission of an overt act, which can be legal or illegal, in furtherance of the conspiracy to complete the formation of the conspiracy. At common law, no overt act was required for the conspiracy to be complete.

EXAM NOTE: Remember, unless the question specifically indicates that the majority rule is being tested, apply the rule of common-law conspiracy on the MBE. The common-law rule does not require the commission of an overt act in furtherance of the conspiracy for the crime to be complete.

---

1. Agreement

The agreement need not be a formal document, or even in writing; an oral agreement is sufficient. An agreement need not be specifically articulated but can be inferred from a concerted action by the defendants.

2. Number of Conspirators

At common law, there is no such thing as a unilateral conspiracy because two or more persons are required to form a conspiracy. This is often referred to as a "bilateral" approach to or theory of conspiracy.

However, the modern trend and the MPC is to allow a "unilateral" conspiracy. Under this approach, the focus of liability is on the individual defendant and his agreement to the object of the conspiracy. A unilateral conspiracy may be formed when *only one party* actually agrees, such as when another party merely feigns agreement, or if the alleged co-conspirators are ultimately acquitted.

a. Feigned agreement

When only one conspirator has the intent to agree, such as when the other conspirator is a governmental agent or pretends to go along with the crime to warn police, there is a conspiracy under the "unilateral" approach but there is no conspiracy at common law unless another participant is involved.

b. Protected by statute

When the purpose of a criminal statute is to protect a type of person (e.g., a statutory rape statute protects the underage participant), there is no conspiracy between the protected party and the targeted defendant.

c. Wharton Rule

Under the Wharton Rule, if a crime requires two or more participants (e.g., adultery) there is no conspiracy unless more parties than are necessary to complete the crime agree to commit the crime. Although there is no conspiracy, the participants may be found guilty of the underlying crime itself. Because the MPC does not require the participation of at least two conspirators, this rule does not apply to conspiracies under the MPC.

d. Corporation and its agents

A corporation can conspire with its own agents with some limitations. In some jurisdictions, there can be no conspiracy between a corporation and a single agent of that corporation. A conspiracy between the corporation and multiple agents of the same corporation may, in most jurisdictions, satisfy the plurality requirement. A corporation or its agents can enter into a conspiracy with another corporation or agents of that corporation.

e. Prosecution of other conspirators

A conspirator cannot be convicted of conspiracy if all other conspirators are acquitted at the same trial. In other circumstances, such as when co-conspirators are never tried or apprehended, a conspirator may be convicted of conspiracy if the prosecution proves the existence of a conspiracy.

f. Spouses as co-conspirators

Common law did not consider husband and wife as co-conspirators because the law viewed them as a single entity. However, they could, as an entity, conspire with a third person. Nearly every jurisdiction has abolished this common-law concept.

3. Unlawful Purpose

Under federal law and the modern trend, "unlawful purpose" is limited to criminal conduct. In some states, even the achievement of a lawful purpose through illegal means can be the subject of a conspiracy.

4. Specific Intent

Conspiracy is a specific-intent crime. A conspirator must have the intent to agree and the intent to commit the criminal objective. The intent to agree may be inferred from the conduct of the parties.

Example: Conspiracy to commit arson requires specific intent, even though the substantive offense of arson only requires malice. Similarly, a conspiracy to commit a strict-liability crime requires intent.

Because intent to agree and to commit the crime are elements of conspiracy, criminal liability for a conspiracy cannot be based solely on knowledge of the existence of the conspiracy. For example, a merchant who supplies goods to a conspirator knowing that the conspirator intends to use the goods in furtherance of the objective of the conspiracy is not a member of the conspiracy simply because the merchant possessed such knowledge. Instead, the merchant must take an additional step to show such intent, such as selling the goods at an exorbitant price, basing the price of the goods on a percentage of the conspiracy's "take," or ordering specially manufactured goods that the merchant does not normally sell.

5. Overt Act Requirement

An overt act was not required at common law, but it is now a required element of a conspiracy under federal law, the MPC, and in a majority of states. When an overt act is required, the conspiracy crime is not complete until the overt act is performed in furtherance of the conspiracy. The overt act can be performed by any co-conspirator, with or without the knowledge of all co-conspirators. The overt act can be lawful or unlawful. However, the MPC does not require an overt act if the conspiratorial crime is a felony in the first or second degree.

Contrast attempt: To constitute attempt, the defendant must have taken a substantial step toward commission of the crime. A mere preparatory act is insufficient for attempt.

6. Scope of Conspiracy

a. Crimes committed by co-conspirators

Under the *Pinkerton* Rule, a conspirator can be convicted of both the offense of conspiracy and all substantive crimes committed by any other co-conspirators acting in furtherance of the conspiracy. Under the MPC, the minority view, a member of the conspiracy is not criminally liable for such crimes unless that member aids and abets in the commission of the crimes.

b. Multiple crimes, single conspiracy

A single conspiracy may have numerous criminal objectives. Not all of the co-conspirators even need to know the identities of all of the other co-conspirators or all of the details of the criminal organization. It is only necessary that all co-conspirators agree to further the common scheme or plan. Multiple conspiracies arise when the objectives and/or crimes are not committed in furtherance of the same agreement, common scheme, and plan.

c. Unknown conspirators, single conspiracy

1) Chain relationship

Persons who do not know each other can be members of the same conspiracy if there is a **community of interest** in the achievement of the object of the conspiracy. A community of interest is usually found when the activities of each person resemble links of a chain, such as a scheme to acquire and distribute drugs. In such a conspiracy, all of the members of the community of interest are liable for the acts of the others in furtherance of the conspiracy.

2) Hub-spoke relationship

A scheme that resembles a hub with spokes, such as the processing of fraudulent loans by one person that were submitted by numerous other individuals, is less likely to have a community of interest. In such a case, the "hub" and each "spoke" are usually treated as having formed a separate conspiracy from all of the other hub-spoke combinations. Thus, the common hub will be liable for all of the conspiracies, but the spoke members are not liable for the acts of the other conspirators.

7. Impossibility

Factual impossibility (that it was factually impossible to complete the intended crime) is not a defense to conspiracy. Legal impossibility (that the intended act is not criminal in nature) may be a defense if the object of the agreement is not a crime.

8. Withdrawal

a. Effect on liability for conspiracy

At common law, withdrawal was not a defense to conspiracy because the conspiracy is complete as soon as the parties enter into the agreement. Under the federal rule, which is also the majority rule, a conspiracy does not come into existence until an overt act has been committed. Consequently, after there has been an agreement but before an overt act has been committed, a person may avoid criminal liability for conspiracy by communicating notice of his intent not to participate to the other potential co-conspirators or by informing the police about the agreement. Upon completion of the overt act, the conspiracy is formed, and withdrawal is no longer possible. Under the MPC and the minority view, subsequent withdrawal is possible only if the defendant acts voluntarily to "thwart the success" of the conspiracy.

b. Effect on liability for substantive crimes

A defendant may limit his liability as a co-conspirator for the substantive crimes that are the subject of the conspiracy by withdrawing from the conspiracy at any time after it is formed. For this purpose, he may withdraw by giving notice to his co-conspirators or timely advising legal authorities of the existence of the conspiracy even though such an action does not thwart the conspiracy.

> While a defendant is not liable as a co-conspirator for crimes committed in furtherance of the conspiracy after an effective withdrawal from the conspiracy, the defendant may nevertheless be liable as an accomplice for subsequent crimes committed by his former co-conspirators for which he has given aid. (*See* I.D.2.c. "Withdrawal," *supra*.)

9. Termination

It is important to determine when a conspiracy ends for the purposes of determining the statute of limitations and the admissibility of acts or declarations made by the conspirators in furtherance of the crime. Generally, the act of concealing the conspiracy is not treated as a part of the conspiracy.

10. Punishment

Jurisdictions vary widely with respect to penalty provisions for conspiracies. Some jurisdictions make conspiracy a misdemeanor regardless of the objective, while other jurisdictions provide maximum sentencing depending on the objective. Still others allow for a permissible maximum sentence, regardless of the objective. Nevertheless, sometimes the sentencing for conspiracy is more severe than the punishment for the crime itself.

D. ATTEMPT

An attempt requires:

i) A **substantial step** toward the commission of a crime; coupled with

ii) The **specific intent** to commit the crime.

If the crime is successfully completed, the attempt is merged into the completed crime.

1. Substantial Step Test

A subjective test, called the "substantial step" test, is applied to determine whether an attempt has occurred. Under this test, conduct does not constitute a substantial step if it is in mere preparation; the act must be conduct that tends to effect the commission of a crime.

a. Acts

Any of the following acts may constitute a substantial step if they corroborate the defendant's criminal purpose (from the MPC):

i) Lying in wait, searching for, or following the intended victim;

ii) Unlawful entry into the place contemplated for the commission of the crime;

iii) Enticing the intended victim to go to such place;

iv) Possession of materials specially designed for committing the crime;

v) Possession of materials to be used in the commission of the crime at or near the place of commission; and

vi) Soliciting an innocent agent to engage in criminal conduct.

b. "Dangerous proximity" test

Some states continue to apply the traditional common-law "dangerous proximity" test. Under this test, an attempt does not occur until the defendant's acts result in a dangerous proximity to completion of the crime.

2. Specific Intent

The defendant must possess the specific intent to perform an act or attain a result, which, if completed, would constitute the target crime, even if the target crime is not a specific-intent crime.

Example: Arson is not a specific-intent crime, but attempted arson is. An attempt to commit a strict-liability crime is also a specific-intent crime.

There is no attempt to commit negligent crimes like involuntary manslaughter because a defendant's act cannot be both intentional and negligent.

3. Impossibility

Impossibility is not a defense to attempt if the crime attempted is factually impossible to commit due to circumstances unknown to the defendant. If, however, the act intended is not a crime (i.e., a legal impossibility), then the defendant is not guilty of attempt. In such a case, even when statutes purport to have done away with the impossibility defense, there is always a provision that allows for legal impossibility.

Example: D shoots V, believing that V is sleeping. V actually was already dead. D is guilty of attempted murder, but not murder.

4. Abandonment

At common law, once the defendant has taken a substantial step toward the commission of the offense, the defendant may not legally abandon the attempt to commit the crime because of a change of heart. Upon the completion of a substantial step, the crime of attempt is completed; there can be no abandonment or withdrawal.

Some states do recognize voluntary abandonment as a defense to attempt. Even then, abandonment is not voluntary if it is motivated by a desire to avoid detection, a decision to delay commission of the crime until a more favorable time, or the selection of another similar objective or victim. Abandonment by the defendant does not constitute a defense for an accomplice who did not join in the abandonment or withdrawal.

5. Prosecution and Punishment

A defendant who does not complete a crime may be charged only with attempt of the completed crime. Punishment for attempt is usually less severe than the sentence for the completed offense.

If a defendant completes a crime, he may be charged with both attempt of the completed crime and with the completed crime itself, but he may be convicted of only one.

V. DEFENSES

A. GENERALLY

1. Justification and Excuse

Defenses may be divided into the categories of justification and excuse. When the defendant's actions, despite being criminal, are socially acceptable, the defendant has acted justifiably. Self-defense and defense of others are examples of justification defenses. When the defendant has a disability that makes her not responsible for her actions, the defendant's criminal behavior is excused. Insanity, intoxication, and duress are examples of excuse defenses. This distinction does not affect the applicability or operation of these defenses.

2. Mistake of Fact

When a defendant is factually mistaken (e.g., the defendant thinks that the victim is holding a pistol that instead is a toy gun), the defendant may generally rely on a defense if the mistake is a reasonable one. In determining the reasonableness of the mistake, the defendant's physical characteristics, experiences, and knowledge are taken into account. An unreasonable factual mistake is a defense only to a specific-intent crime.

B. SPECIFIC DEFENSES

1. Self-Defense

One who is not the aggressor is justified in using reasonable force against another person to prevent immediate unlawful harm to himself. The harm to the defendant must be imminent, not a threat of future harm. The defendant can use only as much force as is required to repel the attack.

a. Deadly force

Deadly force is force that is intended or likely to cause death or serious bodily injury. Deadly force may be justified in self-defense only when it is reasonably necessary to prevent death or serious injury or to prevent the commission of a serious felony involving a risk to human life.

b. Nondeadly force

Nondeadly force is force that is not intended or likely to cause death or serious bodily injury and may be used to repel nondeadly force.

c. Retreat

There is never an obligation to retreat before employing nondeadly force. Under the majority view, retreat is not required even when deadly force is used in self-defense. Under the minority view (states that follow the so-called "retreat doctrine"), retreat is required if it can be safely accomplished. Even under the minority view, however, retreat is never required when the person employing deadly force is in his own home (i.e., the "castle doctrine").

d. Imperfect right of self-defense

Imperfect self-defense occurs when the person claiming self-defense unjustifiably kills the attacker. The purpose of the rule is to reduce the charge from murder to voluntary manslaughter. The rule, adopted in most states, is applied when the defendant cannot claim perfect self-defense for some reason. For example, a defendant honestly but unreasonably believes that deadly force is required to prevent death or serious bodily injury.

e. Aggressor's right to use self-defense

It is possible for an initial aggressor to gain the right to act in self-defense in two circumstances: (i) an aggressor using nondeadly force is met with deadly force, or (ii) the aggressor has, in good faith, completely withdrawn from the altercation and has communicated that fact to the victim.

2. Defense of Others

A person has the right to defend others under the same circumstances in which self-defense would be acceptable. Defense of others is not limited to defending family members but extends to anyone the defendant reasonably believes has the right of self-defense.

3. Defense of Property

A person in lawful possession of property that is threatened by the conduct of another, and who has no time to seek assistance from law enforcement, may take reasonable steps, including the use of nondeadly force, to protect the property. To use force, the defender must reasonably believe that the real property is in immediate danger of unlawful trespass or that personal property is in immediate danger of being carried away, and that the use of force is necessary to prevent either. The force cannot be unreasonably disproportionate to the perceived harm.

There is no right to use deadly force in defending property, with one exception. Generally, a person may use deadly force to prevent or terminate forcible entry into a dwelling if the occupant reasonably believes that the intruder intends to commit a felony inside. The use of deadly force against an intruder exiting the dwelling is generally not permissible. A deadly mechanical device cannot be used to protect property, although non-deadly mechanical devices or objects (such as barbed wire) may be used.

4. Arrest

A police officer or a person acting under police direction is justified in using reasonable force to make a lawful arrest or to prevent the escape of one already in lawful custody.

a. Right to arrest

The right of a police officer to arrest a suspect is often specified by statute. A police officer can lawfully arrest a suspect, with or without a warrant, if the suspect has committed a crime in the officer's presence or if the officer has probable cause to believe that the defendant committed a felony offense outside of his presence. A civilian acting without police direction in making an arrest (e.g., a "citizen's arrest") who makes a mistake, even a reasonable mistake, as to the commission of the crime is not entitled to rely on this defense, but may do so if the civilian makes a reasonable mistake as to the identity of the perpetrator of the crime.

b. Use of force to arrest

A police officer can use nondeadly force to arrest a suspect. A police officer can use deadly force to arrest a suspect if the suspect represents a threat to either the officer or third parties.

c. Resisting unlawful arrest

A defendant may use nondeadly force to resist an unlawful arrest, but never deadly force. Some jurisdictions do not permit the use of force at all and require defendants to seek legal redress for an unlawful arrest.

5. Prevention of Crimes

Anyone can use deadly force to prevent the commission of a serious felony involving a risk to human life, and may use nondeadly force to prevent the commission of a felony or a breach-of-the-peace misdemeanor. A private citizen who makes a mistake, even a reasonable mistake, as to the commission of a serious felony by the victim is not entitled to rely on this defense.

6. Public Authority

Actions taken by public officials pursuant to legal authority (e.g., court-ordered seizure of property, state-sanctioned executions) are justified.

7. Parental Authority

The use of reasonable force in the exercise of parental authority (i.e., discipline) by a parent or by a person in charge of a child (e.g., a teacher) is justified if exercised for the benefit of the minor child.

8. Duress

A third party's unlawful threat that causes a defendant to reasonably believe that the only way to avoid death or serious bodily injury to himself or another is to violate the law, and that causes the defendant to do so, allows the defendant to claim the duress defense.

Duress is not a defense to intentional murder. A defendant charged with felony murder may claim duress as a defense to the underlying felony and avoid conviction for felony murder.

9. Necessity

If the forces of nature (e.g., storm, fire) cause the defendant to commit what would otherwise be a crime, the defendant may be justified in doing so based upon necessity. The law prefers that the defendant, when faced with two evils, avoids the greater evil by choosing the lesser evil, e.g., the destruction of property to prevent the spread of a fire.

The defendant is not entitled to assert necessity if he set the natural forces in motion (e.g., set the fire) or if there is a reasonably apparent noncriminal alternative. In addition, economic necessity does not justify theft. For example, an unemployed worker may not steal food from the grocery store.

Necessity is a result of natural forces; duress results from human actions.

Note, though, that the MPC does not explicitly limit the defense of necessity to natural forces.

> **EXAM NOTE:** While the defendant may escape criminal liability, the defendant may be compelled by tort law to reimburse the victim for any losses.

10. Consent

Consent of the victim is not a defense to a crime unless the consent negates a required element of the crime or precludes the harm sought to be avoided by the crime. Such consent must be voluntarily and freely given, involve no fraud, and be given by one competent to consent.

Consent is a defense to rape (unless the woman is a minor), since rape is defined as sexual intercourse without consent. Consent is also a defense to kidnapping if an adult (but not a minor) consents to traveling with the defendant.

a. Bodily injury

Consent to bodily injury or to conduct that may cause bodily injury may constitute a defense when the injury is not serious or, with regard to a sporting event or similar activity, the conduct and injury are reasonably foreseeable (e.g., boxing).

b. Ineffective consent

Consent may be ineffective when given by a legally incompetent person; by a victim who is unable to make a reasonable judgment due to age, mental disease or defect, or intoxication; or by a victim whom the law seeks to protect. Consent obtained by fraud, duress, or deception may also be ineffective.

11. Entrapment

Entrapment is the conception and planning of an offense by a law-enforcement officer, and his procurement of its commission by a defendant who would not have committed that offense except for the trickery, persuasion, or fraud of the officer. If an officer merely offers an already-predisposed person the opportunity to commit a crime, it is not entrapment. In other words, the defendant must lack any predisposition to commit the crime. Entrapment can occur through the use of an undercover agent but not by a private citizen. The modern trend allows a defendant to deny participation in an event, yet still raise the defense of entrapment. Traditionally, the defendant was precluded from using the entrapment defense if he denied his participation in the event.

a. Subjective approach

The majority of states and the U.S. Supreme Court have adopted the subjective test for entrapment. Under this approach, the **focus is on the defendant**. Entrapment occurs when (i) the crime is induced by a government official or agent, and (ii) the **defendant was not predisposed** (i.e., ready and willing) to commit the crime. If a defendant is predisposed to committing the crime, then the entrapment defense is not available, even if the government agent has engaged in misconduct, such as by supplying contraband. *Hampton v. United States*, 425 U.S. 484 (1976).

b. Objective approach

Under the objective approach, which has been advanced by the MPC and adopted by a few states, the **focus is on the government's action** and the effect those actions would have on a hypothetical innocent person. This approach requires the government official or agent to have induced or encouraged the defendant to commit a crime by employing methods of persuasion or inducement that **create a substantial risk** that the crime will be committed by an otherwise law-abiding citizen.

12. Alibi

An alibi is a defense whereby a defendant denies his participation in a crime because he asserts that he was elsewhere when the alleged crime was committed. An alibi is not an affirmative defense; the defendant is not required to prove that he was elsewhere when the crime was committed. Instead, the burden remains on the prosecution to prove that the defendant was the person who committed the crime.

Criminal Procedure

CRIMINAL PROCEDURE

Table of Contents

CRIMINAL PROCEDURE

I. FOURTH AMENDMENT: APPLICATION TO ARREST, SEARCH AND SEIZURE

The Fourth Amendment reads: "The right of the people to be secure in their persons, houses, papers, and effects against unreasonable searches and seizures shall not be violated, and no Warrants shall issue, but on probable cause, supported by Oath or affirmation, and particularly describing the place to be searched, and the persons or things to be seized." This amendment protects persons against unreasonable arrests or other seizures as well as unreasonable searches. In addition, when a warrant is required, it must comply with these constitutional requirements.

A. GENERAL FOURTH AMENDMENT PRINCIPLES

1. Standing

Fourth Amendment rights are personal and may not be asserted vicariously. A defendant cannot successfully challenge governmental conduct as a violation of the Fourth Amendment protection against unreasonable searches and seizures unless the defendant himself has been seized or he has a reasonable expectation of privacy with regard to the place searched or the item seized. It is not enough that the introduction as evidence of an item seized may incriminate the defendant.

Example: Defendants Al and Bob are accused of burglarizing an electronics store. Police found stolen DVD players in Al's apartment after an illegal warrantless search. Only Al has standing to raise the issue of a Fourth Amendment violation; Bob may not raise it in his own defense, as his rights were not violated.

2. The Exclusionary Rule

The right to be free from unreasonable searches and seizures must be distinguished from the remedy. The primary remedy is the "exclusionary rule," which prevents the introduction at a subsequent criminal trial of evidence unlawfully seized. This remedy is judicially created, not constitutionally mandated. The remedy provided by the exclusionary rule generally applies to criminal trials; it **does not apply** in other court proceedings, including federal habeas corpus review of state convictions, grand jury proceedings, preliminary hearings, bail hearings, sentencing hearings, and proceedings to revoke parole. Evidence will also not be excluded at trial when introduced as impeachment evidence against the defendant. Finally, the exclusionary rule is not applicable to civil proceedings. *See* § I.C.6., Exclusionary Rule, *infra,* for an expanded discussion.

3. Standard of Review

The judge, not the jury, resolves suppression issues raised by a pretrial motion to suppress. A pretrial motion to suppress often involves a mixed question of fact and law. On appeal, the judge's rulings as to questions of law are reviewed de novo; factual findings are reviewed only for clear error. *Ornelas v. United States*, 517 U.S. 690 (1996).

4. Threshold of Governmental Action

The Fourth Amendment limits governmental action; it does not restrict the acts of private parties unless the private person is acting as an "instrument or agent of the government." Even if governmental action exists, there still is no constitutional violation unless the individual had a reasonable expectation of privacy and either the police did not have a valid warrant or they executed an invalid warrantless search.

> **EXAM NOTE:** Remember, the Fourth Amendment applies only to searches and seizures conducted by police or someone acting under police direction.

5. Grand Jury Subpoena

Unless a grand jury subpoena is being used for harassment or is extremely broad, requiring a person to appear before the grand jury under such subpoena does not fall under the protection of the Fourth Amendment.

6. Broader Rights Possible Under State Constitution

A state may grant broader rights under its own constitution than are granted by the federal Constitution. *See Michigan v. Long*, 463 U.S. 1032 (1983). Thus, even though the Fourth (or Fifth or Sixth) Amendment may not restrict the state government, state constitutional law may.

B. ARREST: UNREASONABLE SEIZURE OF PERSONS

1. Seizure: Objective Test—Not Free to Leave

A person is seized by the police when the officer physically touches a subject or when the subject submits to the officer's show of authority. *Terry v. Ohio*, 392 U.S. 1 (1968). When the actions of the police do not show an unambiguous intent to restrain or when the individual's submission to a show of governmental authority takes the form of passive acquiescence, a seizure occurs only if, in view of the totality of the circumstances, a **reasonable innocent person would believe he was not free to leave.** The test is whether a reasonable person would feel free to decline the officers' requests or otherwise terminate the encounter.

a. Intentional detention

The police officer must intentionally employ physical force or a show of authority in order for the officer's actions to result in a seizure.

> **Example:** During a high-speed chase, an officer forced the driver of the pursued automobile off the road. The officer's intentional use of deadly force against the driver constituted a seizure. *Scott v. Harris*, 550 U.S. 372 (2007).

> **Compare:** During a high-speed chase, an officer accidentally struck and killed the passenger of the pursued motorcycle when the motorcycle tipped over. The officer's accidental use of deadly force against the passenger did not constitute a seizure. *County of Sacramento v. Lewis*, 523 U.S. 833 (1998).

However, as long as the officer intentionally employs force or makes a show of authority, the officer's purpose need not be to detain the defendant in order for the defendant to be seized. Consequently, when a police officer makes a traffic stop, not only the driver but also any passengers are deemed to be seized. Therefore, the passenger as well as the driver may challenge the constitutionality of the stop. *Brendlin v. California*, 551 U.S. 249, 251 (2007).

2. Contrast Stop and Frisk

A temporary detention for the purpose of a criminal investigation is a "stop," not an arrest, but is still a seizure for Fourth Amendment purposes. The test for a stop is whether the officer, by means of physical force or show of authority (to which the subject has submitted), has in some way restrained the liberty of the citizen. Seizure includes physical restraint or an order to stop so that the officer can frisk and ask questions on the street.

3. Arrest Warrants

An arrest warrant is issued by a detached and neutral magistrate upon a finding of probable cause that a crime has been committed and that this person was involved in committing the particular crime. However, an arrest made pursuant to a warrant that failed to satisfy the probable cause requirement is not illegal when the officer making the arrest independently had probable cause for making the arrest.

a. Entry into home

A warrant to arrest an individual implicitly authorizes entry into the arrestee's home to serve the warrant if the police have reason to believe that the arrestee is present. A police officer may not arrest a person in another person's home without an arrest warrant for the subject and a search warrant for the third party's home, absent exigent circumstances or valid consent to enter the third party's home. *Steagald v. United States*, 451 U.S. 204 (1981).

4. Warrantless Arrests

Unlike searches, police generally do not need a warrant to make a valid arrest **in a public place,** even if they have time to get one. *U.S. v. Watson*, 423 U.S. 411 (1976). The police, however, must have a warrant to arrest an individual in his own home, absent exigent circumstances or valid consent to enter the arrestee's home. *Payton v. New York*, 445 U.S. 573 (1980).

a. Crime committed in the presence of the arresting party

Either a police officer or a private individual has a right to arrest without an arrest warrant if either a felony or a misdemeanor is committed in the arresting party's presence. In determining whether a crime has been committed, the question is whether an officer could conclude—considering all of the surrounding circumstances—that there was a substantial chance of criminal activity. *District of Columbia v. Wesby*, 583 U.S. ___ (2018).

b. Crime committed outside the presence of the arresting party

In situations in which a **felony** has been committed outside the presence of the one making the arrest, a police officer may arrest anyone whom he has probable cause to believe has committed a felony, but a private individual may make an arrest only if (i) a felony has actually been committed and (ii) the private individual reasonably believes that the person being arrested is guilty.

c. Misdemeanor arrest

A warrantless arrest of a person for a misdemeanor punishable only by a fine is not an unreasonable seizure under the Fourth Amendment. *Atwater v. Lago Vista*, 532 U.S. 318 (2001). Note that the misdemeanor must have been committed in the presence of the arresting party; probable cause to believe that a misdemeanor was committed, without actually witnessing the crime, is not sufficient for a valid warrantless arrest.

d. Effect of invalid arrest

An unlawful arrest alone has **no bearing** on a subsequent criminal prosecution, and it is not a defense to the crime charged. If the police have probable cause to detain a suspect, they may do so even if they illegally arrested him (e.g., in his home without a warrant).

An unlawful arrest has legal significance, however, when there is a seizure of evidence. Evidence seized pursuant to an unlawful arrest may be suppressed at trial. A voluntary confession made after an unlawful arrest will not automatically be suppressed. Note, however, that the unlawfulness of the arrest may be considered as a factor when determining whether a confession was truly voluntary. If the confession is too closely tied to the illegal arrest, it may be suppressed. *See Wong Sun v. U.S.,* 371 U.S. 471 (1963).

C. SEARCH AND SEIZURE

1. Governmental Action

Searches conducted by private citizens are not protected by the Fourth Amendment—there must be governmental action. However, the police may not circumvent the Fourth Amendment by intentionally enlisting private individuals to conduct a search of a suspect or areas in which the suspect has a reasonable expectation of privacy.

2. Defining "Search": The Violation of a Reasonable Expectation of Privacy

Only **unreasonable** searches and seizures are subject to Fourth Amendment protections. An unreasonable search occurs when the government (1) invades a place protected by a **reasonable expectation of privacy,** or (2) **physically intrudes** upon a constitutionally protected area (persons, houses, papers, or effects) for the purpose of gathering information. *Katz v. United States,* 389 U.S. 347 (1967); *Florida v. Jardines,* 569 U.S. 1 (2013) (using a drug-sniffing dog on a homeowner's porch for the purpose of investigating the contents of the home constituted a search); *United States v. Jones,* 565 U.S. 400 (2012) (placement of GPS device on defendant's vehicle for the purpose of monitoring the vehicle's movements constituted a search).

> **EXAM NOTE:** Be aware of fact patterns that involve an individual with no expectation of privacy, such as when incriminating evidence is seized at another individual's home. Remember that the government's action is valid unless there is a legitimate expectation of privacy or the government trespassed upon the defendant's private property.

a. Locations searched

1) Home

Although the Supreme Court has stated that "the Fourth Amendment protects people, not places," (see *id.* at 351), the Fourth Amendment, by its terms, protects against an unreasonable governmental search of a "house." This protection extends to persons who have the right to immediate possession of a dwelling, such as the renter of an apartment or a dormitory. *Chapman v. United States,* 365 U.S. 610 (1961).

a) Curtilage

In addition to the home itself, an area immediately surrounding the home known as the "curtilage" may be covered by the "umbrella" of the home's Fourth Amendment protection.

In determining whether the area is protected, the following four-factor test applies:

i) The proximity of the area to the home;

ii) Whether the area is included within an enclosure surrounding the home;

iii) The nature of the uses to which the area is put; and

iv) The steps taken by the resident to protect the area from observation by passersby.

United States v. Dunn, 480 U.S. 294 (1987).

> **Example:** A barn was 60 yards away from the main house and 50 yards away from the innermost fence surrounding the house. The barn was not being used for domestic purposes and, despite being surrounded by a fence, was fenced in a manner that did not prevent persons from observing what lay inside the fence. Consequently, the barn and the area immediately surrounding it lay outside the curtilage. Information of illegal drug activity being conducted within the barn gained by drug enforcement agents while within that area did not constitute an unreasonable search. *Id.*

b) Open fields

Private property that lies outside the curtilage of a home, such as a farmer's field, is not protected by the home's umbrella of Fourth Amendment protection. Under the "open fields" doctrine, governmental intrusion on such property is not a search. The owner does **not** have a reasonable (i.e., objective) expectation of privacy, even though the owner may have a subjective expectation of privacy based on the fact that the land is fenced, protected from public view, and "no trespassing" signs are posted. *United States v. Oliver*, 466 U.S. 170 (1984).

c) Overnight guest in a home

While an overnight guest in a home does not have an ownership interest in the home, such a guest does have a reasonable expectation of privacy, at least as to the areas of the home to which the guest has permission to enter. *Minnesota v. Olson*, 495 U.S. 91 (1990). (As to the ability of the owner or guest to consent to a search of the home, *see* § I.C.4.f, Consent searches, *infra*.)

> **Contrast short-term use of home for illegal business purpose:** Short-term use of a home (e.g., several hours) with the permission of the owner does not give rise to a reasonable expectation of privacy, at least when the home is being used for an illegal business purpose (e.g., bagging cocaine for sale on the streets). *Minnesota v. Carter*, 525 U.S. 83 (1998).

2) Motel room

As with the search of a home, the search of a motel room by a government agent may be an unreasonable search. A motel clerk's consent to a governmental search of a room during the time it is rented is insufficient to justify the search. *Stoner v. California*, 376 U.S. 483 (1964).

3) Business premises

In general, business premises are protected by the Fourth Amendment. *G.M. Leasing Corp. v. United States*, 429 U.S. 338 (1977). However, such premises may be subjected to administrative searches, *see* § I.C.4.g., Administrative searches, *infra*.

4) Prison

A prison inmate has no reasonable expectation of privacy in his cell. The limitations on Fourth Amendment rights are justified by the need to maintain institutional security and preserve internal order and discipline. *Hudson v. Palmer*, 468 U.S. 517 (1984). Unlike a convict, a pretrial detainee may have a limited expectation of privacy in his cell. However, a detainee's cell may be subject to a routine search, and the detainee's person may be subject to a strip search or a full-body search after a contact visit with someone from the outside. *Bell v. Wolfish*, 441 U.S. 520 (1979). Jail administrators may also require all arrestees committed to the general population of a jail to undergo no-touch visual strip searches, even if the arrest was for a minor offense and even in the absence of reasonable suspicion that the arrestee possesses a concealed weapon or other contraband. *Florence v. Board of Chosen Freeholders of County of Burlington*, 566 U.S. 318 (2012).

5) Trespass

While the fact that a governmental agent is on property without permission may make a warrantless search unreasonable (e.g., a search of a home), the fact that a governmental agent is illegally on property does not automatically make the search illegal (*United States v. Oliver, supra*), nor does the fact that a governmental agent is legally in a public place make the search legal (*Katz v. United States, supra*).

b. Objects sought

1) Papers and effects

The Fourth Amendment, by its terms, protects "papers and effects." For example, a person retains a reasonable expectation that items placed within his luggage will be free from a purposeful, exploratory physical manipulation of the luggage. *Bond v. United States*, 529 U.S. 334 (2000).

Compare smell emanating from object. A person does *not* have a reasonable expectation of privacy with regard to a smell emanating from his luggage, at least when the smell arises from an illegal substance. *United States v. Place*, 462 U.S. 696 (1983).

When papers and effects are transferred to a third party, such as checks and deposit slips given by a customer to a bank, a person no longer has a reasonable expectation of privacy in these items. Similarly, financial statements maintained by a bank are bank records in which the customer has no reasonable expectation of privacy. *United States v. Miller*, 425 U.S. 435 (1976).

Example: A defendant who hides drugs in a friend's purse in order to avoid their detection by police has no legitimate expectation of privacy in the purse. *Rawlings v. Kentucky*, 448 U.S. 98 (1980).

2) Automobiles

Although, under the Fourth Amendment, stopping a car constitutes a seizure of the driver and any passengers, *Brendlin v. California*, 551 U.S. 249 (2007) (passenger), *Delaware v. Prouse*, 440 U.S. 648 (1979) (driver), there is a lesser expectation of privacy with regard to the automobile and its contents than with a home. *Wyoming v. Houghton*, 526 U.S. 295 (1999). Even so, officers must have an articulable, reasonable suspicion of a violation of the law in order to stop an automobile. A call to 911 reporting erratic driving may give the police the reasonable suspicion needed to make a traffic stop if the report is reliable. *Navarette v. California*, 572 U.S. 393 (2014). The fact that a person who is in lawful possession of a rental car is not listed on the rental agreement does not defeat his or her otherwise reasonable expectation of privacy. *Byrd v. United States*, 584 U.S. ___ (2018).

a) Checkpoints

Police may stop an automobile at a checkpoint without reasonable, individualized suspicion of a violation of the law if the stop is based on neutral, articulable standards and its purpose is closely related to an issue affecting automobiles. A roadblock to perform sobriety checks has been upheld, while a similar roadblock to perform drug checks has not. *Compare Michigan Dept. of State Police v. Sitz*, 496 U.S. 444 (1990) (sobriety check) *with Indianapolis v. Edmond*, 531 U.S. 32 (2000) (check for presence of illegal drugs).

Compare random stops: Police may generally *not* stop an automobile, even for a driving-related matter, without a reasonable, individualized suspicion of a violation of the law, unless the stop is effected on the basis of neutral, articulable standards. *Delaware v. Prouse*, 440 U.S. 648 (1979) (no random stop of a driver to verify driver's license and car registration).

i) Immigration law enforcement

When the purpose of the stop relates to the enforcement of immigration laws, any car may be stopped on a random basis at the border of the United States without a reasonable suspicion of wrongdoing. *Almeida-Sanchez v. United States*, 413 U.S. 266 (1973). When a search does not occur at the border or its functional equivalent, all cars may be stopped at a fixed checkpoint without a reasonable suspicion of violation of an immigration law, but a car may not be singled out and randomly stopped without a particularized and objective basis. *United States v. Cortez*, 449 U.S. 411 (1981) (holding the stop of one car proper when officers could reasonably surmise that the car was involved in criminal immigration activity); *United States v. Martinez-Fuerte*, 428 U.S. 543 (1976) (affirming convictions based on stops at checkpoints at which all cars were stopped).

ii) Search for witnesses

A checkpoint maintained by police for the purpose of finding witnesses to a crime (rather than suspects) is not per se unreasonable, as long as (i) the checkpoint stop's primary law enforcement purpose is to elicit evidence to help them apprehend not the vehicle's occupants but other individuals; (ii) the stop advanced a public concern to a significant degree; and (iii) the police appropriately tailored their checkpoint stops to fit important criminal investigatory needs and to minimally interfere with liberties protected by the Fourth Amendment. *Illinois v. Lidster*, 540 U.S. 419 (2004).

b) Car's VIN

The driver of a car does not have a reasonable expectation of privacy in the vehicle identification number (VIN) affixed to an automobile. *New York v. Class*, 475 U.S. 106 (1986). Consequently, a police officer's moving of papers that obstructed his view of this number did not constitute a search under the Fourth Amendment, and a gun found while doing so was admissible into evidence.

3) Abandoned property

Abandoned property is not protected by the Fourth Amendment.

> **Example:** There is no reasonable expectation of privacy in garbage set curbside for pickup. *California v. Greenwood*, 486 U.S. 35 (1988).

c. Persons and their attributes

1) Physical characteristics

There is no expectation of privacy in one's physical characteristics; therefore, a demand for a handwriting or voice sample is not a search. *United States v. Mara*, 410 U.S. 19 (1973) (handwriting exemplar); *United States v. Dionisio*, 410 U.S. 1 (1973) (voice exemplar).

Furthermore, DNA identification of arrestees is a reasonable search that can be considered part of a routine booking procedure. When officers make an arrest supported by probable cause and they bring the suspect to the station to be detained in custody, taking and analyzing a cheek swab of the arrestee's DNA is, like fingerprinting and photographing, a legitimate police booking procedure that is reasonable under the Fourth Amendment. *Maryland v. King*, 569 U.S. 435 (2013).

2) Blood samples

Except in unusual situations, blood samples require warrants, but breath samples do not. The involuntary, warrantless blood test of a drunken-driving suspect was appropriate when police could reasonably have believed that the delay necessary to obtain a search warrant would likely result in disappearance of the blood-alcohol content evidence, and the test was administered according to accepted medical practices. *Schmerber v. California*, 384 U.S. 757 (1966). However, the reasonableness of a warrantless blood test is determined case by case, based on the totality of the circumstances. The Fourth Amendment mandates that police officers obtain a warrant before a blood sample can be drawn, if they can reasonably do so without significantly undermining the efficacy of the search. *Birchfield v. North Dakota*, 579 U.S. ___, 136 S. Ct. 2160 (2016); *Missouri v. McNeely*, 569 U.S. 141 (2013).

When a driver is unconscious and cannot be given a breath test, the exigent-circumstances doctrine (discussed *infra*) generally permits a blood test without a warrant. *Mitchell v. Wisconsin*, 588 U.S. ___, 139 S. Ct. 2525 (2019).

3) Government informants

Some surveillance and investigation techniques have been held not to implicate any reasonable expectation of privacy because the targets of the surveillance were regarded as having assumed the risk that the people with whom they were interacting would be government agents. There is no reasonable expectation of privacy in conversations carried on with government informants or undercover officers. Similarly, if one party to a telephone call consents to wiretapping or agrees to record the call at the government's request, such monitoring will not trigger the Fourth Amendment rights of any other party to the call. *United States v. White*, 401 U.S. 745 (1971). A person also runs the risk that a third party to whom she turns over information may disclose such information to the government. *United States v. Miller*, 425 U.S. 435 (1976).

d. Methods used to search

1) Fly-over

An inspection conducted from at least 400 feet in the air, whether by an airplane or a helicopter, does not violate a reasonable expectation of privacy and therefore is not a search for the purposes of the Fourth Amendment. *Florida v. Riley*, 488 U.S. 445 (1989) (helicopter); *California v. Ciraolo*, 476 U.S. 207 (1986) (airplane).

2) Technological device

Attaching a device to a person's body without consent in order to track that person's movements is a search for Fourth Amendment purposes. *Grady v. North Carolina*, 575 U.S. ___, 135 S. Ct. 1368 (2015). Similarly, collection by law enforcement of cell-site location information records from wireless carriers in order to track a suspect's whereabouts requires a warrant. *Carpenter v. United States*, 585 U.S. ___ (2018).

With regard to automobiles, the Fourth Amendment does not prohibit the police from using technological devices to enhance their ability to search (e.g., radar detectors, computers to search license plates, surveillance equipment). *United States v. Knotts*, 460 U.S. 276 (1983) (placement of a tracking device on a car). However, physically intruding upon a suspect's property to install a technological device (e.g., a GPS tracker on a car to gather information) may constitute a search. *United States v. Jones, supra.*

It is important to note the distinction between *Knotts* and *Jones*—in *Knotts*, the device was installed with the permission of the former owner (a person other than the suspect) before the car came into the defendant's possession; defendant Jones, on the other hand, owned the vehicle in question at the time the government installed the GPS device.

The use of a device or sense-enhancing technology (e.g., a thermal sensing device) that is not in use by the general public to explore the details of a dwelling that would previously have been unknowable without physical intrusion constitutes a search. *Kyllo v. United States*, 533 U.S. 27 (2001). Moreover, use of an electronic listening device to eavesdrop on a conversation made from a public phone booth can violate the speaker's reasonable expectation of privacy. *Katz v. United States, supra.*

Flashlight. Because flashlights are ubiquitous, the use of a flashlight at night to illuminate the inside of a car does not constitute a search for Fourth Amendment purposes. *Texas v. Brown*, 460 U.S. 730 (1983).

3) Canine sniff

Use of a trained dog to sniff for the presence of drugs is a search if it involves a **physical intrusion** onto constitutionally protected property. *Florida v. Jardines*, 569 U.S. 1 (2013) (curtilage). In the absence of a physical intrusion, the use of drug-sniffing dogs does not violate a reasonable expectation of privacy. *Illinois v. Caballes*, 543 U.S. 405 (2005) (car); *United States v. Place*, 462 U.S. 696 (1983) (luggage in a public place).

Officer's sense of smell: A police officer may also rely on his own sense of smell in ascertaining the presence of illegal drugs or alcohol. *United States v. Sharpe*, 470 U.S. 675 (1985) (marijuana); *United States v. Ventresca*, 380 U.S. 102, 104, 111 (1965) (alcohol).

4) Field test of substance

A field test performed on a substance to determine if the substance is contraband is not a search for Fourth Amendment purposes. *United States v. Jacobsen*, 466 U.S. 109 (1984).

3. Search Warrant Requirements

When a search occurs, a warrant serves to protect a person's privacy interests against unreasonable governmental intrusion. A valid search warrant must be issued by a neutral and detached magistrate based on probable cause, must be supported by oath or affidavit, and must describe the places to be searched and the items to be seized.

Warrantless searches are per se unreasonable unless the search satisfies one of seven exceptions to the warrant requirement.

a. Probable cause

Facts supporting probable cause may come from any of the following sources:

i) A police officer's personal observations;

ii) Information from a reliable, known informant or from an unknown informant that can be independently verified; or

iii) Evidence seized during stops based on reasonable suspicion, evidence discovered in plain view, or evidence obtained during consensual searches.

1) Right to attack truthfulness of affidavit

Generally, a search warrant that is valid on its face may not be attacked by a defendant as lacking in probable cause. A defendant can challenge a facially valid warrant only when the defendant can establish, by a preponderance of the evidence, that:

i) The affidavit contained **false statements** that were **made** by the affiant **knowingly, intentionally, or with a reckless disregard** for their truth; and

ii) The false statements were **necessary to** the finding of **probable cause.**

Franks v. Delaware, 438 U.S. 154 (1978).

2) Informants

Courts use the **totality of the circumstances** test to determine whether information provided by a police informant is sufficient to create probable cause. The affidavit generally does not need to include any particular information about the informant, including the informant's identity, so long as a neutral magistrate can find that, based on the informant's information and all other available facts, there is probable cause to issue the warrant. *Illinois v. Gates*, 462 U.S. 213 (1983); *McCray v. Illinois*, 386 U.S. 300 (1967).

b. Particularity

A search warrant must describe with particularity the place to be searched and the objects to be seized. *United States v. Grubbs*, 547 U.S. 90 (2006). Warrants that, in addition to describing specific documents to be seized, also refer to "other fruits, instrumentalities and evidence of the crime at this [time] unknown" are not converted into illegal general warrants by the inclusion of such language. The reference to a "crime" has been interpreted as being limited to a particular crime (e.g., false pretenses), rather than any crime. *Andresen v. Maryland*, 427 U.S. 463 (1976). A warrant need not specify the manner of its execution.

c. Anticipatory warrant

Police do not have to believe that contraband is on the premises to be searched at the time the warrant is issued. The probable cause requirement is satisfied when, at the time that the warrant is issued, there is probable cause to believe that the triggering condition will occur and, if that condition does occur, there is a fair probability that contraband or evidence of a crime will be found in a particular place. *United States v. Grubbs, supra*.

d. Third-party premises

A search warrant may be issued to search the premises of a person who is not suspected of a crime. *Zurcher v. Stanford Daily*, 436 U.S. 547 (1978).

e. Execution of warrant

1) By whom

A warrant cannot be executed by a private citizen. Generally, only a police officer may execute a warrant, but administrative warrants may be executed by the appropriate governmental official (e.g., fire inspector).

2) Timing

A warrant that is not timely executed (i.e., an unreasonable delay occurs) may be subject to challenge on the grounds that probable cause ceased to exist.

3) Manner of execution—knock and announce

Most states and the federal government mandate that a police officer, when executing either a search or an arrest warrant, must generally announce his purpose before entering. The knock-and-announce rule gives individuals the opportunity to comply with the law, to avoid the destruction of property occasioned by a forcible entry, and to collect themselves with dignity before answering the door. The rule also serves to protect officers and the inhabitants of the building from physical harm, because an unannounced entry may provoke violence in supposed self-defense by the surprised resident. A state may permit an exception to the rule if the entry is made under exigent circumstances, such as when there is a reasonable belief of danger to the officer or destruction of evidence. *Ker v. California*, 374 U.S. 23, 34 (1963).

Note, however, that the interests protected by the knock-and-announce requirement do not include the shielding of potential evidence from discovery. Thus, violation of the "knock and announce" rule does not trigger the exclusionary rule (*see* § I.C.6., *infra*) with respect to evidence discovered as a result of a search conducted in violation of the "knock and announce" rule. *Hudson v. Michigan*, 547 U.S. 586 (2006).

4) Seizure of evidence not specified

A search warrant confers authority to search only the places and persons named in it. That said, any evidence of a crime, instrumentalities or fruits of a crime, or contraband found in plain view while properly executing the warrant, whether or not specified in the warrant, may be seized (*see* § I.C.4.e., "Plain view" doctrine, *infra*).

5) Treatment of persons not specified in the warrant

Independent justification is needed to search persons not named in a search warrant; mere proximity to a named person does not supply such justification. *Ybarra v. Illinois*, 444 U.S. 84 (1979). However, in conducting a search for contraband pursuant to a warrant, any occupant of the premises to be searched may be detained in a reasonable manner, which may include the use of handcuffs, for a reasonable time while the search is conducted. *Muehler v. Mena*, 544 U.S. 93 (2005); *Michigan v. Summers*, 452 U.S. 692 (1981). Such a detention is only justified for individuals within the immediate vicinity of the premises to be searched. If an individual is not in the immediate vicinity of the premises, then a detention of that individual must be justified by some other rationale. *Bailey v United States*, 568 U.S. 186 (2013) (detaining suspect one mile away from premises was unreasonable).

4. Exceptions to the Warrant Requirement

> **EXAM NOTE:** Warrantless searches are frequently tested on the MBE. Be aware of answer choices that include concepts that apply to one type of warrantless search when another is being tested.

a. Search incident to a lawful arrest

A warrantless search is valid if it is reasonable in scope and if it is made incident to a lawful arrest. If the arrest is invalid, any search made incident to it is likewise invalid. Therefore, if a suspect is stopped for a traffic offense and given a citation but not arrested, then there can be no search incident to lawful arrest. *Knowles v. Iowa*, 525 U.S. 113 (1999).

1) The *Chimel* standard

A lawful arrest creates a situation that justifies a warrantless contemporaneous search of the person arrested and the immediate surrounding area (i.e., his "wingspan") from which a weapon may be concealed or evidence destroyed. *Chimel v. California*, 395 U.S. 752 (1969).

If the arrest occurs in a home, it is permissible to conduct a "protective sweep" for confederates (i.e., people who might launch an attack) in spaces immediately adjacent to the place of arrest, even without probable cause or reasonable suspicion. A "protective sweep" allows a quick and limited visual inspection of those places immediately adjacent to the place of arrest in which a person might be hiding (e.g., adjacent rooms, closets, showers). If the officers have reasonable suspicion that confederates are hiding beyond these immediately adjacent areas, they can broaden their search for people in those places too. *Maryland v. Buie*, 494 U.S. 325, 334 (1990) (finding that after police properly arrested defendant in his home after defendant came up from his basement, the police were permitted to conduct a protective sweep of the basement to ensure their safety).

2) Time limitations (temporal unity)

A search incident to a valid arrest must take place contemporaneously with the arrest in order to be valid.

3) Scope of search

The right to search incident to a lawful arrest includes the right to search pockets of clothing and to open containers found inside the pockets. The right also extends to containers "immediately associated" with the person (such as a shoulder bag or purse).

The search incident to lawful arrest exception does not extend to an arrestee's cell phone or laptop. Absent exigent circumstances, police must obtain a warrant before searching digital information of a person arrested. *Riley v. California*, 573 U.S. 373 (2014).

4) Vehicle search incident to arrest

To justify a warrantless search of an automobile incident to arrest, the Fourth Amendment requires that law enforcement demonstrate either (i) that the arrestee is within reaching distance of the passenger compartment at the time of the search and, as a result, may pose an actual and continuing threat to the officer's safety or a need to preserve evidence from being tampered with by the arrestee or (ii) that it is reasonable that evidence of the offense of arrest might be found in the vehicle. *Arizona v. Gant*, 556 U.S. 332 (2009).

5) Impounded vehicle

A legally impounded vehicle may be searched, including closed containers, such as glove box or a backpack, as part of a routine inventory search. *South Dakota v. Opperman*, 428 U.S. 364, 369–71 (1976). The warrantless search need not take place at the time that the vehicle is seized.

b. Exigent circumstances

Warrantless entry into a home or business is presumed unlawful unless the government demonstrates both probable cause and exigent circumstances. In determining the existence of exigent circumstances, courts use the "totality of circumstances" test. As a corollary to this doctrine, police may also secure the premises for a reasonable time to enable officers to obtain a warrant when the police have reason to believe that the failure to do so could result in the destruction of evidence. *Illinois v. McArthur*, 531 U.S. 326 (2001).

The exigent-circumstances rule does not apply when the police create the exigency by engaging or threatening to engage in conduct that violates the Fourth Amendment. *Kentucky v. King*, 563 U.S. 452 (2011).

1) Hot pursuit

If the police have probable cause to believe that an individual has committed a *felony* and they are pursuing him to arrest him, then they have the right to enter a private building during the pursuit, to search that building for the person or his weapons while they are present on the premises, and to seize evidence found there, even though the material found is "mere" evidence and neither fruits nor instrumentalities of a crime.

No such exigency exists in pursuing someone suspected of a nonjailable traffic offense; the hot-pursuit exception is inapplicable in that instance. *Welsh v. Wisconsin*, 466 U.S. 740 (1984).

2) Emergency situations

A search without a warrant is authorized whenever there is a reasonable apprehension that the delay required in obtaining the warrant would result in the immediate danger of evidence destruction or the threatened safety of the officer or the public, or when a suspect is likely to flee before a warrant can be obtained.

Whether a person is in need of aid is judged on the basis of a police officer's objective reasonable belief that the person needs aid. Aid includes emergency assistance to an injured occupant as well as protection of an occupant from imminent injury. Neither the officer's subjective motive for searching without a warrant nor the seriousness of the crime the officer was originally investigating are relevant in making this determination. *Brigham City v. Stuart*, 547 U.S. 398 (2006).

c. Stop and frisk

1) Stop—limited seizure/detention

A "stop" (also known as a "*Terry* stop") is a limited and temporary intrusion on an individual's freedom of movement short of a full custodial arrest. Merely approaching a person, but not restricting the person's movement in any way, does not constitute a detention. A stop is justified on the **reasonable suspicion,** based upon **articulable facts,** that the detainees are or were involved in criminal activity. *Terry v. Ohio*, 392 U.S. 1 (1968). Whether reasonable suspicion exists is based on the **totality of the circumstances.** It requires more than a vague suspicion, but less than probable cause, and it need not be based on a police officer's personal knowledge.

> **Example:** Police were justified in stopping a suspect who (i) was standing on a street corner in a high-crime area and (ii) fled upon noticing the police, even though neither factor alone would constitute reasonable suspicion to justify a stop. *Illinois v. Wardlow*, 528 U.S. 119 (2000).

Reasonable suspicion can be based on a flyer, a police bulletin, or an informant's tip, but only if the tip is accompanied by sufficient indicia of reliability. *United States v. Hensley*, 469 U.S. 221, 233–34 (1985).

In addition, a police officer's reasonable mistake of law can support reasonable suspicion to conduct a traffic stop. *Heien v. North Carolina*, 574 U.S. 54 (2014).

2) Frisk—limited search

An officer who does not have probable cause to arrest may make a limited search of a person he has lawfully stopped, such as a pat-down of the outer clothing, if he has **reasonable suspicion** that the person was or is involved in criminal activity **and** that the frisk is necessary for the preservation of his safety or the safety of others (i.e., reasonable suspicion that the person has a weapon).

Under the **"plain feel"** exception, if an officer conducting a valid frisk feels with an open hand an object that has physical characteristics that make its identity immediately obvious (i.e., he has probable cause to believe that the item is contraband), then the officer may seize the evidence. Police may also *briefly* seize items if the officers have a reasonable suspicion that the item is or contains contraband.

3) *Terry* stop and frisk of a car

Pursuant to a lawful stop of a vehicle, police may conduct a search of the passenger compartment for weapons, if:

i)   The police possess a reasonable belief that the suspect is dangerous and may gain immediate control of weapons; and

ii)   The search of the passenger compartment is "limited to those areas in which a weapon may be placed or hidden."

Michigan v. Long, 463 U.S. 1032, 1048–50 (1983).

Police may order occupants out of a vehicle that they have lawfully stopped. *Maryland v. Wilson*, 519 U.S. 408 (1997).

When police make a lawful traffic stop, they are automatically detaining both the driver and the passenger. They may only frisk the driver or the passenger if they have reasonable suspicion that the person is carrying a weapon. *Arizona v. Johnson*, 555 U.S. 323 (2009).

4) Limits on time, place, and investigative method

A *Terry* stop must be temporary and last no longer than is necessary to effectuate the purpose of the stop. The investigative methods employed should be the least intrusive means reasonably available to verify or dispel the officer's suspicion in a short time. Police can require that the detained person identify himself. Failure to comply with this request can result in the arrest of the detained person.

After the conclusion of a traffic stop, absent reasonable suspicion, police extension of the stop in order to conduct a dog sniff violates the Fourth Amendment's protection against unreasonable seizures. *Rodriguez v. United States*, 575 U.S. _____, 135 S. Ct. 1609 (2015).

When police hold a suspect beyond the amount of time necessary to effectuate the purpose of a *Terry* stop, the seizure becomes an arrest and must be supported by probable cause.

5) Development of probable cause

If the officer conducting the stop develops probable cause, the officer may then make an arrest and conduct a full search incident to that arrest. If the stop involves a vehicle, the officer may search the passenger compartment and all containers therein, whether open or closed, if the arrestee is within reaching distance of the passenger compartment of the vehicle or if it is reasonable to believe that the vehicle contains evidence of the offense of arrest. *See* § I.C.4.a.4), Vehicle search incident to arrest, *supra,* discussing the *Gant* rule.

d. Automobile exception

The Fourth Amendment does not require police to obtain a warrant to search a vehicle if they have probable cause to believe that it contains contraband or evidence of a criminal activity. The police may search anywhere in a car that they believe there to be contraband, including the trunk and locked containers, so long as they have **probable cause** to do so. *United States v. Ross*, 456 U.S. 798, 825 (1982). The search may also extend to passengers' belongings, *Wyoming v. Houghten*, 526 U.S. 295, 302 (1999), as well as to mobile homes, *California v.*

Carney, 471 U.S. 386, 393–394 (1985). Any other evidence observed in plain view may also be seized.

> Note that the automobile exception does not permit the warrantless entry of a home or its curtilage in order to search a vehicle therein. *Collins v. Virginia*, 584 U.S. ___ (2018).

1) Pretextual stop

Police may use a pretextual stop to investigate whether a law has been violated, even if they have no reasonable suspicion, provided that they have probable cause to believe that the law for which the vehicle was stopped has been violated. *Whren v. United States*, 517 U.S. 806 (1996) (seizure of illegal drugs constitutional even though police stopped a car for a traffic violation as a pretext to investigate a hunch that the occupants possessed drugs).

2) Containers within a car

Probable cause to search a vehicle extends only to containers and compartments that reasonably could hold the evidence they are searching for. If the police have probable cause to search only a particular container, they may search only that container, and not the entire car. *Arkansas v. Sanders*, 442 U.S. 753 (1979); *California v. Acevedo*, 500 U.S. 565, 570 (1991). (Note, however, that what the officers find in one container may give them probable cause to believe evidence is contained elsewhere in the car.)

> **Example:** A driver left a residence holding a closed paper bag, which officers had probable cause to believe contained narcotics, based on an informant's tip. The bag was placed in the trunk, and the driver drove away. Police were authorized to stop the vehicle, open the trunk, and inspect the bag. However, the search was limited to the bag only. If they did not find the bag, they could only open and search containers big enough to store the bag. *Id.* at 579–80.

3) Trunk

If police have probable cause to search the trunk, not just a container placed in the trunk, then they can search the entire trunk and every container in the trunk, even if locked.

e. "Plain-view" doctrine

1) In public view

Items in public view may be seized without a warrant because one cannot have a reasonable expectation of privacy in things that are exposed to the public (e.g., physical characteristics, vehicle identification numbers, or items in open fields).

2) In private view

In situations in which there is a reasonable expectation of privacy, a police officer may seize an item in plain view of the officer, even if the item was not named in the search warrant, as long as (i) the officer is **lawfully on the premises**, (ii) the incriminating character of the item is **immediately apparent**, and (iii) the officer has **lawful access** to the item (e.g., viewing an object through a window is insufficient if the officer does not have lawful access to the inside of the house). The discovery of the item does not need to be inadvertent. *Horton v. California*, 496 U.S. 128 (1990); *Arizona v. Hicks*, 480 U.S. 231 (1987).

Example: Officer Olivia was executing a valid warrant to search Defendant Doug's home for a gun suspected to have been used in a murder. On entering the premises, Olivia saw bags of cocaine piled on Doug's coffee table. Under the "plain view" doctrine, Olivia could properly seize the bags, even though the warrant applied only to a gun.

f. Consent searches

Consent can serve to eliminate the need for police to have probable cause as well as to first obtain a warrant in order to conduct a search.

1) Voluntary

For permission to constitute consent, the permission must be given voluntarily. Permission given under threats of harm or compulsion does not constitute consent. In determining whether a person's response constitutes consent, courts evaluate the **totality of the circumstances** in which the response is made.

a) False assertion of authority

Permission given in acquiescence to lawful authority (e.g., a warrant) is not voluntary. Consequently, if the officer conducting the search erroneously states that he has a warrant, then permission given in reliance on that statement does not constitute consent. *Bumper v. North Carolina*, 391 U.S. 543, 549 (1968).

b) Knowledge of the right to withhold consent

The failure by police to inform the person from whom consent is sought that she has the right to withhold consent does not invalidate the consent. *Schneckloth v. Bustamonte*, 412 U.S. 218, 233 (1973).

c) Consent based on deceit

A government agent pretending to be a narcotics buyer, for example, may accept an invitation to enter the premises for the purposes contemplated by the occupant (i.e., to purchase drugs). The officer or agent may then seize things in plain view. *Lewis v. United States*, 385 U.S. 206 (1966).

2) Third-party consent

When the person from whom consent is sought is not the defendant, in addition to the voluntariness of the permission, the authority of that person to consent can be an issue.

a) Property of a third party

Generally, a third party has the authority to consent to a search of property that she owns or occupies. As such, the defendant cannot suppress evidence seized during such a search on the grounds that he (the defendant) did not consent to the search.

b) Property of the defendant

Generally, a third party does not have the authority to consent to a search of property owned or occupied by the defendant. The defendant can generally suppress evidence seized during such a search unless (i) an agency relationship exists between the third party and the defendant that gives to the third party the right to consent on behalf of the defendant, or (ii) the defendant otherwise gives the third party such rights with respect to the property that the defendant assumes the risk that the third party would allow the property to be searched (e.g., a shared duffle bag). *Frazier v. Cupp*, 394 U.S. 731, 740 (1969).

c) Jointly controlled property

When the property to be searched is under the joint control of the defendant and a third party (e.g., co-tenants of an apartment, a house jointly owned by a husband and wife), the authority of the third party to consent turns on whether the defendant is present at the time of the search.

i) Defendant not present

If the property to be searched is under the joint control of the defendant and a third party, and the defendant is not present at the time of the search, then the third party has authority to consent. The third party has actual authority when she has joint access or control for most purposes. *U.S. v. Matlock*, 415 U.S. 164, 170–171 (1974). In addition, the third party's consent may be valid even though she lacks actual authority if the police reasonably believe that she has such authority. *Illinois v. Rodriguez*, 497 U.S. 177, 184 (1990).

ii) Defendant present

When the property to be searched is under the joint control of the defendant and a third party, and the defendant is present at the time of the search, then the police may not rely on third-party consent if the defendant objects to the search. *Georgia v. Randolph*, 547 U.S. 103, 114–116 (2006). When the defendant is not present, however, a third party may consent to a search even if the defendant previously was present and objected to a search at that time. *Fernandez v. California*, 571 U.S. 292 (2014).

iii) Ownership versus current control

In some instances, ownership of the premises is not sufficient to confer authority to consent to a search. For example, a landlord may not consent to a search of the tenant's premises. *Chapman v. United States*, 365 U.S. 610, 617 (1961). Similarly, a hotel clerk cannot consent to the search of a guest's room until the guest has permanently checked out. *Stoner v. California*, 376 U.S. 483, 489 (1964). However, some circuits have held that the owner of a house can consent to a search of rooms occupied by non-paying guests.

iv) Parental consent

When a child lives with a parent, the parent has the authority to consent to a search of a child's room even if the child is an adult. However, a parent may lack authority to consent to the search of a locked container inside the child's room, depending on the age of the child. *U.S. v. Block*, 590 F.2d 535, 540 (4th Cir. 1979).

3) Scope of consent

Although a search is limited to the area to which the consent applies, the search may extend to areas that a reasonable officer would believe it extends. For example, consent by a driver to search his car for drugs extends to a closed container within the car that could contain drugs. *Florida v. Jimento*, 500 U.S. 248, 252 (1991).

4) Burden of proof

The prosecution must prove that the permission was freely given; the defendant is not required to show that the permission was coerced.

g. Administrative, special needs, and inventory searches

Administrative search warrants are generally required for nonconsensual fire, health, or safety inspections of residential or private commercial property.

1) Probable cause

The probable cause requirement for administrative searches is less stringent than that for a criminal investigation. Evidence of an existing statutory or regulatory violation or a reasonable plan supported by a valid public interest will justify the issuance of a warrant. *Camara v. Mun. Court of San Francisco*, 387 U.S. 523, 533 (1967).

2) Use of administrative searches

The government may not use administrative searches to investigate criminal activity. However, discovery of evidence during the search does not invalidate the search. The following administrative-type searches may be validly made without a warrant:

i) Searches of people entering an **airplane boarding area,** as long as the passenger can prevent the search by not boarding the plane;

ii) Searches of businesses in **highly regulated industries** such as liquor stores, gun shops, strip-mining operations, and automobile junkyards, because of urgent public interest and under the theory that the business impliedly consented to warrantless searches by entering into a highly regulated industry;

iii) Oral statements seized by **wiretaps,** when matters of national security are at issue;

iv) Searches of students by **public school officials,** so long as they are based on reasonable grounds (this standard is lower than probable cause and calls for only a "moderate chance" of finding the expected evidence, rather than a "fair probability" or "substantial chance"), and the measures adopted for the search are reasonably related to the objectives of the search and not excessively intrusive in light of the age and sex of the student and the nature of the infraction. *New Jersey v. T.L.O.*, 469 U.S. 325, 340–341 (1985); *Safford Unified Sch. Dist. #1 v. Redding*, 557 U.S. 364, 370-371 (2009).

v) **Special needs searches,** such as drug testing for railroad employees involved in an accident or student athletes during the athletic season. To be a special need, the state interest must be a real, current, and vital problem that can be effectively addressed through the proposed search. Even if the need exists, it must be balanced against the privacy interest at stake and the character of the intrusion. *Bd. of Educ. v. Earls*, 536 U.S. 822, 829 (2002);

vi) **Inventory searches** of items in official custody, such as impounded vehicles. After lawfully taking custody of property, police may conduct a warrantless search of other property to protect the owner's property while in custody, to protect police from claims of theft, and to protect officers from danger. Inventory searches must be performed according to standardized criteria and procedures. Subjective intent of the officer is irrelevant;

vii) **Routine international border** searches of border crossers and their belongings within the United States, including (i) stops, but not searches, by roving patrols who reasonably suspect that undocumented immigrants may be in an automobile, (ii) opening of international mail if authorities have reasonable cause to suspect contraband in the mail, and (iii) subsequent reopening of mail after the item had been resealed and delivered to the recipient;

viii) **Vehicle checkpoints and roadblocks** set up to stop cars on the basis of a neutral articulable standard and designed to serve a limited purpose closely related to the problem of an automobile's inherent mobility (e.g., to get drunk drivers off the road);

ix) **Factory searches** of the entire work force to determine citizenship of workers;

x) Searches of **government employees' electronically recorded documents and conduct, file cabinets, and desks** if they are justified by a reasonable suspicion of work-related misconduct or a non-investigatory, work-related need;

xi) **Detention of a traveler** whom authorities have reasonable suspicion is smuggling contraband in his stomach;

xii) Searches of **parolees and their homes,** even with no reasonable suspicion, when a parolee agrees to submit to searches by a parole officer or police officer at any time as a condition of his parole. The rationale being that because there is a greater need to search parolees since they are less likely to be law-abiding citizens, a parolee has a lower expectation of privacy;

xiii) Seizure of **contaminated or spoiled food**; and

xiv) Searches for the **cause of a fire** that occurs within a reasonable time after the fire is extinguished, but excluding searches for other evidence unrelated to the cause that would establish that the fire was attributable to arson. *Michigan v. Clifford*, 464 U.S. 287 (1984) (search of home); *Michigan v. Tyler*, 436 U.S. 499 (1978) (search of business (furniture store)).

h. **Wiretapping**

To obtain a warrant authorizing a wiretap, officers must satisfy the below requirements. The warrant must:

i) Be limited to a short period of time;

ii) Demonstrate probable cause that a specific crime has been or is about to be committed;

iii) Name the person or persons to be wiretapped;

iv) Describe with particularity the conversations that can be overheard; and

v) Include provisions for the termination of the wiretap.

Upon termination of the wiretap, the conversations that have been intercepted must be shown to the court. Note that a person assumes the unreliability of those to whom she speaks and has no Fourth Amendment claim if she finds out later that the listener was wired or recording the conversation. *United States v. White*, 401 U.S. 745 (1971). Furthermore, a speaker who makes no attempt to keep his conversation private has no Fourth Amendment claim. *Katz v. United States*, 389 U.S. 347 (1967).

In addition, a wiretap related to domestic security surveillance requires that a neutral and detached magistrate—not the president—make the determination that a wiretapping warrant should issue, and the wiretap must comply with the Omnibus Crime Control and Safe Streets Act. However, there is no requirement for prior authorization when a covert entry is planned to install the electronic equipment, or when a pen register is used.

5. Raising the Issue of Standing

To establish that a search violated his Fourth Amendment rights, a defendant must show a legitimate expectation of privacy with regard to the search (*see* § I.C.2., *supra*). To make such a showing, which is sometimes referred to as "standing," the defendant may have to admit facts that would incriminate him. Consequently, testimony given by the defendant to establish standing cannot be admitted as evidence against the defendant at trial.

6. Exclusionary Rule

Under the exclusionary rule, evidence obtained in violation of the accused's Fourth, Fifth, or Sixth Amendment rights may not be introduced at her trial to prove her guilt. Under the Fourth Amendment, evidence seized during an unlawful search cannot constitute proof against the victim of the search. *Weeks v. United States*, 232 U.S. 383 (1914).

a. Fruit of the poisonous tree

Subject to some exceptions, the exclusionary rule applies not only to evidence initially seized as a result of the primary government illegality, but also to secondary "derivative evidence" discovered as a result of the primary taint, also known as the "fruit of the poisonous tree."

Example: A police officer conducts an unconstitutional search of a home, finds an address book, and uses that address book to locate a witness. The witness will not be allowed to testify, because her testimony would be a "fruit" of the unconstitutional search.

b. Exceptions

Evidence, whether primary or derivative, may still be admissible if one of the following exceptions to the exclusionary rule applies.

1) Inevitable discovery rule

The prosecution can prove that the evidence would have been inevitably discovered in the same condition through lawful means.

2) Independent source doctrine

The evidence was discovered in part by an independent source unrelated to the tainted evidence.

3) Attenuation principle

The chain of causation between the primary taint and the evidence has been so attenuated as to "purge" the taint. Both the passage of time and/or intervening events may attenuate the taint.

> **Example:** An officer makes an unconstitutional investigatory stop, learns during the stop that the suspect was subject to a valid arrest warrant, arrests the suspect, and seizes incriminating evidence during a search incident to that arrest. The evidence the officer seizes as part of the search incident to the arrest is admissible. *Utah v. Strieff*, 579 U.S. ___, 136 S. Ct. 2056 (2016).

4) Good-faith exception

The good-faith exception applies to police officers who act in good faith on either a facially valid warrant later determined to be invalid or an existing law later declared unconstitutional. *Michigan v. DeFillippo*, 443 U.S. 31 (1979). Good faith is limited to the objective good faith of a reasonable police officer.

This exception does **not** apply if:

i)   No reasonable officer would rely on the affidavit underlying the warrant;

ii) The warrant is defective on its face;

iii) The warrant was obtained by fraud;

iv) The magistrate has "wholly abandoned his judicial role"; or

v)   The warrant was improperly executed.

5) Isolated police negligence

Isolated negligence by law-enforcement personnel will not necessarily trigger the exclusionary rule. To trigger the rule, police conduct must be "sufficiently deliberate such that exclusion can meaningfully deter it." The exclusionary rule serves to deter deliberate, reckless, or grossly negligent conduct or, in some circumstances, recurring or systemic negligence. *Herring v. United States*, 555 U.S. 135, 144 (2009).

> **Example:** Defendant Don goes to the police station to pick up an impounded vehicle. Policeman Paul believes that there might be a warrant out from another county for Don's arrest and calls the other county's sheriff to check. The sheriff tells Paul that there is a warrant out for Don's arrest. Paul immediately arrests Don and in a search incident to the arrest finds illegal drugs and an illegal weapon on Don. Minutes later, the sheriff calls back to say that the warrant had actually been recalled and she had made a mistake. The exclusionary rule will not apply to the drugs and the weapon because Paul was relying in good faith on the erroneous information from the sheriff in conducting the arrest. The exclusionary rule should be applied only if there is substantial additional deterrence of police misconduct to be gained. *Herring v. United States*, 555 U.S. 135 (2009).

6) Knock and announce

The exclusionary rule does not apply to evidence discovered as a result of a search conducted in violation of the "knock and announce" rule, if the search was otherwise authorized by a valid warrant. *Hudson v. Michigan*, 547 U.S. 586 (2006).

7) In-court identification

A witness's in-court identification of the defendant is not fruit of an unlawful detention. Thus, the identification cannot be excluded. On the other hand, live testimony may be excluded as fruit of illegal police conduct if there is a sufficient link between the illegal police conduct and the testimony.

c. Harmless error

Even if the trial court wrongfully admitted illegally seized evidence, the appellate court can refuse to order a new trial if it finds that the error was harmless beyond a reasonable doubt, meaning that the erroneously admitted evidence did not contribute to the result.

Note: The denial of the right to counsel is never a harmless error.

d. Enforcement

When the defendant challenges a confession or the admissibility of evidence, by right, a hearing is held to determine whether the confession or evidence is fruit of the poisonous tree. This hearing is held outside the presence of the jury. The defendant has a right to testify at this hearing, and the state bears the burden of establishing admissibility by a preponderance of the evidence.

e. Obtaining evidence by questionable methods

Evidence obtained in a manner that shocks the conscience is inadmissible. Examples of such methods of gathering evidence include inducements by official actions that offend the sense of justice and serious intrusions into the body, such as with surgery to remove a bullet. Contrast that, however, with a cheek swab to obtain a DNA sample, which is a reasonable intrusion because it is quick and painless, and involves no surgical intrusion beneath the skin. *Maryland v. King*, 569 U.S. 435 (2013).

II.   FIFTH AMENDMENT RIGHTS AND PRIVILEGES

A.   THE PRIVILEGE AGAINST COMPULSORY SELF-INCRIMINATION

The Fifth Amendment provides that no person shall be compelled in any criminal case to be a witness against himself. It is applicable to the states through the Fourteenth Amendment.

1.   Persons

A person means an individual. Artificial entities such as corporations, partnerships, and labor unions may not assert the privilege, but a sole proprietorship may. The privilege does not extend to the custodian of corporate records, even if production would incriminate the custodian individually.

2.   Testimonial Evidence

The privilege protects only testimonial evidence. Nontestimonial physical evidence (such as a blood or urine sample, Breathalyzer test result, handwriting exemplar, voice sample, or other evidence of physical characteristics) is not protected.

3.   Compulsory Disclosure

The privilege generally does not apply to an individual's voluntarily prepared business papers or to records required by law to be kept, such as tax returns. *Fisher v. United States*, 425 U.S. 391 (1976). However, a person can refuse to comply with a requirement to register or pay a tax where the requirement is directed at a select group "inherently suspect of criminal activities." *Marchetti v. United States*, 390 U.S.

39, 52 (1968) (occupational tax on bookies); *Leary v. United States*, 395 U.S. 6 (1969) (registration and tax based on transfer of marijuana).

a. Subpoena

A person who is served with a subpoena requiring the production of possibly incriminating documents may invoke the privilege if the act of turning over the documents constitutes self-incriminating testimony. *United States v. Hubbell*, 530 U.S. 27 (2000).

b. Warrant for seizure of documents

The Fifth Amendment does not prevent law-enforcement officials, pursuant to a valid warrant, from searching for and seizing documents that would incriminate a person. *Andresen v. Maryland*, 427 U.S. 463 (1976).

1) Diaries

Generally, the government may not compel **production** of a diary. The contents of a diary are similar to oral testimony, and as such are considered testimonial in nature. Because one cannot be compelled to testify against himself, the government may not compel production of documents that are similarly testimonial in nature. *See, e.g., Schmerber v. California*, 384 U.S. 757 (1966).

Note, however, that if the diary's production is not compelled, e.g., it is found incident to a lawful arrest, its contents likely are admissible (assuming the entries were made voluntarily).

4. Nature of Proceedings

The privilege extends to a witness in any proceeding, whether civil or criminal, formal or informal, if the answers provide some reasonable possibility of incriminating the witness in future criminal proceedings. *McCarthy v. Arndstein*, 266 U.S. 34 (1924). However, the privilege cannot be invoked when the government requires civil records to be maintained and reported on for administrative purposes, because they are public records, unless those records fulfill a registration requirement of a select group of inherently suspect criminal activities and compliance would require self-incrimination. The privilege does not extend to identification requests at *Terry* stops. A violation occurs the moment the compelled statements are used against a person.

5. Invoking the Privilege

a. Defendant's privilege

A defendant who wishes to invoke the privilege simply invokes it by not taking the stand. Included in this right is the state's inability to compel the defendant to testify. The prosecution cannot bring the defendant's failure to take the stand to the jury's attention.

b. Witness's privilege

A witness, on the other hand, may be compelled to take the stand and can invoke the privilege only in response to a specific question when there is some reasonable possibility that answering the question will incriminate the witness. However, such an invocation after testimony has already been made may violate a defendant's right to confrontation, guaranteed by the Sixth and Fourteenth Amendments, if it prevents adequate cross-examination. *Douglas v. Alabama*, 380 U.S. 415 (1965).

6. **Counseling Clients to Invoke the Privilege**

    Attorneys may counsel their clients to invoke the privilege and will not be held in contempt of court. Otherwise, the person invoking the privilege would be denied his Fifth Amendment protection.

7. **Invocation of Privilege Should Not Impose a Burden**

    The state cannot penalize a defendant for invoking his right against self-incrimination by not testifying or cooperating with authorities. The prosecution cannot comment to the jury on the defendant's refusal to speak in accordance with his *Miranda* rights. A violation in this regard by the state triggers the harmless-error test. However, if during trial the defendant claims that he was not allowed to explain his story, then the prosecution may comment on the defendant's failure to take the stand.

8. **Waiving the Privilege**

    A **defendant** waives the privilege by taking the witness stand; a **witness** waives the privilege by disclosing self-incriminating information in response to a specific question. Having taken the stand, the defendant cannot assert the privilege in response to the prosecution's proper cross-examination of his testimony, including impeachment questions.

B. **THE FIFTH AMENDMENT IN A POLICE INTERROGATION CONTEXT**

In the seminal case of *Miranda v. Arizona,* the U.S. Supreme Court held that a suspect has a constitutional right not to be compelled to make incriminating statements in the police interrogation process. *Miranda v. Arizona*, 384 U.S. 436 (1966). *Miranda* once was considered to be necessary in nearly every encounter with police. However, the Supreme Court has been gradually narrowing the scope and limiting the use of *Miranda.*

Any incriminating statement obtained as the result of **custodial interrogation** may not be used against the suspect at a subsequent trial **unless** the police provided procedural safeguards effective to secure the privilege against self-incrimination (i.e., informed the suspect of his *Miranda* rights). An incriminating statement includes not only a confession, but other inculpatory statements, and is subject to suppression even though the defendant intended the statement to be exculpatory.

1. **Custodial Interrogation**

    Custodial interrogation is questioning initiated by a known (as opposed to undercover) law-enforcement officer after a person is in custody.

    a. **"Custodial"**

        Custody is a substantial seizure and is defined for *Miranda* purposes as either a formal arrest or a restraint on freedom of movement to the degree associated with a formal arrest. *New York v. Quarles*, 467 U.S. 649, 655 (1984).

        If there has been no formal arrest, the question is whether a reasonable person would have believed he could leave, given the **totality of the circumstances**. *Thompson v. Keohane*, 516 U.S. 99 (1995). A child's age is a relevant factor in determining whether a reasonable child would have believed he was in custody. *J.D.B. v. North Carolina*, 564 U.S. 261 (2011).

        1) **Police station**

            While police questioning an individual at a police station typically constitutes a custodial interrogation, the fact that the questioning takes place at a police station does not automatically make the encounter custodial.

> **Example:** A woman voluntarily goes to the police station to talk about a crime. As soon as she arrives, she is informed by the officer on the case that she is free to leave at any time and is not under arrest. Even though she is speaking with the police at the police station, the totality of the circumstances establishes that she is not in "custody," and therefore *Miranda* will not apply. *See California v. Beheler*, 463 U.S. 1121 (1983); *Oregon v. Mathiason*, 429 U.S. 492 (1977).

2) Crime scene

The questioning of a person at the scene of a crime or pursuant to a field investigation does not constitute custody for *Miranda* purposes as long as the person questioned is not under restraint equivalent to that of formal arrest and has the **right to leave** the presence of the questioning officer.

3) Traffic stop

Traffic stops generally are not considered custodial because they generally are brief and temporary. *Berkemer v. McCarty*, 468 U.S. 420 (1984).

4) Prison

Imprisonment alone does not necessarily create a custodial situation within the meaning of *Miranda*. The questioning of a prisoner, who is removed from the general prison population, about events that took place outside the prison is not categorically "custodial" for *Miranda* purposes. A standard, objective "totality of circumstances" analysis applies when an inmate is interviewed, including consideration of the language that is used in summoning the prisoner to the interview and the manner in which the interrogation is conducted. *Howes v. Fields*, 565 U.S. 499 (2012) (holding that defendant was not in custody for purposes of *Miranda* during seven-hour interrogation that lasted well into the night, because he was told at the outset of interrogation, and was reminded again thereafter, that he could terminate the interrogation and go back to his cell whenever he wanted).

5) Continuation of custody

The failure of a police agency to provide *Miranda* warnings to a suspect can render inadmissible a statement given to a second policy agency that continues the interrogation of the suspect in the same location immediately after the termination of the interrogation of the suspect by the first police agency, even though the second police agency gave the suspect *Miranda* warnings and questioned the suspect about an unrelated crime. *Miranda v. Arizona*, 384 U.S. 436, 494-497 (1966) (addressing *Westover v. United States*).

b. "Interrogation"

Interrogation refers not only to express questioning, but also to any words or actions that the police know or should know are **reasonably likely to elicit an incriminating response**. *Rhode Island v. Innis*, 446 U.S. 291 (1980).

1) Voluntariness of statement

Volunteered statements are not protected by *Miranda*, as they are, by definition, not the product of interrogation.

A confession is involuntary only if the police coerced the defendant into making the confession. Whether a statement is voluntary or coerced is determined based on the totality of the circumstances (including facts such as the conduct of the police, the characteristics of the defendant, and the time of the statement). A claim that a confession should be excluded because it is involuntary must be decided by the trial judge as a preliminary question of fact, and not by the jury.

a) Trickery

Trickery by the police or false promises made to the accused by the police may render a confession involuntary. However, deceit or fraud by the interrogators (i.e., lying about a co-conspirator's confession) does not itself make the confession involuntary.

b) Character of the defendant

The defendant's age, state of health, education, or intoxication are all factors in determining the coercive nature of the confession. Although a potentially significant factor, the defendant's mental condition alone cannot violate the voluntariness standard. There must be coercive police activity for the confession to be found involuntary. *Colorado v. Connelly*, 479 U.S. 157 (1986).

> **EXAM NOTE:** Remember to apply the *Miranda* warnings only when an individual is subject to a custodial interrogation. If the police have no intention of questioning the individual, or if the individual is not in police custody, then the *Miranda* warnings are not applicable.

2. Compliance

Once a custodial interrogation begins, anything the defendant says is inadmissible until the defendant is informed of the *Miranda* rights **and** the defendant waives those rights.

The failure to give a suspect the *Miranda* warnings does not require suppression of **physical fruits** of the suspect's "unwarned but voluntary statements." *United States v. Patane*, 542 U.S. 630, 640 (2004).

a. Content

The warnings, which must be given before interrogation begins, need not be a verbatim repetition of the language used in the *Miranda* decision.

Law-enforcement officials must inform suspects:

i) Of their right to remain **silent**;

ii) That any statement uttered may be **used in court**;

iii) Of their right to **consult an attorney** and to have the attorney present during an interrogation; and

iv) That an **attorney will be appointed** to represent indigent defendants.

b. Timing

The *Miranda* warning must be given before interrogation begins. If interrogation is stopped for a long duration, the warning must be given again.

c. Right to counsel invoked

The right to counsel under the Fifth Amendment is not the same as the constitutional requirement of the right to counsel under the Sixth Amendment. The right to counsel under the Fifth Amendment is not automatic. To invoke the right to counsel under the Fifth Amendment, a suspect must make a specific, unambiguous statement asserting his desire to have counsel present. If a suspect makes an ambiguous statement regarding the right to counsel, the police are not required to end the interrogation or to ask questions or clarify whether the suspect wants to invoke the right. *Davis v. United States*, 512 U.S. 452 (1994). However, once that right to counsel is invoked, **all** interrogation must stop until counsel is present. *Edwards v. Arizona*, 451 U.S. 477, 484 (1981). If the suspect voluntarily initiates communication with the police after invoking his right to counsel, a statement made by the suspect, such as a statement that the suspect spontaneously blurts out, can be admissible because it is not made in response to interrogation. In addition, police may re-open interrogation of a suspect who has asserted his Fifth Amendment right to counsel if there has been a 14-day or more break in custody (such as the release back into the general prison population of a suspect who has been incarcerated for another crime). In such circumstances, the officers must give fresh *Miranda* warnings and get a valid waiver before beginning questioning. *Maryland v. Shatzer*, 559 U.S. 98 (2010).

d. **Right to silence invoked**

As with the Fifth Amendment right to counsel, the defendant must make a specific, unambiguous statement asserting his desire to remain silent. Merely remaining silent in response to police questioning does not invoke the privilege. *Salinas v. Texas*, 570 U.S. 178 (2013); *Berghuis v. Thompkins*, 560 U.S. 370 (2010). If a defendant invokes his *Miranda* right to remain silent, the interrogator(s) must "scrupulously honor" that request (e.g., immediately cease interrogation, allow for a significant passage of time, give a second set of warnings). However, if after the defendant is released from custody, the defendant indicates a desire to speak to police, then a subsequent interrogation would be lawful, as long as the defendant was not coerced. The defendant must again receive fresh *Miranda* warnings.

e. **Grand jury**

There is no requirement to give *Miranda* warnings to a witness testifying for the grand jury. The witness may, however, consult with an attorney outside the grand jury room.

3. **Exceptions to the *Miranda* Requirement**

a. **Public safety**

When the public's safety is at risk, the police are not required to give *Miranda* warnings before questioning a suspect.

b. **Routine booking**

The "routine booking question" exception allows police to ask a suspected drunken driver routine biographical questions and to videotape the driver's responses without first giving the driver *Miranda* warnings.

c. **Undercover police**

Miranda warnings are not required if the suspect being questioned is not aware that the interrogator is a police officer. *Illinois v. Perkins*, 496 U.S. 292, 294 (1990).

Example: The police placed an undercover officer, posing as a criminal, in the defendant's jail cell, and the undercover officer engaged the defendant in a conversation designed to elicit details of the crime for which the defendant was suspected. Such statements were admissible in the absence of *Miranda* warnings. *Illinois v. Perkins, supra.*

4. Waiver

A defendant may knowingly and voluntarily waive his *Miranda* rights. The burden is on the government to demonstrate by a preponderance of the evidence that the waiver was made knowingly and voluntarily. (Keep in mind that a defendant's mental illness does not necessarily negate the voluntariness requirement; there must be coercive police activity for a confession to be involuntary. *Colorado v. Connelly, supra.*)

There can be no effective waiver, however, until the *Miranda* warnings are properly given. Silence on the part of the suspect is not sufficient to waive his *Miranda* rights. However, a suspect who has received and understood the *Miranda* warnings, and has not invoked his *Miranda* rights, waives the right to remain silent by making an uncoerced statement to the police. *Berghuis v. Thompkins*, 560 U.S. 370 (2010). The police are not required to inform the suspect of the defense counsel's efforts to reach the defendant by telephone and need not inform counsel that the defendant is being questioned.

5. Use of Statements Taken in Violation of *Miranda*

The failure to give *Miranda* warnings is not a violation until a statement obtained without the use of warnings is used at trial. *Chavez v. Martinez*, 538 U.S. 760 (2003).

a. Impeachment purposes

Statements taken in violation of *Miranda* may be used to impeach the credibility of the criminal defendant if he takes the witness stand and gives testimony at variance with his previous admissions. *Harris v. New York*, 401 U.S. 222, 224 (1971). To be admissible for impeachment, the statement must be voluntary and trustworthy. The impeaching admissions may not be used directly in deciding ultimate issues of guilt or innocence; they may only be used in determining the defendant's veracity.

Post-arrest silence by a defendant who has received *Miranda* warnings generally may not be used by the prosecution as either impeachment or substantive evidence without violating the defendant's right to due process. *Doyle v. Ohio*, 426 U.S. 610 (1976); *United States v. Hale*, 422 U.S. 171 (1975). The Supreme Court has never applied the waiver doctrine to allow post-arrest silence to be admitted for impeachment purposes if the silence occurred after the defendant waived his right to remain silent. However, some states require a defendant to re-invoke his right to remain silent after a waiver to prevent the admission of his subsequent silence as impeachment evidence. *Compare Bass v. Nix*, 909 F.2d 297 (8th Cir. 1990), *with Schragin v. State*, 378 S.W.3d 510 (Tex. App. 2012).

b. Involuntary confessions

Involuntary confessions (e.g., those produced by coercion) cannot be used either substantively or for impeachment purposes. If a coerced confession is admitted into evidence, however, reversal is not automatic; the harmless-error test is applied, and the conviction will stand if the prosecution can show other overwhelming evidence of guilt.

C. FRUITS OF A TAINTED CONFESSION

1. Physical Evidence

Derivative **physical evidence** (e.g., a gun) obtained as a result of a non-Mirandized confession (i.e., a confession that is inadmissible due to the police's failure to give

Miranda warnings) is **admissible,** so long as that confession was not coerced. *United States v. Patane*, 542 U.S. 630 (2004).

2. Second Confession

A *Miranda* violation does not automatically require the suppression of incriminating statements made by the defendant after receiving *Miranda* warnings. *Oregon v. Elstad*, 470 U.S. 298 (1985). However, a second confession may be suppressed when the circumstances indicate that the substance of *Miranda* has been drained away. For a plurality of the court, the test is an objective one—a reasonable person in the suspect's position would not have understood the *Miranda* warnings to convey a message that the suspect retained a choice about whether to remain silent. For the justice who cast the deciding vote (Justice Kennedy), the test is a subjective one—did the police act with an intent to circumvent the purpose of the *Miranda* warnings. *Miranda*; *Missouri v. Seibert*, 542 U.S. 600, 611 (2004).

D. FIFTH AMENDMENT IN THE TRIAL CONTEXT

1. Scope of Privilege

A defendant may refuse to testify at a criminal trial. He may also refuse to answer questions in other proceedings (i.e., civil depositions) when the answers might incriminate him in future criminal proceedings.

The privilege does not prevent the prosecutor from using prior conflicting statements to impeach the defendant once the defendant takes the stand. This is called "opening the door" by the defendant.

2. Voluntariness

Admissions of incriminating statements made during a court-ordered psychiatric examination are generally deemed involuntary and not admissible at trial unless the defendant is given *Miranda* warnings before the interview and waives his rights.

Business papers voluntarily prepared by an individual, or required records, such as tax returns, are not protected.

3. Immunity

The prosecution may compel incriminating testimony (at trial or before a grand jury) if it grants immunity to the individual and the individual must testify. The testimony cannot be used against the individual, directly or indirectly, in a subsequent prosecution.

a. Transactional immunity

Often called "blanket" or "total" immunity, "transactional immunity" fully protects a witness from future prosecution for crimes related to her testimony.

b. Use and derivative-use immunity

"Use and derivative-use" immunity only precludes the prosecution from using the witness's own testimony, or any evidence derived from the testimony, against the witness. The Supreme Court has held that the grant of "use and derivative-use" immunity is all that is constitutionally required to compel the testimony of a witness. *Kastigar v. United States*, 406 U.S. 441, 452–453 (1972). Testimony encouraged by a promise of immunity, however, is considered coerced and involuntary.

c. Federal and state immunity

Testimony under a grant of immunity may not be used by another U.S. jurisdiction to prosecute the defendant. *See United States v. Balsys*, 524 U.S. 666 (1998); *Murphy v. Waterfront Comm'n*, 378 U.S. 52 (1964). Thus, a state grant of immunity will preclude admission of the testimony in a federal proceeding.

4. Prosecutorial Comment

The prosecutor may not comment on the defendant's exercise of the privilege against self-incrimination at trial. It is per se reversible error unless the judge immediately instructs the jury that the prosecutor's comment was improper and that the defendant had a constitutional right not to testify. This constitutional violation is subject to the harmless error rule. *U.S. v. Hastings*, 461 U.S. 499 (1983).

III. SIXTH AMENDMENT RIGHT TO COUNSEL

The Sixth Amendment provides that the accused shall have the right to a jury trial, the right to a public trial, the right to confront witnesses against him, the right to cross-examine witnesses, the right to be present at his own trial, and the right to "the assistance of counsel for his defense." The right to assistance of counsel encompasses not only the right to hire private counsel, but also the right to be provided with counsel without charge if the accused is unable to afford counsel.

A. APPLICABILITY: RIGHT TO COUNSEL

1. Types of Proceedings

The Sixth Amendment provides a constitutional right to counsel in any case in which the defendant is sentenced to incarceration, even if that sentence is suspended. *Scott v. Illinois*, 440 U.S. 367 (1979); *Alabama v. Shelton*, 535 U.S. 654 (2002).

2. Applicable Stages

The Sixth Amendment right to counsel applies at all **critical stages** of a prosecution, after formal proceedings have begun. The right automatically **attaches** when **formal judicial proceedings have begun**, whether that be at a post-arrest initial appearance before a judicial officer, or by way of formal charge, preliminary hearing, indictment, information, or arraignment. There is no right to counsel at post-conviction proceedings such as parole and probation hearings or habeas corpus hearings. For a discussion of a defendant's right to counsel on an appeal (*see* § VI.B. Appeal, *infra*).

> **EXAM NOTE:** Unlike the Fifth Amendment right to counsel, the defendant does not need to invoke the Sixth Amendment right to counsel. The failure to provide counsel at trial results in automatic reversal of a conviction.

a. Critical stages

The Supreme Court has summarized its definition of "critical stage" as those proceedings between an individual and an agent of the state that amount to trial-like confrontations, at which counsel would help the accused in coping with legal problems or meeting his adversary. *Rothgery v. Gillespie County*, 554 U.S. 191, 212 (2008).

Generally, the Sixth Amendment right to counsel attaches at the following critical stages:

i) Post-indictment lineups and in-person identifications;

ii) Post-indictment interrogations, whether custodial or otherwise;

iii) Arraignment and preliminary hearing to determine probable cause to prosecute, bail hearings, and pre-trial motions; and

iv) Plea bargaining, guilty pleas, trials, and sentencing.

Note that direct appeals as a matter of right, while not technically covered by the Sixth Amendment, do require that the state provide counsel to the indigent on equal protection grounds. *Douglas v. California*, 372 U.S. 353 (1963).

b. Noncritical stages

The right to counsel generally does not apply to the following events:

i) A witness viewing photos of the alleged defendant;

ii) Pre-charge (investigative) lineups;

iii) Taking of fingerprints, handwriting exemplars, voice exemplars, or blood samples;

iv) Hearings to determine probable cause to detain the defendant (*Gerstein* hearing);

v) Discretionary appeals; and

vi) Post-conviction proceedings, such as parole or probation hearings, including habeas corpus. (The Sixth Amendment does apply, however, to probation revocation hearings that include sentencing.)

3. Indigence—Right to Appointment of Counsel

When the right to counsel exists, an indigent defendant has the right to the appointment of counsel. *Johnson v. Zerbst*, 304 U.S. 458 (1938) (federal trial); *Gideon v. Wainwright*, 372 U.S. 335 (1963) (state trial, Sixth Amendment right to counsel incorporated by Due Process Clause of the Fourteenth Amendment).

4. Right to Counsel of Choice

In general, a defendant who is able to afford a lawyer is entitled to the counsel of his own choosing, while an indigent defendant is not entitled to the appointment of counsel of his own choosing. *United States v. Gonzalez-Lopez*, 548 U.S. 140, 147–148 (2006) (defendant who retains his own counsel has the right to be represented by that attorney); *Wheat v. United States*, 486 U.S. 153, 159 (1988) (indigent defendant has right to an effective advocate, not to an attorney preferred by defendant). However, a defendant cannot compel a lawyer to represent him even if the defendant has the ability to pay the lawyer. *Id.* In addition, the court can deny a defendant his chosen counsel when the lawyer is not a member of the bar or is otherwise disqualified from representing the defendant. *Id.* (person who is not a member of the bar may not represent anyone but himself; court may disqualify a lawyer who has a serious conflict of interest).

5. Waiver

a. In general

The Sixth Amendment right to counsel can be waived so long as relinquishment of the right is voluntary, knowing, and intelligent. *Patterson v. Illinois*, 487 U.S. 285 (1988); *Brewer v. Williams*, 430 U.S. 387 (1977).

Even though *Miranda* rights purportedly arise from the Fifth Amendment, an accused who receives proper *Miranda* warnings will be considered sufficiently apprised of his Sixth Amendment rights and the consequences of abandoning those rights. As long as the defendant is given *Miranda* warnings and voluntarily waives those rights, the defendant's waiver of his Sixth Amendment rights will also be considered knowing and intelligent. *Patterson v. Illinois*, 487 U.S. 285 (1988).

> **EXAM NOTE:** Remember, even if the defendant has made a valid waiver of his right to counsel, statements made during interrogation must be **voluntary** to be admissible at trial, i.e., the police still cannot use compelled statements.

b. Subsequent waivers pursuant to *Edwards* and *Montejo*

Recall that in the Fifth Amendment context, once an individual in custody asserts the Fifth Amendment right to counsel, no subsequent waiver of that right is valid in a police-initiated custodial interrogation unless counsel is present. *Edwards v. Arizona*, 451 U.S. 477 (1981). Under the *Edwards* rule, any subsequent waiver of the Fifth Amendment right to counsel under these circumstances is presumed to be involuntary. *McNeil v. Wisconsin*, 501 U.S. 171 (1991).

A similar presumption used to apply in the Sixth Amendment context, but has been overturned. *See Michigan v. Jackson*, 475 U.S. 625 (1986) (*overturned by Montejo v. Louisiana*, 556 U.S. 778 (2009)). Therefore, if an accused has not actually asserted his right to counsel (e.g., if the court automatically appoints counsel to the accused before trial), there is no presumption that any subsequent waiver of the right to counsel will be involuntary. *Montejo v. Louisiana*, 556 U.S. 778 (2009). The *Edwards* rule will still apply if the accused has actually asserted his right to counsel, but remember that the *Edwards* rule only applies in custodial interactions. *See Edwards v. Arizona*, 451 U.S. 477 (1981). Therefore, even after Sixth Amendment rights attach, the police may initiate non-custodial interactions with the accused outside the presence of his lawyer, and there will be no presumption that any knowing waiver of the right to have counsel present for the interaction is involuntary. *Montejo v. Louisiana*, 556 U.S. 778 (2009).

c. Right to proceed pro se

A defendant has the constitutional right to refuse counsel and proceed pro se at trial. The waiver of the right to counsel must be knowingly and intelligently made. To that end, the court should make the defendant aware of the dangers and disadvantages of self-representation, such as the inability to raise an "ineffective assistance of counsel" defense on appeal. *Faretta v. California*, 422 U.S. 806 (1975). In addition, the court may, even over the defendant's objection, "appoint a 'standby counsel,' to aid the accused if and when the accused requests help, and to be available to represent the accused in the event that termination of the defendant's self-representation is necessary." *Id.* at 834, fn 46. A defendant who is competent to stand trial may nevertheless be found incompetent to represent himself. *Indiana v. Edwards*, 554 U.S. 164 (2009).

6. Withholding Information

The police are under no obligation to inform a suspect that an attorney has been trying to reach him, and may even withhold that information intentionally, so long as the Sixth Amendment right to counsel has not yet attached. *Moran v. Burbine*, 475 U.S. 412 (1986). If the Sixth Amendment right has attached, this sort of interference with the attorney-client relationship might be a violation of that right.

B. OFFENSE-SPECIFIC

Once the Sixth Amendment right to counsel is properly invoked, it applies **only** to the specific offense at issue in those proceedings. *McNeil v. Wisconsin*, 501 U.S. 171, 175–176 (1991).

1. ***Blockburger* Test**

   Two crimes committed in one criminal transaction are deemed to be the same offense for Sixth Amendment purposes unless each offense requires proof of an element that the other does not. *Texas v. Cobb*, 532 U.S. 162 (2001); *Blockburger v. United States*, 284 U.S. 299, 304 (1932).

2. **Compare to *Miranda***

   Unlike under the *Miranda* standard, under the Sixth Amendment standard, the requirement for counsel to be present applies only to interrogations about the offense charged. However, like with *Miranda,* the defendant may make a knowing and voluntary waiver of the right to counsel being present.

   Example: Defendant Dave has been charged with burglary and is out on bail awaiting trial. The police also suspect Dave in an unrelated arson case, and they bring him to the police station to question him about the arson. Dave is given the *Miranda* warnings and waives his right to remain silent, but he asks to see his attorney. The police do not call Dave's attorney but continue to interrogate Dave until he confesses to the arson. While the police did violate Dave's Fifth Amendment right to have an attorney present during questioning, they did not violate his Sixth Amendment right to counsel, as the arson was unrelated to the burglary, and he hadn't been charged with the arson.

C. **REMEDIES FOR DENIAL OF COUNSEL**

   1. **Effect on Conviction**

      If a right to counsel at a trial proceeding under the Sixth Amendment is denied, the defendant's conviction should be automatically reversed, even without a specific showing of unfairness. *Gideon v. Wainwright*, 372 U.S. 335, 339 (1963). Automatic reversal also applies to a conviction obtained after a court has erroneously refused to permit an attorney chosen by the defendant to represent him, when that attorney is not supplied by the state. *United States v. Gonzalez-Lopez*, 548 U.S. 140 (2006).

   2. **Effect on Guilty Plea**

      If the defendant has pleaded guilty at a preliminary hearing, without being given the opportunity to have counsel, then the defendant has the right to withdraw the plea, and it may not be used against the defendant as an evidentiary admission. *White v. Maryland*, 373 U.S. 59, 60 (1963).

   3. **Effect on Denial of Counsel at Nontrial Proceedings**

      A denial of counsel at a nontrial proceeding, such as a lineup, is subject to harmless-error analysis. *United States v. Wade*, 388 U.S. 218, 223 (1967).

   4. **Admissibility of a Defendant's Statements to Informants**

      Post-indictment statements that a defendant makes to a police informant are inadmissible when the police intentionally create a situation likely to induce the defendant into making incriminating statements about the crime for which he was indicted without the assistance of counsel. *United States v. Henry*, 447 U.S. 264, 274–275 (1980). There is no Sixth Amendment violation, however, if the police place an informant in the defendant's cell simply to listen and report the defendant's statements, without questioning the defendant. *Kuhlmann v. Wilson*, 477 U.S. 436, 456 (1986).

5. **Exclusionary Rule Under the Sixth Amendment**

    a. **Fruits doctrine**

        The fruit of the poisonous tree doctrine is applicable to violations of the Sixth Amendment right to counsel. *Nix v. Williams*, 467 U.S. 431 (1984). Both statements and physical evidence obtained as a result of a Sixth Amendment violation are inadmissible.

    b. **Impeachment**

        If the police initiate a conversation with an accused individual who has requested counsel, any incriminating statements made by the defendant may still be used for impeachment purposes, despite the fact that the improper police conduct precludes admission of the statements as part of the prosecution's case in chief. *Michigan v. Harvey*, 494 U.S. 344, 350–351 (1990).

D. **INEFFECTIVE ASSISTANCE OF COUNSEL**

1. **Standard of Competence**

    The right to counsel encompasses the right to be assisted by a reasonably competent attorney and is presumed. The right to effective counsel extends to the defendant's first appeal. To reverse a conviction on the ground of ineffective counsel, the claimant has the burden to show that:

    i) Counsel's representation fell below an objective standard of reasonableness; and

    ii) Counsel's deficient performance prejudiced the defendant, resulting in the reasonable probability that the outcome would have been different.

    Strickland v. Washington, 466 U.S. 668, 687 (1984). Counsel's mere inexperience, strategy, choice of appellate issues, or even failure to produce mitigating evidence have all been found insufficient to rise to the level of ineffective counsel. *Bell v. Cone*, 535 U.S. 685 (2002); *Jones v. Barnes*, 463 U.S. 745 (1988); *United States v. Cronic*, 466 U.S. 648 (1984). The failure of defense counsel to raise a federal constitutional issue that was law at the time of the trial, but was later overruled, does not constitute ineffective assistance of counsel. *Lockhart v. Fretwell*, 506 U.S. 364 (1993).

2. **Conflict of Interest**

    The representation of defendants with conflicting interests may amount to ineffective assistance of counsel. In general, to overturn a conviction on the basis of a conflict of interest, a defendant must show that there was an actual conflict of interest and that such conflict adversely affected the attorney's performance.

    a. **Actual conflict**

        To find an actual conflict, a court must determine that the defense attorney is subject to an obligation or unique personal interest that, if followed, would lead her to adopt a strategy other than that most favorable to the defendant.

    b. **Adverse impact**

        Adverse impact can be established by demonstrating that some plausible alternative defense strategy or tactic might have been pursued and such strategy or tactic was inherently in conflict with, or not undertaken, due to the attorney's other loyalties or interests. The conflicting character of the strategy is not sufficient if the strategy actually was rejected because another strategy was viewed as even more favorable to the accused.

c. Knowledge of the court

If an attorney representing codefendants makes a timely motion for appointment of separate counsel based on a potential conflict of interest, then the trial judge must either grant the motion or at least conduct a hearing to determine whether appointment of separate counsel is warranted under the circumstances. Failure of the judge to do so requires automatic reversal of a subsequent conviction. *Holloway v. Arkansas*, 435 U.S. 475, 484 (1978). Actual conflict and prejudice are presumed under such circumstances.

Unless the trial court knows or reasonably should know that a conflict exists, however, the court is not required to inquire about multiple representations. *Cuyler v. Sullivan*, 446 U.S. 335, 347–348 (1980). Actual conflict (rather than potential conflict) is required to be shown on appeal if the issue of separate trials was not brought up during the trial, and the defendant must show that the conflict adversely affected counsel's performance. *Mickens v. Taylor*, 535 U.S. 162, 173 (2002).

d. Rule 44(c)

When co-defendants are represented by the same attorney, Rule 44(c) of the Federal Rules of Criminal Procedure requires the court to conduct a prompt inquiry into potential conflicts of interest and advise the defendants of the right to separate representation. Failure to comply with the Rule, though, will not constitute a per se reversible error, and an appellate court will likely ask whether the end result was representation by counsel under an actual conflict.

e. Disqualification despite waiver

A trial court has the authority to disqualify a defense attorney, even over the objection of the defendant, if the court concludes that there is serious potential of a conflict of interest. *Wheat v. United States*, 486 U.S. 153, 158–159 (1988).

3. Communication of Formal Plea Offer

The right to effective assistance of counsel extends to the plea bargaining stage. Defense counsel must accurately communicate to the defendant any formal offer from the prosecution to accept a plea on terms and conditions that may be favorable to the defendant. To show prejudice once a plea offer has lapsed or has been rejected because defense counsel failed to accurately communicate the offer, a defendant must demonstrate a reasonable probability that she would have accepted the plea offer had it been accurately communicated by defense counsel. A defendant must also demonstrate a reasonable probability that the prosecutor and trial court would have accepted the plea if they had the discretion to reject it under state law. *Missouri v. Frye*, 566 U.S. 134 (2012). Ineffective assistance of counsel at the plea bargaining stage may constitute reversible error even if the subsequent trial and conviction are fair. *Lafler v. Cooper*, 566 U.S. 156 (2012).

IV. PRETRIAL PROCEDURES

A. EYEWITNESS IDENTIFICATION PROCEDURES

1. Types

There are two types of eyewitness identification procedures: corporeal and non-corporeal. Corporeal identifications are "in-person," as in lineups or show-ups. Non-corporeal identifications are not in-person and involve police officers using photo arrays for a witness to identify the perpetrator of the crime.

2. **Post-Indictment Identifications—Sixth Amendment Right to Counsel**

A defendant is entitled to have counsel present at any post-indictment lineup or show-up in which the defendant is required to participate. *United States v. Wade*, 388 U.S. 218 (1967); *Gilbert v. California*, 388 U.S. 263 (1967). The prosecution bears the burden of establishing that counsel was present. The right to counsel does not apply to any pre-indictment lineup, even if it takes place after the defendant has been arrested for another unrelated crime. *Kirby v. Illinois*, 406 U.S. 682, 690–691 (1972).

a. **Waiver**

The defendant can waive the right to have counsel present at the lineup, provided that waiver is made knowingly and intelligently. The prosecution bears the burden of demonstrating that the waiver was valid.

b. **Remedy for violation**

Testimony about a post-indictment, pre-trial identification in the absence of counsel is inadmissible at trial, but the witness may still identify the defendant at trial if the prosecution can show that the identification has independent reliability. *United States v. Wade*, 388 U.S. 218 (1967).

c   **Non-corporeal identification procedures**

There is no right to counsel during an identification through a photo array, regardless of when the photo array is conducted.

3. **Impermissibly Suggestive Identification Procedures—Due Process Rights**

A defendant also has a due process right pursuant to the Fifth Amendment (for federal prosecutions) and the Fourteenth Amendment (for state prosecutions) with regard to a witness's identification based on an identification procedure arranged by the police that was impermissibly suggestive. This right exists whether the identification procedure was corporeal or non-corporeal, and whether the identification took place before or after the indictment of the defendant. *Perry v. New Hampshire*, 565 U.S. 228 (2012).

a. **Two-prong test**

Courts use a two-prong test to determine the admissibility of a pre- or post-indictment corporeal or non-corporeal identification. To prevail, the defendant must demonstrate that the procedure was **impermissibly suggestive and** that there was a **substantial likelihood of misidentification**. In order to have the identification admitted, the prosecution can offer evidence that the identification was **nonetheless reliable**.

In making its ruling, the court is to consider the following factors:

i)   The witness's **opportunity to view** the defendant at the time of the crime;

ii) The witness's **degree of attention** at the time of the crime;

iii) The **accuracy of the witness's description** of the defendant prior to the identification;

iv) The **level of certainty** at the time of the identification; and

v)   The **length of time** between the crime and the identification.

Neil v. Biggers, 409 U.S. 188, 199–200 (1972). Only when the indicators of a witness's ability to make an accurate identification are outweighed by the corrupting effect of law enforcement suggestion should the identification be suppressed on due process grounds. *Perry v. New Hampshire, supra*, at 725, quoting from *Manson v. Brathwaite*, 432 U.S. 98, 114 (1977). This test applies both to an out-of-court identification and an in-court identification that is based on a prior out-of-court identification.

1) Impermissibly suggestive

Police identification procedures that are highly suggestive usually are also impermissibly suggestive. However, even when such procedures are highly suggestive, they may not be impermissibly so, if they are necessary. For example, an identification made by a witness of defendant brought in handcuffs to the witness's hospital room by uniformed police officers was not impermissible suggestive because the witness was the only person who could identify the perpetrator, the witness could not leave her hospital room, and it was uncertain whether the witness would survive. *Stovall v. Denno*, 388 U.S. 293 (1967).

In addition, a defendant's due process rights are violated only if it is the police who have arranged the identification procedure to be impermissibly suggestive. For example, when a witness, asked by a police officer to describe the perpetrator of an automobile break-in, pointed out her window to the man standing next to the police officer, the identification—although made as a consequence of suggestive circumstances—was not due to identification procedures arranged by the police. *Perry v. New Hampshire, supra.*

b. Suppression hearing

A defendant who has moved to suppress an identification is entitled to a suppression hearing. This hearing usually is held outside the presence of the jury, although exclusion of the jury is not constitutionally required.

c. Remedy for violation

A conviction as the result of a trial in which an illegal identification was admitted will be overturned **unless,** under the doctrine of harmless error, the appellate court is convinced beyond a reasonable doubt that the improperly admitted identification did not contribute to the verdict.

B. PRELIMINARY PROCEEDINGS

Subsequent to the defendant's arrest, various court proceedings may be held. These pretrial proceedings, which take various forms depending on the jurisdiction, can include a hearing to determine probable cause to detain (a *Gerstein* hearing), an initial appearance, an arraignment, a detention or bail hearing, and a preliminary hearing to determine probable cause to prosecute the defendant. Some of these proceedings may be combined, and some may not be required. In addition, the defendant may make various motions, including motions to suppress evidence obtained in violation of the defendant's constitutional rights.

1. Probable Cause to Detain (*Gerstein* Hearing)

Under the Fourth Amendment, a preliminary hearing must be held after the defendant's arrest to determine whether probable cause exists to hold the defendant, unless such determination has already been made before the defendant's arrest through a grand jury indictment or the judicial issuance of an arrest warrant. *Gerstein v. Pugh*, 420 U.S. 103 (1975). This hearing, known as a *Gerstein* hearing, need not be adversarial. There is no right to counsel at this hearing, and hearsay evidence may be introduced, but a hearing not held within 48 hours after arrest is presumptively unreasonable. *County of Riverside v. McLaughlin*, 500 U.S. 44 (1991). However, the failure to hold this hearing does not affect the prosecution of the defendant for the charged offense, other than the exclusion of any evidence discovered as a consequence of the unlawful detainment. Under the Fifth Amendment, all felony charges must be by indictment of a federal grand jury, unless waived by the defendant.

2. **Initial Appearance**

    Soon after the defendant is arrested, the defendant must be brought before a judge who advises the defendant of the charges against him and of his rights and who appoints counsel if the defendant is indigent. During this initial appearance, which may be held in conjunction with a *Gerstein* hearing, the judge may also determine whether the defendant should be released prior to trial and the conditions of the release (e.g., bail), accept a plea from the defendant, and set a date for a preliminary hearing.

3. **Arraignment**

    At an arraignment, the court informs the defendant of the crime with which the defendant has been charged and elicits the defendant's response (i.e., plea) to those charges. At this time, the court may appoint counsel for an indigent defendant. These events may also take place at the initial appearance.

4. **Detention Hearing**

    In conjunction with the defendant's initial appearance or at a separate hearing, the court may determine whether to release the defendant and any conditions upon such release. At such time, the court may set bail (*see* § C. Right to Bail, *infra*).

5. **Preliminary Hearing to Determine Probable Cause to Prosecute**

    Subsequent to the defendant's initial appearance, a preliminary hearing may be held to determine whether there is probable cause to believe that the defendant has committed a specific crime. At this hearing, which is an adversarial proceeding, the defendant has the right to counsel. *Coleman v. Alabama*, 399 U.S. 1 (1970). A defendant who has been indicted by a grand jury is not entitled to this hearing.

C. **RIGHT TO BAIL**

    There is no explicit constitutional right to bail. However, any denial of bail must comply with the Due Process Clause. Therefore, the setting of excessive bail or the refusal to set bail is immediately appealable. Furthermore, bail set higher than an amount reasonably calculated to ensure the defendant's presence at trial is "excessive" under the Eighth Amendment.

1. **Statutory Bail Provisions**

    The Bail Reform Act of 1984 governs release or detention determinations in federal courts in criminal proceedings. Many states have modeled similar statutory bail provisions on the Act.

2. **Presumptions Pre- and Post-Conviction**

    There is a presumption in favor of pre-trial release. A detention hearing must be held at the initial appearance for there to be a release. However, there is a presumption against bail post-conviction, pending appeal. The Federal Rules of Evidence do not apply at detention hearings.

3. **Pre-Trial Detention**

    Certain pretrial detention practices that are reasonably related to maintaining jail security are permissible and do not violate due process or the Fourth Amendment. These include routine inspections of inmates' cells, prohibiting receipt of outside food or personal belongings, body-cavity searches, and double bunking.

D. COMPETENCY

Incompetency is a bar to trial. The judge has a constitutional duty to investigate and determine the competence of the defendant to stand trial if such evidence is apparent to the judge. A separate hearing is held to assess the defendant's competency. The test for whether a defendant is competent to stand trial is the same test for determining whether the defendant is competent to plead guilty: whether the defendant comprehends the nature of the proceedings against him and has the ability to consult with a lawyer with a reasonable degree of rational understanding.

If the defendant is declared mentally incompetent to stand trial, and the charge is a serious criminal offense, then the government may administer antipsychotic drugs. Three conditions must be met before the defendant can receive these drugs:

i) The treatment should not cause serious side effects that would affect the fairness of the trial;

ii) The treatment is necessary and there is no less intrusive method to further the government's important interest; and

iii) The treatment is medically appropriate.

Sell v. United States, 539 U.S. 166 (2003).

Insanity Defense Distinguished: The insanity defense considers the defendant's mental condition at the time of the crime, whereas incompetence concerns the defendant's mental condition at the time of the trial. Detention also varies depending on whether it is based on incompetency or insanity. In a successful insanity defense, the defendant may be detained in a mental hospital for a longer term than incarceration requires. If a defendant is found to be incompetent, confinement in a mental hospital must be limited to a brief period of time for evaluation.

The conviction of a legally incompetent defendant or the failure of the trial court to provide an adequate competency determination violates due-process principles by depriving the defendant of the constitutional right to a fair trial. State courts may place the burden of proving incompetence on the defendant, but they may not require the defendant to prove it by clear and convincing evidence.

E. GRAND JURIES

1. Indictment

After hearing the prosecution's evidence, the grand jury decides whether there is probable cause to charge a particular defendant with a particular crime and, if so, returns a "true bill" of indictment. (This formal charging process is mandated by the Fifth Amendment under the federal system for felonies and is used in most eastern states, but a state is not constitutionally required to use this process, as the Fifth Amendment Grand Jury Clause has not been incorporated by the Fourteenth Amendment. In most western states, the charging process is initiated by filing an information by a prosecutor.)

2. Grand Jury Proceedings

a. Defendant's rights

The grand jury is a non-adversarial proceeding. The proceedings are conducted in secret, and the defendant has no right to present or confront witnesses or to introduce evidence. The defendant is not entitled to a dismissal due to a procedural defect in grand jury proceedings, unless the defect substantially impacted the grand jury's decision to indict. However, the defendant (or any other witness) may make a motion to seal the grand jury report if he believes that he has been defamed.

1) Double jeopardy

Because jeopardy does not attach until a trial begins, the Double Jeopardy Clause does not apply to grand jury proceedings. The refusal of a grand jury to indict a defendant with respect to a specific crime does not prevent the indictment of the defendant for the same crime by another grand jury. *United States v. Williams*, 504 U.S. 36, 49 (1992). (*See* § VI.A., Double Jeopardy, *infra*.)

b. Role of the prosecutor

The prosecutor is the advisor to the grand jury. As such, the prosecutor's role is to advise the grand jury with respect to the law and assist the grand jury in its job of issuing subpoenas for witnesses and evidence. The prosecutor has no legal obligation to present evidence exculpating the defendant to the grand jury. Thus, a grand jury indictment cannot be dismissed for the prosecutor's failure to present exculpatory evidence, unless the prosecutor violated a preexisting constitutional or legislative rule. The prosecutor is subject to the grand jury secrecy rules.

c. Witness's rights

A grand jury witness has no right to counsel in the grand jury room. The witness may request permission to consult with counsel outside of the jury room before answering a grand jury question. A prosecutor's failure to give a *Miranda* warning to a witness who then lies to a grand jury does not prevent the prosecution of the witness for perjury. *United States v. Wong*, 431 U.S. 174 (1977). Further, a witness who is a target of an investigation and may become a defendant is not entitled to a warning of his putative defendant status; the failure to receive such a warning does not protect a lying witness from a perjury conviction. *United States v. Washington*, 431 U.S. 181 (1977).

d. Grand jury's role

The grand jury has subpoena power to investigate matters before it or to initiate criminal proceedings. The subpoena can be quashed by the opposing party if he can demonstrate that the evidence sought is not relevant to the investigation. However, the witness or defendant cannot attack the subpoena based on the grand jury's lack of probable cause. The grand jury is not restricted to hearing evidence that would be admissible at trial; an indictment may generally be based on hearsay or illegally obtained evidence. *United States v. Calandra*, 414 U.S. 338, 348 (1974) (illegally seized evidence admissible in grand jury proceeding); *Costello v. United States*, 350 U.S. 359 (1956) (hearsay evidence admissible in grand jury proceeding). (Note: By federal statute, information obtained from an illegal wiretap cannot be presented to a grand jury. 18 U.S.C. 2515.) The grand jury may not exclude members of minority races, regardless of whether they are the same race as the defendant. Such exclusion will lead to a reversal of the indictment without regard to the harmlessness of the error. *Campbell v. Louisiana*, 523 U.S. 392 (1998); *Vasquez v. Hillery*, 474 U.S. 254 (1986).

F. STATE'S DUTY TO DISCLOSE

The prosecution has an affirmative duty to disclose any material evidence favorable to the defendant and relevant to the prosecution's case in chief that would negate guilt or diminish culpability or punishment. *Brady v. Maryland*, 373 U.S. 83 (1963). Failure to make such a disclosure violates the Due Process Clause and is grounds for reversal, regardless of whether the failure to disclose was intentional, if the defendant can show that (i) the evidence is favorable to the defendant (i.e., is exculpatory or impeaches) and (ii) the failure to disclose caused prejudice against the defendant (i.e., there is a reasonable probability of a different outcome had the evidence been disclosed earlier). *Strickler v. Green*, 527 U.S. 263, 281-282 (1999); *United States v. Bagley*, 473 U.S. 667, 675 (1985). This duty does not extend to disclosure of impeachment evidence prior to a plea bargain agreement, *United States v. Ruiz*, 536 U.S. 622 (2002), or to post-conviction proceedings.

V. TRIAL

A. JURY TRIAL

In the federal system, the Sixth Amendment provides the right to jury trials. States are obligated under the Fourteenth Amendment to provide jury trials in criminal cases involving only serious offenses. *Duncan v. Louisiana*, 391 U.S. 145 (1968). States have wide latitude, though, to determine the conduct and details of jury use.

Criminal defendants, with some exceptions, are entitled to be present at initial arraignments, at every trial stage (including jury empanelment and the reading of the verdict) and at sentencing. *Lewis v. United States*, 146 U.S. 370; *Diaz v. United States*, 223 U.S. 442, 455. Organizational defendants, defendants accused of misdemeanors, and defendants who persist in disruptive behavior, after being warned by the judge that such behavior could result in removal, need not be present.

1. Maximum Sentence to Exceed Six Months

There is a constitutional right to a jury trial for **non-petty offenses**—those that carry an authorized sentence of **more than six months of imprisonment,** regardless of the actual penalty imposed. *Baldwin v. New York*, 399 U.S. 66 (1970). The right to a jury trial attaches for crimes punishable by six months of imprisonment or less only if additional statutory or regulatory penalties make the offense a "non-petty offense." *United States v. Nachtigal*, 507 U.S. 1 (1993) (a misdemeanor for which the maximum punishment was six months in prison and a $5,000 fine or probation not to exceed five years was not a serious offense). There is no right to trial by jury for multiple petty offenses (those that carry a combined total maximum term exceeding six months); the prison terms imposed for such convictions are not aggregated.

a. Contempt

In a civil contempt case, there is no jury trial requirement if the witness can avoid the punishment by complying with the court order. In a criminal contempt case that has no statutorily authorized punishment, the right to a jury trial is determined by the actual penalty imposed. Thus, a sentence of over six months would trigger the right to a jury trial. However, an alleged contemnor is not entitled to a jury trial simply because a strong possibility exists that upon conviction he will face a substantial term of imprisonment regardless of the punishment actually imposed. Moreover, if a sentence is imposed for contempt and it is more than six months, an appellate court may reduce the sentence to six months or less to protect the conviction against constitutional attack for lack of a jury. There is no right to a jury trial when the sentence imposed is probation, regardless of the length of the probation, at least when imprisonment following revocation of probation does not exceed six months.

2. Waiver

A defendant may waive the right to a jury trial and opt for a trial by judge, known as a "bench trial," if the waiver is freely and intelligently made. *Adams v. United States ex rel McCann*, 317 U.S. 269 (1942). However, the defendant does not have an absolute right to a bench trial. The court or prosecutor may compel the defendant to submit to a jury trial, unless the defendant would be denied a fair trial. *Singer v. United States*, 380 U.S. 24 (1965).

3. **Compliance**

   a. **Jury size and unanimity**

   A jury of less than six members is a denial of due process, and a unanimous verdict is constitutionally required if a jury is made up of only six members. For state-court juries of seven or more, the vote need not be unanimous, but there is no strict rule as to how many votes are required for conviction. *Apodaca v. Oregon*, 406 U.S. 404 (1972).

   The Federal Rules of Criminal Procedure require a unanimous vote by a 12-member jury in federal criminal trials, unless waived in writing and approved by the court. A verdict by 11 jurors is permitted if the 12th juror is excused for good cause after deliberations begin.

   b. **Composition of the jury**

      1) **Representative cross-section of the community**

      The Equal Protection Clause bars racial discrimination in the selection of juries, including grand juries. The requirement that a jury be selected from a representative cross-section of the community also extends to gender discrimination. However, the actual jury selected need not represent a fair cross-section of the community. *Holland v. Illinois*, 493 U.S. 474, 480 (1990).

      2) **All defendants may challenge jury selection discrimination**

      The defendant has standing to challenge the jury-selection process, regardless of any showing of actual bias. *Powers v. Ohio*, 499 U.S. 400, 410–411 (1991).

      3) **Prima facie case**

      The prima facie case for absence of a representative cross-section can be established by showing that:

         i) The group allegedly excluded is a **"distinctive" group** in the community;

         ii) The group was not **fairly represented** in the venire from which the jury was chosen; and

         iii) The underrepresentation resulted from a **systematic exclusion** of the group in the jury-selection process.

      To rebut, the prosecution must show that the disproportionate exclusion manifestly and primarily advances a significant governmental interest.

      4) **State's right to use neutral principles**

      In response to a claim of intentional racial discrimination in jury selection, the state has the right to apply neutral, nonracial principles to jury selection, even though it results in a smaller percentage of minorities on juries. The state must prove "absence of discriminatory intent."

      5) **Peremptory challenges**

      Peremptory challenges are requests by both parties during the voir dire jury-selection process to disqualify potential jurors without the need to show cause.

a) Discriminatory use

The Fourteenth Amendment Equal Protection Clause prohibits both the criminal defendant and the prosecutor from exercising peremptory challenges solely based on race, ethnicity, or gender. *J.E.B. v. Alabama*, 511 U.S. 127 (1994) (gender); *Batson v. Kentucky*, 476 U.S. 79, 84 (1986) (race); *Hernandez v. New York*, 400 U.S. 352 (1991) (ethnicity). The defendant need not be a member of the excluded group in order to have standing to contest the prosecution's use of its peremptory challenges.

If the explanation for striking a juror is deemed pretextual, then it gives rise to an inference of discriminatory intent that makes it difficult for the challenge to survive. *Snyder v. Louisiana*, 552 U.S. 472, 485 (2008).

The United States Supreme Court has set forth a three-prong test (the "*Batson*" test) to determine whether a **peremptory challenge** has been exercised on the basis of race, in violation of the Equal Protection Clause of the Fourteenth Amendment. The test requires that:

i) The moving party establishes a **prima facie case of discrimination**;

ii) The party who exercised the challenge provides a **race-neutral explanation** for the strike;

iii) The moving party carries her burden of **proving that the other party's proffered reason was pretextual** and that the strike was indeed motivated by purposeful discrimination.

Once the party who exercised the challenge offers a race-neutral explanation and the trial court has ruled on the ultimate question of intentional discrimination, the preliminary issue becomes moot. **The ultimate burden of persuasion regarding racial motivation rests with the opponent of the strike.**

b) Not constitutionally required

The loss of a peremptory challenge does not violate the right to an impartial jury. *Ross v. Oklahoma*, 487 U.S. 81, 88 (1988). A defendant's exercise of peremptory challenges does not violate this right when the defendant chooses to use such a challenge to remove a juror who should have been excused for cause. *United States v. Martinez-Salazar*, 528 U.S. 304, 307 (2000).

c) Harmless-error doctrine

The Constitution allows states to choose between harmless-error review and automatic reversal when a judge, acting in good faith, erroneously denies a defendant's peremptory challenge. *Rivera v. Illinois*, 556 U.S. 148 (2009). Thus, if state law permits harmless-error review of the erroneous seating of the juror, there is no constitutional requirement for automatic reversal of the defendant's conviction.

c. Impartial jury

The Sixth Amendment provides that an accused person is entitled to a trial by an impartial jury. Claims of juror bias and misconduct are subject to the harmless-error rule.

1) Views on race

A defendant is entitled to inquire on voir dire into ethnic or racial prejudice of possible jury members only when the issues to be tried involve allegations of racial or ethnic prejudice, or whenever race is "inextricably bound up in the case." *Ristiano v. Ross*, 424 U.S. 589, 597 (1976).

2) Views on capital punishment

Prospective jurors who are opposed to the death penalty may be removed for cause if their opposition to the death penalty is so strong as to prevent or substantially impair the performance of their duties at the sentencing phase of the trial. *Wainwright v. Wirr*, 469 U.S. 412, 424–425 (1985); *Adams v. Texas*, 448 U.S. 38, 44 (1980).

An improper exclusion of a juror from a jury that imposed a death sentence is subject to automatic reversal. *Gray v. Mississippi*, 481 U.S. 648, 668 (1987).

d. Sentencing

1) Enhancements

When a sentence may be increased if additional facts are established, a jury must determine the existence of such facts. Enhancement of a defendant's sentence by a judge without such a determination violates the defendant's right to a jury trial. *Apprendi v. New Jersey*, 530 U.S. 466, 476 (2000). This limitation on a judge's ability to impose an enhanced sentence also applies when the defendant has entered a guilty plea. *Blakely v. Washington*, 542 U.S. 296 (2004). However, the harmless-error test applies to determine whether a sentence enhanced in violation of a defendant's right to a jury trial must be reversed. *Washington v. Recuenco*, 548 U.S. 212 (2006).

2) Concurrent versus consecutive sentences

Judges can decide whether sentences for multiple crimes run concurrently or consecutively without violating this right. *Oregon v. Ice*, 555 U.S. 160 (2009).

e. Inconsistent verdicts

If a jury renders a verdict that a defendant is guilty of certain offenses but not guilty of other related offenses, then the verdict is not reviewable on the grounds of inconsistency, even when the jury acquits the defendant of an offense that is a predicate offense to an offense for which the same jury finds the defendant guilty. *United States v. Powell*, 469 U.S. 57 (1984). This rule, which permits inconsistent verdicts, is also applicable when a defendant is convicted of an offense for which a co-defendant, who is tried at the same time, is acquitted, even though the facts would logically dictate the same verdict for each defendant. *United States v. Dotterweich*, 320 U.S. 277 (1943). This rule extends to bench as well as jury trials. *Harris v. Rivera*, 454 U.S. 339 (1981). (Note: The defendant may challenge a jury verdict on the grounds that there was insufficient evidence to establish the defendant's commission of a crime.)

B. GUILTY PLEAS

A guilty plea is an admission of facts contained in the charging document (e.g., indictment, information).

1. Knowing and Voluntary

Because a guilty plea constitutes both a confession and a waiver of various constitutional rights, the plea must be both intelligent and voluntary. *Boykin v.*

Alabama, 395 U.S. 238 (1969); *McCarthy v. United States*, 394 U.S. 459 (1969). The record must reflect that the judge has determined that the defendant knows and understands the following:

i) The nature of the charges and their essential elements;

ii) The consequences of the plea (e.g., the maximum and minimum possible sentences, possible immigration consequences); and

iii) The rights that the defendant is waiving (e.g., right to a trial).

(Note: The judge does not personally need to explain each element of the crime. It is sufficient for the defendant's counsel to explain the nature and elements of the crime to him. *Bradshaw v. Stumpf*, 545 U.S. 175 (2005).) The judge must also determine that the plea did not result from force or improper threats or from promises other than those contained in the plea agreement.

a. Factual basis for plea

The U.S. Constitution does not forbid criminal sentencing of defendants who are willing to waive their trial and accept a plea while maintaining their innocence. Therefore, because an express admission of guilt is not a constitutional requisite for the imposition of a criminal penalty, a judge may accept pleas that result in a criminal sentence without violating the Constitution, even if the defendant maintains his factual innocence. However, Rule 11(b)(3) of the Federal Rules of Criminal Procedure requires a judge to ascertain that there is factual basis for a defendant's plea in order to accept a guilty plea. Therefore, when the defendant asserts his innocence despite entering a guilty plea, the judge must determine that there is a factual basis for the plea in order to accept the plea. *North Carolina v. Alford*, 400 U.S. 25, 37 (1970).

b. Effect of violation

When the court fails to ensure that the plea was knowing and voluntary, the defendant is entitled to withdraw his plea.

2. Right to Counsel

In entering a plea, a defendant has the right to counsel. *White v. Maryland*, 373 U.S. 59 (1963).

3. Plea Bargain

A plea bargain between the prosecutor and the defendant is treated as a contract. The bargain may involve the crimes with which the defendant has been charged, such as a promise by the prosecutor to drop specific charges in exchange for the defendant's promise to plead guilty to other charges, or the defendant's sentence, such as a promise by the prosecutor to recommend a particular sentence in exchange for the defendant's guilty plea.

a. No right to bargain

A defendant cannot compel the prosecutor to bargain; the defendant does not have a constitutional right to plea bargain. *Weatherford v. Bursey*, 429 U.S. 545 (1977).

b. Pressure to bargain

A defendant's plea made in response to the prosecution's threat to bring more serious charges does not violate the protection of the Due Process Clause against prosecutorial vindictiveness, at least when the prosecution has probable cause to believe that the defendant has committed the crimes. *Bordenkircher v. Hayes*, 434 U.S. 357 (1978). Similarly, the bringing of felony charges against a defendant after the defendant asserted his right to a jury trial for misdemeanor offenses related to the same incident does not in itself constitute prosecutorial vindictiveness. *United States v. Goodwin*, 457 U.S. 368 (1982).

c. No duty to disclose impeachment information

The prosecution is not required to disclose impeachment information or information related to an affirmative defense to a defendant when the defendant enters into a plea bargain agreement prior to trial. The failure to disclose such information does not render the defendant's plea bargain involuntary. *United States v. Ruiz*, 536 U.S. 622 (2002).

d. Enforcement of the bargain

1) Court

When entering into a plea bargain, the agreement is enforceable against the defendant and the prosecutor, but not against the judge. If the judge is not satisfied with the bargain, he can reject the plea. A defendant does not have a constitutional right to have his plea accepted by the court.

2) Prosecution

Should the prosecution violate the provisions of the plea bargain, the judge decides whether specific performance of the plea is required or whether the defendant can withdraw his plea. *Santobello v. New York*, 404 U.S. 257 (1971).

3) Defense

If a defendant fails to abide by the plea agreement (e.g., fails to testify in another trial), then the prosecution can have the sentence vacated and reinstate the original charge. *Ricketts v. Adamson*, 483 U.S. 1 (1987).

4. Effect of the Plea on the Defendant's Rights

Generally, a defendant, by entering a guilty plea, waives his constitutional rights, such as the right to a trial, the privilege against self-incrimination, and the right to confront his accusers. However, a defendant may challenge a guilty plea on the due-process grounds that it was not a knowing and voluntary waiver of such rights. *Boykin v. Alabama*, 395 U.S. 238 (1969). In addition, a guilty plea does not constitute a waiver of a double jeopardy challenge unless the waiver is agreed to in the plea agreement. *Menna v. New York*, 423 U.S. 61 (1975). A defendant may also attack a guilty plea that is due to ineffective assistance of counsel. *Hill v. Lockhart*, 474 U.S. 52 (1985). (Note: A defendant may also challenge a guilty plea on the grounds that the court lacked jurisdiction. *Menna v. New York, supra.*)

C. SPEEDY TRIAL

The Due Process Clause and federal and state statutes protect defendants from intentional and prejudicial **pre-accusation** delay. The Sixth Amendment speedy trial guarantee, the Fourteenth Amendment, the Speedy Trial Act of 1974, and other federal and state statutes protect defendants from undue **post-accusation** delay.

1. Commencement of the Right

Statutes of limitations are the primary safeguards against pre-accusation delay. However, the Due Process Clause may be violated if the delay was used to obtain a tactical advantage for the prosecution or to harass the defendant. *United States v.*

Marion, 404 U.S. 307 (1971). Delay resulting from an investigation conducted in good faith does not violate the Due Process Clause. *United States v. Lovasco*, 431 U.S. 783 (1977).

Under the Sixth and Fourteenth Amendments, the time period commences at the time of arrest or formal charge, whichever comes first. The defendant need not know about the charges against him for the right to attach.

2. Balancing Test

The factors to be considered in determining whether the defendant has been deprived of a speedy trial post-accusation are the:

i) Length of the delay;

ii) Reason for the delay;

iii) Defendant's assertion of a right to a speedy trial; and

iv) Prejudice to the defendant.

Courts weigh these factors and determine whether the state made a "diligent, good-faith effort" to bring the defendant to trial. *Barker v. Wingo*, 407 U.S. 514, 530 (1972). A delay caused by the inaction of an attorney assigned by the state to represent the defendant may be attributable to the defendant, but a delay caused by the court's failure to promptly appoint replacement counsel when an assigned attorney withdraws or by a breakdown in the public-defender system is attributable to the state. *Vermont v. Brillon*, 556 U.S. 81 (2009).

3. Remedy

If the defendant's right to a speedy trial is violated, the charges are dismissed with prejudice.

D. PUBLIC TRIAL

1. Defendant's Right

The Sixth Amendment guarantees a criminal defendant the right to a public trial. The defendant may waive the right and request a closed proceeding. However, because the request also implicates the First Amendment right of access of the press and the public, the court must consider several factors, and the likelihood of a closed proceeding is slight. The court may even allow the proceedings to be televised over the defendant's objection.

The right to a public trial extends to preliminary hearings and suppression hearings. A suppression hearing may be closed if (i) there is an overriding interest likely to be prejudiced by an open trial, (ii) the closure is not in excess of the interest, (iii) other alternatives have been considered, and (iv) the court enters adequate findings to support closure.

2. Public's Right

Regardless of the wishes of the defendant or prosecutor, a trial must be public unless there is either a *substantial likelihood* of prejudice to the defendant or a need to limit access to ensure an orderly proceeding. This right extends even to voir dire and many other preliminary matters. *Press-Enterprise Co. v. Superior Court of CA (Press-Enterprise I)*, 464 U.S. 501, 509–10 (1984).

E.   FAIR TRIAL

1.   Impartial Judge

Due process requires that a judge possess neither actual nor apparent bias. If actual or apparent bias exists, the judge must follow a recusal process in the federal or state jurisdiction.   The impermissible bias or prejudice usually must stem from an extrajudicial source.

2.   Fair Conduct by the Prosecutor

a.   Examples of misconduct

A prosecutor may not:

i)   Make material misstatements of law or fact;

ii)   Elicit information from the defendant outside the presence of his counsel;

iii)   Express opinions about the defendant's guilt or innocence;

iv)   Make unfair or improper remarks about the defendant, his counsel, or witnesses;

v)   Comment on the defendant's failure to testify at trial; or

vi)   Make improper remarks to the jury to inflame their passions to convict for an improper reason.

b.   No use of false testimony

A prosecutor may not knowingly use perjured or false testimony for the case in chief, for sentencing, or to impeach the credibility of a witness.

c.   No suppression of favorable evidence

As discussed in IV.F., *supra,* due process requires the prosecution to disclose evidence favorable to the accused (i.e., exculpatory or impeaching) when such evidence is material to guilt or punishment. Evidence is material if there is a "reasonable probability" that disclosure would have changed the outcome of the proceeding; a reasonable probability is "a probability sufficient to undermine confidence in the outcome." *United States v. Bagley*, 473 U.S. 667, 682 (1985). The prosecution's failure to disclose evidence in its possession both favorable and material to the defense entitles the defendant to a new trial. *Brady v. Maryland*, 373 U.S. 83 (1963). Under *Bagley*, the prosecution's failure to turn over specifically requested evidence will seldom, if ever, be excused.

Similarly, police violate due process when, in bad faith, they destroy evidence that would have been useful to the defendant at trial. The defendant does not, however, have the right to require police to preserve all evidence if it is not certain that the evidence would have been exculpatory.

F.   RIGHT TO CONFRONTATION

1.   Trial

The accused has the right to directly encounter adverse witnesses, to cross-examine adverse witnesses, and to be present at any stage of the trial that would enable the defendant to effectively cross-examine adverse witnesses as guaranteed by the Sixth and Fourteenth Amendments. Not only does this right allow the defendant to cross-examine the adverse witness, but it also allows the defendant to observe the demeanor of the adverse witness. A witness may invoke the right against self-incrimination; however, such an invocation after testimony has already been made may violate the defendant's right to confrontation, guaranteed by the Sixth and Fourteenth Amendments, because the witness's invocation will prevent adequate cross-examination by the defendant.

2. Compliance

a. Face-to-face confrontation

Face-to-face confrontation is not an absolute right. A criminal defendant has the right to confront witnesses against him under the Sixth Amendment, unless preventing such confrontation is necessary to further an important public policy and the reliability of the testimony is otherwise assured. A defendant who voluntarily leaves the courtroom or a disruptive defendant whom the judge removes from the courtroom has not had his right to confrontation violated. This is to be determined on a case-by-case basis.

The state's interest in protecting child witnesses from more than *de minimis* trauma as a result of testifying in the defendant's presence is considered an important public purpose under this rule. *Maryland v. Craig*, 497 U.S. 836, 855–856 (1990).

b. Cross-examination of witnesses

The right to confrontation means more than being allowed to confront the witness physically. The principal purpose of confrontation is to secure for the defendant the opportunity of cross-examination of the prosecution's witnesses.

1) Impeachment for bias

A denial of the opportunity to cross-examine a prosecution witness with regard to bias violates the Confrontation Clause. *Delaware v. Van Arsdall*, 475 U.S. 673, 679 (1986). However, such denial is subject to harmless-error analysis. Moreover, trial judges retain wide latitude to impose reasonable limits on such cross-examination based on concerns about, among other things, harassment, prejudice, confusion of the issues, the safety of the witness, or interrogation that is repetitive or only marginally relevant. *Id.*

2) Memory loss by the witness

The fact that a witness has a memory loss does not by itself violate the Confrontation Clause. *Delaware v. Fensterer*, 474 U.S. 15, 19–20 (1985). The Supreme Court has held that the Confrontation Clause does not bar testimony concerning a prior out-of-court identification when the identifying witness is unable, because of memory loss, to explain the basis for the identification. A defendant may conduct an effective cross-examination if given the opportunity to address the very fact of the poor memory of the witness. *United States v. Owens*, 484 U.S. 554, 564 (1988).

3) Confrontation Clause and the hearsay rule

The Confrontation Clause limits the use of hearsay evidence in a criminal trial. Out-of-court statements by witnesses that are "testimonial" are barred under the Confrontation Clause, unless the witnesses are unavailable and the defendant had a prior opportunity to cross-examine those witnesses, regardless of whether such statements are deemed reliable by the court. If, however, the declarant appears for cross-examination at trial, then the Confrontation Clause places no constraints at all on the use of the declarant's prior out-of-court testimonial statements. *Crawford v. Washington*, 541 U.S. 36, 59 (2004).

Out-of-court testimonial statements are not barred by the Confrontation Clause when they are used for a purpose other than establishing the truth of the matter asserted (i.e., when they are not used for a hearsay purpose). *Id.* *See also Tennessee v. Street*, 471 U.S. 409, 417 (1985).

The Confrontation Clause has no application to "non-testimonial" out-of-court statements. *Whorton v. Bockting*, 549 U.S. 406, 420 (2007).

a) **Testimonial statements**

A statement is considered "testimonial" if the declarant would reasonably expect it to be used in a prosecution. Such statements include affidavits, custodial examinations, prior testimony, and statements given in response to police interrogation. *Crawford v. Washington*, 541 U.S. 36, 40 (2004). The Supreme Court has also held that certificates of analysis, which state the results of state laboratory tests, are testimonial evidence that may not be admitted without accompanying live testimony by the analyst who conducted the tests. *Melendez-Diaz v. Massachusetts*, 557 U.S. 305, 340 (2009). It is not sufficient to substitute the testimony of another analyst who is familiar with the testing protocol but did not perform or observe the tests or sign the report. *Bullcoming v. New Mexico*, 564 U.S. 647 (2011).

b) **Non-testimonial statements**

The Confrontation Clause permits the admission of non-testimonial statements, even if they lack indicia of reliability. *Whorton v. Bockting*, 549 U.S. 406, 411 (2007). Statements made for the primary purpose of assisting the police in the investigation of an ongoing emergency are not testimonial. Examples of non-testimonial statements include statements made to a 911 operator during a domestic dispute, *Davis v. Washington*, 547 U.S. 813, 822 (2006), and statements made to police officers by the victim of a mortal gunshot wound as he lay in a gas-station parking lot. *Michigan v. Bryant*, 562 U.S. 344 (2011).

4) **Witness unavailable**

The right of confrontation is satisfied if the defense counsel had a right to cross-examine the witness at an earlier hearing, provided that the prosecution failed in a good-faith effort to produce the witness at the trial and the declarant is now unavailable. However, if the witness is unavailable because the defendant acted with a purpose to prevent the witness from testifying, then testimonial hearsay is admissible. *Giles v. California*, 554 U.S. 353, 373 (2008).

5) **Confession of a non-testifying co-defendant at a joint trial**

a) *Bruton* **rule**

The admission of a confession by a non-testifying co-defendant at a joint trial against the defendant violates the Sixth Amendment, even when it merely corroborates the defendant's own confession. *Bruton v. United States*, 391 U.S. 123, 132 (1968). A limiting instruction will not cure the defect. If the co-defendant testifies, then the rule does not apply. The rule does not apply at a bench trial. *Lee v. Illinois*, 476 U.S. 530, 539 (1986). It also does not apply to the statements of an accomplice who is not tried as a co-defendant or to a co-defendant who takes the stand and denies making such a statement. *Nelson v. O'Neil*, 402 U.S. 622, 629–630 (1971); *Dutton v. Evans*, 400 U.S. 74, 88–89 (1970).

b) Harmless error

Admission of a co-defendant's statement in violation of *Bruton*, however, is subject to harmless-error analysis. *Schneble v. Florida*, 405 U.S. 427, 430 (1972).

c) Severance

The accused may assert a demand for a severance of the trial of his case from a co-defendant's case whenever the prosecution intends to introduce a confession that is hostile to one co-defendant, and the confession:

  i) Implicates the confessing defendant but is not admissible against the non-confessing defendant; and

  ii) Cannot be edited to exclude inculpation of the non-confessing defendant.

Bruton v. United States, 391 U.S. 123, 132 (1968). The prosecutor may avoid severance if the court denies the use of the statement or the prosecutor chooses not to use it at trial.

G.   DUE PROCESS

1.   Right to Testify

A defendant has a right to testify and to present evidence on his own behalf.

2.   Burden of Proof

a. Presumptions

1) Presumption of innocence

While a defendant is not automatically entitled to a jury instruction apprising the jury of the presumption of innocence doctrine, the presumption is a basic tenet of a fair trial, and it may be required when necessary for a fair trial. *Kentucky v. Whorton*, 441 U.S. 786, 789 (1979).

2) Presumptions of facts

a) Permissive presumption

A permissive presumption (i.e., a presumption that the trier of fact is not compelled to accept and that does not shift the burden of proof) regarding an element of an offense does not violate the due-process requirement that the prosecution must prove each element of an offense unless the presumption is irrational. A presumption is not irrational if it is more likely than not to flow from the proven fact on which it depends. *County Court v. Allen*, 442 U.S. 140, 163–164 (1979) (upholding the statutory presumption that the occupants of a car in which firearms are found are in possession of the firearms).

b) Mandatory presumption

A mandatory presumption regarding an element of an offense violates the due-process requirement. *Sandstrom v. Montana*, 442 U.S. 510, 522 (1979) (jury instruction that a person intends the ordinary consequences of his voluntary acts constituted a mandatory presumption when the crime—deliberate homicide—required proof of intent). This could include either a conclusive presumption that cannot be rebutted (which would relieve the prosecution of having to prove an element of their case), or a rebuttable mandatory presumption (which shifts the burden of proof regarding the element of the offense). To the extent that these presumptions require the trier of fact to accept a fact as proving an element of the crime and disallow the trier of fact from rejecting it, or shift the burden of an element to the defense, they are unconstitutional. *County Court,* 442 U.S. at 159; *Sandstrom,* 442 U.S. at 524.

b. Elements of the prosecution's case

The Due Process Clause requires that the prosecution prove all of the elements of the case beyond a reasonable doubt. Due process does not require the court to use any particular words to advise the jury of the government's burden of proof. In some jurisdictions, the failure to instruct on reasonable doubt may result in reversible error, whereas in other jurisdictions, the lack of such an instruction is per se reversible error.

Sentencing factors need not be proved beyond a reasonable doubt unless the fact is being used to increase the penalty beyond the proscribed statutory maximum, in which case proof beyond a reasonable doubt is required. *Apprendi v. New Jersey,* 530 U.S. 466, 492 (2000).

c. Affirmative defenses

The state is not forbidden by the Due Process Clause from placing the burden of proving an affirmative defense—such as insanity, self-defense, entrapment, or duress—on the defendant. *Dixon v. United States,* 548 U.S. 1, 13 (2006).

d. Directed verdict

In a criminal case, a judge may order a directed verdict only for acquittal; the power to convict is reserved to the jury.

H. SENTENCING

1. Applicable Rights

Sentencing is considered a critical stage triggering the Sixth Amendment right to counsel. A defendant may have the right to confrontation and cross-examination at sentencing, particularly in death-penalty cases, or when a sentence is based upon a finding of new facts beyond those necessary to prove the offense charged. *Gardner v. Florida,* 430 U.S. 349, 358 (1977); *Specht v. Patterson,* 386 U.S. 605, 610 (1967).

2. Enhancement Over the Statutory Maximum

Any fact, other than a prior conviction, that can be used to increase a sentence beyond the statutorily prescribed maximum must be charged in an indictment, submitted to a jury, and established beyond a reasonable doubt. A fact is considered an element of a crime, as opposed to a sentencing enhancement, when it can increase the maximum sentence imposed. The failure to abide by the above procedure is a violation of the defendant's due-process rights under the Fifth Amendment and Sixth Amendment rights to notice and a jury trial, both of which are incorporated against the states through the Fourteenth Amendment. *Apprendi v. New Jersey,* 530 U.S. 466, 476 (2000).

It is not a Sixth Amendment violation for a judge to impose consecutive sentences based on facts that were not found by the jury, but rather by the judge. *Oregon v. Ice,* 555 U.S. 160 (2009). The rule of *Apprendi v. New Jersey, supra,* is thus limited to sentencing for single crimes, not to the arrangement for punishing multiple offenses. However, a sentencing judge, sitting without a jury, may not find the facts necessary to impose the death penalty. *Ring v. Arizona*, 536 U.S. 584 (2002). Similarly, a state law allowing a jury to issue an "advisory sentence," but allowing the judge alone to ultimately weigh the facts to decide whether to impose the death penalty, is unconstitutional. *Hurst v. Florida*, 577 U.S. ___, 136 S. Ct. 616 (2016).

Harmless-error analysis applies in deciding whether or not to overturn a sentence for a judge's failure to submit a sentencing factor to the jury. *Washington v. Recuenco*, 548 U.S. 212, 222 (2006).

I. CRUEL AND UNUSUAL PUNISHMENT

1. Applicability

The Eighth Amendment to the U.S. Constitution prohibits the federal government from imposing cruel and unusual punishment for federal crimes, or "such punishment as would amount to torture or barbarity, any cruel and degrading punishment not known to the common law, or any fine, penalty, confinement, or treatment so disproportionate to the offense as to shock the moral sense of the community." U.S. Const. amend. VIII. The Eighth Amendment's protections are especially important when the sentences imposed are the highest form of punishment under a state's sentencing law.

2. Compliance

a. Non-death penalty

1) Physical conditions of incarceration

The physical conditions of incarceration amount to cruel and unusual punishment only if the prisoner can show that prison officials had actual knowledge of a substantial risk to the prisoners.

2) Physical force

A prisoner need not show serious injury to recover for a violation of the Eighth Amendment prohibition against cruel and unusual punishment. The inquiry is whether the physical force was applied in a good-faith effort to maintain or restore discipline, rather than applied maliciously and sadistically to cause harm.

3) Sentence proportionality

A sentence that is grossly disproportionate to the crime constitutes cruel and unusual punishment. However, a lengthy sentence does not necessarily violate the Eighth Amendment. *Compare Weems v. United States*, 217 U.S. 349 (1910) (reversing punishment of 20 years' imprisonment for falsifying a public record) *with Harmelin v. Michigan*, 501 U.S. 957 (1991) (upholding punishment of life imprisonment without the possibility of parole for drug dealing based on possession of more than 650 grams of cocaine) *and Ewing v. California*, 538 U.S. 11 (2003) (upholding punishment of an indeterminate sentence of 25 years to life for theft of merchandise valued at about $1,200 after conviction of at least two other felonies, at least one of which was serious or violent).

4) Equal protection limitations on punishment

A jail sentence is impermissible if it is imposed only because the defendant was unable to pay a fine. If a defendant has made reasonable bona fide efforts to pay the fine, then revocation of probation without consideration of alternative punishments is fundamentally unfair under the Fourteenth Amendment.

5) Repeat offenders

Some jurisdictions have statutes imposing mandatory indeterminate life sentences (e.g., 25 years to life) on defendants who commit three felonies, even if the felonies are non-violent property-related offenses. These recidivist statutes are not unconstitutional under either the Double Jeopardy Clause of the Fifth Amendment or the Cruel and Unusual Punishment Clause of the Eighth Amendment. *Ewing v. California*, 538 U.S. 11 (2003).

6) Defendant's perjured testimony

If a trial judge believes that the defendant perjured himself during the trial, then the judge may take this belief into consideration when determining the sentence.

b. Capital punishment

The death penalty may be imposed only under a statutory scheme that provides:

i) Clear and objective standards;

ii) Specific and detailed guidance; and

iii) An opportunity for rational review of the process.

1) Homicide crimes

a) Aggravating circumstances

A defendant in a homicide case cannot be sentenced to death unless the trier of fact convicts the defendant of murder and finds at least one "aggravating circumstance" at either the guilt phase or penalty phase. *Brown v. Sanders*, 546 U.S. 212, 218–19 (2006). The aggravating circumstance must meet two requirements:

i) It must not apply to every defendant convicted of murder; and

ii) It must not be unconstitutionally vague. (For example, "especially heinous, atrocious, or cruel" conduct definition is unconstitutionally vague.)

The trier of fact can consider both statutory and non-statutory aggravating circumstances, but the death penalty cannot be imposed without one statutorily defined aggravating factor being found.

b) Mitigating circumstances

A death sentence violates the Eighth and Fourteenth Amendments if the sentencing judge refuses to review or admit mitigating evidence. Mitigating evidence must be presented if it meets a low threshold test for relevance. *Woodson v. North Carolina*, 428 U.S. 280, 316 (1976).

Note: When the death penalty is not imposed (e.g., when the defendant receives a sentence of life in prison without parole), a mandatory sentence may be imposed without the presentation of mitigating evidence. *Harmelin v. Michigan*, 501 U.S. 957, 965 (1991).

Capital-sentencing courts are not required to instruct juries that the defendant need not prove mitigating circumstances beyond a reasonable doubt. *Kansas v. Carr*, 577 U.S. ___, 136 S. Ct. 633 (2016).

c) Felony murder

In felony-murder cases, the death penalty may not be imposed if the defendant, acting as an accomplice, did not kill, attempt to kill, or intend to kill, unless the defendant significantly participated in the commission of the felony and acted with reckless indifference to human life. *Compare Enmund v. Florida*, 458 U.S. 782 (1982) (death penalty not permitted) *with Tison v. Arizona*, 481 U.S. 137 (1987) (death penalty imposed).

2) Non-homicide crimes

Punishment that is disproportionately excessive in relation to the crime committed is prohibited by the Eighth Amendment. The death penalty is considered excessive in rape cases, whether the victim was an adult woman or a child, *Coker v. Georgia*, 433 U.S. 584 (1977); *Kennedy v. Louisiana*, 554 U.S. 407 (2008).

3) Defendant insane

The Eighth Amendment prohibits states from inflicting the death penalty on a prisoner who is insane or can "demonstrate a severe mental disorder." *Panetti v. Quarterman*, 551 U.S. 930, 960 (2007).

4) Intellectual disability of the defendant

The Eighth Amendment prohibits execution of an individual with intellectual disabilities (formerly referred to as "mental retardation"). *Atkins v. Virginia*, 536 U.S. 304 (2002). In determining whether an individual has intellectual disabilities, a state cannot impose a strict cutoff that precludes a finding of intellectual disability if an individual has an IQ of more than 70 or ignore current medical guidelines in defining an intellectual disability because either approach creates "an unacceptable risk that persons with intellectual disability with be executed." *Hall v. Florida*, 572 U.S. 701 (2014) (IQ cutoff); *Moore v. Texas*, 581 U.S. ___, 137 S. Ct. 1039, 1044 (2017) (nonmedical and out-of-date medical factors).

5) Age of the defendant

The Eighth Amendment prohibition against "cruel and unusual punishment" prohibits the execution of a defendant who was younger than 18 years of age at the time of the commission of a crime. *Roper v. Simmons*, 543 U.S. 551, 569 (2005). In addition, the Eighth Amendment prohibits the imposition of a sentence of life without the possibility of parole on a defendant who was younger than 18 years of age at the time of the commission of the crime if the crime was not a homicide. *Graham v. Florida*, 560 U.S. 48 (2010). If the crime was a homicide, the juvenile cannot be subject to a **mandatory** sentence of life imprisonment without the possibility of parole. When sentencing a juvenile, the sentencing judge must take the defendant's youth and other relevant circumstances into consideration. *Miller v. Alabama*, 567 U.S. 460 (2012).

6) Fairness of sentencing proceedings

To minimize the risk of arbitrary action, a capital sentencing process must satisfy, at a minimum, two general requirements:

i) The process must channel or limit the sentencer's discretion in order to genuinely narrow the class of persons eligible for the death penalty and reasonably justify the imposition of a more severe sentence on the defendant compared to others found guilty of murder; and

ii) The court must allow the jury to consider any relevant mitigating evidence that might lead the sentencer to decline to impose the death penalty. The sentencer is also allowed to take into consideration victim impact statements.

If the state puts a capital defendant's future dangerousness at issue, the defendant has the right to inform the jury that the only possible sentence besides death is life imprisonment without parole. *Lynch v. Arizona*, 578 U.S. ___, 136 S. Ct. 1818 (2016).

7) Racial discrimination claims

Under *McCleskey v. Kemp*, 481 U.S. 279 (1987), the Supreme Court held that despite serious statistical evidence of racial disparity in the imposition of the death penalty (e.g., African-American defendants who kill white victims are more likely to receive the death penalty), it was not imposed as a result of unconstitutional discrimination.

8) Lethal injection

Lethal injection is not considered cruel and unusual punishment because there is only a mere possibility that the condemned may receive an improperly administered shot that would cause him unnecessary pain.

c. Adequate medical care

Although prison inmates have a right to adequate medical care, such care constitutes "cruel and unusual punishment" under the Eighth Amendment only when there is a deliberate indifference to the serious medical needs of an inmate. Mere negligence in assessing an inmate's medical condition or in providing treatment is not sufficient to trigger a constitutional violation. *Estelle v. Gamble*, 429 U.S. 97, 104–105 (1976).

VI. POST-TRIAL CONSIDERATIONS

A. DOUBLE JEOPARDY

The Fifth Amendment protection against double jeopardy applies to the federal government. It has been incorporated by the Due Process Clause of the Fourteenth Amendment, and consequently it also applies to the states. *Benton v. Maryland*, 395 U.S. 784 (1969).

1. Protection Against Prosecution and Punishment

The Fifth Amendment Double Jeopardy Clause provides three protections:

i)   Protection against a second prosecution for the same offense after acquittal;

ii) Protection against a second prosecution for the same offense after conviction; and

iii) Protection against multiple punishments for the same offense.

a. **Definition of "same offense"**

1) **Shared elements**

If a defendant's conduct may be prosecuted as two or more crimes, then the *Blockburger* test is applied to determine whether the crimes constitute the same offense for double jeopardy purposes. Under this test, each crime must require the proof of an element that the other does not in order for each to be considered as a separate offense. *Blockburger v. United States*, 284 U.S. 299, 304 (1932).

> **Example 1—No Jeopardy:** A defendant robs a store and shoots and kills the store clerk. The state prosecutes the defendant for premeditated murder. The defendant is acquitted. The state then brings charges against the defendant for robbery. The protection against double jeopardy does not apply because robbery and murder each require the proof of an element that the other does not. Robbery requires, among other elements, the proof that the defendant took the victim's personal property; murder requires, among other elements, the death of the victim.

> **Example 2—Jeopardy:** A defendant robs a store and shoots and kills the store clerk. The state prosecutes the defendant for felony murder based on the robbery. The defendant is acquitted. The state then brings charges against the defendant for robbery. The protection against double jeopardy applies because the state, in order to prove felony murder in the first trial, had to prove that the defendant committed a robbery. *Harris v. Oklahoma*, 433 U.S. 682, 683 (1977).

As a consequence of *Blockburger,* the Double Jeopardy Clause generally bars successive prosecutions for greater and lesser included offenses. A lesser included offense is one that does not require proof of an element beyond those required by the greater offense.

2) **Occurrence of a necessary subsequent event**

When jeopardy has attached with respect to a lesser included offense prior to the occurrence of an event necessary to establish the greater offense, the defendant may be subsequently tried for the greater offense.

> **Example:** A defendant physically harms a victim. He is tried for battery and convicted. The victim subsequently dies as a consequence of the defendant's conduct. The defendant may be tried for murder without running afoul of the Double Jeopardy Clause. *Diaz v. United States*, 223 U.S. 442, 449 (1912).

3) **Statutory offenses**

At a single trial, a defendant may be convicted of two offenses, one of which is a lesser included offense of the other, if both offenses are statutory and the legislature has specifically authorized cumulative punishment. *Missouri v. Hunter*, 459 U.S. 359, 368–369 (1983) (first-degree robbery and armed criminal action).

4) **Conspiracy**

An offense and the conspiracy to commit that offense are not the same offense for double-jeopardy purposes because each requires proof of different elements. *United States v. Felix*, 503 U.S. 378, 389 (1992).

5) Sentence enhancement use

The use of a defendant's prior conviction to enhance the sentence imposed on a defendant for a current conviction does not violate the Double Jeopardy Clause. *Witte v. United States*, 515 U.S. 389, 400 (1995).

b. Acquittal

A defendant who has been acquitted of a crime generally may not be retried for the same crime. A grant of a demurrer or motion to dismiss in favor of the accused at the close of the state's case is the equivalent of an acquittal. *Smalis v. Pennsylvania*, 476 U.S. 140 (1986) (court, having dismissed charge, could not permit prosecution to reinstate charge later in the same trial based on defendant's testimony). There must be a final verdict of acquittal, however, for the Double Jeopardy Clause to apply. *See Blueford v. Arkansas*, 566 U.S. 599 (2012) (holding that defendant could be retried for murder even though jury in first trial had announced in open court that they had unanimously voted against murder charges, because declaration in open court was not equivalent to verdict of acquittal since jury was sent back to deliberate on lesser-included charges of manslaughter and negligent homicide and might have revisited decision on murder charges). An acquittal based on an error of law is nonetheless an acquittal for Double Jeopardy purposes. *Evans v. Michigan*, 568 U.S. 313 (2013) (retrial following court-decreed acquittal barred even though the court misconstrued the statute under which defendant was charged).

2. Attachment of Jeopardy

The protection against double jeopardy is not triggered until jeopardy attaches. In a jury trial, jeopardy attaches when the jury is empaneled and sworn in. In a bench trial, jeopardy attaches when the first witness is sworn in.

3. Different Jurisdictions

Under the dual-sovereignty doctrine, the protection against double jeopardy does not preclude prosecution of a crime by both federal and state governments. Consequently, a defendant may be charged and convicted for the same type of crime in a federal court and a state court. Similarly, a defendant may be prosecuted by two different states for the same conduct. However, a state and state-created entity, such as a municipality, cannot both prosecute a defendant for the same conduct. *Waller v. Florida*, 397 U.S. 387, 394 (1970) (municipality's conviction of defendant for violation of city ordinance for destruction of city property precluded state prosecution for grand larceny).

4. Civil Actions

The Double Jeopardy Clause does not preclude a criminal punishment and civil penalty for the same conduct. Therefore, even if a defendant has been found guilty in a criminal action, the state may still bring a civil action against the defendant that arises out of the same conduct. The protection does not apply to administrative proceedings such as a disciplinary hearing stemming from criminal conduct, nor does it apply to a parole, probation, or bond-revocation hearing related to a criminal charge or punishment.

A civil penalty may be treated as a criminal punishment when the penalty amount is grossly disproportionate to governmental loss and it serves only a deterrent or retributive purpose. *Dep't of Revenue of Montana v. Kurth Ranch*, 511 U.S. 767, 783 (1994) (tax imposed on possession of illegal drugs after satisfaction of state and federal fines and forfeitures). However, a civil forfeiture proceeding is typically not punitive in nature. *United States v. Ursery*, 518 U.S. 267, 275 (1996) (forfeiture of property used in the commission of drug crimes).

Note: Juvenile adjudicatory proceedings are criminal, not civil, actions for purposes of the Double Jeopardy Clause. A minor who is subject to an adjudicatory hearing regarding conduct that would constitute a crime if committed by an adult cannot subsequently be tried as an adult for a crime based on such conduct. *Breed v. Jones*, 421 U.S. 519, 541 (1975).

5. Guilty Plea

A defendant does not automatically waive her double-jeopardy rights by entering a guilty plea, but the plea agreement may include a provision that the charges against the defendant may be reinstated if the defendant breaches the agreement. *Ricketts v. Adamson*, 483 U.S. 1, 11 (1987). A guilty plea to a lesser included offense does not preclude prosecution for a greater offense if the greater offense has been charged before the plea is entered. *Ohio v. Johnson*, 467 U.S. 493, 501 (1984).

6. Mistrial

The Double Jeopardy Clause does not prohibit a retrial following a mistrial if "taking all the circumstances into consideration, there is a manifest necessity for [declaring a mistrial]." Although the decision to declare a mistrial is left to the sound discretion of the judge, the power should be used with "the greatest caution, under urgent circumstances, and for very plain and obvious causes." *United States v. Perez*, 22 U.S. 579, 580 (1824). If the trial judge fails to exercise sound discretion or "acts for reasons completely unrelated to the trial problem which purports to be the basis for the mistrial ruling," the trial court's decision is not entitled to absolute deference, and close appellate scrutiny is appropriate. *Renico v. Lett*, 559 U.S. 766 (2010). A mistrial for the death or illness of a judge or juror, or because of a hung jury, generally constitutes manifest necessity and permits a retrial.

If the judge grants an acquittal instead of declaring a mistrial after there has been a hung jury, then a retrial is not permitted. Moreover, if the prosecution asks for a mistrial because of its inability to locate a witness, then double jeopardy prevents a retrial.

If the defendant asks for or consents to a mistrial, then she generally can be retried, unless the request is based on bad-faith conduct by the prosecutor or judge directed toward goading the defendant into seeking a mistrial. The manifest necessity standard does not apply when the defendant requests a mistrial. *United States v. Dinitz*, 424 U.S. 600, 606–607 (1976).

7. Appeal

a. By the prosecution

The government may appeal an adverse ruling in a criminal case only when authorized by statute. If the trial judge grants an acquittal on an issue that does not relate to the defendant's guilt or innocence, such as the failure to give the defendant a speedy trial, then the prosecution may appeal and, if the appeal is successful, the defendant may be retried. In addition, a prosecutor may appeal an order dismissing an indictment or suppressing evidence, a bail determination, the sentence imposed on a defendant, and a post-verdict new-trial order.

b. By the defendant

The Double Jeopardy Clause generally does not prevent the retrial of a defendant after an appeal on the basis of an error made at trial, such as the admission of improper hearsay evidence or improper jury instructions. *Lockhart v. Nelson*, 488 U.S. 33, 38 (1988). This is true even when a conviction is overturned due to the weight of the evidence. *Tibbs v. Florida*, 457 U.S. 31, 42 (1982). However, a retrial after reversal of a conviction due to **insufficiency** of the evidence is barred by the Double Jeopardy Clause. A conviction is based upon insufficient evidence if the evidence presented, when viewed in the light most favorable to the prosecution, is such that **no rational fact-finder** could have found the defendant guilty beyond a reasonable doubt. *Burks v. United States*, 437 U.S. 1, 18 (1978).

8. **Retrial Offenses**

A defendant who was tried for a crime but convicted only of a lesser included offense may not be retried on the originally charged crime even if the conviction is reversed. *Price v. Georgia*, 398 U.S. 323, 329 (1970).

Example: A defendant on trial for murder is found guilty of voluntary manslaughter. The conviction is overturned on appeal due to trial error. The defendant's retrial for murder violates the Double Jeopardy Clause, even if on retrial the defendant again is convicted only of voluntary manslaughter.

9. **Retrial Punishment**

The Double Jeopardy Clause generally does not preclude a greater sentence from being imposed on a defendant upon reconviction after a successful appeal. However, the Due Process Clause does prevent the imposition of a greater sentence upon reconviction if the greater sentence is imposed as a penalty for the exercise of a statutory right to appeal or to seek a collateral remedy. Consequently, when imposing a greater sentence upon reconviction, the judge must articulate reasons for the greater sentence that are based on objective information concerning identifiable conduct by the defendant that occurred after the original sentencing proceeding. *Alabama v. Smith*, 490 U.S. 794 (1989). In a jurisdiction where a jury rather than the judge determines the sentence, the jury in the retrial may impose a greater sentence unless it has been told of the defendant's original sentence. *Chaffin v. Stynchcombe*, 412 U.S. 17, 24 (1973).

a. **Capital sentencing procedures**

The Double Jeopardy Clause is applicable to capital sentencing proceedings when there is a determination that the government failed to establish an aggravating factor that would justify the death penalty. Consequently, if a jury imposes a life sentence rather than the death penalty, then the defendant, upon retrial, may not be sentenced to death. *Bullington v. Missouri*, 451 U.S. 430, 445 (1981).

10. **Collateral Estoppel**

The Double Jeopardy Clause recognizes the doctrine of collateral estoppel. For collateral estoppel to apply, the earlier decision must have necessarily determined the issue on which collateral estoppel is sought by the defendant.

Example 1: Several victims were robbed at the same time. The defendant is initially tried for the crime with respect to only one of the victims. The sole contested issue at the trial is whether the defendant was a perpetrator of the crime. The defendant is acquitted of the crime. The acquittal prevents the defendant's prosecution for the robbery with respect to any other victim. The fact that the jury determined that the defendant was not a perpetrator of a robbery estops the government from trying the defendant for robbery of any of the other victims. *Ashe v. Swenson*, 397 U.S. 436 (1970).

If a jury acquits a defendant on one crime but deadlocks on another crime that contains the same element, then the jury's verdict may serve to prevent retrial on the crime over which the jury was deadlocked. In such a case, issue preclusion applies to the issue(s) that the jury did determine.

> **Example 2:** A defendant was charged with both insider trading and fraud. An element of both crimes is the possession of insider information. The jury acquitted the defendant of fraud but deadlocked over insider trading. By acquitting the defendant, the jury determined that the defendant did not possess insider information. Consequently, under the doctrine of collateral estoppel, the government could not retry the defendant for insider trading. *Yeager v. United States*, 557 U.S. 110 (2009).

The burden is on the defendant to prove that the jury's verdict **necessarily** determined the issue that the defendant seeks to foreclose. Because a jury usually renders a general verdict in a criminal trial, it is rare that a defendant will be able to meet this burden.

B. APPEAL

The Constitution neither provides for nor guarantees an individual the right to appeal. Nevertheless, appeals are commonplace in the U.S. justice system. When a defendant is entitled to a first appeal as of right, the defendant is guaranteed certain rights, among them equal protection and the right to counsel pursuant to the Fifth and Fourteenth Amendments. *Douglas v. California*, 372 U.S. 353 (1963) (indigent entitled to appoint of counsel). However, despite this latter right, if an attorney believes that the appeal is frivolous, she may withdraw so long as the appellant's right to appeal is protected. *Anders v. California*, 386 U.S. 738 (1967). There is also no right of self-representation during an appeal. *Martinez v. Court of Appeal*, 528 U.S. 152 (2000). When an appeal is discretionary, an indigent defendant does not have the right to the appointment of counsel unless the conviction was based on a plea of guilty or *nolo contendere*. *Ross v. Moffitt*, 417 U.S. 600, 610, 612 (1974); *Halbert v. Michigan*, 545 U.S. 605, 616-17 (2005).

Errors generally must be preserved by a timely objection to be considered on appeal, and even if properly preserved, any error, defect, irregularity, or variance that does not affect substantial rights (i.e., a "harmless" error) will not serve as grounds for reversal. However, under the plain-error doctrine, a defendant who has failed to preserve a claim of error in district court is still entitled to appellate relief when (i) the district court committed error under the law in effect at the time the appeal is heard, (ii) the error is obvious under that law, and (iii) the error affected the defendant's substantial rights. Fed. R. Crim. P. 52(b). A constitutional error is harmless only when it appears beyond a reasonable doubt that the error did not contribute to the verdict obtained. *Mitchell v. Esparza*, 540 U.S. 12 (2003).

C. CONVICTIONS

1. Writ of Habeas Corpus

Convicts may attack their convictions, even if their appeal was unsuccessful or not available, by challenging the lawfulness of the detention under a writ of habeas corpus. The convict does not have to be in custody; she may be out on probation or parole. However, if the defendant's sentence has expired and her prior conviction is being used to enhance a later one, then the defendant does not satisfy the in-custody requirement to petition for the habeas writ.

A writ of habeas corpus proceeding is civil in nature. Therefore, the "beyond a reasonable doubt" standard is not applicable. The petitioner must demonstrate only the unlawfulness of the detention by a preponderance of the evidence. If the petitioner is granted the writ, then the state may appeal, and double jeopardy does not apply to either the appeal or the retrial after the granting of the writ. An indigent person does not have a right to have counsel appointed to assist in perfecting her habeas petition.

2. Parole and Probation

If a new sentence can be imposed upon the revocation of parole, then the right to counsel is activated, and the parolee is entitled to representation to the same extent as a trial. On the other hand, if an already-imposed sentence is triggered by parole revocation, then the right to counsel is limited. The right to counsel applies only if it is necessary for a fair hearing.

3. Access to Courts

Reasonable access to courts, with no unreasonable limitations on presenting arguments, is a right of prison inmates. In addition, inmates cannot be prohibited from consulting with other inmates if there is no reasonable alternative in the prison, such as a law library.

4. Disenfranchisement

Some states disenfranchise a convicted felon. This prohibition on voting does not violate the Fourteenth Amendment, even when it applies to felons who have been released from incarceration. *Richardson v. Ramirez*, 418 U.S. 24, 54 (1974).

Evidence

EVIDENCE

Table of Contents

EVIDENCE

EXAM NOTE: Watch out for MBE questions with answer choices that would be correct under common law but are inconsistent with the Federal Rules. Remember, aside from the rules related to evidentiary privileges and constitutional limitations, the Federal Rules govern the MBE.

I. PRESENTATION OF EVIDENCE

With some exceptions, the Federal Rules apply to all civil and criminal proceedings before United States district courts, courts of appeal, Bankruptcy Court, and Claims Court, and in proceedings before United States magistrates. Fed. R. Evid. 1101(a).

The Federal Rules, except for the rules on privilege, do not apply to:

i) The court's determination of a preliminary question of fact governing admissibility (*see* § I.A.1.a. Judge, *infra*);

ii) Grand jury proceedings; and

iii) Criminal proceedings for the following purposes:

    a) The issuance of a search or arrest warrant or a criminal summons;

    b) A preliminary examination in a criminal case;

    c) Extradition or rendition;

    d) Consideration of bail or other release;

    e) Sentencing; and

    f) Granting or revoking probation or supervised release.

Fed. R. Evid. 1101(c), (d).

A. INTRODUCTION OF EVIDENCE

1. Role of Judge and Jury

In a jury trial, the jury is traditionally the trier of fact and the judge the trier of law.

a. Judge

The trial judge generally decides **preliminary questions** regarding the competency of evidence, including the admissibility of evidence, whether privilege exists, and whether a person is qualified to be a witness. The court is not bound by the Federal Rules in deciding these questions, except with respect to privileges, and it may consider otherwise inadmissible evidence. Fed. R. Evid. 104(a). With respect to preliminary questions, the party offering the evidence ordinarily bears the burden to persuade the trial judge by a preponderance of the evidence. *Bourjaily v. United States*, 483 U.S. 171 (1987) (confession of co-conspirator as admission of party opponent); *Daubert v. Merrell Dow Pharm.*, 509 U.S. 579 (1993) (expert opinion); Rule 702, Notes of Advisory Committee (2000).

Hearings on preliminary matters must be conducted outside the presence of the jury when the hearing involves the admissibility of confessions, when a defendant in a criminal case is a witness and so requests, or when justice requires it. Fed. R. Evid. 104(c).

b. Jury

A party has the right to present evidence (e.g., bias) that is relevant to the weight and credibility of other evidence (e.g., the testimony of a witness). Once evidence has been admitted, it is the role of the jury to determine the **weight and credibility** of the evidence. Fed. R. Evid. 104(e).

2. Challenge to Evidence Ruling

A party may challenge an evidentiary ruling as erroneous only if the ruling affects a substantial right of a party, and the party notifies the judge of the error. There are two ways to call the court's attention to the error—objection and offer of proof. Fed. R. Evid. 103(a). (Note: While the judge in a jury trial must permit a party to challenge the court's ruling, the judge must also conduct the trial to the extent practicable so that inadmissible evidence is not suggested to the jury. Fed. R. Evid. 103(d).)

a. Objection to admission of evidence

If the ruling **admits** evidence, a party must make a timely **objection** or motion to strike and must usually state the specific ground for the objection or motion in order to preserve the admissibility issue for appeal. A party is not required to state the ground if it is apparent from the context. Fed. R. Evid. 103(a)(1).

b. Offer of proof for exclusion of evidence

If the ruling **excludes** evidence, a party must make an **offer of proof** in order to preserve the evidence for appellate review of the ruling. An offer of proof is an oral or written explanation of the relevance and admissibility of the evidence made on the record. The court may direct that an offer of proof be made in question-and-answer form. An offer of proof is not necessary if the substance of the evidence is apparent from the context. Fed. R. Evid. 103(a)(2),(c).

c. Consequence of a definitive ruling

Once a judge has made a definitive ruling on the admissibility of evidence, a party need not renew an objection or offer of proof, even if the ruling was made before the trial began. Fed. R. Evid. 103(b).

d. Plain error rule

A plain error is one that is obvious to a reviewing court. A plain error that affects a substantial right is grounds for reversal, even if no objection or offer of proof was made. Fed. R. Evid. 103(e). A court may take notice of a plain error to prevent a miscarriage of justice or to preserve the integrity and the reputation of the judicial process.

3. Limited Admissibility

Evidence may be admissible for one purpose but not for another (e.g., for impeachment but not substantive purposes), or against one party but not against another. In these cases, if a party makes a timely request, the court must restrict the evidence to its proper scope and instruct the jury accordingly. Fed. R. Evid. 105.

4. Completeness Rule

Under the rule of completeness, when a party introduces part of a writing or recorded statement, an adverse party may compel the introduction of an omitted portion of the writing or statement if, in fairness, it should be considered at the same time, such as when the omitted portion explains or clarifies the admitted portion. This rule also applies to a separate writing or recorded statement that relates to the introduced writing or recorded statement, such as the original letter when the reply letter has been introduced. Fed. R. Evid. 106. The rule of completeness does not require the admission of irrelevant portions of a statement. *United States v. Kopp*, 562 F.3d 141 (2d Cir. 2009).

Timing of introduction of omitted evidence: While the rule of completeness permits an adverse party to compel the immediate introduction of evidence during the presentation of related evidence, the rule does not *require* the adverse party to do so. The adverse party may instead choose to present the omitted evidence subsequently, such as during cross-examination.

5. Judicial Notice

Judicial notice is the court's acceptance of a fact as true without requiring formal proof. The Federal Rules only address judicial notice of adjudicative facts, which are the facts of the case at hand—those that relate to the parties and their activities, and that typically are decided by the jury. The Federal Rules do not apply to judicial notice of legislative facts, which are policy facts related to legal reasoning and the lawmaking process. Fed. R. Evid. 201.

Example (adjudicative fact): A witness testifies that an accident happened on a Saturday. The accident report indicates that the accident happened on July 21, 2007. Whether July 21, 2007, was indeed a Saturday is an adjudicative fact.

Example (legislative fact): A judge must decide whether to recognize an exception to the common-law marital privilege. The fact that allowing the exception would undermine the sanctity of marriage is a legislative fact.

a. Facts subject to judicial notice

Not all adjudicative facts are subject to judicial notice. Judicial notice may be taken of an adjudicative fact only if it is **not subject to reasonable dispute** because (i) it is **generally known** within the territorial jurisdiction of the trial court, or (ii) it can be **accurately and readily determined** from sources whose accuracy cannot reasonably be questioned. Fed. R. Evid. 201(b).

1) Generally known facts within jurisdiction

A fact does not need to be known by everyone to be "generally known"; it must only be well known within the community. Fed. R. Evid. 201(b).

Example: A judge could take judicial notice that a bank provides a checking account customer with a monthly account statement. *Kaggen v. IRS*, 71 F.3d 1018 (2d Cir. 1995).

Despite being termed "judicial notice," a judge may not take notice of a fact based solely on his own personal knowledge.

Example: A judge could not take judicial notice of informal judicial procedures for the issuance of court orders within a jurisdiction. *Switzer v. Coan*, 261 F.3d 985 (10th Cir. 2001).

2) Accurately and readily determined facts

A fact that can be accurately and readily determined need not be generally known as long as it can be determined from a source whose accuracy cannot be reasonably questioned, such as a geographic and historical fact obtained from a respected reference source.

> **Example:** A judge could take judicial notice of the state's statutory rate for post-judgment interest in determining the appropriate interest rate for pre-judgment interest. *Fox v. Kane-Miller Corp.*, 398 F. Supp. 609 (D. Md. 1975).
>
> **Contrast:** A judge could not take judicial notice of information about a company found on the company's website, because such information is often self-serving and subject to puffery. *Victaulic Co. v. Tieman*, 499 F.3d 227 (3d Cir. 2007).

b. Procedure

A court may take judicial notice at any time during a proceeding, including on appeal, whether upon request of a party or by the court's own initiative. Note, however, that a court may not take judicial notice against a criminal defendant for the first time on appeal. *U.S. v. Jones*, 580 F.2d 219 (6th Cir. 1978). If a party makes a request and the court is supplied with the necessary information, then the court must take notice of the fact. Fed. R. Evid. 201(c), (d).

1) Party's opportunity to be heard

When a party makes a timely request, the judge must give the party an opportunity to be heard on the propriety of taking judicial notice and the nature of the fact to be noticed. This right to be heard exists even if the court has taken judicial notice of a fact before notifying the party. Fed. R. Evid. 201(e).

2) Instructing the jury

a) Civil case

In a civil case, the jury must be instructed to accept the noticed fact as **conclusive**. Fed. R. Evid. 201(f).

b) Criminal case

In a criminal case, the jury must be instructed that it **may or may not accept** any judicially noticed fact as conclusive. Fed. R. Evid. 201(f).

B. MODE AND ORDER OF PRESENTATION OF EVIDENCE

1. Trial Process

A trial traditionally begins with the plaintiff's/prosecutor's case-in-chief, followed by the defendant's case, followed by the plaintiff's/prosecutor's rebuttal.

a. Judicial control of process

Subject to the evidentiary rules, a party is generally free to present evidence in the manner and order that the party feels is most effective. The order of the witnesses and presentation of the case, however, are within the discretion of the court, in order to effectively determine the truth, avoid wasting time, and protect witnesses from harassment. Fed. R. Evid. 611(a).

b. Judicial presentation of evidence

A judge may question, or even call, a witness. If the judge calls a witness, all parties may cross-examine that witness. A party objecting to the judge's calling or interrogation of a witness may wait to object until the next opportunity when the jury is not present. Fed. R. Evid. 614.

2. Examination of Witness

A party who calls a witness may examine the witness subject to the evidentiary rules. Another party may then cross-examine that witness.

a. Scope of cross-examination

The scope of cross-examination generally is limited to the subject matter of the direct examination and the credibility of the witness; however, the court may allow inquiry into additional matters. Fed. R. Evid. 611(b).

b. Additional examination

After cross-examination, the party who called the witness may engage in redirect examination, ordinarily to reply to any significant new matter raised on cross-examination. Recross-examination is also generally permissible with respect to significant new matters brought up during redirect examination. For both redirect and recross, the court has discretion to permit inquiry into other matters.

c. Examination of a defendant

The Fifth Amendment privilege against self-incrimination protects a defendant in a criminal case from being compelled to testify. A defendant in a criminal case who testifies as to a preliminary question, such as the voluntariness of the defendant's confession, has not opened himself up to cross-examination on other issues in the case. Fed. R. Evid. 104(d).

d. Motions to strike

During trial testimony, objections should be made after an improper question is asked but before the witness responds. If it is the witness's answer that makes the testimony improper (i.e., unresponsive to the question, hearsay, etc.), counsel should move to strike the answer as inadmissible.

> **EXAM NOTE:** Unresponsive answers are only subject to motions to strike by the examining counsel.

3. Form of Questions

a. Leading questions

1) Direct examination

On direct examination of a witness, a leading question—that is, a question that suggests the answer within the question—generally is not permitted. Fed. R. Evid. 611(c).

> **Example:** The question "Didn't you start the fire at 10:00?" suggests when the person being questioned started the fire. In contrast, the question "When did you start the fire?" does not suggest the answer.

a) Exceptions

A leading question is permitted on direct examination when it is necessary to develop the witness's testimony. For example, a leading question is usually permitted to elicit preliminary background information that is not in dispute. In addition, a leading question is typically permitted on direct examination of a witness who has difficulty communicating due to age or a physical or mental condition. Finally, when a party calls a witness who is likely to be antagonistic, such as an adverse party or a person associated with an adverse party, or a witness who presents adverse testimony (i.e., a hostile witness), even if such testimony is unanticipated, then the party ordinarily is permitted to use leading questions.

2) Cross-examination

There is generally no restriction on the use of leading questions during cross-examination. Fed. R. Evid. 611(c). If questions concerning matters beyond the subject matter of the direct examination are permitted, however, those inquiries must be made as if on direct examination. Fed. R. Evid. 611(b). The use of leading questions may also be restricted when the cross-examination is one of form rather than fact, such as when a party is cross-examined by his own lawyer after having been called as a witness by an opposing party. Fed. R. Evid. 611, Notes of Advisory Committee on Rules.

b. Improper questions

1) Compound question

A question that requires answers to multiple questions is compound and is not permitted.

Example: "Didn't you leave the house at 7:00, lock the door behind you, get in your car, and drive away?" (A "no" answer could mean that the witness did not leave at all, left at a time other than 7:00, did not lock the door, etc.)

2) Assumes facts not in evidence

A question that assumes as true facts that have not been established is not permitted.

Example: "When did you stop beating your wife?" (The question assumes that the witness is married and used to beat his wife. If neither fact has been established, this question is objectionable.)

3) Argumentative

A question that is intended to provoke an argument, rather than elicit a factual response, is not permitted.

Example: "You don't really expect the jury to believe you, do you?"

4) Calls for a conclusion or opinion

A question that requires the witness to draw a conclusion or state an opinion that he is not qualified to make is not permitted.

Example: "How did your mother feel after you told her the news?" (The witness cannot know how her mother felt and would have to give an opinion to answer the question.)

5) Repetitive

The repetition of a question that has been asked and answered is generally not permitted, although judges may allow some repetition, particularly on cross-examination.

4. Exclusion of Witnesses

At a party's request or upon the court's own initiative, the court must exclude witnesses from the courtroom so that they do not hear the testimony of other witnesses.

Some witnesses, however, may not be excluded under this rule, including:

i) A party who is a natural person;

ii) An officer or employee of a party that is not a natural person, after the individual has been designated as the party's representative by its attorney;

iii) A person whose presence is essential to a party's presentation of its case, such as a police officer in charge of the investigation in a criminal case; or

iv) A person, such as a victim, whose presence is permitted by statute.

Fed. R. Evid. 615. Note that a victim may be excluded if the court determines, by clear and convincing evidence, that the victim's testimony would be materially altered by the victim hearing other testimony. 18 U.S.C. § 3771.

C. BURDENS AND PRESUMPTIONS

1. Burden of Proof

The burden of proof comprises two distinct burdens: the burden of production and the burden of persuasion.

a. Burden of production

The party with the burden of production (or burden of going forward) must produce legally sufficient evidence as to each element of a claim or defense, so that a reasonable trier of fact could infer that the alleged fact has been proved. In meeting this burden, a plaintiff or prosecutor has made a **prima facie** case. Failure to meet this burden can result in a directed verdict against the party bearing the burden. The determination of whether it has been met rests with the court. The burden of production may shift during trial.

> **Example:** In a negligence action in which the plaintiff produces uncontroverted evidence of the defendant's negligence, the defendant who does not have an affirmative defense bears the burden of producing evidence that challenges the case made by the plaintiff.

b. Burden of persuasion

The burden of persuasion (or standard of proof) is the degree to which legally sufficient evidence must be presented to the trier of fact. For example, in a civil case, this burden usually lies with the plaintiff to prove the allegations in the complaint and with the defendant to prove any affirmative defenses. This burden does not shift. Typically, determination of whether it has been met rests with the trier of fact.

1) Civil standards

The standard in most civil cases is a **preponderance of the evidence.** A fact is proven by a preponderance of the evidence if it is more likely to exist than not.

A higher standard used in some civil cases (such as fraud) is **clear and convincing evidence.** Under this standard, the existence of a fact must be highly probable or reasonably certain.

2) Criminal standard

In criminal cases, the prosecution must prove each element of a crime **beyond a reasonable doubt** to overcome the defendant's presumption of innocence. *In re Winship*, 397 U.S. 358 (1970).

2. Presumptions

A presumption is a conclusion that the trier of fact is required to draw upon a party's proof of an underlying fact or set of facts (i.e., basic facts). A rebuttable presumption may be overcome by evidence to the contrary; a conclusive presumption may not.

> **Example:** A presumption arises that a person is dead when a party establishes that the person has been missing and not heard from for more than seven years.

> **Example:** A presumption arises that a letter has been received by the intended recipient when the sender places a properly addressed, stamped envelope into an outgoing mailbox.

a. Rebuttable

A rebuttable presumption shifts the burden of production, but not the burden of persuasion, to the opposing party. Under the "bursting bubble" approach followed by the Federal Rules in a civil case, a presumption "bursts" (i.e., no longer has a preclusive effect) after the introduction of sufficient evidence by the opposing party to sustain a contrary finding. If no contrary evidence is introduced, the judge must instruct the jury to accept the presumption. If contrary evidence is introduced, the burden of persuasion remains on the party who had it originally. While the presumption no longer has preclusive effect after the introduction of contrary evidence, a judge may instruct the jury that it may, but is not required to, draw the conclusion (e.g., a person is dead) from the basic facts (e.g., the person has been missing for seven years). Fed. R. Evid. 301.

> **Limitation:** The "bursting bubble" approach does not apply when a federal statute or another Federal Rule of Evidence, such as Federal Rule 302 (*see* § c. Diversity cases, *below*), provides otherwise.

b. Conclusive

Conclusive (or irrebuttable) presumptions are treated as rules of substantive law and may not be challenged by contrary evidence, no matter how strong the proof. One example is the presumption in some states that a child under the age of four lacks the ability to form the intent necessary to commit an intentional tort; no evidence to the contrary is permitted to disprove this assumption.

c. Diversity cases

In a federal diversity action, the federal court generally applies the Federal Rules to determine the resolution of evidentiary issues. However, when state substantive law is determinative of the existence of claim or defense under the *Erie* doctrine, then state law, rather than the Federal Rules, also governs the effect of a presumption related to the claim or defense. Fed. R. Evid. 302.

3. Destruction of Evidence

In general, the intentional destruction of evidence relevant to a case raises a presumption or inference that such evidence would have been unfavorable to the party that destroyed the evidence. To be entitled to such an inference, the alleged victim of the destruction of the evidence must establish that (i) the destruction was intentional, (ii) the destroyed evidence was relevant to the issue about which the party seeks such inference, and (iii) the alleged victim acted with due diligence as to the destroyed evidence. The presumption that arises from the destruction of evidence is rebuttable.

II. RELEVANCE

A. GENERAL CONSIDERATIONS

As a rule, evidence must be relevant to be admissible, and all relevant evidence is admissible unless excluded by a specific rule, law, or constitutional provision. Fed. R. Evid. 402. Evidence is relevant if:

i)   It has any tendency to make a fact more or less probable than it would be without the evidence (i.e., **probative**); and

ii) The fact is of consequence in determining the action (i.e., **material**).

Irrelevant evidence is generally inadmissible. Fed. R. Evid. 401.

> **Sufficiency Distinguished:** To be relevant, evidence need not, by itself, establish an element that a party must prove (e.g., the death of an individual in a homicide prosecution) or serve to refute such an element (e.g., a defendant's lack of a duty in a negligence action). The test of sufficiency of a party's evidence focuses on all evidence submitted by a party and admitted by the court. By contrast, under the test of relevancy, evidence is admissible even if it is only a single brick that is part of a wall of evidence establishing a party's position. Fed. R. Evid. 401, Notes of Advisory Committee, referring to Professor McCormick's famous statement, "A brick is not a wall."

1. Direct and Circumstantial Evidence

a. Direct evidence

Direct evidence is identical to the factual proposition that it is offered to prove. An eyewitness who testifies that she saw the defendant shoot the victim dead is an example of direct evidence that the defendant committed a homicide.

> **Conviction without direct evidence:** There is no rule that requires the presentation of direct evidence in order to convict a defendant. In other words, a defendant can be convicted solely upon circumstantial evidence.

b. Circumstantial evidence

Evidence that tends to indirectly prove a factual proposition through inference from collateral facts is circumstantial. An eyewitness who testifies that, moments before entering a room, she heard a shot, and upon entering the room saw the defendant standing over the body of the victim holding a smoking gun is circumstantial evidence that the defendant committed a homicide.

> **Compare direct evidence:** While it is sometimes said that direct evidence is better than circumstantial evidence, circumstantial evidence may have greater probative value. For example, testimony as to the identity of a thief based on a fleeting glimpse by an eyewitness with poor vision may not be as persuasive as testimony that the stolen item was found in the defendant's home.

2. Exclusion of Relevant Evidence

Relevant evidence may be excluded if its probative value is **substantially outweighed** by the danger of unfair prejudice, confusing the issues, misleading the jury, undue delay, wasting time, or needlessly presenting cumulative evidence. This exclusion is often denominated by the applicable rule; that is, it is referred to as a "Rule 403" exclusion. Fed. R. Evid. 403.

> **Matter of degree:** Evidence may be admissible even if the danger of prejudice or other factors outweigh the probative value, so long as the danger does not do so **substantially.**

3. Relevance Dependent on Existence of Fact

When the relevance of evidence depends upon whether a fact exists, proof must be introduced sufficient to support a finding that the fact does exist. The court may admit the proposed evidence on the condition that the proof is introduced later. Fed. R. Evid. 104(b). In making its determination that sufficient evidence has been introduced, the court must examine all of the evidence and decide whether the jury could reasonably find the conditional fact by a preponderance of the evidence; the court itself is not required to find that the conditional fact exists by a preponderance of the evidence. *Huddleston v. United States*, 485 U.S. 681 (1988).

4. Admission of Inadmissible Evidence—Curative Admission

When a court erroneously admits evidence, the court may permit the introduction of additional inadmissible evidence to rebut the previously admitted evidence. Known as a curative admission, such evidence can be admitted at the court's discretion when necessary to remove unfair prejudice. The failure of a party to object to the admission of the initial inadmissible evidence is one factor to be considered in determining whether the party was unfairly prejudiced by it. Curative admissions are generally used when a motion to strike or curative jury instruction would not suffice. *Nguyen v. Sw. Leasing & Rental, Inc.*, 282 F.3d 1061 (9th Cir. 2002); *United States v. Hall*, 653 F.2d 1002 (5th Cir. 1981); *Crawford v. United States*, 198 F.2d 976 (D.C. Cir. 1952).

5. Laying a Foundation

Various types of evidence are admissible subject to the existence of a necessary predicate (i.e., a foundation), such as the authentication of tangible evidence. The failure of the proponent of the evidence to establish that foundation may be challenged by an objection for lack of proper foundation.

B. CHARACTER EVIDENCE

Character evidence, which is generalized information about a person's behavior—such as information that the defendant is a criminal, a bad parent, or an inattentive driver—is generally inadmissible.

1. Civil Cases

a. Inadmissible to prove conforming conduct

In a civil case, evidence of a person's character (or character trait) generally is inadmissible to prove that the person acted in accordance with that character (or character trait) on a particular occasion. Fed. R. Evid. 404(a)(1).

> **Example:** A plaintiff cannot introduce evidence that the defendant is a reckless driver to prove that the defendant drove recklessly on the day in question.

Evidence concerning past sexual assault or child molestation by a *defendant* in a case in which the claim for relief is based on the defendant's sexual misconduct is admissible. This includes evidence of specific acts. Fed. R. Evid. 415. Evidence concerning the past sexual behavior of a victim of sexual misconduct (e.g., rape) is admissible in limited circumstances (*see* § V.B.6. Sexual Conduct, *infra*).

b. Character at issue

Character evidence is admissible, however, when character is an **essential element** of a claim or defense, rather than a means of proving a person's conduct. Character is most commonly an essential element in defamation (character of the plaintiff), negligent hiring or negligent entrustment (character of the person hired or entrusted), and child-custody cases (character of the parent or guardian). Fed. R. Evid. 404(b); 405.

2. Criminal Cases

a. Defendant's character

1) By prosecution—defendant's bad character

In general, the same rule that applies in a civil action applies to the prosecution in a criminal case. The prosecution is not permitted to introduce evidence of a defendant's **bad character** to prove that the defendant has a **propensity** to commit crimes and therefore is likely to have committed the crime in question. Fed. R. Evid. 404(a)(1).

Example: A defendant is charged with brutally murdering his wife. The prosecution may not present evidence of the defendant's violent nature.

2) By defendant—defendant's good character

A defendant is **permitted** to introduce evidence of his **good character** as being inconsistent with the type of crime charged.

Example 1: A defendant is charged with brutally murdering his wife. The defendant may present evidence of his peaceable nature.

The defendant's character evidence must be pertinent to the crime charged.

Example 2: A defendant is charged with embezzling money from her employer. The defendant may not present evidence of her peaceable nature.

3) Defendant "opens the door"

Although the prosecution cannot introduce evidence of the defendant's bad character, the defendant makes his character an issue in the case if he offers evidence of his good character. When the defendant **"opens the door,"** the prosecution is free to rebut the defendant's claims by attacking the defendant's character. Fed. R. Evid. 404(a)(2)(A).

Defendant as witness: The defendant does not "open the door" to character evidence merely by taking the stand, but as a witness, the defendant is subject to impeachment.

In addition, the defendant "opens the door" for the prosecution to introduce evidence of his bad character by introducing evidence of the victim's bad character. The prosecution's evidence regarding the defendant must relate to the same character trait (e.g., violence) that the defendant's evidence about the victim did. Fed. R. Evid. 404(a)(2)(A).

b. Victim's character

1) By defendant—victim's bad character

A criminal defendant may introduce reputation or opinion evidence of the alleged victim's character when it is relevant to the defense asserted. Fed. R.

Evid. 404(a)(2)(B). (Note: The introduction of evidence of the character of an alleged victim of sexual misconduct in a criminal case, however, is subject to significant limitations (*see* § V.B.6. Sexual Conduct, *infra*).)

> **Example:** A defendant is charged with assault. The defendant may offer evidence of the alleged victim's character trait of violence to support a claim of self-defense by showing that the alleged victim was the aggressor.

2) By prosecution—victim's good character

Generally, the prosecution may offer rebuttal evidence of the alleged victim's good character only after the defendant has introduced evidence of the alleged victim's bad character. Fed. R. Evid. 404(a)(2)(B).

> **Example:** A defendant is charged with assault. The defendant presents evidence of the alleged victim's character trait of violence to support a claim of self-defense. The prosecution may then rebut the defendant's evidence with evidence of the alleged victim's character trait of peacefulness. Note: The prosecution may also offer evidence of the defendant's character trait of violence.

In a homicide case, the prosecution may also offer evidence of the alleged victim's trait for peacefulness to rebut evidence that the alleged victim was the first aggressor. Fed. R. Evid. 404(a)(2)(C).

3. Methods of Proving Character

Proof of character, whether good or bad, offered by any party generally must be in the form of **reputation** testimony or **opinion** testimony. Reputation evidence is defined as a defendant's reputation in the community. "Community" includes people with whom the defendant engages on a regular basis. Fed. R. Evid. 405(a). For use of specific instances of conduct, *see* § II.C.2. Introduction of Specific Acts as Character Evidence, *infra*.

4. Impeachment

Character evidence is admissible for impeachment purposes. Character evidence about the witness may be introduced to show that the witness is not a person whose testimony should be believed. In such instances, the witness's character for untruthfulness is relevant. When permitted, the witness's testimony may be supported by testimony as to the witness's character for truthfulness. Fed. R. Evid. 404(a)(3). *See* § III.B. Impeachment, *infra*.

C. SPECIFIC (BAD) ACTS

In addition to general evidence of a person's character (or character trait), evidence of a specific act is not admissible to prove a person's character in order to show that the person acted in accordance with that character on a particular occasion. Fed. R. Evid. 404(b)(1).

> **Example 1:** A driver is sued to recover for injuries inflicted on the plaintiff allegedly due to the driver's negligent failure to stop at a stop sign. The plaintiff cannot introduce testimony by a witness that the driver failed to stop at the same stop sign the day before the accident in question for the purpose of proving that the driver failed to stop at the stop sign on the day of the accident.

However, evidence of a person's conduct (e.g., crime, other bad act) is admissible for another purpose, such as proving motive, opportunity, intent, preparation, plan, knowledge, identity, absence of mistake, or lack of accident. Fed. R. Evid. 404(b)(2).

Example 2: A defendant is charged with murder. Evidence that the defendant was previously convicted of robbery is likely admissible if the murder victim was the prosecutor on the robbery case against the defendant. Such evidence establishes the defendant's motive for killing the victim.

MIMIC evidence: This type of evidence is sometimes referred to as "MIMIC" evidence (**M**otive, **I**ntent, absence of **M**istake, **I**dentity, or **C**ommon plan), but it is important not to treat this list as all-inclusive. Subject to the other restrictions on the admissibility of evidence (e.g., relevancy, Rule 403 exclusion), a defendant's bad act may be introduced for any purpose so long as that purpose is not to prove that, because the defendant had a propensity to commit crimes, the defendant committed the charged crime.

1. Advance Notice

When a criminal defendant requests, the prosecution must provide reasonable notice of the general nature of such evidence that the prosecution intends to offer at trial. Such notice must generally be given before trial, but it can be given during trial when the court, for good cause, excuses the lack of pretrial notice. Fed. R. Evid. 404(b)(2).

2. Introduction of Specific Acts as Character Evidence

a. Civil cases

When character evidence is admissible as evidence in a civil case (e.g., evidence that is an essential element of a claim or defense), it may be proved by specific instances of a person's conduct as well as either by testimony about the person's reputation or by testimony in the form of an opinion. Fed. R. Evid. 405(b).

b. Criminal cases

Generally, when character evidence is admissible as evidence in a criminal case (e.g., evidence of good character introduced by the defendant), specific instances of a person's conduct are not admissible. Character must be proved by either reputation or opinion testimony. Fed. R. Evid. 405(a).

Non-propensity use: When a defendant's bad act is not used to show the defendant's criminal propensity but for another purpose (e.g., motive, identity), such instance of conduct may be admissible for that purpose.

Essential element of the crime charged: When character or a character trait is an essential element of the crime charged, the defendant may introduce relevant specific acts inconsistent with the crime. Fed. R. Evid. 405(b).

c. Cross-examination of character witness

When a character witness is cross-examined, the court may allow a party to inquire into specific acts committed by the person about whom the witness is testifying. Fed. R. Evid. 405(a).

Rule 403: Keep in mind that evidence of a bad act that is otherwise admissible is especially subject to challenge under Federal Rule 403, which permits the court to exclude evidence when its probative value is substantially outweighed by the danger of unfair prejudice, etc. (*see* § II.A.2. Exclusion of Relevant Evidence, *supra*).

D. HABIT EVIDENCE

Evidence of a **person's habit** or an **organization's routine** is admissible to prove that the person or organization acted in accordance with the habit or routine on a particular occasion. A habit is a person's particular routine reaction to a specific set of circumstances.

> **Example:** A person drives the same route to work and parks in the same spot every day.

Habit evidence may be admitted without corroboration and without an eyewitness. Fed. R. Evid. 406.

> **EXAM NOTE:** Habit is more specific than character evidence. On the MBE, words like "always" or "every time" generally refer to habit, whereas "often" or "frequently" are more likely to imply character evidence.

III. WITNESSES

A. COMPETENCE

Generally, every person is presumed to be competent to be a witness. Common-law prohibitions on a witness's ability to testify because of a lack of religious belief or conviction of a crime are inapplicable in proceedings governed by the Federal Rules. Questions of mental competence generally go to the weight rather than the admissibility of the testimony. However, in cases that turn on state law, such as diversity cases, a witness's competency is determined by state law. Fed. R. Evid. 601. When a question of witness's competency is raised, the issue is one for the judge to decide. Fed. R. Evid. 104, Notes of the Advisory Committee on Rules.

1. Personal Knowledge

A non-expert witness must have personal knowledge of a matter in order to testify about that matter. Personal knowledge may be established by the witness's own testimony as well as through other means. Fed. R. Evid. 602.

2. Oath or Affirmation

A witness must give an oath or affirmation to testify truthfully. The oath or affirmation must be in a form designed to impress that duty on the witness's conscience. Fed. R. Evid. 603. An interpreter must give an oath or affirmation to make a true translation. Fed. R. Evid. 604.

3. Judge as Witness

The presiding judge is absolutely barred from testifying as a witness in the trial. A party is not required to object in order to preserve the issue. Fed. R. Evid. 605.

4. Juror as Witness

a. At trial

A juror may not testify as a witness at trial in front of the members of the jury. If a juror is called to testify, the opposing party must be given the opportunity to object outside the presence of the jury. A juror may be called to testify outside the presence of the other jurors as to matters that occur during the trial, such as the bribery of a juror or a juror's failure to follow the court's instruction (e.g., discussing the case with family members). Fed. R. Evid. 606(a).

b. After trial—"no impeachment" rule

During an inquiry into the validity of a verdict, a juror generally may not testify about:

   i)   Any statement made or incident that occurred during the jury's deliberations (e.g., refusal to apply the court's instructions);

   ii) The effect of anything upon that juror's, or any other juror's, vote; or

iii) Any juror's mental processes concerning the verdict.

Fed. R. Evid. 606(b).

1) Exceptions

A juror may testify about whether:

i) Extraneous prejudicial information was brought to the jury's attention (e.g., the circulation of a newspaper article not introduced into evidence about the trial and the defendant's guilt);

ii) An outside influence was improperly brought to bear on a juror (e.g., a threat on the life of a juror's spouse); or

iii) A mistake was made in entering the verdict onto the verdict form.

The mistake exception, item iii above, does not extend to mistakes about the consequences of the agreed-upon verdict. Fed. R. Evid. 606(b).

Grand jury: The same rule applies regarding a challenge to the validity of an indictment by a grand jury.

2) Right to an impartial jury

There is a constitutional right to an impartial jury in civil as well as criminal cases. U.S. Const. amend. VI; *Warger v. Shauers*, 574 U.S. 40 (2014). This right overrides the "no impeachment" rule when a juror makes a clear post-verdict statement that he relied on racial stereotypes or animus to convict a criminal defendant, and that the animus was a significant motivating factor in the juror's vote to convict. *Pena-Rodriguez v. Colorado*, 580 U.S. ___, 137 S. Ct. 855 (2017). However, this right does not override the "no impeachment" rule when a juror's post-verdict statement reveals that some jurors were under the influence of alcohol and drugs during the trial, *Tanner v. United States*, 483 U.S. 107 (1987), or that a juror failed to disclose a pro-defendant bias during voir dire. *Warger, supra*.

5. Child as Witness

The competence of a child depends on her intelligence, her ability to differentiate between truth and falsehood, and her understanding of the importance of telling the truth. *Wheeler v. United States*, 159 U.S. 523 (1895) (finding a five-year-old child competent to testify at a capital murder trial). A child who is unable to understand the requirement to tell the truth is incompetent to be a witness. There is, however, no specific age at which a person becomes competent. Under federal law, a child who has suffered abuse or witnessed a crime is rebuttably presumed to be competent to testify. 18 U.S.C.S. § 3509.

6. Dead Man's Statutes

At common law, a party with a financial interest in the outcome could not testify in a civil case about a communication or transaction with a person whose estate was party to the case and the testimony was adverse to the estate, unless there was a waiver. Dead Man's Statutes do not apply in criminal cases.

The Federal Rules do not include such a restriction, but most jurisdictions have adopted such "Dead Man's Statutes," which may be applicable in federal cases when state law applies (i.e., diversity cases).

a. Protected parties

The rationale of a Dead Man's Statute is to protect a decedent's estate from parties with a financial interest in the estate. Therefore, protected parties generally include an heir, a legatee, a devisee, an executor, or an administrator of an estate.

b. Disqualified witnesses

Any person directly affected financially by the outcome of the case may be disqualified as a witness under a Dead Man's Statute. A predecessor in interest to the party may be disqualified in order to prevent circumvention of the statute by transference of property to a relative or friend.

c. Interested person

A personal representative of the decedent or a successor in interest may also be protected under a Dead Man's Statute as an interested person.

d. Waiver

An interested person or protected party may waive the protection afforded by a Dead Man's Statute in several ways, including (i) failing to object to the introduction of testimony by a disqualified witness or (ii) introducing evidence of a conversation or transaction to which the statute applies.

B. IMPEACHMENT

A witness may be impeached by calling into question her credibility. Typically, a witness's testimony is challenged based on her character for untruthfulness, bias, ability to perceive or testify accurately, or prior statement that contradicts the witness's testimony at trial. Impeachment evidence may be presented through the witness's own testimony, by the testimony or another witness, or by other extrinsic evidence that contradicts the witness's testimony.

1. Who May Impeach a Witness

Any party, including the party that called the witness to testify, may attack the credibility of a witness. Fed. R. Evid. 607.

2. Witness's Character for Truthfulness

a. Reputation and opinion testimony

A witness's credibility may be attacked by testimony regarding the witness's character for untruthfulness. Generally, this testimony must be about the witness's **reputation** for having a character for untruthfulness or in the form of an **opinion** of the witness's character for untruthfulness. Fed. R. Evid. 608(a).

b. Truthful character evidence

The credibility of a witness may not be bolstered. Evidence of the truthful character of the witness is admissible only after the witness's character for truthfulness has been attacked. Evidence that impeaches the witness but does not specifically attack the witness's character for truthfulness, such as testimony that the witness is biased, does not constitute an attack. As with evidence regarding a witness's character for untruthfulness, evidence as to a witness's character for truthfulness is generally admissible only in the form of reputation or opinion testimony. Fed. R. Evid. 608(a).

c. Specific instances of conduct

Generally, a specific instance of conduct (e.g., lying on a job application) is not admissible to attack or support the witness's character for truthfulness. However, on cross-examination, a witness may be asked about specific instances of conduct if it is probative of the truthfulness or untruthfulness of (i) the witness or (ii) another witness about whose character the witness being cross-examined has testified. Fed. R. Evid. 608(b).

1) Limitations

The judge may refuse to allow such questioning of a witness under either Federal Rule 403 (the probative value is substantially outweighed by the danger of unfair prejudice) or Federal Rule 611 (protection of the witness from harassment or undue embarrassment). In addition, the lawyer who examines the witness must have a good-faith basis for believing that the misconduct occurred before asking the witness about it. *United States v. Davenport*, 753 F.2d 1460 (9th Cir. 1985).

2) Arrest

Because an arrest for misconduct is not itself misconduct, a witness may not be cross-examined about having been arrested solely for the purpose of impeaching the witness's character for truthfulness; however, the witness may be cross-examined about the underlying conduct that lead to the arrest. *See Michelson v. United States*, 335 U.S. 469 (1948).

3) Use of extrinsic evidence

When, on cross-examination, the witness denies a specific instance of conduct, extrinsic evidence is not admissible to prove that instance in order to attack or support the witness's character for truthfulness. This prohibition also bars references to any consequences that a witness may have suffered because of the conduct (e.g., suspension from a governmental job for improper personal use of governmental property). (An exception exists for criminal convictions, *see* § 3. Criminal Conviction, *below*.)

Note, however, that extrinsic evidence of specific conduct can be admissible to impeach the witness on other grounds, such as bias. Fed. R. Evid. 608(b), Notes of Advisory Committee (2003).

While a document is generally considered to be extrinsic evidence, *United States v. Elliott*, 89 F.3d 1360, 1368 (8th Cir. 1996), when the foundation for the document is established through the witness being impeached, it is possible that the document might be admissible to impeach the witness's character for truthfulness. Kevin C. McMunigal & Calvin W. Sharpe, *Reforming Extrinsic Impeachment*, 33 Conn. L. Rev. 363, 372–73 (2001).

4) Privilege against self-incrimination

By testifying on another matter, a witness does not waive the privilege against self-incrimination for testimony that relates only to the witness's character for truthfulness. Fed. R. Evid. 608(b).

3. Criminal Conviction

A witness's character for truthfulness may be impeached with evidence that the witness has been convicted of a crime, subject to the limitations discussed below. It does not matter whether the conviction is for a state or federal crime. Fed. R. Evid. 609.

a. **Crimes involving dishonesty or false statement**

Subject to the 10-year restriction (*see below*), **any witness** may be impeached with evidence that he has been convicted of **any crime**—felony or misdemeanor—**involving dishonesty or false statement,** regardless of the punishment imposed or the prejudicial effect of the evidence. A crime involves dishonesty or false statement if establishing the elements of the crime requires proof (or admission) of an act of dishonesty or false statement, such as perjury, fraud, embezzlement, or false pretense. Crimes of violence, such as murder, assault, and rape, are not crimes involving dishonesty or false statement, even though the perpetrator acted deceitfully in committing the crime of violence. Fed. R . Evid. 609(a)(2).

b. **Crimes not involving dishonesty or false statement**

Subject to the 10-year restriction (*see below*), a conviction for a crime not involving fraud or dishonesty is admissible to impeach a witness only if the crime is **punishable by death or imprisonment for more than one year** (typically, a felony). Fed. R. Evid. 609(a)(1).

1) **Criminal defendant**

When the witness is a criminal defendant, evidence of a felony conviction for a crime not involving dishonesty or false statement is admissible **only if** its probative value outweighs the prejudicial effect to that defendant. This stricter-than-usual balancing test gives extra protection to a criminal defendant who takes the stand in his own defense.

2) **Other witnesses**

For witnesses other than a criminal defendant, such evidence generally must be admitted. The court does have the discretion, however, to exclude the evidence when the party objecting to the impeachment shows that its probative value is **substantially outweighed** by its prejudicial effect (i.e., the Rule 403 standard).

c. **Convictions more than 10 years old**

If more than 10 years have elapsed since the conviction (or release from confinement, whichever is later), then evidence of the conviction is admissible only if:

i) The probative value of the conviction, supported by specific facts and circumstances, **substantially outweighs** its prejudicial effect; and

ii) The proponent gives an adverse party reasonable written notice of the intent to use such evidence so that the adverse party has a fair opportunity to contest the use of such evidence.

Fed. R. Evid. 609(b).

d. **Effect of pardon**

Evidence of a witness's conviction is not admissible if the conviction has been the subject of a pardon, annulment, or other action based on a finding of innocence. This rule also applies to an action based on a finding that the witness has been rehabilitated, provided that the witness has not been convicted of a later crime punishable by death or imprisonment in excess of one year (typically, a felony). Fed. R. Evid. 609(c).

e. Juvenile adjudications

Evidence of a juvenile adjudication is not admissible to impeach a defendant. When the witness is not the defendant, evidence of a juvenile adjudication can be used to impeach the witness's character for truthfulness only if:

i) It is offered in a criminal case;

ii) An adult's conviction for that offense would be admissible to attack the adult's credibility; and

iii) Admitting the evidence is necessary to fairly determine guilt or innocence.

Fed. R. Evid. 609(d).

Used to show bias: Under the Sixth Amendment Confrontation Clause, evidence of a witness's juvenile adjudication can also be used by a criminal defendant to impeach a witness's credibility by showing bias, such as when the witness's juvenile adjudication could provide a motive for the witness to lie. *Davis v. Alaska*, 415 U.S. 308 (1974).

f. Manner of proof

Evidence of a prior conviction may be produced by way of an admission by the witness, whether during direct testimony or on cross-examination, as well as by extrinsic evidence (e.g., a record of the conviction). Fed. R. Evid. 609, Notes of Advisory Committee (1990).

g. Pendency of appeal

A witness's conviction may be used for impeachment purposes even if an appeal is pending. Evidence of the pendency is also admissible. Fed. R. Evid. 609(e).

4. Prior Inconsistent Statements

A witness's prior statement that is inconsistent with a material part of the witness's testimony may be used to impeach the witness.

a. Disclosing the statement to the witness

A party who is examining a witness about the witness's prior statement is not required to show it or disclose its contents to the witness, but the statement must be shown, or its contents disclosed, to an adverse party's attorney upon request. Fed. R. Evid. 613(a).

b. Extrinsic evidence

Extrinsic evidence (i.e., evidence other than the witness's own testimony) of a witness's prior inconsistent statement may be introduced only if the witness is given the opportunity to **explain or deny** the statement, and the opposing party is given the opportunity to **examine the witness** about it. The witness's opportunity to explain or deny the statement need not take place before the statement is admitted into evidence.

1) Exceptions to the opportunity to explain

The opportunity to explain or deny a prior inconsistent statement does not apply when the statement (i) impeaches a hearsay declarant (*see* § 7. Impeachment of a Hearsay Declarant, *below*) or (ii) qualifies as an opposing party's statement under Rule 801(d)(2) (*see* § VI.B.2., Opposing Party's Statement, *infra*). Fed. R. Evid. 806, 613(b).

2) Collateral matter

Extrinsic evidence of a prior inconsistent statement cannot be used to impeach a witness regarding a collateral (i.e., irrelevant) matter; the questioning party is bound by the witness's answer.

5. Bias or Interest

Because a witness may be influenced by his relationship to a party (e.g., employment), his interest in testifying (e.g., avoidance of prosecution), or his interest in the outcome of the case (e.g., receipt of an inheritance), a witness's bias or interest is always relevant to the credibility of his testimony, and consequently, a witness may be impeached on that ground.

Although the Federal Rules do not expressly require that a party ask the witness about an alleged bias before introducing extrinsic evidence of that bias, many courts require that such a foundation be laid before extrinsic evidence of bias can be introduced.

> **EXAM NOTE:** MBE questions typically test bias in the form of witnesses who are employed by one of the parties, or witnesses for the prosecution who testify in exchange for reduced or dropped charges.

6. Sensory Competence

A witness may be impeached by showing a deficiency in her testimonial capacities to perceive, recall, or relate information. This can be achieved by demonstrating that the witness is physically or mentally impaired, or through evidence of outside interference with the witness's abilities, such as thunder impeding the ability to hear or darkness impeding the ability to see.

7. Impeachment of a Hearsay Declarant

When a hearsay statement is admitted into evidence, the credibility of the declarant may be attacked (and, if attacked, supported) by any evidence that would be admissible if the declarant had testified as a witness. The declarant need not be given the opportunity to explain or deny any inconsistent statement or conduct, whether such statement or conduct occurred before or after the hearsay statement. If the party against whom a hearsay statement has been admitted calls the declarant as a witness, then the party is entitled to examine the declarant on the statement as if under cross-examination. Fed. R. Evid. 806.

Similar impeachment treatment is accorded a nonhearsay statement made by a co-conspirator, agent, or authorized spokesperson for an opposing party that has been admitted into evidence.

8. Rehabilitation of a Witness

A witness who has been impeached may be "rehabilitated" by the introduction of rebuttal evidence by either party to support the witness's credibility. Rehabilitation may be accomplished by:

i)   **Explanation** or clarification on redirect examination;

ii) Reputation or opinion evidence of his **character for truthfulness,** if the witness's character was attacked on that ground under Fed. R. Evid. 608(a); or

iii) A **prior consistent statement** offered to rebut an express or implied charge that the witness lied due to improper motive or influence.

Fed. R. Evid. 801(d)(1)(B).

9. Religious Opinions and Beliefs

Evidence of a witness's religious opinions or beliefs is not admissible to attack or support a witness's credibility. Fed. R. Evid. 610. However, such evidence may be admissible to show bias or interest, such as when the witness is affiliated with a church that is a party to a lawsuit.

10. Impeachment by Contradictory Evidence

A witness may be impeached by evidence that contradicts the witness's testimony. Impeachment may be by extrinsic evidence as well as by cross-examination.

Example: The plaintiff in a negligence action based on a car accident testifies that, due to the defendant's reckless driving, the plaintiff's car was damaged. The defense may introduce a record of an insurance claim filed by the plaintiff prior to the accident for such damage due to another incident. Alternatively, the defense attorney may cross-examine the plaintiff about that claim.

11. Collateral Issues

While the Federal Rules do not explicitly prohibit impeachment on collateral issues, a court may refuse to admit evidence related to a collateral issue under the Rule 403 balancing test. Generally, a party may not impeach the credibility of a witness by introducing extrinsic evidence of a collateral matter. Instead, the party must accept the witness's testimony.

Example: A defendant is charged with assault. A prosecution witness testifies that the defendant assaulted the victim, who was wearing a plaid shirt. The defense may not call another witness to testify that the victim was wearing a striped shirt in order to establish the type of shirt that the victim was wearing.

C. RECOLLECTION REFRESHED

1. Present Recollection Refreshed

A witness may examine any item (e.g., writing, photograph) to "refresh" the witness's present recollection. The witness's testimony must be based on the witness's refreshed recollection, not on the item itself (e.g., the witness cannot read from the refreshing document).

a. Adverse party's options

When the item used to refresh a witness's recollection is a writing, the adverse party is entitled to have the document produced, to inspect the document, to cross-examine the witness about it, and to introduce any relevant portion into evidence. If the producing party claims that the document contains unrelated matter, the court may examine the document in camera and delete any unrelated portion before ordering that the rest be delivered to the adverse party. The adverse party may object to the deletion, in which case the deleted portion must be preserved in the record. Fed. R. Evid. 612(b).

Evidentiary purpose: When an adverse party seeks to introduce a writing used to refresh a witness's memory, the writing typically will be admissible for only the purpose of impeaching the witness's credibility. It will be admissible for substantive purposes only if it satisfies the other restrictions on admissibility, such as the hearsay rule.

When the refreshing of a witness's memory with a writing takes place before the witness testifies, the court may permit an adverse party to utilize these options, if justice so requires. Fed. R. Evid. 612(a).

b. Failure to produce or deliver the writing

In a criminal case, if the prosecution refuses to comply with a court order to produce or deliver a writing, the court must strike the witness's testimony, or may, when justice requires, declare a mistrial. In other circumstances, the court is free to issue any appropriate order. Fed. R. Evid. 612(c).

2. Past Recollection Recorded

A memorandum or record about a matter that a witness once had knowledge of but now has insufficient recollection of to testify to it may be admissible under a hearsay exception (*see* § VII.B.5. Recorded Recollection, *infra*). Although the record may be read into evidence, it is received as an exhibit only if offered by an adverse party.

Refreshed and recorded recollections distinguished: The item used to refresh a witness's present recollection is generally not admitted into evidence, but a document introduced under the recorded recollection hearsay exception may be.

D. OPINION TESTIMONY

1. Lay Witness

A lay (non-expert) witness is permitted to testify as to the witness's opinion if the opinion is:

i) Rationally **based on the perception** of the witness;

ii) Helpful to a **clear understanding** of the witness's testimony or the determination of a fact in issue; and

iii) **Not** based on scientific, technical, or specialized knowledge.

Fed. R. Evid. 701. Typically, a lay witness may state an opinion as to matters such as appearance, emotion, intoxication, and speed of a vehicle.

If the opinion is based on scientific, technical, or specialized knowledge, then the witness must be qualified as an expert before giving that opinion. By contrast, if a lay witness has gained familiarity with a matter that the general public does not have but could acquire without a specialist's training, then a lay witness may state an opinion. Fed. R. Evid. 701, Notes of Advisory Committee on 2000 amendments.

Example: A frequent user of heroin can identify a substance as heroin, but cannot testify as to the process for manufacturing heroin without qualifying as an expert.

2. Expert Witness

a. Subject matter of testimony

Before an expert witness may testify, the court must first determine that the subject matter of the witness's testimony:

i) **Is scientific, technical, or other specialized knowledge,** which focuses on the *reliability* of the testimony; and

ii) Will **help the trier of fact** understand the evidence or determine a fact in issue, which focuses on the *relevance* of the testimony.

Some courts have held that expert testimony that goes to the credibility of a witness improperly invades the province of the jury to determine whether the witness is telling the truth. *Compare Nimely v. City of N.Y.*, 414 F.3d 381, 397 (2d Cir. 2005) (expert testimony that defendant witnesses had not lied inadmissible) *with United States v. Shay*, 57 F.3d 126 (1st Cir. 1995) (expert testimony that defendant witness suffered from pseudologia fantastica, a mental disorder that caused him to lie pathologically admissible).

b. **Qualified expert**

Once the testimony is determined to be reliable and relevant, an expert witness may testify as to her opinion, provided:

i) The witness is **qualified as an expert** by knowledge, skill, experience, training, or education;

ii) The testimony is based on **sufficient facts or data**;

iii) The testimony is the product of **reliable principles and methods** (i.e., the factual data, principles, and methods used as a basis for the testimony are of the type reasonably relied on by experts in the field, although the data need not be admissible itself); and

iv) The witness **applied the principles and methods reliably to the facts** of the case.

Fed. R. Evid. 702. The expert must also possess a reasonable degree of certainty in her opinion, which may be expressed using language such as "probably." *United States v. Mornan*, 413 F.3d 372 (3d Cir. 2005); *see also*, *Kumho Tire Co. v. Carmichael*, 526 U.S. 137 (1999); *Daubert v. Merrell Dow Pharm.*, 509 U.S. 579 (1993).

c. **Ultimate issue**

Generally, an opinion of a witness, whether lay or expert, may be admissible even though the opinion embraces an ultimate issue in the case (including the defendant's state of mind). However, an expert **may not** state an opinion about whether a criminal defendant had the **requisite mental state** of any element of the crime charged or of a defense. That determination lies in the province of the trier of fact. Fed. R. Evid. 704.

d. **Basis of opinion**

The expert's opinion may be based on facts and data that the expert has personally observed or about which the expert has been made aware. When such facts and data are not admissible, the opinion itself may nevertheless be admissible if experts in the particular field would reasonably rely on those kinds of facts and data in forming an opinion on the subject. If such facts are inadmissible, the proponent nevertheless may disclose them to the jury if their probative value in helping the jury evaluate the opinion substantially outweighs their prejudicial effect. Fed. R. Evid. 703.

1) **Disclosure of underlying facts and data**

An expert may state an opinion and give the reasons for it without first testifying as to the underlying facts or data, unless the court orders otherwise. Another party, when cross-examining the expert, may, of course, require the expert to disclose those facts or data. Fed. R. Evid. 705.

2) **Use of hypothetical**

In making facts known to the expert at trial, use of a hypothetical question is not required.

3) Lack of knowledge

A party can challenge the credibility of an expert witness on cross-examination by attacking the adequacy of the expert's knowledge, both their general knowledge in their field of expertise and their specific knowledge of the facts underlying their testimony.

e. Court-appointed expert

The court may appoint an expert witness and must inform the expert, either orally or in writing, of the expert's duties. Such a witness must advise each party of any findings. Each party may depose the witness, call the witness to testify, and cross-examine the witness. The court may authorize disclosure to the jury that the court appointed the expert. In a criminal case, the expert is paid by funds provided by law; in most civil cases, the expert's compensation is paid by the parties. Fed. R. Evid. 706.

f. Interpreter

An interpreter is subject to the rules for expert witnesses. Fed. R. Evid. 604.

E. PAYMENT OF WITNESS

A lawyer may not offer or pay a witness any consideration:

i)   In excess of the reasonable expenses of the witness incurred and the reasonable value of the witness's time spent in providing evidence, except that an expert witness may be offered and paid a noncontingent fee;

ii) Contingent on the content of the witness's testimony or the outcome of the litigation; or

iii) Otherwise prohibited by law.

Restatement (Third) of the Law Governing Lawyers, § 117.   The prohibition against contingent compensation does not apply to an expert retained only to consult and not to testify or otherwise provide evidence. Id., at § 117, cmt c. Any witness in attendance in federal court or a deposition pursuant to federal rule or court order is entitled to an appearance fee as well as a travel allowance. 28 U.S.C. § 1821.

IV. TANGIBLE EVIDENCE

Tangible evidence is evidence that is not presented in the form of testimony by a witness; it includes both documentary evidence (e.g., a written contract, a letter) and physical objects (e.g., a gun, torn clothing, an injured foot, a sound recording).

A. AUTHENTICATION

All tangible evidence must be authenticated. To authenticate an item, the proponent must produce sufficient evidence to support a finding that the thing is what its proponent claims it is. This is a lesser standard than a preponderance of the evidence. Fed. R. Evid. 901(a).

Satisfaction of the standard for authentication by a proponent of an item does not conclusively establish that the item is what the proponent claims. Admission of the item into evidence does not preclude the opponent from presenting evidence challenging the proponent's claim. For example, a party may introduce evidence that contradicts the other party's authentication of a signature on an instrument.

1. **Physical Objects**

   a. **Personal knowledge**

   A physical object may be authenticated by testimony of **personal knowledge** of the object. Fed. R. Evid. 901(b)(1).

   Example: The owner of a stolen pocket watch may authenticate the watch by simply identifying it, "Yes, that is my pocket watch that was stolen."

   b. **Distinctive characteristics**

   A physical object may be authenticated by testimony of its **distinctive** characteristics. Fed. R. Evid. 901(b)(4).

   Example: An electronically stored document may be authenticated by its metadata (e.g., filename, file type, creation date, permissions).

   c. **Chain of custody**

   Authentication by chain of custody must be used with respect to a physical object that could easily be tampered with or confused with a similar item, such as a blood sample. The witness testifying must account for the whereabouts of the item from the time it was obtained up until its introduction at the trial.

   d. **Reproductions and explanatory evidence**

   When reproductions (e.g., photographs, diagrams, maps, movies) are introduced into evidence, they may be authenticated by the testimony of a witness with personal knowledge that the object accurately depicts what its proponent claims it does. It is generally not necessary to call the person who created the reproduction to authenticate it. However, the creator may be called to authenticate the reproduction and may do so by testifying that the reproduction method produces an accurate result. Fed. R. Evid. 901(b)(9).

   e. **X-ray images and electrocardiograms**

   X-ray images, electrocardiograms, and similar items are physical representations of things that cannot otherwise be seen (i.e., the inner workings and functionality of a human body), and, as such, unlike other reproductions, they cannot be authenticated merely by the testimony of a witness that they are accurate reproductions of the facts. To authenticate such an item, it must be shown that an accurate process was used, that the machine used was working properly, and that the operator of the machine was qualified to operate it. The chain of custody must also be established.

2. **Documentary Evidence**

   Documentary evidence is commonly authenticated by stipulation, testimony of an eyewitness, or handwriting verification.

   a. **Ancient documents and data compilations**

   A document or data compilation, including data stored electronically, is considered authentic if it is (i) at least **20 years old,** (ii) in a **condition unlikely to create suspicion** as to its authenticity, and (iii) **found in a place where it would likely be** if it were authentic. Fed. R. Evid. 901(b)(8).

b. Public records

A public record may be authenticated by evidence that the document was recorded or filed in a public office as authorized by law or that the document is from the office where items of that kind are kept. Fed. R. Evid. 901(b)(7).

c. Reply letter doctrine

A document may be authenticated by evidence that it was written in response to a communication, so long as it is unlikely, based on the contents, that it was written by someone other than the recipient of the first communication.

d. Handwriting verification

There are two methods by which handwriting verification may be used to authenticate a writing.

1) Comparison

An expert witness or the trier of fact may compare the writing in question with another writing that has been proven to be genuine in order to determine the authenticity of the writing in question. Fed. R. Evid. 901(b)(3). This method may also be used for authenticating other items, such as fingerprints, cloth fibers, and hair.

2) Non-expert opinion

A lay witness with personal knowledge of the claimed author's handwriting may testify as to whether the document is in that person's handwriting. The lay witness must not have become familiar with the handwriting for the purposes of the current litigation. Fed. R. Evid. 901(b)(2).

e. Self-authenticating documents

The following items of evidence are self-authenticating—they do not require extrinsic evidence (i.e., evidence outside the document) of authenticity in order to be admitted:

i) Public documents bearing a governmental seal and a signature of an authorized governmental official or that are not sealed but are signed by an authorized governmental official and certified by another authorized governmental official;

ii) Certified copies of public records;

iii) Official publications issued by a public authority;

iv) Newspapers and periodicals;

v) Trade inscriptions (e.g., labels affixed in the course of business that indicate origin, ownership, or control);

vi) Notarized (acknowledged) documents;

vii) Commercial paper (including the signature thereon, and related documents);

viii) Any document, signature, or other item declared by federal statute to be authentic; and

ix) Records of a regularly conducted activity (e.g., a business) certified by a custodian of the records.

Although a proponent of a self-authenticating document generally is not required to give an adverse party advance notice of the intent to introduce the document, the proponent of business records (item ix, *above*) must give an adverse party reasonable written notice prior to the trial or hearing of the intent to offer the record and must make the record available for inspection so that the party has a fair opportunity to challenge them. Fed. R. Evid. 902.

f. Attesting witness

The testimony of a witness who attests or subscribes to a document generally is not required to authenticate a document. However, such testimony may be required by state law, such as to authenticate a will. Fed. R. Evid. 903.

3. Oral Statements

Oral statements may need to be authenticated as to the identity of the speaker in cases in which that identity is important (e.g., an opposing party's statement).

a. Voice identification

A voice can be identified by **any person** who has heard the voice **at any time** (including one made familiar solely for the purposes of litigation, in contrast to the rule for handwriting verification). It makes no difference whether the voice was heard firsthand or through mechanical or electronic transmission or recording. Fed. R. Evid. 901(b)(5).

b. Telephone conversations

A party to a telephone conversation may authenticate statements made during that conversation as having been made by a particular individual by testifying that:

i) The caller recognized the speaker's voice;

ii) The speaker knew facts that only a particular person would know;

iii) The caller dialed a number believed to be the speaker's, and the speaker identified himself upon answering; or

iv) The caller dialed a business and spoke to the person who answered about business regularly conducted over the phone.

Fed. R. Evid. 901(b)(4)–(6).

B. BEST EVIDENCE RULE

The best evidence rule (also known as the original document rule) requires that the original document (or a reliable duplicate) be produced to prove the contents of a writing, recording, or photograph, including electronic documents, x-rays, and videos. A "writing" is defined as "letters, words, numbers or their equivalent set down in any form." A "recording" and "photograph" are similarly broadly defined. Fed. R. Evid. 1001(a)–(c).

This rule applies only when the **contents of the document are at issue** or a witness is **relying on the contents of the document** when testifying. Fed. R. Evid. 1001–08.

Caution: Despite its name, the best evidence rule does not require a party to present the most persuasive evidence, nor does it require the presentation of documentary evidence instead of a witness's testimony simply because a document is available.

Example: A witness writes down her observations of an accident immediately after it happens. The best evidence rule does not prevent the witness from testifying about the event simply because a writing of her observations exists.

1. **Contents at Issue**

   The contents of a document are at issue when:

   i) The document is used as proof of the happening of an event, such as with a photograph of a bank robbery;

   ii) The document has a legal effect, such as with a contract or a will; or

   iii) The witness is testifying based on facts learned from the writing (as opposed to personal knowledge), such as with an x-ray image.

   Fed. R. Evid. 1002, Notes of Advisory Committee.

2. **"Original"**

   An original of a writing or recording includes any counterpart intended to have the same effect as the original by the person who executed or issued it. If the information is stored electronically, any legible printout (or other output readable by sight) that reflects the information accurately is an original. An original of a photograph includes the negative and any print made from it. Fed. R. Evid. 1001(d).

3. **Exceptions**

   a. **Duplicates**

      A duplicate is a counterpart produced by any process or technique that accurately reproduces the original. Fed. R. Evid. 1001(e). A duplicate is admissible to the same extent as an original unless:

      i) There is a genuine question as to the authenticity of the original; or

      ii) The circumstances make it unfair to admit the duplicate, such as may be the case when only part of the original is duplicated.

      Fed. R. Evid. 1003.

      Handwritten copies: Handwritten copies of an original are not duplicates and are admissible only when the original or duplicate is lost, destroyed, or in the possession of an adversary who fails to produce it.

   b. **Original unavailable**

      The original is not required, and other evidence of its contents is admissible if:

      i) All of the originals are lost or destroyed, and not by the proponent acting in bad faith;

      ii) The original cannot be obtained by any available judicial process;

      iii) The party against whom the original would be offered (a) had control of the original, (b) was at that time put on notice that the original would be the subject of proof at the trial or hearing, and (c) failed to produce it at the trial or hearing; or

      iv) The writing, recording, or photograph is not closely related to a controlling issue (i.e., it is a collateral matter).

      In such cases, once the party has accounted for the absence of an original, the party may prove the contents of the writing, recording, or photograph by other means. Fed. R. Evid. 1004.

c. Public records

The contents of a public record (i.e., an official record or a document recorded or filed in a public office as authorized by law) may be, and generally are, proved by a certified copy rather than by the original record. Alternatively, a public record may be proved by a copy of the record plus the testimony of a person who has compared the copy with the original. If a certified or compared copy cannot be obtained by reasonable diligence, the contents may be proved by other evidence. Fed. R. Evid. 1005.

d. Summaries

The contents of voluminous writings, recordings, or photographs may be presented in the form of a chart, summary, or calculation, if such contents cannot be conveniently examined in court. The proponent must make the originals or duplicates available for examination and copying by other parties at a reasonable time and place. The court may order the proponent to produce the originals or duplicates in court. Fed. R. Evid. 1006.

e. Admission by party

The proponent may prove the contents of a writing, recording, or photograph by the testimony, deposition, or written statement of the party against whom the evidence is offered. In such a case, the proponent does not need to account for the original. Fed. R. Evid. 1007.

Oral out-of-court statement: If a party against whom a document is offered admits to the contents of the document in an oral statement made out of court (other than during a deposition), the best evidence rule applies. The proponent must account for the original before using the adverse party's oral statement to prove the contents of the document.

4. Role of Court and Jury

Ordinarily, the court determines whether the proponent has fulfilled the conditions for admitting other evidence of the content of a document. In a jury trial, however, the jury determines any issue as to whether:

i) An asserted writing, recording, or photograph ever existed;

ii) Another writing, recording, or photograph produced at trial is the original; or

iii) Other evidence of content correctly reflects the content.

Fed. R. Evid. 1008.

C. PAROL EVIDENCE RULE

1. General Rule

The parol evidence rule operates to exclude evidence that, if introduced, would change the terms of a written agreement. The rule is based on the assumption that a written contract represents the complete agreement between the parties.

a. Complete integration

If a written agreement is a complete integration (i.e., contains all of the terms to which the parties agreed), then the parol evidence rule is in effect, and no extrinsic evidence may be introduced.

b. Partial integration

A contract that contains some, but not all, of the terms to which the parties agreed is a partial integration. In this case, extrinsic evidence that **adds to** the writing may be admitted. Evidence that **contradicts** the writing may not be admitted.

2. Exceptions

Extrinsic evidence can always be admitted for the following purposes:

i) To clarify an ambiguity in the terms of the writing;

ii) To prove trade custom or course of dealings;

iii) To show fraud, duress, mistake, or illegal purpose on the part of one or both parties; or

iv) To show that consideration has (or has not) been paid.

3. Applicable Evidence

Only evidence of **prior or contemporaneous negotiations** is subject to the parol evidence rule. In other words, evidence of negotiations conducted **after** the execution of the written contract is not prohibited by the parol evidence rule and may be offered to prove subsequent modifications of the agreement.

D. DEMONSTRATIVE AND EXPERIMENTAL EVIDENCE

A court may allow demonstrations and experiments to be performed in the courtroom. This may include exhibition of injuries in a personal injury or criminal case. A court has discretion to exclude evidence of personal injuries if the demonstration of such severe injuries would result in unfair prejudice. A court may also exclude a demonstration that cannot be effectively cross-examined. Science experiments are permitted but may be excluded if they will result in undue waste of time or confusion of the issues.

V. PRIVILEGES AND OTHER POLICY EXCLUSIONS

A. PRIVILEGES

The Federal Rules have no specific privilege provisions but instead defer to common-law privileges, except in diversity cases, when state rules generally apply. Fed. R. Evid. 501. A claim of privilege applies at all stages of a case or proceedings. Fed. R. Evid. 1101(c).

1. Confidential Communication

For a privilege to apply, there must be a confidential communication.

a. Presence of third party

Generally, if the communication is overheard by a third party, the privilege is destroyed. However, the presence of the third party does not destroy the privilege if:

i) The first two parties do not know that the third party is present (e.g., an unknown eavesdropper); or

ii) The third party is necessary to assist in the communication (e.g., a translator).

b. Waiver

A privilege may be waived if the person who holds the privilege:

i) Fails to assert the privilege in a timely manner (i.e., when the testimony is offered);

ii) Voluntarily discloses, or allows another to disclose, a substantial portion of the communication to a third party, unless the disclosure is privileged; or

iii) Contractually waives the privilege in advance.

A wrongful disclosure without the privilege holder's consent does not constitute a waiver. For limitations on waiver of the attorney-client privilege due to inadvertent disclosure, *see* § 3.c. Effect of disclosure on waiver, *below*.

2. Spousal Privilege

"Spousal privilege" comprises two distinct privileges: spousal immunity and confidential marital communications.

a. Spousal immunity

The general rule is that the spouse of a **criminal defendant** may not be called as a witness by the prosecution. Nor may a married person be **compelled** to testify against his spouse in any criminal proceeding, including a grand jury proceeding, regardless of who is the defendant.

1) Holder of the privilege

a) Federal courts

In federal courts (and a majority of states), the **witness spouse** holds the privilege and may choose to testify but cannot be compelled to do so.

b) State courts

In a minority of jurisdictions, the **party spouse** (as opposed to the witness spouse) holds the privilege and may prevent the witness spouse from testifying, even if the witness spouse wants to testify.

2) Period to which the privilege applies

The spousal immunity privilege applies to testimony about events that occurred **before and during the marriage.**

3) Time limit on assertion of the privilege

The spousal immunity privilege can be asserted **only during a valid marriage.** The right to assert the privilege expires upon divorce or annulment.

b. Confidential marital communications

Communication made between spouses **while they were married** is privileged if the communication was made **in reliance on the sanctity of marriage.**

1) Holder of the privilege

The majority view, which is followed by most federal courts, is that the privilege is held by **both** spouses. E.g., *United States v. Porter*, 986 F.2d 1014, 1018 (6th Cir. 1993). Under the majority view, **either spouse** may assert the privilege and refuse to testify about the communication or prevent the other spouse from testifying. Waiver of the privilege by one spouse does not affect the other spouse's right to claim the privilege. Some courts, however, have taken the position that only the communicating spouse can assert the privilege. *See* 1 Kenneth S. Broun et al., McCormick on Evidence § 83 (6th ed. 2006).

2) Scope of the privilege

This privilege applies only to communications made **during marriage.** This privilege applies to both **civil and criminal cases.**

3) Lack of time limit on assertion of the privilege

The time for asserting this privilege extends **beyond the termination of the marriage.** Thus, either party may assert the privilege—by refusing to testify or by preventing the other party from doing so—at any time, even after divorce or the death of one spouse.

> **Comparison of timing:** Spousal immunity applies to events occurring before marriage but ends when the marriage does, whereas the confidential communication privilege begins with marriage but continues after the marriage has ended.

c. Exceptions

Spousal privileges are subject to limitations in cases in which one spouse is suing the other, or when one spouse is charged with a crime against the other spouse or the children of either. For example, a defendant-spouse accused of battery of a witness-spouse would not be able to prevent the witness-spouse from testifying as to confidential marital communications.

3. Attorney-Client Privilege

A confidential communication between a client and an attorney for the purpose of seeking legal advice or representation is privileged.

a. Elements

1) Confidential

The communication must be intended to be confidential in order to be privileged. A communication made in the presence of a third party generally is not privileged, but the presence of, or communication by or through, a representative of the client or the attorney does not destroy the attorney-client privilege.

2) Communication

The communication must be **for the purpose of seeking legal advice or representation,** but the attorney does not need to give advice or agree to the representation for the privilege to exist.

a) Non-privileged statements

A statement made to an attorney that is not about legal advice or services sought by the client is not privileged. This includes statements regarding the fact of employment, the identity of the client, and the fee arrangements for the representation. If providing such information would divulge a confidential communication or incriminate the client, then it may be protected.

Furthermore, the attorney-client privilege does not protect disclosure of the underlying facts. A client cannot be compelled to answer the question "What did you say to your attorney?" but cannot refuse to reveal a fact within her knowledge merely because she told that fact to her attorney. *Upjohn Co. v. United States*, 449 U.S. 383 (1981) (quoting *Philadelphia v. Westinghouse Electric Corp.*, 205 F.Supp. 830, 831 (E.D. Pa. 1962)).

Finally, communications are not privileged when they are made to an attorney who is acting in a capacity other than as an attorney, such as a tax preparer, business partner, or witness to a will.

b) Corporate client

When an attorney represents a corporation, some states limit the privilege to communications received by the attorney from a member of the "control group" of the corporation (employees in a position to control or take a substantial part in a decision). *See, e.g., Consolidation Coal Co. v. Bucyrus-Erie Co.*, 432 N.E.2d 250 (Ill. 1982). However, in cases in which federal law controls, the privilege extends to communications by a non-control-group employee about matters within the employee's corporate duties made for the purpose of securing legal advice for the corporation. *Upjohn Co. v. United States*, 449 U.S. 383 (1981) (protecting communications by lower-level employees who were directed by their superiors to communicate with the corporation's attorney).

3) Client holds the privilege

The client holds the privilege and only the client, guardian, or a successor-in-interest (e.g., the personal representative of a deceased client's estate) may waive it. The attorney, however, must assert the privilege on the client's behalf to protect the client's interests. The privilege exists until it is waived, and it can survive termination of the attorney-client relationship, and even the client's death.

b. Exceptions

The attorney-client privilege does not protect these confidential communications:

i)   Communications made to enable or aid the commission of what the client **knew or should have known** was a crime or fraud;

ii)   Communications relevant to a dispute between attorney and client (e.g., a malpractice allegation);

iii)   Communications relevant to a dispute between parties who claim through the same deceased client; and

iv)   Communications between former co-clients who are now adverse to each other.

> **Work product documents:** Documents prepared by an attorney for his own use in connection with the client's case are not covered by the attorney-client privilege because **they are not communications.** However, such documents are protected under the "work product" doctrine and are not subject to discovery unless the party seeking disclosure (i) demonstrates a substantial need for the information, and (ii) cannot obtain the information by any other means without undue hardship. The mental impressions, conclusions, and trial tactics of an attorney are always protected from discovery. Fed. R. Civ. P. 26(b)(3).

c. Effect of disclosure on waiver

Although the Federal Rules generally do not address the existence or scope of common-law privileges, there is one exception. Federal Rule 502 addresses the effect that a litigation-related disclosure of protected information has on the waiver of the attorney-client privilege, drawing a distinction between an intentional disclosure and an unintentional disclosure. The rule applies to confidential communications as well as material protected by the work-product doctrine. Fed. R. Evid. 502.

1) Inadvertent disclosure—no waiver

When made during a federal proceeding, the inadvertent disclosure of privileged communication or information does not waive the privilege if the holder of the privilege:

i)   Took reasonable steps to prevent disclosure; and

ii) Promptly took reasonable steps to rectify the error.

Fed. R. Evid. 502(b). In determining whether the holder took reasonable steps to prevent disclosure, factors such as the number of documents to be reviewed, the time constraints for production, or the existence of an efficient records-management system may be relevant.

2) Intentional disclosure—limitation on the scope of waiver

When made during a federal proceeding, the intentional disclosure of privileged material operates as a waiver of the attorney-client privilege. The waiver extends to undisclosed information only in those unusual situations in which (i) the disclosed and undisclosed material concern the same subject matter and (ii) fairness requires the disclosure of related information because a party has disclosed information in a selective, misleading, and unfair manner. Fed. R. Evid. 502(a).

3) Effect of disclosure made in a state proceeding

When privileged material is disclosed in a state proceeding and the state and federal laws are in conflict as to the effect of the disclosure, the disclosure does not operate as a waiver in a subsequent federal proceeding if the disclosure (i) would not be a waiver had it been made in a federal proceeding or (ii) is not a disclosure under the law of the state where it was made. In other words, the federal court must apply the law that is most protective of the privilege. This rule does not apply if the state court has issued an order concerning the effect of the disclosure; in such a case, the state-court order would be controlling. Fed. R. Evid. 502(c).

4) Controlling effect of a federal confidentiality order

A federal court may order that the privilege or protection is not waived by disclosure connected with the pending litigation (i.e., a confidentiality order). In such a case, the disclosure does not constitute a waiver in any other federal or state proceeding. Fed. R. Evid. 502(d).

5) Parties' agreement

An agreement between the parties regarding the effect of a disclosure binds only the parties unless the agreement is incorporated into a court order. Fed. R. Evid. 502(e).

4.   Physician-Patient Privilege

Although there is no common-law privilege covering statements made by a patient to a physician, most states protect such communications by statute, so long as the communications were made for the purpose of obtaining medical treatment. The patient holds the privilege; thus, only the patient may decide whether to waive it.

The privilege does not exist if:

i) The information was acquired for **reasons other than treatment**;

ii) The patient's **physical condition is at issue**;

iii) The communication was made as part of the **commission of a crime or tort**;

iv) A **dispute exists** between the physician and the patient;

v) The patient contractually **agreed to waive** the privilege; or

vi) A **case is brought in federal court** and state law does not apply (e.g., most cases that involve a federal question).

If an attorney requests that a physician consult with his client, then the physician-patient privilege applies only if treatment is contemplated during the consult.

5. **Psychotherapist-Patient Privilege**

The federal courts and all states recognize some form of privilege for confidential communications between a psychiatrist, psychologist, or licensed social worker and a patient in the course of diagnosis or treatment. The patient holds the privilege, but the psychotherapist must assert the privilege in the patient's absence. *Jaffee v. Redmond*, 518 U.S. 1 (1996).

The privilege does not exist if (i) the patient's mental condition is at issue, (ii) the communication was a result of a court-ordered exam, or (iii) the case is a commitment proceeding against the patient.

6. **Self-Incrimination**

a. **In general**

The Fifth Amendment protection against self-incrimination allows a witness in any proceeding to refuse to give testimony that may tend to incriminate the witness. The protection covers only current (not prior) statements and the fruits derived therefrom, and it does not apply to physical characteristics or mannerisms. The privilege belongs only to human beings. A corporation or other organization is not able to assert the privilege. *Bellis v. United States*, 417 U.S. 85 (1974). The Fifth Amendment only protects against domestic prosecutions; it cannot be invoked out of a fear of foreign prosecution. *United States v. Balsys*, 524 U.S. 666 (1998).

b. **Comment and inference**

In a criminal case, a prosecutor may not comment on the defendant's failure to take the stand and may not argue that the jury should draw a negative inference from the assertion of the privilege. *Griffin v. California*, 380 U.S. 609 (1965).

In a civil case, however, it is proper for the opposing party to ask the jury to draw an adverse inference from a witness's claim of privilege.

c. **Immunity**

A witness may be compelled to provide incriminating testimony if the government grants him immunity from prosecution. The witness is not entitled to "transactional" immunity, i.e., protection against prosecution for the entire transaction about which he was testifying; instead, the government is constitutionally required to offer mere "use" immunity, which prohibits only the use of the compelled testimony against the witness. *Kastigar v. United States*, 406 U.S. 441 (1972). If the government does prosecute the witness in such a case, the government has the burden to show that the compelled testimony did not provide an investigatory lead that was helpful to the prosecution.

A witness may lose the right to invoke the privilege if the danger of incrimination has been removed through acquittal or conviction of the underlying charge. If the questioning about the adjudicated crime can lead to prosecution for other crimes, however, the privilege can be invoked.

7. Other Privileges

a. Clergy-penitent

In some jurisdictions, a confidential communication made by a penitent to a member of the clergy is privileged. The penitent holds the privilege, but the clergy member must assert the privilege on the penitent's behalf.

b. Accountant-client

Although not available at common law, many jurisdictions recognize a privilege for confidential communications made by a client to his accountant. The privilege operates similarly to the attorney-client privilege.

c. Professional journalist

There is no federal privilege protecting a journalist's source of information, but some states have enacted statutes extending some protection to journalists.

d. Governmental privileges

The government, at all levels, is privileged against disclosing:

i)   The identity of an informant in a criminal case; and

ii) The communication of **official information** (i.e., information that relates to the internal affairs of the government and is not open to the public) by or to public officials.

B. PUBLIC POLICY EXCLUSIONS

1. Subsequent Remedial Measures

When measures are taken that would have made an earlier injury or harm less likely to occur (e.g., repairing an area where a customer slipped), evidence of the subsequent measures is **not admissible to prove negligence, culpable conduct, a defective product or design, or the need for a warning or instruction.** However, evidence of subsequent remedial measures may be admissible for other purposes, such as impeachment or—if disputed—ownership or control of the cause of the harm (e.g., a car) or the feasibility of precautionary measures. Fed. R. Evid. 407.

Product liability: The exclusion of evidence of a subsequent remedial measure applies to product liability actions based on negligence and those based on strict liability.

a. Timing of remedial measure

To be excluded, the remedial measure must be undertaken **after** the plaintiff is injured; a remedial measure made after a product was manufactured but **before** the plaintiff was injured is not subject to exclusion under this rule. Fed. R. Evid. 407, Notes of Advisory Committee (1997).

b. Third-party remedial measure

This exclusion does not apply to a remedial measure undertaken by a third party, rather than a defendant. *E.g., Diehl v. Blaw-Knox*, 360 F.3d 426, 430 (3d Cir. 2004).

2. Compromise Offers and Negotiations

Compromise offers made by any party, as well as any conduct or statements made during compromise negotiations, are not admissible to prove or disprove the **validity or amount of a disputed claim,** nor may they be admitted for impeachment by prior inconsistent statement or contradiction. Fed. R. Evid. 408.

Lack of dispute: If the claim is not disputed as to its validity or amount (e.g., a party admits to both), then a statement made in connection with an offer to settle for a lesser amount is admissible. Fed. R. Evid. 408, Notes of Advisory Committee.

a. Exceptions

1) Negotiation with a governmental agency

A person's conduct or statements made during compromise negotiations with a governmental agency (e.g., the IRS) during the exercise of its regulatory, investigative, or enforcement authority may be introduced in a subsequent criminal case against the person.

2) Admissibility for other reasons

Evidence of settlement offers and negotiations is admissible to prove bias or prejudice of a witness, to negate a claim of undue delay, or to prove obstruction of a criminal investigation or prosecution.

b. No immunization of evidence

Evidence may be admissible through means other than as an admission made during compromise negotiations. A party does not immunize (i.e., protect from admission) evidence simply by discussing it during compromise negotiations. Fed. R. Evid. 408, Notes of Advisory Committee (2006).

c. Prohibition on all parties

Compromise evidence is not admissible on behalf of **any party** who participated in the compromise negotiations, even the party who made the settlement offer or statement. The protection of this rule cannot be waived unilaterally. Moreover, when there are more than two parties, a settlement agreement entered into by a party with an adverse party cannot be used by a remaining adverse party to prove or disprove the validity or amount of an unsettled claim. Fed. R. Evid. 408, Notes of Advisory Committee (2006); *Branch v. Fid. & Cas. Co.*, 783 F.2d 1289 (5th Cir. 1986).

3. Offers to Pay Medical Expenses

Evidence of the payment, offer to pay, or promise to pay medical, hospital, or similar expenses resulting from an injury is **not admissible to prove liability for the injury.** Fed. R. Evid. 409.

Compare compromise: Unlike a compromise negotiation, any conduct or statement that accompanies the payment, offer to pay, or promise to pay medical expenses is admissible.

4. Plea Negotiation

In a civil or criminal case, evidence of the following is generally not admissible against the defendant who made the plea or participated in the plea discussions:

i) Withdrawn guilty pleas;

ii) Pleas of no contest (i.e., a *nolo contendere* plea);

iii) Statements made while negotiating a plea with a prosecutor (e.g., an offer to plead guilty); and

iv) Statements made during a plea proceeding (e.g., a Rule 11 proceeding under the Federal Rules of Criminal Procedure). Fed. R. Evid. 410(a).

a. Exceptions

Statements made during pleas or negotiations are admissible, however, if another statement made during the same plea or negotiation has already been admitted, and fairness requires that the statement in question also be admitted. Such statements also are admissible in a subsequent perjury prosecution if they were false statements made under oath, on the record, and with counsel present. Fed. R. Evid. 410(b).

b. Waiver

A defendant may waive the protection of Rule 410 if the waiver is knowing and voluntary. *United States v. Mezzanatto*, 513 U.S. 196 (1995).

5. Liability Insurance

Evidence that a person was or was not insured against liability is not admissible to prove whether the person acted negligently or otherwise wrongfully. However, such evidence may be admissible for another purpose, such as to prove agency, ownership, or control, or to prove a witness's bias or prejudice. Fed. R. Evid. 411.

6. Sexual Conduct

a. Victim's conduct

Under the "rape shield" rule, evidence offered to prove the sexual behavior or sexual predisposition of a victim (or alleged victim) generally is not admissible in any civil or criminal proceeding involving sexual misconduct. The exclusion applies to the use of such evidence for impeachment as well as substantive purposes.

Sexual behavior includes not only sexual intercourse or contact but also activities that imply such sexual intercourse or contact, such as the use of contraceptives or the existence of a sexually transmitted disease. Sexual predisposition can include the victim's mode of dress, speech, or lifestyle. Fed. R. Evid. 412(a), Notes of Advisory Committee (1994).

1) Exceptions

a) Criminal cases

In a criminal case involving sexual misconduct, evidence of specific instances of a victim's sexual behavior is admissible to prove that someone other than the defendant was the source of semen, injury, or other physical evidence. In addition, evidence of sexual behavior with the person accused of sexual misconduct is admissible if offered by the defendant to prove consent or if offered by the prosecution. Fed. R. Evid. 412(b)(1).

Note that, in contrast with the general preference under the Federal Rules for reputation or opinion testimony over evidence of specific acts, in criminal cases involving sexual misconduct, reputation or opinion evidence of a victim's sexual behavior or predisposition is not admissible.

Finally, any evidence whose exclusion would violate the defendant's constitutional rights is admissible under Rule 412. For example, under the Sixth Amendment Confrontation Clause, a defendant in a rape case may be able to cross-examine an alleged victim who testified that she lived with her mother about her cohabitation with another man in order to show that the alleged victim denied having consensual sex with the defendant in order to protect her relationship with the other man. *Olden v. Kentucky*, 488 U.S. 227 (1988).

b) Civil cases

In a civil case, evidence offered to prove a victim's sexual behavior or predisposition is admissible if its probative value **substantially outweighs** the danger of harm to any victim and of unfair prejudice to any party. Evidence of a victim's reputation is admissible only when it has been placed in controversy by the victim. Fed. R. Evid. 412(b)(2).

The restriction on evidence of a victim's sexual behavior or predisposition applies only when the party against whom the evidence is offered can be characterized as a victim of sexual misconduct. For example, a plaintiff in a defamation action based on a statement about the plaintiff's sexual behavior is not a victim of sexual misconduct. By contrast, a plaintiff who brings a Title VII sexual harassment action can be characterized as a victim of sexual misconduct. Fed. R. Evid. 412, Notes of Advisory Committee (1994).

c) Procedure for admission

In a criminal or civil case, the party intending to offer evidence of the victim's sexual behavior or predisposition must file a motion describing the evidence and stating the purpose for its introduction. The motion must be filed at least 14 days before trial unless the court sets a different time. The motion must be served on all parties, and the victim (or the victim's guardian or representative) must be notified. The court must conduct an *in camera* hearing and give the victim and the parties the right to attend and to be heard. Unless the court orders otherwise, the record of the hearing is sealed. Fed. R. Evid. 412(c).

b. Defendant's conduct

In a criminal case in which a defendant is accused of sexual assault, attempted sexual assault, or conspiracy to commit sexual assault, evidence that the defendant committed any other sexual assault is admissible to prove any relevant matter. Similarly, in a criminal case in which a defendant is accused of child molestation, evidence that the defendant committed any other child molestation is admissible to prove any relevant matter. A similar rule applies in civil cases alleging sexual assault or child molestation. Fed. R. Evid. 413–15.

Propensity evidence: Unlike Federal Rule 404(b), which applies to other crimes or bad acts committed by a defendant, these rules permit the use of a defendant's previous commission of a sexual assault or child molestation as evidence of the defendant's propensity to commit the charged sexual assault or child molestation.

Consequently, for example, a defendant's prior conviction for rape can be used as evidence of the defendant's propensity to commit the charged rape, but a defendant's prior conviction for robbery cannot be used as evidence of the defendant's propensity to commit the charged robbery.

The court does have discretion to exclude such evidence under Rule 403 when the probative value is substantially outweighed by the danger of unfair prejudice. *United States v. Kelly*, 510 F.3d 433 (4th Cir. 2007); *Johnson v. Elk Lake Sch. Dist.*, 283 F.3d 138 (3d Cir. 2002).

1) Not limited to convictions

An arrest or even testimony of an incident that was unreported to the authorities may be admitted as evidence that a defendant has committed sexual assault or child molestation. Moreover, unlike Rule 609 regarding the use of a conviction to impeach a witness, there is no specific time restriction on the use of such evidence. *See, e.g., United States v. Horn*, 523 F.3d 882 (2008).

2) Pretrial disclosure

The prosecutor or plaintiff who intends to introduce such evidence must disclose it to the defendant at least 15 days before trial unless the court, for good cause, allows a later disclosure. Fed. R. Evid. 413(b), 414(b), 415(b).

VI. HEARSAY

A. WHAT IS HEARSAY

Hearsay is a statement that the declarant makes at a time other than while testifying at the current trial or hearing (i.e., an out-of-court statement) that is offered to prove the truth of the matter asserted. Fed. R. Evid. 801(c). Hearsay evidence generally is inadmissible unless it falls within an exception or exclusion set out in the Federal Rules, a federal statute, or a Supreme Court rule. Fed. R. Evid. 802.

1. Declarant—Person

The declarant (i.e., the maker of the statement) must be a person. Evidence generated by a machine or an animal is not hearsay. Fed. R. Evid. 801(b). Examples of such nonhearsay evidence include:

i) A dog's bark;

ii) An automatically generated time stamp on a fax;

iii) A printout of results of computerized telephone tracing equipment; and

iv) Raw data (such as blood-alcohol level) generated by a forensic lab's diagnostic machine.

Witness as declarant: A witness's own prior statement may be hearsay, and if hearsay, the witness may be prohibited from testifying as to her own statement unless an exception or exclusion applies.

2. Statement—Assertion

A statement is a person's oral or written assertion, or it may be nonverbal conduct intended as an assertion. Fed. R. Evid. 801(a). An example of assertive conduct is a defendant nodding his head up and down to indicate a "yes" answer to a question.

Contrast nonassertive conduct: Nonassertive conduct is not hearsay. An example of nonassertive conduct is a pilot's act of flying an airplane, when such evidence is offered as evidence of the plane's safety.

3. **Offered to Prove the Truth of the Matter Asserted**

   Statements offered to prove something other than the truth of the matter asserted are not hearsay.

   > **EXAM NOTE:** A statement that is not hearsay is not automatically admissible. For exam purposes, it is important to keep in mind that the statement must be admissible under the other rules restricting admission, such as the rules on privileges.

   a. **Legally operative facts**

      A statement offered to prove that the statement was made, regardless of its truth, is not hearsay.

      Example: In a slander action, the defendant's statement that the plaintiff is a murderer may be admissible to prove that the defendant made the statement but not to prove that the plaintiff is a murderer.

   b. **Effect on recipient**

      A statement offered to show the effect on the person who heard it is not hearsay.

      Example: In a negligence action, the defendant's statement to the plaintiff that the sidewalk in front of the defendant's house was icy may be admissible to show that the plaintiff had notice of the danger but not to show that the sidewalk was actually icy.

   c. **State of mind**

      A statement offered as circumstantial evidence of the declarant's mental state is not hearsay.

      Example: A testator's statement, "I am the queen of England," is not admissible to show its truth, but it is admissible to prove that the testator is not of sound mind.

   d. **Identification**

      A statement that is used as circumstantial evidence linking a person with an event, place, or object is not being introduced for its truth and therefore is not hearsay.

      Example: A hotel receipt found on defendant's person is circumstantial evidence that the defendant had been to the hotel and therefore is not hearsay. *United States v. Mejias*, 552 F.2d 435, 446 (2d Cir. 1977).

   e. **Impeachment and Rehabilitation**

      A statement offered solely to impeach or rehabilitate a witness is not being introduced for its truth and therefore is not hearsay (*see* III.B.4. Prior Inconsistent Statement, *supra*).

4. **Multiple Hearsay**

   A statement that contains hearsay within hearsay may be admissible as long as each part of the combined statement conforms to a hearsay exception. Fed. R. Evid. 805.

Example: A plaintiff sues a defendant for battery, claiming that the defendant struck the plaintiff's kneecaps with a baseball bat. At trial, the plaintiff seeks to introduce as evidence a hospital record, which consists of a note from a physician that the plaintiff told the physician that the plaintiff's injury was caused by being struck with a baseball bat. Both the plaintiff's statement to the physician and the note are hearsay; they are out-of-court statements being offered to prove the truth of the matter asserted—the cause of the plaintiff's injury. However, because each part of the statement falls within a hearsay exception (the plaintiff's statement is a statement made for the purpose of obtaining medical treatment, and the doctor's note is a business record), the hospital record may be admissible.

B. WHAT IS NOT HEARSAY

The following types of statements, which otherwise would qualify as hearsay, are expressly defined as nonhearsay. Fed. R. Evid. 801(d).

1. Declarant-Witness's Prior Statements

The Federal Rules identify three types of prior statements that are not hearsay. In all three cases, the witness who made the statement (declarant witness) must testify at the present trial or hearing and be subject to cross-examination concerning the statement in order for it to be admissible. Fed. R. Evid. 801(d)(1).

a. Prior inconsistent statements

A prior inconsistent statement **made under penalty of perjury** at a trial, hearing, or other proceeding, or in a deposition may be admissible to **impeach** the declarant's credibility and as **substantive evidence.** Statements made in a prior legal action that is unrelated to the current action may be admitted under this rule. Fed. R. Evid. 801(d)(1)(A).

Statement not made at a former proceeding: An inconsistent statement that was not made under penalty of perjury may be admissible to impeach a witness but is not admissible under this provision as substantive evidence.

b. Prior consistent statements

A prior consistent statement, whether made under oath or not, may be admissible (i) to rebut an express or implied charge that the declarant recently fabricated it or acted from a recent improper influence or motive in testifying, only if it was made **before the declarant had reason to fabricate or the improper influence or motive arose;** or (ii) to rehabilitate the declarant's credibility as a witness when attacked on another ground. Fed. R. Evid. 801(d)(1)(B).

c. Prior statement of identification

A previous out-of-court identification of a person after perceiving that person (e.g., lineup) is not hearsay and may be admissible as substantive evidence. Fed. R. Evid. 801(d)(1)(C). Even if the witness has no memory of the prior identification, it will be admissible because the witness is subject to cross-examination about the prior identification. *United States v. Owens*, 484 U.S. 554 (1988).

> **EXAM NOTE:** Beware of fact patterns involving prior out-of-court identifications by a witness who is not testifying at the current trial and therefore is not subject to cross-examination. This rule cannot apply, for instance, if the witness is dead or otherwise unavailable to testify.

2. **Opposing Party's Statement**

A statement made by a **party to the current litigation** is not hearsay if it is offered by an opposing party. The statement may have been made by the party in his individual or representative capacity (e.g., trustee). Fed. R. Evid. 801(d)(2)(A). This type of statement traditionally was known as an admission of a party-opponent.

Contrast statement against interest exception: Unlike with the statement against interest hearsay exception (*see* § VII.A.4. Statement Against Interest, *infra*), an opposing party's statement need not have been against the party's interest at the time that it was made.

Unlike most testimony by a lay witness, an opposing party's statement may be admitted even if it is not based on personal knowledge. In addition, an opposing party's statement in the form of an opinion may be admitted, even if the statement is about a matter that normally would be beyond the scope of lay witness opinion testimony. Fed. R. Evid. 801(d)(2), Notes of Advisory Committee.

a. **Judicial admission**

An admission made during the discovery process or a stipulation otherwise made during a proceeding is conclusive evidence, as is a statement made in a pleading, unless amended. Otherwise, although a statement in a pleading or an admission or stipulation made in another proceeding is usually admissible, it may generally be rebutted.

Note: A *withdrawn* guilty plea is generally not admissible in a subsequent civil or criminal proceeding (*see* § V.B.4. Plea Negotiation, *supra*.)

b. **Adoptive admission**

An adoptive admission is a statement of another person that a party expressly or impliedly adopts as his own. Fed. R. Evid. 801(d)(2)(B). Silence in response to a statement is considered an adoptive admission if:

   i) The person was present and heard and understood the statement;

   ii) The person had the ability and opportunity to deny the statement; and

   iii) A reasonable person similarly situated would have denied the statement.

Post-arrest silence by a defendant who has received *Miranda* warnings may not be used as an adoptive admission of a statement made by another person (e.g., a police officer). *Doyle v. Ohio*, 426 U.S. 610 (1976).

c. **Vicarious statements**

A statement made by one person may be imputed to another based on the relationship between them. In determining whether a statement constitutes an opposing party's statement, the statement is considered, but the statement itself cannot establish the necessary relationship between the parties.

1) **Employee or agent**

A statement made by a party's agent or employee constitutes an opposing party's statement if it was made concerning a matter **within the scope of and during the course of the relationship.** Fed. R. Evid. 801(d)(2)(D).

2) Authorized speaker

A statement about a subject that is made by a person who is **authorized** by a party to make a statement on the subject constitutes an opposing party's statement. Fed. R. Evid. 801(d)(2)(C).

3) Co-conspirators

Although a statement made by one co-party is not admissible against another co-party based solely on their status as co-parties, a statement made by a co-conspirator **during and in furtherance of** the conspiracy is admissible as an opposing party's statement against other co-conspirators. Fed. R. Evid. 801(d)(2)(E). A statement made by a co-conspirator after being arrested generally is not admissible, since it was not made during the conspiracy.

VII. HEARSAY EXCEPTIONS

Although hearsay generally is inadmissible, the Federal Rules identify some situations in which hearsay is allowed, either because of necessity (i.e., the declarant is unavailable) or because the statements are inherently trustworthy, in which case the declarant's availability is immaterial.

A. DECLARANT UNAVAILABLE AS A WITNESS

There are five exceptions to the hearsay rule that apply only if the declarant is unavailable as a witness: former testimony, dying declaration, statement against interest, statement of personal or family history, and statement offered against a party that wrongfully caused the declarant's unavailability.

1. Unavailable Declarant

An unavailable declarant is a person who:

i)   Is exempt on the grounds of privilege;

ii) Refuses to testify despite a court order to do so;

iii) Lacks memory of the subject matter of the statement;

iv) Is unable to testify due to death, infirmity, or physical or mental disability; or

v)   Is absent and cannot be subpoenaed or otherwise made to be present.

A declarant is not deemed unavailable if the unavailability is due to the procurement or wrongdoing of the proponent of the statement in order to prevent the declarant from testifying at or attending the trial. Fed. R. Evid. 804(a).

2. Former Testimony

Testimony that was given **as a witness** at a trial, hearing, or lawful deposition is not excluded as hearsay if the party against whom the testimony is being offered (or, in a civil case, a party's predecessor-in-interest) had an **opportunity and similar motive** to develop the testimony by direct examination, redirect examination, or cross-examination. This exception applies whether the testimony was given during the current proceeding or during a different one, but the witness who gave the testimony must now be unavailable. Fed. R. Evid. 804(b)(1).

Grand jury testimony generally does not fall within the former testimony exception, but it may be admissible nonhearsay evidence as a prior inconsistent statement.

3. Dying Declaration

A statement qualifies as a "dying declaration" if:

i) The declarant **believes that her death is imminent**; and

ii) The statement pertains to the **cause or circumstances** of the death she believes to be imminent.

Under this exception to the hearsay rule, although the declarant must be unavailable, the declarant need not have actually died in order for the statement to avoid exclusion as hearsay. The dying-declaration exception applies **only in homicide prosecutions and civil cases.** Fed. R. Evid. 804(b)(2).

4. Statement Against Interest

A statement made by a declarant who is unavailable to testify is not excluded as hearsay if the statement:

i) Was against the declarant's interest at the time it was made; and

ii) Would not have been made by a reasonable person unless he believed it to be true.

Under this exception to the hearsay rule, the statement must have been against the declarant's proprietary or pecuniary interest, have invalidated the declarant's claim against someone, or have exposed the declarant to civil or criminal liability. A statement that would subject the declarant to criminal liability is not admissible unless corroborating circumstances clearly indicate the trustworthiness of the statement. Fed. R. Evid. 804(b)(3).

Opposing party's statement distinguished: A **statement against interest** may be made by a non-party, the declarant must be unavailable, and the statement must have been against the declarant's interest at the time it was made. An **opposing party's statement,** on the other hand, must have been made by a party, and the statement need not have been against the party's interest when it was made (*see* § VI.B.2. Opposing Party's Statement, *supra*).

5. Statement of Personal or Family History

A statement concerning the unavailable declarant's own birth, adoption, marriage, divorce, legitimacy, familial relationship, or other similar fact of personal or family history is not excluded as hearsay. Fed. R. Evid. 804(b)(4).

6. Statement Against Party That Caused Declarant's Unavailability

Formerly known as the "forfeiture against wrongdoing" exception, a statement offered against a party that wrongfully caused the declarant's unavailability is not excluded as hearsay. Under this exception, the wrongful party forfeits the right to object to the admission of the declarant's statement as hearsay. The wrongdoing, which need not be criminal, may be accomplished by a deliberate act or by acquiescing to another's act, but must be done with the intent of preventing the witness from testifying. This exception applies to all parties, including the government. Fed. R. Evid. 804(b)(6).

Note: For the effect of the Confrontation Clause on this exception, *see* § VIII.A.1.b. Unavailability of the declarant, *infra*.

B. DECLARANT'S AVAILABILITY AS A WITNESS IMMATERIAL

The following hearsay exceptions do not require that the declarant be unavailable because the circumstances under which the statements were made suggest that the statements are inherently trustworthy. Fed. R. Evid. 803.

1. Present Sense Impression

A statement describing or explaining an event or condition that is made **while or immediately after the declarant perceived it** is not excluded as hearsay. Fed. R. Evid. 803(1).

a. Res gestae

A common-law hearsay exception labeled "res gestae" (meaning "things done") existed for a statement that was precipitated by an event or was about a contemporaneous condition. The Federal Rules do not contain a general res gestae exception but instead recognize several distinct, related exceptions, including exceptions for a present sense impression; an excited utterance; a dying declaration; a statement of mental, emotional, and physical condition; and a statement made for purposes of medical treatment or diagnosis.

2. Excited Utterance

A statement made about a startling event or condition **while the declarant is under the stress of excitement that it caused** is not excluded as hearsay. Under this exception to the hearsay rule, the event must shock or excite the declarant, and the statement must relate to the event, but the declarant need not be a participant in the event (i.e., the declarant can be a bystander). Fed. R. Evid. 803(2).

Present sense impression distinguished: A present sense impression must be a **description** of the event, whereas an **excited utterance** need only **relate to** the exciting event.

Example 1: Adele looks out the window and states, "It sure is raining hard tonight." She has made a statement of present sense impression, which is admissible to prove that it rained on the night in question.

Example 2: Bob discovers that he has a winning lottery ticket and shouts, "I just won a million dollars!" He has made an excited utterance, which is admissible to prove that he won the money.

Note: There is some overlap between these exceptions, and a statement, such as one describing a murder made immediately after the murder took place, could fall into both categories.

3. Statement of Mental, Emotional, or Physical Condition

A statement of the declarant's **then-existing** state of mind or emotional, sensory, or physical condition is not excluded as hearsay. Fed. R. Evid. 803(3).

a. State of mind

A statement of **present intent, motive, or plan** can be used to prove **conduct in conformity** with that state of mind. A statement of a memory or past belief is inadmissible hearsay when used to prove the fact remembered or believed, unless the statement relates to the validity or terms of the declarant's will.

> **EXAM NOTE:** Do not confuse this "state of mind" hearsay exception with circumstantial evidence of the declarant's state of mind, which is not hearsay. (*See* § VI.A.3.c. State of mind, *supra*.) To fall under the hearsay exception, the statement must be offered to prove that the declarant acted in accordance with his stated intent.

b. Physical condition

When a declarant's physical condition at a particular time is in question, a statement of the declarant's mental feeling, pain, or bodily health made **at that time** can be used to prove the **existence** of that condition but not its cause.

In most states, a statement made by a patient to a doctor relating to a **past** condition is not admissible under this exception. Under the Federal Rules, such a statement is admissible under the hearsay exception for statements for purposes of medical diagnosis or treatment (*see* 4. Statement Made for Medical Diagnosis or Treatment, *below*).

4. Statement Made for Medical Diagnosis or Treatment

A statement describing medical history or past or present symptoms is not excluded as hearsay if it is made for medical **diagnosis or treatment.** A statement of the cause or source of the condition is admissible as an exception to the rule against hearsay if it is reasonably pertinent to diagnosis or treatment. Fed. R. Evid. 803(4).

Effect of physician-patient privilege: A statement that falls within this hearsay exception still may be inadmissible if it is protected by the physician-patient privilege.

a. Statement made to a person other than a physician

The statement need not be made to a physician to fall under this exception. Statements to other medical personnel, including hospital attendants and ambulance drivers, or even to family members, may be included. Fed. R. Evid. 803(4), Notes of Advisory Committee.

b. Statement made to nontreating physician

Statements made to a physician consulted only for the purpose of enabling the physician to testify at trial are admissible. Fed. R. Evid. 803(4), Notes of Advisory Committee on Proposed Rules, Exception (4); Fed. R. Evid. 703.

c. Statement made by a person other than the patient

Under this hearsay exception, the statement need not necessarily be made by the patient, so long as it is made for the purpose of medical diagnosis or treatment. The relationship between the declarant and the patient usually determines admissibility—the closer the relationship, the stronger the motive to tell the truth, and, as such, the more presumably reliable the statement. The court must assess the probative value of the statement pursuant to Rule 403, weighing that value against the risk of prejudice, confusion, or waste of time. *See Weinstein's Evidence*, Vol. 4 (1993), p. 803-145.

5. Recorded Recollection

If a witness is unable to testify about a matter for which a record exists, that record is not excluded as hearsay if the following foundation is established:

i) The record is on a matter that the witness once knew about;

ii) The record was made or adopted by the witness when the matter was fresh in the witness's memory;

iii) The record accurately reflects the witness's knowledge; and

iv) The witness states that she cannot recall the event well enough to testify fully and accurately, even after consulting the record on the stand.

Under this exception, the record, if admitted, may be read into evidence, but it may be received as an exhibit only if offered by an adverse party. Fed. R. Evid. 803(5).

Present recollection refreshed distinguished: An item—which need not be a writing—used to refresh a witness's recollection is not admitted into evidence (*see* § III.C.1. Present Recollection Refreshed, *supra*), so there is no hearsay problem.

6. **Records of Regularly Conducted Activity (Business Records)**

A record (e.g., memorandum, report, data compilation) of an act, event, condition, opinion, or diagnosis is not excluded as hearsay if:

i) The record was kept in the course of a regularly conducted activity of a business, organization, occupation, or calling;

ii) The making of the record was a regular practice of that activity; and

iii) The record was made at or near the time by (or from information transmitted by) someone with knowledge.

Although this exception is commonly referred to as the "business records" exception, it extends to any regularly conducted activity of an organization, including a nonprofit organization. Fed. R. Evid. 101(b)(4); 803(6)(A)–(C).

Recorded recollection exception distinguished: Unlike the recorded recollection exception, the business records exception does not require the inability to remember, but it does require that the record be kept in the course of a regularly conducted activity.

a. **Authentication**

For the record to be admissible under the business records hearsay exception, the custodian of the record or other qualified witness may testify that the above requirements have been met. Alternatively, a record may be self-authenticated if properly certified (*see* § IV.A.2.e. Self-authenticating documents, *supra*). Fed. R. Evid. 803(6)(D).

b. **Lack of trustworthiness**

A business record that otherwise qualifies under this hearsay exception is nevertheless inadmissible if the opponent shows that the source of information for the record or the method or circumstances of its preparation indicate a lack of trustworthiness. Fed. R. Evid. 803(6)(E).

Anticipation of litigation: Records prepared in anticipation of litigation, such as an employee's accident report, may not qualify under this exception due to a lack of trustworthiness. *Palmer v. Hoffman*, 318 U.S. 109 (1943).

c. **Medical records**

Medical records are considered business records to the extent that the entries relate to diagnosis or treatment. Statements related to fault associated with the cause of injury generally do not qualify under the business records exception.

d. Police reports

A police report can qualify under the business records exception, but a statement made by a witness that is contained in the report does not generally qualify because the witness is not acting on behalf of the police in making the statement. The statement may, however, qualify under another hearsay exception, such as an opposing party's statement.

e. Absence of a record

Evidence that a **matter is not included in a record** of a regularly conducted activity may be admissible to prove that the matter did not occur or exist, provided that a record was regularly kept for a matter of that kind. The opponent may prevent admission by showing circumstances, including the possible source of the information, that indicate a lack of trustworthiness. Fed. R. Evid. 803(7).

7. Public Records

A hearsay exception applies to a record or statement of a public office or agency that sets out:

i) The **activities** of the office or agency;

ii) An **observation** of a person under a duty to report the observation (except for an observation of a law enforcement officer offered in a criminal case); or

iii) **Factual findings of a legal investigation,** when offered in a civil case or against the government in a criminal case.

Fed. R. Evid. 803(8).

> **Investigative reports:** In addition to factual findings, opinions, evaluations, and conclusions contained in an investigative report that are based on factual findings are included in the public records exception. *Beech Craft Corp. v. Rainey*, 488 U.S. 153 (1988).

a. Lack of trustworthiness

As with the business records exception, the court may exclude any evidence offered under this exception if the opponent shows that the source of the information or other circumstances indicate a lack of trustworthiness. Fed. R. Evid. 803(8)(B).

b. Absence of a record

Similarly, testimony or a certification by a public official that a diligent search failed to disclose a public record or statement may be admitted to prove that the record or statement does not exist, or that a matter did not occur or exist, if the public office regularly kept a record of statements for a matter of that kind. In a criminal case, a prosecutor must provide the defense with written notice of the intent to offer such evidence at least 14 days before trial, and the defendant has seven days from receipt of notice to object in writing. Fed. R. Evid. 803(10), *Melendez-Diaz v. Massachusetts*, 557 U.S. 305 (2009).

c. Public records of vital statistics

A record of a birth, death, or marriage is not excluded as hearsay if the event is reported to a public office in accordance with a legal duty. Fed. R. Evid. 803(9).

8. Learned Treatises

A statement contained in a treatise, periodical, or pamphlet is not excluded as hearsay if:

i) An expert witness **relied on the statement during direct examination** or it was **called to the expert's attention on cross-examination**; and

ii) The publication is established as a **reliable authority** by admission or testimony of the expert witness, by another expert's testimony, or by judicial notice.

If admitted, the statement is read into evidence, but the publication itself may not be received as an exhibit. Fed. R. Evid. 803(18).

9. Judgment of Previous Conviction

Evidence of a final judgment of conviction is not excluded as hearsay if:

i) The judgment was entered after a trial or guilty plea, but not a plea of no contest (i.e., *nolo contendere*);

ii) The conviction was for a crime punishable by death or imprisonment for more than one year; and

iii) The evidence is offered to prove any fact essential to sustain the judgment.

If the prosecutor in a criminal case offers evidence of a final judgment of conviction for a purpose other than impeachment, the judgment must have been against the defendant. The pendency of an appeal may be shown but does not affect admissibility. Fed. R. Evid. 803(22).

Traffic offense: A driver's guilty plea to a traffic offense that is punishable by a fine or imprisonment for one year or less cannot be used as evidence of the driver's negligence under this hearsay exception.

10. Other Exceptions

Other hearsay exceptions for which the declarant's availability is immaterial include:

i) A statement concerning personal or family history, such as a birth, death, marriage, or divorce contained in a regularly kept record of a religious organization (Fed. R. Evid. 803(11));

ii) A statement of fact in a marriage or baptismal certificate (Fed. R. Evid. 803(12));

iii) A statement of fact about personal or family history contained in a family record, such as a Bible or an engraving on a ring (Fed. R. Evid. 803(13));

iv) Records of, and statements in, documents affecting an interest in property (Fed. R. Evid. 803(14), (15));

v) Statements in ancient documents (i.e., authenticated documents prepared before January 1, 1998) (Fed. R. Evid. 803(16));

vi) Market reports and similar commercial publications generally relied upon by the public (Fed. R. Evid. 803(17));

vii) Reputation concerning personal or family history, boundaries or general history, or character (Fed. R. Evid. 803(19)–(21)); and

viii) A judgment admitted to prove a matter of personal, family, or general history or a boundary, if the matter was essential to the judgment and could be proved by evidence of reputation. Fed. R. Evid. 803(23).

C.   RESIDUAL EXCEPTION

There is a "catch-all" exception for a statement that is not otherwise covered by the Federal Rules. A hearsay statement may be admissible under this exception if:

i)   The statement has equivalent circumstantial guarantees of trustworthiness;

ii)   It is offered as evidence of a material fact;

iii)   It is more probative on the point for which it is offered than any other evidence that the proponent can reasonably obtain; and

iv)   Admission will best serve the purposes of the Federal Rules and the interests of justice.

The proponent must give an adverse party reasonable notice before the trial or hearing of the intent to offer the statement as well as its particulars, including the declarant's name and address. Fed. R. Evid. 807.

VIII.   CONSTITUTIONAL LIMITATIONS

A.   HEARSAY EVIDENCE RESTRICTIONS

Hearsay evidence has successfully been challenged on two constitutional grounds.

1.   Sixth Amendment—Confrontation Clause and Hearsay Evidence

In a criminal trial, the Confrontation Clause of the Sixth Amendment requires that, in order to admit an out-of-court testimonial statement of a declarant (i.e., hearsay) against a defendant:

i)   The declarant must be unavailable; and

ii)   The defendant must have had a prior opportunity to cross-examine the declarant.

Crawford v. Washington, 541 U.S. 36 (2004).

Note: The Supreme Court suggested in dicta in *Crawford* that the Confrontation Clause does not preclude the admission of a dying declaration as hearsay, even if the statement is testimonial, since this common-law exception predates the Confrontation Clause. *Crawford v. Washington*, 541 U.S. 36, 56, n.6 (2004).

a.   Testimonial statements

In determining whether a statement is testimonial, an objective analysis of the circumstances, rather than the subjective purpose of the participants, is key. A statement made during a police interrogation that had the primary purpose of ascertaining past criminal conduct is testimonial, as is a certificate of a governmental laboratory analyst that a substance was an illegal drug. *Melendez-Diaz v. Massachusetts*, 557 U.S. 305 (2009).

By contrast, a statement made to police during the course of questioning with the primary purpose of enabling police to provide assistance to meet an ongoing emergency (e.g., a 911 call) is not testimonial, *Davis v. Washington*, 547 U.S. 813 (2006), nor is a statement made by a fatally wounded victim as to the identity of his assailant in response to police questioning, because the statement was made to assist the police in addressing an on-going emergency, *Michigan v. Bryant*, 562 U.S. 344 (2011).

Generally, a statement made to an individual who is not a law enforcement officer, such as a teacher, is much less likely to be testimonial than a statement made to a law enforcement officer, even when the individual is under a duty to report such statements to police (e.g., school personnel's statutory obligation to report suspected child abuse to police). In addition, a statement made by a very young child (e.g., a three-year old) will seldom, if ever, be testimonial.

Example: Statements made by a young child to his teachers in response to questions about physical evidence of abuse that identified the defendant as the child's abuser were not testimonial. *Ohio v. Clark*, 576 U.S. ___, 135 S. Ct. 2173 (2015).

b. Unavailability of the declarant

The Confrontation Clause mandates that the use of hearsay evidence based on the forfeiture-by-wrongdoing exception requires the defendant to have acted with the particular purpose of making the witness unavailable. The mere fact that the declarant is unavailable due to the defendant's act (e.g., murder of the witness) is not sufficient to establish such a purpose when the defendant is on trial for the act that made the witness unavailable. *Giles v. California*, 554 U.S. 353 (2008).

2. Fourteenth Amendment—Due Process Clause

The Due Process Clause of the Fourteenth Amendment may prevent application of a hearsay rule when such rule unduly restricts a defendant's ability to mount a defense.

Example: Application of a state evidentiary rule that prevents a defendant from using a witness's hearsay statements to impeach the witness's in-court testimony operated to deny the defendant the ability to present witnesses in the defendant's own defense. *Chamber v. Mississippi*, 410 U.S. 284 (1973).

B. FACE-TO-FACE CONFRONTATION

The Confrontation Clause reflects a preference for face-to-face confrontation of a defendant and a witness in court.

Example: A defendant who is charged with committing a sex crime against a child can force the child victim to testify in open court rather than from behind a screen that blocks the witness's view of the defendant. *Coy v. Iowa*, 487 U.S. 1012 (1988).

This type of confrontation may be denied, however, if there is an important public interest at stake, such as protecting a child.

Example: A child victim of a sex crime could testify via a one-way closed circuit television when there was a specific finding that the child witness would suffer serious emotional distress if the witness was required to testify in open court. *Maryland v. Craig*, 497 U.S. 836 (1990). The Court in *Coy*, above, refused to recognize a *presumption* of trauma to witnesses who were victims of sexual abuse.

Real Property

REAL PROPERTY

Table of Contents

REAL PROPERTY

I. OWNERSHIP

Ownership of real property may be transferred by sale, by gift, or, upon death, by devise or intestate succession. The seller or donor is called the "grantor," and the buyer or recipient is called the "grantee." This section will discuss both present and future possessory interests in land (which are subject only to the rights of others), and other sections will discuss nonpossessory interests in land (which are subject to specific restrictions as to the use of the land).

A. PRESENT ESTATES

To be categorized as a freehold, an estate must be (i) immobile (either land or some interest derived from or affixed to land) and (ii) for an indeterminate duration (as opposed to a leasehold, which is for a limited duration). The owner of a present estate has the right to currently possess the property.

1. Fee Simple Absolute

Fee simple absolute (or "fee simple") is the most common form of property ownership and the broadest ownership interest recognized by law. It is absolute ownership of potentially infinite duration. It is "freely alienable" because it is able to be transferred inter vivos, by will, or intestacy without restriction. A fee simple absolute has no accompanying future interest. Although common law required words of limitation (e.g., "and heirs"), conveyances that are ambiguous are now considered fee simple by default (e.g., "to B").

Example: A conveys Blackacre "to B and his heirs." C conveys Whiteacre to "B." Both conveyances give B a fee simple absolute estate in the property.

Note that using the limitation "and heirs" does not restrict the ability of the transferee of a fee simple absolute interest or other real property interest to transfer that interest during the transferee's life or to devise that interest by will death, nor limit the people to whom the interest may be transferred to the transferee's heirs.

2. Defeasible Fees

As with a fee simple absolute estate, a defeasible fee is ownership of potentially infinite duration. But, unlike a fee simple absolute estate, a defeasible fee **may be terminated by the occurrence of an event**. Three defeasible fee simples are (i) fee simple determinable, (ii) fee simple subject to a condition subsequent, and (iii) fee simple subject to an executory interest. A defeasible fee is freely alienable by the owner during his life, and upon his death, it is devisable (i.e., transferable by will) and descendible (i.e., transferable by intestacy).

> **EXAM NOTE:** If a statement in a conveyance of real property merely indicates a grantor's desire, intent, or purpose for which the property is to be used rather than imposing a condition on the ownership of the property itself, the property interest is treated as a fee simple absolute, rather than a defeasible fee.

a. Fee simple determinable

A fee simple determinable is a present fee simple estate that is **limited by specific durational language** (e.g., "so long as," "while," "during," "until"), such that **it terminates automatically** upon the happening of a stated event, and full ownership of the property is returned to the grantor (or his successor in interest).

1) Future interest in grantor—possibility of reverter

Upon the occurrence of the stated condition, the estate automatically reverts back to the grantor. This future interest is known as a **"possibility of reverter."** The estate reverts back to the grantor whether or not the language of the grant specifically mentions the grantor as owner of this future interest. A possibility of reverter is freely alienable, devisable, and descendible.

Example: A conveys Blackacre "to B and his heirs, until B gets married." The estate reverts back to A if B gets married. B has a fee simple determinable in Blackacre, and A has a possibility of reverter.

b. Fee simple subject to a condition subsequent

A fee simple subject to a condition subsequent is a present fee simple that is **limited in duration by specific conditional language** (e.g., "provided that," "on condition that," "but if"). Upon the occurrence of the condition, the **grantor** (or his successor interest) **has the right to terminate this estate**.

> **EXAM NOTE:** Unlike a fee simple determinable, termination of a fee simple subject to a condition subsequent is not automatic. Upon occurrence of the stated condition, the present fee simple **will terminate only if the grantor affirmatively demonstrates intent to terminate** (e.g., by bringing an eviction action).

If the language in the conveyance is ambiguous, courts typically adopt a preference for the fee simple subject to a condition subsequent over a fee simple determinable.

1) Future interest in grantor—Right to terminate

In the conveyance, the grantor must explicitly retain the right to terminate the fee simple subject to a condition subsequent (known as the **"right of entry," "right of reentry,"** or **"power of termination"**). In most states, this right is devisable and descendible upon the owner's death. However, under the common law, it cannot be transferred during the owner's lifetime. Modern statutes in some states do allow an inter vivos transfer of a right of entry. The owner may waive this right, but the mere failure to assert it does not constitute a waiver.

Example: A conveys Blackacre "to B and his heirs, but if B gets married, then A can reenter Blackacre." B has a fee simple subject to a condition subsequent in Blackacre, and A has a right of reentry. If B gets married, B will retain his current possessory estate in Blackacre until A exercises his right to terminate B's estate.

> **EXAM NOTE:** In the above example, remember that until A retakes Blackacre, B continues to own the land.

c. Fee simple subject to an executory interest

A fee simple subject to an executory interest is a present fee simple estate that is limited by specific language, whether that language is durational (e.g., "so long as," "while," "during," "until") or conditional (e.g., "provided that," "on condition that," "but if"), such that, upon the occurrence of the specified event or condition, title will automatically pass to a **third party** (i.e., someone other than the grantor or the holder of the present fee). (Note: When the specific language is durational (e.g., "so long as," "while," "during," "until"), the present fee simple interest is sometimes referred to as a "fee simple determinable subject to an executory limitation" to distinguish it from a present fee simple interest limited by conditional language.)

> **EXAM NOTE:** Unlike a present fee simple estate that is associated with a future interest in the grantor, even if the specific language is conditional, the occurrence of the condition stated in an executory interest automatically triggers the passage of title to the third party.

1) Future interest in third party—executory interest

The future interest held by the third party is an executory interest. An executory interest is freely alienable by the owner during his life, and upon his death, it is devisable and descendible

For a more detailed discussion, see § I.B.5. Executory Interests, *infra*.

> **Example (1):** A conveys Blackacre "to B and his heirs, until B gets married, then to C." In Blackacre, B has a fee simple subject to an executory interest (also referred to as a "fee simple determinable subject to an executory interest"), and C has an executory interest. A does not have an interest in Blackacre.
>
> **Example (2):** A conveys Blackacre "to B and his heirs; but if B gets married, then to C." In Blackacre, B has a fee simple subject to an executory interest, and C has an executory interest. A does not have an interest in Blackacre.
>
> (Note: In each example, C's interest is a shifting executory interest (*see* I.B.5.a., Shifting Executory Interest, *infra*). Also, C's interest may be subject to the Rule Against Perpetuities (*see* I.B.8. Rule Against Perpetuities, *infra*).

3. Fee Tail

A fee tail is a freehold estate that limits the estate to the grantee's lineal blood descendants by specific words of limitation (e.g., "heirs of the body"). The fee tail estate has been eliminated in most states; it is treated as a fee simple absolute estate.

4. Life Estate

A life estate is a present possessory estate that is limited in duration by a life. The language must be clear, and must be measured in terms of a life, not a number of years (e.g., "to A for life"). Upon the end of the measuring life, title reverts to the grantor or specified remainderman. This future interest is known as a "reversion."

> **Example 1:** A conveys Blackacre "to B for the life of B." B has a life estate in Blackacre, which terminates upon B's death. A has a reversion; upon B's death, ownership of Blackacre reverts to A.
>
> **Example 2:** A conveys Blackacre "to B for B's life, and then to C." B has a life estate in Blackacre, which terminates upon B's death. C has a remainder; upon B's death, ownership of Blackacre vests in C.

The life estate is not subject to the Rule Against Perpetuities.

a. Measuring life is the grantee

To be a life estate, the interest granted must be measured by the life of a human being and be qualified only by non-time limitations. Unless otherwise specified, the measuring life is the grantee.

> **Example:** A conveys Blackacre to "B for life." B has a life estate that is measured by his own life.

A life estate is fully transferable during the life of the person by whom the life estate is measured. Because the interest terminates at the death of the person by whom the life estate is measured, a life estate measured by the grantee's life is generally neither devisable nor descendible.

In states that continue dower and curtesy, a conveyance from the husband to a bona fide purchaser without the wife's joining in the conveyance does not defeat dower. Similarly, a wife's dower rights are not defeated by the husband's creditors. In the states that have done away with the common-law curtesy and dower custom, a surviving spouse has a statutory right to take a portion of the decedent's estate.

b. Measuring life is a third party

A life estate measured by the life of a third party is called a "life estate *pur autre vie*."

> **Example:** O conveys Blackacre to "A for the life of B, with a remainder to C." O granted a life estate to A for the life of B.

When the measuring life survives the owner of the life estate, the life estate may be devised by the owner or inherited by the owner's heirs.

> **Example:** O conveys Blackacre to "A for the life of B, with a remainder to C." O granted a life estate to A for the life of B. A dies before B and devises the life estate to D. When B dies, D's inherited life estate terminates, and C's remainder becomes possessory.

c. Rights and obligations

A life tenant has the right of possession, the right to all rents from use of the property by another person, and the right to lease, sell, or mortgage his interest in the property (i.e., right of alienation).

Since property taxes are imposed on an annual basis, they are an assessment only against the life estate, not against future interests in the property. Generally, these taxes are a personal obligation of the life tenant only to the extent that she receives a financial benefit from the property. When the life tenant does not occupy the property and instead rents it out to a third party, the amount of the rents collected constitute her financial benefit from the property. When the life tenant occupies the property, her financial benefit is measured by the fair market rental value of the property. Consequently, when the holder of a future interest pays the taxes because the life tenant fails to do so, the holder can bring an action against the life tenant personally to recoup his payment of those taxes only to the extent of the life tenant's personal benefit from the property. Any excess can only be recovered through a foreclosure action against the life tenant's property interest.

As a current obligation, interest payments due on a mortgage of the property granted prior to the creation of a life estate and future interest are subject to a similar treatment. Principal payments due on such a mortgage are allocated to the future interests.

The life tenant is generally under no obligation to insure the land for the benefit of the remainderman and is not responsible for damage caused by third-party tortfeasors.

d. **Waste**

The rights of a holder of a life estate are limited by the doctrine of waste. Under this doctrine, a life tenant must deliver the property in essentially the same condition that it was in when she took possession. The holder of a future interest in the property (e.g., remainder, executory interest, reversion) may enter the land to inspect for waste, and she may seek damages and an injunction to prevent waste.

Other estates: Although the doctrine of waste typically arises in the context of a life estate, it comes into play with abuse, neglect, or improvement of real property by any person who holds a present property interest that is not a fee simple interest (e.g., a defeasible fee).

1) **Affirmative waste**

Affirmative (or voluntary) waste is the result of overt conduct that causes a decrease in the value of the property. The holder of a vested future interest may bring suit for damages, and the holder of any future interest may bring suit for an injunction. Limited exceptions exist for the exploitation of natural resources (e.g., minerals, timber) if such use was authorized by the grantor, was in effect at the time the tenancy began, or is necessary to maintain the property.

2) **Permissive waste**

Permissive waste occurs when the life tenant "permits" the premises to deteriorate through neglect, a failure to preserve the property, or a failure to reasonably protect the property. To maintain the property and avoid permissive waste, the life tenant is required to make reasonable repairs but need not spend more than the amount of income generated by the property, or, if the life tenant is in actual possession of the property, its fair rental value.

3) **Ameliorative waste**

Ameliorative waste occurs when a change in use of the property **increases** the value of the property. At common law, a life tenant was prohibited from engaging in acts that changed the property's value (even those that enhanced the value), unless all future interest holders were known and consented. The current majority rule allows life tenants to physically alter structures on the property when a substantial and permanent change in neighborhood surroundings makes it necessary to continue reasonable use of the property, so long as the property value is not diminished. When determining whether ameliorative waste is non-compensable, courts consider the tenant's expected remaining life, the need for the change, and the good faith of the parties.

e. **Life estate subject to an executory interest—cutting short a life estate**

A life estate can be subject to a condition that cuts it short.

Example: A conveys Blackacre "to B for life, but if B remarries, then to C." B has a life estate subject to an executory interest. C has an executory interest.

B. FUTURE INTERESTS

A future interest is an interest in presently existing property or in a gift or trust, which may commence in use, possession, or enjoyment sometime in the future.

1. Reversion

A reversion (or "reverter") is the future interest held by the grantor who grants a life estate or estate for years but does not convey the remaining future interest to a third party. Reversions are not subject to the Rule Against Perpetuities. A reversion is fully transferable *inter vivos*, devisable by will, and descendible by inheritance

2. Possibility of Reverter

A possibility of reverter is a future interest retained by a grantor when a fee simple determinable is conveyed.

3. Right of Reentry

A right of reentry (also called "right of entry" or "power of termination") is a future interest retained by the grantor after a fee simple subject to a condition subsequent is granted.

4. Remainder

Generally, a remainder is a future interest created in a grantee that is capable of becoming an estate that is presently possessory upon the natural expiration of a prior possessory estate (e.g., a life estate, estate for years) that is created in the same conveyance in which the remainder is created. However, by definition, a remainder interest cannot follow a defeasible fee interest. A remainder can be either vested or contingent.

a. Vested remainder

A vested remainder is an interest that is not subject to any conditions precedent and is created in an ascertainable grantee.

> **Example:** A conveys Blackacre "to B for life, and then to C and his heirs." Here, the grantee, C, is ascertainable.

1) Vested subject to open (class gifts)

A class gift consists of a group of unspecified persons whose number and identity and share of the interest is determined in the future (e.g., at the death of the donor). Usually, the members of a group are children of a specified person.

> **Example 1:** A conveys a present gift of a remainder interest "to my children." Here, A conveys a class gift to an unspecified group because the recipients (i.e., those who will qualify as A's children upon A's death) are not known until A dies.

If a conveyance grants a remainder to a class of grantees and at least one but less than all of the grantees receives a vested remainder at the time of the conveyance, then that vested remainder is subject to open (i.e., the property interest is uncertain because other grantees may become vested and able to share in the grant).

> **Example 2:** A conveys "to B for life, and then to B's children as they turn 18." B has three children upon death, X (10 years old), Y (15 years old), and Z (20

years old). Z has a vested remainder subject to open because the property interest may be shared if Y and/or X become vested (i.e., reach age 18).

Once a class closes, any person who might otherwise have become a class member (e.g., later-born siblings) cannot claim an interest in the property as a class member.

Although those born after the class closes are generally not part of the class, **those already in gestation upon closing are included** in the class.

Absent a closing date, the **rule of convenience** closes the class when any member of the class becomes entitled to immediate possession of the property.

Example: A conveys "to B for life, and then to C's children." If the conveyance does not specify when the class closes, then the class closes when B dies, regardless of any of C's children born after B's death.

2) Vested subject to complete divestment

A vested remainder subject to divestment indicates that the occurrence of a condition subsequent will completely divest the remainder interest.

Example: A conveys "to B for life, and then to C; but if C has no children, then to D's children." C has a vested remainder interest, but if he is not survived by his children at the time of B's death, then C's interest will be divested.

b. Contingent remainder

A remainder is contingent if it is created in a grantee that is unascertainable, or if it is subject to an express condition precedent to a grantee's taking. This situation normally occurs in one of two circumstances: (i) when the property cannot vest because the beneficiary is unknown or (ii) when the property cannot vest because the known beneficiary is subject to a condition precedent that has not yet occurred.

Example: A conveys "to B for life, remainder to C's heirs." If C is alive at the conveyance, then C's heirs are not yet ascertainable, and the remainder is contingent.

Contingent remainders were destroyed at common law if they had not vested by the time the preceding estate terminated. In such a situation in most states today, the grantor's reversion becomes possessory, and the person holding the contingent remainder takes a springing executory interest (see *below*), which becomes possessory if the condition precedent is met.

c. Rule in *Shelley's Case*

At common law, the Rule in *Shelley's Case* prevented contingent remainders in the grantee's heirs by defeating the grantor's intent and changing the interest that the grantor purported to give to the grantee and his heirs to a vested remainder in the grantee. The Rule in *Shelley's Case* changes the state of the title to two successive freehold estates in the grantee only. Under the doctrine of merger, both the present and future interests are merged so that the grantee takes in fee simple absolute. Most jurisdictions have abolished the Rule in *Shelley's Case*, and the parties now take the present and future interests according to the language in the deed.

> **Example:** A conveys "to B for life, remainder to B's heirs." If the Rule in *Shelley's Case* applies, then after the merger, B will receive the property in fee simple absolute. If the Rule in *Shelley's Case* has been abolished, then B has a life estate, and B's heirs have a contingent remainder in the subject property.

d. Doctrine of Worthier Title

The Doctrine of Worthier Title is a rule of construction similar to the Rule in *Shelley's Case*, except that it prevents remainders in the grantor's heirs, and it still applies in only a few states. The presumption is in a reversion to the grantor, rebuttable by a showing of contrary intent.

e. Survivorship contingency

If a survivorship contingency is stated in a conveyance, then the majority view is that the contingency applies at the termination of the interest that precedes distribution of the remainder. A minority approach interprets a survivorship contingency to require surviving only the testator and not the life tenant.

5. Executory Interests

An executory interest is a future interest in a third party that is not a remainder and that generally cuts the prior estate short upon the occurrence of a specified condition. In addition, a future interest that follows a fee simple determinable and is held by a third party (rather than the grantor) is an executory interest, even though it arises naturally out of the termination of the fee simple determinable, because a remainder never follows a defeasible fee and an executory interest is the only other future interest held by a third party.

There are two types of executory interests: shifting executory interests and springing executory interests.

a. Shifting executory interest

A shifting executory interest divests the interest of the grantee by cutting short a prior estate created in the same conveyance. The estate "shifts" from one grantee to another on the happening of the condition.

> **Example:** A conveys "to B and his heirs, but if C returns from Paris, then to C." This conveyance creates a fee simple subject to an executory limitation in B and a shifting executory interest in C.

b. Springing executory interest

A springing executory interest divests the interest of the grantor or fills a gap in possession in which the estate reverts to the grantor.

> **Example:** A conveys "to B for life, and one year after B's death to C and his heirs." This conveyance creates a life estate in B, a one-year reversion in A (in fee simple subject to an executory limitation), and a springing executory interest in C.

6. Transferability of Remainders and Executory Interests

Vested remainders are fully transferable *inter vivos*, devisable by will, and descendible by inheritance. Today, executory interests and contingent remainders are transferable *inter vivos* in most jurisdictions, although under common law they were not transferable; both are devisable and descendible.

It is important to note that most states permit any transferable future interest to be reached by creditors, except for those interests held by unascertainable or unborn persons.

7. Classification of Interests

It is important to classify the various interests in a disposition clause in order (i.e., from left to right) because the characterization of the first interest usually determines the characterizations of the following interests. For example, a contingent remainder can follow a contingent remainder, but it cannot follow a fee simple.

Example 1: A conveys Blackacre "to B for life, then to C if C survives B; but if C does not survive B, on B's death to D."

B has a present life estate. C has a future interest, which is a remainder because it can become possessory upon the termination of the preceding possessory interest (i.e., B's life estate), and it is a contingent remainder because C's taking is conditioned on C surviving B. D also has a future interest, which is a remainder because it can become possessory upon the termination of B's life estate; it is a contingent remainder because D's taking is contingent on C not surviving B.

Now consider the following language that results in the same outcome (i.e., C owns Blackacre if C survives B, and D owns Blackacre if C does not) but different property interests for C and D immediately after the conveyance.

Example 2: A conveys Blackacre "to B for life, and on B's death to C. But if C predeceases B, on B's death to D." B has a present life estate. C has a future interest, which is a remainder because it can become possessory upon the termination of B's life estate. C's remainder is vested because C is ascertainable **and** there is no condition precedent that C must satisfy to take Blackacre. However, C's vested remainder is subject to complete if a condition subsequent (C predeceasing B) occurs. D has a future interest, but it is not a remainder because C's interest is not an estate of a fixed duration but is instead a fee simple estate, which has an unlimited duration. However, if the condition subsequent occurs, then D would be entitled to take possession of Blackacre, thereby cutting short C's interest. Consequently, D has a shifting executory interest.

The above two examples demonstrate the importance of examining each clause independently and classifying each interest in the proper order.

8. Rule Against Perpetuities

Under the Rule Against Perpetuities ("Rule"), specific future interests are valid only if they must vest or fail by the end of a life in being plus 21 years.

Example 1: A conveys Blackacre "to B for life, and then to the first male descendant of B, then to C." This provision violates the Rule because it may be many generations before there is a male descendant of B, if at all.

Example 2: A conveys Blackacre "to B for life, and then to B's first son who reaches the age of 18, then to C." This provision is valid because any son of B will attain age 18 within 21 years after B's death.

Note the difference in the examples above. In Example 1, the opportunity for B to have a male descendant does not end after he dies. Because there is a possibility that the devise will neither vest nor fail within a life in being plus 21 years, the Rule is violated.

On the other hand, in Example 2, once B dies, his opportunity to have children ends, and so the clock starts. If, when he dies, B has at least one son under the age of 18, then it is certain to be less than a life in being plus 21 years before the condition either vests (son reaches 18) or fails (son dies).

a. Affected future interests

The Rule applies only to the following interests: contingent remainders, vested remainders subject to open, executory interests, powers of appointment, rights of first refusal, and options. It does **not** apply to future interests that are held by the grantor (i.e., reversion, possibility of reverter, right of reentry).

1) Trust interests

Even though a beneficiary of a trust holds only an equitable interest in the trust property, such an interest may be subject to the Rule.

b. Measuring lives

The application of the Rule is determined by one or more measuring lives. A measuring life must be human, but there can be more than one measuring life, provided the number of such lives is reasonable. If a measuring life is not specified, then the measuring life is the life directly related to the future interest that is subject to the Rule.

Example 1: A devises Blackacre "to B for life, and then to B's children who reach the age of 25." B's life is the measuring life.

If there is no measuring life, then the applicable vesting period is 21 years from the time that the future interest is created.

Example 2: A devises Blackacre "to a charity for so long as the property is used as an animal shelter, and then to C." Because there is no measuring life, C's interest must vest or fail within 21 years of the creation of C's interest in order to satisfy the Rule. Since there is no guarantee regarding the future use to which Blackacre is put, C's interest violates the Rule.

c. Creation events

The Rule tests the future interest as of the time that it is created. For example, a future interest created by a will is tested as of the testator's death.

d. "Vest or fail" requirement

The Rule requires that the future interest either vest or fail to vest within the applicable time period. If there is **any possibility** that it will not be known whether the interest will vest or fail within that period, then the Rule has not been satisfied.

e. Effect of violation

If a future interest fails to satisfy the Rule, then **only the offending interest fails**. In the rare case when the voiding of the future interest undermines the grantor's intent, the entire transfer is voided.

f. Special rule for transfer to a class (class gifts)

If the transfer of a future interest is made to a class, and the Rule voids a transfer to any member of a class, then the transfer is void as to all class members, even those whose interests are already vested (i.e., "bad as to one, bad as to all").

Example: A devises Blackacre "to B for life, and then to B's children who graduate from college." At the time of A's death, B had two children: X, who had graduated from college, and Y, who had not. X has a vested remainder subject to open; Y, as well as any afterborn children of B, has a contingent remainder. At the time of B's death, Y has also graduated from college, and B has had a third child, Z, who is in elementary school. Because it may take Z more than 21 years to graduate college and thereby vest his interest, not only is Z's interest void under the Rule, but X and Y's interests are also void.

1) Rule of convenience as a savior

The rule of convenience, which is a rule of interpretation, can operate to prevent the application of the Rule to a class transfer. Under this rule, membership in a class closes whenever any member of the class is entitled to immediate possession of a share of the class gift.

Example 1: A conveys Blackacre "to B for life, and then to B's grandchildren." At the time of the conveyance, B has one grandchild, X. X has a vested remainder subject to open. Although B may have grandchildren born more than 21 years after B's or X's death, the class will close upon B's death because B has a grandchild, X. Consequently, X and any other grandchildren born prior to B's death will take Blackacre. The Rule will not apply to void their interests in Blackacre.

Since the rule of convenience is a rule of interpretation, it does not apply when the grantor specifies that the class should remain open even though a member of the class is entitled to immediate possession of a share of the class gift. In addition, the application of the rule of convenience to a class transfer does not automatically forestall the application of the Rule.

Example 2: Assume the same facts as those in Example (1), except that B has no grandchildren at the time of the conveyance. After the conveyance, B has a child, C. Then, A, B, and all of B's children die themselves childless, except C. Twenty-two years later C has a child, G. Since G's interest will not vest within a life in being plus 21 years, and there is no member of the class who was entitled to immediate possession of a share of the class gift on B's death, the contingent remainder in B's grandchildren is void under the Rule and is not saved by the rule of convenience.

EXAM NOTE: Beware of fact patterns with class gifts to grandchildren of an *inter vivos* grantor instead of a testator. An *inter vivos* transfer is more likely to violate the Rule because the donor may have more children, while a deceased testator most likely will not.

2) Exceptions

There are two main exceptions to the "bad as to one, bad as to all" rule for class transfers. Both transfers of a specific dollar amount to each class member (e.g., "$50,000 to each grandchild who survives his parent") and transfers to a subclass that vests at a specific time (e.g., "to the children of B, and upon the death of each, to that child's issue") are tested separately. Any person who is entitled to the transferred interest is not prohibited from taking that interest simply because there are other members of the class who are prohibited from taking the interest.

g. Exceptions to the Rule Against Perpetuities

1) Charity-to-charity exception

If property passes from one charity to another charity, then the interest of the receiving charity is not subject to the Rule.

Example: Blackacre is conveyed "to charity B, as long as the premises are used for a school, and then to charity C." The executory interest of charity C may not vest within the time allotted by the Rule, but, because the Rule does not apply to charity-to-charity transfers, C's executory interest is valid.

EXAM NOTE: The Rule applies to property that passes between a charity and a non-charity.

2) Option and right of first refusal exception

The Rule does not apply to an option to purchase the property or a right of first refusal that is held by a current leasehold tenant. If the current tenant can transfer such an option, then this exception does not apply to a subsequent holder of the purchase option. In addition, the Rule does not apply to an option contract or a right of first refusal when the property right is created in a commercial transaction. (See III.E.3., *infra*).

h. Common violations

1) Class transfers—"survival beyond age 21" condition

If a transfer to a class is conditioned on the class members surviving to an age beyond 21 and the class is open, then the transfer to the class violates the Rule.

Example: A conveys Blackacre "to B for life, and then to B's children who reach the age of 30." At the time of the conveyance, B has one child, X, who is 35 years old. X has a vested remainder subject to open; B's potential children have a contingent remainder. The contingent remainder violates the Rule because it is possible that B could have another child who would not attain the age of 30 until more than 21 years after B's death. Because the contingent remainder is invalid, X's vested remainder subject to open is also invalid as a consequence of the "bad as to one, bad as to all" rule for class transfers.

2) Fertile octogenarian

Anyone, regardless of age or physical condition, including an 80-year-old woman (i.e., the fertile octogenarian) is deemed capable of having children for the purposes of the Rule. Some states have set an age limit (e.g., 55 years old) beyond which it is rebuttably presumed that a woman cannot have a child.

Example: A conveys Blackacre "to B for life, then to B's children who reach the age of 30 years old." At the time of the conveyance, B is 90 years old, with one child, X, who is 35 years old. X has a vested remainder subject to open, since B, despite her age, is assumed to be capable of having another child. Because the contingent remainder in that child would violate the Rule, X's interest is also void under the "bad as to one, bad as to all" rule.

3) Unborn spouse

If an interest following a widow's life estate cannot vest until the widow dies, then it violates the Rule.

> **Example:** A conveys Blackacre "to B for life, then to B's widow for life, then to B's children who are then living." The contingent remainder in B's children violates the Rule because B's widow may be someone who is not yet alive at the time of the conveyance. The contingent remainder would not violate the Rule if the life estate was conveyed to a particular person (e.g., B's current spouse) instead of "B's widow."

4) Defeasible fee followed by an executory interest

An executory interest that follows a defeasible fee violates the Rule, unless there is a time limit on the vesting of the executory interest that satisfies the Rule.

If the limit on the defeasible fee is durational (e.g., "so long as," "while"), then the striking of the executory interest leaves the grantor with the possibility of reverter. If the limit on the defeasible fee is a condition subsequent (e.g., "but if," "upon the condition that"), then the striking of the executory interest leaves the holder of the defeasible fee with a fee simple absolute interest in the property.

> **Example 1:** A conveys Blackacre "to B so long as the property is used for residential purposes; if it is not, then to C." B has a fee simple subject to an executory interest; C has an executory interest. Because C's executory interest could become possessory after the expiration of the testing period for the Rule, C's interest is stricken, and A has a possibility of reverter in Blackacre.
>
> **Example 2:** A conveys Blackacre "to B; but if the property is used for residential purposes, then to C." B has a fee simple subject to an executory interest; C has an executory interest. Because C's executory interest could become possessory after the expiration of the testing period for the Rule, C's interest is stricken, and B owns Blackacre in fee simple absolute.

5) Conditional passage of interest

If there is a condition imposed on the passing of a future interest subject to the Rule that is not confined to a specified time limit that meets the Rule's testing period, such as probating the will or termination of a current military conflict, then the future interest runs afoul of the Rule.

i. Statutory changes

1) "Wait and see" stance

A majority of the states have adopted the Uniform Statutory Rule Against Perpetuities, which adopts a "wait and see" stance with respect to the applicability of the Rule. Under this stance, an otherwise invalid interest is valid if it does in fact vest within 90 years of its creation. A few states have simply repealed the Rule altogether.

2) *Cy pres* doctrine

Some states permit a court to reform a conveyance to prevent it from violating the Rule by applying the *cy pres* doctrine. Under this doctrine, the court makes changes to the conveyance, such as reducing a time limit for a future interest to take effect to 21 years after the expiration of the last measuring life, in order to come "as near as possible" to the intent of the transferor while staying within the bounds of the Rule. Restatement (Second) of Property: Donative Transfers § 1.5.

C. CONCURRENT ESTATES

A concurrent estate (i.e., co-tenancy) arises when two or more persons own real property simultaneously. The most common concurrent estates are tenancy in common, joint tenancy, and tenancy by the entirety.

1. Tenancy in Common

A tenancy in common exists when two or more co-owners have an **equal right to possess** property (unity of possession) but **do not have a right of survivorship** with respect to the property interest held by another co-owner. In most states, there is a rebuttable presumption that a conveyance of property to two or more persons as joint owners creates a tenancy in common rather than a joint tenancy. Each co-tenant holds an undivided interest with unrestricted rights to possess the whole property, regardless of the size of the co-tenant's interest. Each tenant can unilaterally transfer, devise, mortgage, or lease his interest to a third party, without affecting the interest of the other tenants in common. .

2. Joint Tenancy

A joint tenancy exists when two or more persons own property **with the right of survivorship** (i.e., upon the death of a joint tenant, the interest terminates and automatically goes to the surviving joint tenants). Modern law calls for a clear expression of intent along with survivorship language.

> **EXAM NOTE:** To determine if a joint tenancy was created, look for survivorship language.

a. Four unities

In addition to the right of survivorship, each joint tenant must not only have an equal right to possess or use the property (unity of **p**ossession), but each interest must be equal to the other interests (unity of **i**nterest) and have been created at the same time (unity of **t**ime) and in the same instrument (unity of **t**itle). [*Mnemonic–"**PITT**"*].

Unlike a joint tenancy, a tenancy in common requires only the unity of possession.

b. Severance

The severance of joint tenancy may occur in several ways. The severance of a joint tenancy converts it into a tenancy in common. However, if there are more than two joint tenants, a severance does not automatically affect the joint tenancy of all joint tenants.

Example 1: X and Y hold Greenacre as joint tenants. X gives his interest in Greenacre to Z. X's action results in a severance of the joint tenancy. After the severance, X and Z hold Greenacre as tenants in common.

Example 2: X, Y, and Z hold Greenacre as joint tenants. X gives his interest in Greenacre to A. X's action results in a severance of the joint tenancy with respect to X's interest. After the severance, A holds a one-third interest in Greenacre as a tenant in common with Y and Z, who each still hold a one-third interest in Greenacre as joint tenants between themselves.

1) **Conveyance**

a) **At death**

A devise (i.e., a conveyance by will) by a joint tenant of his property interest is not given effect. Instead, the property passes automatically to the remaining joint tenants due to the right of survivorship.

> **Example 3:** Assume the same facts as those in Example 2. Y dies and leaves all of his property to B. B is not entitled to Y's one-third interest in Greenacre. Instead, Z, by virtue of his right of survivorship, owns a two-thirds interest in Greenacre as a tenant in common with A, who continues to hold her one-third interest in Greenacre.

b) **Lifetime transfer**

A lifetime (*inter vivos*) transfer by a joint tenant of his property interest effects a severance of the joint tenancy.

> **Example 4:** Assume the same facts as those in Example 2. Y, while alive, sells his interest in Greenacre to C. This effects a severance of the remaining joint tenancy that existed between Y and Z. A, C, and Z each hold a one-third interest in Greenacre as tenants in common.

i) **Contract to transfer: one joint tenant**

In most states, a joint tenant may effect a severance by executing a contract to convey his property interest.

ii) **Contract to transfer: all joint tenants**

In some states, a contract to convey property held in a joint tenancy that is executed by all of the joint tenants does not effect a severance. Severance occurs only upon the transfer of the property. In other states, severance occurs upon the execution of a contract to convey by all of the joint tenants.

2) **Mortgages**

A joint tenant may grant a mortgage in her joint tenancy interest. In **lien theory** states (the majority), the mortgage is only a lien on the property; the granting of a mortgage does not sever the joint tenancy, and severance occurs only upon a foreclosure sale following a default. In **title theory** states (the minority), the granting of a mortgage by a joint tenant constitutes a transfer of title; the joint tenancy is between the mortgagee and the other joint tenants, and it is severed and converted into a tenancy in common; if there is more than one remaining joint tenant, however, they continue to hold their property interests with each other as joint tenants.

3) **Judicial lien**

A judicial lien is typically imposed as a consequence of an adverse judgment against a joint tenant stemming from a contractual or tort liability. In most states, a judicial lien imposed on the property interest of a joint tenant does not sever the joint tenancy. There must be a levy and sale of the property interest to effect a severance. If the joint tenant against whose property interest the lien is imposed dies prior to the sale, the remaining joint tenants are entitled to that property interest by right of survivorship.

4) Leases

There is a split among jurisdictions with respect to how to handle joint tenancies when one joint tenant leases his interest. Some jurisdictions hold that the lease destroys the unity of interest and thus severs the joint tenancy, while other jurisdictions believe that the lease merely temporarily suspends the joint tenancy, which resumes upon expiration of the lease.

5) Intentional killings

When one co-tenant intentionally kills the other co-tenant, some states allow the felonious joint tenant to hold the property in constructive trust for the deceased joint tenant's estate. This means that the surviving joint tenant does not profit from the felony but can keep his interest in the property. Other jurisdictions have statutes that sever the joint tenancy upon a felonious killing of one joint tenant by another joint tenant.

3. Tenancy by the Entirety

Tenancy by the entirety is a joint tenancy between married persons with a right of survivorship. The same rules for joint tenancy apply to tenancy by the entirety, plus the joint tenants must be married when a deed is executed or the conveyance occurs (the fifth unity—**unity of person**). Neither spouse can alienate or encumber the property without the consent of the other. Tenancy by the entirety is recognized in about half of the states. In states in which it is recognized, a majority rebuttably presume that a conveyance to a married couple creates a tenancy by the entirety, and, upon divorce, that the property is held in a tenancy in common.

4. Rights and Obligations

a. Possession

Unless there is an agreement to the contrary, each co-tenant has the right to possess all of the property; one co-tenant may not bind another co-tenant to a boundary line agreement with a neighbor. A co-tenant is generally not required to pay rent to the other co-tenants for the value of her own use of the property, even when the other co-tenants do not make use of the property. Similarly, a co-tenant is generally not required to share profits earned from the use of the property, such as from a business conducted on the property.

Because of each tenant's right to possess the entire property, a co-tenant's exclusive use of the property does not, by itself, give rise to adverse possession of the interest of another co-tenant.

1) Ouster

When a co-tenant refuses to allow another co-tenant access to the property, the ousted co-tenant may bring a court action for ouster (e.g., seek an injunction) to gain access to the property and to recover the value of the use of the property for the time during which the co-tenant was denied access to the property.

2) Natural resources

A co-tenant is entitled to the land's natural resources (e.g., timber, minerals, oil, gas) in proportion to her share.

b. Third-party rents

A co-tenant must account to other co-tenants for rent received from third parties, but she can deduct operating expenses, including necessary repairs, when calculating net proceeds. Third-party rents are divided based on the ownership interest of each tenant.

c. Operating expenses

A co-tenant can collect contribution from the other co-tenants for paying more than his portion of necessary or beneficially spent operating expenses (e.g., taxes, mortgage interest payments). A co-tenant in sole possession of the property can collect only to the extent that those expenses exceed the rental value of the property.

d. Repairs and improvements

A co-tenant cannot compel other co-tenants to share in the expenses for repairs made to the property, unless (i) those repairs are necessary and (ii) the co-tenant brings an action for accounting or partition. A co-tenant may, in some jurisdictions, maintain a separate action for contribution, only if the other co-tenants were notified of the need for the repair.

Similarly, except in an action for accounting or partition, a co-tenant does not have a right to reimbursement from other co-tenants for improvements made to the property.

e. Fiduciary obligation

Although co-tenants owe a duty of fair dealing to each other, co-tenants generally do not owe fiduciary duties to each other. However, a fiduciary obligation can be imposed on co-tenants who jointly purchase the property in reliance on each other or acquire their interests at the same time from a common source, such as by gift, will, or inheritance. Typically, these co-tenants will be related or in a confidential relationship. The primary situation in which such a co-tenant is found to have a fiduciary obligation arises when the property is sold at a tax or mortgage foreclosure sale and a co-tenant acquires the property. In such a situation, the other co-tenants have the right to reacquire their original interests by paying their due contributions within a reasonable time.

Example: A brother and sister inherit land from their mother as tenants-in-common, each holding a one-half interest in the land. Neither pays the taxes on the property. The local government secures a lien on the property for the unpaid taxes and the property is sold at a tax sale. The brother purchases the property at the sale for $100,000. The brother has a fiduciary obligation to his sister to permit her to reacquire her one-half interest in the property by paying him $50,000, her share of the purchase price, within a reasonable time.

A fiduciary obligation is not imposed with respect to a property right acquired by a co-tenant prior to the creation of the co-tenancy (e.g., a mortgage).

f. Partition

1) Who may partition

A tenant in common or a joint tenant generally has the right to unilaterally partition the property, but a tenant by the entirety **does not** have this right. Property can be partitioned either voluntarily (if the co-tenants agree in writing on the division of land) or involuntarily (by court action).

The holder of a future interest who shares that interest with another (e.g., jointly held remainder interest) does not have the right to immediate possession and therefore cannot maintain an action for involuntary partition.

2) Effect of partition

In a "partition in kind" action, the court divides the jointly owned property into distinct physical portions. If physical division of the property is not practicable or fair, the court may order a partition by sale and distribute the proceeds among the co-tenants in accordance with their ownership interests. Courts prefer a partition in kind.

3) Agreement not to partition

An agreement by co-tenants not to seek partition is enforceable. However, the agreement must be clear, and the time limitation must be reasonable.

D. SPECIAL REAL PROPERTY ISSUES

1. Fair Housing and Discrimination

The federal Fair Housing Act (FHA) (Title VIII of the Civil Rights Act of 1968), 42 U.S.C. § 3601 *et seq.*, prohibits discrimination in the sale, rental, and financing of homes and in other housing-related transactions (such as advertising, homeowner's insurance, and zoning). Owner-occupied buildings with no more than four living units (including the owner's living unit), single-family housing sold or rented without the use of a broker, and housing operated by religious organizations and private clubs that limit occupancy to members are generally exempted from the FHA.

a. Protected classes

The FHA prohibits discrimination on the basis of race, color, religion, national origin, sex, disability, and familial status. Protected familial status includes having or securing custody of children under the age of 18 and being pregnant. Exemption from familial status protection exists for certain housing for older persons.

b. Prohibited practices

The FHA prohibits taking any of the following actions on the basis of a protected characteristic:

i) Refusing to rent or sell housing;

ii) Making housing unavailable;

iii) Providing different housing services or facilities;

iv) Setting different terms for sale or rental of a dwelling;

v) Falsely denying that housing is available;

vi) Refusing to make a mortgage loan or imposing different terms or conditions on a loan;

vii) Refusing to allow a disabled tenant to make reasonable modifications to the dwelling or common-use areas at his own expense;

viii) Refusing to make reasonable accommodations in rules, policies, practices, or services if necessary for the disabled person to use the housing (e.g., refusing to allow a visually impaired tenant to keep a guide dog in an apartment with a "no pets" policy);

ix) Threatening, coercing, intimidating, or interfering with anyone exercising a fair housing right; and

x) Advertising or making any statement that indicates a limitation or preference based on protected characteristics.

The exemptions for owner-occupied buildings with no more than four living units (including the owner's living unit) and single-family housing sold or rented without the use of a broker, do not generally apply to the advertising restriction (item x), above). A religious community or private club whose membership is not restricted based upon race, color, or national origin may restrict tenancy only to its members in a property that it owns, and may advertise to that effect.

c. Enforcement and compliance

The U.S. Department of Housing and Urban Development (HUD) plays the lead role in administering the FHA. A person who believes that a violation of the FHA has occurred may file a complaint with HUD and/or file suit in federal court (a court-appointed attorney may be available). Available relief includes actual damages (including humiliation, and pain and suffering), injunctive or other equitable relief (such as making the housing available), and reasonable attorney's fees and costs. If the case is resolved by an administrative hearing, then a civil penalty to vindicate the public interest may be assessed. A federal court may award punitive damages.

d. Complaint process

Complaints filed with HUD are first investigated by the Office of Fair Housing and Equal Opportunity (FHEO). There must be a causal connection between the prohibited behavior and the alleged violation. If FHEO finds reasonable cause to believe that discrimination occurred, then the case goes to an administrative hearing within 120 days, unless either party elects for the case to be heard in federal court.

Before an administrative hearing is ordered, HUD attempts to reach an agreement among the parties, and any conciliation agreement will cease action on the complaint. For a conciliation agreement to cease action on the complaint, however, it must protect both the complainant and the public interest. The breach of a conciliation agreement may result in suit by the attorney general.

e. Proof of discrimination

1) Racial discrimination

To establish racial discrimination under the FHA, the plaintiff need only show a disparate racial impact, not a racial intent or purpose. In showing a disparate racial impact, the plaintiff must establish that the defendant's policy caused the disparate impact; statistical evidence of disparate impact is not in itself sufficient. *Tex. Dep't of Hous. & Cmty. Affairs v. Inclusive Cmtys. Project, Inc.*, 135 S.Ct. 2507 (2015).

Compare constitutional discrimination: To establish a violation of the Fourteenth Amendment's Equal Protection Clause, the plaintiff must show a racial intent or purpose; a racial impact is not sufficient. *Arlington Heights v. Metropolitan Hous. Dev. Corp.*, 429 U.S. 252 (1977).

2) Occupancy restrictions

Although the FHA prohibits discrimination on the basis of familial status, it does exempt reasonable zoning restrictions based on maximum occupancy. However, this statutory exemption is limited to a strict numerical maximum occupancy restriction (e.g., "no more than eight persons may occupy a dwelling"); a zoning restriction that defined "family" for purposes of an area zoned for single families to permit an unrestricted number of family members to live together while restricting the number of unrelated persons who could live together did not qualify for this exemption. *City of Edmonds v. Oxford House, Inc.*, 514 U.S. 725 (1995). (Note that this case involved an attempt by a locality to prevent a group home for those with disabilities from being located in an area zoned for one-family residences. The holding was confined to a decision about the statutory exemption for a maximum occupancy restriction, and did not address the larger issue of the degree to which or the means by which a locality may accomplish that goal.)

Compare constitutional discrimination: Under the Fourteenth Amendment, a local occupancy restriction on unrelated individuals is only subject to the rational-basis test. *Village of Belle Terre v. Boraas*, 416 U.S. 1 (1974); *but see Moore v. City of East Cleveland*, 431 U.S. 494 (1977) (related persons, including extended family members, have a fundamental right to live together in a single household).

2. Conflict of Laws

When significant aspects of a legal action are divided between two or more states (e.g., parties who are residents of different states), the forum court must determine the law to be applied in deciding a particular issue. The decision as to which state's law should govern is determined under conflict-of-laws principles.

a. General rule

1) Law of the situs

In a case involving real property, if there is a conflict as to which state's law should be applied to resolve the issue, the general conflict-of-laws rule is that the law applied by the forum court should be determined by the conflict-of-laws rule that would be applied by the courts of the state where the property is located (i.e., the situs). Usually, the conflict-of-laws rule of the situs state directs the application of its own local law on that issue (i.e., the **law of the situs**) in resolving the matter.

Compare jurisdiction: To hear a case, the forum court must have both subject-matter jurisdiction and personal jurisdiction over the parties. If an action involves interests in land located in the state, such as an action for partition or to quiet title, then a state court has in rem jurisdiction to decide those interests, even if the court lacks personal jurisdiction over the parties claiming an interest in the property. Restatement (Second) of Conflict of Laws § 59.

2) Issues governed by general rule (i.e., law of the situs)

The following real property issues are usually governed by the general rule:

i) The validity of and rights created by a contract for the transfer of an interest in land by sale or lease;

ii) Whether a conveyance (e.g., a deed) transfers an interest in land, and the nature of the interest transferred (e.g., fee simple absolute, easement, real covenant);

iii) Whether there has been a transfer of an interest in land by operation of law (e.g., adverse possession, prescription), and the nature of the interest transferred;

iv) Whether a lien (e.g., a mortgage) creates an interest in land, and the nature of the interest created;

v) The method for foreclosure of a mortgage on land and the resulting interests;

vi) Whether an interest in land has been transferred by the exercise of a power created by the operation of law (e.g., transfer of land by the executor of a will) or a power of attorney, and the nature of the interest transferred;

vii) The existence and extent of an equitable interest in land;

viii) The passage of an interest in land upon the death of the owner by intestate succession; and

ix) Whether an interest in land escheats to the state.

Restatement (Second) of Conflict of Laws §§ 189, 223, 225–236, 241–243.

b. Exceptions to the general rule

1) Documents that specify applicable law

If **an instrument** that conveys an interest in land or **a will** that devises an interest in land designates the application of a specific jurisdiction's laws, then those laws generally apply. Restatement (Second) of Conflict of Laws §§ 224, 240.

If parties to a **contract for the transfer of an interest in land** designate applicable law, that law will apply with regard to the validity of the contract as well as the rights and duties created by the contract. Otherwise, if a state has a more significant relationship to the transaction and the parties than the situs state, that other state's laws should be applied. This modified rule also applies to covenants of title, real covenants that directly affect the transferred land, or an agreement to assume a mortgage. Restatement (Second) of Conflict of Laws §§ 189, 190.

2) Effect of marriage

The effect of marriage on an interest in land owned by a spouse at the time of the marriage or acquired by a spouse during the marriage is generally governed by the conflict-of-laws rules of the situs state.

The law of the situs generally governs interests in land owned by a spouse at the time of the marriage. When dealing with property acquired during marriage, the law of the spouses' domicile when the property was acquired determines whether the property is marital or separate property, and the law of the situs determines the rights of a third party (e.g., a creditor) to the property. Restatement (Second) of Conflict of Laws §§ 233, 234; *Powell on Real Property* § 53.06.

With regard to the existence and extent of a common-law or statutory interest, including a forced share interest, of a surviving spouse in the land of the deceased spouse, the general rule applies. Restatement (Second) of Conflict of Laws §§ 241, 242.

3) Collateral issues

If an action regarding real property rights involves a collateral issue, then the conflict-of-laws rule of the situs state may apply the law of the state with the most significant interest when determining the collateral issue. Restatement (Second) of Conflict of Laws § 223, cmt. i.

Example: The owner of land located in State A transfers title to the land. The buyer, who lives in State B, subsequently files suit in State A to cancel the deed, alleging that the transfer was due to a fraud perpetrated by the transferor in State B. The conflict-of-laws rule of State A may direct that the law of State B be applied to determine whether the transferor's conduct constituted fraud.

c. Other issues

When the action does not directly relate to an interest in land, the general rule does not apply.

1) Mortgage note

Typically, a mortgage is given as security for a debt obligation, evidenced by a promissory note. Issues regarding the note (e.g., the validity of the note, interpretation of its terms, whether the note is in default) are determined by the local law of the state where the contract requires that repayment be made, unless some other state has a more significant relationship to the transaction and the parties. Restatement (Second) of Conflict of Laws § 195, cmt. a.

2) Foreclosure-related rights

Similarly, issues that relate to a foreclosure but do not affect an interest in land (e.g., the mortgagee's right to hold the mortgagor liable for any deficiency remaining after foreclosure, or to bring suit upon the underlying debt without having first proceeded against the mortgaged land) are determined by the law that governs the debt for which the mortgage was given, which is the law of the state that has the most significant relationship to the transaction and the parties. Restatement (Second) of Conflict of Laws §§ 188; 229, cmt. e.

II. LANDLORD AND TENANT

The relationship between a landlord and a tenant can create four kinds of estates. This relationship is generally governed by a contract, called the lease, that contains the covenants (i.e., promises) of the parties. The promises are generally independent of each other. In other words, each party must perform his promises regardless of whether or not the other party performs his promise.

A. TYPES OF TENANCIES

There are four types of landlord-tenant estates:

i) Tenancy for years;

ii) Periodic tenancy;

iii) Tenancy at will; and

iv) Tenancy at sufferance.

1. **Tenancy for Years**

   A tenancy for years is an estate measured by a fixed and ascertainable amount of time.

   a. **Term**

   A tenancy for years may be any length of time (e.g., one week, six months, five years).

   b. **Creation**

   A tenancy for years is created by an agreement between the landlord and the tenant.

   1) **Statute of Frauds**

   The Statute of Frauds applies to a tenancy for years that is **longer than one year**. Restatement (Second) of Property: Landlord and Tenant § 2.1, Statutory Note 1.

   a) **Requirements**

   The lease agreement must be in a writing that:

   i) Identifies the **parties**;

   ii) Identifies the **premises**;

   iii) Specifies the **duration** of the lease;

   iv) States the **rent** to be paid; and

   v) Is **signed by the party to be charged**.

   Restatement (Second) of Property: Landlord and Tenant § 2.2.

   b) **Determination of time period**

   In most jurisdictions, when a lease is to commence in the future, it is the period of the lease itself that must exceed one year for the Statute of Frauds to apply to the lease. Restatement (Second) of Property: Landlord and Tenant § 2.1, cmts. c, f. In most jurisdictions, when a lease is subject to an option to renew, the option is disregarded when considering whether the lease must comply with the Statute of Frauds. Restatement (Second) of Property: Landlord and Tenant § 2.1, Reporter's Notes on cmt. c.

   c) **Effect of noncompliance**

   A lease subject to the Statute of Frauds that does not comply with it (e.g., an oral lease) is invalid unless the tenant takes possession of the premises with the acquiescence of the landlord, in which case a tenancy at will is created. If the rent is then paid by the tenant and accepted by the landlord, a periodic tenancy is created. If the tenant further makes substantial improvements to the premises and thereby indicates that the parties contemplated a lease for more than a year, the oral lease is given full effect. Restatement (Second) of Property: Landlord and Tenant § 2.3.

c. Termination

1) At end of term

Termination occurs automatically upon the expiration of the term; no notice is required. Any right to renew the agreement must be explicitly set out in the lease.

2) Prior to end of term

Termination may also occur before the expiration of the term, such as when the tenant surrenders the leasehold (i.e., the tenant offers and the landlord accepts return of the leasehold). In addition, although at common law the doctrine of independent covenants usually prevented the breach of a covenant in the lease by a tenant or landlord from giving the other party the right to terminate the lease, most states recognize that the breach of certain leasehold covenants (i.e., the tenant's payment of the rent and the landlord's covenants of quiet enjoyment and implied warranty of habitability) can give rise to a right to terminate the lease.

2. Periodic Tenancy

A periodic tenancy is a repetitive, ongoing estate measured by a set period (e.g., a month, a year) but with no predetermined termination date. It automatically renews at the end of each period until one party gives a valid termination notice.

a. Term

The term of a periodic tenancy may be fixed by the parties (e.g., "The premises are rented on a month-to-month basis.") or determined by their actions (e.g., the tenant pays rent each week and the landlord accept the payment). When the lease states that the rent is a specific amount for specific period, but also states that a portion of the rent is payable at intervals throughout that period, most jurisdictions treat the term of the periodic tenancy as the longer specific period. Restatement (Second) of Property: Landlord and Tenant § 1.5.

> **Example:** The lease states, "The premises are rented at an annual rate of $120,000, payable at $10,000 on the first of each month." The lease is a year-to-year lease.

b. Creation

A periodic tenancy can be created by express agreement, implication (e.g., the failure of an express agreement to mention a termination date), or operation of law (e.g., a holdover tenant, *see* § II.B.5.c. Holdover tenant, *below*). The Statute of Frauds applies to a periodic tenancy only if the initial term of the tenancy exceeds one year. Restatement (Second) of Property: Landlord and Tenant § 2.1, cmt. d.

c. Termination

Because a periodic tenancy automatically renews, notice is generally required to terminate this tenancy.

1) Notice—timing

Notice of termination must be given before the beginning of the intended last period of the periodic tenancy.

Example 1: A landlord who wants to terminate a month-to-month tenancy as of March 31st must give notice of the termination to the tenant before the first day of March.

For a year-to-year periodic tenancy, notice must be given at least six months (rather than one year) in advance. Many states have further reduced the advance notice period for a periodic tenancy of more than a month (e.g., one month for a year-to-year tenancy). Notice that is given late is generally treated as effective to terminate the tenancy as of the end of the following period.

Example 2: A landlord who wanted to terminate a month-to-month tenancy that began on January 1st as of March 31st gave notice of the termination to the tenant on March 5th. The notice is effective to terminate the month-to-month tenancy as of the end of April.

A notice of termination is generally effective only as of the last day of the period (e.g., the end of the month for a month-to-month tenancy that began on the first day of the month).

Example 3: A landlord wanted to terminate a month-to-month tenancy that began on January 1st as of March 15th. The landlord gave notice of the termination to the tenant on February 14th. The notice is effective to terminate the month-to-month tenancy as of the end of March.

2) Notice—writing

An oral notice of termination is sufficient under the common law to terminate a periodic tenancy. Under modern statutes, most states require some form of written notice. However, the application of these statutes varies. For example, some statutes apply only to residential leases, while others apply to all leases. In addition, some statutes place the writing requirement on the landlord only, while others place the writing requirement on both the landlord and the tenant.

3) Other ways to terminate

The same circumstances discussed with regard to a tenancy for years may also give rise to the termination of a periodic tenancy prior to the end of a term (*see* 1.c.2) Prior to end of term, *supra*).

3. Tenancy at Will

a. Term

A tenancy at will is a leasehold estate that does not have a specific term and continues so long as the landlord and the tenant desire.

b. Creation

A tenancy at will can be created by the express agreement of the parties or by implication if the owner permits the tenant to occupy the premises, such as when the parties are negotiating the extension of an expired lease. Unless this tenancy is expressly created, the payment of rent by the tenant and acceptance by the landlord converts a tenancy at will into a periodic tenancy.

c. Termination

A tenancy at will can be terminated by either the landlord or the tenant. It can also be terminated by operation of law upon the death of either party, because of waste or assignment by the tenant, or upon transfer or lease of the property to a third party by the landlord. Restatement (Second) of Property: Landlord and Tenant § 1.6.

1) Notice

At common law, a tenancy at will could be terminated by either party without advance notice, but the tenant had to be given a reasonable time in which to vacate the premises. Restatement (Second) of Property: Landlord and Tenant § 1.6, cmt. c. By statute, most states now require that a party give advance notice (e.g., 30 days) in order to terminate a tenancy at will. Restatement (Second) of Property: Landlord and Tenant § 1.6, Statutory Note 3.

2) Right of only one party to terminate

When the parties agree that only one party has the right to terminate, some courts do not treat the leasehold estate as a tenancy at will but instead as a determinable leasehold (e.g., a tenancy for years determinable, a periodic tenancy determinable). (Note: If the estate is measured by the life of the tenant, the estate is a determinable life estate.) When the agreement is unconscionable, some courts treat the leasehold estate as a tenancy at will that may be terminated by either party. Restatement (Second) of Property: Landlord and Tenant § 1.6, cmt. g.

4. Tenancy at Sufferance

A tenancy at sufferance (holdover tenancy) exists for the period after the expiration of a lease during which the tenant remains on the premises without the landlord's permission.

> **EXAM NOTE:** Know the difference between a tenancy at will, which is created by the agreement of the landlord and the tenant, and a tenancy at sufferance, which is created by the actions of the tenant alone.

A tenancy at sufferance is terminated if the tenant vacates the premises or the landlord evicts the tenant. In such case, the tenant is obligated to pay the reasonable value of his use and occupancy of the premises, which typically is a daily rate determined by reference to the previous rent. In addition, the tenant is liable for reasonably foreseeable special damages that result from his holding over, such as the cost of evicting the tenant. Alternatively, the landlord can terminate the tenancy at sufferance by binding the tenant to a new tenancy (*see* II.B.5.c. "Holdover tenant," *below*).

B. DUTIES OF THE TENANT

The tenant has two basic duties: to pay rent and to avoid waste. The duty to pay rent arises as a consequence of the agreement between the tenant and the landlord (i.e., a lease), which usually takes the form of a written contract. The duty to avoid waste is the same duty imposed on any holder of a current possessory property interest with respect to the holders of other interests in the same property. The duty to avoid waste may be modified by contractual or other legal obligations regarding repair of the premises.

1. Duty to Pay Rent

Although a tenant may enjoy a leasehold estate without having to pay rent (e.g., a tenancy at will), most tenants are required to pay rent. Although rent was not apportionable under common law, most states today allow the tenant to pay a proportionate amount of the rent if the leasehold terminates prematurely. In addition, the landlord may require a deposit (either as security or a future rent payment) prior to commencing the leasehold.

This duty to pay rent is subject to two major exceptions: destruction of the premises and a material breach by the landlord.

a. Destruction of the premises

The lease is terminated, and the tenant is excused from paying rent if the premises are destroyed, such as by flood, as long as the tenant is not at fault for the destruction. At common law, the tenant's duty to pay rent was not excused simply because the leasehold premises were destroyed.

b. Material breach of the lease by the landlord

At common law, the doctrine of independent covenants usually prevented the tenant from avoiding the obligation to pay rent despite the landlord's material breach of the lease. However, even at common law, a landlord's breach of the covenant of quiet enjoyment gave the tenant the right to terminate the lease and cease paying rent. Currently, most states give tenants various options with regard to the payment of rent if a landlord violates the implied warranty of habitability **in a residential lease** (e.g., establishment of an escrow account into which the rent is paid, deducting the cost of repairs incurred by the tenant from the rent paid).

2. Duty to Avoid Waste

At common law, a tenant was held to the same standards of waste imposed on a life tenant, including the duty not to commit affirmative waste (i.e., damage to the property), ameliorative waste (i.e., alterations to the property, even if the value of the property increases), or permissive waste (i.e., failure to prevent or repair damage).

a. Affirmative waste

A tenant is prohibited from committing voluntary waste.

b. Ameliorative waste

A tenant is entitled to make changes to the physical condition of the leased property that increase the property value if reasonably necessary for the tenant to use the property in a reasonable manner, unless the landlord and tenant agree otherwise. Restatement (Second) of Property: Landlord and Tenant § 12.2(a). Landlords usually require advance permission.

c. Permissive waste

A tenant has a duty, unless relieved by the terms of the lease, state statute, or local ordinance, to repair the premises to the extent necessary to maintain the premises in its pre-rental condition. An exception exists for **normal wear and tear**, unless the tenant contracts otherwise.

3. Contractual Duty to Repair

If a **nonresidential lease** specifies that the tenant must "repair and maintain" the property, then the tenant is generally liable for all damage to the property, unless the landlord caused the damage. If the damage is significant (e.g., structural damage due to a fire) and such damage was not caused by the tenant, then the modern trend is to narrowly read the tenant's duty to repair and to find that it does not cover such damage.

A **residential lease** provision that places the burden of repair on the tenant is generally void, but the tenant may be required to notify the landlord of the need for such repairs.

4. Other Duties

A tenant may have other duties or restrictions imposed by the lease, such as a duty to avoid excessive noise, a prohibition on pets, or a non-compete clause that precludes the tenant from operating a business that competes with the landlord's business). In addition, a tenant may face implied duties, such as a prohibition on the use of the premises for illegal purposes (e.g., drug distribution).

5. Landlord's Remedies for the Tenant's Breach

At common law, under the doctrine of independent covenants, a landlord could not regain possession of the premises or terminate the lease if a tenant breached a duty imposed by the lease. Most jurisdictions now statutorily recognize the right of a landlord to terminate a lease for nonpayment of rent. In addition, most leases themselves contain a forfeiture clause that permits a landlord to regain possession of the premises and terminate the lease if the tenant breaches a duty owed to the landlord.

a. Tenant on the premises during the term of the lease

1) Failure to pay rent

If the tenant remains in possession of the premises but fails to pay rent, then the landlord can sue for damages resulting from the breach as well as to remove the tenant from the property and terminate the lease.

a) Future rents

In determining the landlord's damages, the majority rule is that the doctrine of anticipatory repudiation does not apply to leases and the landlord is not entitled to damages with respect to future rents that would have been due under the lease. In states that do apply the doctrine of anticipatory repudiation to leases, damages are generally measured by the difference between future rent that would be owed under the unexpired term and either (i) the reasonable rental value of the premises for such term or (ii) the actual rent collected on a re-letting of the premises for such term. This means that the landlord could collect, at most, the value by which the future rents would have exceeded a reasonable rental value for the property. *See, e.g., Stableford v. Schulingkamp*, 67 So. 2d 306 (Miss. 1953).

2) Late payment of rent

If a tenant pays the rent but fails to do so on time, the landlord is entitled to damages. Whether the landlord can also sue to remove the tenant depends on whether the delay constitutes a material breach of the lease. Moreover, if a landlord accepts late payment of rent, the landlord is treated as waiving his right to regain possession of the premises and terminate the lease at least with regard to that breach of the lease..

b. Abandonment

If a tenant unjustifiably abandoned the leasehold, then the tenant is treated as having made an offer to surrender his rights under the lease.

1) Acceptance of surrender—termination of the lease

If the landlord accepts this offer, the lease is terminated, and the tenant is not liable for any future rent. A landlord's retaking possession of the premises coupled with the landlord's own use of the premises or re-renting the premises to a third-party may be treated as acceptance of the tenant's offer unless the landlord notifies the tenant otherwise.

2) Continuation of the lease

The landlord who does not accept the tenant's offer (e.g., notifies the tenant of such) retains the right to continue to enforce the lease, which means that the tenant remains obligated to continue paying the rent.

a) Duty to mitigate

Under the majority rule, a landlord must mitigate damages by making a reasonable effort to re-rent the premises. The landlord who re-rents the premises on the tenant's behalf may hold the tenant liable for any deficiency. The minority rule does not require the landlord to mitigate damages. Under the minority rule, a landlord who learns of the tenant's abandonment of the premises need not take any action.

c. Holdover tenant

When a tenant continues to occupy the premises without the landlord's agreement after the original lease expires, the tenant is a "holdover tenant."

1) Eviction

The landlord may evict a holdover tenant though legal action if the tenant remains after receiving a written notice to vacate the premises. All jurisdictions no longer allow a landlord to use self-help in a residential tenancy; in a commercial tenancy, only a minority of jurisdictions permit the use of self-help. Of those that do, some prohibit the use of force, while others permit the use of reasonable force to regain possession of the premises.

2) New periodic tenancy

The landlord may instead bind the holdover tenant to a new periodic tenancy. This may be accomplished by specifically informing the tenant or by accepting rent from the holdover tenant. The length of this new periodic tenancy is determined by the period on which rent was calculated under the prior lease. For a commercial lease, the maximum period of new tenancy is one year. For a residential lease, the maximum period is generally a month.

a) Modification of terms

A landlord can modify the terms of this new tenancy (e.g., increase the rent) if the landlord informs the tenant of the new terms prior to the expiration of the prior lease. The tenant who fails to object is deemed to have accepted the new terms.

b) Exceptions

For purposes of binding a tenant to a new lease, a tenant is not considered to be a holdover tenant if the tenant leaves a few articles of personal property behind, the tenant's occupation extends a few hours beyond the termination time, or circumstances out of the tenant's control (e.g., severe illness) prevent the tenant from leaving. In addition, a landlord cannot make this election with regard to a seasonal lease.

C. DUTIES OF THE LANDLORD

1. Give Possession

In most states, a tenant is relieved of the obligation to pay rent if the landlord fails to deliver actual physical possession of the leasehold premises. The minority rule requires only that the landlord deliver legal possession.

2. Duty to Repair

Under the common law, there was no implied duty on the part of the landlord to repair leased premises. However, the majority of jurisdictions today enforce an implied duty upon the landlord to repair under a residential lease, even when the lease attempts to place the burden on the tenant, except for damages caused by the tenant. Failure to make these repairs may constitute a constructive eviction or violate the implied warranty of habitability.

In contrast, courts are reluctant to imply a landlord's duty to repair in commercial leases because the implied warranty of habitability does not apply in commercial leases. Therefore, absent some statutory or contractual obligation, a landlord only has a duty to make a repair if (i) the repair is so substantial that it would not ordinarily fall within the tenant's common law repair duty, or (ii) the value of the repair would primarily inure to the landlord's reversionary interest. *See, e.g., Brown v. Green,* 884 P.2d 55 (Cal. 1994).

3. Warranty of Habitability

There is an implied warranty of habitability in most **residential** leases, particularly when the dwelling is multi-family. The landlord must maintain the property such that it is reasonably suited for residential use. The landlord's failure to comply with housing code requirements may serve as evidence of a breach of this warranty, particularly if the violations substantially threaten the tenant's health and safety. This warranty generally cannot be waived by the tenant, either by express language in the lease or by taking possession of the property with knowledge of the conditions.

If the premises are not habitable, then the tenant may choose to (i) refuse to pay rent, (ii) remedy the defect and offset the cost against the rent, or (iii) defend against eviction. Generally, before the tenant can withhold the rent or remedy the defect, she must first notify the landlord of the problem and give him a reasonable opportunity to correct it. The tenant is not required to vacate the premises.

4. Covenant of Quiet Enjoyment

Every lease (both commercial and residential) contains an implied covenant of quiet enjoyment. This covenant is a promise by the landlord not to interfere with the tenant's possession of the leased premises. It is breached only when the conduct of the landlord or someone with superior title prevents the tenant from possessing the leased premises.

The landlord is not liable for acts of other tenants, but he has a duty to take action against a tenant's nuisance-like behavior and to control the common areas. Off-premises actions of third parties will not suffice.

Any actions by the landlord that breach this covenant may amount to an **actual or constructive eviction** of the tenant.

a. Actual eviction

If the landlord removes the tenant from the premises, then the total eviction terminates the lease and ends the tenant's obligation to pay rent.

1). Partial eviction

If the tenant is prevented from possessing or using a portion of the leased premises, then the tenant may seek relief for a partial actual eviction. The type of relief granted depends on who prevented the possession.

a) Landlord

The tenant is completely excused from paying rent for the entire premises if the landlord is responsible for partial eviction.

b) Third parties

The tenant must pay the reasonable rental value of the premises occupied if the partial eviction is by a third party with a superior claim to the property.

The tenant is not excused from paying rent if a third-party adverse possessor/trespasser partially evicts the tenant.

b. Constructive eviction

If the landlord breaches a duty to the tenant, such as failing to make a repair, that substantially interferes with the tenant's use and enjoyment of the leasehold (e.g., fails to provide heat or water), then the tenant's obligation to pay rent is excused due to constructive eviction **only if the tenant gives notice and adequate time to permit the landlord to fulfill his duty and vacates** the property within a reasonable amount of time.

Not every interference with the use and enjoyment of the premises amounts to a constructive eviction. Temporary or *de minimis* acts not intended to amount to a permanent expulsion do not amount to constructive eviction.

5. Retaliatory Eviction Doctrine

Under the doctrine of retaliatory eviction, a landlord may not evict a residential tenant as retaliation for the tenant's reporting a housing code violation to the appropriate authorities or for refusing to pay rent when the landlord breaches the warranty of habitability. This doctrine also prevents a landlord from retaliating against a residential tenant by refusing to renew a periodic tenancy. This doctrine is not available to a tenant whose rental payments are in arrears.

6. Security Deposit

A landlord may require a security deposit from a tenant as a guarantee of the tenant's fulfillment of the tenant's lease obligations.

a. Amount of the security deposit

In about half of the states, the maximum amount of a security deposit is set by statute and generally ranges from one to two months' rent. Some states permit an additional amount to be collected from tenants with pets, or a set a lower maximum amount if the tenant is a senior citizen. Typically, the landlord is required to give the tenant a receipt for the security deposit.

The landlord is often required to maintain the security deposit in an escrow account, and, in some states, interest earned on the account belongs to the tenant, not the landlord.

b. Use of the security deposit

Generally, a landlord is required to promptly return a security deposit at the end of the lease or to notify the tenant of the amount retained by the landlord and the reasons for doing so. Monetary penalties may be imposed on the landlord for failing to comply with the statutory requirements of security deposits.

The landlord may retain some or all of a security deposit when a tenant breaches the lease, usually by failing to pay the rent. The landlord may also retain some or all of a security deposit for damage to the premises that are in excess of normal wear and tear.

D. TORT LIABILITIES

1. Tenant

The tenant is the possessor of the leasehold who owes a duty of care to invitees, licensees, and foreseeable trespassers and may be liable for dangerous conditions or activities on the leased property.

2. Landlord

Under common law, the landlord is responsible for injuries occurring only in **common and public areas** or in non-common areas under the landlord's control, or those occurring as a result of a **hidden defect** or **faulty repair** completed by the landlord or the landlord's agent.

The modern trend is to hold landlords to a general duty of reasonable care. This means that a landlord may be liable for (i) existing defects prior to the tenant's occupation of the premises, (ii) failure to make repairs required by a housing code, and (iii) at times, the criminal activity of third persons who injure tenants.

See the Themis Torts outline for a further discussion of the liability of owners and possessors of land.

E. ASSIGNMENT AND SUBLETTING

Absent any language to the contrary, a lease can be freely assigned or sublet. Because a lease is both a contract and a conveyance, each can be an independent ground for liability.

1. Assignment versus Sublease

An assignment is a complete transfer of the tenant's remaining lease term. Any transfer for less than the entire duration of the lease is a sublease. A transfer of a physical portion of leased property for the tenant's remaining lease term is a partial assignment.

2. Assignee's Rights and Liabilities

An assignee-tenant is in privity of estate with the landlord, and thus he is liable to the landlord for the rent and any other covenants in the lease that run with the lease. However, if the assignee-tenant reassigns the leasehold to a subsequent tenant, then the assignee-tenant's privity of estate with the landlord ends. In that case, the initial assignee-tenant is no longer liable to the landlord based on privity of estate because the subsequent tenant is now in privity of estate with the landlord.

3. Sublessee's Rights and Liabilities

Because the sublessee is not in privity of estate or contract with the landlord, the sublessee is not liable to the landlord for the rent or any other covenants in the lease, but he is liable to the lessee. However, if the sublessee expressly assumes the rent covenant (or any other covenants), then he becomes personally liable to the landlord.

Although the sublessee can enforce all covenants made by the original lessee in the sublease, the sublessee cannot enforce any covenants made by the landlord.

4. Original Tenant's Rights and Liabilities

The privity of estate held by the original tenant terminates upon a successful assignment by the tenant to the assignee (but does not terminate upon a sublease). Because the original tenant remains in privity of contract with the landlord (both are parties to the lease agreement), however, the original tenant remains liable for all the covenants in the lease—even after a successful assignment. Absent an agreement by the landlord to release the original tenant from liability (i.e., a **novation**), the original tenant remains liable to the landlord for the entire duration of the lease.

5. Landlord Assignments

Unless the lease provides otherwise, a landlord may assign his rights under the lease, usually as part of a transfer of the landlord's ownership interest in the property, to a third party without the tenant's consent. The tenant owes rent, as well as any other burden imposed by a covenant in the lease that runs with the land, to the assignee landlord. Likewise, the assignee landlord is obligated to the tenant to perform any burden imposed by a covenant that runs with the land. The assignor landlord remains liable to the tenant for all covenants in the lease.

a. Attornment

Attornment is the tenant's acknowledgment of a new landlord. Although a tenant can do so formally in a writing, a tenant's payment of rent to the new landlord is deemed an attornment. At common law, the tenant's obligations under the lease did not come into existence until attornment. Today, a tenant's obligations to an assignee landlord arise automatically upon notice of the assignment, and attornment occurs primarily in the context of the transfer of ownership of leased commercial property. For example, a tenant in a commercial lease may be obligated under an attornment clause to acknowledge the tenant's lease obligations to a person who gains ownership of the property through a foreclosure sale.

6. Limitations on Assignment and Subletting

a. Prohibition

When a lease prohibits the tenant from assignment or subletting the leasehold, the tenant may nevertheless assign or sublet the premises. However, the landlord generally can then terminate the lease for breach of one of its covenants and recover any damages.

b. Landlord's permission

When a lease prevents assignment or subletting without the permission of the landlord, and the lease is silent as to a standard for exercising that permission, the modern trend imposes a requirement that the landlord may withhold permission only on a **reasonable ground in relationship to the property being leased** and not on a whim or personal prejudice. The traditional rule is that the landlord may withhold permission at his discretion. Non-assignment and non-sublease clauses are valid but narrowly construed.

A clause that prohibits assignment does not automatically also prohibit subleasing.

c. Waiver by the landlord

An assignment or sublease may be waived if the landlord knows of either the assignment or sublease and does not object. When a landlord consents to an assignment or waives her right to object, she cannot then object to a subsequent assignment. This prohibition on an objection to a subsequent assignment does not apply to subsequent subleases, and a minority of jurisdictions do not impose such a prohibition even on a subsequent assignment.

F. CONDEMNATION

Condemnation is the taking of land for public use or because it is unfit for use. The right of a tenant upon condemnation depends upon whether the condemnation is partial or complete. If the condemnation is partial, meaning that only a portion of the leased property is condemned or the property is temporarily condemned, then the tenant must continue to make his rent payments. The tenant is entitled to compensation for the portion of the property that was condemned or the time he was dispossessed from the leased property. If the condemnation is complete, meaning that the entire leased property is taken for the balance of the lease term, then the tenant is discharged from his rent obligation and is entitled to compensation for the taking.

III. THE LAND SALE CONTRACT

A. FORMATION

A contract for the sale of real property is subject to the same requirements as any other contract (i.e., offer, acceptance, and consideration), and it is also subject to the Statute of Frauds.

1. Real Estate Broker

In many instances, the sale of real property involves a real estate broker. The rights and duties of the broker are generally governed by contract, although state law requires a person to be licensed in order to serve as a broker and often imposes various requirements. All states also recognize and license real estate salespersons (typically referred to as "real estate agents") who generally serve as a subagent of a real estate broker. Generally, when a person who is required to be licensed fails to obtain a license, the person is not entitled to a commission on the sale of the real property.

a. Types of agents

In general, a real estate broker, as an agent, owes his principal the duties that any agent owes to a principal, including the duties of loyalty, disclosure, and confidentiality.

1) Seller's agent

Typically, a real estate broker serves as the seller's agent. There is usually a listing broker, who deals directly with the seller and who may help to set the asking price and assume primary responsibilities for advertising the property for sale. There is usually also a selling broker, who serves as a subagent of the listing broker and finds a buyer for the property. Generally, the listing broker and the selling broker share in the commission paid by the seller.

2) Buyer's agent

More recently, a real estate broker may serve as the buyer's agent. Typically, such an agent also receives a commission-based fee in an amount similar to the selling agent.

3) Dual agent

A dual agent serves as agent for both the buyer and the seller of real property. This situation may arise when the real estate agents who represent the buyer and the seller of a residence are themselves each agents of the same real estate broker. It may also arise when a real estate broker represents a seller regarding the sale of the seller's residence and the buyer of that transaction regarding the sale of the buyer's own residence, which typically is a condition of the buyer's purchase of the seller's residence. Many states prohibit a person from serving as a dual agent, due to the likelihood of a conflict of interest. In states that permit a person to serve as a dual agent, the person is required to disclose the dual agency to the buyer and the seller and obtain the informed consent of each.

4) Non-agent—transaction broker

Many states recognize a broker who does not serve as an agent of either the buyer or the seller, but instead offers to facilitate the sale by performing various functions, such as finding a lender who is willing to finance the transaction. This type of broker, who is generally referred to as a transaction broker, owes each party the duty to perform the broker's tasks with the necessary skill, care, and diligence and to deal fairly with each party, but does not owe either party a duty of loyalty.

> When a real estate broker facilitates the leasing of real property (i.e., leasing broker) as an agent for a party, the broker typically is acting as an agent for the landlord. When a real estate broker facilitates the acquisition of a mortgage loan (i.e., mortgage broker) for a party, the broker is typically the agent of the borrower.

b. Types of listings

If the listing agreement between the seller of real property and the real estate broker does not address the issue of what is required of the broker for her to earn a commission, or if the agreement provides that the broker has a nonexclusive agency, the broker's efforts must be the **procuring cause** for the buyer's purchase of the property for the broker to be entitled to a commission (i.e., the resulting sale must be induced primarily by those efforts). However, if the agreement provides that the broker has an exclusive agency, then the broker is entitled to a commission if her effort (or that of any other broker) is the procuring cause for the buyer's purchase of the property. Moreover, if the agreement provides that the broker has an exclusive right to sell the property, then the broker is entitled to a commission if the efforts of anyone, even the seller himself, are the procuring cause for the buyer's purchase of the property.

Most listing agreements provide for payment of a commission to the real estate broker upon the procurement of **a buyer who is ready, willing, and able** to purchase the property on terms that are agreeable to the seller. Consequently, a broker generally has a right to a commission when the contract of sale is executed or, if the contract is subject to conditions, when the conditions are satisfied, even if the sale does not take place. However, in a minority of states, the broker is not entitled to a commission if the buyer defaults ("no sale, no commission" rule), though a listing agreement may provide the broker with a share of any recovery gained by the seller from the defaulting buyer (e.g., retention of a deposit).

c. Preparation of contract of sale

Most states recognize that a real estate agent or broker who is not an attorney may prepare a contract for the sale of real property. Many states limit the types of contracts that a real estate agent or broker may prepare to standard form contracts that can usually be completed by filling in blanks in the form. *Commonwealth v. Jones & Robins, Inc.*, 41 S.E.2d 720 (Va. 1947)(preparation of simple contract of sale permitted); 4 Colo. Code Regs. § 725-1 E-4,33. In some states, the focus is on whether the agent or broker charges a separate fee for preparing the contract and whether it is incident to the agent's or broker's regular course of business. In some states, the real estate agent or broker is required to provide a written notice or require that the contract itself contain a contingency regarding attorney review or approval. *In re Op. No. 26 of the Comm.*, 654 A.2d 1344 (N.J. 1995) (notice must spell out who the broker represents and give the parties three days in which to seek the advice of an attorney and to cancel the contract); *Duncan & Hill Realty v. Dep't of State*, 405 N.Y.S.2d 339 (App. Div. 1978); Opinion of N.Y.S. Attorney General 96-F11, dated November 14, 1996 (the contract must contain a clause that the contract is subject to the approval of the parties' attorneys).

d. Written agency contract

Under the equal dignities rule, many states require a contract to pay a commission to a real estate agent or broker to be in writing because the underlying contract to sell the real property must be in writing. Restatement (Third) of Agency § 3.02, cmt. e.

2. Statute of Frauds

The land sales contract must:

i) Be in writing;

ii) Be signed by the party to be charged; and

iii) Contain all of the essential terms (i.e., parties, property description, terms of price and payment).

> **Other real property instruments:** The Statute of Frauds also applies to a promise to create an interest in real property, the assignment of a right to purchase real property, an option contract for the sale of an interest in real property, and a promise to give a mortgage or other lien as security.
>
> Although leases, as property interests, are generally subject to the Statute of Frauds, a lease for one year or less is usually not covered by the Statute. In addition, licenses and assignments of mortgages are typically not within the Statute.
>
> Note that a deed (the document that conveys a real property interest) need not satisfy the Statute of Frauds, but must be in writing, signed by the grantor, contain a description of the property, and identify the grantee; in addition, the deed must contain words of transfer (*see* § IV.B.2. Deed, *infra*, regarding the requirements for a valid deed).

3. Exceptions to the Statute of Frauds

a. Part performance

Under the doctrine of part performance, either party may seek specific performance when the acts of performance constitute persuasive evidence of the existence of a contract. Among the acts that may constitute such evidence are:

i) Payment of all or part of the purchase price;

ii) Possession by the purchaser; or

iii) Substantial improvement of the property by the purchaser.

Most jurisdictions require at least two of the above three acts to establish sufficient part performance.

b. Full performance

When a party to an oral contract who has promised to convey real property performs, that party can enforce the other party's oral promise unless the promise is itself the transfer of a real property interest.

Example: During a face-to-face conversation, a seller agrees to transfer land to a buyer in exchange for the buyer's promise to pay $50,000 to the seller. The seller tenders the deed to the buyer and the buyer accepts the deed. The seller can enforce the buyer's oral promise to pay $50,000 to the seller.

c. Detrimental reliance

Specific performance may also be permitted when the party seeking enforcement has reasonably relied on the contract and would suffer such hardship that the other party will be estopped from asserting the Statute of Frauds as a defense to the contract.

d. Admission

A party may be able to enforce an oral land sales contract when the other party admits the existence of the contract.

4. Rescission of a Contract

Although a writing is generally required to create an enforceable land sales contract, most states permit the oral rescission of a land sales contract.

B. PERFORMANCE

1. Marketable Title

Absent contrary language, an implied covenant of marketable title (i.e., a title free from defects) is part of a land sales contract, regardless of the type of deed created. Marketable title is a title that is free from an unreasonable risk of litigation.

a. Defects

Defects in title rendering title unmarketable include:

i) Title acquired by adverse possession that has not yet been quieted (i.e., supported by a judicial decree);

ii) Future interests wherein the holders of such interests have not agreed to the transfer;

iii) Private encumbrance (e.g., mortgage, covenant, option, or easement);

iv) Violation of a zoning ordinance; or

v) Significant physical defect (e.g., an encroachment that is incurable).

The above defects may be waived by the buyer in the contract of sale or subsequently.

b. Timing

Unless otherwise agreed, the seller is not required to deliver marketable title until the closing (i.e., termination of the real estate sale, when ownership transfers and the deed is delivered to the buyer). With regard to an outstanding mortgage, the seller is permitted to apply the proceeds from the sale of the property to the mortgage obligation. If the sale proceeds exceed the amount of the outstanding mortgage, the seller, by doing so, can eliminate this title defect.

In the case of an installment land contract, marketable title is not required to be given until delivery occurs.

c. Remedies for unmarketable title

A buyer may rescind and recover out-of-pocket costs and earnest money payments, sue for breach, or bring an action for specific performance with an abatement of the purchase price (e.g., a price adjustment to compensate the buyer for the defect), but she usually cannot do so until the date of closing.

2. Time of the Essence

Generally, a court will assume that time is not of the essence in a real-estate contract, unless the contract specifically states that time is of the essence, circumstances indicate that this was the intention of the parties, or one party gives the other party notice that time is of the essence. Such notice must be given at a reasonable time before the date designated for closing.

If time is not of the essence, strict adherence to the closing date set in the contract will not be required in equity. Thus, a failure to perform will generally not be grounds for rescission of the contract. A party can sue for specific performance, though, as long as the party was ready to perform within a reasonable time from the date set for performance.

Regardless of whether time is of the essence in a real-estate contract, though, the party that fails to render performance on the date set for closing in the contract will be in breach and liable for damages in an action at law for incidental losses such as taxes, interest, etc.

3. Implied Warranty of Fitness or Suitability (New Homes)

Replacing the doctrine of *caveat emptor* ("let the buyer beware"), a warranty of fitness or suitability (or a warranty of quality, workmanlike construction, performance, or habitability) is implied in almost all jurisdictions in a contract for the sale of a newly constructed residence. In some jurisdictions, the warranty extends to the repair or remodeling of an existing residence and even to related structures (such as a detached garage or a retaining wall).

a. Good workmanship/habitability

In some states, the warranty parallels the warranty of merchantability given by a merchant of goods under Article 2 of the Uniform Commercial Code. Under this type of warranty, the seller warrants that he used adequate materials and good workmanship in working on the residence. The implied warranty generally covers latent construction defects (i.e., defects that cannot be discovered by reasonable observation or inspection), such as a defective electrical, plumbing, or mechanical system, or a leaky roof or drainage problem that does not manifest itself until after the sale. Although the buyer has a duty to conduct a reasonable inspection of the residence for patent defects, the buyer is not required to employ an expert home inspector. In other states, the warranty parallels the warranty of habitability given by a landlord to a residential tenant. Under this type of warranty, the focus is on whether the defect significantly affects the ability of the buyer to live in the residence. Some states recognize both prongs of this warranty.

b. Parties

1) Defendants

Generally, the warranty is implied against commercial builders, developers, and contractors of residences.

2) Plaintiffs

A majority of jurisdictions permit not only the initial homeowner-purchaser but also subsequent purchasers who do not contract directly with the commercial developer or builder to recover damages. However, a subsequent purchaser of the residence may be subject to defenses that the commercial developer or builder can raise against the initial purchaser.

c. Timing

Generally, a suit for breach of this warranty must be brought within a reasonable time. When the warranty is statutory, a fixed time is generally specified (generally from one year to 10 years), and may vary with the type of defect (e.g., structural defects, foundation problems). Many states apply both a statute of limitations that typically begins to run when the buyer discovered or should have discovered the defect, and also a statute of repose that typically begins to run with the completion of the residence or the initial buyer's possession of it. Some of these states provide a short extension of the time in which to bring a claim if the defect is discovered toward the end of the statute of repose.

Example: A state sets a three-year statute of limitations for claims brought under a tort or contract theory. However, the state also has a six-year statute of repose that begins to run upon completion of the home. If a buyer discovers a defect in the fourth year after construction is completed, the buyer would have to bring the claim within the two years that remain under the statute of repose, rather than the longer three-year period for bringing tort or contract claims, generally.

d. Damages

Damages are generally based on the cost of repairs to bring the residence into compliance with the warranty. However, when the defects cannot be corrected without substantial destruction of the residence, damages may be based on the difference between the value of the residence with the warranty and the value of the residence as built.

e. Disclaimer, waiver, and notice

This implied warranty may be disclaimed by the builder or waived by the homeowner if done so with language that is clear and unambiguous, but a general disclaimer (e.g., "property is sold as is") is typically not sufficient. Some jurisdictions require the homeowner to give the builder notice of the defect and an opportunity to correct it before bringing suit.

4. Duty to Disclose Defects (All Homes)

In a majority of jurisdictions, a seller of a residence has a duty to disclose all known material physical defects to the buyer. The defect must not be readily observable or known to the buyer. To be material, the defect must substantially affect the value of the residence, impact the health or safety of a resident, or affect the desirability of the residence to the buyer. When a seller fails to make such disclosures, the buyer may rescind the sale or seek damages. Some states limit this duty to commercial sellers (e.g., builders); other states impose this duty on all sellers.

Even in a jurisdiction that does not require an affirmative disclosure by the seller, a buyer can sue the seller for misrepresentation or fraudulent concealment. General disclaimers (e.g., "property is sold as is") that, in some states, are sufficient to disclaim this duty are not sufficient to preclude the seller's liability for misrepresentation or fraudulent concealment.

5. Tender of Performance

The seller's and the buyer's performance are concurrent conditions. Therefore, one is not obligated to perform without the other's performance. When one party, either the buyer or the seller, repudiates the contract, the non-repudiating party is excused from performing. However, if both parties fail to perform, then the closing date is usually extended until one of the parties performs or repudiates the contract. On the other hand, the inability of the seller to produce a marketable title does not automatically create a material breach; rather, the buyer must give the seller sufficient time to cure the title defect unless time is of the essence and the defect cannot be cured before the time fixed for closing.

6. Merger

Under the common law doctrine of merger, obligations contained in the contract of sale, such as the seller's duty to deliver marketable title, or a description of the size or location of the property, are merged into the deed and cannot thereafter be enforced unless the deed contains the obligation. However, this doctrine generally is not applicable to obligations that are collateral to and independent of the conveyance itself, such as the obligation of the buyer to perform some act on the property after acquisition or the obligation of the seller to remove the seller's personal property. In addition, the merger doctrine does not prevent a buyer from bringing a fraud claim against the seller for fraudulent assertions in the land sale contract, even after closing.

Note that the term "merger" is used in other real property contexts, such as the merger of property interests (e.g., acquisition of both the land that is subject to and the land that is benefited by a restrictive covenant). Such a merger results in the extinguishment of the property right (e.g., the restrictive covenant).

C. REMEDIES FOR BREACH

1. Damages

Both the buyer and the seller can recover expectation damages based on the difference between the contract price and the market value on the date of performance. In some jurisdictions (about half), if the seller's breach resulted from an inability to deliver marketable title, but the seller acted in good faith, then the buyer's damages are limited to the buyer's out-of-pocket expenses. In addition, a buyer or seller can recover incidental damages, such as expenses associated with a title search or survey of the property.

a. Buyer's deposit as liquidated damages

A real property contract usually requires the buyer to make a deposit of a portion of the purchase price (sometimes referred to as "earnest money"). In addition, the contract typically contains a liquidated damages clause that provides for the seller to retain the buyer's deposit in the event that the buyer breaches the contract and refuses to purchase the property. In general, for a liquidated damages clause to be enforceable, the amount of liquidated damages must be reasonable. Traditionally, many courts have found a deposit of no more than 10 percent of the purchase price to be reasonable as a liquidated damages amount. However, courts may consider factors such as the sophistication of the buyer and the nature of the transaction (commercial versus residential) in determining the reasonableness of the seller's retention of the buyer's deposit. In addition, a court may refuse to enforce a liquidated damages clause when the seller suffers no actual loss. When the contract is silent as to dispensation of the deposit in the event of a default by the buyer, courts consider the same factors, and usually allow the seller to retain the deposit when reasonable.

2. Specific Performance

The buyer is entitled to specific performance for a seller's breach of a contract to sell a real property interest because the buyer's remedy at law is considered inadequate due to the unique nature of land. Under the theory of **mutuality of remedies**, the seller is also permitted to seek specific performance and force the buyer to purchase a real property interest, although some courts have rejected this theory because the seller typically receives money rather than real property. When the buyer seeks specific performance with respect to property for which there is a title defect (e.g., an encumbrance), the buyer may also obtain an abatement in the purchase price to compensate the buyer for the defect.

D. EQUITABLE CONVERSION

Under the doctrine of equitable conversion, although the seller retains legal title to real property during the pendency of the sales contract, equitable title passes to the buyer upon entering the contract. The seller effectively holds the property in trust for the buyer, and he has a duty to keep up the property. However, as the holder of legal title, the seller has the right to possess the property. Equitable conversion does not apply if the contract is not specifically enforceable.

1. Action Against the Seller

When an action is maintained against the seller for a claim that arose prior to the execution of the contract, a judgment obtained against the seller after the execution of the contract is not enforceable against the real property. Under the doctrine of equitable conversion, the seller's interest is converted by the contract into an interest in the proceeds from the sale; it is no longer an interest in the real property itself.

2. Risk of Loss

Most states, following the logic of the doctrine of equitable conversion, place the risk of loss during the time between the execution of the contract and the closing **on the buyer**, regardless of whether the buyer takes possession of the property. An exception is recognized when the loss is attributable to the seller's intentional or negligent actions. The Uniform Vendor and Purchaser Risk Act (adopted by a minority of jurisdictions) keeps the risk of loss with the seller, unless and until the buyer takes possession, or title is transferred. For the Act to apply, a material part of the property must be destroyed.

3. Insurance

Unless the contract requires otherwise, the seller does not have a duty to carry casualty insurance. Because the buyer has an equitable interest in the property, the buyer may obtain such insurance. When the risk of loss is on the buyer and the seller has casualty insurance, the seller is generally required to give the buyer credit against the purchase price in the amount of the insurance proceeds when a casualty occurs.

4. Effect of the Buyer's or Seller's Death

When one of the contracting parties dies prior to the performance date of the contract, the seller's interest may be treated as personal property and the buyer's interest may be treated as a real property interest for the purposes of distributing the property pursuant to either's will.

a. Seller's death

When the seller-decedent has devised his real property interests, the proceeds from the sale of the property under contract are treated as personal property that passes to the devisee of the seller-decedent's personal property. The devise of the real property itself is treated as having been adeemed. In jurisdictions that have adopted an anti-ademption statute, the devisee of the seller-decedent's real property is entitled to the sale proceeds.

b. Buyer's death

The person entitled to the buyer-decedent's real property, such as the devisee of the buyer-decedent's real property pursuant to the buyer-decedent's will, can compel the transfer of the property to herself.

E. OPTIONS AND RIGHTS OF FIRST REFUSAL

An option to purchase real property (or a right of first refusal with respect to the transfer of property) involves special considerations. As an interest in property, each is subject to the Statute of Frauds and the applicable recording act.

1. Option Contract

In an option contract, one party acquires the right to purchase property, typically during a specific time period, in exchange for consideration.

a. Protection against revocation and termination

An option contract removes the ability of a grantor to revoke the option. Otherwise, an offeror is free to withdraw the offer, despite a promise to the contrary, unless the offeree has detrimentally relied on the offer. In addition, as a contract, the option does not terminate upon the death or incapacity of the grantor of the option, unlike the termination of an offer upon the death of the offeror.

b. Counteroffer without rejection

The holder of an option can make an offer to the grantor of the option that otherwise would constitute a counteroffer (and thereby a rejection of the original offer) without losing the right to exercise the option.

c. Acceptance

The holder of an option must exercise the option pursuant to the terms of the contract. The mailbox rule, which treats an acceptance as valid when mailed, does not apply. The holder's decision to exercise the option must be received by the grantor of the option within any time period specified in the contract.

2. Right of First Refusal

A right of first refusal is a preemptive right that gives its holder the opportunity to acquire property prior to its transfer to another, and it is valid unless it is unreasonable. The right may be limited in various ways, such as the time period during which the right exists, the transactions to which it applies, and its transferability to another person.

3. Rule Against Perpetuities

The Rule Against Perpetuities does not apply to an option or right of first refusal granted in a lease to a current leasehold tenant. At common law, the Rule would apply to options in gross, but the Third Restatement states that the Rule does not apply to options at all. In addition, under the Uniform Statutory Rule Against Perpetuities, which has been adopted by a majority of jurisdictions, the Rule does not apply to an option contract or a right of first refusal when the property right is created in a commercial transaction. (*See* § I.B.8. Rule Against Perpetuities, *supra.*)

4. Restraints Against Alienability

Although direct restraints on the alienability of property are invalid, both an option contract and a right of first refusal are only partial restraints. In determining whether to enforce each, the rule of reasonableness applies. Under this rule, the utility of the purpose served by the restraint is balanced against the likely harm that would result from its enforcement. In most cases, each is enforceable. Restatement (Third) of Property: Servitudes § 3.4, cmt. c.

5. Marketable Title

A right of first refusal as well as an option contract can constitute an encumbrance that prevents the seller of property from providing marketable title.

IV. TITLES

A. ADVERSE POSSESSION

Under the doctrine of adverse possession, ownership of real property is transferred to a person who exercises exclusive physical possession of that property for a certain amount of time. Title acquired by adverse possession is as good as title transferred by a prior record owner. For possession to ripen into title, possession must be continuous, actual, open and notorious, hostile, and exclusive. Government-owned land cannot be adversely possessed.

1. Continuous

Possession must be continuous and uninterrupted for a specific period (e.g., 10, 15, or 20 years). Seasonal or infrequent use may be sufficiently continuous if it is consistent with the type of property that is being possessed (e.g., a vacation residence, a hunting camp).

a. Tacking

An adverse possessor may tack on his predecessor's time in order to satisfy the statutory period, as long as there is privity between successive possessors. Privity is satisfied if the possessor takes by any non-hostile means (such as descent, devise, contract, or deed). The periods of possession must pass directly from one possessor to the next without any gaps.

Tacking is not allowed when there is an actual, wrongful exclusion of a party entitled to possession from the property (ouster).

b. Disability of an owner

The statute of limitations will not run against a true owner who is afflicted with a disability (e.g., insanity, infancy, imprisonment) at the inception of the adverse possession.

2. **Actual, Open, and Notorious**

Possession must be open and notorious, such that a reasonable true owner would become aware of the claim. Uses that are hidden are insufficient to satisfy this requirement.

3. **Hostile**

The adverse possessor must possess the land without the owner's permission. The majority of jurisdictions do not require that the possession be hostile in the sense that the possessor purposefully seeks to defeat the owner's title. Instead, the possessor, by possessing the land, must objectively demonstrate an intent to claim the land as his own, regardless of his subjective intent. In jurisdictions that consider the possessor's subjective intent, some require a possessor to believe, in good faith, that he has the legal right to possess (i.e., believes that the property is not owned or thinks that he owns the property). Others require the possessor to act in bad faith (i.e., aggressive trespass).

4. **Exclusive**

Possession cannot be shared with the true owner, although two or more people can join together to create a tenancy in common by adverse possession.

5. **Scope of Possession**

a. **Constructive adverse possession**

If a person enters property under color of title (a facially valid will or deed) and actually possesses only a portion of the property, then constructive adverse possession can give title to the whole. The amount possessed must be a reasonable portion of the whole.

b. **Below the surface area**

The adverse possessor acquires the rights to the subsurface (e.g., mineral rights), unless those rights belong to a third party.

c. **Future interests**

The adverse possessor acquires the estate held by the person who has legal possession at the time that the adverse possession began. The adverse possession period does not run against a future interest that exists at the time that the adverse possession begins, but it does begin to run against a future interest created from a fee simple absolute estate after the adverse possession has begun.

B. **DELIVERY AND RECORDING OF A DEED**

A deed is the legal instrument that transfers the ownership of real property. To transfer a real property interest, the grantor must demonstrate the intent to make a present transfer of the interest (e.g., delivery of the deed), and the grantee must accept the interest. In addition, pursuant to the Statute of Frauds, the transfer of a real property interest must be evidenced by a writing (e.g., a written contract or deed satisfying the Statue of Frauds). Finally, the grantee may be able to protect his property interest against others' claims by recording the deed.

1. **Intent to Transfer (Delivery)**

The grantor must, at the time of transfer, intend to make a present transfer of a property interest to the grantee. Note that the interest itself may be a future interest, such as when a parent retains a life estate in a residence and transfers a remainder interest to an adult child.

Typically, this intent is manifested by delivery of the deed. Delivery may be completed by physically handing or mailing the deed to the grantee or the grantee's agent. In addition, the execution and recording of a deed create a **rebuttable presumption** that the deed is to be presently operative. Restatement (Third) Property: Wills and Other Donative Transfers, § 6.3, cmt. e.

Although it is often stated that a deed must be delivered in order for a real property interest to pass (i.e., a delivery requirement), the term "delivery" is used as shorthand for the existence of the necessary grantor intent. Physical transfer of a deed is not required and is not conclusive evidence of the grantor's intent.

a. **Retention of the deed by the grantor**

When the grantor keeps the deed, intent to transfer is not presumed. Instead, parol evidence is admissible to establish whether the grantor had the intent to make a present transfer of the property interest.

b. **Transfer of the deed to the grantee**

Transfer of a deed to the grantee creates a presumption that the grantor intended to make a present transfer of the property interest. Parol evidence is admissible to show that the grantor lacks such intent (e.g., the grantor intended only to create a mortgage, not to effect an outright transfer). However, when the grantor transferred the deed to the grantee subject to an oral condition (i.e., a condition that does not appear in the deed), parol evidence is not admissible, and the condition is not enforceable.

Although physical transfer of a deed is not conclusive evidence of the grantor's intent to transfer a real property interest, a grantor without the intent to transfer real property who nonetheless allows the grantee to obtain physical possession of the deed may be estopped from asserting that the delivery was invalid against a bona fide purchaser from the grantee.

c. **Transfer of the deed to a third party**

1) **Grantor's agent**

When the grantor transfers the deed to her own agent (e.g., an attorney), the transfer is treated as if the grantor had retained the deed, even when the grantor has instructed the agent to deliver the deed to the grantee at some future time or upon the happening of an event. Until the grantor's agent delivers the deed to the grantee, the grantor can demand that the agent ignore the prior instruction and return the deed to the grantor.

2) **Grantee's agent**

When the grantor transfers the deed to the grantee's agent, the transfer is treated as if it had been made to the grantee herself.

3) **Independent agent—gift**

If the grantor purportedly gives property to a grantee through a third party and places a condition on the transfer of the deed by the third party to the grantee, whether delivery has taken place depends on the grantor's language. If the grantor retains an absolute right to recover the deed, then no valid delivery exists because transfer of title was not clearly intended.

Example 1: A executes a deed that transfers real property to B. The deed itself contains no conditions. A gives the deed to C to hold and says, "Give this deed to B on his 21st birthday, unless I ask for the deed back before then."

Because A retained an absolute right to recover the deed, A did not have the intent to make a present transfer.

If the grantor does not retain a right to retrieve the deed, then the key is whether the grantor intends to make a present gift of a property interest. If so, the grantor cannot later void the gift. Instead, the conditional transfer is treated as creating a future property interest in the grantee.

Example 2: A executes a deed that transfers real property to B. The deed itself contains no conditions. A gives the deed to an independent third party, C, and says, "I want B to have this property when she has her first child. Please give the deed to her then." Since A gave C the deed with the intent of presently creating an executory interest in B, B currently has an executory interest in the real property.

When the third party's transfer of the deed to the grantee is conditioned on the death of the grantor, the grantor's transfer of the deed to the third party must evidence the intent to make a present gift. When the grantor's intent is that the gift itself be effective only upon the grantor's death, the transfer can be ineffective due to a failure to comply with the requirements for a testamentary transfer (i.e., the Statute of Wills).

Example 3: A executes a deed that transfers real property to B. The deed itself contains no conditions. A gives the deed to an independent third party, C, saying, "I want B to have this property upon my death. Please give the deed to her then." Because A gave C the deed with the intent of presently creating a remainder interest in B, the transfer is effective.

Example 4: A executes a deed that transfers real property to B. The deed itself contains no conditions. A gives the deed to an independent third party, C, saying, "I want B to have this property if she outlives me. Please give the deed to her then." Because A gave C the deed with the intent of making a testamentary transfer (i.e., requiring that B survive A in order to take the property), the transfer is ineffective unless the requirements for a testamentary transfer were satisfied.

4) **Independent agent—contract**

When a contract for the sale of real property calls for the seller to give the deed to an independent third party (i.e., an escrow agent) and conditions the release of the deed to the buyer on the happening of an event, typically payment of the purchase price, the escrow agent is obligated to transfer the deed to the buyer if and when the condition occurs.

a) **Retrieval by the grantor**

When there is a written contract, the grantor cannot require the escrow agent to return the deed prior to the failure of the condition to occur. When the contract is oral, the grantor can reclaim the deed from the escrow agent because the Statute of Frauds requires a writing for a land sales contract to be enforceable.

b) **Escrow agent**

When the escrow agent delivers the deed to the buyer prior to the performance of the condition, title to the property remains with the seller. This is true even when the buyer then transfers the property to a third party, even a person who purchases the property in good faith (i.e., a bona fide purchaser). An exception exists when the seller permits the buyer to possess the property.

c) Time of transfer

In general, title to the property remains in the seller until the condition is satisfied. Once the condition is satisfied, title automatically vests in the buyer. The date of transfer can relate back to the date that the grantor deposited the deed in escrow when, before the condition is satisfied, the grantor dies, the grantor becomes incapacitated or marries, or the grantee dies.

d. Acceptance

Acceptance is required for a transfer to be complete, and the grantee is generally presumed to have accepted any beneficial conveyance. Acceptance relates back to the time the deed was transferred, unless a bona fide purchaser or creditor of the grantor would be negatively affected by doing so.

If the grantee rejects the deed, no title passes and the grantor holds the title.

If the grantee accepts the deed and then changes his mind even a moment later, his return, destruction, or cancellation of the deed is ineffective to transfer ownership of the property back to the grantor. A new, valid deed must be executed in order for the grantee to convey the property back to the original grantor.

2. Deed

a. Drafting, review, and negotiation of a deed and other closing documents

In general, the giving of legal advice and counsel to others, as well as the preparation and approval of legal instruments such as deeds and mortgages for someone else, constitutes the practice of law. *See, e.g.,* N.Y. Judiciary Law § 484; *Countrywide Home Loans, Inc. v. Ky. Bar Ass'n*, 113 S.W.3d 105, 112 (Ky. 2003). However, a non-attorney who is acting on his own behalf may select and draft a legal document. *Wash. State Bar Assn. v. Great W. Union Fed. Sav. & Loan Assn.*, 586 P.2d 870 (Wash. 1978). (*See* III.A.1.c. "Preparation of the contract of sale," *supra*, regarding the completion of a standard form contract by a real estate agent or broker.)

1) Mortgage lenders—lending documents

The completion of standard mortgage loan documents by non-attorney employees of the mortgage lender is not the practice of law, even if the lender charges the borrower a reasonable fee for preparation of such documents, so long as the employees are not exercising legal discretion in completing the documents. *Perkins v. CTX Mortg. Co.*, 969 P.2d 93 (Wash. 1999).

2) Conduct of the settlement

A slight majority of states do not require an attorney to conduct a settlement (i.e., closing). *In re Op. No. 26 of the Comm.*, 654 A.2d 1344 (N.J. 1995) (if notice is provided, the closing may be conducted by the real estate agent or broker or by an officer of a title insurance company instead of an attorney). However, although a non-attorney may conduct a settlement, the non-attorney may not answer legal questions that arise or otherwise give legal advice. *Countrywide Home Loans, Inc. v. Ky. Bar Ass'n*, 113 S.W.3d 105 (Ky. 2003).

b. Contents of the deed

A valid deed must include all necessary terms: the identity of the grantor and the grantee, words of transfer, a description of the property interest being transferred, and the grantor's signature. Unlike in a contract, **consideration is not required**.

1) Parties

The **grantor** and **grantee** must be identified. A deed that does not identify the grantee is ineffective until the grantee's name is added or determined. A deed to a nonexistent grantee is void as to the nonexistent grantee.

Example: A grantor executed a deed conveying Blackacre "to my neighbors." Until the intended neighbors are determined by extrinsic evidence, the deed has no effect.

2) Words of transfer

The portion of a deed that contains the words that transfer an interest from the grantor to the grantee is called a "granting clause" (e.g., "do grant and convey"). Any language evidencing a present intent to transfer will suffice.

3) Description of property

The description of the property must be reasonably definite, but extrinsic evidence is admissible to clarify. A habendum clause (e.g., "to have and to hold") in a deed defines the interest conveyed. When there is an irreconcilable difference between the granting clause and the habendum clause, the granting clause prevails.

Descriptions by metes and bounds or by street address are acceptable but not required to sufficiently describe the property. When there is a conflict between descriptions of the property in the deed, descriptions based on monuments (e.g., "from oak tree east to the tool shed") are given priority over area descriptions (e.g., "100 acres").

4) Execution of the deed

A grantor's signature on the deed is generally required, but in most states, it need not be witnessed or acknowledged (notarized). Although a grantee's signature is not required (a deed that is not signed by the grantee is sometimes referred to as a "deed poll"), the grantee's acceptance of the deed is sufficient to make easements and covenants in the deed enforceable against the grantee.

a) Forgery of deed itself or grantor's signature

A deed that contains a forged grantor's signature is void, even if relied upon by a bona fide purchaser. Similarly, a deed that has been forged is void. However, a deed that has been procured by fraud is merely voidable and may be enforced by a bona fide purchaser without notice of the fraud.

b) Execution by an agent

An agent may execute a deed on behalf of a principal-grantor.

i) Equal-dignities rule

While the creation of an agency relationship does not generally require a writing, under the equal-dignities rule, when the act performed by an agent on behalf of the principal is required to be in writing by law, the agent's authority must also be in writing. Restatement (Third) of Agency § 3.02. Consequently, when an agent signs a deed (or a real property instrument that is subject to the Statute of Frauds, such as a contract for the sale of real property), the agent's authority must also be in writing.

(a) Exceptions

An officer of an entity such as a corporation who has the authority to act on behalf of the entity by virtue of the officer's status may sign a deed without specific authorization of the corporation to do. In addition, a person whose only act is signing a specific deed at the grantor's request (i.e., an amanuensis) may do so without written authorization. Restatement (Third) of Agency § 3.02, cmt. c.

(b) Estoppel of a principal

A principal-grantor may be estopped from asserting the lack of writing as a defense when the principal has made a manifestation of an agent's authority that induces detrimental reliance by a third party. Restatement (Third) of Agency § 3.02.

ii) Signature on the deed

A deed is valid if an agent with authority signs only the principal's name. A deed is not valid at law if an agent with authority signs only her own name, but the deed may be enforced in equity as between the parties and subsequent purchasers with notice of the existence of the agency.

c) Grantor's lack of capacity and other defenses

A grantor who conveys a real property interest is subject to the same capacity requirements as a person who enters into a contract (*see* MBE Contracts outline I.E.6. Capacity to Contract). In addition, a deed may be subject to reformation or rescission on the same grounds as a contract (e.g., fraud, undue influence, duress) (*see* MBE Contracts outline I.E.1.–5.).

d) Conveyance of jointly owned property

Generally, a co-tenant in a joint tenancy or a tenancy in common can convey only his interest in jointly owned property. A deed executed by a co-tenant that purports to be a conveyance of the entire jointly owned property has the effect of conveying only that co-tenant's interest. A purported conveyance of a physical portion of jointly owned property is void.

3. Recording Act

While a deed need not be recorded to be valid and convey good title, all states have enacted recording acts, which establish priorities among conflicting claims to real property interests and promote certainty of title. Nearly all instruments affecting real property interests may be recorded, including easements, covenants, leases, contracts to convey, and mortgages. Some states also require the grantor to acknowledge the deed before a notary public before accepting it for recording, in an attempt to prevent fraudulent transfers. Unless the recording act governs, the common law rule of "first in time, first in right" generally applies to determine priorities.

a. Types of statutes

The three types of recording statutes are notice, race, and race-notice.

> **EXAM NOTE:** Notice and race-notice statutes are the most frequently tested types of recording statutes on the MBE.

1) Notice statute

A purchaser need only purchase without notice of the prior interest to prevail under a notice statute. (See *infra* for a discussion of what constitutes notice.) Notice statutes tend to protect subsequent purchasers against interest holders who could have but failed to record documents describing their interests.

> **EXAM NOTE:** Notice statutes are commonly tested on the MBE and usually contain words such as "in good faith" or "without notice."

> **Example of a notice statute:** "No conveyance or mortgage of real property shall be good against subsequent purchasers for value and *without notice* unless the same be recorded according to law."

> **EXAM NOTE:** Remember that a bona fide purchaser need not record in order to prevail over a prior interest in a notice jurisdiction, but he must record to prevail against a subsequent purchaser.

2) Race statute

A minority of states have race statutes, under which a purchaser who records first prevails, regardless of his knowledge of any prior conflicting interests.

> **Example of a race statute:** "No conveyance or mortgage of real property shall be good against subsequent purchasers for value unless the same be *first recorded* according to law."

3) Race-notice statute

A race-notice statute requires a subsequent purchaser to take the interest without notice of a prior conflicting interest **and** be the first to record.

> **EXAM NOTE:** Look for words in the statute such as "in good faith" in conjunction with phrases such as "first duly recorded," which are present in a race-notice statute.

> **Example of a race-notice statute:** "No conveyance or mortgage of real property shall be good against subsequent purchasers for value and *without notice* who shall *first record*."

> **EXAM NOTE:** The recording acts provide that prior conveyances and mortgages that would prevail under the common-law rule may be defeated by certain "subsequent purchasers for value" who meet the requirements of the recording act (e.g., took without notice, recorded first, or both). In other words, the recording acts operate by protecting the claim of certain subsequent purchasers who would have lost under the common law "first in time, first in right" rule. Remember that when a recording act does not apply, the common law "first in time, first in right" rule applies.

b. Paid value

Only a grantee who pays value for an interest in real property is entitled to protection under the recording statutes.

> **EXAM NOTE:** Many questions have the grantee clearly paying value for the property, but be on the lookout for situations involving mortgages, judgment liens, and donees.

1) Mortgages

Mortgagees are considered to have "paid value" and are protected by the recording acts, unless the mortgage is not given simultaneously with a loan.

2) Donees, heirs, and devisees

Grantees who acquire title of property by gift, intestacy, or devise are not protected by the recording act against prior claims to the same property, even when those claims are not recorded.

Example: A sells Blackacre to B, who forgets to record the deed. In the interim, A gives a deed to his daughter, C, who promptly records her deed. C will not defeat B's ownership because C did not pay value for the property.

3) Judgment liens

Creditors are protected only against claims that arise after a judgment against the debtor is recorded, unless otherwise indicated by statute. Note that a lawsuit may be pending that could affect title to the property. In such case, any party to the action may record a **lis pendens** (a notice of pending action), which serves as notice to third parties of the claims pending in the lawsuit.

Example: B makes a loan to A and A grants B a mortgage interest in Blackacre as security for the loan. C, a creditor of A, not knowing of the deed to B, then records a judgment lien against Blackacre. C is not protected against B's unrecorded interest because it preceded the recording of C's lien.

4) Judicial sale

Most jurisdictions protect a purchaser of property at a judicial sale against all unrecorded interests subject to the recording act.

Example: Assume the same facts as those in the example in 3), above. C obtains an order requiring a sheriff to levy on the lien and Blackacre is sold at a judicial sale. D purchases Blackacre at the sale. D takes Blackacre free of B's mortgage interest.

5) Shelter rule

Grantors who are protected by the recording act protect (or "shelter") their grantees who would otherwise be unprotected. The **exception** to the shelter rule is that a purchaser who is not a bona fide purchaser cannot convey to a bona fide purchaser and then buy back the property to obtain the status of a bona fide purchaser.

c. Notice

As discussed *supra*, only purchasers who give value in good faith and without notice of a prior claim will prevail in notice or race-notice jurisdictions. "Notice" can be actual, by inquiry, or constructive. Whether a purchaser has notice is tested as of the time of the conveyance of the property to the purchaser. Notice obtained by the purchaser after the conveyance does not prevent the purchaser from enjoying the benefit of the recording act.

1) Actual notice

A grantee possessing actual, personal knowledge of a prior interest cannot prevail under a notice or race-notice recording statute.

2) Inquiry notice

If a reasonable investigation would have disclosed the existence of prior claims, then the grantee is considered to possess inquiry notice, and she cannot prevail against those prior claims. The purchaser is charged with whatever knowledge a reasonable inspection of the property would have disclosed. In most states, taking a quitclaim deed does not in itself create inquiry notice of prior claims.

> **EXAM NOTE:** Examples of situations that typically give rise to inquiry notice on the MBE are (i) when someone other than the grantor has possession of the property (e.g., a tenant) or (ii) when documents are referenced in the chain of title.

> **Example:** A's deed to B references a restrictive covenant entered into by A and B at the time of the deed. The deed is recorded, but the covenant is not contained in the deed. Any purchaser in A's chain of title will be charged with knowledge of the covenant and its contents.

3) Constructive notice

Grantees are held to have constructive notice of all prior conveyances that were properly recorded.

a) Tract index

All properties in a tract index system are listed by location on a separate page that includes all conveyances and encumbrances.

b) Grantor-grantee indexes

Each yearly index is usually alphabetized by the last names of grantors and grantees.

When searching the chain of title, the potential purchaser must first search for the grantor's name as a grantee (to ensure good title) in the grantee index, and he must then search for the name of the grantor's grantor as a grantee, and so on, until the title has been searched back to its inception (common-law rule) or as far back as the recording statute provides. Some states have enacted a marketable title act that establish search cutoff dates (e.g., 40 years). Then, the grantors are searched as grantors to verify the chain of title.

c) Related searches

Title searches also should include a search of tax assessment and judgment lien records, as well as the marriage, divorce, and probate records for every named grantor and grantee.

d. Priorities

Interests are placed in order of priority based on the relevant statute (notice, race, and race-notice). The protected interest that is first in time is satisfied first, followed by the junior interests in order of time.

e. Rule application

Example 1: First, O sells Blackacre to A, but A does not record. Second, O then sells Blackacre to B, who has no notice of the earlier conveyance to A. Next, A records. Then, B records. B sues A to quiet title in Blackacre. What is the result?

i) Under a race statute, the first in time to record prevails. In the situation above, A wins because A was the first to record.

ii) Under a notice statute, regardless of who records first, those who in good faith purchase without notice prevail. So, in the above scenario, B wins because B took without notice.

iii) In a race-notice jurisdiction, B is unable to prove that he had both no notice **and** recorded first. Because A recorded first, A wins.

Example 2: First, O sells an easement in Blackacre to A, but A does not record. Second, O then sells Blackacre in fee simple absolute to B, who knows of the earlier conveyance to A. Next, B records. Then, A records. B sues A to quiet title to Blackacre. What is the result?

i) Under a race statute, B wins, and the easement is extinguished because B recorded first.

ii) Under a notice statute, A wins because B had notice of A's rights at the time of purchase.

iii) In a race-notice jurisdiction, A prevails and can enforce the easement against B because B is unable to show that he both recorded first **and** purchased without notice of A's prior claim.

Example 3: First, O promises A in writing that O will use Blackacre only for residential purposes, and the parties intend that this burden will run with the land. A does not record the promise. O then sells Blackacre in fee simple absolute to B, who has no notice of O's earlier promise to A. Next, B records. Then, A records the promise. B then sells a fee simple absolute estate in Blackacre to C, who has actual knowledge of O's promise to A. C uses Blackacre for nonresidential purposes. A sues C to enforce O's promise to A, seeking damages and an injunction. What is the result?

i) Under a race statute, C wins, even though C records after A. In this situation, A's recording is outside C's chain of title, so it does not constitute "winning the race" for the purposes of a race statute. Also, because B's interest in Blackacre "wins" over A's, and C relies on B's title, C wins.

ii) Under a notice statute, C wins even though C had notice. The shelter doctrine shelters C by making B's title marketable, because B was a good-faith purchaser. Therefore, B passes his title to C, and C takes B's status as a good-faith purchaser.

iii) In a race-notice jurisdiction, C wins because the shelter doctrine applies.

f. Chain-of-title problems

1) Wild deed

Although an instrument is recorded and indexed in the recording office, it may not be recorded in such a way as to give notice to subsequent purchasers (i.e., the deed may not be in the "chain of title"). A recorded deed that is not within the chain of title is a "wild deed."

Example 1: First, O sells Blackacre to A, but A does not record. Second, A sells Blackacre to B, and B records. O then conveys Blackacre to C, who has no notice of the earlier conveyances to A or B. Next, C records. Then, A records the deed from O to A. B sues C for title to Blackacre. What is the result?

  i) Under a race statute, C prevails even though B recorded the deed from A to B before C recorded the deed from O to C, because the deed from A to B was a "wild deed," outside C's chain of title. In performing a standard title search, C would have searched in the grantor index for deeds listing O as the grantor from the date the deed granting Blackacre to O was recorded to the date C recorded the deed from O to C. No deed from O to A would have been discovered in such a search, and without finding a deed from O to A, C would not be expected to look for a deed from A to B.

  ii) Under a notice statute, C prevails because he had no actual notice of the conveyances from O to A and from A to B, and the deed from A to B did not give him constructive notice because it was a wild deed.

  iii) In a race-notice jurisdiction, C prevails for a combination of the two reasons above: C had no actual or constructive notice of O's deed to A, and B's prior recording of the deed from A to B does not count because it is a wild deed.

2) Deed recorded late

Example 2: O sells Blackacre to A, but A does not record. Next, O sells Blackacre to B, who has actual notice of the conveyance from O to A, and B records. Then, A records. Next, B conveys to C, who has no actual notice of the O-to-A conveyance. C sues A for title to Blackacre. What is the result?

  i) Under a race statute, C prevails even though A recorded the deed, because A's deed was recorded outside C's chain of title. Remember that under the standard title search, C would research the grantor index only under O's name until the date that B recorded the deed from O to B. Because O's deed to A was filed after that date, it is not considered "duly recorded" for the purposes of a race statute.

  ii) Under a notice statute, C wins because C had no notice and because A's deed was recorded outside C's chain of title.

  iii) In a race-notice jurisdiction, C wins because both race and notice requirements are met.

3) Estoppel by deed (after-acquired title)

Under the "estoppel by deed" doctrine, a grantor who conveys an interest in land by warranty deed before actually owning it is estopped from later denying the effectiveness of her deed. Consequently, when the grantor does acquire ownership of the land, the after-acquired title is transferred automatically to the prior grantee.

However, under the majority rule, a subsequent purchaser from the same grantor who takes without notice can obtain good title—despite the doctrine of estoppel by deed—in a notice or race-notice jurisdiction. The purchaser is generally required to search the grantee index for a grantor's name only as far back as the date on which the grantor's name appears as a grantee (i.e., the date on which the grantor acquired the property). That date is the earliest date that a grantor's name must be searched on the grantor index for a conveyance by the grantor. The recording of a transfer made by the grantor before that date is not treated as giving the purchaser constructive notice of the transfer.

4) Title insurance

a) Process

After conducting a title search, a title insurance company typically issues a title commitment that binds the company to provide title insurance to the purchaser of real property or a mortgagee. The commitment may list matters, such as an outstanding mortgage, that must be corrected before the company will issue a policy. After closing, the deed and any new mortgages are recorded and the title insurance policy is issued.

b) Insured defects

Title insurance typically protects not only against defects that could have been uncovered by a careful title search, such as recorded easements, covenants, mortgages, and tax or judgment liens, but also title defects resulting from forged instruments, undelivered deeds, or deeds executed by a person without legal capacity or authority. Defects that typically are not covered in a standard policy include off-record matters, such as claims for adverse possession or a prescriptive easement, or violations of zoning ordinances.

c) Types of policies

(1) Owner's policy

An owner's policy protects the owner of the property (i.e., the mortgagor or the mortgagee) as the named insurer from the insured defects. It does not protect subsequent transferees, but can protect an insured from a defect that is not discovered until after the insured has transferred the property to someone else. Coverage is typically based on the purchase price of the property.

(2) Lender's policy

A lender's policy protects the mortgage lender as well as an assignee of the mortgage loan, but does not protect the mortgagor. The focus is defects that affect the validity, priority, and enforceability of the mortgage. Coverage is based on the amount of the mortgage loan and typically is reduced as the mortgage obligation is reduced.

d) Protection

An insurance policy protects the policy holder, up to the amount of coverage provided, against actual monetary loss due to an insured defect.

The policy holder is not required to prove fault, but is required to prove that the defect occurred before the policy took effect.

g. Interests acquired adversely

1) Adversely acquired property interests

A recording act does not protect a subsequent purchaser for value from a property interest acquired by operation of law, such as a property interest acquired by adverse possession or prescriptive easement. Since generally such ownership arises automatically upon the expiration of the statutory period, there is no documentation to be recorded. However, with regard to an unrecorded easement, including an easement created by prescription, implication, estoppel, or oral grant, the Restatement (Third) has taken the position that these easements are subject to extinguishment under a recording act, unless the easement is reasonably necessary for the enjoyment of the dominant estate, relates to an underground utility, or, at least when the recording act is a race-notice or notice type act, the easement would be discovered by reasonable inspection or inquiry. Restatement (Third) of Property; Servitudes § 7.14.

2) Invalid deed

When a deed would not be given effect due to the grantee's actions, such as a forged deed or a deed with a forged grantor's signature, the recording act does not validate such a deed.

Example: An owner of land promises to transfer it to her nephew. The owner prepares a deed but does not deliver it to the nephew. After the owner's death, the nephew finds the deed among the owner's papers and records it. The deed is ineffective to transfer ownership to the nephew because it was not delivered to the nephew during the owner's lifetime. The nephew's recording of the deed does not validate this deed.

4. Types of Deeds

a. General warranty deed

The grantor of a general warranty deed guarantees that he holds six covenants of title, which are discussed below.

1) Present covenants

The three present covenants embodied in the general warranty deed are the covenant of seisin, the covenant of the right to convey, and the covenant against encumbrances. The statute of limitations begins to run at the time of conveyance.

The covenant of seisin warrants that the grantor owns the land as it is described in the deed. The covenant of the right to convey guarantees that the grantor has the right to transfer title. The covenant against encumbrances guarantees that the deed contains no undisclosed encumbrances.

2) Future covenants

The three future covenants embodied within a general warranty deed are the covenants of quiet enjoyment, warranty and further assurances. Future covenants run with the land and can be enforced by remote grantees. The statute of limitations does not begin to run until the grantee's rights are encroached.

The covenant of quiet enjoyment guarantees that the grantee's possession will not be interfered with by a third party's lawful claim for title. The covenant of warranty guarantees that the grantor will defend against a third party's lawful claim for title. The covenant for further assurances guarantees that the grantor will do whatever is necessary to perfect title should it turn out to be defective, though this covenant is not recognized in all states.

3) Breach of covenant

a) Time of breach

Breach of the present covenants occurs at the time of conveyance. In most states, the present covenants do not run with the land and cannot be enforced by subsequent grantees.

Conversely, breach of a future covenant occurs only upon interference with possession by a third party. Future covenants run with the land and can be enforced by subsequent grantees.

b) Requirements for breach

A breach of the covenants of seisin and right to convey arises when the grantor is not the owner of the described estate (e.g., another party owns a portion of the property). A breach of the covenant against encumbrances occurs when a property is encumbered by a mortgage, lease, easement, or covenant not specified in the deed. Even if the deed is silent, some states do not recognize a breach if the grantee had knowledge of the encumbrance, if it was visible, or if it benefitted the land. Most states do not find a breach from a violation of a zoning restriction or housing code.

A breach of a future covenant occurs when the grantee has been sued or evicted by someone with a valid superior interest. The grantor is not required to defend against a third party's wrongful claim or eviction.

c) Recovery of damages

A buyer can recover for breach of the covenant against encumbrances the lesser of the difference in value between title with and without the defect, or the cost of removing the encumbrance.

To recover for the covenants of enjoyment or warranty, the grantee must notify the grantor of the interference, and the grantor must refuse to defend the title. Recovery is the lesser of the purchase price or the cost of defending the defective title.

Recovery for the covenants of seisin, right to convey, or further assurances is the lesser of the purchase price or the cost of perfecting title.

d) After-acquired title

When a person who purports to transfer real property that he does not own subsequently becomes the owner of that property, the after-acquired title doctrine provides that title to the property automatically vests in the transferee. Most often, this doctrine is applied to the grantor of a warranty deed. A related doctrine, estoppel by deed, prevents the grantor from asserting ownership of the after-acquired property. For the interplay of estoppel by deed and the recording acts, *see* § IV.B.3.f.3. Estoppel by deed (after-acquired title), *supra*.

b. Special warranty deed

A special warranty deed contains the same covenants of title as a general warranty deed but only warrants against defects arising during the time the grantor has title.

c. Quitclaim deed

Unlike a warranty deed, a quitclaim deed promises **no covenants of title**.

A common form of quitclaim deed is the tax deed, which is used by government authorities when selling properties seized for nonpayment of taxes.

The grantee in a quitclaim deed (or a grant deed or warranty deed) receives no better title than what the grantor possessed.

Recording a quitclaim deed may give the grantee priority over an earlier unrecorded general warranty deed.

C. CONVEYANCE BY WILL, TRUST, AND OPERATION OF LAW

Real property can be conveyed by will and by statutes that govern intestate succession for property that does not pass by will.

1. Conveyance by Will and Operation of Law

A transfer of ownership of real property at death through a will can take effect through a specific devise (e.g., "I leave my residence to my son") or a residuary clause (e.g., "I leave all other property to my daughter") when the property is not specifically mentioned in the will.

When a decedent does not leave a valid will or the will does not govern the real property, the property is transferred pursuant to the applicable state law of intestate succession. While the intestacy rules vary by state, preference is typically given to the decedent's immediate family (e.g., spouse, children). When a decedent has no heir, as determined under state law, the property typically escheats to the state.

While typically a beneficiary under a will (i.e., devisee) or the intestacy rules (i.e., heir) desires the property, a beneficiary may renounce ownership of the real property by disclaiming it.

a. Ademption

A devise of real property may fail (or be "adeemed") because the testator no longer owns the property upon death (i.e., because the property was sold, destroyed, or given away before death). If the testator gives the property to the intended beneficiary while the testator is still alive, then the devise is adeemed by satisfaction. Once a devise is adeemed, the beneficiary named in the will takes nothing.

> **EXAM NOTE:** Remember that ademption can occur only with a specific devise, such as real property, and not with a general devise, such as money.

Example: A executes a will under which Blackacre is devised to B, but then he sells Blackacre to C. When A dies, the gift is adeemed, and B takes nothing.

b. Lapse and anti-lapse

Under common law, a devise of real property can also fail (lapse) if the beneficiary under a will dies before the testator and no alternate beneficiary is named. When the testator indicates a clear intent that the devise survive the death of the beneficiary, the devise will not fail. In addition, all jurisdictions have anti-lapse statutes, which prevent a gift from lapsing if the gift is made to parties specified by the statute (usually immediate relatives of the testator) and they leave issue who survive the testator. In most jurisdictions, the anti-lapse statute is limited to grandparents or a descendant of a grandparent of the testator (e.g., aunts, uncles, parents, siblings, children.) A lapsed gift becomes part of the residuary estate.

Example: By will, A devises her car to B, Blackacre to C, and the remainder of her property (the residuary estate) to D. A does not name any alternate beneficiaries. If C dies before A and the devise does not qualify for protection under the anti-lapse statute, then Blackacre becomes part of the residuary estate and passes to D, along with all of A's property other than the car, which goes to B. If C is related to A such that the anti-lapse statute applies, then Blackacre passes to C's descendants.

When a devise is made to a class (e.g., "my children") and one member of the class dies before the testator, only the surviving class members take the property. However, if an anti-lapse statute applies because the class members were related to the testator, then the descendants of the predeceased class member also share in the devise. Most states apply the anti-lapse rule first, before applying the class gift rule.

c. Exoneration of liens

Under the common-law exoneration of liens doctrine, if a testator makes a specific devise of real property that is subject to an encumbrance, such as a mortgage or a lien, then the devisee is entitled to have the land "exonerated" by payment of the encumbrance from the remaining assets in the testator's estate. Most states have abolished this doctrine. In such states, the property passes subject to the encumbrance unless the will specifically requires payment of the encumbrance.

2. Conveyance by Trust

A trust is essentially a situation in which property is managed by one person or entity for the benefit of another.

a. Private trusts

The parties to a trust include the settlor (the person who creates the trust), the trustee (the person who holds legal title to the property), and the beneficiary (the party who holds equitable title). A valid trust must have:

i) **Intent**, the settlor must intend to make a gift in trust;

ii) **Valid purpose**, any purpose not illegal or against public policy;

iii) **Res**, the property that is subject to the trust; and

iv) **Beneficiaries**, those **identifiable** persons for whose benefit the trust is created and who hold equitable title to the property.

An *inter vivos* trust is created when the settlor conveys his property (res) to the trustee while the settlor is alive. Alternatively, the settlor may simply declare that he is holding certain property in trust for certain beneficiaries, without there being an actual conveyance of the property. Remember that any conveyance of real property must include a writing that satisfies the Statute of Frauds.

Another form of conveyance occurs when the settlor creates a trust by language in his will and transfers the property by devise in his will. This type of trust is called a "testamentary trust" and comes into being only on the death of the settlor.

Finally, the settlor may create an *inter vivos* trust but not fund the trust until his death, by devise in his will. In this case, property "pours over" into the trust.

b. Charitable trusts

A charitable trust is one with a stated charitable purpose made to benefit the community at large or a particular segment of the community. A differentiating factor between a private trust and a charitable trust is the beneficiaries. As noted above, a private trust must have identifiable beneficiaries, whereas in a charitable trust, the beneficiaries must be reasonably numerous and unidentifiable.

Another important distinction is that the Rule Against Perpetuities does not apply to trusts that are entirely charitable. Moreover, if a charitable trust can no longer serve the purpose for which it was created, the court can apply the doctrine of *cy pres* and redirect the trust to a similar charity or purpose. The attorney general of the state also has the power to enforce a charitable trust but not a private trust.

D. RESTRAINTS ON ALIENATION

1. Restraints on Legal Interests

A direct restraint on alienation is a restriction on transferring property and may be void as against public policy. If the restraint is void, then the restraint is rejected, and the property can be alienated in violation of the void restraint. If the restraint is valid, then any attempt to alienate the property in violation of the restraint is null and void. Restatement (Second) of Property; Donative Transfers § 4.1.

a. Forms of restraint

1) Disabling restraint

A disabling restraint is a prohibition on the transfer of the property interest by its owner. Such a restraint is always void.

2) Forfeiture restraint

A forfeiture restraint effects the loss of property (i.e., the property is forfeited) if the interest owner attempts to transfer his interest. Such a restraint on a future interest or a life estate can be valid.

3) Promissory restraint

A promissory restraint is a promise by the property interest holder not to transfer the property interest. Such a restraint is enforceable by an injunction against the transferor/promisor to prevent the transfer or by a suit seeking damages from the transferor/promisor for having violated the promise. Such a restraint on a life estate can be valid.

b. Prohibited restraints

An absolute restraint on alienation of a fee simple is void. In addition, any restraint based on a person's race, ethnicity, or religion is not enforceable. Further, such discriminatory restraints are considered state actions and are forbidden by the Fourteenth Amendment. Moreover, the federal Fair Housing Act prohibits housing discrimination on the basis of race, color, religion, gender, disability, familial status, and national origin. Among the prohibited activities are refusing to rent or sell housing or setting different terms or conditions for the sale or rental of a dwelling on a prohibited basis. There are various exceptions, including an exemption for a residential sale by an owner and a lease of an owner-occupied dwelling with four or fewer units.

c. Permissible restraints

A restraint that is limited in time and purpose may be valid. In addition, a right of first refusal, which gives the holder of the right the opportunity to purchase the property interest if sold, is usually upheld, as are restrictions on the transfer of a lease (e.g., a prohibition on assignment). Other permissible restraints are those found in commercial transactions when the basis for the restraint is found in the parties' contractual obligations.

> **Compare restraints on use:** Unlike restraints on the transfer of legal property interests, restraints on the **use** of property (e.g., covenants) are generally permissible. Such indirect restraints on alienation are invalid only if they lack rational justification. Restatement (Third) of Servitudes §3.5.

2. Restraints on Equitable Interests

A restriction on the transferability of an equitable property interest (e.g., a beneficial property interest held in trust), such as a spendthrift clause, is valid.

V. MORTGAGES AND SECURITY INTERESTS

The owner of an interest in real property may convey or retain that interest as security for the payment of an obligation, usually a loan. The obligation typically takes the form of a promissory note, which sets out the terms of the transaction. This document reflects only the personal obligation of the debtor and need not be filed in order to enforce the mortgage. If the obligation is not repaid when due, then the holder of the security interest may sell the property and use the proceeds to satisfy the outstanding obligation.

The two main forms that a security interest may take are a mortgage and a deed of trust.

A. MORTGAGES

1. Mortgages Generally

A mortgage is an interest in real property that serves as security for an obligation. The obligation may be owed by the person who conveys the interest (i.e., the **mortgagor)** or a third party. The **mortgagee** is the person with the security interest in the real property, typically a bank.

> As a conveyance of an interest in real property, the mortgage must satisfy the Statute of Frauds.

2. Lien Theory versus Title Theory States

In a **majority** of the states, the mortgagor (borrower) is treated as the owner of the real property interest, and the mortgagee (lender) is treated as the holder of a lien on that interest. These states are referred to as "lien states." By contrast, in a **minority** of states, the mortgagee is treated as the owner of the real property interest, and the mortgagor possesses the right to regain ownership of the real property upon satisfaction of the obligation. These states are referred to as "title states."

a. Effect on joint tenancy

In a lien state, a mortgage interest is treated as a lien that does not affect a joint tenancy until foreclosure. In a title state, the joint tenancy is severed upon the granting of a mortgage, and the interest is converted into a tenancy in common. In either case, upon foreclosure, the mortgagee may only foreclose on the undivided tenancy in common interest of the mortgagor, and the interests of other co-tenants to the property are not affected.

B. MORTGAGE ALTERNATIVES

1. Deed of Trust

In some states, a deed of trust (or trust deed) is used in place of a mortgage. The borrower (landowner) delivers title to real property to a third-party trustee (typically the lender's lawyer) as security for the payment of the note to the beneficiary (lender), with the condition that the trustee re-conveys the title to the borrower upon payment of the note. If the borrower fails to pay the note (defaults), then the beneficiary instructs the trustee to sell the land to repay the note. When the property is transferred by trustee in violation of the trust, an equitable lien may be imposed on the transferred property in favor of the lender.

For most purposes, a deed of trust is treated the same as a mortgage. However, a primary reason for using a deed of trust instead of a mortgage is that while, upon default, a mortgagee-lender who conducts a non-judicial foreclosure sale cannot purchase the property at the sale, a beneficiary-lender of a deed of trust can purchase the property at a similar sale held by the trustee.

2. Installment Land Contract

An installment land contract (i.e., a contract for deed) is a contract whereby the seller retains title until the buyer makes the final payment under an installment payment plan. Traditionally, an installment land contract allowed the seller to keep all installment payments and retake possession if the buyer failed to make a single payment, even if the buyer had made almost all of the installment payments.

States vary in their methods to assist a buyer in default. Some states treat an installment land contract as a mortgage, requiring the seller to foreclose on the property to gain clear title. Other states offer the buyer the equitable right of redemption. Still others allow the seller to retain ownership of the property but require some form of restitution to the buyer.

3. Absolute Deed

An absolute deed (also known as a "deed of absolute sale") is free of all liens and encumbrances and is used to transfer unrestricted title to property. When there is an obligation created prior to or contemporaneously with this transfer, the grantor may prove that the transfer was not actually a sale but instead a disguised mortgage. If proven, a court treats the transfer as an equitable mortgage.

a. Evidentiary issues

The grantor must prove the existence of such an agreement by clear and convincing evidence. Parol evidence is admissible to establish the existence of such an agreement because the deed was not intended to be a complete integration of the parties' agreement. In addition, the Statute of Frauds does not prevent the introduction of oral evidence to explain or interpret the written deed (i.e., to show that the deed was subject to an agreement that the property serve as security for an obligation).

b. Grantee's sale to a bona fide purchaser

If the grantee sells the property to a bona fide purchaser, the grantor cannot recover the property from the bona fide purchaser. However, the grantor may be able to recover the difference between the value of the property and the amount of the outstanding obligation from the grantee.

4. Conditional sale and repurchase

When real property is sold and then leased back to the seller, usually for a long period of time with the option to repurchase the property, the transaction may constitute the creation of a security interest in the property, a disguised mortgage, rather than a sale-leaseback arrangement. Among the factors the court will take into account when determining the true character of the transaction are the equivalency of the lease payments to the fair market rental value of the property and the likelihood that the seller-lessee will exercise his right to repurchase the property at the end of the lease period.

C. TRANSFER

1. By the Mortgagor

The transfer by the mortgagor of mortgaged property can have significant ramifications for both the mortgagor and the transferee. Restatement (Third) of Property §§ 5.1–5.5.

a. Mortgagor's liability

Unless the mortgagee-lender agrees to release the mortgagor-borrower from liability for the loan, the mortgagor-borrower remains personally liable on the loan obligation after the transfer of the mortgaged property. If the transferee assumes the mortgage obligation, then the transferee as well as the mortgagor-borrower is personally liable to the mortgagee-lender to pay the loan obligation. In the event the mortgagor-borrower makes mortgage payments, she can immediately seek reimbursement from the transferee, since as between the mortgagor-borrower and the transferee, the transferee is primarily liable to the pay the mortgage obligation. However, if the mortgage obligation is unpaid, the lender may sue either the mortgagor-borrower or the transferee-buyer personally and if there is still a deficiency, sue the other. Restatement (Third) of Property: Mortgages, § 5.1.

1) Lender's modification or release of the transferee's obligation

As transferor, the original mortgagor-borrower is relieved of personal liability when the mortgagee-lender impairs the original mortgagor-borrower's right of recourse against the transferee by modifying the terms of the loan or releasing the transferee from personal liability on the obligation. For example, a complete release from liability granted by the mortgagee-lender to the transferee usually results in the discharge of the mortgagor-borrower's personal liability on the mortgage obligation. The traditional rule is that the original mortgagor-borrower is completely relieved of personal liability by a modification in the terms of the loan. Some states and the Restatement limit the relief to the amount that original mortgagor-borrower's right of recourse is impaired. Restatement (Third) of Property: Mortgages, § 5.3, cmt. b.

2) Lender's release or impairment of property subject to mortgage

The original mortgagor-borrower is also relieved of personal liability if the mortgagee-lender releases or impairs the property subject to the mortgage. Some states provide that a release completely discharges the mortgagor-borrower's personal liability. Other states and the Restatement provide that the mortgagor's personal liability is discharged only to the extent of the value of the property released. Restatement (Third) of Property: Mortgages, § 5.3, cmt. c.

Note: The reason that the mortgagor-borrower is "let off the hook" (i.e., released from personal liability to the mortgagee-lender) is that the mortgagee-lender's release of the mortgage eliminates the mortgagor-borrower's ability to be subrogated to the mortgagee-lender's mortgage interest. If the mortgagor-borrower were not released from personal liability, the mortgagor-borrower would remain liable to the mortgagee-lender, but would not have the protection of the mortgage in seeking to recoup from the transferee the amount paid to the mortgagee-lender.

3) Due-on-sale clause

Most mortgages contain a due-on-sale clause. This clause provides that, upon the transfer of mortgaged property, the lender has the option to demand immediate payment of the full amount of the outstanding obligation, including interest, unless the lender has given its written permission for the transfer. In exchange for this permission, the lender may increase the interest rate on the loan or demand an "assumption fee." Due-on-sale clauses are federally enforceable. 12 USC § 1701j–3.

Other transfers: Although labeled a "due-on-sale" clause, the clause typically covers any type of transfer (e.g., gift), and can be found in an installment sale contract as well as a mortgage. 12 CFR 191.5(b)(1)(i).

a) Residential property exception

Residential real property, which includes property containing fewer than five dwelling units, is not subject to federal enforcement of a due-on-sale clause with respect to a variety of transfers, including the automatic "transfer" of a joint tenancy interest upon the death of the borrower, a transfer by will or intestacy to a relative upon the death of the borrower, a transfer to the spouse or child of the borrower, a transfer to an ex-spouse due to a divorce, and a transfer to the borrower's living trust. 12 USC § 1701j–3(d).

4) Due-on-encumbrance clause

Similar to a due-on-sale clause, a due-on-encumbrance clause gives the lender the right to accelerate a mortgage obligation upon the mortgagor's obtaining a second mortgage or otherwise encumbering the property. A due-on-encumbrance clause is generally enforceable to the same extent as a due-on-sale clause. Restatement (Third) of Property: Mortgages, § 8.1, cmt. b.

b. Transferee's liability

1) Assuming a mortgage obligation—personal liability

If the transferee-buyer assumes the mortgage obligation, then the transferee-buyer, as well as the mortgagor-borrower, is personally liable to the lender to pay the mortgage obligation. If the mortgage obligation is unpaid, the lender may sue either the mortgagor-borrower or the transferee-buyer personally and if there is still a deficiency, sue the other.

Most jurisdictions do not require that the assumption agreement be in writing; if proven, an oral agreement is enforceable.

2) "Subject to" mortgage obligation—no personal liability

If the transferee-buyer takes title "subject to" an existing mortgage obligation, then upon default the transferee-buyer is not personally liable, but the property may be sold at a foreclosure sale to satisfy the outstanding mortgage loan obligation. If there a deficiency after distribution of the sale proceeds, only the transferor-seller is personally liable for it. If a deed is silent or ambiguous as to the transferee-buyer's liability, then the transferee-buyer is considered to have taken the property subject to the mortgage obligation. However, a minority of jurisdictions imply an assumption of the mortgage when the transferee-buyer pays the seller the difference between what the house was worth and the outstanding balance on the mortgage obligation. *Heid v. Vreeland*, 30 N.J. Eq. 591 (1879).

2. By the Mortgagee

a. Proper party to pay

If the promissory note given by the mortgagor-borrower is a negotiable instrument, then the mortgagor-borrower is generally obligated to pay the holder of the note. This is true even when the mortgagor-borrower does not have notice that the original mortgagee has transferred the note to a third party and mistakenly pays the original mortgagee. However, a promissory note given in connection with a mortgage may not be a negotiable instrument because the note does not contain the words of negotiability (i.e., "pay to the order of" or "pay to bearer") or payment is subject to the conditions that prevent negotiability. In such cases, the mortgagor may pay the original mortgagee until the mortgagor receives notice of the transfer. Restatement (Third) of Property: Mortgages § 5.5.

b. Method of transfer

If the promissory note is nonnegotiable, ownership of the note may be transferred by a separate document that assigns the mortgagor's rights to the transferee. If the promissory note is a negotiable instrument, it may be transferred only by negotiation, which may require not only delivery of the note, but also its indorsement.

c. Transfer of mortgage and note

The promissory note and the mortgage that serves as security for the note are typically transferred together.

1) Transfer of mortgage without note

Jurisdictions are split with regard to the effect of transferring a mortgage without the note. Because the note is the principal evidence of the debt, many states treat a transfer of the mortgage alone as void. Other jurisdictions, however, treat the note as having automatically been transferred along with the mortgage, unless the parties to the transfer agree otherwise.

2) Transfer of note without mortgage

When the note is transferred without the mortgage, the mortgage is treated as having been automatically transferred along with the note, unless the parties to the transfer agree otherwise. Although it is customary for the transferee to obtain and record a mortgage assignment, no separate written assignment of the mortgage is necessary for the transferee to be entitled to enforce the mortgage. Restatement (Third) of Property: Mortgages § 5.4.

D. PRE-FORECLOSURE RIGHTS AND DUTIES

1. Mortgagee's Right to Possession

Whether the mortgagee may take possession of the real property depends on the theory of title that the jurisdiction follows.

In a **lien theory state**, the mortgagee cannot take possession prior to foreclosure because the mortgagor is considered to be the owner of the real property until foreclosure.

In a **title theory state**, legal title is in the mortgagee until the mortgage has been fully satisfied. Thus, the mortgagee is theoretically entitled to take possession at any time, although the mortgagee is typically prohibited by the terms of the mortgage from taking possession of the property before default occurs. The mortgagee-in-possession can make repairs, take rent, prevent waste, and lease out vacant space. While in practice this may seem advantageous, few mortgagees take advantage of this right because of the liability risks involved. A mortgagee-in-possession assumes a duty to take reasonable care of the property, and she incurs liability as if she were the owner. Some mortgagees instead opt to have the court appoint a receiver to manage the property and intercept the rents prior to foreclosure.

A minority of jurisdictions follow the **intermediate title theory**, which in practice operates similar to the title theory. Under this theory, the mortgagor retains legal title until default, and, upon the mortgagor's default, it vests legal title in the mortgagee.

Regardless of the theory adhered to by a jurisdiction, the mortgagee may take possession of the real property if the mortgagor abandons the property.

2. Waste

A mortgagor in possession has a duty not to commit waste at least to the extent that the waste impairs the mortgagee's security. This duty exists even if the mortgagor is not otherwise in default.

3. Equity of Redemption

After default on the obligation, but **prior to** a foreclosure sale, the mortgagor may retain the property under the doctrine of equity of redemption by paying the amount of the loan obligation currently owed, which, if there is an acceleration clause (*see* E.1.a. Acceleration clause, *below*), can be the full amount of the unpaid loan obligation, plus any accrued interest. Many states recognize a statutory right of redemption that permits the mortgagor to reclaim the property after a foreclosure sale (*see* § V.E.3.a.1. Statutory right of redemption, *below*).

a. Deed in lieu of foreclosure

In lieu of foreclosure, a mortgagor may convey all interest in the property to the mortgagee ("deed in lieu of foreclosure"). This permits the mortgagee to take immediate possession of the property without any further legal formalities, but it requires the consent of both the mortgagor and the mortgagee. The mortgagee generally may reserve the right to pursue a deficiency as measured by the difference between the outstanding mortgage obligation and the fair market value of the property against the mortgagor, but the mortgagor may bring an equitable action to set aside the conveyance if it is not reasonable and fair.

b. Clogging the equity of redemption

A mortgagor may waive his right to redeem after the mortgage is executed in exchange for consideration. However, courts routinely reject attempts by the mortgagee to deny the mortgagor this right (i.e., to "clog" the equity of redemption) prior to default, such as by the inclusion of a waiver clause in the mortgage.

c. Redemption by others

In addition to being exercised by the mortgagor, the right of redemption may also be exercised by anyone whose right to mortgaged property stems from the mortgagor's interest in the property, such as an heir, a devisee, a purchaser, a donee, or a tenant, as well as a junior lienholder to whom the mortgagor has granted a second mortgage that is subordinate to the mortgage that is redeemed.

E. FORECLOSURE

1. Foreclosure Methods

A mortgagee may generally foreclose on a mortgage when the obligation to which the mortgage relates is in default. Typically, this occurs when the mortgagor fails to make timely loan payments.

a. Acceleration clause

Although a mortgagee may bring a foreclosure action whenever a mortgage obligation is in default, the mortgagee is entitled to collect only the amount of the obligation that is currently due and owing, unless the mortgage contains an acceleration clause. An acceleration clause provides that the full amount of the mortgage obligation becomes due upon default.

b. Notice of foreclosure

For a mortgagee to foreclose on a mortgage, she must give the mortgagor prior notice. In addition, if foreclosure is conducted by a judicially supervised sale, the mortgagee must give notice to the holders of any junior interest in the property. The mortgagee may join others who have an interest in the property (e.g., the holder of a senior mortgage) or who are liable on the debt (e.g., a guarantor) as proper, but not necessary, parties.

c. Foreclosure methods

1) Judicially supervised sale

All states permit a mortgagee to foreclose on a mortgage through a judicially supervised public sale of the mortgaged property. In about half of the states, this is the primary method of foreclosure and in some states, it is the only method permitted.

2) Privately supervised sale

More than half of the states also permit a mortgagee to foreclose on a mortgage through a privately conducted public sale of the mortgaged property when the mortgage contains a "power-of-sale" clause. This method is more common in states that recognize a deed of trust as the security instrument, and in such states, it is typically conducted by the trustee pursuant to the power-of-sale clause in the deed of trust. Typically, this method is faster and less expensive than a judicially supervised sale.

3) Strict foreclosure

In a very few states the strict foreclosure method is the primary method of foreclosure, although other states permit its use in certain situations. Under this method, the mortgagee brings an equity action for a court order requiring the mortgagor to pay the mortgage obligation within a specified time period. If the mortgagor does not pay within the time period, then the mortgagor forfeits his equity of redemption, and the mortgagee takes title to the property.

d. Timing of enforcement of note and foreclosure of mortgage

Most states permit the mortgagee to elect whether to bring an action to enforce the mortgage obligation (e.g., note) against the mortgagor-borrower personally or to initiate an action to foreclose on the mortgage. To the extent that the obligation is not satisfied by pursuing one type of action, the mortgagee may then be able to pursue the other enforcement action. A few states require that the action to foreclose on the mortgage and the action on the mortgage obligation be maintained as a single action.

2. Priority of Interests

If there is more than one interest (e.g., two or more mortgages) in the property being foreclosed, a valid foreclosure terminates any interest in the foreclosed property that is junior to the interest being foreclosed, but it has no effect on any senior interest.

In determining the priority of interests (i.e., whether an interest is junior or senior to another interest), the basic "first in time, first in right" rule is applied. However, this rule is subject to various exceptions.

a. Purchase-money mortgage exception

A purchase-money mortgage is a mortgage granted to (i) the seller of real property or (ii) a third-party lender, to the extent that the loan proceeds are used to acquire title to the real property or construct improvements on the real property if the mortgage is given as part of the same transaction in which title is acquired. A purchase-money mortgage has priority over mortgages and liens created by or that arose against the purchaser-mortgagor prior to the purchaser-mortgagor's acquisition of the property, whether or not recorded. This priority of a purchase-money mortgage generally exists with respect to a judgment lien against the purchaser-mortgagor that pre-dates the purchaser-mortgagor's acquisition of the property and an after-acquired property clause in a mortgage of other property granted by the purchaser-mortgagor prior to the purchaser-mortgagor's acquisition of the property in question. (*see* § V.E.2.f. After-acquired property, *below*). In addition, a purchase-money mortgage has priority over a vendor's lien, such as an equitable vendor's lien that arises when the seller of real property takes a promissory note for part of the purchase price but does not take a mortgage.

A seller's purchase-money mortgage generally has priority over a purchase-money mortgage given to a third-party lender by a buyer to aid the buyer in acquiring the property from the seller. The priority of third-party purchase-money mortgages is determined chronologically, subject to any other applicable exception. Restatement (Third) of Property: Mortgages §§ 7.2, 7.5.

b. Recording act exception

A mortgage, as an interest in property, is subject to the state's recording act. Consequently, a subsequent mortgage that satisfies the requirements of the applicable recording act has priority over an unrecorded prior mortgage. For example, in a notice jurisdiction, the mortgagee who receives her mortgage without knowledge of a prior unrecorded mortgage has priority over the holder of the unrecorded mortgage.

c. Subordination agreement between mortgagees

The holder of a prior mortgage can agree to subordinate his interest to the holder of a subsequent mortgage. This agreement is enforceable unless the mortgage is not sufficiently described or specified.

d. Mortgage modifications and replacements

A senior mortgagee who enters into an agreement with the mortgagor to modify the mortgage or the obligation it secures subordinates his interest to a junior mortgagee's interest to the extent that the modification is materially prejudicial to the junior mortgagee's interest. The senior mortgagee's interest otherwise remains superior to the junior mortgagee's interest. Similarly, when a senior mortgagee releases a mortgage and, as part of the same transaction, replaces it with a new mortgage, the new mortgage retains the same priority as the former mortgage, except to the extent that any change in the terms of the mortgage or the obligation it secures is materially prejudicial to the holder of a junior interest in the real estate. Restatement (Third) of Property: Mortgages § 7.3(a)(1), (b).

e. Future-advances mortgages

A **future-advances mortgage** is a mortgage given by a borrower in exchange for the right to receive money from the lender in the future. This type of mortgage is also known as a "line of credit." It is often used for home-equity, construction, business, and commercial loans, and it can provide for obligatory advances or optional advances. If advances are obligatory, the future-advances mortgage has priority with respect to amounts loaned both before and after the future-advances mortgagee has notice of a subsequent mortgage. If, however, the advances under a future-advances mortgage are optional, then a subsequent mortgage has priority over amounts loaned after the future-advances mortgagee has notice of the subsequent mortgage.

There is a split among the states as to whether actual notice is required or whether constructive notice is sufficient. In a majority of states, the mortgagee must have actual notice of a subsequent mortgage to lose priority for that loan amount. The reasoning is that the mortgagee should not be required to conduct a title search each time it disburses an amount on the loan. In a minority of states, however, constructive notice (i.e., record notice) is sufficient for the mortgagee to lose priority for later loan disbursements. In addition, the modern trend is to treat a mortgagee as having priority with respect to all future advances, including optional advances, over a subsequent mortgagee.

f. After-acquired property

A mortgagor may grant a mortgagee rights to property that the mortgagor acquires in the future. For the mortgagor to have such rights, the mortgage must clearly state that it applies to after-acquired property. A provision in a mortgage that the mortgage applies to "all my property" is not sufficient. In addition, to be enforceable against third parties, the mortgagee must properly record his interest in the property subsequently acquired by the mortgagor in the place where interests in that property must be recorded (e.g., the county in which the after-acquired property is located). Even when properly recorded, an interest in after-acquired property is junior to a purchase-money mortgage. Restatement (Third) of Property: Mortgages § 7.5.

3. Effect on Various Parties

a. Mortgagor

A foreclosure sale eliminates the mortgagor's interest in the property.

1) Statutory right of redemption

Many states permit the mortgagor to reclaim the property after a foreclosure sale. In these jurisdictions, during a fixed period of time (typically between three months and two years), the mortgagor has the right to compensate the party who purchased the property at the foreclosure sale and reclaim the property.

b. Purchaser of property

The purchaser of property at a foreclosure sale takes the property free and clear of any junior mortgage and subject to any senior mortgage. In addition, the purchaser may be subject to the mortgagor's statutory right of redemption.

c. Senior interest

The rights of the holder of a senior interest are generally not affected by a foreclosure sale.

d. Junior interests

All interests that are junior to the mortgage that is foreclosed are generally destroyed.

1) Omitted party

If the foreclosure is a judicial foreclosure, the holder of a junior interest must be given notice of the foreclosure and made a party to the foreclosure action. This provides the junior interest with an opportunity to redeem the property by paying off a senior interest. If the holder of a junior interest is not made party to the action, her interest is not affected by the foreclosure action.

If the foreclosure is a "power of sale" foreclosure, most states that recognize this form of foreclosure do not require the foreclosing mortgagee to give notice to the holder of a junior interest, even though the sale will result in the destruction of the junior interest. However, the holder of a junior interest (as well as the mortgagor) can challenge a "power of sale" foreclosure that does not comply with the statutory procedures for such sales. A failure to adhere to these procedures may result in the voiding of the sale, even if the challenger does not establish harm that results from the failure.

2) "Marshalling of assets"

Generally, a creditor whose debt is secured by a mortgage on multiple properties can elect which property to subject to a foreclosure sale. However, when a senior mortgage is foreclosed and the mortgage covers multiple properties, the holder of a junior mortgage on some but not all of these properties can petition the court to apply the equitable doctrine of **"marshalling of assets."** Under this doctrine, the holder of the senior mortgage may be compelled to first foreclose on the properties for which only that holder possesses a mortgage in order to protect the security interest of the holder of the junior mortgage, so long as it does not prejudice the interest of the holder of the senior mortgage or a third party. If there are multiple junior interests, then property subject to the more recently created interests is subject to foreclosure prior to property subject to the more remotely created interests (i.e., **the "inverse order rule"**).

4. **Distribution of Proceeds**

   a. **Generally**

   The proceeds from a foreclosure sale are applied first to the costs associated with the sale, second to the mortgage obligation being foreclosed, and third to the mortgage obligations owed to junior interest holders in the order of the priority of their interests. Any remainder is paid to the debtor-mortgagor.

   b. **Improvement to mortgaged property**

   A mortgage generally includes improvements made to the property. Consequently, in satisfaction of the mortgage obligation, a mortgagee is entitled to the proceeds from the sale of the property, including the amount attributable to an improvement of the property by the mortgagor. This right does not extend to an improvement made by a mortgagor's tenant, such as a trade fixture, to which the tenant has a superior right. (Note: If an improvement has been funded by a second mortgage, the second mortgagee may have rights in the property that are superior to the rights of the first mortgagee in the property.)

5. **Deficiency**

   After bringing a foreclosure action, the mortgagee is permitted by many states to bring a deficiency action against the mortgagor and/or any party who has assumed the mortgage if the foreclosure sale proceeds are insufficient to satisfy the mortgage obligation. Some states disallow this action when the mortgagee forecloses via a privately supervised foreclosure sale or when the mortgage is a purchase-money mortgage. In addition, in some states, the total amount that may be recovered by a mortgagee through the foreclosure sale and the deficiency action is limited to the fair market value of the property. In all states, if the mortgagee has granted the mortgagor a nonrecourse loan, then the mortgagor does not have personal liability for the loan and thus is not liable for any deficiency.

6. **Subrogation (Payment by a Third Party)**

   A person who pays off another person's mortgage obligation may become the owner of the obligation and the mortgage to the extent necessary to prevent unjust enrichment. Among the circumstances in which the equitable remedy of subrogation is appropriate is when the payor (i.e., the subrogee) is under a legal duty to pay the obligation, or when the payor does so to protect his own interest or on account of misrepresentation, mistake, duress, fraud, or undue influence. Restatement (Third) of Property: Mortgages § 7.6.

   a. **Amount paid**

   Subrogation is not permitted when the full obligation secured by the mortgage is not discharged. (Note: An obligation may be fully discharged even though the payor pays less than the face value of the obligation if the payor does so as a result of a negotiated settlement with the obligee.) In the case of a partial discharge, a payor who is a subordinate mortgagee may be able to add the amount paid to the balance of the subordinate mortgage and recover the amount upon foreclosure.

7. **Defenses**

   A mortgage is generally enforceable only to the extent that the underlying obligation is enforceable. A mortgage is subject to the same defenses as the underlying obligation secured by the mortgage (e.g., mistake, duress, failure of consideration, fraud, or lack of capacity). In addition, when the interest on the mortgage obligation violates state usury law, the lender will forfeit the interest, but generally not the principal due on the loan.

a. Transferee who assumes a mortgage

A donee who takes property that has been mortgaged is entitled to assert the donor's defenses against the mortgagee. However, a transferee who purchases real property and agrees to assume an existing mortgage obligation generally may not raise defenses that the mortgagor-transferor could have raised against enforcement of the mortgage obligation, such as statute of limitations, forgery, lack of capacity, or failure of consideration. Restatement (Third) of Property: Mortgages § 5.1, cmt. g.

b. Transferor's right to raise the transferee's defenses

In general, a mortgagor who becomes a surety with respect to a mortgage obligation upon the transfer of the property to a person who assumes that obligation is entitled to the benefit of any favorable modification of the obligation, such as a lower interest rate or an extension of time to pay (*see* § V.C.1.a. Mortgagor's liability, *supra*). The mortgagor-transferor may raise such a modification as a defense to the mortgagee's attempt to enforce the original terms of the mortgage obligation. However, the mortgagor-transferor is not entitled to raise defenses that are personal to the transferee, such as lack of capacity or a discharge in bankruptcy. Restatement (Third) of Property: Mortgages § 5.3, cmt. i.

F.   DISCHARGE

A mortgage obligation may be discharged by payment of the debt secured by the mortgage or by acceptance by the mortgagee of a deed in lieu of foreclosure. In addition, the doctrine of merger may be applied to eliminate a mortgage.

Generally, since a mortgage interest serves as security for an obligation to the mortgagee, the cancellation of the obligation results in the termination of the mortgage interest unless the parties agree otherwise. However, the mortgagee's mortgage interest may continue despite the cancellation of the mortgage obligation when there are other mortgages or liens on the property. Restatement (Third) of Property: Mortgages § 8.5, illus. 1.

1.   Mortgagor's Right of Prepayment

Traditionally, in the absence of a clause permitting a mortgagor to prepay a mortgage obligation, the mortgagor had no such right. Applying the "perfect tender in time" rule, the courts concluded that the lender had the right to insist upon performance specified in the loan agreement. Under the modern trend, the presumption is reversed, and prepayment, in part as well as in whole, is permitted unless the mortgage note contains a clause prohibiting prepayment. Restatement (Third) of Property: Mortgages § 6.1.

Generally, a lender may enforce a provision in a mortgage note that prohibits or restricts prepayment (i.e., a "lock-in" clause) or imposes a prepayment penalty unless the provision is unconscionable or enforcement would run counter to the duty of good faith and fair dealing. Restatement (Third) of Property: Mortgages § 6.2. However, if the mortgage is on a mortgagor-occupied residence, about half of the states require the lender to permit prepayment or place restrictions of various sorts on the imposition of a prepayment penalty (e.g., limitation on the interest rate of the loan, limitation on the amount or rate of the penalty, limitation of the penalty to the first few years of the mortgage). E.g., Iowa Code § 535.9. In addition, home mortgage notes issued by the Federal National Mortgage Association and the Federal Home Loan Mortgage Corporation specifically permit prepayment without a fee.

2. Merger

Under the doctrine of merger, when a mortgagee's interest in real property and the interest in the same property retained by the mortgagor are acquired by the same person, the mortgage is treated as having merged into a fee ownership of the property. Under this doctrine, the mortgagee, by accepting a deed in lieu of foreclosure, loses the ability to eliminate junior mortgages. However, most jurisdictions generally treat the mortgagee who receives a deed in lieu of foreclosure as reserving the right to foreclose on its mortgage and thereby eliminate any junior mortgages, finding either an express or implied intent by the mortgagee not to merge its mortgage interest with its title to the property. In contrast, some jurisdictions, adopting the Restatement position that the merger doctrine should not be applied to mortgages, nevertheless achieve a similar result when the mortgagee who takes a deed in lieu of foreclosure has actual knowledge of a junior mortgage. In such case, the mortgagee loses the right to foreclose on its mortgage, irrespective of the existence of an intent to merge. Restatement (Third) of Property: Mortgages § 8.5.

VI. DISPUTES ABOUT THE USE OF LAND

The most commonly tested disputes about the use of land revolve around use of another's land (by easement, profit, or license) or restriction of use of one's own land (by covenants running with the land or equitable servitude). Other disputes concern who has the right to own or possess land; ownership is decided by a quiet-title action, while possession (often between a landlord and a tenant) is decided by an action for ejectment or summary proceedings (e.g, forceable entry and detainer proceedings).

A. EASEMENTS

An easement is the right held by one person to make specific, limited use of land owned by another. The land that is subject to the easement is the **servient estate**, whereas the land that benefits from an easement on a servient estate is the **dominant estate**.

> **EXAM NOTE:** When a fact pattern involves the use of another's land, consider three questions:
>
> 1. Was an easement created?
>
> 2. If so, what is the scope of the easement?
>
> 3. Was the easement terminated?

1. Classification of Easements

Easements are either tied to the land (appurtenant) or are personal to the holder (in gross), and they will give the holder a right that is either affirmative (the right to do something) or negative (the right to prevent another from doing something).

a. Easements appurtenant

Easements are presumed to be appurtenant (i.e., tied to the land) unless there are clear facts to the contrary. The benefits of an easement must correspond directly to the use and enjoyment of the possessor of the dominant estate.

b. Easements in gross

An easement is in gross if it was granted to benefit a particular person (as opposed to the land).

Example: A owns lakefront property and grants B, who lives in a town across the lake, an easement to gain access to the lake at a certain point on A's property. A created an easement in gross because it benefits B, not any land owned by B.

c. Affirmative easements

Most easements are affirmative, giving the holder the right to make affirmative use of another's property (e.g., the right to cross another's land to access a highway).

d. Negative easements

A negative easement (or "restrictive covenant") prevents the owner from using land in particular ways in order to benefit the land of the holder of the easement. To be valid, a negative easement must be expressly created by a writing signed by the grantor, and it is typically recognized only in relation to restricting use of light, air, support, or stream water from an artificial flow.

Example: A conveys a lot adjacent to his own to B, with an agreement that no structure will be built that would obstruct the light and air of A's land. This is a negative easement of light and air because it deprives B from enjoying the property to the fullest extent. Negative easements are really restrictive covenants (see full discussion, *infra*).

2. Creation

a. Express easements

An express easement arises when it is affirmatively created by the parties in a writing that satisfies the Statute of Frauds.

1) By grant

An easement by grant is created when the owner of the servient estate grants another person an easement in the servient estate.

2) By reservation

An easement by reservation is created when the owner of the servient estate conveys the servient estate to another person but reserves an easement in that property for his own use and benefit. At common law, a grantor could not convey property but reserve an easement in the property for the use and benefit of a third party. The modern trend permits the reservation of an easement in a third party. Even in jurisdictions that continue to follow the common law, the reservation of an easement in a third party is often recognized when the third party made similar use of the land prior to its conveyance (i.e., a quasi-easement existed). Restatement (Third) of Property: Servitudes § 2.6(2).

b. Easements by necessity and implication

1) Easement by necessity

An easement by necessity is generally created only when property is virtually useless (e.g., landlocked) without the benefit of an easement across neighboring property. In addition, for an easement by necessity to be created, both the dominant and servient estates must have been under common ownership in the past. Also, the necessity must have arisen at the time that the property was severed and the two estates were created. However, unlike with an easement by implication, a quasi-easement need not have existed at the time that both estates were under common ownership (i.e., there need not be a showing of prior use). Restatement (Third) of Property: Servitudes § 2.15.

Example 1: B owns an undeveloped parcel of land, which B subdivides into two lots. B sells one of the lots to A and retains the other lot for himself. The only access to a public road from the lot purchased by A is through the lot retained by B. Even though the deed makes no mention of an easement across B's lot and there has not been a prior path from A's lot across B's lot to the public road, A has an easement by necessity across B's lot to the road.

In judging the existence of an easement by necessity, typically the property must be inaccessible without the easement. However, the existence of access involving other property does not preclude the creation of an easement by necessity when the owner of dominant estate does not have a legal right of access through the other property. *Noll v. Plosky*, 484 So. 2d 1345 (Fla. Dist. Ct. App. 1986).

Example 2: B owns an undeveloped parcel of land, which B subdivides into two lots. B sells one of the lots to A and retains the other lot for himself. B's lot abuts the only public road in the area, while A's lot does not have direct access to the road. However, A can purchase, for a reasonable price, an easement from C, the owner of another lot that adjoins A's lot and, like B's lot, has access to the public road. A has an easement by necessity across B's lot to the road because, while A has the opportunity to acquire access to public road, A does not have a legal right to access the public road through C's lot.

2) Easement by implication

If the owner of two parcels of land previously used one parcel to benefit the other, then the court may find that, upon the sale of the dominant parcel, the parties intended the easement to continue if the prior use was continuous, apparent (open and obvious), and reasonably necessary to the dominant land's use and enjoyment (as distinguished from an easement by necessity, which requires strict necessity).

a) Quasi-use

Because an owner cannot have an easement on his own land, the prior use is considered a "quasi-easement." The scope of an easement by implication is determined by the prior use. The scope can change over time if the change is reasonably foreseeable at the time of the conveyance.

b) Recorded plat

Easements may also be implied without an existing use in a conveyance of lots sold in a subdivision with reference to a recorded plat or map that details streets leading to lots. An easement may be implied from a subdivision map or plat, may be created through eminent domain, and may arise by actual or implied dedication. Individuals who buy lots have an implied easement to be able to get to their lots that does not expire even if a public easement held by the city or county is vacated in the future.

c. Easements by prescription

Easements can be obtained by prescription similarly to the way land can be acquired by adverse possession. There must be continuous, actual, open, and hostile use for a specific period (e.g., 10, 15, or 20 years). Unlike with adverse possession, the use need not be exclusive (such as a public easement to access a beach).

The scope of an easement by prescription is limited to the nature and extent of the adverse use.

d. Easements by estoppel

Good-faith, reasonable, detrimental reliance on permission by a servient estate holder to make a limited use of her property can create an easement by estoppel. Restatement (Third) of Property: Servitudes, §§ 2.9, 2.10.

Example: A allows B to use a road on A's land to gain access to B's land, and B builds his house with the road being its main access point, improving the road with pavement and foliage. Thereafter, A tells B that he can use the road only if B pays $500; A closes off the road when B refuses. B likely has an easement by estoppel because he relied on the ability to use the road when he built his house, and unjust enrichment may otherwise result.

Distinguish this example from an easement by prescription, which requires that the use be hostile (i.e., A does not give permission to B to use the road).

3. Transfer

a. Easement appurtenant

An easement appurtenant is transferred with the land to which it relates. Consequently, the benefit is transferred automatically with the transfer of the dominant estate, and the burden likewise is transferred automatically with the transfer of the servient estate.

b. Easement in gross

Traditionally, an easement in gross could not be transferred, but most courts now allow transfer if it is for commercial use or if the parties intended it to be transferable. However, like easements appurtenant, the burden of an easement in gross is transferred automatically with the transfer of the servient estate.

Whether a transferable easement in gross can be apportioned turns on whether the easement in gross is exclusive or non-exclusive. A non-exclusive easement may not be divided up, but an exclusive easement may be. However, the division of an exclusive easement in gross is subject to the "one stock" rule. Under this rule, the use that the transferees make of the easement collectively is limited by the use that the transferor made of the easement (i.e., his "stock").

4. Scope of Easement

a. Express easements

The scope of an express easement is defined in the first instance by its terms. If the terms are ambiguous, then courts look to the intent of the parties, which may be indicated by the post-creation conduct of the parties and what is reasonable in light of the easement's purpose. If the location of the easement is not specified, then the owner of the servient estate may fix the location, provided it is reasonable.

b. Other easements

The scope of an easement by necessity is determined by the extent of the necessity. The scope of an easement by implication is determined by the existing quasi-easement. The scope of an easement by prescription is limited to the nature and extent of the adverse use.

c. Change in easement

The owner of the servient estate may thwart a change in the scope of an express easement that conflicts with the terms of the easement. Otherwise, a change in the scope of an existing easement is tested under a reasonableness standard in light of the purpose of the easement.

5. Termination

In addition to terminating in accord with its express terms, an easement may also be terminated in the following ways.

a. Release

An easement can terminate by a writing that expressly releases the easement right and complies with the Statute of Frauds.

b. Merger

An easement is terminated if the owner of the dominant or servient estate acquires fee title to the other estate; the easement is said to "merge" into the title. The easement is not automatically revived on the separation of the property into the previous dominant and servient estates.

Note that the easement does not merge if the owner acquires less than fee title.

c. Severance

Any attempt to convey an appurtenant easement separate from the land it benefits terminates (or "severs") the easement.

d. Abandonment

An easement can be terminated if the owner of the easement acts in an affirmative way that shows a clear intent to relinquish the easement right.

Mere statements of intent without affirmative conduct are insufficient to constitute abandonment but may constitute estoppel (*see* § VI.A.5.g. Estoppel, *infra*). Mere nonuse of the easement is also not sufficient to extinguish the easement right.

Example: B is the owner of an easement across A's land for access to a beach. B does not like the beach and builds a brick wall across his land, blocking the entranceway to the easement. B's easement is terminated by abandonment.

e. End of necessity, destruction of related structure, and condemnation of estate

An easement by necessity terminates when the necessity ceases to exist. In addition, destruction of a structure on the servient estate by natural forces can terminate an easement if the easement is related to the structure (e.g., access to a lighthouse). Condemnation of the servient estate also terminates an easement. Note that some courts permit the holder of the easement to receive compensation because of the condemnation.

f. Prescription

If an easement holder fails to protect his easement against a trespasser for the statutory period, then his easement right may be terminated by prescription.

g. Estoppel

If the servient estate owner changes position to his detriment in reliance on statements or conduct of the easement holder that the easement is abandoned, then the easement holder may be estopped from asserting the easement.

h. Sale to a bona fide purchaser

If an **express easement** is granted but not recorded, then, depending on the applicable recording act, the easement may not be enforceable against a subsequent bona fide purchaser of the servient estate. The easement itself is not terminated, but rather cannot be enforced against the purchaser.

6. Duty to Maintain

The owner of the easement has the right as well as the duty to maintain the easement for its purpose unless the parties otherwise agree, and may be liable for damages caused to the servient estate for negligent or intentional violations of this duty, but is not strictly liable for any damage suffered by the servient estate from the use of the easement. If the easement is shared, the owner who maintains or repairs the easement may seek contribution from the other owners of the easement after adequate notice and an opportunity to participate in repair decisions. The owner of the servient estate also has an obligation to contribute to repair or maintenance of an easement if the servient estate owner uses the easement. Restatement (Third) of Property: Servitudes § 4.13 (2000).

7. Profit

A profit (also known as a profit à prendre) is a nonpossessory right to enter another's land and remove specific natural resources (such as oil, gas, minerals, timber, or game). Profits are created and analyzed similarly to easements, except that profits cannot be created by necessity.

Although a profit can be either exclusive or non-exclusive, most are construed as non-exclusive. If the profit is exclusive, then the holder of the profit has an unlimited and exclusive right to take the subject matter of the profit from the land. If the profit is non-exclusive, then the right to take the natural resource is either limited by quantity, time, or use, or it is shared with another. Exclusive rights may be assigned or otherwise transferred and apportioned, as long as the apportionment is not wholly inconsistent with the original agreement.

Non-exclusive rights can be assignable or otherwise transferred, but apportionment is not permitted when the burden on the servient estate is increased. Under the "one stock" rule, the transferees are limited to the amount of material taken by the transferor (i.e., his "stock"), and this quantity is divided up by transferees taking the profit.

8. License

As with an easement, a license is a nonpossessory right to use another's land for a specific purpose. Unlike an easement, a license is freely revocable unless coupled with an interest or detrimentally relied upon, in which case the license is irrevocable. An irrevocable license based on detrimental reliance is the functional equivalent of an easement by estoppel with one exception: an easement continues to bind successors to the servient estate while a license only binds the licensor. When the language of the permission is ambiguous, courts prefer to interpret the language as granting a license.

A license coupled with an interest occurs when, for example, a grantor creates a life estate for A with the remainder to B. During A's life tenancy, B has an irrevocable license to enter the land and inspect for waste, because of his future interest in the land.

A license may be created without consideration or a writing. Because no writing is required, a license is created when there is an oral attempt to create an easement or a written attempt otherwise fails due to the Statute of Frauds. If the licensee then expends money or otherwise detrimentally acts in reliance on the license, a court may recognize an easement by estoppel.

In addition to a specific revocation by the licensor, a license is revoked when the licensor dies or the servient estate is transferred. Usually, a license cannot be transferred by the licensee, and the attempt to do so results in the loss of the license.

Tickets to sporting stadiums, theaters, and other public venues are sometimes characterized as licenses in that the owner of the facility may revoke the ticketholder's right to be on the premises. However, if the owner does so, the owner may incur contractual liability to the ticketholder depending on the terms of the agreement between the two.

B. COVENANTS RUNNING WITH THE LAND

Unlike easements, profits, and licenses, which generally grant affirmative rights to use real property, real covenants and equitable servitudes restrict the right to use real property or impose obligations on the owners of real property. When damages are sought to enforce the covenant, the covenant is called a "real covenant." When an injunction is sought to enforce a covenant, it is called an "equitable servitude."

1. Real Covenants

While the enforceability of a covenant by the original parties to the covenant is governed by contract law, a covenant linked to real property may also be enforced by and against subsequent landowners as a matter of property law. Such a covenant is known as a "real covenant," i.e., a covenant that runs with the land.

EXAM NOTE: The requirements for a covenant to run with the land have been tested on nearly every MBE.

a. Requirements

The requirements discussed below are necessary for both the benefit and the burden of a covenant to run with the land, unless otherwise indicated.

1) Writing

For a covenant to be enforceable as a real covenant, it must first comply with the Statute of Frauds.

Note that if any covenants are contained in the deed itself, even if the successor in interest does not sign the deed, acceptance of the deed satisfies the Statute of Frauds as though the successor in interest had signed the covenants himself.

2) Intent

The parties must intend for the rights and duties to run with the land.

Look for either explicit language, such as "and his heirs and assigns," or implication from the totality of the document and circumstances.

3) Touch and concern

The covenant must "touch and concern the land," which generally means that the person seeking enforcement must establish that the benefit or burden affects both the promisee and the promisor as owners of land and not merely personally.

The modern trend shifts the burden to the person challenging the enforceability of the covenant. The covenant is presumed valid unless it is illegal, unconstitutional, contrary to public policy, imposes an unreasonable restraint on alienation or trade, or is unconscionable. Restatement (Third) of Property: Servitudes § 3.2.

a) Negative covenants

Negative covenants run with the land if they restrict the owner's use or enjoyment of the land (e.g., a covenant not to use the property for vacation rentals).

b) Affirmative covenants

Affirmative covenants run with the land if they require the owner to do something related to use and enjoyment of the land (e.g., a covenant to maintain a fence). Traditionally, a covenant to pay money was held not to touch and concern because it did not physically affect the land, but today such a covenant, which typically involves the payment of fees to a common-interest ownership community (e.g., a homeowners' or condominium association), is generally enforceable.

4) Notice—burden only

A purchaser without notice of a burdening covenant is not bound by it if protected by the recording act.

Remember that notice can be constructive (recorded in the chain of title) as well as actual (knowledge that the covenant exists).

5) Privity

a) Horizontal privity—burden only

For the burden to run, the original parties to the covenant must have privity of estate at the time the agreement creating the covenant is entered into. This means that there must be some shared property interest apart from the covenant itself. (Note: Horizontal privity is not required for the benefit to run.)

b) Vertical privity

"Vertical privity" refers to the relationship between the original party and the successor to the property interest. The burden of the covenant runs if the successor holds an estate of the same duration as the original party. The benefit of the covenant runs if the successor holds some portion of the property interest held by the original party. Consequently, a covenant granted by the holder of a fee simple interest cannot be enforced against a successor interest that holds only a life estate, but the life estate holder can enforce a covenant given to the holder of the fee simple interest.

Unlike an easement, a real covenant cannot be created by necessity, implication, prescription, or estoppel.

b. Specific types of covenants

There are certain burdens that come with their own specific problems. With **covenants not to compete**, although the burden of restricting land use touches and concerns the land, some courts have refused to permit the benefit to run with the land because the covenant does not affect the land's physical use. A **racially based covenant** that prevents an owner from transferring his property to another because of the transferee's race is never enforceable because to enforce it would violate the Fourteenth Amendment.

c. Remedy

As an action at law, the remedy for breach of a real covenant is damages.

2. Equitable Servitudes

Equitable servitudes are agreements about land use that are enforced at equity by injunction. The requirements for enforcement of an equitable servitude are not as stringent as those for enforcement of a real covenant.

a. Requirements

For a servitude to be enforced at equity, it meet the following requirements:

i)   It must be **in writing**;

ii) There must be **intent** for the restriction to be enforceable by and against successors;

iii) The servitude must **touch and concern** the land; and

iv) If the person against whom the servitude is to be enforced is a purchaser, he must have **notice** (whether actual, record, or inquiry notice) of the servitude.

Regarding the need for a writing (item i, *above*), there is an exception for an implied reciprocal servitude (*see* b. Implied reciprocal servitudes, *below*). The requirement of notice (item iv, *above*), which is based on the principle that the acquisition of legal title by an innocent purchaser defeats a prior equitable claim, is independent of the effect of the recording act on the enforcement of an equitable servitude.

> **EXAM NOTE:** When a party has established the existence of a real covenant entitling him to money damages, remember that the promise may also be enforced as an equitable servitude entitling the party to equitable relief. However, since an equitable servitude does not require privity, the reverse is not necessarily true.

b. Implied reciprocal servitudes

Implied reciprocal servitudes (also called "mutual rights of enforcement" and "reciprocal negative servitudes") arise typically in planned subdivisions. Most jurisdictions impose the following requirements to enforce an implied reciprocal servitude:

i)   There must be **intent to create** a servitude on all plots (i.e., a common scheme);

ii) The servitude must be **negative** (i.e., a promise to refrain from doing something); and

iii) The party against whom enforcement of the servitude is sought must have actual, record, or inquiry **notice**. Reciprocal negative covenants are implied from the common scheme.

Note that a writing is **not** required for an implied equitable servitude.

> **EXAM NOTE:** Implied reciprocal servitudes are typically tested in a situation involving an owner subdividing a large tract of land into smaller lots to create a common scheme of development by:
>
> i)   **Recording a map** showing the scheme;
>
> ii) **Telling purchasers** of the lots about the plan; or
>
> iii) Including a **common building restriction** in most of the lot deeds.

c. Remedy

The remedy for breach of an equitable servitude or an implied reciprocal servitude is an injunction.

d. Defenses

1) Changed circumstances

If a restriction (i.e., real covenant or equitable servitude) on a property no longer makes sense to enforce due to drastic changes in the surrounding area, the restriction may not be enforceable. A good indication that the neighborhood has changed is a change in zoning to permit what the covenant would deny.

Example: A small subdivision restricts lots to residential use. Forty years later, the subdivision is next to a major thoroughfare, and the land in the surrounding area is largely commercial and industrial. The restriction for residential use will likely be unenforceable on the theory that its value was lost with the drastic change of the neighborhood.

2) Laches

An unreasonable delay in pursuing equitable relief can give rise to an affirmative defense. To bar an equitable claim, the delay must be shown to have either worked to the defendant's disadvantage or warranted the presumption that the plaintiff has waived his right.

For plaintiff's delay to constitute a waiver, the plaintiff must have knowledge of his rights and an awareness of the facts giving rise to those rights. Actions by the defendant that prevent the plaintiff from having such knowledge and awareness, such as concealment or fraud, can result in the court refusing to recognize laches as a defense.

3) "Unclean hands"

A plaintiff who seeks equitable relief may be denied such relief when he himself has engaged in the same conduct of which he is complaining, in this circumstance, breached the same servitude or a closely related one. The plaintiff's misconduct is often characterized as "unclean hands." The plaintiff's breach must have been intentional or undertaken in bad faith, but it need not have caused direct injury to the defendant himself or his property. Previous inequitable conduct by the plaintiff that does not relate to the current claim does not prevent the plaintiff from asserting this defense.

4) Acquiescence

Equitable relief may be denied by a party's acquiescence in the other party's conduct. Since acquiescence is viewed as implied permission, acquiescence presupposes knowledge. There can be no acquiescence with regard to something about which a party lacks knowledge.

5) Estoppel

Equitable estoppel prevents a person who has induced reliance by another from benefiting from a change in his position at the expense of the other.

3. Transfer of Covenants, Equitable Servitudes

Covenants, equitable servitudes, and implied reciprocal servitudes create real property rights and obligations that are transferred along with the real property interest itself to a subsequent owner when the requirements discussed above at § VI.B.1. Real Covenants and § VI.B.2. Equitable Servitudes are met.

For a covenant or equitable servitude to be enforceable against a subsequent owner, the key often is whether that owner had **notice** of the covenant or servitude. However, notice is not required for the burden to run against a transferee who is not a bona fide purchaser.

4. Termination of Covenants, Equitable Servitudes

Covenants, equitable servitudes, and implied reciprocal servitudes terminate as easements do, upon written release, merger of title, abandonment, estoppel, condemnation, or sale to a bona fide purchaser who can assert the protection of a recording act.

5. Common-Interest Ownership Communities

A common-interest ownership community is a real estate development in which individually owned lots or units are burdened by a covenant that imposes an obligation to pay dues to an association that:

i) Provides services or facilities to the common property or to the individually owned property, or

ii) Enforces other covenants or easements that burden the property in the development or neighborhood.

The dues must be required regardless of use of the services or facilities or withdrawal from the association. Restatement (Third) of Property: Servitudes § 6.2.

a. Types

The two main types of common-interest ownership communities are residential communities with mandatory membership associations and condominiums. In addition, cooperatives, which involve leasehold property interests, are treated as a common-interest ownership community.

1) Property owners' associations

In general, a property owners' association is a common-interest ownership community only if the property owners are required as a consequence of their property ownership to belong to the association and pay dues to it.

A real estate development in which property owners are required to pay for the use of, or to contribute to the maintenance of, property held in common by the individual owners is also a common-interest ownership community, even though membership in the association itself is optional. Restatement (Third) of Property: Servitudes § 6.2, cmt. c.

2) Condominiums

Typically, a condominium is created pursuant to a state statute by filing a declaration (or master deed) and a plat with the real property recording office for the locality in which the condominium is located. The declaration, together with any bylaws, sets out the rights and obligations of the unit owners with respect to each other, and it fixes each owner's share of the condominium for the purposes of allocating expenses, taxes, and voting rights. The plat typically describes the physical boundaries of each unit and the common areas.

A condominium may contain solely residential or commercial units or a mixture of the two.

a) Condominium units

Condominium unit ownership is fee ownership. In a condominium, each unit owner typically owns the interior of his unit, including the interior surfaces of the common elements (e.g., walls, ceilings, and floors).

Each unit owner is responsible for the taxes, insurance, and maintenance expenses related to his unit, and, as owner of a fee interest in his unit, may mortgage that interest.

b) Common areas

Each unit owner also owns the common areas of the building (e.g., lobby, hallways, stairs, elevators, swimming pool) together with the other unit owners as tenants in common. A unit owner has the non-exclusive right to access and use the common areas, but, unlike other tenants in common, does not have the right of partition with respect to the common areas. Each unit owner's tenancy-in-common ownership of the common areas is inseparable from his ownership of the unit itself.

Each unit owner is assessed a fee for the maintenance expenses of the common areas that is paid to the association. In addition, each unit owner is allocated a portion of taxes attributable to the common areas, which is imposed directly on each unit owner by the taxing authority.

3) Cooperatives

Unlike a condominium, a cooperative typically consists of land and one or more buildings owned by a corporation that leases individual residential units (e.g., apartments) to its shareholders. A resident is a tenant who also owns one or more shares of stock in the corporation, and is prohibited from transferring her interest in the corporation separately from the lease.

Unlike a condominium, in which each owner is responsible for his own mortgage, a cooperative has a blanket mortgage. This mortgage generally has priority over occupancy leases. A default on the mortgage can result in foreclosure proceedings on the property, which can in turn terminate all leases. Each shareholder-tenant is assessed a fee that is paid to the association that represents a share of the taxes and maintenance expenses of the cooperative.

b. Governance

1) Declaration and other governing documents

The recorded document (or documents) that imposes the covenants and easements creating the common-interest ownership community is typically referred to as the "**declaration**." The declaration, together with other documents, such as the articles of incorporation, bylaws, and rules and regulations adopted by the association, serves to govern the operation of the association and determine the rights and obligations of the members of the common-interest ownership community. Collectively, these documents are known as the "**governing documents**." Because the declaration is ordinarily recorded before common-interest community members purchase their properties, greater weight is often given to the terms of the declaration than the terms of other governing documents that are not recorded. Restatement (Third) of Property: Servitudes § 6.2(5, 6), cmts. e, f.

2) Association

The **association** that is created to manage the affairs and property of a common-interest ownership community, including the enforcement of covenants and easements, may take various forms, such as an unincorporated association, trust, or partnership, but it is typically a corporation. Restatement (Third) of Property: Servitudes § 6.2(3), cmt. c.

3) Board

Regardless of the legal form, the association is typically governed by a **board**. Unless a statute or a governing document provides otherwise, the board exercises the powers of the common-interest ownership community. The board is elected by the members of the association, who are the owners of the individual lots, units, or leasehold interests. The board may maintain day-to-day control over the maintenance of the property or may employ a manager to do so. Restatement (Third) of Property: Servitudes § 6.16. Members generally have the right to vote in elections for the board of directors and on other matters properly presented to the members, to attend and participate in meetings of the members, and to stand for election to the board of directors. Restatement (Third) of Property: Servitudes § 6.18.

4) Developer

Unless exempt by statute, the developer of a common-interest ownership community has a duty to create an association to manage the common property and enforce the servitudes. Unless fixed by statute, which is often the case, after a reasonable time, the developer has a duty to transfer the common property to the association and to turn over control of the association to the members other than the developer. Factors such as the percentage of units or lots that have been sold, the interval since the first unit or lot was sold, and the level of the developer's construction and marketing activities are relevant in determining a reasonable time. Restatement (Third) of Property: Servitudes § 6.19(1, 2).

Once a developer has relinquished control, the association has the power to terminate without penalty any contract or lease between the association and the developer or an affiliate of the developer.

In addition, the association can terminate any contract or agreement for management or maintenance services, any lease of recreational or parking facilities, or any other contract or lease that was not bona fide or was unconscionable to the members other than the developer at the time it was entered into. Restatement (Third) of Property: Servitudes § 6.19(3).

Federal law also provides for the cancellation of any contract for a period of more than three years for the operation, maintenance, or management of the property that is between the unit owners or association and the developer (or an affiliate) that was entered into while the developer or affiliate had control of the association. The unit owners generally have a two-year window after the association gains control in which to vote to terminate the contract, and they must do so by a two-thirds vote of all unit owners other than the developer or affiliate. The federal law applies only to condominiums and cooperatives that have been created by conversion of existing residential rental property. 15 U.S.C. § 3607.

The developer may not use the power to amend or modify the declaration in a way that would materially change the character of the development or the burdens on the existing community members unless the declaration fairly apprises purchasers that the power could be used for the kind of change proposed. Restatement (Third) of Property: Servitudes § 6.21.

c. Powers of the community

A common-interest ownership community, typically acting through its board, has the powers reasonably necessary to manage the common property, administer the covenants, and carry out other functions set out in the governing documents or granted by statute. Restatement (Third) of Property: Servitudes § 6.4. Included are the following powers to the extent not limited or prohibited by the governing documents or statute.

1) Levy assessments and charge fees

The community has the power to levy assessments against individually owned property and charge reasonable fees for services or for the use of common property. This power tends to be specifically granted by statute or by covenants in the declaration and is enforceable without regard to common-law rules regarding privity or the relationship of these covenants to ownership of the land (i.e., "touch and concern" requirements).

The assessments may be allocated among the individually owned properties on any reasonable basis and are secured by a lien against those properties. An assessment generally survives a foreclosure sale and is not terminated by a tax sale or a sale in bankruptcy proceedings. An assessment may be invalid if the board fails to comply with required procedures, but a community member is not entitled to withhold payment of assessments to offset a default by the association in fulfilling its duties to the member or to use an agreement with a developer as a defense to nonpayment of the assessment. Restatement (Third) of Property: Servitudes § 6.5(1), (2), cmts. a, e.

2) Manage, acquire, and improve common property

The community has the power to manage and protect common property, including making substantial alterations, improvements, and additions to common property. Restatement (Third) of Property: Servitudes § 6.6.

3) Adopt rules governing use of property

Unless limited by statute or the governing documents, the community has the implied power to adopt reasonable rules to govern the use of common property, and the use of individually owned property to protect the common property. In addition, when the declaration grants a general power to adopt rules, the community has the power to adopt reasonable rules designed to protect a community member from unreasonable interference in the enjoyment of her individual property, as well as to protect her enjoyment of the common property against interference caused by another's use of other individually owned property. In determining the validity of a rule, the primary test is whether the regulation is reasonably related to furthering a legitimate purpose of the association. Unless specifically authorized by the declaration, the community does not have the power to adopt other rules that restrict the use or occupancy of, or behavior within, individually owned property. Restatement (Third) of Property: Servitudes § 6.7.

> **Contrast with declaration:** The restrictions imposed by the declaration are not subject to a reasonableness requirement. These restrictions are valid unless illegal, unconstitutional, or against public policy.

> **Design control:** Unless authorized by statute or the governing documents, which frequently is the case, a community may **not** impose restrictions on the structures or landscaping that it places on individually owned property, or on the design, materials, colors, or plants that may be used. Restatement (Third) of Property: Servitudes § 6.9.

4) Enforce governing documents and rules

The community has the power to enforce governing documents, adopted rules and regulations, and assessments and fees, judicially and extrajudicially. To encourage compliance, the community may adopt reasonable rules and procedures, such as:

i) Imposing fines, penalties, and late fees;

ii) Withdrawing privileges to use common recreational or social facilities;

iii) Requiring prior submission of plans for projects (e.g., construction) to ensure compliance with existing restrictions;

iv) Conducting reasonable inspections of property for covenant violations, if there is a reasonable belief that such violations exist; and

v) Denying voting privileges or board positions to those not current with assessment payments.

Restatement (Third) of Property: Servitudes § 6.8, cmt. b.

5) Litigate in its own name

The association has the power to litigate or to be involved in administrative proceedings in its own name on behalf of itself or on behalf of members in matters affecting the community. Restatement (Third) of Property: Servitudes § 6.11.

6) Amend the declaration

Members may amend the declaration, except as expressly limited by a statute or the declaration. Restatement (Third) of Property: Servitudes § 6.10.

d. Duties associated with the community

1) Duties of the community to members

A common-interest ownership community has the following duties to its members:

   i) To use ordinary care and prudence in managing the property and financial affairs of the community that are subject to its control;

   ii) To treat members fairly;

   iii) To act reasonably in the exercise of its discretionary powers, including rulemaking, enforcement, and design-control powers; and

   iv) To provide members with reasonable access to information about the association, the common property, and the financial affairs of the association.

A change in an association rule triggered by changed circumstances may not be applied retroactively if it would be impractical or cause substantial hardship to do so.

A member who challenges an action of the association has the burden of proving a breach of duty by the association. In addition, unless the breach involves ultra vires action by the association, the member must prove that the breach has caused or threatens to cause injury to the member individually, or to the interests of the community. Restatement (Third) of Property: Servitudes § 6.13.

2) Duties of directors and officers of an association

The members of the board (e.g., directors) and officers of the association, who often serve without compensation, have a duty to act in good faith, to act in compliance with the law and the governing documents, to deal fairly with the association and its members, and to use ordinary care and prudence in performing their functions. The degree of care required is that of an ordinary, reasonable director of a common-interest ownership community. Many courts apply the business-judgment rule to insulate a director or an officer from liability for an honest but mistaken business decision. Restatement (Third) of Property: Servitudes § 6.14, cmt. c.

3) Liability of members for association torts

Members are not jointly and severally liable for torts that occur on or that are caused by the commonly held property. They are liable only for their proportionate share of the association's tort liability as determined by their share of liability for common expenses. Restatement (Third) of Property: Servitudes § 6.15.

C. FIXTURES

A fixture is tangible personal property (i.e., chattel) that is attached to real property in such a manner that it is treated as part of the real property when determining its ownership. (Note: By contrast, accessions are goods that are attached to other goods rather than real property, such as a radio installed in a car. Accessions are governed by Article 9 of the Uniform Commercial Code.) A trade fixture is chattel used in a trade or business that is attached to real property, such as a display counter in a retail store or a stove in a restaurant.

1. **Structures and Items Incorporated Into Structures**

   Structures built on real property (e.g., walls, dams) and materials incorporated into a structure (e.g., bricks used in making a wall) become part of the realty. The owner of the real property is generally also the owner of the structure on the real property (e.g., an improvement), including any materials used in constructing the structure. Once incorporated into the structure, such materials become an integral part of the real property and are not subject to a separate security interest. UCC § 9-334(a).

2. **Attachment of Chattel**

   The fee simple owner of real property is free, subject to governmental land-use restrictions, to make improvements to the real property, including fixtures. For the holder of a life estate or a tenant, the right to make improvements to real property (ameliorative waste) is somewhat circumscribed. (*See* § I.A.4.d.3. Ameliorative waste, *supra*, regarding life estate holders, and § II.B.2. Duty to Avoid Waste, *supra*, regarding tenants.)

3. **Removal of Chattel**

   a. **Fee simple owner of real property**

      A fee simple owner of real property typically intends for the chattel to become a fixture by attaching chattel to real property. Such intent is judged by applying an objective, reasonable person standard that examines such factors as the importance of the chattel to the real property, whether the chattel was specially designed for use on the real property, and the amount of damage to the real property that removal of the chattel would cause.

      When the chattel is a fixture, the buyer of the real property is generally entitled to the chattel unless the seller reserves the right to remove the fixture in the contract of sale. Similarly, the mortgagee is entitled to the chattel upon foreclosure of the mortgage unless the mortgage provides otherwise.

   b. **Other possessors of real property**

      1) **Permissive removal of fixtures**

         Absent an agreement to the contrary, a non-freehold tenant, such as a tenant under a tenancy for years or a periodic tenancy, can remove a fixture that the tenant has attached to the leased property if (i) the leased property can be and is restored to its former condition after the removal, and (ii) the removal and restoration is made within a reasonable time. If the leased premises cannot be restored to its former condition, then the tenant can remove the fixture only with the consent of the landlord. This rule generally applies to commercial tenants and the removal of trade fixtures, as well as to residential tenants and the removal of personal items, such as bookshelves attached to the wall. Restatement (Second) of Property: Landlord and Tenant § 12.2(4), (5).

         A licensee and a life tenant are generally also subject to this rule.

         A reasonable time for removal generally does not extend beyond the termination of the lease, but it may do so when (i) the termination is not due to a breach by the tenant, and (ii) the date of termination is not foreseeable by the tenant sufficiently far enough in advance to permit removal before the termination of the lease or unless equitable factors (such as illness of the tenant) justify an extension. Restatement (Second) of Property: Landlord and Tenant § 12.3.

2) Required removal of fixtures

In general, a tenant who has made permitted alterations in the premises, including the installation of fixtures, does not have to restore the property to its original condition unless the lease specifically requires such action. Therefore, unless the lease provides otherwise, the tenant cannot be required to remove fixtures that do not constitute a breach of the lease. 52A C.J.S. Landlord and Tenant § 884 (2005); *see Wilder Cos., Ltd. v. Cal. Pizza Kitchen, Inc.*, 32 Mass. L. Rep. 505 (2015).

c. Trespassers

Under common law, a trespasser (such as a holdover tenant) is prohibited from removing a fixture attached to the land. Many jurisdictions now allow a trespasser to remove a fixture that was attached in good faith or at least to recover the value added to the property by the improvement.

d. Sale of fixtures by the property owner

A contract for the sale of a structure or its materials is a contract for the sale of goods governed by the UCC when the structure or material is to be severed by the seller. A contract for the sale of other things that are attached to real property and are capable of severance without material harm to the real property is a contract for the sale of goods regardless of whether the seller or buyer effects the severance. UCC § 2-107(1), (2).

D. EMBLEMENTS (CROPS)

Fructus industriales and *fructus naturales* are two types of crops that, with some exceptions, are conveyed along with the land. *Fructus industriales* are produced through cultivation and are considered personalty. *Fructus naturales* are perennial; they do not require planting because they are produced by nature alone. Title to *fructus naturales* passes automatically with the land because this crop is considered real property.

1. Conveyance of Crops

Generally, both *fructus naturales* and *fructus industriales* are conveyed along with the land because the owner of the land is presumed to be the owner of both types of crops. Because this presumption is based on the intent of the parties, a contrary intent may be shown to rebut the presumption.

2. Exceptions

Harvested crops, or crops that have been severed from the land, are not conveyed with the land. Thus, the prior owner can remove the crops and has the right to reenter the land.

Some courts also treat ripened *fructus industriales* as being constructively severed from the land because they no longer draw sustenance from the soil. Thus, in some jurisdictions, these crops are not conveyed with the land.

When crops are planted by a tenant, if the tenant's lease is for an uncertain duration and the lease is terminated through no fault of the tenant, then the tenant has a right to reenter the land to remove, harvest, and cultivate crops planted prior to the termination of his tenancy. This "doctrine of emblements" applies unless there is a provision to the contrary in the lease, or the one who planted the crops is a trespasser. However, adverse possessors who plant under a claim of right are entitled to the same rights as tenants.

E.   GOVERNMENTAL REGULATION OF LAND—ZONING

Zoning is governmental regulation of land use.

1.   Authority

a.   Federal authority

There is no specific federal constitutional authority for Congress to pass zoning legislation, or for other federal agencies or entities to promulgate zoning rules and regulations. Instead, the federal government is limited to zoning statutes and regulations that are authorized by its exercise of another power, such as its Article I, Section 8 power over the District of Columbia or its Article IV, Section 3 power over federal lands.

b.   State authority

Each state, pursuant to its police power, can enact laws for the general welfare (e.g., health, safety, morals), including zoning laws that regulate land use. States have mostly delegated this power to local government entities.

c.   Local authority

Almost all states currently have in force a version of the Standard State Zoning Enabling Act, which was drafted by the U.S. Department of Commerce in the 1920s. The enabling act grants local governments the power to enact zoning and other land-use ordinances. Both the state's power to enact zoning laws and the state's ability to delegate that power to the local governments have withstood constitutional challenges based on the Fourteenth Amendment's Substantive Due Process and Equal Protection Clauses. *Euclid v. Ambler Realty Co.*, 272 U.S. 365 (1926).

1)   Lack of authority

A local zoning ordinance that is unauthorized or that exceeds the authority possessed by the local government can be challenged as ultra vires. Such an ordinance is void. In most states, while the state may permit a local government entity to adopt more stringent regulations than those imposed by the state, state statutes or regulations may instead preempt a local zoning ordinance. *E.g., Lakeside Lodge v. Town of New London*, 960 A.2d 1268 (N.H. 2008). In some states, local governments (e.g., municipalities) are recognized as possessing the power of home rule. *E.g.*, Ohio Const. art. XVIII, § 3. In such states, the local government has broader authority over local zoning.

2)   Irrational or arbitrary zoning

A local zoning ordinance must also be rationally related to a legitimate governmental purpose. An ordinance that is irrational or arbitrary, either on its face or as applied to particular property, may be struck down. *Euclid v. Ambler Realty Co., supra*.

3)   Referendum zoning

Typically, zoning rules are promulgated by an elected, local government entity (e.g., city council, board of supervisors). Zoning imposed by popular vote (i.e., referendum zoning) rather than a local government body does not violate the Due Process Clause of the Fourteenth Amendment. *Eastlake v. Forest City Enters., Inc.*, 426 U.S. 668 (1976) (any change in proposed land use agreed to by the city council had to be approved in a referendum by a 55 percent vote). Zoning by referendum does not violate substantive due process under the U.S. Constitution, even if the local governmental decision is characterized as an administrative rather than legislative act.

2. Types of Zoning Laws

Traditionally, zoning laws have focused on the property's use. The three primary categories of use have been residential, commercial, and industrial, with subdivisions within each category (e.g., single-family residential, multi-family residential). Traditionally, zoning laws have been based on cumulative zoning, with residential uses being permitted in all zones, commercial uses limited to some zones, and industrial uses limited to the fewest zones. Alternatively, zoning laws have adopted mutually exclusive zoning in which only one or more types of use is permitted within each zone. Under this type of zoning, residential use is not necessarily permitted in all zones.

Zoning laws have also imposed restrictions on the development of property apart from its use (e.g., building setback and height restrictions, or density regulations, such as restriction on the minimum size or number of dwellings on a lot).

Zoning laws may also address special concerns, such as environmental protection, historical preservation, and aesthetics. Although zoning for these purposes was initially subject to challenge as beyond the police power of the government, such zoning is now widely regarded as a proper exercise of that power. *E.g., Penn Cent. Transp. Co. v. New York City*, 438 U.S. 104 (1978) (a New York City landmark law that prohibited the construction of an office tower on Grand Central Terminal was upheld).

3. Challenges to Restrictive Zoning

A zoning ordinance by its very nature subjects some property owners to different restrictions than other property owners. These restrictions may run afoul of various constitutional and statutory protections.

a. Fifth Amendment Takings Clause

Zoning regulations typically do not rise to the level of a taking that requires compensation of the adversely affected property owners. However, if a regulation results in the elimination of any economically viable use of real property, a taking may occur. For an extended discussion of constitutional restrictions on regulatory takings, see the Themis Constitutional Law Outline § XV. Takings Clause.

b. Fourteenth Amendment Substantive Due Process

Unless a fundamental right has been violated, a Fourteenth Amendment substantive due process challenge to a zoning ordinance need only satisfy the rational-basis test (i.e., a rational relationship to a legitimate governmental interest). The right to housing is not a fundamental right. *Belle Terre v. Boraas*, 416 U.S. 1, 7 (1974) (a zoning ordinance that restricted land use to single-family dwellings and defined "family" as excluding more than two unrelated individuals was upheld); *Lindsey v. Normet*, 405 U.S. 56, 74 (1972) (expedited eviction procedures for a tenant's failure to pay rent were subject to the rational-basis test). However, the right of family members to live together is a fundamental right. *Moore v. E. Cleveland*, 431 U.S. 494 (1977) (an ordinance that prevented second-generation family members such as grandparents and grandchildren from living together was struck down).

c. Fourteenth Amendment Equal Protection Clause

A zoning ordinance that discriminates against a suspect class (e.g., race, national origin) is subject to strict scrutiny. However, for the challenger to establish discrimination, the ordinance must have a discriminatory purpose or intent; it is not sufficient for a challenger to show a discriminatory effect. *Vill. of Arlington Heights v. Metro. Hous. Dev. Corp.*, 429 U.S. 252 (1977) (denial of a rezoning request to permit multiple-family, subsidized housing was sustained absent a showing of discriminatory purpose or intent).

Although persons who are disabled do not constitute a quasi-suspect class, the requirement that a group home for mentally disabled persons obtain a special-use permit when a similar permit was not required of other multiple-resident dwellings lacked a rational relationship to a legitimate purpose. *City of Cleburne v. Cleburne Living Ctr.*, 473 U.S. 432 (1985).

d. First Amendment Free Speech Clause

A zoning ordinance that restricts the location of adult entertainment businesses but does not outright ban such businesses does not violate the First Amendment's Free Speech Clause. The government has a substantial interest in regulating the secondary effects that result from the operation of these businesses, such as increased crime. *Renton v. Playtime Theatres*, 475 U.S. 41 (1986). By contrast, an ordinance that prohibited a resident from displaying a sign with a political message in her front yard violated the First Amendment's Free Speech Clause. *City of Ladue v. Gilleo*, 512 U.S. 43 (1994).

e. Federal Fair Housing Act

The federal Fair Housing Act (FHA) prohibits discrimination on the basis of race, color, religion, national origin, sex, disability, and familial status. *See* § I.D.1. Fair Housing and Discrimination, *supra*.

f. Federal Religious Land Use and Institutionalized Persons Act

The federal Religious Land Use and Institutionalized Persons Act prohibits a land-use regulation that imposes a substantial burden on the exercise of religion unless the government proves that the burden is in furtherance of a compelling governmental interest and is the least-restrictive means of furthering that interest. In addition, this Act prohibits a land-use regulation that discriminates against a religious assembly or institution, totally excludes religious assemblies from a jurisdiction, or unreasonably limits religious assemblies, institutions, or structures within a jurisdiction. 42 U.S.C. § 2000cc.

g. State constitutional and statutory challenges

A state constitution may provide a property owner with greater protection than the federal constitution does. In addition, a property owner may challenge a zoning ordinance for its failure to conform to any state statutory protections.

Example: New Jersey prohibits zoning that precludes housing for moderate- and low-income individuals as a violation of the state due process and equal protection constitutional provisions. A locality is required to provide its fair share of the housing needs of the region. *S. Burlington Cty. NAACP v. Mt. Laurel (Mt. Laurel I)*, 336 A.2d 713 (1975); *S. Burlington Cty. NAACP v. Mt. Laurel (Mt. Laurel II)*, 510 A.2d 612 (1986).

4. Treatment of Existing Nonconforming Property

When a zoning ordinance is enacted or modified, there are often properties within a zone that do not conform to the requirements for that zone (i.e., a nonconforming use). A zoning ordinance must generally make provision for property with an existing nonconforming use. *See*, Mass. Laws. ch. 40A, § 6; *see Nectow v. City of Cambridge*, 277 U.S. 183 (1928) (a zoning ordinance that restricted property to residential uses violated substantive due process with respect to property that, when the zoning ordinance was adopted, was under contract to be sold to a buyer who planned to use the property for nonresidential purposes). A zoning ordinance that permits an existing nonconforming use of property to continue is sometimes said to have "grandfathered" the nonconforming use.

a. Time for testing

Unless the ordinance provides otherwise, the time for testing whether the nonconforming use is protected by a grandfather provision is the date that the zoning ordinance (or its modification) takes effect.

1) Vested right

In determining whether a property owner has acquired a vested right in the nonconforming use, most courts require that, at the time that the zoning ordinance takes effect, the property owner must, in good faith, have secured any necessary permit from the proper local authority (e.g., a building permit) and also have made substantial progress toward achieving the nonconforming use. In a few states, securing a permit by itself is sufficient.

2) Zoning estoppel

Some states also recognize the concept of zoning estoppel. A local government entity is estopped from exercising its zoning power when a property owner, relying in good faith on the entity's conduct, has substantially changed its position, such as by incurring significant expenses and obligations, so that it is unjust to deny the property owner the right to use his property in a manner that conflicts with the zoning ordinance. Some states limit zoning estoppel to situations in which the local government entity acts in bad faith, such as when a building permit is issued and then a zoning ordinance is specifically enacted to preclude the property owner from erecting or finishing the building for which the permit was granted.

b. Time limit on nonconformity

Most states permit the imposition of a reasonable time limit on the existence of the nonconformity, after which the nonconformity must cease. This type of limitation is often characterized as an **amortization ordinance** because it is based in part on amortizing the property owner's investment over time. In assessing the reasonableness of an amortization period, both the burden placed on the property owner and the benefit to the public are taken into account. *AVR, Inc. v. City of St. Louis Park*, 585 N.W.2d 411 (Minn. Ct. App. 1998); *Cf. Tahoe Reg'l Planning Agency v. King*, 233 Cal. App. 3d 1365 (1991).

The ordinance may set a specific time period for different classes of property or may establish criteria that a designated officer or entity is to apply on a case-by-case basis to determine the appropriate amortization period. Some states do not permit the imposition of a time limit on an existing nonconformity, finding it an impermissible taking of private property. *Cf. Pa. Nw. Distribs. v. Zoning Hearing Bd.*, 526 Pa. 186 (1991).

c. Subsequent events

1) Expansion of the nonconforming use

Generally, a property owner whose nonconforming use has been grandfathered is not entitled to subsequently increase the nonconforming use, such as by enlarging a building that houses a nonconforming use or acquiring and developing adjacent property in accord with the nonconforming use. However, the owner may be permitted to increase the frequency of the nonconforming use to upgrade the means to accomplish the nonconforming use, so long as the nature and character of the use does not constitute a substantial change. *Trip Assocs. v. Mayor & City Council*, 898 A.2d 449 (Md. 2006) (an increase in the number of nights that adult entertainment was presented at a club was allowed); *Union Quarries, Inc. v. Bd. of Cty. Comm'rs*, 478 P.2d 181 (Kan. 1970) (use of modern equipment in the operation of a rock quarry was permitted). Similarly, repair of an existing structure is generally permitted. *Granger v. Bd. of Adjustment*, 44 N.W.2d 399 (Iowa 1950).

2) Change to another use

Generally, a property owner whose nonconforming use has been grandfathered is not entitled to switch to another nonconforming use.

3) Failure to register the nonconforming use

A zoning ordinance may require the property owner who has the right to use the property in a nonconforming manner to register that nonconforming use with the local zoning entity. Failure to do so can result in the loss of this right. *Bd. of Zoning Appeals v. Leisz*, 702 N.E.2d 1026 (Ind. 1998).

4) Termination of a nonconformity

a) Voluntary

A property owner whose nonconforming use has been grandfathered may lose the right to use the property in that manner if the owner abandons the nonconforming use. Most states require both a voluntary cessation of the nonconforming use and an intent to abandon such use. *E.g., City of Univ. Place v. McGuire*, 30 P.3d 453 (Wash. 2001). Some states provide that the nonconforming use right terminates after a specific time period of nonuse (e.g., six months), regardless of intent. *Purich v. Draper Props.*, 912 A.2d 598 (Md. 2006).

b) Involuntary

A property owner whose nonconforming use has been grandfathered may suffer termination of the nonconforming use due to natural forces (e.g., fire, flood). Although involuntary termination of a nonconforming use does not constitute abandonment, the zoning ordinance may deny the property owner the right to resume the nonconforming use after an involuntary termination. *State ex rel. Brizes v. De Pledge*, 162 N.E.2d 234 (Ohio Ct. App. 1958).

5) Transfer of nonconforming property

Most courts permit a property owner whose nonconforming use has been grandfathered to transfer not only the property itself, but also the right to use the property in the nonconforming manner. *E.g., Budget Inn of Daphne, Inc. v. City of Daphne*, 789 So. 2d 154 (Ala. 2000); *Contra Vill. of Valatie v. Smith*, 632 N.E.2d 1264 (N.Y. 1994).

5. Treatment of a Post-Ordinance Nonconformity

Usually, the property owner will request either a special exception permit or a zoning variance from a special entity, such as the board of zoning appeals.

a. By ordinance—special exception

The ordinance itself may recognize that particular future uses of the property are permissible if a permit is obtained. For example, some businesses such as gas stations or funeral homes may require special-use permits even in a commercially zoned area.

Issues frequently raised with regard to special uses include whether the ordinance provides sufficient guidance for the entity charged with granting the permit to prevent an arbitrary or irrational decision, whether the entity has complied with the procedures for determining whether to issue a permit, whether the property owner has complied with procedures for obtaining a permit, and whether the property owner has established entitlement to the special-use permit.

b. By administrative action—variance

A property owner may also seek approval to use his property in a manner that is not in conformity with a zoning ordinance (i.e., a variance). To be entitled to a variance, the owner must establish that:

i) Compliance with the zoning ordinance would result in an **unnecessary hardship**;

ii) The hardship arises from circumstances that are **unique** to the property;

iii) The hardship was **not created by the owner**;

iv) Granting the variance would be **in keeping with** the overall **purpose of the ordinance**; and

v) Granting the variance would **not result in substantial harm** to the general welfare.

1) Unnecessary hardship

The hardship must arise from the characteristics of the property itself, not from the financial circumstances of the property owner.

2) Hardship not self-induced

A property owner may not create the need for the variance, such as by selling a portion of the property so that the remaining portion cannot satisfy the zoning ordinance (e.g., is less than the minimum size). There is a split among the states as to whether a property owner who purchased property with the knowledge that the zoning ordinance prohibits the use or development of the property sought as a variance is entitled to a variance.

3) Types of variances

Variances fall into one of two general categories—use variances and area variances.

a) Use variance

A use variance is sought to obtain the right to use the property in a manner not permitted by the zoning ordinance (e.g., operating a business in a residential neighborhood). A reduction in the value of the property as a consequence of being unable to use it in the manner sought is not sufficient to justify a use variance. In fact, the absence of any reasonable permitted use is sometimes required before a use variance is granted.

b) Area variance

Area variances focus on restrictions on the manner in which the property is developed (e.g., a structure may not be built within 20 feet of the boundary of the property or may be no more than two stories high) rather than the use to which the property is put. Such a variance, which often arises due to the odd shape of the property, is generally more likely to be granted than a use variance.

4) Conditional variance

A variance may be granted subject to reasonable conditions, particularly when those conditions are designed to minimize the impact of the variance on the surrounding area.

5) Variance and subsequent owners

Although a variance is requested by a particular owner, it is granted with respect to the property itself. Consequently, it may be transferred along with ownership of the property to subsequent owners of the property.

6. Procedural Due Process Rights

When a property owner seeks a permit to build in conformity with the zoning ordinance, a special-use permit, or a variance, the property owner has procedural due process rights. The owner has the rights to receive a hearing before an impartial decision maker, to present evidence to the decision maker, and to receive an explanation of the decision. *Johnson v. City of Seattle*, 335 P.3d 1027 (Wash. App. 2014). Typically, when a property owner is denied a permit or a variance, the owner also has the right to appeal this denial to a reviewing entity (e.g., a board of zoning appeals).

Compare legislative zoning: In contrast to local administrative actions that affect a particular property owner, such rights (e.g., notice, opportunity to be heard) do not exist with regard to adoption of a comprehensive zoning ordinance by the local legislative body.

7. Alternative Forms of Zoning

In addition to zoning in which a locality is divided into geographic areas (zones) with particular uses permitted in each area (i.e., Euclidian zoning), there are other approaches to zoning that have generally been upheld even though they give the local government greater discretion with regard to the development of real property.

a. Contract zoning

A local government may enter into an agreement with a developer to permit the development of property in exchange for specific promises by the developer with regard to that property (i.e., an exaction). For the applicability of the Fifth Amendment's Takings Clause to an exaction, see the Themis Constitutional Law outline § XV.B.5. Exaction as a Taking.

b. Floating zones

A local government, determining that a particular use is desirable, may adopt rules regarding such a use, but not link the use to a particular area. Instead, the zone for this use is said to "float" until a property owner applies to have the zone apply to her property.

c. Cluster zoning

A local government may, by ordinance, permit the development of a tract of land, typically for residential purposes, in a manner that meets the zoning requirements when considered as a whole, but that fails to do so when considered on a lot-by-lot basis. Such zoning, also known as density zoning, focuses on controlling the overall density of a development, while providing flexibility with regard to the size and location of structures within the development.

d. Planned-unit development

A planned-unit development is similar to cluster zoning, but it typically involves a larger tract of land and a mixture of residential and other uses of the land. As with cluster zoning, the focus is on maintaining the same density of development that would otherwise be permitted but allowing flexibility in the development of individual parcels of land.

8. Zoning and Comprehensive Plan

The Standard State Zoning Enabling Act, which has been adopted in some form by almost all states, requires a comprehensive zoning plan. The Act specifies that a planning or zoning commission should be established to prepare this plan and to recommend a zoning ordinance to implement it.

a. Lack of a planning commission or a comprehensive plan

Despite the Act, a zoning ordinance passed by a local government that has not created a planning commission or developed a comprehensive plan has generally been upheld. Usually, the ordinance itself has been viewed as a comprehensive plan.

b. Adherence to a comprehensive plan

A comprehensive plan as developed by a planning commission does not itself have legal effect, though a zoning ordinance generally must conform to the plan. To the extent that the ordinance varies significantly from the plan, the ordinance is subject to challenge as ultra vires.

c. Regional or statewide plan

A few states have adopted a general plan for a particular region, for a particular type of development (e.g., an enterprise zone), or for the state as a whole. In such case, the local zoning ordinance is usually required to conform to this plan.

9. Zoning Changes

Zoning changes are generally made by legislative act. As such, they are not subject to procedural due process restrictions, but they may be challenged on other constitutional grounds, such as a violation of substantive due process if irrational or arbitrary.

a. Burden of proof

In general, a property owner who challenges the validity of a zoning change bears the burden of proof. A few states provide that there is a presumption that the original zoning was proper and the proponent of the change must establish a justification for the change (e.g., mistake, changed conditions).

b. Spot zoning

"Spot zoning" is arbitrary discrimination against or in favor of the owner of rezoned property.

A rezoning that affects a small number of parcels of land (often a single parcel) in manner that is inconsistent with the zoning of the neighboring land and the comprehensive plan (if one exists) and that usually benefits the owner of the parcels to the detriment of the neighboring land constitutes impermissible "spot zoning."

A similar change in the comprehensive plan that results in a change in the zoning for a particular parcel or only a few parcels is also susceptible to challenge as "spot zoning" due to the lack of uniformity in zoning similarly situated properties.

10. Subdivision Development

Development of a large tract of land that is to be subdivided into parcels, typically for residential use, is subject to special governmental controls. Developers must submit and get approval on the development plan, including a plat (map), before development can take place. The plan must conform generally to regulations regarding, for example, the location and size of streets and sidewalks, water and sewer mains, and, if the development is large enough, parks and schools. The developer is usually required to construct the infrastructure (e.g., streets, sidewalks) as part of the process of developing the property, and then it is usually required to donate or dedicate the infrastructure to the local government or to pay a fee in lieu of doing so. Generally, such a requirement has been upheld unless it fails to bear a reasonable relationship to the size of the development.

11. Relationship to Covenants

Compliance with a zoning restriction does not protect an owner from a suit for breach of a covenant and compliance with a covenant does not protect an owner from a zoning violation action.

Example 1: A real covenant that requires each owner in a subdivision to maintain a six-foot high fence around his back yard can be enforced by the other owners in the neighborhood, even though the zoning ordinance only requires a four-foot high fence. Compliance with the ordinance does not protect a property owner from a breach of covenant suit brought by a neighbor.

Example 2: Assume the zoning ordinance requires an eight-foot high fence. The property owner who has a six-foot high fence cannot escape compliance with the ordinance on the grounds that his fence complies with the covenant.

F. DEDICATION

Dedication is the giving of land by the lawful owner to the government for use by the public. The owner still retains the fee, but the public essentially holds an easement in trust such that the owner does not retain any rights that are inconsistent with the complete exercise and enjoyment of the public uses to which the property has been committed. The dedication may be express (through a deed) or implied, but it must be accepted by the public entity (which can be implied by use).

G. NUISANCE

See a more detailed discussion of Nuisance in the Themis Torts outline.

1. Private Nuisance

A private nuisance is a **substantial, unreasonable** interference with another individual's use or enjoyment of his property. The interference may be intentional, negligent, reckless, or the result of abnormally dangerous conduct. Anyone with possessory rights in the property may bring a nuisance claim.

a. Substantial

A substantial interference is one that would be offensive, inconvenient, or annoying to an average person in the community.

b. Unreasonable

The interference is unreasonable if the injury caused outweighs the usefulness of the defendant's actions.

2. Public Nuisance

A public nuisance is an unreasonable interference with the health, safety, or property rights of the community. To recover for a public nuisance, a plaintiff must show that he suffered a different kind of harm than that suffered by the rest of the community.

3. Remedies

a. Damages

The usual remedy for nuisance is damages. Damages include any depreciation in the value of the property, and they may be apportioned among multiple defendants. All resulting harm is recoverable, including personal harm (e.g., diseases acquired from inhaling fumes) and harm to property.

b. Injunctive relief

If money damages are inadequate or unavailable, courts may impose injunctive relief. In determining whether an injunction is appropriate, the courts will balance the potential hardships of the two parties. However, the court need not consider the relative hardships if the defendant's conduct was willful.

H. OTHER PROPERTY RIGHTS—WATER, AIR, SUPPORT

1. Water Rights

a. Riparian rights

Riparian rights deal with the right of an owner to take and use water from a watercourse that flows through or adjacent to the owner's land, as well as the ability of the landowner to transfer those rights to another.

1) Reasonable-use doctrine

The riparian doctrine, favored in the eastern region, states that water belongs to those who own the land bordering the watercourse (riparians). Most states apply the **reasonable-use doctrine**, allowing the owner to make any reasonable use of the water. One riparian is liable to another for unreasonable interference with the other's use. Domestic ("natural") use trumps commercial ("artificial") use and can be unlimited. The water right cannot be sold or transferred separate and apart from the adjoining land.

2) Prior-appropriation doctrine

Most western states have adopted the doctrine of prior appropriation, which states that the water rights are determined by priority of beneficial use. The norm for allocation is first in time, first in right. Subsequent users must not infringe upon the rights of the prior user. Any productive or beneficial use of the water, including use for agriculture, is sufficient to create appropriation rights. The water rights are unconnected to the adjoining land and can be sold or transferred separately.

b. Navigable waterways

Rights in navigable waters are controlled by the government's right to protect the use of the waterway for transportation and public access. Rights to nonnavigable water vary depending on the theory to which the jurisdiction subscribes (primarily reasonable use or prior appropriation).

c. Groundwater

Groundwater is natural water that flows or lies under the surface and either percolates to the surface naturally or is tapped by a well. Most western states follow the prior-appropriation doctrine, though a few states apply the correlative-rights doctrine. Under correlative rights, each landowner above a common groundwater source has an equal right to use a reasonable amount of water for beneficial use. Most eastern states follow the reasonable-use doctrine, though a few apply the common-law doctrine of absolute ownership. Under absolute ownership, the surface owner has total and complete discretion over water extraction and use.

d. Surface water

Surface water is water that lies on the surface of the land but that is not part of a lake or waterway. Usually, the water derives from rain or melted snow. In about half of the states, the landowner may make changes or improvements to his land to combat the flow of surface water ("common-enemy doctrine"), though some jurisdictions will hold landowners liable in negligence for harm to another's land. On the other hand, about half of the states prevent the landowner from altering the rate or natural flow of water ("natural flow theory"), though the rule has been modified to permit **reasonable** changes in water flow determined by balancing the harm against the utility. The growing trend is to take a negligence-based approach and apply the reasonable-use doctrine.

2. Support Rights

A landowner has the right to have the land supported in its natural state.

a. Lateral support

A landowner has a right to lateral support from adjoining land. When adjoining land is in its natural state (i.e., undeveloped), a landowner who excavates on his own land is strictly liable for any damage to the adjoining land caused by the excavation. If the adjoining land has been improved (i.e., is not in its natural state), the excavating landowner is strictly liable for any damage caused by the excavation only if the land **would have collapsed in its natural state** (regardless of the improvement). If the improvement contributed to the collapse, then the adjoining landowner may recover only if the excavating landowner was negligent.

Example 1: Owner and Neighbor have adjoining parcels of land. Owner excavates on his land, causing Neighbor's undeveloped land to collapse. Owner is strictly liable.

Example 2: Owner and Neighbor have adjoining parcels of land. Owner's excavation of his land causes Neighbor's barn and the land under it to collapse. Owner is strictly liable unless the weight of Neighbor's barn contributed to the collapse. In that case, Neighbor may recover only if Owner was negligent in his excavation.

b. Subjacent support

The right to subjacent support (i.e., support from beneath the surface of the land) arises when the owner of land grants the right to mine on his land to a third party. The owner of the mineral rights is strictly liable for any failure to support the land and any buildings on the land at the time the rights were conveyed. The owner is liable only for negligence for damage to any improvements built after the conveyance of the rights.

3. Air Rights

A landowner has the right to reasonable use and enjoyment of the airspace above his land as long as it does not interfere with another's reasonable use and enjoyment of land. The amount of airspace is not unlimited as it was at common law, and it is now restricted by the state and federal governments. A landowner has the right to have the air above his land be free from excessive noise and aircraft transit. This is not an exclusive right, but such intrusions may constitute a trespass, a nuisance, or a governmental taking under the Takings Clause of the Fifth Amendment. The right to airspace is transferable and may be conveyed to another (e.g., condominiums).

Note: A landowner has no similar right to sunlight or to a view. A neighbor is free to cultivate a plant or to construct a structure that blocks a landowner's access to sunlight or interferes with the landowner's scenic view, unless the neighbor's sole purpose is to cause that result. *See, e.g., Chatsworth Realty 344 LLC v. Hudson Waterfront Co.,* 2003 N.Y. Misc. LEXIS 166 (N.Y. Sup. Ct. Mar. 4, 2003); *Kruger v. Shramek,* 5 Neb. App. 802 (Neb. Ct. App. 1997) (a neighbor's landscaping blocking another landowner's view is not actionable as a nuisance).

Torts

TORTS

Table of Contents

TORTS

I.   INTENTIONAL TORTS INVOLVING PERSONAL INJURY

A.   GENERALLY

A prima facie case for any intentional tort, including those not involving personal injury, must include proof of an **act, intent, and causation**.

1.   Act

The act must be voluntary, meaning that the defendant must have directed the physical muscular movement.

2.   Intent

The defendant acts **intentionally** if:

i)   He acts with the **purpose** of causing the consequences of his act; or

ii)   He acts knowing that the consequence is **substantially certain** to result.

Restatement (Third) of Torts: Liability for Physical and Emotional Harm § 1 (2010).

a.   Children and the mentally incompetent

A majority of courts hold that both **children** and those who are **mentally incompetent** can be held **liable for intentional torts** if they either act with a purpose or know the consequences of their acts with a substantial certainty.

b.   Transferred intent

Transferred intent exists when a person intends to commit an intentional tort against one person but instead commits:

i)   A **different intentional tort** against that person;

ii)   The intended tort **against a different person**; or

iii)   A different intentional tort against a different person.

> **Example 1:** When the defendant throws a hardball in the direction of the plaintiff, intending only to scare her (assault), but the ball strikes the plaintiff, the defendant is liable to the plaintiff for the battery. **The intent to commit one intentional tort** (the assault) **suffices to satisfy the intent requirement for another intentional tort**, the battery. Conversely, if the defendant intends to strike the victim and cause contact but instead misses and scares the plaintiff, the intent to cause the battery suffices for the intent required for the assault.
>
> **Example 2:** If the defendant throws a punch intending to strike the man standing next to him, but he misses and instead strikes a third party, then the intent to commit a battery on the man suffices to complete the intent requirement for the battery to the third party under the doctrine of **transferred intent**.

Example 3: If the defendant throws a punch intending to strike the man standing next to him, and he misses both that man and a third party who is standing nearby, but he causes that third party to experience apprehension of an imminent harmful or offensive bodily contact, then the intent to commit a battery on the man "transfers" and suffices to complete the tort of assault against the third party.

EXAM NOTE: Transferred intent applies only to the following intentional torts: battery, assault, false imprisonment, trespass to chattels, and trespass to land. It generally **does not apply** to intentional infliction of emotional distress or conversion.

B. BATTERY

1. Elements

A defendant is liable to the plaintiff for **battery** when he:

   i) Causes a **harmful or offensive contact** with the person of another; and

   ii) Acts **with** the **intent** to cause such contact or the apprehension of such contact.

2. Lack of Consent

There is no battery if the plaintiff consented to the act, either expressly or by virtue of participating in a particular event or situation (such as being bumped on a crowded subway or playing in a football game). *See* § II.A. Consent, *infra*.

3. Harmful or Offensive Contact

Contact is harmful when it causes injury, physical impairment, pain, or illness.

Contact is **offensive when a person of ordinary sensibilities** (i.e., a reasonable person) would find the contact offensive (objective test).

Note that a **defendant may be liable if he is aware that the victim is hypersensitive but proceeds to act nonetheless**. In such a case, the fact that a reasonable person would not find the contact offensive is not a defense.

The plaintiff need not be aware of the contact when it occurs in order to recover.

Example: If an operating room attendant inappropriately touches the patient while she is under the effect of anesthesia, there may be a battery even though the patient was not aware of the touching.

4. Plaintiff's Person

Contact with anything **connected to** the plaintiff's person qualifies as contact with the plaintiff's person for the purposes of battery (e.g., a person's clothing, a pet held on a leash, a bicycle ridden by the plaintiff).

5. Causation

The act must in fact result in contact of a harmful or offensive nature. A defendant who sets in motion a chain of events that causes contact with the plaintiff, whether the contact is direct or indirect, is liable (e.g., a tripwire set by the defendant that causes the plaintiff to fall).

6. Intent

To act intentionally, a defendant must act with either (i) the purpose of bringing about the consequences of that act or (ii) the knowledge that the consequences are substantially certain to occur.

Depending on the jurisdiction and the factual context, a defendant may be liable if he intends merely to bring about the contact. In many jurisdictions, while the contact must be harmful or offensive, the defendant need not intend that result (single-intent rule). In other jurisdictions, a defendant may be required not only to intend to bring about a contact, but also to intend that the contact be harmful or offensive (dual-intent rule). Although the few jurisdictions that have addressed this issue directly are divided, a majority of jurisdictions appear to prefer the single-intent rule.

The doctrine of transferred intent applies to battery.

7. Damages

No proof of actual harm is required; the plaintiff may recover nominal damages even though no actual damage occurred (to vindicate his right to physical autonomy).

Many states allow recovery of **punitive damages** if the defendant acted outrageously or with malice (i.e., a wrongful motive, or a conscious or deliberate disregard of a high probability of harm). *See* § IV.F.7. Punitive Damages, *infra*.

Under the **thin-skull rule** (also known as the "eggshell-plaintiff" rule), the defendant is not required to foresee the extent of damages in order to be held liable for all damages.

Example: If the defendant inappropriately pinches a stranger on a bus, he will be liable for battery. If it turns out that the victim is a hemophiliac and bleeds to death, the defendant will be liable for all damages appropriately awarded for the wrongful death.

C. ASSAULT

An assault is the plaintiff's reasonable apprehension of an imminent harmful or offensive bodily contact caused by the defendant's action or threat with the intent to cause either the apprehension of such contact or the contact itself.

1. Bodily Contact

Bodily contact is not required for assault.

The prototypical assault occurs when the plaintiff sees the defendant throw a punch at him. Regardless of whether the punch connects (and therefore causes a battery), the apprehension of the contact is sufficient for assault.

2. Reasonable Apprehension

A plaintiff's apprehension must be reasonable. Unlike with battery, the plaintiff must be aware of or have knowledge of the defendant's act or threat.

The defendant's apparent ability to cause harm (e.g., a "real-looking" toy gun) can be sufficient to place the plaintiff in apprehension of harm.

Even if the victim is confident that he can prevent the threatened harm, there may still be an assault.

3. Imminence

The threatened bodily harm or offensive contact must be **imminent**, i.e., without significant delay. Threats of future harm are insufficient, as are threats made by a defendant too far away to inflict any harm.

Example: If the defendant calls and threatens the plaintiff from across the city, then the threat is not imminent and therefore there is no assault.

4. Mere Words

It is sometimes said that "**mere words alone do not constitute an assault**." However, words coupled with conduct or other circumstances may be sufficient. If the defendant is able to carry out the threat imminently and takes action designed to put the victim in a state of apprehension, then there may be an assault.

Example: If the defendant sneaks up behind the plaintiff in a dark alley and utters in a menacing voice, "Your money or your life," then an assault may be complete.

5. Intent

The defendant must intend to cause the plaintiff's apprehension of an imminent harmful or offensive contact or intend to cause harmful or offensive bodily contact with the victim.

The defendant's own words, however, can negate the intent.

Example: If the defendant says, "If you were not such a good friend, I would punch you," then there is no assault.

The doctrine of transferred intent applies to assault.

6. Damages

No proof of actual damages is required. The victim can recover **nominal damages** and, in appropriate cases, **punitive damages**. If the plaintiff sustains **damages from physical harm**, such as a heart attack resulting from the assault, then he may recover these as well.

D. INTENTIONAL INFLICTION OF EMOTIONAL DISTRESS

A defendant is liable for intentionally or recklessly acting with **extreme** and **outrageous conduct** that causes the plaintiff severe emotional distress.

1. Intent

The defendant must intend to cause severe emotional distress or must act with recklessness as to the risk of causing such distress. The traditional doctrine of transferred intent does not apply to intentional infliction of emotional distress when the defendant intended to commit a **different** intentional tort (such as a battery) against a different victim. Instead, this situation is governed by the rules for third-party victims. See Section 4, below. However, transferred intent **may** apply to intentional infliction of emotional distress if, instead of harming the intended person, the defendant's extreme conduct harms another.

2. Extreme and Outrageous Conduct

Conduct is extreme and outrageous if it **exceeds the possible limits of human decency**, so as to be entirely intolerable in a civilized society. The character of the conduct must be outrageous and the conduct must be sufficiently unusual to be extreme.

Example: As a practical joke, the defendant tells the plaintiff that his wife was killed in an accident.

While liability generally does not extend to mere insults, threats, or indignities, a defendant's abusive language and conduct may be sufficiently "extreme and outrageous" if either:

i) The defendant is in a position of **authority or influence** over the plaintiff, such as a police officer, employer, or school official, or traditionally an innkeeper or an employee of a common carrier; or

ii) The plaintiff is a member of a group with a **known heightened sensitivity** (e.g., young children, pregnant women, or elderly persons).

3. Public Figures

Public figures and public officials may not recover for the tort of intentional infliction of emotional distress by reason of publication without showing in addition that the publication contains a false statement of fact that was made with "actual malice," i.e., with knowledge that the statement was false or with reckless disregard as to whether or not it was true. *Hustler Magazine v. Falwell*, 485 U.S. 46, 56 (1988).

In addition, the U.S. Supreme Court has suggested that private plaintiffs cannot recover for IIED if the conduct at issue was speech on a matter of public concern because that conduct may be protected by the First Amendment. *Snyder v. Phelps*, 562 U.S. 443 (2011).

4. Third-Party Victims

A defendant may be liable to a third-party victim if he intentionally or recklessly causes severe emotional distress to:

i) A member of the victim's **immediate family** who contemporaneously perceives the defendant's extreme and outrageous conduct, whether or not such distress results in bodily injury; or

ii) Any other bystander who contemporaneously perceives the conduct, if the distress **results in bodily injury**.

If the defendant's **design or purpose** was to cause severe distress to the third-party victim, the victim need not have contemporaneously perceived the conduct.

Example: If the defendant draws a pistol and threatens to shoot a woman in her husband's presence, and the husband suffers severe emotional distress, he may recover.

5. Causation

The plaintiff may establish causation by a showing that the defendant's actions were a **factual cause** of the plaintiff's distress.

6. Damages

The plaintiff must prove severe emotional distress beyond what a reasonable person could endure.

In many cases, the very extreme and outrageous character of the defendant's conduct itself provides evidence that the plaintiff experienced severe mental distress. In other words, the more extreme the defendant's conduct, the less evidence is required of the severity of the plaintiff's emotional distress.

If the plaintiff is **hypersensitive**, however, and experiences severe emotional distress unreasonably, then there is no liability **unless the defendant knew** of the plaintiff's heightened sensitivity.

Most courts do not require the plaintiff to prove physical injury except in the case of bystander recovery when the plaintiff is not a member of the immediate family of the person toward whom the defendant's extreme and outrageous conduct is personally directed (*see* § I.D.3. Acts Directed Toward Third Parties, *above*).

> **EXAM NOTE:** The distinction between intentional and negligent infliction of emotional distress (*see* § IV.G.1. Negligent Infliction of Emotional Distress, *infra*) is often tested on the MBE.

E. FALSE IMPRISONMENT

False imprisonment results when a defendant acts:

i) Intending to **confine or restrain** the plaintiff within boundaries fixed by the defendant;

ii) Those actions directly or indirectly **result in such confinement**; and

iii) The plaintiff is **conscious of the confinement** or is **harmed by it**.

1. Confined Within Boundaries

The plaintiff must be confined within a bounded area in which the plaintiff's freedom of movement in all directions is limited. The bounded area may be large and need not be stationary. An area is not bounded if there is a **reasonable** means of safe escape.

2. Methods of Confinement

The defendant may confine or restrain the plaintiff by the use of physical barriers, physical force, direct or indirect threats (to the plaintiff, a third party, or the plaintiff's property), or by the invalid use of legal authority, duress, or the failure to provide a reasonable means of safe escape.

Shopkeeper's Privilege: A shopkeeper's reasonable (in both duration and manner) detention of a suspected shoplifter is **not** an invalid use of authority and hence is not a false imprisonment.

Furthermore, a court may find that the defendant has confined the plaintiff when he has refused to perform a duty to release the plaintiff from an existing confinement or provide a means of escape.

Example: If a child accidentally locks herself in a restroom in a restaurant, the restaurant may be liable if it intentionally fails to assist her in unlocking the door to obtain her release.

The defendant's use of moral pressure or future threats does not constitute confinement or restraint. The plaintiff is not imprisoned if she submitted willingly to confinement.

3. Time

The length of time of the confinement or restraint is immaterial, except as to the determination of the extent of damages.

4. Intent

The defendant must act with the purpose of confining the plaintiff or act knowing that the plaintiff's confinement is substantially certain to result.

If the confinement is due to the defendant's negligence rather than his intentional acts, then the defendant may be liable under the rules governing negligence but not under the intentional tort of false imprisonment. If the imprisonment occurs by pure accident and involves neither the defendant's intent nor his negligence, then there is no recovery.

The doctrine of transferred intent applies to false imprisonment.

5. Damages

It is not necessary to prove actual damages (except when the plaintiff is unaware of the confinement). Punitive damages may be imposed in appropriate cases.

II. DEFENSES TO INTENTIONAL TORTS INVOLVING PERSONAL INJURY

A. CONSENT

1. Express Consent

The plaintiff expressly consents if she, by words or actions, manifests the willingness to submit to the defendant's conduct. The defendant's conduct may not exceed the scope of the consent.

a. Mistake

Consent by mistake is valid consent unless the defendant **caused** the mistake or **knew** of it and **took advantage** of it.

b. Fraud

Consent induced by fraud is invalid if it goes to an **essential** matter. If the fraud that induced the consent goes only to a collateral matter, then the consent is still valid.

c. Duress

Consent given while under duress (physical force or threats) is not valid. The threat, however, must be of **present action**, not of future action.

2. Implied Consent

The plaintiff's consent is implied when the plaintiff is silent (or otherwise nonresponsive) in a situation in which a reasonable person would object to the defendant's actions.

a. Emergency situation

When immediate action is required to save the life or health of a patient who is incapable of consenting to treatment, such consent is ordinarily unnecessary. Courts generally say that consent is "implied in fact," but it probably is more accurate to say that the treatment is privileged.

Even in an emergency situation, however, a competent and conscious patient's right to refuse treatment cannot be overridden.

b. Injuries arising from athletic contests

Consent may also be implied by custom or usage (e.g., participation in a contact sport). The majority of jurisdictions that have considered the issue of when a participant in an athletic contest can recover have concluded that the injured player can recover only for a reckless disregard of a player's safety, such as a violation of a safety rule designed primarily to protect participants from serious injury.

c. Mutual consent to combat

In the case of boxing or prizefighting, most courts hold that the plaintiff consents to intentional torts when he engages in the fighting, and he is therefore precluded from recovering for any injuries sustained.

In the case of street fighting and other illegal activities, the courts are divided. A majority holds that consent to such acts is not a defense because one cannot consent to a criminal act. The Second Restatement and a significant minority of courts now hold to the contrary, however. Restatement (Second) of Torts § 60 (1965).

3. Lack of Capacity

A plaintiff's lack of capacity due to youth, intoxication, or incompetence may negate the validity of her consent.

B. SELF-DEFENSE

1. Use of Reasonable Force

A person may use **reasonable force** to defend against an offensive contact or bodily harm that he **reasonably believes** is about to be intentionally inflicted upon him. The force used in self-defense must be reasonably proportionate to the anticipated harm. A person's mistaken belief that he is in danger, so long as it is a **reasonable mistake**, does not invalidate the defense.

2. Use of Deadly Force

The defendant may use deadly force only if he has a reasonable belief that force sufficient to cause serious bodily injury or death is about to be intentionally inflicted upon him.

3. No Obligation to Retreat

In a majority of states, by judicial decision or a "stand your ground" statute, a person is **not required to retreat** before using force, including deadly force, in defense. In a minority of states, a person has a duty to retreat before she may use deadly force in defense, if she can do so safely, but this duty does not apply if the defendant is in (or within the curtilage of) her own home. Restatement (Second) of Torts § 65.

4. Initial Aggressor

The initial aggressor is not entitled to claim self-defense unless the other party has responded to nondeadly force with deadly force.

5. Third-Party Injuries

The actor is **not liable** for injuries to **bystanders** that occur while he is acting in self-defense, so long as those injuries were accidental, rather than deliberate, and the actor was not negligent with respect to the bystander.

C. DEFENSE OF OTHERS

One is justified in using **reasonable force** in defense of others upon a reasonable belief that the **defended party would be entitled to use self-defense**. It is no longer required that the force be used to defend a member of the defendant's own family or someone otherwise under the defendant's legal protection. The defender may use force that is proportionate to the anticipated harm to the other party. He is not liable for acting on a mistaken belief that the third party is in danger as long as his belief is reasonable.

D. DEFENSE OF PROPERTY

1. Reasonable Force Allowed

A person may use reasonable force to defend her property if she reasonably believes it is necessary to prevent tortious harm to her property.

2. Use of Deadly Force Not Allowed

Deadly force **may not be used** merely in defense of property. A person may never use a deadly mechanical device (e.g., a spring-loaded gun) to defend her property.

3. Reasonable Force to Prevent Intrusion Upon Real Property

A possessor of land generally may use reasonable force to prevent or terminate another's intrusion upon her land. However, the possessor may not use force to prevent or terminate the visitor's intrusion on her land if the visitor is acting under necessity (*see* § III.C.6. Necessity as a Defense, *infra*). In addition, a landowner is generally entitled to use reasonable force only after making a request that the trespasser desist and the trespasser ignores the request. Such a request is not required if the landowner reasonably believes that a request will be useless or that substantial harm will be done before it can be made. Restatement (Second) of Torts § 77.

The land possessor is not liable for using force if she makes a reasonable mistake with respect to an intrusion occurring on her land.

4. Recapture of Chattels

A person may use reasonable force to reclaim her personal property that another has wrongfully taken. Before using reasonable force, the person must request the return of the chattel unless the request would be futile. If the original taking was lawful (e.g., a bailment) and the current possessor of the property has merely retained possession beyond the period of time to which the owner consented, then only peaceful means may be used to reclaim the chattel. Restatement (Second) of Torts § 104.

5. Force to Regain Possession of Land

At common law, an owner or a possessor of land was permitted to use reasonable force to regain possession of that land from one who had wrongfully taken possession of it. However, modern statutes provide procedures for recovery of realty; therefore, the use of force is no longer allowed.

E. PARENTAL DISCIPLINE

A parent may use reasonable force or impose reasonable confinement as is necessary to discipline a child, taking into consideration the age of the child and the gravity of the behavior. An educator has the same privilege unless the parent places restrictions on that privilege.

F. PRIVILEGE OF ARREST

1. Felony

a. Arrest by private citizen

A private citizen is privileged to use force (e.g., commit a battery or false imprisonment tort) to make an arrest in the case of a felony if the felony has in fact been committed and the arresting party has reasonable grounds to suspect that the person being arrested committed it.

It is a defense to make a reasonable mistake as to the **identity of the felon** but not as to the **commission of the felony**.

b. Arrest by police officer

A police officer must reasonably believe that a felony has been committed and that the person she arrests committed it. Unlike a private citizen, a police officer who makes a mistake as to the commission of a felony is not subject to tort liability.

2. Misdemeanor

In the case of a misdemeanor, a police officer may make an arrest if the misdemeanor is being committed or reasonably appears about to be committed **in the presence** of the officer. When the person effecting the arrest is a private citizen, the misdemeanor must also be a breach of the peace.

III. HARMS TO PERSONAL PROPERTY AND LAND

A. TRESPASS TO CHATTELS

1. Definition

A defendant is liable for trespass to chattels (i.e., tangible personal property) if he **intentionally interferes with the plaintiff's right of possession** by either:

i) **Dispossessing** the plaintiff of the chattel; or

ii) **Using or intermeddling with** the plaintiff's chattel.

Trespass to chattels requires that the plaintiff show **actual harm** to or deprivation of the use of the chattel for a substantial time.

2. Intent

Only the intent to do the interfering act is necessary; the defendant need not have intended to interfere with another's possession of tangible property.

The doctrine of transferred intent applies to trespass to chattels.

3. Appropriate Plaintiffs

An action for trespass to chattels may be brought by **anyone with possession or the immediate right to possession** of the chattel.

4. Mistake

Mistake of law or fact by the defendant about the legality of his actions is not a defense.

5. Damages

In a case of dispossession, a plaintiff may recover for:

i) The **actual damages caused** by the interference; and

ii) The **loss of use**.

In circumstances of use or intermeddling, the plaintiff may recover only when there are **actual damages**.

6. Remedy

The plaintiff may be entitled to compensation for the **diminution in value** or the **cost of repair**.

B. CONVERSION

1. Definition

A defendant is liable for conversion if he **intentionally** commits an act **depriving the plaintiff of possession** of her chattel or **interfering** with the plaintiff's chattel in a manner **so serious as to deprive the plaintiff of the use of the chattel**. The plaintiff's damages are the chattel's full value at the time of the conversion.

Only personal property and intangibles that have been reduced to physical form (e.g., a promissory note) can be converted.

2. Intent

The defendant must only intend to commit the act that interferes; intent to cause damage is not necessary. Mistake of law or fact is no defense (e.g., a purchaser of stolen goods is liable to the rightful owner). Transferred intent does not apply to conversion. The defendant must have intended to exercise control over the particular piece of property.

Accidentally damaging the plaintiff's chattel is not conversion if the defendant had permission to use the property.

3. Interference

The defendant interferes with the plaintiff's chattel by exercising **dominion or control** over it. Examples of acts of conversion include wrongfully acquiring, transferring, or detaining; substantially changing; severely damaging or destroying; or misusing the chattel.

Note that if the original acquisition of the chattel was not wrongful, then the plaintiff must demand the return of the chattel before she sues for conversion.

4. Distinguishing Conversion From Trespass to Chattels

There is no specific rule as to what behavior constitutes conversion, as opposed to trespass to chattels; it is a matter of degree of seriousness. The following factors are considered:

i) The **duration and extent** of the interference;

ii) The defendant's **intent to assert a right inconsistent** with the rightful possessor;

iii) The defendant's **lack of good faith**;

iv) The **expense or inconvenience** to the plaintiff; and

v) The **extent of the harm** to the chattel.

Generally, the greater the degree of these factors, the greater the likelihood that a conversion has occurred. Conversion is an exercise of dominion or control over the plaintiff's personal property such that the court is justified in requiring the defendant to pay the plaintiff the full value of the property.

Example: If an embittered defendant steals his ex-girlfriend's car and drives it into a lake, then that is conversion. If he merely hits the hood of her car once with a hammer, that is trespass to chattels.

5. Damages

The plaintiff may recover **damages in the amount of the full value of the converted property** at the time of the conversion. Alternatively, the plaintiff may bring an action for replevin to recover the chattel.

C. TRESPASS TO LAND

Trespass to land occurs when the defendant's **intentional** act causes a **physical invasion** of the plaintiff's land.

1. Intent

The defendant need only have the **intent to enter the land** (or to cause a physical invasion), not the intent to commit a wrongful trespass. In other words, the defendant

need not know that the land belongs to another. Mistake of fact is not a defense.

> **Example:** An erroneous survey of the defendant's property leads the defendant to believe that an annoying cherry tree is on her property when in fact it is on her neighbor's property. She intentionally enters her neighbor's land and cuts down the tree. Even though she reasonably believed that the tree was on her property, she is liable for trespass to land.

The doctrine of transferred intent applies to trespass to land.

2. Physical Invasion

The defendant need not personally enter onto the plaintiff's land; intentionally flooding the plaintiff's land, throwing rocks onto it, or intentionally emitting particulates into the air over the land will each suffice.

Additionally, the defendant's failure to leave the plaintiff's property after his lawful right of entry has expired constitutes a physical invasion.

A trespass may be committed on, above, or below the surface of the plaintiff's land.

3. Appropriate Plaintiffs

Because it is the right to possession that is being protected, **anyone in actual or constructive possession of land may bring an action for trespass** (e.g., owner, lessee, adverse possessor).

4. Distinguished From Nuisance

Trespass always requires an invasion or intrusion of land; nuisance may or may not involve intrusion.

Trespass protects the possessor's interests in the land; nuisance protects the use and enjoyment of land. *See also* § III.D. Nuisance, *infra*.

If no physical object enters onto the plaintiff's land (e.g., the defendant's floodlights project onto the plaintiff's land, or damage results from the defendant's blasting), then the case is generally treated as a nuisance or strict liability action (discussed in III.D. Nuisance and V. Strict Liability, *infra*).

5. Damages

No proof of actual damages is required.

6. Necessity as a Defense

The privilege of necessity is available to a person who enters or remains on the land of another (or interferes with another's personal property) to prevent serious harm, which typically is substantially more serious than the invasion or interference itself. The privilege of necessity applies only to intentional torts to property, including trespass to land, trespass to chattels, and conversion.

a. Private necessity

Private necessity is a **qualified** privilege to protect an interest of the defendant or a limited number of other persons from serious harm. The privilege applies if the interference was **reasonably necessary** to prevent a serious injury from nature or another force not connected with the property owner. A defendant is not entitled to exercise this privilege on behalf of another if the defendant knows or has reason to know that the other person is unwilling for the defendant to take such action. Despite this privilege, the property owner is entitled to recover **actual**

damages, but cannot recover nominal or punitive damages nor use force to eject the defendant. Restatement (Second) of Torts § 197.

> **Example:** During a severe storm, the owner of a boat secures the boat to a dock to prevent the destruction of the boat. The storm winds knock the boat against the dock, causing damage to the dock. The defendant is not liable as a trespasser to the plaintiff for nominal damages, but is liable to the dock owner for the actual damages to the dock.

> **EXAM NOTE:** Private necessity, often referred to simply as "necessity," has been tested frequently on the MBE.

b. Public necessity

Under the doctrine of public necessity, private property may be intruded upon or destroyed when necessary to protect a large number of people from public calamities, such as the spread of a fire, the spread of a disease, or the advance of a hostile military force.

The privilege is **absolute**. As long as the defendant acts reasonably, he is not liable for any damage to the property. He is not liable even if the original entry was not necessary, as long as he **reasonably believed** that the necessity existed. The privilege lasts only as long as the emergency continues.

The privilege is available to private citizens or public officials, should the plaintiff seek to hold a public official personally liable.

D. NUISANCE

> **EXAM NOTE:** Although most Torts classes devote little time to this topic, the law of nuisance, particularly private nuisance, is tested frequently on the MBE.

1. Private Nuisance

a. Definition

A private nuisance is a thing or activity that **substantially and unreasonably interferes** with another individual's **use or enjoyment** of his land.

b. Nature of the defendant's conduct

The interference must be intentional, negligent, reckless, or the result of abnormally dangerous conduct to constitute nuisance.

c. Appropriate plaintiffs

Anyone with **possessory** rights in real property may bring a nuisance claim.

d. Substantial interference

A substantial interference is one that would be **offensive, inconvenient, or annoying to a normal, reasonable person in the community**. A person with special sensitivities can recover only if the average person would be offended, inconvenienced, or annoyed. Conversely, a "thick-skinned" plaintiff who is not offended, inconvenienced, or annoyed is nevertheless entitled to recover if an average reasonable person would be, although the amount of damages may be affected.

e. Unreasonable interference

The interference is unreasonable if the injury caused by the defendant **outweighs the usefulness** of his actions.

f. Distinguished from trespass

1) Physical invasion

Trespass requires a **physical invasion** of the plaintiff's property. Nuisance does not require physical invasion, but **physical invasion may constitute a nuisance**.

> **Example:** If the defendant's factory emits particulates that settle on the plaintiff's property, then the defendant may be liable for both trespass and private nuisance.

2) Substantial interference

Private nuisance requires **substantial interference** with the plaintiff's use and enjoyment of her property. Trespass, however, does not require a substantial intrusion.

> **Example:** A defendant's merely walking onto the plaintiff's land, if unprivileged and not consented to, is a trespass.

3) Duration

Generally, a nuisance is continuous. A trespass may be a one-time event, episodic, or continuous.

g. Access to light

Historically, courts have refused to find the obstruction of sunlight as creating a private nuisance.

h. Defenses to private nuisance

Apart from challenging the elements of nuisance, the defenses available to a defendant turn on whether the defendant's conduct is intentional, reckless, negligent, or abnormally dangerous. For example, the plaintiff's negligence or assumption of the risk may be a defense to a nuisance (or reduce recovery in a comparative-fault jurisdiction).

1) Regulatory compliance

The fact that a defendant complies with a statute, local ordinance, or administrative regulation is not a complete defense to a nuisance action. However, such statutory or regulatory compliance may be admitted as evidence as to whether the interference with the plaintiff's use and enjoyment of her land is unreasonable. For example, zoning regulations are typically regarded as admissible evidence in actions for nuisance, but they are not determinative.

2) Coming to the nuisance

It is generally **not a defense** that the plaintiff "came to the nuisance" by purchasing property in the vicinity of the defendant's premises with knowledge of the nuisance operated by the defendant. However, the fact that the plaintiff moved to the nuisance is not irrelevant; it may be considered by the jury in determining whether the plaintiff can recover for the nuisance.

> In other words, the plaintiff's coming to the nuisance **does not entitle the defendant to judgment** as a matter of law, but it is **evidence that the jury may consider**.

Conversely, ownership of land prior to the defendant's entry into the neighborhood will not, by itself, make the defendant's action a nuisance. The test is whether the defendant's action is unreasonable.

2. Public Nuisance

a. Definition

A public nuisance is an unreasonable interference with a right common to the general public. (Note: Public nuisance does not necessarily involve land, but it is included in this part of the outline because of its common historical roots with private nuisance.) Typical examples of public nuisance include air pollution, pollution of navigable waterways, interference with the use of public highways, and interference with the public's use of parks or other public property.

A private citizen has a claim for public nuisance only if she suffers harm that is **different in kind** from that suffered by members of the general public.

Example 1: If the defendant pollutes a river, a plaintiff who fishes in the river cannot bring a claim for public nuisance. However, a plaintiff who operates a fishing camp on the banks of the river and suffers a substantial economic loss may do so.

Example 2: A dynamiting operation causes rocks to block a public highway. All members of the community are harmed by the nuisance. Consequently, a driver who suffers economic harm, such as a loss of business, due to the blockage cannot recover.

Example 3: Same facts as in Example 2, but in this case, a rock strikes the driver's car, cracking the windshield. The driver has suffered harm different from the general community and may bring an action in public nuisance.

In most instances, state statutes or local ordinances specifically declare something to be a public nuisance, such as running a house of ill repute or a disorderly tavern, gambling on Sundays, or growing certain types of thorny bushes.

Public authorities can either (i) seek injunctive relief to abate (prevent the continuation of) the public nuisance or (ii) criminally prosecute the defendant.

b. Applying principles derived from the law of private nuisance

The law of public nuisance is extremely vague and varies greatly from one jurisdiction to another. However, the modern trend is to transpose much of the law governing private nuisance onto the law of public nuisance, including the required nature of a defendant's conduct and available defenses.

3. Remedies for Nuisance

a. Damages

The usual remedy for nuisance is damages. All resulting harm is recoverable, including damages for reduction in the value of real property, personal injury, and harm to personal property.

1) Utility of the defendant's conduct

Even if the utility of the defendant's conduct outweighs the gravity of the harm, damages (but not injunctive relief) may be available if the harm is serious and the financial burden of compensating for the harm would not make the defendant's continuing conduct unfeasible. In other words, while it may be reasonable for the defendant to engage in the conduct, it is unreasonable for the defendant to do so without paying for the harm done.

2) Continuing nuisance

If the nuisance is a continuing one and the court deems it "permanent," then the court will award the plaintiff all past and future damages, which prevents plaintiffs from returning to the court to collect damages in the future.

Occasionally, courts award **temporary damages** measured by the damages that have occurred prior to trial and within the statute of limitations. In these instances, plaintiffs may return to the court in the future to collect additional temporary damages if the nuisance continues.

b. Injunctive relief

If monetary damages are inadequate and the nuisance would otherwise continue, then courts may grant injunctive relief. In determining whether an injunction is appropriate, the courts will "**balance the equities**"; that is, weigh the social utility of the defendant's conduct against the harm caused to the plaintiff and others. However, the court need not consider the relative hardships if the defendant's sole purpose was to cause harm to the plaintiff or to violate the common standards of decency (sometimes called a "spite nuisance").

4. Abatement

a. Private nuisance

A person may enter another's land to abate a private nuisance after giving the defendant notice of the nuisance and the defendant refuses to act. The amount of force used may be only that which is reasonable to abate the nuisance; the plaintiff is liable for any additional damage.

b. Public nuisance

One who is entitled to recover for a public nuisance has the right to abate that nuisance by self-help, as one would with a private nuisance. However, in the absence of unique injury, a public nuisance may be abated only by a public authority.

IV. NEGLIGENCE

> **EXAM NOTE:** Approximately half of the Torts questions on the MBE test the topic of negligence.

A. DEFINITION

Negligence is **conduct** (the commission of an act or failure to act), without wrongful intent, that falls below the minimum degree of ordinary care imposed by law to protect others against unreasonable risk of harm.

A prima facie case of negligence consists of four elements:

i) **Duty**, the obligation to protect another against unreasonable risk of injury;

ii) **Breach**, the failure to meet that obligation;

iii) **Causation**, a close causal connection between the action and the injury; and

iv) **Damages**, the loss suffered.

The plaintiff must establish all four elements of negligence by a preponderance of the evidence.

EXAM NOTE: When analyzing answer choices to negligence questions, look for the threshold elements. For instance, if there is no duty, then you can dismiss answer choices involving breach, causation, or damages.

B. DUTY

In general, a duty of care is owed to all foreseeable persons who may foreseeably be injured by the defendant's failure to act as a reasonable person of ordinary prudence under the circumstances. Generally, there is no duty to act affirmatively, even if the failure to act appears to be unreasonable. (*See* § IV.B.4. Affirmative Duty to Act, *below*.)

1. Foreseeability of Harm

While the foreseeability of harm alone does not create a duty, most courts emphasize the foreseeability of harm to the plaintiff when evaluating the existence of a duty. The foreseeability of the type of harm is also relevant to proximate cause. *See* § IV.E.3. Proximate Cause (Legal Cause), *infra*.

2. Foreseeability of the Plaintiff

a. Cardozo (majority) view

The majority rule is that a duty of care is owed to the plaintiff only if she is a member of the class of persons who might be foreseeably harmed (sometimes called "foreseeable plaintiffs") as a result of the defendant's negligent conduct. According to Judge Cardozo's majority opinion in *Palsgraf v. Long Island R. R. Co.*, 162 N.E. 99 (N.Y. 1928), the defendant is liable only to plaintiffs who are **within the zone of foreseeable harm**.

b. Andrews (minority) view

The minority view (and the Restatement approach), articulated in Judge Andrews's minority opinion in *Palsgraf*, states that if the defendant can foresee harm to **anyone** as a result of his negligence, then a duty is owed to **everyone (foreseeable or not) harmed** as a result of his breach. The issue of whether the plaintiff is foreseeable is reserved for proximate cause. *See* § IV.E.3. Proximate Cause, *infra*. Restatement (Third) of Torts: Liability for Physical and Emotional Harm § 29 cmt. n (2010).

3. Specific Classes of Foreseeable Plaintiffs

a. Rescuers

A person who comes to the aid of another is a foreseeable plaintiff. If the defendant negligently puts either the rescued party or the rescuer in danger, then he is liable for the rescuer's injuries. To the extent that a rescuer's efforts are unreasonable, comparative responsibility may reduce the rescuer's recovery, but does not automatically bar it. Restatement (Third) of Torts: Liability for Physical and Emotional Harm § 32 (2010).

An emergency professional, such as a police officer or firefighter, is barred from recovering damages from the party whose negligence caused the professional's injury if the injury results from a risk inherent in the job ("firefighter's rule").

b. Intended beneficiaries

A defendant is liable to a third-party beneficiary if the legal or business transaction that the beneficiary is a part of is prepared negligently, and the defendant could foresee the harm of completing the transaction.

c. Fetuses

Fetuses are owed a duty of care if they are viable at the time that the injury occurred. *See* § IV.G.4. "Wrongful Life" and "Wrongful Birth" Claims, *infra*.

d. Anticipated victim of a crime

The special relationship between a psychotherapist and a patient can impose upon the therapist an affirmative duty to act to protect a third party. Generally, a psychotherapist owes a duty only to her patient. For example, a psychiatrist who fails to correctly diagnose a suicidal patient is liable only to the patient if the patient commits suicide.

However, when a patient has made credible threats of physical violence against a third party, the psychotherapist has a duty to warn the intended victim. *Tarasoff v. Regents of the University of California*, 551 P.2d 334 (Cal. 1976). The threat must be a serious threat of physical violence against an ascertainable intended victim, determined by the objective standard of a reasonable psychotherapist in the same circumstance.

4. Affirmative Duty to Act

In general, there is no affirmative duty to act. However, a duty is imposed in the following situations.

a. Assumption of duty

A person who voluntarily aids or rescues another has a duty to act with reasonable ordinary care in the performance of that aid or rescue.

Note that some states have enacted "Good Samaritan" statutes to protect doctors and other medical personnel when they voluntarily render emergency care. These statutes exempt medical professionals from liability for ordinary negligence; however, they do not exempt them from liability for gross negligence.

b. Placing another in peril

A person who places another in peril is under a duty to exercise reasonable care to prevent further harm by rendering care or aid.

c. By contract

There is a duty to perform contractual obligations with due care.

d. By authority

One with actual ability and authority to control another, such as parent over child and employer over employee, has an affirmative duty to exercise reasonable control. Generally, this duty is imposed upon the defendant when the defendant knows or should know that the third person is apt to commit the injuring act.

Example: A parent may be liable for failing to control the conduct of a child who uses a dangerous instrumentality to injure a plaintiff.

e. By relationship

A defendant with a unique relationship to a plaintiff, such as business proprietor–patron, common carrier–passenger, innkeeper-guest, employer-employee, or parent-child, may have a duty to protect, aid, or assist the plaintiff and to prevent reasonably foreseeable injury to her from third parties.

f. By statute that imposes an obligation to act for the protection of another

A statute that imposes an obligation to act for the protection of another but does not expressly or impliedly create or reject a private cause of action may give rise to an affirmative duty to act.

> **Example:** A municipality adopts an ordinance that requires all citizens to report suspected animal abuse or neglect to a particular state agency. Failure to report can result in criminal liability, but the ordinance is silent as to civil liability. A woman worked next to an animal boarding facility and could see the play area from her office window. After witnessing several incidents, the woman had reason to believe the dogs at the facility were subjected to physical abuse. Nevertheless, the woman did not comply with the ordinance and never reported her suspicions.
>
> If one of the dogs was injured as a result of the abuse, the owner of the dog might bring a negligence action against the woman based on her failure to report her suspicions of physical abuse.
>
> **Compare negligence per se:** In the case of negligence per se based on the violation of a statutory standard, the defendant owes a duty of reasonable care to the plaintiff and the statutory standard is used in determining whether the defendant's conduct was reasonable.

C. THE STANDARD OF CARE

1. Reasonably Prudent Person

In most cases, the standard of care imposed is that of a **reasonably prudent person under the circumstances**. This standard is an **objective** one, measured by what a reasonably prudent person would do, rather than whether a particular defendant is acting in good faith or using her best efforts. A defendant is required to exercise the care that a reasonable person under the same circumstances (i.e., in her position, with her information and competence) would recognize as necessary to avoid or prevent an unreasonable risk of harm to another person.

a. Mental and emotional characteristics

Under this standard, the defendant is presumed to have average mental abilities and the same knowledge as an average member of the community. The defendant's own mental or emotional disability is not considered in determining whether his conduct is negligent, unless the defendant is a child. In other words, **a mentally disabled person is held to the standard of someone of ordinary intelligence and knowledge**.

Most courts hold that if a defendant possesses special skills or knowledge, she is held to a higher standard, i.e., she must exercise her superior competence with reasonable attention and care.

b. Physical characteristics

A defendant's particular physical characteristics (e.g., blindness) are taken into account and the reasonableness of the conduct of a defendant with a physical disability is determined based upon a reasonably careful person with the same disability. Restatement (Third) of Torts: Liability for Physical and Emotional Harm § 11 (2010). For example, a blind pedestrian must act as any other reasonable blind person would act under the circumstances.

c. Intoxication

Intoxicated individuals are held to the same standards as sober individuals unless their intoxication was involuntary.

d. Children

The standard of care imposed upon a child is that of a **reasonable child of similar age, intelligence, and experience**. Unlike the objective standard applied to adult defendants in negligence actions, the standard applicable to minors is more subjective in nature because children are unable to appreciate the same risks as an adult.

However, a child engaged in a high-risk activity that is characteristically undertaken by adults, such as driving a car, is held to the same standard as an adult. Courts regard children of a particularly young age as incapable of negligent conduct. Under the Third Restatement, children under the age of five are generally incapable of negligent conduct. Restatement (Third) of Torts: Liability for Physical and Emotional Harm § 10 (2010).

2. Standards of Care for Specific Classes of Defendants

A discussion of the traditional standards of care for special defendants follows, but note that the modern trend has been to move away from distinctions in the level of care and instead measure the parties' conduct in light of what is reasonable under the circumstances.

a. Common carriers and innkeepers

Under the common law, a majority of jurisdictions held both common carriers (e.g., planes, trains, buses) and innkeepers to the highest duty of care consistent with the practical operation of the business. Under this approach, common carriers and innkeepers could be held liable for "slight negligence."

A majority of courts continue to hold **common carriers** to this higher standard. However, most courts today hold that an **innkeeper** (hotel operator) is liable only for **ordinary negligence**.

Note, however, that the Third Restatement approach is slightly different: common carriers and innkeepers are treated alike and must exercise reasonable care toward their passengers and guests. Although generally there is no affirmative duty to act, common carriers and innkeepers have a duty to act based upon the special relationship they have with their customers. Restatement (Third) of Torts: Liability for Physical and Emotional Harm § 40 (2010).

> **EXAM NOTE:** Be certain to apply these standards only with regard to customers of a common carrier or guests of an innkeeper.

b. Automobile drivers

In most jurisdictions, automobile drivers owe ordinary care to their guests as well as their passengers (those who confer an economic benefit for the ride). However, a minority of jurisdictions distinguish between the two with "guest statutes," which impose only a duty to refrain from gross or wanton and willful misconduct with a guest in the car. Proof of simple negligence by the driver will not result in recovery by the plaintiff-guest.

c. Bailors and bailees

A bailment occurs when a person (the bailee) temporarily takes possession of another's (the bailor's) personal property, such as when a driver leaves his car with a valet. The duty of care that must be exercised by a bailor or bailee varies depending on the type of bailment.

1) Bailor's duty

A gratuitous bailor (e.g., the owner of a power saw who lends it without charge to a friend) has a duty to inform the bailee only of **known** dangerous defects in personal property, but a compensated bailor (e.g., a commercial entity that leases a power saw to a customer) must inform a bailee of defects that are known or **should have been known** by the bailor had he used reasonable diligence.

2) Bailee's duty

When a bailor receives the sole benefit from the bailment, the bailee has a lesser duty to care for the property and is liable only if he has been grossly negligent. In contrast, when a bailee receives the sole benefit from the bailment, he must exercise extraordinary care for the bailor's property. Slight negligence on the bailee's part will result in liability for any injuries to the property from failure to properly care for or use it. In a bailment for mutual benefit, the bailee must take reasonable care of the bailed property.

d. Emergency situations

The applicable standard of care in an emergency is that of a reasonable person in the same situation. In other words, less may be expected of the reasonably prudent person who is forced to act in an emergency, but only if the defendant's conduct did not cause the emergency.

3. Possessors of Land

The term "possessors of land" includes owners, tenants, those in adverse possession, and others in possession of land. The fact that a plaintiff is injured while on someone else's land does not affect the liability of a defendant other than the land possessor. Only land possessors are protected by the rules limiting liability to trespassers or licensees. Everyone else—for example, easement holders (e.g., a utility company with power lines on the land) or those licensed to use the land (e.g., hunters)—must exercise reasonable care to protect the trespasser or the licensee.

In general, possessors of land owe a duty only to those within the boundaries of their land. The duty to entrants on the land includes:

i)   **Conduct** by the land possessor that creates risks;

ii) **Artificial conditions** on the land;

iii) **Natural conditions** on the land; and

iv) Risks created when any of the **affirmative duties** discussed in § IV.B.4. Affirmative Duty to Act, *supra*, are applicable.

a. Two approaches

1) Traditional approach

Approximately one-half of all jurisdictions continue to follow traditional rules that provide that the standard of care owed to land entrants depends upon the status of the land entrant as an invitee, a licensee, or a trespasser.

2) Modern trend

Courts in the other half of jurisdictions (as well as the Third Restatement) require that a standard of reasonable care applies to all land entrants except trespassers, abolishing the distinction between invitees and licensees. (In the case of the Third Restatement, the rule applies to all land entrants except for "flagrant" trespassers (*see* b.2) Modern and Third Restatement approach, *below.*)

The land possessor must use reasonable care to prevent harm posed by artificial conditions or conduct on the land. As for natural conditions, the general rule is that there is no duty to remove or protect against the condition, although there is an exception for rotting trees in densely populated areas.

a) Known or obvious dangers

A land possessor must take reasonable precautions for known or obvious dangers when the possessor should anticipate the harm despite such knowledge or obviousness. However, when the danger is open and obvious to the entrant, a warning will ordinarily not provide additional protection against harm. Consequently, if the only purpose of a warning would be to provide notice of a danger that is open and obvious, there is no liability for failing to provide such a warning. In addition, even when a warning is required, an entrant who encounters an obviously dangerous condition and fails to exercise reasonable self-protective care is contributorily negligent.

b. Trespassers

A trespasser is someone who enters or remains upon the land of another **without consent or privilege** to do so.

1) Traditional approach

A landowner is obligated **to refrain from willful, wanton, reckless, or intentional misconduct** toward trespassers.

a) Spring-guns and other traps

The use of a spring-gun or other trap set to expose a trespasser to a force likely to inflict death or grievous bodily injury will lead to liability for the land possessor. The land possessor cannot do indirectly what he would be forbidden to do directly (e.g., shoot the trespasser).

b) Discovered trespassers

Land possessors owe a duty toward **discovered or anticipated trespassers** to warn or protect them from **concealed, dangerous, artificial conditions**. There is no duty to warn of natural conditions or artificial conditions that do not involve risk of death or serious bodily harm. Land possessors also have a duty to use reasonable care while conducting activities on their land, as well as to control the activities of third parties on their property.

When a land possessor **should reasonably know** that trespassers are consistently entering his land (e.g., frequent trespassers using a footpath to cut across the corner of the property), the possessor owes a duty to the **anticipated trespasser**, regardless of the land possessor's actual knowledge of the trespasser's presence.

c) Undiscovered trespassers

Land possessors generally owe no duty to undiscovered trespassers, nor do they have a duty to inspect their property for evidence of trespassers.

d) Attractive nuisance

> **EXAM NOTE:** Attractive nuisance has been heavily tested on the MBE.

Under the "attractive nuisance" doctrine, a land possessor may be liable for **injuries to children** trespassing on the land if:

i) An artificial condition exists in a place where the land possessor knows or has reason to know that **children are likely to trespass**;

ii) The land possessor knows or has reason to know that the condition poses an **unreasonable risk** of death or serious bodily injury to children;

iii) The children, because of their youth, do not discover or **cannot appreciate the danger** presented by the condition;

iv) The utility to the land possessor of maintaining the condition and the burden of eliminating the danger are **slight compared to the risk of harm** presented to children; and

v) The land possessor fails to exercise **reasonable care** to protect children from the harm.

Restatement (Second) of Torts § 339 (1965).

2) Minority and Third Restatement approach

A few states now take the approach that land possessors owe trespassers, like all other land entrants, a reasonable standard of care under all the circumstances. Of course, the fact that the land entrant is trespassing, particularly if he is undiscovered, is one fact that the jury may consider in deciding whether the land possessor has exercised reasonable care.

The Third Restatement § 52 provides that although a duty of reasonable care is generally owed to trespassers, only the duty not to act in an intentional, willful, or wanton manner to cause physical harm is owed to **flagrant trespassers** who are not imperiled and unable to protect themselves. A burglar in a home would be a flagrant trespasser, but someone injured while walking in a public park at midnight, despite the presence of a posted notice that the park was closed after dusk, would not be. This distinction has not been widely adopted by the courts.

c. Invitees: traditional approach

An invitee is either:

i) A **public invitee**—someone invited to enter or remain on the land for the purposes for which the land is held open to the public; or

ii) A **business visitor**—someone invited to enter or remain on the land for a purpose connected to business dealings with the land possessor.

A land possessor owes an invitee the duty of reasonable care, including the duty to use reasonable care to **inspect** the property, **discover** unreasonably dangerous conditions, and **protect** the invitee from them.

However, the duty of reasonable care owed to an invitee does not extend beyond the scope of the invitation, and the invitee is **treated as a trespasser** in areas beyond that scope.

1) Non-delegable duty

The land possessor's duty to invitees is a non-delegable duty. For example, even if a store owner hires an independent contractor to maintain the escalator in her store, she will remain liable if the contractor negligently fails to properly maintain the escalator. This same principle of non-delegable duty applies under the modern approach (*see* 5.a.2) Modern Trend, *above*), under which the land possessor owes most land visitors a duty of reasonable care.

2) Recreational land use

In some jurisdictions, a land possessor who opens his land to the public for recreational purposes is not liable for injuries sustained by recreational land users so long as he does not charge a fee for the use of his land, unless the landowner acts willfully and maliciously or, in some jurisdictions, with gross negligence.

d. Licensees: traditional approach

A licensee is someone who enters the land of another with the express or implied permission of the land possessor or with a privilege.

Examples of licensees include:

i) **Social guests**—note, they may be "invited," but they are still licensees, not invitees;

ii) Those whose presence is **tolerated** by the land possessor such as children who routinely cut across the land on their way home from school; and

iii) **Emergency personnel** such as police, firefighters, and emergency medical technicians.

The land possessor has a duty to either **correct or warn** a licensee of **concealed dangers** that are either **known** to the land possessor or that **should be obvious** to her. The land possessor **does not have a duty to inspect** for dangers. In addition, the land possessor must exercise **reasonable care** in conducting activities on the land.

e. Liability of landlords and tenants

Because the obligations associated with property are owed by the possessor of the land, a lessee assumes any duty owed by the lessor once the lessee takes possession.

1) Landlord's liability

The landlord remains liable for injuries to the tenant and others occurring:

i) In **common areas** such as parking lots, stairwells, lobbies, and hallways;

ii) As a result of **hidden dangers** about which the landlord **fails to warn** the tenant;

iii) On premises **leased for public use**;

iv) As a result of a hazard caused by the landlord's **negligent repair**; or

v) Involving a hazard that the landlord has **agreed to repair**.

2) Tenant's liability

As an occupier of land, the tenant continues to be liable for injuries to third parties arising from dangerous conditions within the tenant's control, regardless of whether the land owner has liability.

f. Off-premises victims

A landowner generally does not owe a duty to a person not on the premises (e.g., passerby, owner of adjacent land) who is harmed by a **natural condition** on the landowner's premises. An exception exists, however, with respect to trees in urban areas.

With respect to an **artificial condition**, the landowner generally owes a duty to prevent an unreasonable risk of harm to persons who are not on the premises. Similarly, with respect to an activity conducted on the premises by the owner or by someone subject to the owner's control, the landowner generally owes a duty of reasonable care to persons who are not on the premises.

g. Sellers of real property

Sellers of real property owe a duty to disclose to buyers those concealed and unreasonably dangerous conditions known to the seller. These are conditions that the buyer is unlikely to discover upon reasonable inspection. The seller's liability to third parties continues until the buyer has a reasonable opportunity, through maintenance and inspection, to discover and remedy the defect.

D. BREACH OF DUTY

1. Generally

A breach of duty occurs when the defendant departs from the required standard of care, such as failure to act as a reasonable person, an unexcused violation of a statute, or, if there is no direct evidence, through res ipsa loquitur.

There are two approaches for determining negligent conduct (breach of the general standard of care).

a. Traditional approach

Most courts determine breach of the standard of care by comparing the defendant's conduct with what a **reasonably prudent person** under the circumstances would or would not have done (applying an objective standard).

b. Cost-benefit analysis

The modern trend and the Third Restatement approach set out the primary factors to consider in determining whether the defendant has acted in accordance with the standard of care as follows:

i) The foreseeable **likelihood** that the defendant's conduct would cause harm;

ii) The foreseeable **severity** of any resulting harm; and

iii) The defendant's **burden** (costs or other disadvantages) in avoiding the harm.

The Third Restatement defines negligence using these terms rather than the reasonably prudent person standard. Restatement (Third) of Torts: Liability for Physical and Emotional Harm § 3.

2. Custom

a. Within a community or an industry

Evidence of a custom in a community or an industry is admissible as evidence to establish the proper standard of care, but such evidence is not conclusive. The entire community or industry may be negligent.

b. Safety codes

Safety codes promulgated by industries, associations, and government bodies for the guidance of operations within their respective fields of interest are admissible to prove custom.

c. Professionals

A professional person (e.g., doctor, lawyer, or electrician) is expected to exhibit the **same skill, knowledge, and care as an ordinary practitioner in the same community**. A specialist may be held to a higher standard than a general practitioner because of his superior knowledge.

Establishing negligence by a professional person generally requires expert testimony to establish both the applicable standard of care and the defendant's deviation from that standard. However, when the defendant's negligence is so apparent that a layperson can identify it, expert testimony will not be required. *See, e.g., Palmer v. A.H. Robins Co.*, 684 P.2d 187 (Colo. 1984) (Because the standard of care was regarded as within the common knowledge of a layman when the surgeon amputated the wrong leg, no expert testimony was required to establish the standard of care.).

With regard to professionals, deviation from the relevant custom is dispositive evidence of a breach. Similarly, compliance with the relevant custom is dispositive evidence that the professional did not breach a duty of care.

d. Physicians

1) Local versus national standard

Traditionally, physicians were held to the "same or similar locale" rule of custom: did the physician's actions comport with those customarily employed by doctors in the same locale or in similar localities? While some jurisdictions have retained the traditional rule, the majority of jurisdictions now apply a national standard to physicians, including physicians who are specialists.

2) Informed consent

Physicians are under a specific obligation to explain the risks of a medical procedure to a patient in advance of a patient's decision to consent to treatment. Failure to comply with this "informed consent" doctrine constitutes a breach of the physician's duty owed to the patient and is actionable as medical malpractice (medical negligence).

A **majority** of jurisdictions hold that the required level of disclosure of risks is governed by custom among medical practitioners. However, a significant **minority** holds that the physician must disclose any "material risk"; that is, any risk that might make a difference to a reasonable person in deciding whether to proceed with the surgery or other medical treatment.

Doctors are **not** under an obligation to disclose when:

i) The risk is a **commonly known** risk;

ii) The patient is **unconscious** or otherwise incapable of giving consent (e.g., emergency treatment);

iii) The patient **waives or refuses** the information;

iv) The patient is **incompetent** (although the physician must make a reasonable attempt to secure informed consent from a guardian); or

v) The disclosure would be **detrimental** to the patient (e.g., would upset the patient enough to cause extreme illness, such as a heart attack).

3. Negligence Per Se

EXAM NOTE: Negligence per se has been heavily tested on the MBE.

The standard of care can sometimes be determined by statute. In most jurisdictions, the violation of such a statute establishes negligence as a matter of law (a conclusive presumption as to duty and breach). A minority of jurisdictions hold that violation of the statute is merely evidence of negligence (a rebuttable presumption as to duty and breach).

a. Elements

i) A criminal or regulatory statute (or an administrative regulation or municipal ordinance) imposes a specific duty for the protection of others;

ii) The defendant violates the statute by failing to perform that duty;

iii) The plaintiff is in the class of people **intended to be protected** by the statute; and

iv) The harm is of the type the statute was **intended to protect against**.

Once negligence per se is established, in order for the defendant to be liable, the plaintiff must prove that his injuries were proximately caused by the defendant's violation of the statute.

b. Effect of a defendant's compliance

Generally, compliance with a statute, a regulation, or an ordinance does not prove the absence of negligence. However, if the defendant's conduct complies with a federal regulatory statute, such as a statute that is part of comprehensive regulatory schemes, compliance with the federal requirements may preempt common-law tort actions.

c. Defenses

An excused violation of an applicable statute can be a defense to negligence per se under the following circumstances.

1) Greater risk of harm

The defendant may be able to avoid liability by proving that compliance would have involved a greater risk of physical harm to the defendant or others than noncompliance would have (e.g., it was an emergency).

2) Incapacity

The violation of a statute may not be negligence if the violation is reasonable in light of the defendant's **physical disability** or incapacitation, or if the defendant is a **child**.

3) Reasonable care

It is a defense that the defendant exercised **reasonable care** in attempting to comply with the statute.

4) Vagueness

If the requirements of the statute at issue were presented to the public in a **confusing** manner (e.g., extremely vague or ambiguous), then the defendant's violation is excused.

5) Reasonable ignorance

If the statute imposes an obligation only under certain factual circumstances that are not usually present, and the defendant is **not aware** that these circumstances are present and further proves that his ignorance was reasonable, then the defendant's violation of the statute is excused for the purposes of negligence per se.

d. Violation by a plaintiff

The violation of a statute, a regulation, or an ordinance by a plaintiff may constitute contributory negligence per se. The same requirements apply.

4. Res Ipsa Loquitur

Under the doctrine of res ipsa loquitur, the trier of fact may infer the existence of the defendant's negligent conduct in the absence of direct evidence of such negligence. Res ipsa is **circumstantial evidence** of negligence that does not change the standard of care.

> **EXAM NOTE:** Res ipsa loquitur does not apply if there is direct evidence of the cause of the injury.

a. Traditional requirements

Under the traditional standard for res ipsa loquitur, still used in many jurisdictions, the plaintiff must prove that:

i) The accident was of a kind that **ordinarily does not occur** in the absence of negligence;

ii) It was caused by an agent or instrumentality within the **exclusive control** of the defendant; and

iii) It was not due to any action **on the part of the plaintiff**.

In establishing that the accident was of a kind that ordinarily does not occur in the absence of negligence, the plaintiff need not conclusively exclude all other possible explanations. It is enough that the facts proved reasonably permit the conclusion that negligence is the more probable explanation. Restatement (Second) of Torts § 328D.

b. Modern trends

Even under the traditional requirements, courts often generously interpret the "exclusive control" requirement.

Example: The defendant hires an independent contractor to clean and maintain his store premises. The plaintiff is injured when she slips on a floor negligently left wet by an independent contractor. Courts will find that the duty to maintain the premises open to the public is a non-delegable duty, such that the defendant continued to be in "exclusive control." Therefore, res ipsa loquitur can be used to find that the defendant breached a duty of reasonable care.

1) Medical malpractice

In medical malpractice cases when several physicians, nurses, and other medical personnel have access to the plaintiff during surgery, a small number of jurisdictions apply res ipsa loquitur, finding that each defendant has breached a duty of care unless he can exonerate himself. In the absence of such exonerating evidence, the courts hold all defendants jointly and severally liable. *See, e.g., Ybarra v. Spangard*, 25 Cal. 2d 486 (1944).

2) Products liability

In negligence cases involving products, even if the product passes through many hands—those of the manufacturer, the distributor, the retail store, and the consumer/user—if the manufacturer wrapped the package or it is clear that any negligence took place during the production process, **many courts ignore the exclusivity requirement**.

3) Comparative-fault jurisdictions

Courts in the vast majority of jurisdictions that have adopted comparative fault also are inclined to loosely apply the third requirement—that the harm must not be due to any action on the part of the plaintiff (whether such action constitutes contributory negligence or not)—because such a requirement would otherwise be in tension with the law holding that the plaintiff's contributory negligence is no longer a total bar to recovery.

c. Third Restatement

In light of the fact that the majority of jurisdictions generously apply the traditional requirements for res ipsa loquitur, the Third Restatement has rearticulated the requirements of the doctrine in the following manner.

The fact-finder may infer that the defendant has been negligent when:

i) The accident that caused the plaintiff's harm is a type of accident that ordinarily happens as a result of negligence of a class of actors; and

ii) The defendant is a relevant member of that class of actors.

Note that a group approach to res ipsa loquitur is generally supportable only if the parties in the group have an ongoing relationship pursuant to which they share responsibility for a dangerous activity. Restatement (Third) of Torts: Liability for Physical and Emotional Harm § 17.

However, because the Third Restatement was only recently adopted, few courts have adopted this precise articulation of the doctrine.

d. Procedural effect of res ipsa loquitur

If the plaintiff establishes a prima facie case of res ipsa, then the trial court should deny the defendant's motion for a directed verdict, and the issue of negligence must be decided by the trier of fact. In most jurisdictions, res ipsa does not require that the trier of fact find negligence on the defendant's part. It simply establishes an inference of negligence sufficient to avoid dismissal of the plaintiff's action.

E. CAUSATION

The plaintiff must prove that the defendant's actions were both the actual cause (also known as the "factual cause" or "cause in fact") and the proximate cause (also known as the "legal cause" or, under the Restatement, the "scope of liability") of the plaintiff's injury.

1. Actual Cause (Cause in Fact)

a. "But for" test

If the plaintiff's injury would not have occurred **but for** the defendant's tortious act or omission, then the defendant's conduct is a factual cause of the harm. If the injury would have occurred despite the defendant's conduct, then there is no factual cause.

b. Multiple and/or indeterminate causes

The but-for test of causation often will not work if:

i) There are multiple tortfeasors and it cannot be said that the defendant's tortious conduct necessarily was required to produce the harm;

ii) There are multiple possible causes of the plaintiff's harm, but the plaintiff cannot prove which defendant caused the harm; or

iii) The defendant's negligent medical misdiagnosis increased the probability of the plaintiff's death, but the plaintiff probably would have died even with a proper diagnosis.

1) Substantial factor

When but-for causation does not work, most courts substitute a substantial-factor test. In cases in which the conduct of a defendant together with some other cause (e.g., another defendant or an independently occurring event) may have contributed to a plaintiff's indivisible injury, each of which alone would have been a factual cause of that injury, the test is whether the defendant's tortious conduct was a **substantial factor** in causing the plaintiff's harm.

Under the minority rule of the Third Restatement, each such cause or act is regarded as a factual cause of the harm. Together they are designated as "multiple sufficient causes." Restatement (Third) of Torts: Liability for Physical and Emotional Harm § 27.

2) Alternative causation

If the plaintiff's harm was caused by (i) one of a small number of defendants—usually two and almost never more than four or five, (ii) each of whose conduct was tortious, and (iii) all of whom are present before the court, then the court may shift the burden of proof to each individual defendant to prove that his conduct was not the cause in fact of the plaintiff's harm.

3) Concert of action

If two or more tortfeasors were **acting pursuant to a common plan or design** and the acts of one or more of them tortiously caused the plaintiff's harm, then all defendants are jointly and severally liable.

> **Example:** Two defendants agree to a drag race and one of them injures another driver or a passenger during the race. Both are jointly and severally liable to the plaintiff.

c. Loss of chance of recovery

Some jurisdictions apply the "loss of chance" doctrine. The doctrine is usually applied in a medical malpractice case (e.g., failure to diagnose) when a plaintiff cannot meet the preponderance standard (i.e., more likely than not) for causation because the chance of recovery was already less than 50% before the defendant's negligent conduct.

Under this doctrine, courts allow the plaintiff to recover reduced damages, often measured by an amount equal to the total damages recoverable as a result of the decedent's death multiplied by the difference in the percentage chance of recovery before the negligent misdiagnosis and after the misdiagnosis.

> **Example:** The plaintiff's total damages are $1,000,000, and his chances of survival were 40% without the negligent misdiagnosis and 25% after the misdiagnosis. The plaintiff will recover $150,000 ($1,000,000 × (40% − 25%)).

2. Causal Linkage

Most often, when the plaintiff proves that the defendant's tortious conduct was a **but-for cause** of his injury, he also implicitly proves that the defendant's conduct increased the probability that the plaintiff would be harmed.

However, a defendant is not the proximate (legal) cause of harm when the tortious aspect of the defendant's conduct was of a type that does not increase the risk of that harm. In such cases, it is purely coincidental that the defendant's tortious conduct was the but-for cause of the plaintiff's injury.

> **Example:** A passenger in a car is injured because the wind blows down a tree and the car is positioned under the tree at the moment it falls only because the driver has been traveling at an unreasonably unsafe speed. While the passenger would not have been injured but for the driver's negligent speeding, most courts would find that the driver should not be found to be a cause of the accident under the doctrine of causal linkage, i.e., the driver's conduct did not increase the probability that the plaintiff would be harmed.

3. Proximate Cause (Legal Cause)

In addition to proving actual causation, the plaintiff must prove that the defendant's tortious conduct was a proximate cause of her harm. Proximate cause is a legal limitation on actual cause, focusing on foreseeability. Some courts and the Third Restatement prefer the phrase "scope of liability." The majority rule for proximate cause requires that the plaintiff suffer a foreseeable harm that is not too remote and is within the risk created by the defendant's conduct.

a. Foreseeability of harm

1) Majority rule

A defendant is liable for **reasonably foreseeable consequences** resulting from his conduct. The type of harm must be foreseeable, though the extent of harm need not be foreseeable, *see* §IV.E.3.c. Extent of damages, *below*. A defendant's liability is limited to those harms that result from the risks that made the defendant's conduct tortious, within the scope of liability of the defendant's conduct. Restatement (Third) of Torts: Liability for Physical and Emotional Harm § 29.

2) Minority rule

Some courts follow the **Andrews test** from *Palsgraf* and find proximate cause for all consequences that flow directly from the defendant's conduct, considering factors including the number of intervening causes and the remoteness of the cause from the effect. Other courts find proximate cause if the defendant's conduct was a **direct cause** of the plaintiff's injury, regardless of foreseeability.

b. Indirect causation

The second proximate cause issue is whether the injury resulted without any unforeseeable or extraordinary events that will serve to break the chain of the defendant's liability.

1) Direct cause

A plaintiff can recover when the defendant's tortious acts are the **direct cause** of the plaintiff's harm **without the intervention of independent contributing acts**.

2) Indirect cause

An indirect cause results from an act or event occurring after the defendant's tortious act and before the plaintiff's injury (i.e., an **intervening** event). A **superseding** cause is any intervening event that **breaks the chain** of proximate causation between the defendant's tortious act and the plaintiff's harm. Whether an intervening cause will be superseding depends upon its **foreseeability**. The fact that an intervening cause occurred at all is considered to be foreseeable.

A defendant is liable if the type of harm is foreseeable, even if it occurred in an unforeseeable manner.

a) Foreseeable intervening causes

A foreseeable intervening cause will not cut off a defendant's liability. Examples of foreseeable intervening forces include subsequent medical malpractice, disease, or accident; negligence of rescuers; normal forces of nature; or efforts to protect a person or property.

As a general guideline, **negligent intervening acts are usually regarded as foreseeable** and do not prevent the original defendant from being held liable to the plaintiff.

Example: The defendant negligently injures the plaintiff in an auto accident. The plaintiff seeks treatment for the resulting broken leg, and the treating physician commits malpractice that results in the amputation of the leg. Because the original driver-defendant's negligence was a but-for cause of the amputated leg and because medical malpractice is foreseeable, the driver's negligence is also a proximate cause of the amputated leg, and the driver may be held liable for the damages caused by the entire injury, including the consequences of the amputation.

b) Unforeseeable intervening causes

Most courts hold that an **unforeseeable** intervening cause is a superseding cause that therefore breaks the chain of causation between the defendant and the plaintiff. Examples of unforeseeable superseding causes include extraordinary acts of nature ("act of God") and criminal acts and/or intentional torts of third parties.

Criminal acts of third parties are generally regarded as **unforeseeable superseding causes** and therefore break the chain of causation between the original defendant's negligence and the plaintiff's harm.

However, if the duty breached by the defendant is one of **failing to use reasonable care to protect the plaintiff** and the plaintiff is harmed by a **criminal act**, then the original defendant remains liable.

Example: A middle-school student is assaulted during a field trip. Her teacher failed to use reasonable care to protect her. The fact that the intervening cause of her harm, the assault, was criminal will not preclude the student and her parents from holding the school liable.

c) Effect of non-superseding intervening causes

If the intervening negligent act is not a superseding cause, then the original defendant and the actor responsible for the intervening negligent act can be held jointly and severally liable to the plaintiff.

> **EXAM NOTE:** Remember that the original tortfeasor remains liable unless the results of an intervening act are **unforeseeable**. In particular, keep in mind that negligence (e.g., medical malpractice) is foreseeable, and therefore it is not a superseding cause that breaks the chain of causation and insulates the defendant from liability.

c. Extent of damages

Under the "thin-skull" or "eggshell-skull" rule, the **extent of the damages need never be foreseeable**. The defendant is liable for the full extent of the plaintiff's injuries that may be increased because of the plaintiff's preexisting physical or mental condition or vulnerability, even if the extent is unusual or unforeseeable.

F. DAMAGES

1. Actual Damages

The plaintiff must prove actual harm, i.e., personal injury or property damage, in order to complete the requirements of liability for negligence. Unlike in actions for intentional torts, nominal damages are not recoverable in negligence actions.

a. Emotional distress damages

A plaintiff who is the victim of a tort that causes physical injury may also add emotional distress as an element of damages (sometimes known as "parasitic" damages).

Most jurisdictions do not allow a plaintiff to recover in negligence for pure emotional distress, though a plaintiff with a physical manifestation of the distress (e.g., nausea) may be able to recover through a claim for negligent infliction of emotional distress. *See* § IV.G.1. Negligent Infliction of Emotional Distress, *infra.*

b. Attorney's fees

Attorney's fees and interest from the date of damage are not recoverable in a negligence action.

2. Compensatory Damages

The general measure of compensatory damages is compensation that would make the victim whole, as if she had never suffered the injury.

3. Mitigation of Damages, Avoidable Consequences

The plaintiff must take reasonable steps to mitigate damages. Although sometimes phrased as a "duty to mitigate," this "duty" is not an obligation that the plaintiff owes to the defendant but instead is a limitation on the plaintiff's recovery due to the failure to avoid harm that could have been avoided by the use of reasonable effort after the tort was committed.

For example, if the victim fails to use reasonable care to treat a wound, resulting in infection and the loss of a limb, that failure to mitigate her damages likely will reduce or even eliminate her recovery, depending on the jurisdiction's approach to contributory negligence.

4. Personal Injury: Categories of Damages

The typical categories of damages recoverable in a personal injury action include:

i) Medical and rehabilitative expenses, both past and future;

ii) Past and future pain and suffering (e.g., emotional distress); and

iii) Lost income and any reduction in future earnings capacity.

5. Property Damage

a. General rule

When the plaintiff's real or personal property is injured or destroyed by the defendant's tortious conduct, the general rule is that the plaintiff may recover the difference between the fair market value of the property immediately before the injury and immediately after the injury.

b. Cost of repairs

In the case of tortious harm to personal property, most courts also allow the cost of repairs as an alternative measure of damages, provided that the cost of repairs does not exceed the value of the property.

c. Household items

In the case of household items, such as clothing and appliances, courts often hold that replacement value is the measure of damages.

6. Collateral-Source Rule

a. Traditional rule

Under the traditional rule, benefits or payments provided to the plaintiff from outside sources (such as the plaintiff's medical insurance) are not credited against the liability of any tortfeasor, nor is evidence of such payments admissible at trial. Even under the traditional rule, payments made to the plaintiff by the defendant's insurer are not considered payments from a collateral source, and such payments are credited against the defendant's liability.

b. Modern trend

A majority of states have passed statutes that either eliminate the collateral-source rule entirely or modify its application (e.g., not applicable in medical malpractice cases).

7. Punitive Damages

The plaintiff may be entitled to punitive damages if he can establish by clear and convincing evidence that the defendant acted willfully and wantonly, recklessly, or with malice. Torts that inherently involve a malicious state of mind or outrageous conduct (such as intentional infliction of emotional distress) may often result in punitive damages for the plaintiff.

Note that in many states the availability of punitive damages as a remedy is determined by statute. There are also constitutional limitations on the amount of a punitive damages award. The U.S. Supreme Court has held that an award for punitive damages should be within a single-digit ratio to any compensatory damages in order to comply with due process. *State Farm v. Campbell*, 538 U.S. 408 (2003).

G. SPECIAL RULES OF LIABILITY

1. Negligent Infliction of Emotional Distress

There are three types of cases in which a defendant may breach the duty to avoid negligently inflicting emotional distress upon a plaintiff. Whether a duty exists may depend upon whether the harm and the plaintiff are reasonably foreseeable. Some states deny recovery because one or the other is too speculative and thus not foreseeable.

a. Zone of danger

A plaintiff can recover for negligent infliction of emotional distress from a defendant whose tortious conduct placed the plaintiff in harm's way if the plaintiff demonstrates that:

i) He was within the "**zone of danger**" of the threatened physical impact—that he feared for his own safety because of the defendant's negligence; and

ii) The threat of physical impact caused emotional distress.

1) Proof of emotional distress

The majority rule is that the emotional distress must be manifested by **physical symptoms** (e.g., nightmares, shock, ulcers). The severity of symptoms required varies by jurisdiction. A few states as well as the Restatement allow recovery for serious emotional disturbance without a physical manifestation of harm. Restatement (Third) of Torts: Liability for Physical and Emotional Harm § 4, comment d.

Compare to intentional infliction of emotional distress, under which the plaintiff must prove more than negligence (intentional or reckless extreme or outrageous conduct) but need not prove any physical injury.

b. Bystander recovery

Most states allow a bystander plaintiff outside the zone of danger to recover for emotional distress if that plaintiff:

i) Is closely related to the person injured by the defendant;

ii) Was present at the scene of the injury; and

iii) Personally observed (or otherwise perceived) the injury.

A majority of jurisdictions have not expanded liability to an unmarried cohabitant. However, some jurisdictions do allow engaged cohabitants to recover.

1) Proof of emotional distress

As with a plaintiff who is in the zone of danger, for a plaintiff who is a bystander, the majority rule is that the emotional distress must be manifested by **physical symptoms** (e.g., nightmares, shock, ulcers).

c. Special relationship

The duty to avoid negligent infliction of emotional distress exists without any threat of physical impact or physical symptoms in cases in which there is a special relationship between the plaintiff and the defendant. The most common examples are a mortician mishandling a corpse or a common carrier mistakenly reporting the death of a relative.

Example: A physician negligently misdiagnoses a patient with a terminal illness that the patient does not have, and the patient goes into shock as a result.

2. Pure Economic Loss

A plaintiff who suffers only economic loss without any related personal injury or property damage cannot recover such loss through a negligence action. However, once a plaintiff has proven non-economic injury, he is entitled to recover both economic and non-economic damages.

3. Wrongful-Death Actions and Survival Actions

a. Wrongful-death actions

A decedent's spouse, next of kin, or personal representative may bring suit to recover **losses suffered as a result of a decedent's death** under wrongful-death actions created by state statutes. Under typical statutes, the recoverable damages include the **loss of support** (income) as a result of the decedent's death, as well as the **loss of companionship, society, and affection** experienced by the surviving family members, **but not pain and suffering**. Recovery, however, is limited to what the deceased would have recovered had he lived. Additionally, the decedent's creditors have no right to institute a claim against the amount awarded.

b. Survival actions

Survival statutes typically enable the personal representative of a decedent's estate to pursue **any claims the decedent herself would have had at the time of her death**, including claims for damages resulting from both personal injury and property damage. Such claims often involve damages resulting from the tort that injured the decedent and later resulted in her death.

Example: If the decedent was negligently injured by the driver of another automobile and lingered—out of work, in the hospital, and in extreme pain—for one year before passing away, his estate would be able to recover for his **medical expenses** from the time he was injured until his death, for his **loss of income** during this time, and for the **pain and suffering** he experienced.

Most states do not allow survival of tort actions involving intangible personal interests (such as defamation, malicious prosecution, or invasion of privacy) because they are considered too personal to survive the decedent's death.

If a jurisdiction recognizes both wrongful-death actions and survival actions, there is no double recovery.

4. **Recovery for Loss Arising From Injury to Family Members**

   a. **Spouses**

   One spouse may recover for loss of consortium and services as a result of injuries to the other spouse resulting from the defendant's tortious conduct.

   b. **Parent-child**

   A parent may recover damages for loss of services if a child is injured due to the defendant's tortious conduct. Many jurisdictions allow a parent to recover for loss of the child's companionship in a wrongful-death action if the child is killed, but only a few jurisdictions allow a parent to recover for such damages if the child is injured but lives.

   Similarly, many jurisdictions allow a child to recover for loss of the parent's companionship in a wrongful-death action, but most do not allow the child to recover such damages if the parent is injured but lives. In a wrongful-death action, the child's claim for loss of support resulting from the decedent's death will be brought by the statutorily designated adult family member as part of the wrongful-death action.

   c. **Limitations**

   The amount of damages recoverable in a derivative action (an action arising solely because of tortious harm to another) for interference with family relationships is reduced in a comparative-fault jurisdiction (and eliminated in a contributory-negligence jurisdiction) by the injured family member's contributory negligence. Thus, if the damages recovered in the injured family member's own action are reduced by the plaintiff's comparative fault, then the damages recoverable by his family members in their derivative action will also be reduced.

5. **"Wrongful Life" and "Wrongful Birth" Claims**

   a. **Wrongful life**

   Most states do not permit actions by a child for "wrongful life" based on the failure to properly perform a contraceptive procedure or failure to diagnose a congenital defect, even if the child is born with a disability. A few states permit a "wrongful life" action, but they limit the child's recovery to special damages attributable to the disability.

   b. **Wrongful birth**

   Conversely, many states do permit parents to recover for "wrongful birth" (failure to diagnose a defect) or "wrongful pregnancy" (failure to perform a contraceptive procedure). Generally, the mother can recover damages for the medical expenses of labor as well as for pain and suffering. In the case of a disabled child, the parents may be able to recover damages for the additional medical expenses of caring for that child, and, in some states, may recover for emotional distress as well.

H.   VICARIOUS LIABILITY

Vicarious liability is a form of strict liability in which one person is liable for the tortious actions of another. It arises when one person has the right, ability, or duty to control the activities of another, even though the first person was not directly liable for the injury. It is, of course, a defense to vicarious liability that the conduct of the person subject to the plaintiff's conduct was not tortious.

1.   Liability of an Employer for an Employee's Torts (Respondeat Superior)

a.   Employer's right of control

As a rule, a person is an employer if the person has the right to control the means and methods by which another performs a task or achieves a result. The person subject to this right is an employee. Absent a right to control, the person is likely an independent contractor (*see* 2. Torts Committed by Independent Contractors, *below*).

b.   Scope of employment

An employer is liable for the tortious conduct of an employee that is within the **scope of employment**. Conduct within the scope of employment includes acts that the employee is employed to perform or that are intended to profit or benefit the employer.

> Careful instructions directed to the employee do not insulate the employer from liability—even when the employee acts counter to the instructions—if the employee is acting within the scope of employment.

1)   Intentional torts

As with negligence, an employer's vicarious liability for an employee's intentional tort depends on whether the employee was acting within the scope of employment. Generally, an employer is not liable for the intentional tort of an employee. For example, if an employee, acting on a personal grudge, punches a customer, the employer probably will not be held liable. There are two exceptions, however. Restatement (Third) of Agency § 7.07.

a)   Force is inherent

When force is **inherent** in the employee's work (e.g., a bouncer at a bar), the employer may be responsible for injuries the employee inflicts in the course of his work.

b)   Position of authority

If the employer **authorizes** the employee to act on his behalf, and the employee's position provides the opportunity to commit an intentional tort, the employer may be liable. For example, if an employee with the power to sign contracts enters into a fraudulent contract with a third party, the employer may be liable.

2)   Detour and frolic

An employer may be liable for a tort committed by the employee during an employee's detour (a minor and permissible deviation from the scope of employment) but not for an employee's frolic (an unauthorized and substantial deviation).

The employer and employee are jointly and severally liable (*see* § IV.J.1. Joint and Several Liability, *infra*) for torts committed by the employee within the scope of employment.

c. Direct liability

In addition to vicarious liability for torts committed by an employee within the scope of employment, an employer is liable for its own negligence in the hiring, training, supervising, or entrustment of an employee. Generally, the employer's liability extends only to actions taken by the employee within the scope of the employment.

2. Torts Committed by Independent Contractors

a. Generally no vicarious liability

Those who engage an independent contractor are generally not vicariously liable for the torts of the independent contractor.

b. Distinguished from employee

An independent contractor is one engaged to accomplish a task or achieve a result but who is not subject to another's right to control the method and means by which the task is performed or the result reached.

   i)   Independent contractors tend to have specialized skills or knowledge, e.g., physicians and plumbers; and

   ii) Independent contractors tend to work for many employers, while employees more often work for a single employer.

c. Non-delegable duties

A person who hires an independent contractor is vicariously liable for certain conduct, including:

   i)   Inherently dangerous activities;

   ii) Non-delegable duties arising out of a relationship with a specific plaintiff or the public (i.e., activities that are inherently risky or that affect the public at large, such as construction work adjacent to a public highway);

   iii) The duty of a storekeeper or other operator of premises open to the public to keep such premises in a reasonably safe condition; and

   iv) In a minority of jurisdictions, the duty to comply with state safety statutes.

d. Apparent agency

Under the rule of apparent agency, a person who hires an independent contractor to perform services is subject to vicarious liability for physical harm if (i) the services are accepted in the reasonable belief that the person or the person's employees are rendering the services, and (ii) the independent contractor's negligence is a factual cause of harm to one who receives the services, and such harm is within the scope of liability. The reasonable belief must be traced to manifestations of the person, but the injured person need not be the person who accepts the services based on that belief.

Example: On a hot summer day, a brother and sister are walking on a city sidewalk in the neighborhood in which they live. The sister passes out. The brother hails a taxi. Painted on the taxi is the name of a taxi company that owns the taxi. The driver of the taxi is an independent contractor. The brother places his sister into the taxi, enters himself, and directs the taxi to drive them home. On the way there, the taxi, as a result of the driver's carelessness, hits a car. Both the brother and sister are injured. The taxi company is vicariously liable to the sister, as well as the brother, for the negligence of the taxi driver, even though only the brother relied on the identification of the taxi company as the provider of the taxi services.

e. Negligence in selection or supervision

A party who selects or supervises an independent contractor may be liable for his own negligence in selecting or supervising the independent contractor.

3. Business Partners and Joint Enterprise Participants

Partners in a partnership are jointly and severally liable for torts committed within the scope of the partnership. Participants in a joint enterprise, in which each has a common purpose with the other participants and there is a mutual right of control, may be liable for the tortious acts of each other that are committed within the scope of the business purposes.

By contrast, a member of a limited liability company (LLC) is generally not personally liable for torts committed by another member of the LLC.

4. Automobile Owners

a. Negligent entrustment

The owner of a vehicle (or any other object that carries the potential for harm, such as a gun or lawn mower) may be liable for the negligent acts of a driver or user to whom the car or other property was entrusted if the owner knew or should have known of the user's negligent propensities.

b. Family-purpose doctrine

Many jurisdictions, through either legislative enactments or judicial decisions, have adopted the family-purpose doctrine, providing that the owner of an automobile may be liable for the tortious acts of **any family member** driving the car with permission.

c. Owner liability statutes

Many jurisdictions have enacted statutes that provide that the owner of an automobile may be liable for the tortious acts of **anyone** driving the car with permission.

5. Parents and Their Children

a. No vicarious liability

The general rule is that parents are not vicariously liable for their minor child's torts. **Exceptions** to this general rule include situations in which:

i) The child commits a tort while acting as **the parent's agent**;

ii) State statutes provide for the liability of parents when children commit specified acts such as **vandalism or school violence**; or

iii) State statutes require that a parent, when he signs for the child's driver's license application, assumes liability for any damages caused by negligent acts that the child commits while driving a car.

b. Negligence of the parents

Parents, however, are liable for their own negligence with respect to their minor child's conduct. A parent is under a duty to exercise reasonable care to prevent a minor child from intentionally or negligently harming a third party, provided the parent:

   i) Has the ability to control the child; and

   ii) Knows or should know of the necessity and opportunity for exercising such control.

In such circumstances, a parent who fails to exercise control may be liable for harm caused by the child, even though the child, because of his age, is not liable. Restatement (Second) of Torts § 316 (1965).

Example: A father gives a gun to his six-year-old son. Although the son lacks the necessary maturity and judgment to operate the gun independently in a safe manner, the father allows the son to use the gun when the father is not present. The son, while aiming the gun at a toy in his yard, misses and accidentally shoots a neighbor. The father, because of his failure to properly supervise his son, can be liable for the injury suffered by the neighbor that is directly attributable to the son's conduct, even though the son himself will not be liable because of his age.

6. Liability for Another's Alcohol Consumption

a. Dram-Shop liability

Many states recognize, either by statute (a "dram-shop act") or by judicial decision, a cause of action against the seller of intoxicating beverages when a third party is subsequently injured due to the buyer's intoxication. Most states limit liability to situations in which the buyer was a minor or was intoxicated at the time of the sale. The states are divided as to whether the cause of action is grounded in negligence or strict liability.

b. Social host liability

Many states extend liability to a social host who serves intoxicating beverages (or substances) to a guest. Liability may be for the intoxicated person's injuries as well as those of a third party injured by the intoxicated person. Laws vary, and some are specifically directed to a person who serves alcohol (or makes it available) to a minor. Liability often extends to the intoxicated guest's torts that occur off premises (e.g., an intoxicated guest hits a pedestrian on the way home from the host's party).

7. Bailment Liability

A bailor may be liable for his own negligent actions but generally is not vicariously liable for the tortious acts of his bailee, except for those limited situations described above, such as bailments involving automobiles or parents and children.

I. IMMUNITIES FROM TORT LIABILITY

Traditionally, government entities, charities, and family members were immune from liability. Today, these immunities have been largely eliminated, but the rules governing the liability of these defendants continue to differ from those governing other tortfeasors.

1. **Liability of the Government and Its Officers**

    a. **Federal government**

    Under the Federal Tort Claims Act (FTCA), the U.S. government waives immunity in tort actions, with the following exceptions:

    i)   Certain enumerated torts (assault, battery, false imprisonment, false arrest, malicious prosecution, abuse of process, libel and slander, misrepresentation and deceit, and interference with contract rights), although intentional torts committed by law-enforcement officers are not excepted;

    ii) Discretionary functions (i.e., planning or decision making, as opposed to operational acts);

    iii) Assertion of the government's immunity by a government contractor in a products-liability case if the contractor conformed to government specifications and warned the government of any known dangers in the product; and

    iv) Certain traditional governmental activities (i.e., postal, tax collection or property seizure, admiralty, quarantine, money supply, and military activity).

    When the U.S. government waives its sovereign immunity under the FTCA, it is liable in the same manner and to the same extent that a private person under the same circumstances would be liable, but it is not liable for punitive damages.

    b. **State governments**

    Most states have waived sovereign immunity, at least partially, through legislation. Simultaneously, however, they have imposed limits on the amount of recovery and the circumstances under which the state can be held liable. They also have created procedural barriers to recover that do not exist in claims against private defendants. **State tort claims acts vary greatly** and therefore each act must be read carefully.

    Unless otherwise provided in the legislation, the same terms and conditions apply to the liability of state agencies—including prisons, hospitals, and educational institutions—as to the state itself.

    c. **Municipalities**

    1) **Usually governed by the state's tort claims act**

    Today, the liability of municipalities, other local governments, and their agencies usually is governed by the provisions of state tort claims acts.

    2) **Governmental versus proprietary functions**

    Traditionally, immunity attached to the performance of traditional governmental functions (such as police and court systems) but did not attach when a municipality was performing a "proprietary" function that often is performed by a private company (such as utilities and parking lots).

    3) **Public-duty rule**

    The public-duty rule provides that there is no liability to any one citizen for the municipality's failure to fulfill a duty that is owed to the public at large, unless that citizen has a special relationship with the municipality that creates a special duty. A special relationship can be shown by:

i) Promises or actions on the part of the municipality demonstrating an affirmative duty to act on behalf of the injured party;

ii) Knowledge by the municipality's agents that failure to act could lead to harm;

iii) Direct contact between the municipality's agents and the injured party; and

iv) The injured party's justifiable reliance on the municipality's affirmative duty.

d. Government officials

1) Discretionary functions

When a government official is personally sued, immunity applies if she is performing **discretionary functions** entrusted to her by law so long as the acts are done without malice or improper purpose.

2) Ministerial functions

There is no tort immunity for carrying out ministerial acts, such as driving while on government business.

3) Highly ranked officials

Many highly ranked government officials, such as legislators performing their legislative functions, judges performing their judicial functions, prosecutors, and some upper-echelon officials of the executive branches, are usually absolutely immune from personal liability.

4) Federal immunity

Under the so-called "Westfall Act," 28 U.S.C. § 2679(b)(1), the remedy against the United States under the FTCA for torts committed by federal employees precludes any personal liability on the part of a federal employee under state tort law.

2. Intra-family Immunity

Intra-family immunity applies only to personal injuries, not to property damage.

a. Interspousal immunity

Traditionally, interspousal immunity prevented one spouse from suing the other in a personal-injury action. In most jurisdictions today, however, interspousal immunity has been extinguished, and either spouse can now institute a cause of action for personal injury against the other spouse.

b. Parent-child immunity

Traditionally, parents were immune from tort claims brought by their children. In recent decades, however, there has been a clear trend toward abolishing or greatly restricting parental immunity, but abrogation has proceeded more slowly than in the case of interspousal immunity.

Courts generally allow parents to be held liable in areas other than **core parenting activities**. For example, most states allow children to sue parents:

i) For injuries arising from **automobile accidents**;

ii) In extreme cases, such as those involving **sexual abuse and intentional tortious conduct**; and

iii) When the parent is acting in a **dual capacity**, such as when the parent is a physician treating the child for an injury (medical malpractice claim allowed).

3. Charitable Immunity

Most states have either totally or partially eliminated the common-law rule of charitable immunity. Some states cap the amount of damages recoverable from a charitable institution.

J. SHARING LIABILITY AMONG MULTIPLE DEFENDANTS

1. Joint and Several Liability

a. Definition

Under the doctrine of joint and several liability, each of two or more tortfeasors who is found liable for a single and indivisible harm to the plaintiff is subject to liability to the plaintiff **for the entire harm**. *See* Restatement (Third) of Torts: Apportionment of Liability § A18. The plaintiff has the choice of collecting the entire judgment from one defendant, the entire judgment from another defendant, or portions of the judgment from various defendants, as long as the plaintiff's entire recovery does not exceed the amount of the judgment.

> **EXAM NOTE:** Always apply joint and several liability on the MBE unless the facts instruct you to apply a different test.

b. Application

Examples of when joint and several liability applies include, among other instances, when:

i) The tortious acts of two or more tortfeasors combine to produce an indivisible harm (*see* § IV.E.1.b.2. Concurrent tortfeasors contributing to an individual injury, *supra*);

ii) The harm results from the acts of one or more tortfeasors acting in concert (*see* § IV.E.1.b.4. Concert of action, *supra*);

iii) Alternative liability applies (*see* § IV.E.1.b.3. Alternative causation, *supra*);

iv) Res ipsa loquitur is used against multiple defendants (such as in a surgical setting), and the plaintiff is unable to identify the tortfeasor whose acts were negligent (*see* § IV.D.2. Res Ipsa Loquitur, *supra*); and

v) The employer and the employee are both held liable (*see* § IV.H.1. Liability of an Employer for an Employee's Torts (Respondeat Superior), *supra*).

c. Limitations

Most states limit the application of joint and several liability (e.g., to a defendant more than 10% at fault), and a few have eliminated it altogether. *See* § IV.J.3. Several (Proportionate) Liability, *below*.

2. Contribution

If two or more tortfeasors are subject to liability to the same plaintiff, and one of the tortfeasors has paid the plaintiff more than his fair share of the common liability, then he generally may sue any of the other joint tortfeasors for contribution and recover anything paid in excess of his fair share. A person seeking contribution must prove that the person against whom contribution is sought would have been liable to the plaintiff in an amount and share equal to or greater than the amount sought as contribution. *See* Restatement (Third) of Torts: Apportionment of Liability § 23.

a. Determining fair shares

In most jurisdictions, each party's fair share is determined by comparing how far each tortfeasor departed from the standard of reasonable care.

b. Intentional tortfeasor

Generally, a party who has committed an intentional tort may not seek contribution from another tortfeasor.

3. Several (Proportionate) Liability

A majority of states now restrict or reject joint and several liability and instead recognize **pure several liability**, under which **each tortfeasor is liable only for his proportionate share** of the plaintiff's damages. In most of these jurisdictions, each defendant's share of liability is determined in accordance with how far each deviated from the standard of reasonable care. In other words, the more culpable defendant pays the higher proportion of the damages.

4. Satisfaction and Release

Once a plaintiff has recovered fully from one or a combination of defendants, she is barred from pursuing further action against other tortfeasors. The plaintiff generally may not receive double recovery.

If the plaintiff has not been wholly compensated, it is now the usual rule that a release of one tortfeasor does not release the others but instead diminishes the claim against the others, ordinarily by the amount of compensation received from the released tortfeasor. However, a release may bar claims against other tortfeasors if either (i) the release agreement so provides or (ii) the plaintiff has been entirely compensated for his losses.

5. Indemnification

Indemnification is the shifting of the entire loss from one person to another.

a. Vicarious liability

Indemnification generally applies when a person is vicariously liable for the other's wrongdoing. The person who has discharged the liability is entitled to indemnity from the actual wrongdoer who was primarily responsible for the harm (e.g., an employer who pays a judgment for the tort of an employee because of the employer's vicarious liability).

b. Other instances of indemnification

A tortfeasor can seek complete reimbursement (indemnity) from another tortfeasor when:

i) There is a **prior indemnification agreement** between the parties (e.g., in the construction industry, a contractor may agree to indemnify a subcontractor for the latter's negligence that may occur in the future);

ii) There is a significant difference between the blameworthiness of two defendants such that **equity requires a shifting of the loss** to the more blameworthy defendant; or

iii) Under **strict products liability**, each supplier has a right of indemnification against all previous suppliers in a distribution chain.

Note: Indemnity in degree of blameworthiness is rejected in jurisdictions with comparative-negligence systems. These states apportion damages based on relative fault, although indemnification is allowed in other instances when it is not based on degree of fault.

K. DEFENSES TO NEGLIGENCE

1. Contributory Fault

Contributory fault occurs when a plaintiff **fails to exercise reasonable care** for her own safety and thereby **contributes to her own injury**. Note that when a plaintiff is suing a defendant for the negligent rendering of services, such as medical services, the plaintiff's negligent conduct in creating the condition that the defendant has been employed to remedy is not considered.

a. Contributory negligence: traditional rule

At common law, and in a handful of states, the plaintiff's contributory negligence (i.e., failure to exercise reasonable care for her own safety) is a **complete bar to recovery**, regardless of the percentage that the plaintiff's own negligence contributed to the harm.

Examples of contributory negligence include:

i) A plaintiff-pedestrian's crossing the street against the light; and

ii) A plaintiff driving at an unreasonable speed that deprived him of the opportunity to avoid a traffic accident.

A rescuer who takes significant risks when attempting a rescue may also be permitted to recover, despite the rescuer's negligence.

Contributory negligence is not a defense to an intentional tort, gross negligence, or recklessness.

b. Last clear chance

In contributory-negligence jurisdictions, the plaintiff may mitigate the legal consequences of her own contributory negligence if she proves that the defendant had the last clear chance to avoid injuring the plaintiff but failed to do so. This doctrine has been abolished in most comparative-fault jurisdictions.

1) Helpless plaintiff

A plaintiff who, due to his own contributory negligence, is in peril from which he cannot escape is in helpless peril. In such cases, the defendant is liable if she **knew or should have known** of the plaintiff's perilous situation and could have avoided harming the plaintiff but for her (the defendant's) own negligence.

2) Inattentive plaintiff

A plaintiff who, due to his own contributory negligence, is in peril from which he could escape if he were paying attention is an inattentive or oblivious plaintiff. The defendant is liable only if she has **actual knowledge** of the plaintiff's inattention.

c. Comparative fault

Almost all jurisdictions have adopted some form of comparative fault (comparative negligence). There are two basic forms of comparative fault.

1) Pure comparative negligence

In jurisdictions that have adopted the doctrine of pure comparative negligence, a plaintiff's contributory negligence is not a complete bar to recovery. Instead, the plaintiff's full damages are calculated by the trier of fact and then reduced by the proportion that the plaintiff's fault bears to the total harm (e.g., if the plaintiff's full damages are $100,000, the plaintiff is 80% at fault, and the defendant is 20% at fault, then the plaintiff will recover $20,000).

> **EXAM NOTE:** Always apply pure comparative negligence on the MBE unless the facts instruct you to apply a different test.

2) Modified or partial comparative fault

A majority of comparative-fault jurisdictions apply modified comparative fault. In these jurisdictions:

i) If the plaintiff is **less at fault than the defendant**, then the plaintiff's recovery is **reduced by his percentage of fault**, just as in a pure comparative-fault jurisdiction;

ii) If the plaintiff is **more at fault than the defendant**, then the plaintiff's **recovery is barred**, just as in a contributory-negligence jurisdiction;

iii) In the vast majority of modified comparative-fault jurisdictions, if the plaintiff and the defendant are **equally at fault**, then the **plaintiff recovers 50% of his total damages**. In a few modified comparative-fault jurisdictions, the plaintiff recovers nothing when the plaintiff and the defendant are equally at fault.

3) Multiple defendants

In either a pure comparative-fault or a modified comparative-fault jurisdiction, the plaintiff's degree of negligence is compared to the total negligence of all defendants combined.

4) Relationships to other defenses

i) Last clear chance no longer applies as a separate doctrine in comparative-fault jurisdictions.

ii) Comparative fault will reduce the plaintiff's recovery even if the defendant's conduct is willful, wanton, or reckless, but it will not reduce the plaintiff's recovery for intentional torts.

iii) The impact of comparative fault on assumption of risk is considered in § IV.K.2.c. Unreasonably proceeding in the face of known, specific risk, *below*.

5) Illustrations

i) Single defendant, pure comparative—The defendant is 55% negligent and the plaintiff is 45% negligent in causing the accident. They each have $100,000 in damages. The plaintiff will recover $55,000 from the defendant ($100,000 minus $45,000, which represents the plaintiff's proportionate fault of 45%), and the defendant will recover $45,000 from the plaintiff. The plaintiff will have a net recovery of $10,000 because the defendant's damages will be offset against the plaintiff's damages.

ii) **Single defendant, modified or partial comparative**—Same facts as above, except that the defendant will not recover anything because he was more than 50% at fault.

iii) **Multiple defendants, modified or partial comparative**—Two defendants are negligent: Defendant 1 is 20% negligent; Defendant 2 is 45% negligent. Combined, their negligence is 65%. The plaintiff is 35% negligent. The plaintiff can recover $65,000 from either Defendant 1 or Defendant 2 under the theory of joint and several liability. The paying defendant can then seek contribution from the nonpaying defendant. If either defendant suffered damages, he also has a right of recovery against either of the other two negligent parties because each one's negligence is less than the total negligence of the other two.

d. Imputed contributory negligence

Imputed contributory negligence occurs when another person's fault is "imputed" to the plaintiff to prevent or limit his recovery due to the other person's fault. For example, an employee's negligent driving may prevent or reduce an employer's recovery from a third party if the employer's car is damaged by the third party's negligence. The fault of one business partner can be imputed to another business partner as contributory negligence when the second party is suing a third party.

Imputed contributory negligence is disfavored. Imputed contributory negligence does not apply to:

i) A married plaintiff whose spouse was contributorily negligent in causing the harm, in a suit against a third party;

ii) A child plaintiff whose parent's negligence was a contributing cause of her harm, in a suit against a third party;

iii) An automobile passenger suing a third-party driver if the negligence of the driver of the car in which the passenger was riding also contributed to the accident; or

iv) An automobile owner in an action against a defendant driver for negligence when the driver of the owner's car also was negligent.

e. Distinguishing comparative fault, contribution, and several liability

Comparative fault, contribution, and several liability all involve comparing the level of egregiousness of fault of parties in tort litigation. However, each of these concepts operates in a different context:

i) Comparative fault always involves comparing the fault of a plaintiff with the fault of one or more defendants;

ii) Contribution involves comparing the degrees of fault of co-defendants in an action or as the result of a motion by one co-defendant against another co-defendant; it does not affect the liability of any of the defendants to the plaintiff;

iii) Several liability, in the jurisdictions where it operates, involves comparing the levels of fault of the co-defendants; however, unlike with contribution, the issue is how much the plaintiff will receive from each defendant.

2. **Assumption of the Risk**

   a. **Express: Exculpatory clauses in contracts**

   In general, parties can contract to disclaim liability for negligence. But courts **will not** enforce exculpatory provisions:

   i) Disclaiming liability for reckless or wanton misconduct or gross negligence;

   ii) When there is a gross disparity of bargaining power between the parties;

   iii) When the party seeking to apply the exculpatory provision offers services of great importance to the public that are a practical necessity for some members of the public such as medical services;

   iv) If the exculpatory clause is subject to typical contractual defenses such as fraud or duress; or

   v) When it is against public policy to enforce agreements that insulate people from the consequences of their own negligence.

   Some jurisdictions require that the contract explicitly state that claims "based on negligence" are disclaimed.

   Generally, **common carriers, innkeepers, and employers cannot disclaim liability for negligence**. State statutes often provide that certain additional businesses cannot disclaim liability for negligence.

   Many courts now hold that **disclaimer of liability by contract negates** the fact that the defendant owes a **duty of care** to the plaintiff in the first place. This causes the plaintiff's prima facie case for negligence to fail, rather than acting as an affirmative defense of assumption of the risk.

   b. **Implied: Participants in and spectators of athletic events**

   In a negligence claim brought by a spectator of or a participant in an athletic event or similar activity, the spectator or participant necessarily subjects himself to certain risks that are usually incident to and inherent in the game or activity. Some courts hold that the other players or facility owners therefore do not owe the spectators a duty of care; others allow the defendant to defend against the claim using the affirmative defense of assumption of the risk.

   c. **Implied: Unreasonably proceeding in the face of known, specific risk**

   Traditionally, and in many jurisdictions today, a plaintiff's **voluntarily encountering a known, specific risk** is an affirmative defense to negligence that affects recovery. Most courts hold that the voluntary encountering must also be **unreasonable**.

   In the few **contributory negligence** jurisdictions and in a minority of comparative-fault jurisdictions, this form of assumption of the risk remains a **total bar** to recovery.

   In most **comparative fault** jurisdictions, this form of assumption of the risk has been merged into the comparative-fault analysis and merely **reduces recovery**. The plaintiff's awareness of the risk is considered in determining the degree to which the plaintiff is at fault, but it also can be considered in determining the reasonableness of the plaintiff's or the defendant's actions.

Consent distinguished: Consent is a defense to intentional torts, whereas assumption of the risk applies to negligence actions and actions alleging strict liability.

V.   STRICT LIABILITY

A prima facie case for strict liability requires (i) an absolute duty to make the plaintiff's person or property safe, (ii) actual and proximate causation, and (iii) damages.

The three general situations in which strict liability is imposed are:

i)   **D**angerous activities;

ii)   **A**nimals; and

iii)   **D**efective or dangerous products.

MNEMONIC: **DAD**

EXAM NOTE: The "DAD" situations are the only situations in which a defendant can be liable without fault. Otherwise, strict liability is generally the wrong answer choice.

A.   ABNORMALLY DANGEROUS ACTIVITIES

1.   Basic Rule

A defendant engaged in an abnormally dangerous activity may be held strictly liable—without any proof of negligence—for personal injuries and property damage caused by the activity, regardless of precautions taken to prevent the harm. Restatement (Third) of Torts: Liability for Physical and Emotional Harm § 20.

The concept was first introduced in the English case, *Rylands v. Fletcher*, LR 3 HL 330 (1868), holding an owner of property with a dam on it strictly liable for the harm caused by the release of water due to the bursting of the dam.

2.   Definition of "Abnormally Dangerous"

Abnormally dangerous means that an activity:

i)   Creates a **foreseeable and highly significant risk** of physical harm even when reasonable care is exercised; and

ii)   The activity is **not commonly engaged in**.

In addition to these requirements, in evaluating whether an activity is abnormally dangerous, courts often consider the **gravity of the harm** resulting from the activity, the **inappropriateness of the place** where the activity is being conducted, and the **limited value** of the activity to the community.

EXAM NOTE: The focus is on the inherent nature of the activity, not on how careful the defendant may or may not be in conducting the activity.

Common abnormally dangerous activities include mining, blasting, using explosives, fumigating, crop dusting, excavating, disposing of hazardous waste, storing gasoline in residential areas, storing toxic chemicals and gases, and storing large quantities of water and other liquids.

Jurisdictions are split as to whether fireworks displays constitute an abnormally dangerous activity. Some compare the activity to blasting, finding that fireworks displays are not commonly engaged in and present substantial risks that cannot be eliminated with the exercise of reasonable care. Other jurisdictions, relying on the Second Restatement of Torts, have found that their value to the community outweighs the risks, and do not find the activity abnormally dangerous.

Damage or injury caused by flying aircraft is no longer subject to strict liability, though a few states still apply the doctrine to ground damage from an airplane crash.

3. Scope of Risk

Strict liability for an abnormally dangerous activity exists **if the harm that occurs results from the risk that made the activity abnormally dangerous in the first place**.

Example: If the defendant's employee drops a heavy package of explosives, hitting the plaintiff's head and causing a concussion, the plaintiff's claim is for negligence, not strict liability. The concussion is not the type of harm (i.e., an explosion) that makes the use of explosives an abnormally dangerous activity.

As in the case with negligence, the defendant's liability can be cut off by unforeseeable intervening causes. *See* § IV.E.3.b.2.b) Unforeseeable intervening causes, *supra*.

B. ANIMALS

1. Wild Animals

A wild animal is an animal that, **as a species or a class**, is not by custom devoted to the service of humankind in the place where it is being kept. For example, a wild elephant that has been tamed and exhibited as part of a circus remains categorized as a wild animal. Many states have passed legislation to protect those who display wild animals to the public (e.g., a public zoo), applying a negligence standard instead of strict liability.

a. Dangerous propensity

The possessor of a wild animal is strictly liable for harm done by that animal, in spite of any precautions the possessor has taken to confine the animal or prevent the harm, if the harm arises from a **dangerous propensity** that is **characteristic of such a wild animal** or of which the owner **has reason to know**.

b. Plaintiff's fearful reaction

Strict liability applies to an injury caused by a **plaintiff's fearful reaction to the sight of an unrestrained wild animal**, in addition to injuries caused directly by the wild animal.

c. Liability to trespassers

Licensees or invitees injured by a wild animal may recover in strict liability. A landowner is **not** strictly liable for injuries inflicted by his animals against a **trespasser**, except for injuries inflicted by a **vicious watchdog**. Remember, however, that a landowner may be liable on a negligence theory.

2. Domestic Animals

a. Known to be dangerous

A domestic animal's owner is strictly liable for injuries caused by that animal if he **knows or has reason to know** of the animal's **dangerous propensities**, and the harm results from those dangerous propensities. Otherwise, at common law, the owner of a domestic animal is liable only for negligence.

b. "Dog-bite" statutes

Many states have enacted "dog-bite" statutes that hold owners of dogs or other domestic animals designated in the statute strictly liable for damages resulting from personal injuries.

3. Trespassing Animals

The owner of any animal, wild or domestic (other than household pets), is strictly liable for any reasonably foreseeable damage caused by his animal while trespassing on the land of another. The exception for household pets (the Third Restatement specifically mentions dogs and cats) does not apply if the owner knows or has reason to know that the dog or cat is intruding on another's property in a way that has a tendency to cause substantial harm. The general negligence standard applies if an animal strays onto a public road and contributes to an accident there. Restatement (Third) of Torts: Liability for Physical and Emotional Harm § 21.

4. The Landlord's Liability

In most jurisdictions, the landlord is not liable for harms caused by animals owned by his tenants. The landlord lacks the required element of control over the animal. Some jurisdictions impose liability on the landlord based on negligence if the landlord is aware of the dangerous propensities of the dog or other animal.

C. DEFENSES TO STRICT LIABILITY

1. Contributory Negligence

In contributory-negligence jurisdictions, the plaintiff's contributory negligence is not a defense to strict liability, i.e., it does not bar recovery.

2. Comparative Fault

Courts are divided, and in some comparative-fault jurisdictions, the plaintiff's contributory negligence does not reduce the plaintiff's recovery under a strict-liability claim. Other jurisdictions and the Third Restatement would allow recovery to be reduced by the comparative fault of the plaintiff.

3. Assumption of the Risk

The plaintiff's assumption of the risk bars his recovery in a strict-liability action. This defense is also referred to as "knowing contributory negligence." With animals, if the plaintiff is aware of the dangerous propensity of an animal and taunts the animal, he may be prohibited from recovering under the doctrine of assumption of the risk.

4. Statutory Privilege

Performance of an essential public service (e.g., construction of utility or sewer lines) exempts one from strict liability; however, liability may still exist under a negligence theory.

VI. PRODUCTS LIABILITY

A product may be defective because of a defect in its **design** or **manufacture** or because of a **failure to adequately warn** the consumer of a hazard related to the foreseeable use of the product.

When a plaintiff files a products-liability case, he generally has at least three possible claims on which to base an action: **negligence, strict products liability**, and **breach of warranty**. Each type of claim requires different elements. (The Third Restatement provides for only a single cause of action in the absence of additional facts, and some courts have begun to adopt this approach.)

If, however, the defendant intended or knew with substantial certainty the consequences of the defect, then the cause of action could be based on an intentional tort. As with any intentional tort claim, punitive as well as compensatory damages are recoverable. The same defenses germane to each type of tort are applicable.

A. NEGLIGENCE

As with any negligence action, the plaintiff must prove duty, breach, causation, and damages to prevail.

1. Duty

The commercial manufacturer, distributor, retailer, or seller of a product owes a duty of reasonable care to **any foreseeable plaintiff** (i.e., a purchaser, user, or bystander).

2. Breach

Failure to exercise **reasonable care** in the inspection or sale of a product constitutes breach of that duty. The plaintiff must establish not only that the defect exists, but also that the defendant's negligent conduct (lack of reasonable care) led to the plaintiff's harm. In other words, had the defendant exercised reasonable care in the inspection or sale of the product, the defect **would have been discovered**, and the plaintiff would not have been harmed. The plaintiff also has the option of invoking res ipsa loquitur if the defect could not have occurred without the manufacturer's negligence.

The individual defendant must have breached his duty to reasonably inspect or sell. Unlike in strict products liability, the negligence of others in the supply chain cannot be imputed. Rather, the plaintiff has the burden of proving fault on the part of any particular defendant.

3. Causation

The plaintiff must prove factual and proximate causation. *See* IV.E. Causation, *supra*.

When a retailer sells a product with a known defect and without giving adequate warnings about the defect, the failure to warn may be a superseding cause, breaking the chain of causation between the manufacturer and the injury.

4. Damages

The plaintiff is entitled to recover damages resulting from any personal injury or property damage. A claim for purely economic loss (including a claim for harm to the product itself) is generally not allowed under either a negligence theory or a strict-liability theory, but it must be brought as a breach-of-warranty action.

5. Defenses

The standard negligence defenses of contributory/comparative negligence and assumption of the risk apply.

B. STRICT PRODUCTS LIABILITY

Under strict liability, the manufacturer, retailer, or other distributor of a defective product may be liable for any harm to persons or property caused by such product.

EXAM NOTE: Strict products liability is only one way that a manufacturer or supplier of a product can be held liable for a plaintiff's injuries. Remember also to consider breach of warranty and negligence.

1.   **Elements of a Claim**

To recover, the plaintiff must plead and prove that:

i)   The product was **defective** (in manufacture, design, or failure to warn);

ii) The defect existed at the time the product left the defendant's control; and

iii) The defect **caused the plaintiff's injuries** when the product was used in an **intended or reasonably foreseeable way**.

2.   **Defective Product**

A product is defective when, at the time of the sale or distribution, it contains a manufacturing defect, a design defect, or inadequate instructions or warnings (i.e., failure to warn).

a.   **Manufacturing defect**

A manufacturing defect is a **deviation from what the manufacturer intended** the product to be that causes harm to the plaintiff. The test for the existence of such a defect is whether the product **conforms to the defendant's own specifications**.

b.   **Design defect**

Depending on the jurisdiction, courts apply either the **consumer-expectation test** or the **risk-utility test** to determine whether a design defect exists. Many jurisdictions use various hybrids of the two tests, and some states allow the plaintiff to prove a design defect under either test.

i)   **Consumer-expectation test:** Does the product include a condition not contemplated by the ordinary consumer that is **unreasonably dangerous** to him?

ii) **Risk-utility test:** Do the risks posed by the product **outweigh its benefits**?

Under the risk-utility test, in a majority of jurisdictions and under the Third Restatement, the plaintiff must prove that a **reasonable alternative design** was available to the defendant and the failure to use that design has rendered the product not reasonably safe. The alternative design must be economically feasible.

Merely providing a warning does not necessarily prevent a product from being unreasonably dangerous.

c.   **Failure to warn**

An action brought under a failure-to-warn theory is essentially the same as a design-defect claim, but the defect in question is the manufacturer's failure to provide an adequate warning related to the risks of using the product. A failure-to-warn defect exists if there were **foreseeable risks of harm, not obvious to an ordinary user** of the product, which risks could have been reduced or avoided by providing reasonable instructions or warnings. The failure to include the instructions or warnings renders the product not reasonably safe.

1)   **Prescription drugs**

Under the "learned-intermediary" rule, the manufacturer of a prescription drug typically satisfies its duty to warn the consumer by informing the prescribing physician of problems with the drug rather than informing the patient taking the drug. Restatement (Third) of Torts: Products Liability § 6 (1998). There are several exceptions, including, most importantly:

i) If the manufacturer is aware that the drug will be dispensed or administered without the personal intervention or evaluation of a healthcare provider, such as when a vaccine is administered through a mass inoculation; and

ii) As a result of a federal statute, in the case of birth control pills.

d. Inference of defect

A plaintiff is entitled to a res ipsa loquitur–like inference that a product defect existed if the harm suffered by the plaintiff:

i) Was of a kind that ordinarily occurs as a result of a product defect; and

ii) Was not solely the result of causes other than a product defect existing at the time of sale or distribution.

Restatement (Third) of Torts: Products Liability § 3 (1998).

This inference is frequently applied in cases involving a manufacturing defect when the product is lost or destroyed as a consequence of the incident that caused the plaintiff's harm.

3. Plaintiffs

To bring a strict-liability action, a plaintiff is not required to be in privity of contract with the defendant. **Anyone foreseeably injured** by a defective product or whose property is harmed by the product may bring a strict-liability action. Appropriate plaintiffs include **not only purchasers**, but also **other users** of the product and even **bystanders** who suffer personal injury or property damage.

4. Defendants

> **EXAM NOTE:** MBE questions frequently involve the viability of claims against various defendants and the possibility of cross-claims among these defendants.

a. Business of a seller

To be subject to strict liability for a defective product, the defendant must be in the **business of selling** or otherwise distributing products of the type that harmed the plaintiff.

b. Chain of distribution

Included as a seller are the **manufacturer** of the product, its **distributor**, and its **retail seller**.

c. Even if not responsible for the defect

As long as the seller is a commercial supplier of the product, she is subject to strict liability for a defective product, even if the revenue from sales of the product is not a significant portion of her business. The seller is strictly liable even if the seller was not responsible for the defect in any way and even when the product is not purchased directly from the seller.

d. Seller of a component part

The commercial supplier of a component, such as sand used in manufacturing cement or a switch used in an electrical device, is subject to liability if the component itself is defective, but not when the component is incorporated into a product that is defective for another reason. However, the commercial supplier of a component may be liable if that supplier substantially participates in the process of integrating the component into the design of the assembled product and that product is defective due to the integration.

e. Indemnification

Ordinarily, if the plaintiff recovers from the retailer solely for a product defect that existed at the time the product left the manufacturer's control, the retailer is able to recover from the manufacturer in an indemnification action.

f. Lessor

Generally, a lessor of a commercial product (e.g., car, boat, tools) is subject to strict liability for a defective product.

g. Products and services

A product is tangible personal property distributed commercially for use or consumption. A service is not a product. A seller that provides both products and services generally is **liable if the defective product is consumed**, such as food at a restaurant, but not if the product is only used, such as the vendor of a balloon ride when the balloon itself is defective. Hospitals and doctors generally are treated as providing a service, rather than a product, in cases in which the defective product is used as a tool, loaned to the patient, or even implanted in the patient.

h. Exclusions

1) Casual seller

Because the seller must be in the business of selling similar products, a casual seller, such as an individual car owner who sells a car to his neighbor or an accountant who sells her office furniture to another businessperson, is not subject to strict liability.

2) Auctioneer

Similarly, an auctioneer of a product generally is not subject to strict liability with respect to the products auctioned.

3) Employer

The immunity created by workers' compensation statutes protects the plaintiff's employer from most tort claims brought by the victim. It does not provide any immunity for other defendants. Frequently, the plaintiff-employee is injured while working with a defective machine tool or with a toxic substance, such as asbestos insulation. Workers' compensation does not bar a claim against the manufacturer of these products.

5. Damages

As with negligence claims, the plaintiff is entitled to recover damages for any personal injury or property damage. A claim for **purely economic loss generally is not allowed under a strict-liability theory** but must be brought as a breach-of-warranty action, as must a claim for harm to the product itself and any consequential damages arising therefrom.

6. **Defenses**

a. **Comparative fault**

In most states and under the Third Restatement, the plaintiff's own negligence reduces his recovery in a strict-products-liability action in the same manner as in a negligence action. In those jurisdictions, a plaintiff's conduct that amounts to an "assumption of the risk" is treated as comparative negligence in order to reduce but not eliminate recovery. In some comparative-fault jurisdictions, the plaintiff's recovery in strict products liability is not reduced by the percentage that the plaintiff's fault contributed to causing her injury.

b. **Contributory negligence**

In a contributory-negligence jurisdiction, the plaintiff's negligence generally is not a defense to a strict-products-liability action when the plaintiff negligently failed to discover the defect or misused the product in a reasonably foreseeable way, but it generally is when the plaintiff's fault consisted of unreasonably proceeding in the face of a known product defect.

Suppliers are required to anticipate reasonably foreseeable misuses of their products.

c. **Assumption of the risk**

Assumption of the risk is a subjective standard. The plaintiff must be aware of the danger and knowingly expose himself to it. Voluntary and knowing assumption of the risk is a complete bar to recovery in contributory-negligence jurisdictions and in a small number of comparative-fault jurisdictions. Because traditional assumption of the risk has been eliminated in most comparative-fault jurisdictions, in those states, a plaintiff's assumption of a risk reduces his recovery in proportion to his degree of fault, but it is not a complete bar to recovery.

d. **Product misuse, modification, or alteration by the user**

The misuse, alteration, or modification of a product by the user in a manner that is neither intended by nor reasonably foreseeable to the manufacturer typically negates liability. On the other hand, foreseeable misuse, alteration, or modification usually does not preclude recovery.

A majority of comparative-fault jurisdictions treat product misuse as a form of fault that reduces, but does not eliminate, the plaintiff's recovery. A significant minority of comparative-fault jurisdictions, and most contributory-negligence jurisdictions, hold that product misuse totally bars recovery.

EXAM NOTE: Product misuse has been tested frequently on the MBE.

e. **Substantial change in the product**

If the product substantially changes between the time it is distributed by the manufacturer and the time it reaches the consumer (e.g., a part is reconditioned), then this change may constitute a **superseding cause** that cuts off the liability of the original manufacturer.

f. **Compliance with governmental standards**

Most often, compliance with governmental safety standards is not conclusive evidence that the product is not defective. On the other hand, the jury can consider evidence introduced by the defendant that the product complied with governmental standards and also evidence offered by the plaintiff on the product's failure to comply with these standards in deciding whether the product is defective.

However, if a product complies with federal safety statutes or regulations, a state tort claim act may be "preempted" if (i) Congress has explicitly so indicated, (ii) Congress has comprehensively regulated the field (i.e., "field preemption"), or (iii) it would be impossible for the manufacturer to comply with both the federal regulation and the requirements of state tort law.

g. "State of the art"

In failure-to-warn and design-defect cases, the manufacturer may introduce as evidence the level of relevant scientific, technological, and safety knowledge existing and reasonably feasible at the time of the product's distribution. In most jurisdictions, compliance with this "state of the art" standard does not bar recovery against the manufacturer as a matter of law. However, many states have enacted statutes providing that compliance with the state-of-the-art standard is a total bar to recovery.

h. Statute of limitations issues

The statute of limitations begins to run against the plaintiff with a personal injury whenever he discovers, or in the exercise of reasonable care should discover, his injury and its connection to the product. As a result, the statute of limitations may not preclude an action against a manufacturer or other seller until many decades after the manufacture and distribution of the product. For example, asbestos-related diseases may not manifest themselves until decades after the distribution of the asbestos insulation and the plaintiff's exposure to it.

i. Contract disclaimers, limitations, and waivers

A **disclaimer** or limitation of remedies or other contractual exculpation (i.e., waiver) by a product seller or other distributor **does not generally bar** or reduce an otherwise valid products-liability claim for personal injury.

j. Unforeseeable intervening causes

As in the case with negligence, the defendant's liability can be cut off by unforeseeable intervening causes. *See* § IV.E.3.b.2.b) Unforeseeable intervening causes, *supra*.

C. WARRANTIES

Products-liability actions brought under warranty theories generally may be brought not only against a retailer of a product, but also against a manufacturer or distributor of goods, at least when damages are sought for personal injury or property damage.

1. Implied Warranties

a. Two types

1) Merchantability

The implied warranty of merchantability warrants that the product being sold is **generally acceptable and reasonably fit for the ordinary purposes for which it is being sold**. The seller must be a merchant with respect to the kind of goods at issue.

2) Fitness for a particular purpose

The implied warranty of fitness warrants that a product is fit for a particular purpose, but only if the **seller knows the particular purpose** for which the product is being purchased and the buyer **relies on the seller's skill or judgment in supplying the product**.

b. Damages

Any product that fails to live up to either of the above warranties constitutes a breach of the defendant's warranty; the **plaintiff need not prove any fault** on the defendant's part.

The buyer may recover damages for personal injury and property damage, as well as for **purely economic loss**.

c. Privity requirement

As for recovery by an injured party other than the buyer, the Uniform Commercial Code (UCC) includes three alternative provisions governing privity requirements of the plaintiff. The majority of states have adopted Alternative A, which is the most restrictive provision. It allows only the purchaser or a member of her family or household to recover for personal injury, but not property damage or pure economic loss. Alternative B allows anyone reasonably expected to use, consume, or be affected by the product to recover for personal injury. Alternative C is similar to Alternative B but also allows for recovery of property damage and economic loss. Some states have not adopted any alternative while others have adopted a modified version.

2. Express Warranties

An express warranty is a guarantee—an **affirmation of fact or a promise**—made by the seller regarding the product that is part of the **basis of a bargain**. A seller is liable for any breach of that warranty, regardless of fault. Damages for personal injury or property damage are recoverable.

3. Defenses to Warranty Claims

a. Disclaimers

Although the seller generally can disclaim warranties, in the case of **consumer goods, any limitation of consequential damages for personal injury is prima facie unconscionable**.

Disclaimer clauses that conflict with the express warranties, such as "all warranties, express or implied, are disclaimed," are ignored. UCC § 2-316. In the case of express warranties, a disclaimer is valid only if it is consistent with the warranty, which it usually is not.

b. Tort defenses

1) Assumption of the risk

The plaintiff's unreasonable, voluntary encountering of a known product risk affects recovery in the same way as it would in a strict-products-liability claim.

2) Comparative fault

Most comparative-fault jurisdictions reduce recovery based on warranty claims in the same way they would strict-products-liability claims.

3) Contributory negligence

In contributory-negligence jurisdictions, most courts hold that contributory negligence does not bar a plaintiff's warranty claim, except when the contributory negligence consists of the unreasonable encountering of a known risk (i.e., the overlap between contributory negligence and assumption of the risk).

4) Product misuse in implied warranty claims

With or without using the language of "product misuse," most courts find that product misuse prevents recovery under the implied warranty of merchantability when the product is warranted to be fit for ordinary purposes.

5) Failure to provide notice of breach

A warranty claim generally fails if the plaintiff fails to provide the seller with notice of the breach of warranty within the statutorily required time period (when applicable) or a reasonable period of time.

VII. DEFAMATION, INVASION OF PRIVACY, AND BUSINESS TORTS

A. DEFAMATION

A plaintiff may bring an action for defamation if:

i) The defendant's **defamatory language**;

ii) Is **of or concerning** the plaintiff;

iii) Is **published** to a third party who **understands** its defamatory nature; and

iv) It **damages** the plaintiff's reputation.

For **matters of public concern**, the plaintiff is constitutionally required to prove **fault** on the part of the defendant. If the plaintiff is either **a public official or a public figure**, then the plaintiff must prove **actual malice**. If either (i) the defamatory statement relates to a matter of public concern or (ii) the plaintiff is a public official or a public figure, then the plaintiff must prove that the **defamatory statement is false** as part of her prima facie case.

1. Defamatory Language

Language that harms a person's reputation by diminishing respect, esteem, or goodwill toward the plaintiff, or deterring others from associating with the plaintiff, is defamatory. The plaintiff may introduce extrinsic facts to establish defamation by innuendo.

An opinion is actionable if the defendant implies that there is a factual basis for that opinion. *See Milkovich v. Lorian Journal Co.*, 497 U.S. 1 (1990); *Gertz v. Welch, Inc.*, 418 U.S. 323 (1974).

Example: If the defendant said, "In my opinion, John Jones is a thief," the statement could be regarded as defamatory because it implies the fact that John Jones stole something. On the other hand, the statement, "In my opinion, John Jones is a lousy artist," cannot be the basis for a defamation action because people can disagree regarding the quality of an artist's paintings.

2. "Of or Concerning" the Plaintiff

A reasonable person must believe that the defamatory communication refers to this particular plaintiff and holds him up to scorn or ridicule in the eyes of a substantial number of respectable members of the community.

If the defamatory language applies to a group, then a member of the group can maintain a defamation action only if the group is so small that the matter can reasonably be understood to refer to that member, unless there is other evidence that the language refers to that particular member.

A deceased individual cannot be defamed. A corporation, partnership, or unincorporated association may be defamed if the language prejudices it in conducting its activities or deters others from dealing with it.

3. **Publication**

   a. **To a third party**

   Publication of defamatory matter is its **intentional or negligent** communication to a **third party** (i.e., to someone other than the person being defamed) who **understands** its defamatory nature.

   Example: If an employer confronts her employee in a face-to-face conversation during which no one else is present and no one can overhear the conversation and tells him that he is being fired because he embezzled company funds, then there is no publication and no defamation.

   > **EXAM NOTE:** MBE questions on defamation often center on the publication requirement. Remember that the statement must be **intentionally or negligently made to a third party**. Beware of fact patterns in which the publication requirement is not met, such as those involving a third party learning about the statement through no fault of the defendant's, a third party who doesn't understand the statement to be defamatory, or when no third party hears the statement.

   b. **Republication**

   A person who **repeats** a defamatory statement may be liable for defamation even though that person identifies the originator of the statement and expresses a lack of knowledge as to the truthfulness of the statement. In addition, a person who repeats a defamatory statement may be liable for defamation even though the communication of the statement to that person was privileged.

   c. **Internet service providers**

   A federal statute provides that Internet service providers are not publishers for the purpose of defamation law.

4. **Constitutional Requirements**

   Since the Supreme Court's opinion in *New York Times v. Sullivan*, 376 U.S. 254 (1964), which held that the First Amendment affects the plaintiff's right to recover under the common-law tort of defamation, constitutional requirements now underlie many aspects of defamation law. These constitutional requirements affect fundamental aspects of defamation law in various ways depending on (i) the category into which the plaintiff fits and (ii) the nature of the defamatory communication.

   a. **Public official**

   A public official is someone in the hierarchy of government employees who has, or appears to have, **substantial responsibility for or control over the conduct of government affairs**. **Candidates for public office** are also treated as public officials.

b. Public figure

The constitutional requirements are the same when the plaintiff is a public figure as when she is a public official.

There are two ways in which a plaintiff may be categorized as a public figure:

   i)   **General purpose public figures**—plaintiffs who occupy positions of such **persuasive power and influence in society** that they are deemed public figures for all purposes; and

   ii) **Limited purpose or special purpose public figures**—plaintiffs **who thrust themselves to the forefront of particular public controversies** in order to influence the resolution of the issues involved. These plaintiffs are treated as public figures **if the defamatory statement relates to their participation in the controversy**, but they are treated as private figures if the defamation relates to any other matter.

c. Private person

1) Matter of public concern

If the plaintiff is a **private person** (neither a public figure nor a public official) and the statement involves a matter of **public concern**, then the defendant is entitled to **limited constitutional protections**, though not as significant as those available when the person being defamed is either a public official or a public figure.

2) Not a matter of public concern

If the plaintiff is a **private person** and the statement is **not a matter of public concern**, then there are **no constitutional restrictions** on the law of defamation. However, many states now apply the same principles of defamation law to all cases involving private persons as plaintiffs.

5. Falsity

a. Matters of public concern

If either (i) the defamatory statement relates to a matter of public concern or (ii) the plaintiff is a public official or a public figure, then the plaintiff must prove that the **defamatory statement is false** as part of her prima facie case.

b. Private person plaintiff/not a matter of public concern

At common law and in some states today, a private person plaintiff suing for defamation regarding a statement that does not involve a matter of public concern is **not required to prove falsity** as part of her prima facie case. However, the defendant may prove the truth of the statement as an affirmative defense.

6. Fault

a. Public official or public figure

If the plaintiff in a defamation action is either a public official or a public figure, then the plaintiff is required to prove that the defendant acted with **actual malice**; that is, he either had **knowledge that the statement was false or acted with reckless disregard as to the truth or falsity of the statement**. To establish a reckless disregard for the truthfulness of a statement, the plaintiff must prove that the defendant entertained **serious doubts** about its truthfulness; mere failure to check facts is not sufficient. *New York Times Co. v. Sullivan*, 376 U.S. 254 (1964); *St. Amant v. Thompson*, 390 U.S. 727 (1968).

b. Private person/matter of public concern

If the plaintiff in a defamation action is a private person and the defendant's statement involves a matter of public concern, then the plaintiff is constitutionally required to prove that the **defendant acted with fault—either negligence or actual malice**. *Gertz v. Robert Welch, Inc.*, 418 U.S. 323 (1974). The level of fault will determine what damages may be recovered.

c. Private person/not a matter of public concern

If the plaintiff in a defamation action is a private person and the defendant's statement does not involve a matter of public concern, then the constitutional requirements do not apply. At common law, the defendant was strictly liable. Most states today require **at least negligence** by the defendant for all defamation actions, and some now require actual malice in all defamation actions.

7. Libel and Slander Distinguished

a. Libel

Defamation by words **written, printed, or otherwise recorded** in permanent form is libel.

1) Television and radio

Today, it is generally—though not universally—accepted that defamatory **radio and television broadcasts are libel**, regardless of whether they are spoken from a script.

2) E-mail and other electronic communication

Most courts addressing the issue have held that e-mail messages are categorized as **libel**. It is not yet clear whether courts will hold that tweets and text messages are libel or slander.

3) General and presumed damages

Subject to the constitutionally imposed limits on damages recoverable in a defamation action, the libel plaintiff need only prove **general damages** in order to complete the prima facie tort of libel. General damages are any damages that **compensate the plaintiff for harm to her reputation**. Under the common law, the plaintiff was entitled to recover "presumed damages" as part of general damages. The plaintiff did not need to prove that she actually incurred any damages; her lawyer only needed to invite the jury to award the damages that it believed flowed from the defendant's defamatory communication.

4) Libel per quod

In some jurisdictions, under the doctrine of libel per quod, if the nature of the defamatory statement requires proof of extrinsic facts to show that the statement is defamatory, then the plaintiff must prove either special damages or that the statement fits into one of the four categories of statements that satisfy the requirements of slander per se.

b. Slander

Defamation by **spoken word, gesture, or any form other than libel** is slander. To recover for slander, the plaintiff must plead and prove one of the following.

1) Special damages

Special damages require the plaintiff to prove that a third party **heard** the defendant's defamatory comments and **acted adversely** to her. Most often, special damages involve an economic loss to the plaintiff, e.g., loss of employment or loss of business, but they also would include such things as the plaintiff's fiancé breaking off the engagement or a friend refusing to host the plaintiff in her home after hearing the defamatory comments.

2) Slander per se

Under the doctrine of slander per se, a plaintiff alleging slander need not plead and prove special damages if the statement defaming her fits into one of four categories.

To qualify as slander per se, the defamatory statement must accuse the plaintiff of one of the following.

i) **Committing a crime.** In many jurisdictions, the crime must be one involving moral turpitude or one that subjects the criminal to imprisonment.

ii) **Conduct reflecting on the plaintiff's lack of fitness to conduct his business, trade, or profession.** A general disparaging statement (e.g., the plaintiff "is a drunk") must be particularly harmful to one engaged the plaintiff's business, trade, or profession.

iii) **Having a loathsome disease.** Traditionally, loathsome diseases included illnesses such as leprosy or a sexually transmitted disease.

iv) **Sexual misconduct.** In modern times, examples of cases falling within this subcategory, as well as the previous one, are very rare. A few courts have held that trading sex for drugs constitutes sexual misconduct.

3) Parasitic damages

Once the plaintiff satisfies the requirements of the slander per se prima facie tort by proving either special damages or slander per se, at common law, she could recover general damages as parasitic damages.

4) Constitutional constraints

Damages recoverable in a slander action, as well as damages recoverable in a libel action, are subject to the constitutional limitations discussed below.

8. Constitutional Limitations on Damages

If the plaintiff is a private figure and the matter is one of public concern, presumed and punitive damages may not be awarded if the plaintiff establishes the defendant's fault without proving actual malice. *Gertz v. Robert Welch Inc., supra.* However, if the plaintiff is a private figure and the matter is not one of public concern, presumed and punitive damages may be awarded even if the plaintiff establishes the defendant's fault without proving actual malice. *Dun & Bradstreet, Inc. v. Greenmoss Builders, Inc.,* 472 U.S. 749 (1985).

9. Defenses

a. Truth

Truth is an absolute defense to a claim of defamation.

Falsity as an element of a cause of action: For a defamation action brought by a public official or figure, by a limited public figure, or by a private figure regarding a statement about a matter of public concern, the falsity of the statement is an element that the plaintiff must prove.

Common-law distinction: The plaintiff need not prove fault or falsity for common-law defamation. Defamatory statements are presumed to be false, and the defendant must assert truth as a defense.

A truthful statement is not defamatory. A statement that contains slight inaccuracies may nevertheless be considered to be true and therefore not defamatory. A statement that a person has engaged in conduct that is substantially different from the conduct in which the person did in fact engage is not considered to be true, even if the person's actual conduct was equally or more morally reprehensible.

> **EXAM NOTE:** If a statement is true but seems like defamation, consider whether it constitutes intentional infliction of emotional distress or invasion of privacy.

b. **Consent**

Consent by the plaintiff is a defense, but as with other torts, a defendant cannot exceed the scope of the plaintiff's consent.

c. **Absolute privileges**

Statements made under the following circumstances are shielded by absolute privilege:

i)   In the course of **judicial proceedings** by the participants to the proceeding (e.g., witnesses, parties, lawyers, judges);

ii) In the course of **legislative proceedings** (e.g., committee hearings) by the participants to the proceeding (e.g., witnesses, legislators);

iii) In the course of the performance of legislative duties by a legislator and official duties by any federal official or a state executive official;

iv) Between **husband and wife**; and

v)   **Required publications** by radio, television, or newspaper (e.g., statements by a political candidate that a station must carry and may not censor).

Statements made by participants in the course of judicial proceedings must be related to the proceedings in order to be privileged. A similar limitation applies to statements made by witnesses in the course of a legislative proceeding, but not to statements made by legislators in such proceedings, whose statements need not be related to a matter of legislative concern.

d. **Qualified (conditional) privilege**

Statements made under the following circumstances are subject to a conditional privilege:

i)   In the **interest of the publisher** (defendant), such as defending his reputation;

ii) In the **interest of the recipient of the statement** or a third party; or

iii) Affecting an important **public interest**.

Qualified privileges most often occur in the contexts of employment references, credit reports, and charges and accusations within professional societies and among members of religious and charitable organizations.

1) Abuse of privilege

A qualified privilege may be lost if it is abused. Generally, a privilege is abused by making statements outside the scope of the privilege or by acting **with malice**. Traditionally, the malice required was **express** malice—hatred, ill will, or spite. Today, most jurisdictions hold that **actual malice**, i.e., knowledge that a statement is false or acting with a reckless disregard as to the truth or falsity of the statement, will defeat a qualified privilege.

2) Burden of proof

The burden is on the defendant to prove that the privilege exists. It is, therefore, an **affirmative defense**. The burden is then on the plaintiff to prove that the privilege has been abused and therefore lost.

B. INVASION OF PRIVACY

The right of privacy **does not extend to corporations**, only to individuals. Additionally, because the right of privacy is a personal right, in most instances, this right terminates upon the death of the plaintiff and does not extend to family members.

Invasion of privacy is not a single tort but includes four separate causes of action.

MNEMONIC: **I FLAP** (**I**ntrusion, **F**alse **L**ight, **A**ppropriation, **P**rivate facts)

1. Misappropriation of the Right to Publicity

A majority of states recognize an action for the misappropriation of the right to publicity, which is based on the right of an individual to control the commercial use of his identity. The plaintiff must prove:

i) **The defendant's unauthorized appropriation of the plaintiff's name, likeness, or identity** (Most often, commercial appropriation cases involve the use of the plaintiff's name or picture, but this is not required. A television or radio production might mimic the plaintiff's distinctive vocal patterns. Also, an action may be maintained when the defendant uses other items closely associated with the plaintiff, such as a specially designed car with unique markings associated with a racecar driver.);

ii) For the **defendant's advantage**, commercial or otherwise;

iii) **Lack of consent**; and

iv) Resulting **injury**.

The states are split as to whether this right survives the death of the individual, with some states treating it as a property right that can be devised and inherited.

2. Intrusion Upon Seclusion

Many states recognize an action for unreasonable intrusion upon the plaintiff's private affairs (also referred to as "intrusion upon seclusion"). The defendant's act of **intruding**, physically or otherwise, into the plaintiff's private affairs, solitude, or seclusion in a manner or to a degree **objectionable to a reasonable person** establishes liability. Eavesdropping on private conversations by electronic devices is considered an unreasonable intrusion. Photographing a person in a public place generally is not, unless the photograph is taken in a manner that reveals information about the person that the person expects to keep private even in a public place.

Unlike the other forms of invasion of privacy, no publication is required to establish liability.

3. **Placing the Plaintiff in a False Light**

A majority of jurisdictions recognize a separate tort of false light. The plaintiff must prove that the defendant (i) **made public** facts about the plaintiff that (ii) placed the plaintiff in a **false light**, (iii) which false light would be **highly offensive to a reasonable person**. Most jurisdictions require that the plaintiff prove **actual malice** by the defendant. As considered in the discussion of defamation, this may be constitutionally required in many instances.

Attributing to the plaintiff **views** that he does not hold or **actions** that he did not take may constitute placing him in a false light. Similarly, falsely asserting that the plaintiff was a victim of a crime or once lived in poverty may be sufficient for the false light tort.

This false light does not necessarily involve an absolute falsity; rather, the presentation of the truth in a misleading way can be sufficient to sustain this claim. Consequently, truth is not a defense if the resulting implication is still false or misleading, but it may be a defense if the resulting implication is true.

4. **Public Disclosure of Private Facts**

a. **Elements**

To recover, the plaintiff must show that:

i) The defendant **gave publicity to a matter concerning the private life** of another; and

ii) The matter publicized is of a kind that:

a) Would be **highly offensive** to a reasonable person; and

b) Is not of **legitimate concern** to the public.

b. **Publicity**

The requirement of publicity in the public disclosure tort requires far broader dissemination of the information than is required under the "publication" requirement of defamation. The information must be communicated at large or to so many people that it is substantially certain to become one of public knowledge.

c. **Disfavored tort**

Because the public disclosure tort involves the dissemination of true facts, it clearly is in tension with the First Amendment's freedoms of speech and the press. Accordingly, the tort is disfavored in the modern era.

d. **Disclosure of dated material**

Today, most courts hold that the public disclosure of even dated material—for example, a criminal conviction from decades ago—is a matter of public interest and therefore does not create liability.

5. Damages

The plaintiff need not prove special damages for any of the invasion of privacy torts. Emotional distress and mental distress are sufficient.

6. Defenses

a. Defamation defenses

The defenses of absolute and qualified privilege that are applicable in defamation actions also apply to privacy actions brought on "false light" or "public disclosure of private facts" grounds. These defenses are not applicable if the defendant was intrusive.

b. Consent

Consent is a defense to invasion of privacy actions. Mistake as to consent negates this defense, no matter how reasonable the mistake.

> **EXAM NOTE:** Remember that truth generally is not a defense to invasion of privacy, whereas it is a complete defense to defamation.

C. INTENTIONAL MISREPRESENTATION

A prima facie case of intentional misrepresentation (also called "fraud" or "deceit") is established by proof of the following six elements.

1. A Defendant's False Representation

The misrepresentation must be of **a material fact**, not an opinion. Usually, the defendant actively misrepresents the facts, such as through deceptive or misleading statements or pictures. Sometimes, the misrepresentation occurs through the active concealment of a material fact, such as when the seller of a house places paneling over the basement walls to conceal that the foundation is in terrible condition.

There generally is no duty to disclose a material fact or opinion to the other party. However, there may be an affirmative duty to disclose a fact when the plaintiff is:

i) In a fiduciary relationship with the defendant;

ii) Likely to be misled by statements previously made by the defendant ("partial disclosure"); or

iii) (In a minority of jurisdictions) Under a mistaken belief about a basic fact of the transaction that the defendant is aware of and should disclose.

2. Scienter

The defendant must have known the representation to be false or must have acted with reckless disregard as to its truthfulness.

3. Intent to Induce Reliance

The defendant must have intended to induce the plaintiff to act (or refrain from acting) in reliance on the misrepresentation.

4. Causation

The misrepresentation must have caused the plaintiff to act or to refrain from acting. That is, the plaintiff must have actually relied on the misrepresentation.

5. **Justifiable Reliance**

The **plaintiff's reliance must have been justifiable**. Reliance is not justifiable if the facts are obviously false or if the defendant is stating a lay opinion. However, the plaintiff is under no duty to investigate the truth or falsity of the statement.

6. **Damages**

The plaintiff **must prove actual damages** to recover; nominal damages are not awarded. Consequential damages may also be awarded.

In a majority of jurisdictions, the measure of recovery in misrepresentation cases is the "benefit of the bargain" rule (the difference between the actual value received in the transaction and the value that would have been received if the misrepresentation were true).

The Second Restatement and a handful of states allow the plaintiff to choose between the benefit of the bargain and the out-of-pocket loss measures of damages.

A small minority of states limit the plaintiff's recovery to his out-of-pocket losses (similar to the typical tort law measure of recovery).

In all jurisdictions, the plaintiff is not permitted to recover damages for emotional distress.

D. **NEGLIGENT MISREPRESENTATION**

This tort is based upon a breach of the duty to supply correct information and often arises in the context of accountants and other suppliers of commercial information.

1. **Elements and Scope**

In a majority of jurisdictions and under the Second Restatement, the elements are:

i) The defendant provides **false information**;

ii) As a result of the defendant's **negligence**;

iii) During the **course of his business** or profession;

iv) Causing the plaintiff to **justifiably rely** upon the information; and

v) The plaintiff either is in a **contractual relationship** with the defendant or is a third party known by the defendant as one for whose benefit the information is supplied.

Under this rule, the accountant who regularly conducts audits and furnishes financial statements and opinions routinely required by lenders, investors, purchasers, or others is not liable unless she is informed that an identified third party or identified third parties will be using the statement for a particular purpose.

2. **Defenses**

Unlike in intentional misrepresentation, in negligent misrepresentation, negligence defenses can be raised.

3. **Damages**

The plaintiff can recover reliance (out-of-pocket) damages, as well as any other consequential pecuniary damages, if negligent misrepresentation is proven with sufficient certainty.

4. Distinguished From Ordinary Negligence

The ordinary rules of negligence apply when physical harm is a foreseeable result of a negligent misrepresentation.

> **Example:** A defendant air traffic controller is liable for ordinary negligence when he negligently gives the pilot of an airplane incorrect information about the plane's location and speed and, as a result, the passenger-parachutist jumps to his death in a lake instead of at the target airfield.

E. INTENTIONAL INTERFERENCE WITH BUSINESS RELATIONS

1. Intentional Interference With a Contract

a. Elements

To establish a prima facie case for intentional interference with a contract, the plaintiff must prove that:

i) A **valid contract** existed between the plaintiff and a third party;

ii) The defendant **knew** of the contractual relationship;

iii) The defendant **intentionally interfered** with the contract, causing a breach; and

iv) The breach caused **damages** to the plaintiff.

b. Nature of the contractual relationship

In the majority of states, the contract in question **must be valid and not terminable at will**. However, a minority of states will allow the cause of action to be brought for interference with a contract that is terminable at will.

A contract that is voidable by one of the parties to the contract, such as due to a violation of the Statute of Frauds, may be the subject of tortious interference unless the party elects to void the contract.

c. Interference with performance other than inducing breach

The defendant may be liable whenever he prevents a party from fulfilling its contractual obligations or adds to the burden of a party's performance, even if the defendant does not induce the party to breach its contractual obligation. To be considered tortious, a defendant's actions must **substantially exceed** fair competition and free expression, such as persuading a bank not to lend money to a competitor.

d. Justification defense

A defendant's interference usually will be found to be justified if it is not motivated by an improper purpose. Some courts require the plaintiff to prove that the breach was induced by an improper purpose. Considerations of health, safety, morals, or ending poor labor conditions are proper purposes. For example, a defendant who tries to convince a U.S. clothing store to stop buying fabrics from a foreign textile manufacturer known for its inhumane labor conditions will not be liable for interference with a contract.

A defendant might claim that the interference is within the privilege of fair competition. If the contract is terminable at will, the defendant's attempt to induce a third party to breach its contract with the plaintiff can be justified if the defendant is a business competitor of the plaintiff who is in an existing contractual relationship with the third party.

2. Interference With a Prospective Economic Advantage

A defendant may be liable for intentionally interfering with a prospective business relationship or economic benefit between the plaintiff and a third party, even in the absence of an existing contract.

The other elements remain the same, but without an existing contract, some jurisdictions require that the defendant's conduct be wrongful, either "independently tortious" (e.g., consisting of fraud or assault) or a violation of federal or state law. Other jurisdictions and the Second Restatement engage in a more open-ended balancing process to decide whether the defendant's conduct is improper.

Absent proof of wrongful conduct (e.g., defamation), a defendant who is the business competitor of the plaintiff will not be held liable for encouraging the third party to switch his business to the defendant.

3. Theft of Trade Secrets

The plaintiff must own a valid trade secret (i.e., information that provides a business advantage) that is not generally known. The owner of the secret must take reasonable precautions to protect the secret, and the defendant must have taken the secret by improper means.

F. INJURIOUS FALSEHOODS

1. Trade Libel

Trade libel imposes tort liability for **statements injurious to a plaintiff's business or products**. Unlike defamation, it is not intended to compensate for harm to the personal reputation of the owner/manager of the business. Proof of special damages is required. Damages for mental suffering are not available. The plaintiff must prove:

i) Publication;

ii) Of a false and derogatory statement;

iii) With malice;

iv) Relating to the plaintiff's title to his business property, the quality of his business, or the quality of its products; and

v) Causing special damages as a result of interference or damage to business relationships.

Defenses include truth as well as the privilege of fair competition (e.g., making general comparisons to a competitor's product).

2. Slander of Title

Similar to trade libel, slander of title protects against false statements that harm or call into question the plaintiff's ownership of real property. The plaintiff must prove:

i) Publication;

ii) Of a false statement;

iii) Derogatory to the plaintiff's title;

iv) With malice;

v) Causing special damages;

vi) As a result of diminished value in the eyes of third parties.

G.   WRONGFUL USE OF THE LEGAL SYSTEM

1.   Malicious Prosecution

A person is liable for malicious prosecution when:

   i)   He **intentionally and maliciously** institutes or pursues, or causes to be instituted or pursued;

   ii) For an **improper purpose**;

   iii) A legal action that is brought **without probable cause**; and

   iv) That **action is dismissed** in favor of the person against whom it was brought.

Most jurisdictions have extended malicious prosecution to include civil cases as well as criminal actions. The civil action is sometimes known as wrongful institution of civil proceedings.

The plaintiff may recover for any damage proximately caused by the malicious prosecution, including legal expenses, lost work time, loss of reputation, and emotional distress.

Note that judges and prosecutors enjoy absolute immunity from liability for malicious prosecution.

2.   Abuse of Process

Abuse of process is the misuse of the power of the court. To recover for abuse of process, the plaintiff must prove:

   i)   A legal procedure set in motion in proper form;

   ii) That is "perverted" to accomplish an ulterior motive;

   iii) A willful act perpetrated in the use of process that is not proper in the regular conduct of the proceeding;

   iv) Causing the plaintiff to sustain damages.

For abuse of process, unlike malicious prosecution, the existence of probable cause—and even whether the defendant ultimately prevails on the merits—is not determinative in precluding liability. Rather, **the essence of the tort is using the legal process for an ulterior motive, such as extorting payment or recovering property**.

Example: A local school board of education sued a teacher's union and subpoenaed 87 teachers for a hearing in order to prevent the teachers from walking a picket line during a labor dispute between the union and the board of education.

Note that abuse of process, like malicious prosecution, does not require ill will or spite, but it does require proof of damages.

Final Review Outlines

FINAL REVIEW OUTLINE: CIVIL PROCEDURE

I. **Subject Matter Jurisdiction (SMJ)**

   A. **In general**—a court's competence to hear and determine cases of general class and subject to which proceedings in question belong

   B. **Federal question (FQ)**

   1. District courts have original jurisdiction (JX) of all civil actions arising under the Constitution, laws, or treaties of the U.S.

   2. **Concurrent/exclusive JX**—state courts and federal courts have concurrent JX of FQ claims, except when Congress expressly provides that JX of the federal courts is exclusive

   3. **Scope**

      • **Express**—FQ exists if cause of action (c/a) in question is expressly created by federal law and federal law provides the underlying right

      • **Implied**—FQ likely to be found if right is created by federal law, and a c/a can be fairly implied and was intended by Congress

      • **Not express/implied**—complaint must involve a state claim that is (1) necessarily raised, (2) actually disputed, (3) substantial, and (4) capable of resolution in federal court without disrupting the federal-state balance approved by Congress

   4. **Well-pleaded complaint**—FQ exists only when federal issue is presented on the face of the complaint (P's c/a—not defenses, answers or counterclaims)

   5. **No amount-in-controversy or diversity requirement**

   C. **Diversity jurisdiction (DJ)**

   1. Federal courts have JX when parties are citizens of different states or citizens of a state and citizens of a foreign state, and amount in controversy exceeds $75,000

   2. **Complete diversity**—no diversity if any P is a citizen of the same state or citizen of the same foreign country as any D in the case

   3. **Citizenship of parties**

      • **Individuals**—domicile is state in which an individual is present and intends to reside for an indefinite period; an individual can only have one domicile at a time; and domicile determined when action is commenced

      • **Corporations**—citizenship is state of incorporation and state where it has its principal place of business ("nerve center" from which the high-level officers direct, control, and coordinate the activities of the corporation)

   4. **Amount in controversy**

      • **Standard of proof**—P's good-faith assertion in complaint is sufficient unless there is legal certainty that P cannot recover alleged amount

      • **Aggregation of claims**—permitted for multiple Ps with common/undivided interest (counterclaims generally not counted in determining whether P has met amount)

      • Permissive counterclaim must meet jurisdictional amount requirement; compulsory counterclaim need not

   5. **Creating/destroying diversity**—assignment of claims, failure to name indispensable parties, voluntary change of state citizenship, and replacement of parties

D. Supplemental jurisdiction (SJ)

1. Federal court with JX may exercise SJ over additional claims which court would not independently have SMJ (usually state law claims against a nondiverse D), but that arise out of a "common nucleus of operative fact" such that all claims should be tried in a single judicial proceeding

2. **FQ**—additional claims against same party can be heard through SJ if common nucleus of operative fact test is met (same requirements for pendent JX over claims involving joinder or intervention of additional parties)

3. **DJ**

    - **Permissive joinder**—addition of a plaintiff asserting additional claim cannot violate complete diversity rule (and not required to satisfy jurisdictional amount)

    - **Counterclaims**—compulsory counterclaims need not satisfy jurisdictional amount, but permissive counterclaims must satisfy both DJ requirements

    - **Cross-claims**—may be asserted by a D against another D or by a P against another P, if the cross-claim arises out of the same transaction or occurrence as the initial claim; no amount in controversy or citizenship requirement if the court has SMJ

E. Removal jurisdiction

1. D may generally remove case from state court to federal district court having SMJ

    - Removal must be to the district court for the district and division in which the state court action is pending

    - Removal to the wrong district court is subject to a motion to remand (or transfer to the proper federal court)

2. **Determination**

    - **Generally**—right to remove determined by pleadings filed when petition to remove is filed

    - **DJ**—diversity must exist at time of filing of original action as well as at time notice of removal is filed

3. **DJ**—if removal based solely on DJ, claim may be removed only if no D is a citizen of the state in which the action was filed

4. **FQ**—if FQ claims are joined with claims that aren't independently removable, entire case may be removed

5. **Notice**

    - D must file notice within 30 days after receipt by or service on D of the initial pleading

    - **FQ**—only Ds against whom federal claim is filed must consent/join in removal

    - **Removal based on DJ**—cannot occur more than one year after action is commenced (unless P acted in bad faith)

6. **Remand**

    - **Lack of SMJ**—any time before final judgment is rendered

    - **Other reasons**—motion to remand for any defect other than SMJ must be within 30 days after filing of notice of removal

II. **Personal Jurisdiction (PJ)**

A. **In general**

1. **Three types**—in personam, in rem, and quasi-in-rem JX

2. A federal court will look to state long-arm statutes to determine if it has PJ over the parties

3. **Due process**—federal court may not exercise PJ over a D unless the D has "minimum contacts" with the forum state and the exercise of JX would be fair and reasonable

4. **Consent**—a party may expressly, impliedly, or voluntarily consent to PJ

5. **Defenses**—lack of JX, insufficiency of process or service of process must be asserted in responsive pleading (or motion before it is submitted), and failure to object waives the objection

B. **In personam**

1. Generally required whenever judgment sought that would impose personal obligation on D

2. **Bases for in personam JX**

- **Voluntary**—appearance alone does not waive right to object to PJ

- **Domicile**—if authorized by statute, a state has JX over person domiciled in state (person with capacity intends to make that state his home)

- **Consent**—D can expressly consent to JX by K or once an action is brought, impliedly through conduct, or voluntarily through appearance in court (unless to object to JX)

- **Long-arm statute**—authorizes PJ over nonresidents who engage in some activity in state or cause some action to occur within state to extent permissible under Due Process Clause

- **Attachment of property**—if claim is not related to ownership of attached property, there must be minimum contacts between D and forum state to establish JX

3. **Due-process requirements**—satisfied if nonresident D has certain minimum contacts with the forum state such that the maintenance of the action does not offend traditional notions of fair play and substantial justice

- **Minimum contacts** (MC)

  o **Purposeful availment**—D's contacts with forum state must be purposeful and substantial, such that D should reasonably anticipate (foresee) being taken to court there

  o **Specific and general JX**

    ▪ **Specific**—when c/a arises out of or closely relates to a D's contact with forum state, even if it's the only contact; specific personal JX is for that action only

    ▪ **General**—requires that D be domiciled in or have continuous and systematic contacts with the forum state; confers personal JX even when c/a has no relationship with D's contacts with the state

  o **Imputed contacts**

    ▪ **Partnerships**—each partner is generally an agent of partnership

    ▪ **Corporations**—out-of-state corporation's contacts with forum state doesn't automatically establish JX over wholly-owned subsidiary unless it is parent's alter ego or acting as agent

- **Employees/agents**—contacts by nonresident employer's agents/employees imputed to employer if acting within the scope of agency/employment (not usually applicable to independent contractors)
  - **Fair play and substantial justice**—once minimum contacts are established, a court must still examine the facts to determine if maintenance of the action would "offend traditional notions of fair play and substantial justice." Factors include:
    - Interest of forum state in adjudicating matter
    - Burden on D of appearing in case
    - Interest of judicial system in efficient resolution of controversies, and
    - Shared interests of the states in promoting common social policies

4. **In personam JX over corporations**
   - **Resident** (i.e., incorporated in the forum state)—any action may be brought against a resident corporation
   - **Foreign** (i.e., not incorporated in the forum state)
     - Minimum contacts and substantial fairness rules apply
     - Test is whether a corporation's affiliations with the forum state are so "continuous and systematic" as to render the corporation essentially "at home" in the forum state
     - A corporate D is always at home in the state of incorporation and the state of its principal place of business (and, in exceptional cases, a state in which D's operations are so substantial and of such a nature as to render the corporation at home there as well)

5. **Internet website**—JX over a nonresident's website is based on the degree of interactivity between the website and the forum, ranging from passive sites to those that are integral to D's business

6. **Suits based on K**—K can be a significant factor in determining whether MC exist, and choice-of-law provisions are a significant factor as they establish that the nonresident purposefully availed herself to benefits of forum state's laws

C. **Jurisdiction over things**

   1. **In rem**
      - **Definition**—gives court authority to determine issues concerning rights to real/personal property
      - **Due process**—proceedings against property must still satisfy due-process requirements for PJ and property must generally be present within the forum state

   2. **Quasi in rem**
      - **Definition**—determines only the interests of the parties to the action regarding property located in forum state (e.g., lien foreclosure or quiet title action), and not personally binding against D
      - **Due process**—if disputes are unrelated to ownership of property and no close relationship is formed, in addition to having property located in forum state, MC must be shown between D and forum state

D. **Notice and opportunity to be heard**

1. **Notice**

   - **Rule**—must be reasonably calculated, under all the circumstances, to apprise interested parties of pending action and afford them the opportunity to object

   - **Form**—via in-person delivery, registered mail, etc. if identity/address known or obtainable through reasonable efforts

2. **Opportunity to be heard**—for D whenever there is state-sponsored interference with a D's property interest

E. **Defenses to jurisdictional claims**—special appearance to challenge PJ (abolished under FRCP) and collateral attacks

III. Venue

A. **Venue in federal court**

1. **General rule**—venue proper in judicial district where any D resides in state where all Ds reside; or where substantial part of the events/omissions occurred; or where property that is subject of the action is located (otherwise where any D is subject to PJ)

2. **Residence**—judicial district where D is domiciled for individual; where D subject to PJ for an entity; or, when entity is P, where principal place of business is located

B. **Change of venue in federal court**

1. **Original venue proper**

   - **General rule**—transfer permitted to any district where case might have been brought or to which all parties consent

   - **DJ**—new district court must apply law from previous court

   - **FQ**—new district court in another appellate circuit will apply federal law as interpreted by its court of appeals (not the appellate circuit of the transferring district court)

2. **Original venue improper**

   - **General rule**—dismiss case or transfer case to proper district if it's in the interest of justice

   - **DJ**—district court to which the case is transferred applies the choice-of-law rules of the state in which it is located (not the state law of the court transferring the case)

   - **FQ**—new court will apply its own court of appeals' interpretation of law (not the appellate circuit of the transferring district court)

   - **No PJ**—a court lacking PJ over the D may transfer the case to a different venue

C. **Forum non conveniens**

1. **Federal**—only used when forum that is deemed most appropriate for the action is a state or foreign court

   - Burden generally on D, but if forum selection clause designates a state or foreign court, burden shifts to P

IV. Choice of Law: The *Erie* Doctrine

A. **In General**

1. **FQ**—federal substantive and procedural law controls, as well as federal common law

2. **DJ**—state substantive law and applicable federal procedural law

B. **Substance or procedure**—determination is unclear

   1. **Valid federal statute on point when state and federal laws conflict**

      - Apply federal law

      - Before applying a Federal Rule (rather than a federal statute), court must determine the Rule is valid under the Rules Enabling Act: does the Federal Rule abridge, enlarge, or modify any substantive right?

         o If **no**, then apply the Federal Rule

         o If **yes**, then apply the Federal Rule if it only incidentally affects a litigant's substantive rights

   2. **No federal rule on point**—apply state law if failure to do so would lead to different outcomes in state and federal court

   3. **Substantive law**—elements of claim or defense, statute of limitations (S/L) and tolling provisions, and burden of proof

   4. **Procedural law**—judge/jury allocation, assessment of attorney's fees, equitable/legal determination

C. **Federal common law**

   1. **In general**

      - Created when there is no applicable federal statute or constitutional provision

      - There is no **general** federal common law; general areas that federal common law is applicable to will be limited

   2. **FQ**—apply federal common law in the following instances:

      - Admiralty cases

      - When the U.S. is a party to the case

      - Interstate disputes

      - Cases implicating relations with foreign countries

      - Cases in which the government acts in a proprietary role (e.g. enters into contracts, issues commercial paper, and oversees regulatory programs), and

      - When Congress has left a gap in a statutory scheme

   3. **DJ**—when a "uniquely federal interest" is at stake and a significant conflict exists between that interest and the operation of state law

   4. **State court cases**—if state JX is concurrent with FQ JX and federal common law would have applied in federal court, then it will also apply in state court

D. **State conflict-of-law rules**—federal court must apply state's conflict-of-law rules

   1. **DJ**—district court bound by conflict-of-laws rules of state in which the district court is located, but only to extent that state's rules are valid under Full Faith and Credit and Due Process Clause

   2. **Procedural or substantive law**—states apply their own procedural laws and sometimes apply the substantive law of a foreign JX

V. **Pleadings**

   A. **Service of process**

1. **Timing**—within 90 days after filing of complaint

2. **Methods of service for individual**

   - Personally

   - At D's usual place of abode with a person of suitable age/discretion who resides there, or

   - Delivering to D's agent

3. **Service on corporations/associations**—to officer or agent, or by following state law

4. **Waiver of service**

   - Request for waiver must be in writing and addressed to individual D, or officer/agent of corporation, and must give D reasonable time of at least 30 days after request sent to return waiver

   - **Effect**—extends time to serve answer from 21 (after service of process) to 60 days (after waiver request sent—90, if foreign)

B. **Injunctions**

   1. **Temporary restraining order** (TRO)

      - Preserves the status quo until an opportunity for a full hearing

      - Effective for a limited time (no longer than 14 days unless good cause exists or adversary consents)

      - May be issued without notice to adverse party if immediate and irreparable injury will result and movant's attorney certifies efforts made to give notice and the reason why notice should not be required

      - Not generally immediately appealable

      - **Motion to dissolve**—if issued without notice, the adverse party may appear and move to dissolve or modify the TRO (must give two days' notice unless the court sets a shorter time)

   2. **Preliminary injunction (PI)**

      - Issued prior to a full hearing on the merits, upon notice to the defendant

      - May be issued to a P if:

        o P is likely to succeed on the merits

        o P is likely to suffer irreparable harm in the absence of relief

        o Balance of equities is in P's favor, and

        o Injunction is in the public interest

   3. **Permanent injunction**

      - Once issued, it continues until dissolved by the court, but any affected person may move for modification or dissolution

      - Same standard as for PI but P must show actual success on the merits

C. **Complaint**

   1. **Federal rule**—short/plain statement of court's SMJ, P's entitlement to relief, and demand for judgment (notice pleading)

   2. **Timing**—filing generally occurs before service; service generally within 90 days of filing

D. **Motions against the complaint** (within 21 days of service)

1. **Rule 12(b) motion to dismiss**

   - Lack of SMJ (can be raised at any time)

   - Lack of PJ, improper venue, insufficient process or service (can be raised in pre-answer motion or answer, or within time to amend answer as of right; otherwise waived)

   - "Omnibus motion" rule (motion raising one of these defenses but omitting the others waives the excluded defenses)

   - Failure to state a claim upon which relief can be granted and failure to join necessary/indispensable party (can be raised in any pleading, motion for judgment on pleadings, or at trial)

2. **Rule 12(b)(6) motion to dismiss**

   - Claim will be dismissed if it fails to assert legal theory of recovery cognizable at law or allege facts sufficient to support cognizable claim; and court treats well-pleaded facts as true, resolves doubts/inferences in P's favor, and views pleading in light most favorable to P

   - **Strength of facts**—must raise right to relief above speculation, assuming that allegations in complaint are true; and raise reasonable expectation that discovery will reveal evidence of necessary element

   - **Court can consider**—only allegations and attached exhibits in the complaint

   - **Court's two-step analysis**

     o Identify and reject legal conclusions unsupported by factual allegations

     o Assume truth/veracity of well-pleaded facts and include context specific analysis that draws on court's judicial experience and common sense to determine if allegations plausibly give rise to relief

3. **Motion for judgment on the pleadings [Rule 12(c)]**—after answer filed, allows court to dispose of a case when material facts are not in dispute and judgment on merits can be achieved based on content of pleadings

4. **Motion for more definite statement**—responding party may move for more definite statement if claim for relief is so vague or ambiguous that party cannot reasonably draft responsive pleading

5. **Motion to strike**

   - **Federal rule**—when pleading contains insufficient defense, or redundant, immaterial, impertinent, or scandalous material – court may order such defense or material stricken; can be used to avoid unnecessary time and money in litigating invalid issues

6. **Amending a motion**—not specifically provided for in the Rules, but generally allowed by courts if the party acts promptly

E. **Answer**

1. **Admission/denial**—answer must admit/deny P's allegations, or plead lack of sufficient knowledge (with reasonable investigation)

2. **Affirmative defenses**—D must state them or they are deemed waived

3. **Timing**

   - **Service under Rule 5**—service to party w/ attorney must be made to attorney in accordance w/ Rule 5

- **No motion to dismiss**—21 days after being served with summons and complaint (or 60 days if D timely waived service)
- **Motion to dismiss**—no filing while motion is pending, and within 14 days after notice of court's action

F. **Reply**

1. **Response**—by P to D's answer within 21 days after being served with order to reply

G. **Amendments**

1. **Rule**
   - Party may amend a pleading once as of right within 21 days if no responsive pleading is required, or after being served with an answer or 12(b) motion; otherwise during/after trial if it conforms to evidence and opposing party has opportunity to prepare
   - Court should freely give leave to amend a pleading when justice so requires and will not result in undue prejudice to opposing party

2. **Relation back**
   - **New claim**—relates back to date of original pleading if amendment asserts claim/defense that arose out of same conduct, transaction, or occurrence as original pleading
   - **New party**
     o Relates back to date of original pleading if amendment asserts claim/defense that arose out of same conduct, transaction or occurrence as original pleading
     o New party receives notice of action within 90 days after original complaint filed
     o D knew or should have known about action but for mistake concerning proper party's identity

3. **Time to respond**—within 14 days after service of amended pleading or time left on original pleading, whichever is later

H. **Supplemental pleadings**—to describe events occurring after filing of earlier pleading

I. **Rule 11 sanctions**

1. Court may impose sanctions limited to what suffices to deter repetition of conduct by others similarly situated

2. **Types**—nonmonetary directives, penalties to court or payments to movant for attorney's fees and other expenses directly resulting from violation

VI. **Multiple Parties and Claims**

A. **Joinder of parties**

1. **Permissive joinder**
   - Ps and Ds may join/be joined in one action if any right to relief is asserted jointly, severally, or with respect to or arising out of same transaction, occurrence or series of them and question of law or fact common to all Ps or Ds will arise
   - **SMJ**—need SMJ:
     o **Ds**—SJ doesn't apply so there must be complete diversity between Ps and Ds and each claim must exceed $75,000

- o **Ps**—SJ is permitted for JX amount less than or equal to $75,000 but there must still be complete diversity
- **In personam JX**—court needs in personam PJ over D for proper joinder
- **Venue**—joinder subject to applicable venue requirements

2. **Compulsory joinder**
   - **Necessary parties**—necessary for just adjudication:
     - o Complete relief cannot be provided to existing parties in absence of that person, or
     - o Disposition in absence of that person may impair person's ability to protect his interest, or
     - o Absence of that person would leave existing parties subject to substantial risk of multiple or inconsistent obligations
   - **SMJ**—need SMJ, so if exclusive basis for JX is DJ, party can't be added if it would destroy diversity
   - **In personam JX**—court needs in personam PJ over D for proper joinder
   - **Venue**—if a joined party objects to venue and the joinder would make venue improper, the court must dismiss that party
   - **Indispensable parties**—if parties cannot be joined because of JX or venue, court may dismiss case and will consider following factors:
     - o Extent to which judgment without party would prejudice them or existing parties
     - o Extent to which protective measures could prevent prejudice
     - o Whether judgment rendered in necessary party's absence would be adequate, and
     - o Whether P would have adequate remedy if action were dismissed

B. **Intervention**
   1. **Intervention as of right** (if not through federal statute)
      - Nonparty has interest in property or transaction that is subject matter or action
      - Disposition of action may impair nonparty's interest
      - Nonparty's interest not adequately represented by existing parties
   2. **Permissive intervention**—court must consider undue delay/prejudice to rights of original parties
      - Movant has conditional right to intervene under federal statute, or
      - Movant's claim/defense and original action share common question of law or fact
   3. **Timeliness**—court will consider following factors:
      - Length of time movant knew or reasonably should have known that its interest was threatened before moving to intervene
      - Prejudice to existing parties if intervention is permitted, and
      - Prejudice to movant if intervention is denied
   4. **SMJ**—cannot be joined in a case based exclusively on DJ if the exercise of JX inconsistent with requirements of DJ

C. **Interpleader**—allows person holding property (stakeholder) to force all potential claimants into single lawsuit

1. **Federal interpleader rule**
   - **Rule:**
     o **Ps**—persons with claims that may expose P to multiple liability may be joined as Ds and required to interplead claims though they lack common origin or are adverse and independent rather than identical or P denies liability
     o **Ds**—exposed to similar liability may seek interpleader through a cross-claim or counterclaim
   - **SMJ**—court must already have JX over all parties, and for DJ, only stakeholder needs to be diverse from claimants (claimants need not be diverse among themselves)
   - **In personam JX**—court needs in personam PJ over claimants in order to join them
   - **Venue**—interpleader subject to venue requirements

2. **Federal statutory interpleader**
   - **SMJ**—DJ met if any two adverse claimants are citizens of different states, and property at issue must merely exceed $500
   - **In personam JX**—nationwide PJ and service of process permitted
   - **Venue**—proper in any district where a claimant resides

D. **Joinder of claims**

1. **Permissive joinder**
   - A party may join independent or alternative claims of whatever nature against opposing party
   - **SMJ:**
     o **DJ**—P may aggregate all diversity claims to satisfy amount-in-controversy requirement
     o **FQ**—nonfederal claims can be joined only if DJ exists or if claims are part of same case/controversy as federal claim so SJ applies
   - **Venue**—joinder subject to venue requirements

2. **Counterclaims** (must be answered within 21 days of service)
   - **Compulsory:**
     o At time of service, counterclaim is compulsory if it arises out of same transaction/occurrence that is subject matter of opposing party's claim and doesn't require adding another party over whom court has no JX
     o **SMJ**—by definition court will have SJ so don't need independent SMJ from original claim
   - **Permissive:**
     o Party has discretion if counterclaim isn't compulsory
     o **SMJ**—need DJ or FQ
   - **Third parties**—can assert counterclaims against original P or D, and governed by requirements for counterclaims and joinder

3. **Cross-claims** (must be answered within 21 days of service)

- A claim against coparty may be asserted if they arise out of same transaction or occurrence that is subject matter of original action or counterclaim and new parties subject to joinder rules

- **SMJ**—by definition court will have SJ so don't need independent SMJ from original claim

- **In personam JX and venue**—PJ satisfied because parties are already before the court; proper venue over original claim, party cannot object to venue over cross-claim

4. **Third-party claims (impleader)**

- **Definition**—defending party (third-party P) can implead nonparty (third-party D) for liability on original claim

- **Timing**—can be asserted any time after complaint is filed, but third-party P must get court permission if filed more than 14 days after service of original answer

- **SMJ**— by definition court will have SJ so don't need independent SMJ from original claim, but if original claim is based only on DJ, claims by P against third-party D must meet DJ or FQ JX requirements on its own

- **In personam JX**—court needs in personam PJ over third parties

E. **Class actions**

1. **Basic requirements**

- **Numerosity**—class is so numerous that joinder of all members is impracticable

- **Commonality**—must be questions of law or fact common to class

- **Typicality**—claims/defenses of representatives must by typical of class, and

- **Adequacy**—representatives must fairly and adequately protect the interests of class

2. **Three situations when class can be certified:**

- **Risk of prejudice**—separate actions would create risk that the class opponent would be subject to inconsistent adjudications or if separate actions would impair the interests of class members

- **Final equitable relief**—the class shares a general claim and injunctive or declaratory relief is sought; a single, indivisible remedy would provide relief to each class member (therefore monetary damages not available)

- **Common legal/factual questions**—must predominate over questions affecting individual members and class action is superior method for bringing about fair and efficient adjudication of controversy; class representatives need not establish likelihood of success on common question of law

3. **SMJ**—FQ, DJ (class representatives must be diverse from class opponents and at least one P must meet $75,000 jurisdictional amount), or Class Action Fairness Act of 2005

4. **Venue**—when there is a defendant class, venue requirements must be met and residence of class representatives (not class members) is what matters

VII. **Pretrial Procedure and Discovery**

A. **Mandatory disclosures**

1. **Initial disclosures**

- **Generally**—subject to certain exceptions, must disclose information regarding individuals having discoverable information, documents supporting claims/defenses, computation and backup of damages, or relevant insurance agreement for satisfying judgment

- **Standard**—information reasonably available to it, and party not excused for not fully investigating case, challenges to insufficiency of another party's disclosures, or because another party failed to disclose

- **Timing**—within 14 days after the parties' discovery conference

2. **Expert testimony**

- **Generally**—identify expert witnesses and produce expert report subject to certain requirements

- **Timing**—at least 90 days before trial or 30 days after disclosure of opposing party's expert evidence on same subject matter

3. **Pretrial** (evidence to be presented at trial other than for impeachment)

- **Generally**—witness list by testimony or deposition, and documents and exhibits

- **Timing**—at least 30 days before trial

- **Objections**—within 14 days after disclosures are made or else waived unless excused by court for good cause or pursuant to relevance rules of the FRE

B. **Discovery scope and limits**

1. **Scope**

- Generally permitted with regard to any non-privileged matter relevant to any party's claim or defense in action, proportional to the needs of the case

- **Relevance**—information need not be admissible in evidence to be discoverable

- **Privileged information** (not discoverable)—determined under federal common law for FQ cases, and state law for DJ or SJ

2. **Limitations** (balance discovery and privacy interests)

- Generally cannot seek discovery until after discovery conference

- Discovery sought is unreasonably cumulative or can be obtained from a more convenient or less expensive source

- The party seeking discovery had ample opportunity to obtain information by discovery

- The proposed discovery is not relevant and proportional

3. **Trial preparation materials**

- Party may not discover documents and tangible things prepared in anticipation of litigation or for trial, unless other party shows that it has substantial need for the materials to prepare its case and cannot, without undue hardship, obtain their substantial equivalent by other means

- Mental impressions, conclusions, opinions, or legal theories of party's attorney or other representative are protected

4. **Experts**

- Expert witnesses may be deposed, but expert report drafts and disclosure are protected, as well as any communications between the party's attorney and expert witness unless they relate to compensation, facts/data used or assumptions relied upon by expert in forming his opinion

C. **Discovery conference**—Parties must confer at least 21 days before scheduling conference to consider nature and basis of their claims/defenses and possibility of settlement, automatic disclosures, preserving discoverable information, and developing discovery plan; sets the scope and schedule for discovery

D. **Discovery devices**

1. **Oral depositions**—can take place any time after discovery conference and limited to 10 per party (unless showing of good cause to court)

2. **Interrogatories**

   - 25 written interrogatories per party relating to non-privileged matters relevant to any party's claim/defense and proportional to the needs of the case

   - Must be fully and separately answered under oath unless timely objected to with specificity

3. **Requests to produce documents**—a party has 30 days from being served with request or 30 days from the parties' first rule 26(f) conference, if the request was served prior to that conference to respond

4. **Physical/mental exams**—the court may order person to submit to physical/mental exam if physical/mental condition is in controversy

5. **Requests for admission**—a party can serve written request for admission of any relevant, non-privileged matters relating to statements or opinions of fact or to application of law to fact, which once admitted is conclusively established

E. **Enforcement**

1. **Motion to compel**—party can move to compel disclosure or discovery against a party failing to make automatic disclosures, or to respond to discovery requests (including evasive or incomplete disclosure)

2. **Sanctions**—if a party fails to obey a court order regarding discovery, the court may impose sanctions subject to the abuse of discretion standard

3. **Electronically stored information**—if information that should have been preserved is lost because a party failed to take reasonable steps to preserve it, the court may order measures to cure the prejudice or, if the party acted with the intent to deprive the another party of the information, instruct the jury that it may or must presume that the information was unfavorable to the party or dismiss the action or enter a default judgment

F. **Pretrial conferences**—the court may direct counsel and unrepresented parties to appear for pretrial conferences for purposes such as expediting disposition of the action, effective case management, and facilitating settlement

G. **Adjudication without trial**

1. **Dismissal**—of complaint, counterclaim, cross-claim, or third-party claim

   - **Voluntary**

     o By filing notice or by stipulation—P can dismiss action without leave of court any time before opposing party serves answer or motion for summary judgment, or by stipulation of all parties who have appeared; dismissal will usually be without prejudice, but the "two-dismissal" rule applies o By court order—decision to dismiss with or without prejudice is left to court's discretion (usually without prejudice but not a matter of right); court considers whether dismissal without prejudice unfairly affects D; "two-dismissal" rule generally not implicated

- **Involuntary**—when P fails to prosecute or comply with the Rules or court order, D can move to dismiss, which if granted is with prejudice and operates as an adjudication on the merits

2. **Default judgment**—when a party fails to defend an action, P may seek default judgment (after at least seven days' notice to D, if D has appeared), which can be set aside for good cause by the court, depending upon whether D's failure to act was willful, setting aside default would prejudice P, and D presented a meritorious claim

3. **Summary judgment**

- **Standard**—no genuine dispute as to any material fact and the movant is entitled to judgment as a matter of law; court will construe all evidence in the light most favorable to the nonmoving party and resolve all doubts in favor of nonmoving party

- **Burden of proof**—the movant has burden of persuasion to show prima facie case before the burden shifts to the opposing party to set forth specific evidence showing the existence of a genuine issue of fact

- **Timing**—may be filed anytime until 30 days after close of all discovery; nonmovant generally must be given sufficient opportunity to obtain discovery

4. **Declaratory judgment**—the court tells the parties their rights and responsibilities without awarding damages or ordering parties to do (or refrain from doing) anything

VIII. Trial Procedure

A. Jury trial

1. **Right to jury trial**—action at law tried on demand to a jury, but for state-law claims in diversity actions, federal law will determine whether there is a right to a jury trial

2. **Jury demand**—must be served within 14 days after service of the last pleading directed to the issue that is to be tried by jury

- A party may specify the issues for which a jury trial is demanded (otherwise, the demand is treated as requesting a jury trial for all issues triable by a jury)

- A party may withdraw a jury trial demand with the consent of the other parties

- **Case removed from state court**—a party who has made a jury trial demand in accord with state law need not renew the demand; if state law does not require a party to make a jury trial demand, a party need not make one after removal (unless the court orders the parties to do so)

3. **Jury size**

- At least six and no more than 12

- Once selected, a juror must participate in the verdict unless dismissed for good cause

- No provisions for alternate jurors

4. **Jury selection**—peremptory challenges may not be made for racial or gender-based reasons; court will allow three for each party in civil cases but an unlimited number of challenges are permitted for cause (e.g., bias or personal relationship to a litigant)

5. **Jury instructions**

- A party may request the court to give specific instructions at the close of evidence (or earlier if ordered by the court)

- Prior to final arguments, the court must inform the parties of any instructions it proposes to give to the jury; the parties may object to the court's proposed instructions on the record and out of the jury's hearing

- Unless a party objects on the record to an erroneous instruction given or proposed to be given by the court or to the court's failure to give an instruction requested by a party, the party generally cannot raise the matter on appeal

6. **Jury verdicts**

- Unless the parties stipulate otherwise:

  o The verdict must be unanimous

  o The verdict must be returned by a jury of at least six jurors

- **Form of verdict**

  o **Special**—written finding made by the jury on each issue of ultimate fact; judge determines the legal consequences of those findings

  o **General**—typically a decision by the jury as to the prevailing party and, if the plaintiff is the prevailing party, the amount of damages

  o **General with special interrogatories**—couples a general verdict with a special verdict; used to ensure that the jury independently considered the material facts of the case in arriving at its verdict

7. **Juror misconduct**

- Concealing facts relating to his qualifications or giving false testimony during voir dire

  o Party must show that the juror failed to answer honestly a material question and that a proper response would have provided a valid basis for a challenge for cause

- **Other forms of juror misconduct**—violating the confidentiality of deliberations, being improperly influenced by non-jurors, or investigating facts outside of those presented at trial

  o Court may dismiss juror or order a new trial

  o A juror may testify about whether extraneous prejudicial information was improperly brought to the jury's attention or whether any outside influence was improperly brought to bear on a juror

B. **Trial by the court**

1. The court must make findings of fact and conclusions of law on the record at the close of evidence or in an opinion or memorandum of decision filed by the court

2. On appeal, a court's findings of fact can be set aside only if clearly erroneous

C. **Consolidation actions and separate trials**

1. **Common question of fact or law**—the court may join any or all matters at issue, consolidate the actions, or issue any other orders to avoid unnecessary cost or delay

2. **Separate trials**—a court may order a separate trial of one or more issues or claims for convenience, to avoid prejudice, or to expedite and economize; any federal right to a jury trial must be preserved

D. **Judgment as a matter of law**

1. **Overview**

    - Challenges the sufficiency of the evidence in a civil jury trial

    - **Prior to submission to jury**—party may file a motion for judgment as a matter of law ("directed verdict")

    - **After verdict and entry of judgment**—party may renew their motion for judgment as a matter of law (motion for "judgment notwithstanding the verdict" or "JNOV")

2. **Motion for judgment as a matter of law ("directed verdict")**

    - The court must view evidence in light most favorable to the opposing party and draw all reasonable inferences from evidence in favor of opposing party

    - **Timing**—any time before the case is submitted to the jury

3. **Renewed motion for judgment as a matter of law ("JNOV")**

    - If the court does not grant a directed verdict, movant can file a JNOV no later than 28 days after entry of judgment (jury discharge, if the issue was not decided by verdict)

    - Can be granted only on grounds raised in the pre-verdict motion

    - Court may: (i) allow judgment on the verdict; (ii) order a new trial; or (iii) direct the entry of judgment as a matter of law

E. **Judgment**—a decree or order by a court that resolves the parties' rights and demands for relief in a manner that permits it to be appealed

1. **Agreement with pleadings**

    - **Generally**—judgment should grant a party the relief to which it is entitled, even if not requested in its pleading

    - **Default judgment**—must not differ in kind or exceed amount demanded in pleadings

2. **Costs**—unless a federal statute, rule, or court order provides otherwise, the prevailing party is allowed court costs, other than attorney's fees, without needing to file a motion

3. **Attorney's fees**—unless a statute or court order provides otherwise, a claim for attorney's fees that is not required by law to be proved at trial as an element of damages must be made by a motion filed within 14 days after entry of judgment

F. **Motion to amend or make additional findings** (nonjury trial)—must be made within 28 days of entry of judgment; may be combined with a new trial motion

G. **Motion to alter or amend a judgment**—must be made within 28 days of the entry of judgment

H. **Motion for new trial**—the court may grant a new trial, with respect to some or all issues, to prevent a miscarriage of justice

IX. **Post-Trial Procedure**

A. **Alteration of or relief from judgment**

1. **Relief from judgment or order**—court can relieve party of final judgment within a reasonable time, and no later than one year following judgment entry for (i) mistake, inadvertence, surprise, or excusable neglect, (ii) newly discovered evidence (not previously discovered through reasonable diligence), or (iii) fraud, misrepresentation, or misconduct by opposing party

2. **Other remedies**—a court may also:

- Entertain an independent action to relieve a party from an order, judgment, or proceeding;

- Grant relief to D who was not personally notified of the action; or

- Set aside a judgment for fraud on the court.

B. **Appeals**—if more than one claim is presented in case, or there are multiple parties, a district court may direct entry of a final judgment as to one or more issues/parties, but only if the court expressly determines that there is no just reason for delay

C. **Full faith and credit**—if valid judgment is rendered by a court that has JX over the parties, and parties receive proper notice of the action and a reasonable opportunity to be heard, judgment will receive the same effect in other states as state where it was rendered

D. **Claim preclusion** (res judicata)

1. **Valid final judgment on the merits**—court must have PJ and SMJ, D must have had proper notice and opportunity to be heard, court must have nothing further to do but order entry of judgment, and decision must be made on merits of claim/defense (rather than technical grounds)

2. **Sufficiently identical claims**—original and later-filed claim must be sufficiently identical to be barred under claim preclusion (federal "transactional" approach)

3. **Sufficiently identical parties**—P and D must be the same, and in the same roles, in both the original action and subsequently filed action

E. **Issue preclusion** (collateral estoppel)—"offensive" use may be permitted

1. **Requirements**

- **Same issue**—facts relevant to particular issue and applicable law must be identical

- **Actually litigated**—the issue must have been actually litigated in the prior action

- **Final, valid judgment**—first determination of issue was within authority of court that decided it and the determination was made in final decision on the merits

- **Essential to judgment**—issue that constitutes a necessary component of the decision reached will be considered essential

2. **Criminal prosecution**

- **In favor of prosecution** (preclusion)—issues determined in a criminal prosecution in favor of the prosecution are generally preclusive in a civil action against D based on the same conduct

- **In favor of D** (no preclusion)—issues determined in a criminal prosecution in favor of D are not preclusive in a civil action against D based on the same conduct because P in the civil action was not a party to the criminal prosecution

FINAL REVIEW OUTLINE: CONSTITUTIONAL LAW

I.   Judicial Power

A. Source and scope

1. **Source**—Article III requires the establishment of a Supreme Court and permits Congress to create other federal courts and place limitations on their jurisdiction

2. **Scope**

- Limited to cases and controversies (partial list):
  - Arising under the Constitution, laws, and treaties of the United States;
  - When the United States is a party;
  - Between two or more states, or between a state and citizens of another state;
  - Between citizens of different states or between citizens of the same state claiming lands under grants of different states; or
  - Between a state, or its citizens, and foreign states, citizens, or subjects.
- Although not enumerated in the Constitution, the judiciary has the power to review:
  - Another branch's act and declare it unconstitutional;
  - The constitutionality of a decision by a state's highest court; and
  - State actions under the Supremacy Clause to ensure conformity with the Constitution.

3. **Limitations—Eleventh Amendment**

- Jurisdictional bar prohibiting citizens of one state from suing another state (not local government) in federal court; immunizes states from suits in federal court for money damages or equitable relief
- Bars suits in federal court against state officials for violating **state** law
- Exceptions to application of 11th Amendment:
  - Consent;
  - Injunctive or declaratory relief;
  - Damages paid by state officer;
  - Congressional enforcement of 13th, 14th, and 15th Amendment rights.

B. Jurisdiction of the Supreme Court

1. **Original**

- "All cases affecting ambassadors, other public ministers and consuls and those in which a State shall be a party"
- Congress cannot expand or limit this jurisdiction

2. **Appellate**

- By certiorari (discretionary) and direct appeal (mandatory)
- A final state-court judgment resting upon adequate and independent state grounds is not reviewable by Supreme Court

C. **Judicial review in operation**

1. **Standing**

- **General rule**—the plaintiff (P) must establish:
  - ○ Injury in fact—concrete and particularized; injury need not be physical or economic; future injury must be actual and imminent
  - ○ Causation—injury caused by the defendant's (D's) violation of a constitutional or other federal right
  - ○ Redressability—relief requested must be likely to prevent or redress the injury
  - ○ "Prudential standing"—P is a proper party to invoke judicial resolution of the dispute
- **Taxpayer status**—generally no standing to challenge government allocation of funds, but a taxpayer has standing to:
  - ○ Litigate how much is owed on her tax bill; and
  - ○ Challenge government expenditures as violating the Establishment Clause.
- **Third-party standing**—generally no standing to bring a lawsuit based on the claims of a third party, but exceptions include:
  - ○ When the third party is unable to assert his own rights;
  - ○ If there is a special relationship between P and the third party; or
  - ○ P's injury adversely affects P's relationship with the third party.
- **Organizational standing**—an organization can sue on its own behalf or on behalf of its members if:
  - ○ Its members would have standing to sue in their own right; and
  - ○ The interests at stake are germane to the organization's purpose.
- **Section 1983 claims**—section 1983 does not provide any substantive rights; it provides a method to enforce the substantive rights granted by the Constitution and other federal laws
  - ○ Proper Ds—individual government employees at any level of government, in their individual capacities; incudes municipalities and local governments
  - ○ Color of state law—P must show that the alleged deprivation was committed by a person acting "under color of state law" (functional identical to "state action")

2. **Timeliness**

- **Ripeness**—P must have experienced a real injury (or imminent threat thereof); an action brought too soon is "unripe"
- **Mootness**—must be a live controversy at each stage of review; an action brought too late is "moot"; a case is **not** moot if:
  - ○ Controversy is "capable of repetition" but is "evading review," i.e., it will not last long enough to work through the judicial system
  - ○ D voluntarily ceases its illegal or wrongful action upon commencement of litigation
  - ○ Named P's claim in a class action suit is resolved (i.e., that fact does not render the entire class action moot)

3. **Justiciability**

    - **Advisory opinions**—no advisory opinions; an actual case or controversy must exist

    - **Declaratory judgments**—not prohibited, but the challenged action must pose "real and immediate danger" to a party's interests

    - **Political questions**—not subject to judicial review when: (i) the Constitution has assigned decision making on this subject to a different branch of the government; or (ii) the matter is inherently not one that the judiciary can decide

4. **Abstention**—a federal court may abstain from deciding a claim when strong state interests are at stake

II. Powers of Congress

A. Commerce

1. **Interstate commerce**

    - The power to regulate: (i) the **channels** and (ii) the **instrumentalities** of interstate commerce, as well as (iii) any activity that **substantially affects** interstate commerce

    - **Construed broadly**—but does not give Congress the power to mandate that individuals not engaged in commercial activities engage in commerce

2. **Substantial economic effect**

    - The power to regulate any activity or combination of activities that has a substantial economic effect on interstate commerce

    - **Aggregation**—even if an intrastate activity has no direct economic impact on interstate commerce, Congress can regulate as long as there is a **rational basis** for concluding that the **"total incidence"** of activity in the aggregate **substantially affects** interstate commerce

3. **Non-economic activity**—to regulate intrastate, non-economic activity that involves an area of traditional state concern, the non-economic activity must have a substantial economic effect on interstate commerce

B. Taxation and Spending

1. **Taxing**

    - Tax by Congress will be upheld if it has reasonable relationship to revenue production

    - Congress has plenary power to impose taxes to raise revenue (i.e., any public purpose) through General Welfare Clause

2. **Spending**—Congress has the power to spend for the general welfare (i.e., any public purpose), including conditional federal funding

C. War and defense powers—power to declare war, raise and support armies, provide and maintain a navy, etc.

1. **Provide for the national defense**—in both wartime and peacetime (e.g., military draft and selective service)

2. **Military courts and tribunals**—to try enemy soldiers, enemy civilians, and current members of the U.S. armed forces; no jurisdiction over U.S. civilians; not all constitutional protections apply (e.g., right to jury trial or grand jury indictment)

3. **National guard**—power to authorize the President to call National Guard units to execute federal laws, suppress insurrections, and repel invasions; constitutional authority extends

to use of National Guard units in domestic situations and non-emergency circumstances (but limited by statute)

D. Property power—no express limit on power to dispose of US property; however, Congress may only take private property for public use with just compensation and to effectuate an enumerated power

E. Power over aliens and citizenship

1. **Aliens**—Congress has plenary power over aliens (subject to Due Process Clause for an alien within the US)

2. **Naturalization—Congress has** exclusive authority over naturalization

F. Necessary and Proper Clause—Congress has the power to enact any legislation necessary and proper to execute any authority granted to any branch of the federal government; not an independent source of power

G. Power to enforce the 13th, 14th, and 15th Amendments

1. **Ban on slavery** (13th)—power to adopt legislation rationally related to eliminating racial discrimination; the only amendment that authorizes Congress to regulate purely private conduct

2. **Equal protection and due process (14th)—permits Congress to pass legislation to enforce equal protection and due process rights** (but not to expand those rights or create new ones); must be "congruence and proportionality" between the injury to be prevented or remedied and the means adopted to achieve that end

3. **Voting** (15th)—prohibits both the state and federal governments from denying any citizen the right to vote on the basis of race, color, or previous condition of servitude; Congress cannot treat states differently and thereby impinge on their "equal sovereignty" unless the different treatment is rationally justified by current circumstances

III. Powers of the President

A. Domestic power

1. **Pardon power for federal offenses** (i.e., not state crimes)—a pardon may be granted at any time after commission of the offense

2. **Veto power**—the President has 10 days to act on proposed legislation; the President may:

   - **Sign the bill**—it becomes law;

   - **Veto the bill**—by sending it back, with objections, to the house in which it originated; Congress can override the veto by two-thirds vote in each house

   - **Do nothing**—result depends on whether Congress is in session at the end of the 10-day period

     o Congress in session—bill becomes law without the President's signature

     o Congress adjourned—bill **does not** become law (pocket veto; cannot be overridden)

3. **Appointment and removal of officials**

   - **Appointment**—the President appoints all "officers of the United States," with the advice and consent of the Senate

   - **Removal**—generally accepted that the President may remove any executive appointee without cause (and without Senate approval)

4. **Authority as chief executive**—the President's authority varies with the degree of congressional authorization of the action

5. **Duty to faithfully execute laws**—the "Take Care Clause" imposes duty on the President to faithfully execute laws, even when the President disagrees

B. Foreign affairs

1. **Commander in Chief**

   - Only Congress can declare war, but the President can take military action without a declaration of war in the case of actual hostilities against the US

   - Congress may limit the President's military activities through exercise of its military appropriation power

2. **Treaties**—the President has the exclusive power to negotiate treaties; a treaty may only be ratified by a two-thirds vote of the Senate

3. **Executive agreements**—the President has the power to enter into executive agreements with foreign nations; Senate approval not required

IV. Federal Interbranch Relationships

A. Congressional limits on the executive

1. **Impeachment**—the House of Representatives may impeach (i.e., bring charges) by a majority vote; the Senate tries the impeached official (two-thirds vote is necessary for conviction)

2. **Appropriation**—if Congress explicitly mandates expenditure of funds, the President cannot impound those funds (e.g., refuse to spend them)

3. **Legislative veto**—it is unconstitutional for Congress to attempt a legislative veto of an executive action

B. Delegation of legislative power—delegation of some of Congress's authority to the executive branch is constitutional if Congress specifies an "intelligible principle" to guide the delegate (nondelegable powers include: impeachment power, power to declare war)

C. Judicial limitation of congressional power—Congress cannot reinstate the right to bring a legal action after the judgment in the action is final

D. Immunities and privileges

1. **Judicial**—a judge has absolute immunity from civil liability for damages resulting from judicial acts (no immunity regarding nonjudicial activities, e.g., hiring and firing court employees)

2. **Legislative**—no civil or criminal liability for statements and conduct made in the regular course of the legislative process by members of Congress

3. **Executive**

   - **Executive privilege**—a privilege with respect to the disclosure of confidential information by the executive branch to the judiciary or Congress

   - **Executive immunity**

     o The President may not be sued for civil damages with regard to any acts performed as part of the President's **official responsibilities**

     o No immunity from a civil action based on conduct alleged to have occurred before the President took office or completely unrelated to carrying out his job

o The President may be subject to such a suit even while in office

V. **Federal and State Powers**

   A. **Exclusive federal powers**—include the powers to coin money, enter into treaties, declare war, and the power over citizenship

   B. **Exclusive state powers**—broad interpretation of the Commerce Clause and the spending power limit the states' exclusive powers

   C. **Concurrent federal and state laws**—under the Supremacy Clause, federal law supersedes conflicting state law

VI. **Intergovernmental Immunities**

   A. **Federal immunity**—the states have no power to regulate the federal government (unless permitted by Congress or not inconsistent with federal policy); the federal government and its instrumentalities are immune from taxation by the states (unless by generally applicable indirect taxes that do not unreasonably burden the federal government)

   B. **State immunity**

   1. **Federal regulation**—the federal government has virtually unlimited power to regulate the states

      • As long as Congress is exercising one of its enumerated powers, Congress generally may regulate the states

      • Congress cannot "commandeer" state legislatures by commanding them to enact specific legislation (or prohibiting a state from enacting new laws); encouragement may not exceed the point at which "pressure turns into compulsion"

   2. **Federal taxation**—the federal government may tax a state, but states have partial immunity from direct federal taxation that would unduly interfere with the performance of the states' "sovereign functions of government"

VII. **State Regulation and Taxation of Commerce**

   A. **Dormant Commerce Clause**

   1. **General rule**—if Congress has not, the states can regulate interstate commerce so long as the regulation does not:

      • Discriminate against out-of-state commerce;

      • Unduly burden interstate commerce; or

      • Regulate wholly out-of-state activity.

   2. **Discrimination against out-of-state commerce**—protecting local economic interests at the expense of out-of-state competitors

      • **Necessary to an important state interest**—a discriminatory state or local regulation may be upheld if: (i) an important local interest being served; and (ii) no other nondiscriminatory means are available to achieve that purpose; rarely upheld

         o Not discriminatory merely because the entire burden of a regulation falls on out-of-state businesses

      • **Market participant exception**

         o A state can favor local commerce or discriminate against nonresident commerce like a private business, if the state is acting as a buyer or seller (i.e., not as a market regulator)

- o This exception does not apply to challenges pursuant to the Privileges and Immunities Clause of Article IV
  - **Traditional government function**—state and local regulations can favor state and local government entities (but not private entities) if the entities are performing a traditional government function (e.g., waste disposal)
  - **Congressionally permitted discrimination**—must be unmistakably clear that Congress intended to permit the otherwise impermissible state regulation
  3. **Undue burden on interstate commerce**
     - A nondiscriminatory state regulation may still be struck down if it imposes an undue burden on interstate commerce
     - **Balancing test**—purpose of state law against burden on interstate commerce and evaluate whether there are less restrictive alternatives

B. **State Taxation of Commerce**
   1. **Interstate commerce**
      - **General rule**—states may tax interstate commerce only if Congress has not already acted in the particular area and the tax does not discriminate against or unduly burden interstate commerce
      - **Four-part test:**
        - o **Substantial nexus**—between the activity being taxed and the taxing state;
        - o **Fair apportionment**—such that interstate commerce does not pay total taxes greater than local commerce;
        - o **Nondiscrimination**—no direct commercial advantage to local businesses over interstate competitors (even if neutral on its face); and
        - o **Fair relationship**—the tax must be fairly related to the services provided by the taxing state.
   2. **Foreign commerce**—states must have congressional consent to impose import or export taxes (except what is absolutely necessary for executing its inspection laws)

VIII. **Federal Preemption of State Law**
   A. **Express preemption**—when the Constitution makes federal power exclusive or Congress has enacted legislation explicitly prohibiting state regulation in the same area
      1. **Narrow construction**—express federal preemption must be narrowly construed
      2. **Savings clause**—may explicitly preserve or allow state laws regulating in the same area
   B. **Implied preemption**
      1. **When applicable**—implied preemption occurs when any of the following exist:
         - Congress intended for federal law to occupy the field;
         - State law directly conflicts with federal law (e.g., impossible to comply with both); or
         - State law indirectly conflicts with federal law (e.g., creating an obstacle to the law's purpose).
      2. **Absence of preemption**
         - If federal law does not preempt state law, a state is free to enact legislation regarding the same issue

- Federal law sets a **floor** below which state law generally cannot go, but it does **not** set a **ceiling** beyond which state law cannot go

IX. **Relations Among States**

A. **Full Faith and Credit Clause**

1. **Judgments**—out-of-state judgments must be given in-state effect if:

- The court rendering judgment had jurisdiction over the parties and subject matter;

- The judgment was on the merits; and

- The judgment was final.

2. **Laws** (public acts)—the Constitution prohibits state courts of general jurisdiction from refusing to hear a case solely because the suit is brought under a federal law, and a state may not discriminate against rights arising under federal laws

X. **State Action**—a prerequisite to triggering constitutional protections

A. **Traditional governmental function**—state action occurs when a private person carries on activities traditionally performed exclusively by the state (e.g., running primary elections)

B. **Significant state involvement**

1. **Definition**

- Sufficient mutual contacts between the conduct of a private party and the government such that the government is pervasively entwined with the entity and (i) constitutional standards should apply to the private actor; or (ii) a mutual benefit results (e.g., joint venture); or

- The state creates a private entity by special law for the furtherance of governmental objectives and retains permanent control of the entity

2. **Guidelines**

- Mere licensing or regulation of a private party is not state action

- The state must act affirmatively to facilitate, encourage, or authorize the activity

C. **Insignificant state involvement—businesses that the government substantially regulates or to which it grants a monopoly**; nursing homes that accept Medicaid; schools receiving government funds but are operated by a private corporation

XI. **Procedural Due Process**—Fifth Amendment (federal government) and Fourteenth (states)

A. **Due process generally**

1. **Procedural due process**—ensures the necessary procedures are followed before depriving individuals and other "persons" (e.g., corporations) of "life, liberty, or property"

2. **Incorporation**—most provisions of the Bill of Rights are applicable against states

3. **Substantive due process**—guarantees fundamental rights to all persons; a "catchall" for rights not explicitly set forth in the Constitution

B. **Procedural due process applied**

1. **General principles**

- Fundamental Fairness—includes the right to be notified of charges or proceedings and the opportunity to be heard; ask: (i) is the threatened interest a protected one? (ii) if so, what process is due?

- **Neutral decision maker**

- **Intentional governmental act**—mere negligence does not trigger due process

2. **Protected Interests**

- **Liberty**—an impingement on liberty is significant governmental restraint on one's physical freedom, fundamental rights, or freedom of choice or action

- **Property**—there must be a legitimate claim of entitlement by virtue of statute, employment contract, or custom

3. **Notice and hearing**—the amount of process due is determined by three factors:

- The private interest affected;

- The risk of erroneous deprivation and value of additional safeguards; and

- The government's interest, including the burden (cost) of additional process.

4. **Court access**—court fees are waived for an indigent person if the fees will deny a fundamental right; counsel is appointed for indigent criminal defendants

XII. Substantive Due Process

A. Standard of review

1. **Strict scrutiny**—if government action infringes upon a fundamental right

- Law must be **least restrictive** means to achieve **compelling** government interest

  o Least restrictive—there cannot be a less restrictive way to achieve the interest and the law should be neither over- nor under-inclusive

  o Compelling interest—generally understood to mean necessary or crucial

- The burden of proof is on the government

2. **Rational basis**—if the interest infringed upon is not fundamental

- Law must be **rationally related** to a **legitimate** state interest (minimal scrutiny)

- The government's stated interest in enacting the law need not be one that it offered when the law was passed; any legitimate reason will suffice

- In practice, applied to laws related to lifestyle, taxation, zoning, and punitive damages

- The burden of proof is on the challenger

B. Fundamental rights

1. **Travel**

- From state to state

- Reasonable residency requirements or waiting periods may be imposed on the receipt of some government benefits

- Once a person qualifies as a resident, she must be treated equally

2. **Voting and ballot access**

- **Right to vote**

  o Applies to all federal, state, and local elections, including primary elections

  o Despite being a fundamental right, strict scrutiny does not apply to all laws that restrict this right o The more significant the government restriction, the greater the degree of scrutiny

- **Public office and ballot access**—no fundamental right to hold office through election or appointment, but all persons do have a constitutional right to be considered for office without the burden of invidious discrimination

3. **Privacy**—includes marriage, contraception, intimate sexual behavior, abortion (undue burden test), parental rights, family relations, obscene material, right to refuse medical treatment, and right to avoid disclosure of personal medical information

4. **Second Amendment**—guarantees an individual's right to possess a firearm, subject to lawful regulations

XIII. Equal Protection

A. General considerations

1. **Constitutional basis**—14th Amendment Equal Protection Clause for states and 5th Amendment Due Process Clause for federal government

2. **Standards of review**—depends on the classification of persons or type of right concerned

   - **Strict scrutiny**
     o **Least restrictive** means to achieve a **compelling** governmental interest
     o Burden of proof is on the government
     o Applies if a fundamental right or a suspect classification is involved

   - **Intermediate scrutiny**
     o **Substantially related** to an **important** governmental interest
     o Burden appears generally to be on the government
     o Applies when a classification is based on gender or legitimacy
     o Gender cases require an "exceedingly persuasive justification" for the classification

   - **Rational basis**
     o **Rationally related** to a **legitimate** governmental interest
     o Burden is on the challenger to show that the law is arbitrary or irrational
     o Applies when higher standards do not apply (e.g., age, wealth, weight)

3. **Proving discrimination**—to trigger strict or intermediate scrutiny, there must be discriminatory intent on the part of the government

   - **Discriminatory on its face**—a law that, by its very language, creates distinctions between classes of persons

   - **Discriminatory application**—a law that is neutral on its face, but applied in a discriminatory fashion

   - **Discriminatory motive**—a law that is neutral on its face and in its application, but results in a disparate impact; proof of discriminatory motive or intent is required

B. Suspect classifications

1. **Race, ethnicity, and national origin**

   - **School integration**—only de jure (intentional) segregation in schools violates the Equal Protection Clause

- **Affirmative action**—programs that favor racial or ethnic minorities are subject to strict scrutiny

2. **Alienage** (in some cases—depends on the level of government and the nature of the classification)

   - A federal classification is likely valid unless it is arbitrary and unreasonable

   - A state classification is generally subject to strict scrutiny and will be struck down

     o Examples—laws prohibiting aliens from owning land, obtaining commercial fishing licenses, or being eligible for welfare benefits or civil service jobs

     o Exception: participation in government functions—rational basis standard applied

C. Quasi-suspect classifications

1. Gender

- There must be discriminatory intent by the government to trigger intermediate scrutiny (not just disparate impact)

- The government must show that an "exceedingly persuasive justification" exists for the gender distinction, and that separate facilities are substantially equivalent

- Affirmative action (benign discrimination) is permissible under intermediate scrutiny as a remedy for past gender-based discrimination

2. Legitimacy—legislation designed to punish nonmarital children will not be upheld

D. Nonsuspect classifications

1. Age

2. Poverty

3. Sexual orientation—the Supreme Court has not resolved the issue of whether discrimination based on sexual orientation is subject to heightened scrutiny

E. Fundamental rights unique to equal protection (i.e., no overlap with substantive due process)

1. "One person, one vote"—when the government establishes voting districts for the election of representatives, the number of persons in each district must be approximately equal

2. Gerrymandering—election districts for public office may not be drawn using race as the predominant factor in determining the boundary lines, unless the district plan can survive strict scrutiny

XIV. Privileges & Immunities Clauses

A. Comity Clause

1. Prohibits state discrimination against nonresident citizens—applies only to "citizens" (i.e., not corporations or aliens)

2. Rights protected—prohibits one state from discriminating against citizens of another state with respect to fundamental rights or essential activities (e.g., pursuit of employment, transfer of property, access to state courts)

3. Exception—substantial justification: discrimination against out-of-state citizens may be valid if the state can show:

- The nonresidents either cause or are a part of the problem that the state is trying to solve; and

- There are no less-restrictive means to solve the problem.

B. **Fourteenth Amendment**—national citizenship

1. Applies only to "citizens" (i.e., not corporations or aliens)

2. Protects citizens from infringement by the states upon the privileges or immunities of **national** citizenship

- Includes the rights to travel interstate, vote for national offices, enter public lands, and peaceably assemble

- This provision is seldom successfully invoked; the rights are redundant to rights provided elsewhere in the Constitution; in practice, applies only to the right to travel

XV. **Takings Clause**—a check on the power of eminent domain

A. **Property interest**

1. **Types of property**—includes real property, tangible personal property, and intangible property

2. **Types of interests**—includes fee simple, easement, leasehold, lien, and the rights of a property owner (e.g., the right to control access to the property)

B. **Types of takings**

1. **Seizure of property**—classic application of the Takings Clause; the primary challenge is whether the owner has received just compensation

2. **Damage to or destruction of property**

3. **Re-characterization of private property as public property**

4. **Regulatory taking**

- Generally, a regulation that adversely affects a person's property interest is not a taking, but it is possible for a regulation to rise to the level of a taking

- **Per se takings**—(i) permanent physical occupation; (ii) when the regulation results in a permanent total loss of the property's economic value

5. **Exaction of promises from developer as a taking**

- Does not violate the Takings Clause if there is:

  o An essential nexus between legitimate state interests and the conditions imposed on the property owner; and

  o A rough proportionality between the burden imposed on the property owner and the impact of the proposed development.

C. **Just compensation**—fair market value at the time of the taking; measured in terms of the loss to the owner (not the benefit to the government)

XVI. **Prohibited Legislation**

A. **Bills of attainder**—a legislative act that declares a person or group of persons guilty of some crime and punishes them without a trial; applies only to criminal or penal measures

B. **Ex post facto laws**—(i) criminalizes an act that was not a crime when it was originally committed; (ii) authorizes a more severe penalty after an act was committed; (iii) deprives D of a defense available when the act was committed; or (iv) decreases the prosecution's burden of proof below that required when the act was committed

C. **Impairment of contracts**—the "Contracts Clause" prohibits the states from passing any law "impairing the obligation of contracts;" applies only to state legislation—not state-court decisions and not federal legislation—that retroactively impairs contractual rights; does not apply to contracts not yet entered into

XVII. Freedom of Religion

A. **Establishment**—when a governmental program shows preference to one religion over another, or to religion over nonreligion, strict scrutiny applies

1. **Standard of review** (*Lemon* test)—a governmental action that benefits religion is valid if:

   - It has a secular purpose;

   - Its primary effect neither advances nor inhibits religion; and

   - It does not result in excessive government entanglement with religion.

2. **Financial aid**

   - **Aid to religiously affiliated institutions**—permitted if the aid is secular in nature, used only for secular purposes, and distributed according to religiously neutral criteria

     o Secular textbooks, computers, transportation, etc. found constitutional

     o The level of government entanglement is not a separate requirement; it is one factor to be considered when deciding whether religion is being advanced or inhibited

   - **Tax exemptions**—valid if equivalent to exemptions to other charitable institutions not advancing or inhibiting religion (i.e., cannot be available only to religious organizations)

   - **Tax deductions and aid for parochial school expenses**

     o Tax deductions—to reimburse tuition expenses only for parents of students in religious schools are invalid (the deduction must be available to all parents)

     o Tuition vouchers—do not violate the Establishment Clause if parents can decide whether to use them at religious or non-religious schools; however, states may deny state funds to a student pursuing a religious career without violating the Free Exercise Clause of the federal constitution

3. **Public school activities**—the following practices have been held invalid as clearly promoting religion**: (i) prayer and Bible reading; (ii) period of silence for "meditation or voluntary prayer" lacking any secular purpose; (iii) nondenominational prayer at school events; (iv) posting the Ten Commandments** on public-school classroom walls; and (v) prohibiting the teaching of Darwinism

4. **Access to public school facilities by religious groups**—if a public school allows student groups or organizations to use its facilities when classes are not in session, allowing a religious organization to use those facilities does not violate the Establishment Clause

5. **Religious displays**

   - **Ten Commandments**—a display on public property is not allowed if it has a predominantly religious purpose

- **Government holiday displays**—generally permissible unless a reasonable observer would conclude that the display is an endorsement of religion; context is key

B. **Free exercise**—includes the freedom to believe and the freedom to act

1. **Religious belief**

- The freedom to believe in any religion or none at all is absolutely protected and cannot be restricted by law

- The government may not: (i) deny benefits or impose burdens based on religious belief; (ii) require affirmation of a belief; or (iv) determine the reasonableness of a belief (although it may determine the sincerity of the person asserting that belief)

2. **Religious conduct**

- Not absolutely protected

- State laws that intentionally target religious conduct are subject to strict scrutiny

- Neutral laws of general applicability that have an impact on religious conduct are subject only to the rational basis test

XVIII. **Freedom of Expression and Association**

A. **Regulation of speech**

1. **Expressive conduct** (symbolic speech)—subject to a lesser degree of protection than speech; a regulation of expressive conduct is upheld if:

- The regulation is within the government's power to enact;

- It furthers an important governmental interest;

- The interest is unrelated to the suppression of ideas; and

- The burden on speech is no greater than necessary.

2. **Overbreadth**

- A law that burdens a substantial amount of speech or other conduct constitutionally protected by the First Amendment is "overbroad" and therefore void (does not apply to commercial speech)

- Overbroad statutes may be challenged as "facially invalid" (even by those who are validly regulated) to prevent a chilling effect on protected speech

3. **Vagueness**—a statute void for vagueness if it fails to provide a person of ordinary intelligence with fair notice of what is prohibited

4. **Prior restraints**—regulation of speech that occurs in advance of its expression

- Generally presumed to be unconstitutional, with limited exceptions

- The limited exceptions require at a minimum that: (i) there is a **particular harm** to be avoided; and (ii) certain **procedural safeguards** are provided to the speaker, e.g.,

   o The standards must be narrowly drawn, reasonable, and definite;

   o The censoring body must promptly seek an injunction; and

   o There must be a prompt and final judicial determination of the validity of the restraint.

- The burden is on the government to prove that the material to be censored is not protected speech

5. **Unfettered discretion**

- A law or regulation that permits a governmental official to restrict speech must provide definite standards as to how to apply the law in order to prevent governmental officials from having unfettered discretion over its application

- A statute that gives officials unfettered discretion is void on its face

6. **Freedom not to speak**

- The First Amendment protects not only freedom of speech, but also the freedom not to speak

- However, a state can compel a private entity (e.g., a shopping mall) to permit individuals to exercise their own free-speech rights when the private entity is open to the public and the message is not likely to be attributable to the private entity

- Although one can be compelled to join or financially support a group with respect to one's employment, one cannot be forced to fund political speech by that group

7. **Government speech**—need not be viewpoint-neutral, but is subject to the Establishment Clause

8. **Campaign related speech**

- **Contributions**—statutes limiting campaign contributions are subject to intermediate scrutiny

- **Expenditures**—in contrast to campaign contributions, restrictions on expenditures by individuals and entities (including corporations and unions) on communications during an election campaign regarding a candidate are subject to strict scrutiny

B. **Regulation of time, place, and manner of expression**

1. **Public forum**

- **Traditional**—historically associated with expression (e.g., sidewalks, streets, parks)

- **Designated** (limited)—not historically used for speech-related activities, but which the government has opened for such use (e.g., civic auditoriums, publicly owned theaters, or school classrooms afterhours)

- In either forum, the restrictions must:

   o Be content-neutral as to both subject matter and viewpoint;

   o Be narrowly tailored to serve a significant governmental interest; and

   o Leave open ample alternative channels for communication of the information.

- **Injunction**—the test for the constitutionality of injunctions in public forums depends on whether the injunction is content-neutral or content-based

   o Content-neutral—whether it burdens no more speech than is necessary to achieve an important governmental interest

   o Content-based—it must be necessary for the government to achieve a compelling governmental interest

2. **Nonpublic forum**—all public property that is not a traditional or designated public forum

- The government may regulate speech-related activities in nonpublic forums as long as the regulation is: (i) viewpoint-neutral and (ii) reasonably related to a legitimate governmental interest

- o Viewpoint-neutral—the government may prohibit speech on certain issues altogether, but it may not allow only one side of an issue to be presented
- o Reasonable—the restriction must be rationally related to a legitimate governmental interest
- **Personal property**—regulation of speech on a person's own private property will rarely be upheld, particularly content-based regulations

C. **Regulation of Content**—whether content-based on its face or in application or intent, is generally subject to strict scrutiny, except:

1. **Obscenity and child pornography**—not protected by 1st Amendment
   - **Obscenity test**—the average person, applying contemporary community standards, must find that the material, taken as a whole:
     - o Appeals to the prurient interest (community standard);
     - o Depicts sexual conduct in a patently offensive way (community standard); and
     - o Lacks serious literary, artistic, political, or scientific value (national standard).

2. **Incitement to violence**—a state may forbid speech that advocates the use of force or unlawful action if:
   - The speech is directed to inciting or producing imminent lawless action; and
   - It is likely to incite or produce such action (i.e., creates a clear and present danger).

3. **Fighting words**—words that by their very nature are likely to incite an immediate breach of the peace
   - Words that are simply annoying or offensive are not fighting words
   - There must be a genuine likelihood of imminent violence by a hostile audience

4. **Defamation**—if P is a public official or public figure, or a defamatory statement involves a matter of public concern, then in addition to the elements of a prima facie case of defamation, P must prove **fault** and **falsity** of the statement
   - **Public figure**—someone who is known to the general public and includes any person who has voluntarily injected herself into the public eye; P must prove D acted with **actual malice**
   - **Public concern**—if P is a private figure but the defamatory statement involves a matter of public concern, then P need only prove **negligence** with respect to the falsity of the statement

5. **Commercial speech**—restrictions on commercial speech are subject to a four-part test:
   - The commercial speech must concern lawful activity and be neither false nor misleading;
   - The asserted governmental interest must be substantial;
   - The asserted regulation must directly advance asserted interest; and
   - The regulation must be narrowly tailored to serve interest (meaning a "reasonable fit" between the government's ends and the means chosen to accomplish those ends).

D. Regulation of the media—the media has no greater First Amendment rights than the general public

1. **General considerations**—regulation of the right to publish about matters of public concern is subject to strict scrutiny

   - **Gag orders**—subject to prior-restraint analysis; rarely upheld

   - **Attending trials**—the right to attend trials may be outweighed if the judge finds an overriding interest that cannot be accommodated by less restrictive means

   - **Illegally obtained private info**—permitted to publish if third party (unknown to publisher) obtained info and involves matter of public concern

   - No constitutional privilege to protect sources

2. **Broadcast**

   - Radio and television broadcasters are said to have a greater responsibility to the public; they can be more closely regulated than print and other media

   - Broadcasters may be sanctioned for airing "patently offensive sexual and excretory speech," even if such speech does not qualify as obscene

3. **Cable television—content-based regulations** of cable broadcasters are subject to strict scrutiny

4. **Internet**—any regulation of Internet content is subject to strict scrutiny

E. Regulation of association

1. **Overview**—freedom of association protects the right to form or participate in any group, gathering, club, or organization virtually without restriction; the right is not absolute

2. **Public employment**

   - An individual generally cannot be denied public employment based simply upon membership in a political organization

   - A person may only be punished or deprived of public employment based on political association if that individual:

     o Is an active member of a subversive organization;

     o Has knowledge of the organization's illegal activity; and

     o Has specific intent to further those illegal objectives.

3. **Bar membership**

   - Admission cannot be denied on the basis of political association unless the candidate knowingly belongs to a subversive organization with specific intent to further its illegal ends

   - The state may deny bar membership to a candidate who refuses to answer questions about political affiliations if that refusal obstructs the investigation of the candidate's qualifications

4. **Elections and political parties**

   - **Voters in primary elections**

     o A state cannot require a local political party to select presidential electors in an open primary when the national party prohibits nonparty members from voting

- A state can require a semi-closed primary system even if the party wants to permit anyone to vote
- A state may not prohibit a political party from allowing independents to vote in its primary

- **Ballot access to general election**—a state may refuse to grant a political party's candidate access to the general-election ballot unless the party demonstrates public support through voter signatures on a petition, voter registrations, or previous electoral success

- **Fusion candidate**
    - A candidate who is nominated by more than one political party
    - A state may prohibit a fusion candidate from appearing on the general-election ballot as a candidate of multiple parties

5. **Criminal penalty**

- A statute that purports to criminally punish mere membership in an association violates the First and Fourteenth Amendments

- Such membership may only be criminalized if: (i) the group is actively engaged in unlawful activity, or is engaging in advocacy that passes the "clear and present danger" test; and (ii) the defendant knows of and specifically intends to further the group's illegal activity

FINAL REVIEW OUTLINE: CONTRACTS & SALES

I. **Formation of Contracts** (Ks)—binding K requires mutual assent, consideration, and lack of valid defenses

    A. **Offer**—objective manifestation of a willingness by offeror to enter into agreement that creates power of acceptance in offeree

        1. **Intent**—a statement is an offer only if:

- Person to whom it is communicated could reasonably interpret it as an offer
- Expresses present intent of a person to be legally bound by a K

        2. **Knowledge**—offeree must know of the offer in order to have the power to accept

        3. **Terms**—must be certain and definite or the K fails for indefiniteness

- **Under common law (CL)**
  - Essential terms (parties, subject matter, price, quantity) must be covered in K
  - If the parties intended to create a K, the court may supply missing terms
- **Under UCC**
  - Only essential term is **quantity**
    - Exception—requirements or output Ks (UCC implies "good faith")
    - UCC "fills the gap" if other terms are missing
  - K formed if both parties intend to K and reasonably certain basis for giving remedy

        4. **Language**—offer must contain words of promise, undertaking, or commitment, and be targeted to a number of people who could actually accept

- If a **return promise** is requested—**bilateral K**
- If an **act** is requested—**unilateral K**

        5. **Invitation to deal**—advertisements are only an invitation to receive offers (but may qualify as an offer if sufficiently specific and limit who can accept or if associated with a stated reward)

    B. **Termination of offers**

        1. **Lapse of time**—specified termination date or reasonable period of time if none stated

        2. **Death/mental incapacity of offeror**

- **General rule**—offer terminates, even if offeree does not learn of offeror's death until after the offeree has sent what he believes is an acceptance
- **Exception**—offers for option Ks do not terminate because consideration was paid to keep the offer open

        3. **Destruction/illegality**—offer terminated

        4. **Revocation**

- Offer can be revoked any time prior to acceptance (even if it states it will be open for specific amount of time)
- Not effective until communicated
- Revocation sent by mail not effective until received

5. **Limitations on revocation**
   - **Option K**—offeree must generally give consideration for option to be enforceable
   - **UCC firm offer rule**
     - Offer irrevocable (for reasonable time but no more than three months) if offeror is a merchant (or any business person), and assurances (in authenticated writing) are made that offer will remain open
     - No consideration needed to keep offer open
   - **Promissory estoppel**—if offeree reasonably and detrimentally relies on offer it may become irrevocable
   - **Partial performance**—for all Ks, offeree must have knowledge of offer when performance begins
     - Unilateral K—offeror cannot revoke once offeree has begun performance
     - Bilateral K—commencement of performance operates as promise to render complete performance

6. **Revocation of general offers** (to large number of people)—revocable only by notice given at least same level of publicity as offer (effective even if potential offeree acts in reliance on offer)

7. **Rejection by offeree**
   - Offeree clearly conveys to offeror that he no longer intends to accept the offer
   - Rejection usually effective upon receipt
   - **Counteroffer**—acts as rejection of original offer and creates new offer

C. **Acceptance**—objective manifestation by the offeree to be bound by the terms of the offer

1. **Bilateral v. unilateral**
   - **Bilateral K**
     - Exchange of promises that render both enforceable
   - **Unilateral K**
     - Promise to do something by one party in return for an act of the other party
     - Starting to perform is not enough, but it will make offer irrevocable for a reasonable period of time to complete performance
     - Offeree must be aware of offer before acting

2. **Means of acceptance**—unless offeror specifies, offeree can accept in any reasonable manner/means
   - **Silence**—is not acceptance unless offeree has reason to believe offer could be accepted by silence or previous dealings make it reasonable to believe that offeree must notify offeror if he does not intend to accept
   - **Shipment of goods**
     - Buyer's request that goods be shipped is inviting acceptance either by seller's promise to ship or by prompt shipment of goods

o Nonconforming goods shipped—both an acceptance and a breach, unless seller seasonably notifies buyer that goods are an accommodation (counteroffer); buyer may then accept or reject the nonconforming goods

3. **Mailbox rule** (applies only to **acceptance**; almost exclusively applies to **bilateral Ks**)

- **Acceptance**—effective when sent (not upon receipt), unless offer provides otherwise

- **Rejection following acceptance**—acceptance will control even if offeror receives rejection first (but if offeror detrimentally relies on rejection then offeree estopped from enforcing K)

- **Acceptance following rejection**—mailbox rule does not apply; first one received (i.e., in possession of offeror or her agent, or deposited in mailbox) will prevail; offeror need not actually read the received communication

- **Revocation**—effective upon receipt

- **Options and other irrevocable offers**—mailbox rule does not apply; acceptance must be received by offeror by a certain date or before offer expires

4. **Notice**

- **Unilateral K**

o Offeree not required to give notice after completing performance, unless:

    ▪ Offeror wouldn't learn of performance with reasonable certainty and promptness; or

    ▪ Offer requires notice.

o Notice required but not provided—offeror's duty is discharged, unless:

    ▪ Offeree exercises reasonable diligence to give notice;

    ▪ Offeror learns of performance within reasonable time; or

    ▪ Offer indicates notice of acceptance is not required.

- **Bilateral K**—offeree must give notice of acceptance

o Mailbox rule—acceptance valid when sent (even though offeror hasn't received it)

o UCC—if acceptance is made by beginning performance, notice is required within a reasonable time; failure to give notice results in offer's lapse

D. **Additional or different terms**

1. **CL mirror-image rule**—acceptance must mirror the terms of the offer, so any change or addition to the terms acts as a rejection and a new counteroffer

- Conditional acceptance terminates the offer and acts as new offer from original offeree

2. **UCC** (no mirror-image rule)—acceptance containing additional or different terms generally treated as acceptance

- **One or both parties not merchants**—definite and seasonable expression of acceptance sent within a reasonable time is usually acceptance of original offer, and new/different terms are treated as proposed additions to the K that must be separately accepted by offeror

o Exception—an acceptance expressly conditioned on assent to new/different terms is treated as a counteroffer

- **Both parties are merchants** (battle of the forms)

- o Additional terms—automatically included in the K, unless:
  - Term materially alters original K (i.e., would result in surprise or hardship);
  - Offer expressly limits acceptance to terms of the offer; or
  - Offeror objects to new terms within a reasonable time after notice of new terms is received.
  - If one of these exceptions is met, original terms of offer control
- **Different terms** ("knock-out" rule)—different terms in offer/acceptance nullify each other, and court uses Article 2's gap-filling provisions to patch holes in K
- **Acceptance based on conduct**—if offer and purported acceptance differ too much to create a contract but the parties begin to perform anyway, then UCC allows for a contract to be recognized with the following terms:
  - o Any terms actually agreed upon in the parties' writings, and
  - o Any supplementary terms filled in by the UCC

E. Consideration

1. **Bargain and exchange**—must be a bargained-for legal detriment to the promisee
   - Legal detriment and bargained-for exchange
     - o To constitute sufficient consideration, must be bargained-for in exchange for the promise, promise must induce the detriment, and detriment must induce the promise
     - o Consideration can be return promise to do or refrain from doing something, or performance of or refraining from doing some act
   - **Gift**
     - o Test to distinguish gift from valid consideration is whether offeree could reasonably believe intent of offeror was to induce the action (if YES, then there is consideration and promise is enforceable)
     - o Promissory estoppel—if promisor/donor knows that promise to make a gift will induce substantial reliance by promisee and failure to enforce it would cause substantial injustice, promise is enforceable

2. **Adequacy of consideration**
   - **Subjective value**—benefit to promisor need not have economic value; if promisor wants it, giving of it will constitute adequate consideration
   - **Preexisting duty rule**
     - o CL—does not qualify as consideration unless promisor gives something in addition to what is owed, or varies preexisting duty in some way
     - o Exception for third party—third-party promise contingent upon performance of another party's contractual obligation is sufficient consideration
   - **Past consideration**—modern trend towards enforcing past promises under the material benefit rule
   - **Modification**
     - o CL—must be supported by consideration, and agreements to modify K are enforceable if:

- Rescission of existing K and entering into of new K
- Unanticipated difficulties arise and modification is fair and equitable, or
- New obligations arise on both sides
  - o UCC
    - Requires only good faith
    - No consideration is necessary
- **Accord and satisfaction**
  - o Accord—one party agrees to accept a different performance from the other party to satisfy the other party's existing duty
  - o Satisfaction—performance of the accord agreement will discharge both the original K and the accord K
  - o Original K not discharged until satisfaction is complete
  - o An unliquidated or disputed claim may be discharged by negotiable instrument (e.g., a check with the note "Payment in full")
- **Illusory promise**—not legally binding because it is vague or promisor can choose whether or not to honor it
- **Voidable/unenforceable promises**—can still constitute consideration
- **Requirements** (buyer agrees to buy all that he requires) and **output** (seller agrees to sell all that she manufactures) Ks
  - o There is consideration because promisor suffers legal detriment
  - o Quantities may not be unreasonably disproportionate to estimates
- **Legal claim settlement**—a promise not to assert (or a release of) a claim or defense is not consideration, unless the claim or defense is doubtful or the party promising not to assert (or releasing) the claim believes in good faith that it is valid

F. **Promises binding without consideration**

1. **Pay a debt barred by statute of limitations** (SoL)—new promise to pay debt after SoL has run is enforceable without new consideration

2. **Perform voidable duty**—new promise to perform voidable duty is enforceable if it doesn't suffer from an infirmity rendering it voidable

3. **Material benefit rule**—when a party performs an unrequested service for another party, the modern trend permits the performing party to enforce the promise of payment for material benefits received to extent necessary to prevent injustice (unless donative intent)

4. **Promissory estoppel** (consideration "substitute")—a promise is binding if:
   - Promisor should reasonably expect it to induce action on the part of the promisee or a third person
   - Promise does induce such action, and
   - Injustice only avoided by enforcement of promise

G. **Enforceability**—a defense to formation or a defense to enforcement may render K void, voidable, or unenforceable

1. **Void Ks**—entire transaction is null, as if no K existed

2. **Voidable Ks**—operates as valid K until/unless one party takes steps to avoid it

3. **Unenforceable Ks**—valid K that cannot be enforced if one party refuses to carry out its terms

H. **Defenses to formation**—no "meeting of minds" due to mistake or misunderstanding, misrepresentation or fraud, undue influence or duress, or lack of capacity

1. **Mistake**

   • **Mutual**

     ○ Both parties mistaken as to essential element

     ○ K generally voidable by party adversely affected if:

       ▪ Mistake existed when K was formed

       ▪ Mistake relates to basic assumption of K

       ▪ Mistake has material impact on transaction, and

       ▪ Adversely affected party did not assume the risk of mistake

     ○ Neither party can avoid K if reformation available to cure mistake

   • **Unilateral**

     ○ One party is mistaken as to essential element of K, but either party can enforce K on its terms

     ○ Mistaken party can void K if he didn't bear risk of mistake and either:

       ▪ Mistake would make enforcement of K unconscionable, or

       ▪ Non-mistaken party caused the mistake, had duty to disclose or failed to disclose mistake, or knew or should have known the other party was mistaken

     ○ Must be absence of serious prejudice to other party to rescind K

   • **Reformation** (mutual mistake)

     ○ Court can reform writing except to extent that rights of third parties who relied on K would be unfairly affected

2. **Misunderstanding**—both parties believe they are agreeing to same material terms, but they in fact agree to different terms

   • **Neither party knows or has reason to know**—no K if material term involved

   • **One party knows or has reason to know**—K formed based upon meaning of material term as understood by unknowing party

   • **Both parties know terms ambiguous at time of K formation**—no K unless both parties intended same meaning

   • **Waiver**—one party can choose to enforce K according to other party's understanding

   • **Subjective determination of misunderstanding**—each party's knowledge or reason to know of the misunderstanding governs (i.e., not what a reasonable person would know)

3. **Misrepresentation**—an untrue assertion of fact (i.e., present event or past circumstance)

   • **Fraudulent misrepresentation**—requires proof that:

     ○ The misrepresentation is **fraudulent**:

       ▪ Knowing or reckless false assertion of fact

- With intent to mislead
  - o The misrepresentation **induced assent** to the K, and
  - o **Justifiable reliance** on the misrepresentation by the adversely affected party
- **Nondisclosure**—conduct to conceal a fact or nondisclosure of a known fact is tantamount to an assertion that the fact does not exist
- **Effect**
  - o Fraud in the factum (execution)—fraudulent misrepresentation prevents party from knowing character/essential term of transaction, so no K is formed and apparent K is **void** unless reasonable diligence would have revealed K's true terms
  - o Fraud in the inducement—fraudulent misrepresentation is used to induce another to enter into a K; K **voidable** by adversely affected party if she justifiably relied on the misrepresentation
- **Nonfraudulent misrepresentation** (innocent/negligent)—renders K voidable by adversely affected party who justifiably relied on **material** misrepresentation and was induced to assent to K because of it
- **Effect of party's fault**—a party's fault in not knowing or discovering facts before entering into the K does not prevent the party's reliance on the misrepresentation from being justified (unless it constitutes a failure to act in good faith)
- **Cure of misrepresentation**—K not voidable if facts cured before deceived party has avoided the K
- **Avoidance/reformation for misrepresentation**—when content/legal effect of K is misrepresented, deceived party can avoid K or reform it to express what was represented

4. **Undue influence**—unfair persuasion of a party to assent to a K
   - **Unfair persuasion**
     - o Relationship between dominant party and dependent party due to lack of expertise or experience, or diminished mental capacity
     - o Persuasion of one party seriously impairs the free and competent judgment of other party
   - **Confidential relationship**—dominant party has burden of proving K was fair (may be held to higher standard of disclosure)
   - **Third party undue influence**—victim may void K unless nonvictim party to K gave value or materially relied on K in good faith and without knowledge of undue influence
   - **Damages**—restitution available

5. **Duress**—improper threat that deprives party of meaningful choice
   - **Improper threat**
     - o Threats of criminal or civil action (made in bad faith), or
     - o Threats to breach K in violation of good faith and fair dealing
   - **Deprivation of meaningful choice**—person has no reasonable alternative such that threat induced his assent
   - **Effect on K**—K is **void** when duress is through physical compulsion and **voidable** in other instances

6. **Capacity to K**

- **Infancy** (under 18)—**voidable by infant** but not by adult (except for reasonable value of necessaries)

- **Mental illness**—K is **void** for one who is adjudicated mentally incompetent, but only voidable if there has been no adjudication

- **Guardianship**—K is **void** for individuals under guardianship (except for reasonable value of necessaries)

- **Intoxication**—K is **voidable** by intoxicated party if she was unable to understand nature/consequences of K and other party knew of intoxication

I. **Defenses to enforcement**

1. **Illegality**

- K is **unenforceable** if consideration/performance under K is illegal

- K is **void** if it contemplates illegal conduct

- Duty to perform is **discharged** if K becomes illegal after formation

- If one party is justifiably ignorant of facts making K illegal or lacks illegal purpose he can recover (assuming guilt of other party)

- **Exceptions:**

  - Ignorance of illegality—a party may recover if the party is justifiably ignorant of the facts making K illegal and the other party had knowledge of the illegality

  - Lack of illegal purpose—a party who has substantially performed may recover if:

    - K does not involve illegal consideration/performance—the party is unaware of the other party's illegal purpose

    - The party knows of the other party's illegal use—unless the party furthered the illegal use or the use involves grave social harm

  - Divisible Ks—if K can easily be divided into legal and illegal parts, a party may recover on the legal part(s)

  - Licensing violation—depends on the purpose of the licensing requirement:

    - Regulatory purpose—the party who fails to comply cannot enforce the K

    - Raise revenue—the party who fails to comply can enforce the K

  - Restitution

    - Not *in pari delicto*—when parties are not equally at fault, the less guilty party may recover under restitution

    - Withdrawal—a party who withdraws from an illegal K before the improper purpose has been achieved may recover under restitution when the party has not engaged in serious misconduct

2. **Unconscionability**—K is unconscionable when it is so unfair to one party that no reasonable person in the position of the parties would agree to it (e.g., hidden, complex boilerplate language, adhesion Ks)

3. **Public policy**—K may be unenforceable if it violates significant public policy

J. **Implied-in-fact Ks and quasi-Ks**

1. **Implied-in-fact**—conduct, not words, indicates assent or agreement

2. **Quasi-Ks**—a plaintiff confers benefit on a defendant and the plaintiff has reasonable expectation of compensation and court implies K to prevent unjust enrichment

    - **Requirements:**
        - ○ Plaintiff conferred measurable benefit on defendant,
        - ○ Plaintiff acted without gratuitous intent, and
        - ○ Unfair to let defendant retain benefit

K. **Warranties in sale-of-goods Ks**

   1. **Express warranty**

       - Any promise, affirmation, description, or sample that is part of the basis of the bargain, **unless it is merely the seller's opinion**

       - **Disclaimers**—disclaimers that unreasonably negate or limit express warranties are inoperative

   2. **Implied warranty of merchantability**

       - Implied whenever seller is a merchant

       - Goods must be fit for their ordinary purpose

       - Warranty can be disclaimed by use of "as is," "with all faults," or similar language

       - Disclaimer may be oral, but must use the term "merchantability" and be conspicuous if in writing

   3. **Implied warranty of fitness for a particular purpose**

       - Implied whenever seller has reason to know (from any source) buyer has particular use for goods and buyer is relying on seller's skill to select the goods

       - Warranty can be disclaimed by conspicuous writing

II. **Discharge**

   A. **Impracticability**—replaces CL doctrine of impossibility

      1. **Defense available if:**

          - Performance becomes illegal after K is made;

          - Specific subject matter of K is destroyed;

          - Performing party to the K dies or becomes incapacitated (personal services K); or

          - Performance becomes impracticable.

      2. **Elements:**

          - Unforeseeable event has occurred;

          - Nonoccurrence of event was basic assumption on which K was made; and

          - Party seeking discharge is not at fault.

      3. **Timing**—usually arises after K formation, but a fact making K performance impractical can exist when K is made if the party has no reason to know of the fact

      4. **Assumption of risk**—impracticability defense not available to a party who assumes the risk of an event happening

5. **Partial impracticability**

   • If seller is able to deliver some of the goods, they must be apportioned among all of the buyers with whom the seller has contracted

   • Buyer may refuse to accept and may cancel K

6. **Failure of a particular source**—if K specifically identifies a source, and source of supply fails, performance is discharged even if other sources are available

B. **Frustration of purpose**

   1. Applies when unexpected events arise that destroy one party's purpose in entering into K, even if performance of K not rendered impossible

   2. Frustrated party entitled to rescind K without paying damages

   3. Unexpected event need not be completely unforeseeable, but must be so severe it's not within assumed risks inherent under K

   4. **Timing**—can arise at the time of K if a party has no reason to know a fact exists

C. **Rescission**—cancelling of K so as to restore parties to their positions before K was made

   1. Parties may seek to rescind for a variety of reasons but grounds for rescission must have existed at the time the K was made

   2. **Rescission also possible by mutual agreement of the parties**—surrender of rights under the original K is consideration for the rescission

      • **Third-party beneficiaries**—K **not** discharged by mutual rescission if third-party rights have already vested

D. **Release**

   1. Writing that manifests intent to discharge another party from an existing duty

      • **CL**—release must be supported by **consideration**

      • **UCC**—written waiver or renunciation signed/delivered by aggrieved party is enough (**no consideration** necessary)

E. **Destruction/damage to identified goods**

   1. **Destruction**—goods identified when K made are destroyed by no fault of either party before risk of loss passes to buyer; K is avoided, both parties are discharged, and neither party is in breach

   2. **Goods damaged but not destroyed**—K avoided or buyer can choose to take goods at reduced price without any other claim against seller

   3. **Risk of loss**—if risk of loss has passed to buyer, K is not avoided and seller may demand performance by buyer

III. **Third-Party Beneficiary Contracts**—when two parties contract with the understanding and intent that performance by one of the parties is to benefit a third person

A. **Intended and incidental beneficiaries**—third party can recover if she is an intended beneficiary

   1. **Intended beneficiary**—one to whom the promisee wishes to satisfy an obligation or otherwise benefit by the promised performance; has the right to bring an action on the K

   2. **Incidental beneficiary**—one who benefits from a K even though there is no contractual intent to benefit that person; no right to enforce K

B. **Vesting of beneficiary's rights**—rights of intended beneficiary vest when beneficiary:

    1. Detrimentally relies on rights created;

    2. Manifests assent to K at one of the party's request; or

    3. Files lawsuit to enforce K.

C. **Defenses**—promisor can raise any defense against third party that he had against original promisee

IV. Assignment of Rights & Delegation of Duties

A. **Assignment of rights**

    1. Not allowed when it materially increases duty or risk of obligor or materially reduces obligor's chance of obtaining performance

    2. Need present intent to transfer the right immediately

    3. If assignment is for consideration, it is irrevocable

    4. Assignee takes all of the rights of assignor as the K stands at time of the assignment, but she takes subject to any defenses that could be raised against the assignor

    5. A prohibition on assignment does not affect the assignment of rights, but bars delegation of duties (unless circumstances indicate otherwise)

B. **Delegation of duties**

    1. Generally allowed, except when other party to K has substantial interest in a specific individual's performance (for example, personal services K involving special skill)

    2. When obligations are delegated, delegator is not released from liability, so he is still liable if delegate doesn't perform (unless there is a novation)

    3. Delegate's acceptance of a delegation constitutes a promise to perform the delegated duties; promise is enforceable if there is consideration or a consideration substitute

    4. Delegation in contracts for the sale of goods may be treated by the other party as creating reasonable grounds for insecurity; the other party may demand assurances from delegate; conforming promises by permitted delegates must be accepted

    5. A prohibition on assignment does not affect the assignment of rights, but bars delegation of duties (unless circumstances indicate otherwise)

C. **Assignment of contract**—assignments not limited to contractual rights (e.g., "this contract is assigned to") are generally treated as both an assignment of rights and a delegation of duties

V. Statute of Frauds (SoF)

A. **Writing required**—memorandum must:

    1. Be in **writing**;

    2. Be **signed** by the party to be charged (i.e., any authentication that identifies the party);

    3. Contain the **essential elements** of the deal.

B. **Types of Ks within the SoF**

    1. **M**arriage—any agreement in consideration of marriage

    2. **S**uretyship—K to answer for debt/duty of another

    3. **O**ne year—K that cannot be performed within one year after K is made

4. **U**CC—when K for the sale of goods is at least $500, memo must indicate that K has been made, identify **parties**, contain a **quantity** term, and be **signed** by the party to be charged

   - **Exceptions**—writing not required under UCC for:
     - Specially manufactured goods,
     - Part payment,
     - Receipt and acceptance,
     - Judicial admission, or
     - Failure to object to memo within 10 days of receipt (when both parties are **merchants**)

5. **R**eal property K—applies to Ks providing for subsequent conveyances of an interest in property (subsequent acts showing existence of K may also make oral Ks for transfers of interest enforceable)

C. **Exceptions**

1. **Promissory Estoppel**

2. **Judicial Admissions**

VI. **Parol Evidence** (P/E)—prevents introduction of prior extrinsic evidence that contradicts terms of written K

A. **Integration**—parties intended writing to be their final agreement (P/E rule applies)

1. **Total integration** (complete expression of all terms of parties' agreement)—parties cannot introduce extrinsic evidence of prior/contemporaneous understandings or negotiations

   - **Partial**—if writing sets forth only some terms, then parties are permitted to introduce supplementary extrinsic evidence of other terms that are **consistent** with writing (not contradictory)

2. **Intent of the parties**—determines if there is total, partial, or no integration

   - **CL** ("four corners" rule)—can only look to writing itself for intent

   - **Second Restatement**—if an extrinsic term of agreement would naturally be omitted from a writing, then term can be introduced so long as it isn't contradictory

   - **UCC**—assumes written K is only a partial integration and allows almost any outside terms

B. **When P/E is inapplicable—does not apply** to communications occurring **after** the execution of the written K and when parties are (partial list):

1. Raising a defense to formation

2. Raising a defense to enforcement

3. Proving condition precedent to existence of the K

4. Interpreting/clarifying ambiguity in K

5. **U**CC—supplementing even apparently unambiguous terms by evidence of trade usage or course of dealing (priority, highest to lowest: express terms, course of performance, course of dealing, trade usage)

VII. Conditions and Performance

A. Condition—future event that must take place before rights or obligations are created, destroyed, or enlarged

1. **Failure of a condition**—relieves a party of the obligation to perform

2. **Express**—K includes words like "on the condition that" or "provided that"
   - Condition must be complied with fully unless excused; substantial performance will not suffice
   - Enforceable even when the failure to meet the condition results in the denial of compensation

3. **Implied**—those deemed to be part of K because agreement suggests that parties truly intended the condition but failed to expressly include it, or because fairness requires its inclusion
   - Only substantial performance required to satisfy condition
   - **UCC**—implies duty of cooperation when performance of one party depends on the cooperation of the other party

B. Timing of conditions

1. **Condition precedent**—condition precedes the obligation to perform

2. **Condition subsequent**—condition excuses the duty to perform after a particular event occurs

3. **Concurrent conditions**—each party's duty to perform is conditioned on the other party's duty to perform (each party must perform simultaneously)

C. Satisfaction of conditions—examined against objective, **reasonable person standard** unless aesthetic taste is involved (then **subjective standard**; the party must use **good faith** when assessing satisfaction; dissatisfaction must be honest, but may be unreasonable)

D. Performance of contractual duty

1. **Order of performance**—unless the language or circumstances indicate otherwise, performance is due:
   - **When one party's performance requires a period of time**—that party must complete his performance before the other party is required to perform
   - **When both parties' performance can be rendered at the same time**—both parties must perform at the same time; one party's failure to perform excuses the other party's performance

2. **Substantial performance** (does not generally apply to Ks for sale of goods)
   - **Express condition precedent**—parties are generally held strictly to the condition; full compliance is required before other party's performance is due
   - **Implied or constructive condition precedent**—a party who substantially complies with the condition can trigger the other party's obligation to perform
   - **Damages**—K price minus any amount it will cost other party to obtain complete performance as promised
     - Even if no substantial performance, potential recovery through restitution
     - Failure to substantially perform is a material breach

- **Willful breach**—more likely to be treated as a material breach (i.e., substantial performance is less likely to be found when the breach is willful)

3. **Perfect tender under the UCC**

   - Seller must **transfer ownership** and **tender goods** conforming to warranty obligations

   - Buyer may **inspect goods** and, upon acceptance, has an **obligation to pay** for them

   - **Perfect tender rule**—substantial performance insufficient (except for installment Ks and when parties agree)

   - **Transferring ownership**

     o Automatic warranty of good title, rightful transfer, and goods free of security interest of which buyer is unaware

     o Actual knowledge of security interest nullifies warranty of title

   - **Seller's obligation to tender goods**—must be in accordance with K provisions or with UCC if K is silent on tender

   - **Method of tender**

     o Seller's place of business—seller must place goods at the disposition of the buyer and give the buyer notice, if necessary

     o Shipment contract (e.g., "F.O.B. seller's place of business")—seller must deliver goods to a carrier and make a contract for their shipment; when the K is silent, a shipment K is presumed when the K requires shipment by third-party carrier

     o Destination contract (e.g., "F.O.B. buyer's place of business")—seller must deliver goods to the place specified in contract and tender them there by holding them at the buyer's disposition

   - **Buyer's obligations**—once conforming tender is made, buyer obligated to accept and pay K price; rejection amounts to breach of K

   - **Buyer's right to inspect before payment**—generally, a right to inspect goods that are tendered, delivered, or identified to the K for sale, unless K provides otherwise

4. **Divisible or installment Ks**

   - **CL**—various units of performance divisible into distinct parts

     o Recovery limited to amount promised for the segment of K performed

     o Damages recoverable for breach of other segments

   - **UCC**—goods delivered in multiple shipments, each to be separately accepted

     o Perfect tender rule does not apply

     o Right to reject determined by "substantial conformity" standard—buyer can only reject if nonconformity **substantially impairs the value** to buyer and cannot be cured

     o Buyer may cancel K only if nonconforming tender **substantially impairs the value** of the entire K

5. **Implied duty of good faith and fair dealing**

   - Imposed on each party in any contract (common law or UCC)

- **"Good faith"**—"honesty in fact and the observance of reasonable commercial standards of fair dealing"

E. Suspension or excuse of conditions

1. **Waiver**—party whose duty is subject to a condition can waive a nonmaterial condition by words or conduct; the condition may be reinstated if:
   - The waiving party communicates the retraction of the waiver before the condition is due; and
   - The other party has not suffered detrimental reliance.

2. **Wrongful interference**—if party whose duty is subject to a condition wrongfully prevents or interferes with occurrence of that condition, then the condition is excused and interfering party has absolute duty to perform (per implied duty of **good faith and fair dealing**)

3. **Election**—a party who chooses to continue with a K after a condition is broken effectively waives that condition

4. **Estoppel**—once a party waives condition, he can be estopped from using that condition as a defense if other party **reasonably relied** on waiver

VIII. Breach of Contract and Remedies

A. Breach of K—once duty to perform exists, nonperformance is a breach unless duty is discharged

1. **CL**
   - **Material breach** (nonbreaching party does not receive substantial benefit of bargain)—allows nonbreaching party to withhold any promised performance and to pursue remedies for breach, including damages
   - **Minor breach** (breaching party has substantially performed)—nonbreaching party entitled to pursue remedies for nonmaterial breach (damages) but must perform under the K

2. **UCC**
   - In general, seller must strictly perform all obligations under K or be in breach
     - Material breach only applies to installment Ks or when parties stipulate it in K

B. Anticipatory repudiation

1. **CL**
   - **Promisor repudiates before time of performance is due**—repudiation must be clear and unequivocal through words or acts
   - **Nonbreaching party's options:**
     - Treat repudiation as a breach, or
     - Ignore repudiation and demand performance of promisor, but suspend any performance by promisee if it would increase promisor's damages
     - If date of performance has not passed and the only performance left is payment, must wait for actual breach before filing suit
   - **Retraction of repudiation**—can be retracted until promisee acts in reliance on repudiation, accepts repudiation, or commences action for breach of K

- **Unilateral Ks**—anticipatory repudiation **does not apply**

    2. **UCC**

    - Anticipatory repudiation occurs when there has been an **unequivocal refusal** of buyer/seller to perform or when reasonable grounds for insecurity arise and the other party fails to provide adequate assurances within reasonable time (not to exceed 30 days)

    - **Retraction of repudiation**—permitted if other party has not canceled the K or materially changed position

    3. **Prospective inability to perform**—party's expectations of performance may be diminished by an event occurring after K formation

    - **UCC**

        o A party can demand assurances if reasonable grounds for insecurity about other party's ability to perform (and may suspend performance until provided); the demand must be in writing

        o Failure to provide adequate assurances within reasonable time (limited to 30 days) treated as repudiation

C. **Remedies**—damages for breach of K

    1. **Expectation damages**

    - **In general**

        o Intended to put nonbreaching party in same position as if K had been performed

        o Must be calculated with reasonable certainty

        o Expectation damages = loss in value + other loss – cost avoided – loss avoided

    - **Partial performance**—partially performing party recovers work performed + expectation damages for work not yet performed

    - **Defective performance**

        o Construction Ks—damages; generally the cost to correct the defect

        o Sale of goods—damages equal to the difference between the value of the goods as warranted and the actual value of the tendered nonconforming goods

        o Real estate—damages for failure to perform = difference between K price and market value; damages for late delivery = fair market rental value

    - **Economic waste**—applies to construction contracts

        o Occurs when the cost to fix or complete construction is clearly disproportional to any economic benefit/utility gained as a result; court can award damages equal to the diminution in the market price of property

        o If the breach is willful and only completion of the K will give the nonbreaching party the benefit of its bargain, court can award damages to fix or complete construction even if it results in economic waste

    - **UCC Breach of warranty damages**—difference between the value of the goods accepted and the value they would have had if they had been as warranted (often, repair costs)

2. **Consequential damages and foreseeability**
   - **Direct damages**—necessary and usual result of D's wrongful act (i.e., "loss of value)
   - **Consequential damages**—damages that result from the breach, but arise out of special circumstances unique to the parties to the contract; must be reasonably foreseeable to the breaching party (but need not be a usual result of D's conduct), caused by the breach, and reasonably certain in value to be recovered
   - **Foreseeability**
     o Unforeseeable—not recoverable unless the breaching party had some reason to know about the possibility of the unforeseeable consequential damages
     o Damages are recoverable if they are natural and probable consequences of breach, or if they were contemplated by the parties at K formation, or if they were otherwise foreseeable
   - **Causation**—D's defense that P's losses would have occurred regardless of D's breach
   - **Reasonable certainty**
     o Dollar amount of damages must be proven with reasonable certainty
     o If lost profits are too speculative, courts may limit recovery to reliance damages (reasonable expenditures made in connection with the K)
   - **UCC breach of warranty**
     o Limitation of consequential damages for personal injury in the case of consumer goods is prima facie unconscionable
     o Limitation of damages when the loss is commercial is **not** prima facie unconscionable

3. **Incidental damages**—compensation for commercially reasonable expenses incurred as a result of other party's breach
   - **Seller's breach**—expenses incurred in inspection, receipt, transportation, care, and custody of goods rightfully rejected; expenses in effecting cover; and any other reasonable expense incident to the delay or other breach
   - **Buyer's breach**—any expenses incurred in stopping delivery; in the transportation, care, and custody of goods after the buyer's breach; in connection with return or resale of the goods; or otherwise resulting from the breach

4. **Liquidated damages and penalties**—damages stipulated by the parties to the K as a reasonable estimation of actual damages to be recovered in the event of a breach
   - **Enforceable if:**
     o Parties intended to agree in advance to damages that might arise from breach
     o Stipulated amount was reasonable at time of K, bearing some relation to damages that might be sustained, and
     o Actual damages would be uncertain in amount and difficult to prove

5. **Punitive damages**—rarely available in K actions but may be available if conduct constituting breach is also recoverable under tort theory

6. **Nominal damages**—when no damages are alleged/proven

7. **Attorney's Fees**—in K, not recoverable absent express agreement or specific law

8. **Mitigating damages**

- Party to K must avoid or mitigate damages to the extent possible by taking steps that do not involve undue risk, expense, or inconvenience

- Nonbreaching party held to standard of **reasonable conduct** in preventing loss

- **Services K**—a party is generally not required to accept any type of employment (only employment of the same type as the party was contracted to perform)

- Failure to mitigate reduces damages that may be recovered by nonbreaching party

D. **Restitution and reliance recoveries**

1. **Restitutionary damages** (restores to a party the benefit conferred on the other party)

- Measured by either the reasonable value of the D obtaining that benefit from another source, or increase in the D's wealth from having received that benefit

- If P has not substantially performed and is in breach, P not permitted to recover

- **Recovery by nonbreaching party**

   o Nonbreaching party may recover for any benefit conferred on breaching party by way of part performance or reliance

   o Nonbreaching party may not recover restitution if he has fully performed and the only remaining performance by the other party is the payment of a definite sum of money

- **Recovery by breaching party**

   o If D has benefitted from P's performance, P can recover for benefit conferred less the D's damages for the breach

   o P generally cannot recover if P's breach was willful or if K provides that nonbreaching party may retain the value of the breaching party's performance as liquidated damages

2. **Reliance damages** (reasonable out-of-pocket expenses incurred by nonbreaching party)

- Recoverable if nonbreaching party incurs expenses in reasonable reliance upon the promise that other party would perform

- Party **cannot recover both** reliance and expectation damages

E. **Specific performance**—an equitable remedy possible when damages are an inadequate remedy

1. **Factors considered** in determining whether damages are adequate

- Difficulty of proving damages with reasonable certainty

- Hardship to D

- Balance of the equities

- Wishes and understandings of the parties

- Practicality of enforcement

- Mutuality of agreement

2. **Real property**—specific performance granted because real property is **considered unique**

3. **UCC**—specific performance may be granted to the buyer when goods are rare or unique

4. **Equitable defenses—laches** (prejudicial delay in bringing the action) or **unclean hands** (nonbreaching party guilty of some wrongdoing in the transaction) may be raised by breaching party

F. UCC remedies

1. **Buyer's remedies**—when seller fails to perform or makes a nonconforming tender

   - **Failure to tender goods**

     o Cancel K—if breach of installment K goes to entire K

     o Recovery of payments—upon cancellation, buyer entitled to recover payments made for tender; on rejection or revoked acceptance, also gets security interest in goods in buyer's possession

     o Damages—market price minus K price plus incidental and consequential damages

     o Cover—buyer may purchase similar goods elsewhere and recover replacement price minus the K price

     o Specific performance—for **unique** goods

     o Replevin—buyer can obtain undelivered goods from seller if at least partial payment is made or the buyer is unable to effect cover

   - **Nonconforming tender**—buyer has right to accept or reject all or part of the goods (and the right to inspect before making that decision)

     o Rejection—buyer can reject goods if he gives notice to seller within a reasonable time and before acceptance, and is then entitled to a return of any payments made or to seek same remedies as if no tender was made

     o Acceptance—buyer accepts goods by expressly stating acceptance, using the goods, or failing to reject the goods; to recover damages, buyer must give seller timely notice of breach; damages measured by difference between value of nonconforming goods and value of conforming tender (usually cost of replacement or repair), plus consequential and incidental damages

     o Right to cure—seller has right to cure defective tender if time of performance under K has not yet elapsed or seller had reasonable grounds to believe that buyer would accept despite the nonconformity

2. **Seller's remedies**

   - **Right to price**—seller may recover the full price if buyer has accepted goods; conforming goods are destroyed or lost after risk has shifted to buyer; seller cannot reasonably sell identified goods

   - **Right to reclaim goods**—from insolvent buyer if he makes a demand within 10 days after buyer receives goods

   - **Stoppage of goods in transit**—permitted if buyer breaches or is insolvent

   - **Wrongful rejection by buyer**—seller can collect damages, resell the goods, or recover the price, and, if the seller is a "lost volume" seller, lost profits; seller can also collect incidental damages

3. **Risk of loss**

   - **Unidentified goods**—if goods are damaged/destroyed and there is no breach, risk of loss is on seller until he satisfies delivery obligations (and then risk shifts to buyer)

- Shipment K—risk of loss passes to buyer when the seller gives possession of the goods to the carrier and makes proper contract for their shipment
- Destination K—risk of loss passes to buyer when the seller tenders the goods at the place specified in the K
- **Identified goods**—seller is excused if goods are totally destroyed through no fault of the seller prior to the risk of loss being shifted to the buyer
- Effect of a breach of K
  - Seller's breach—if seller delivers nonconforming goods, risk of loss remains on the seller until buyer accepts or there is cure
  - Buyer's breach—if buyer breaches/repudiates after goods have been identified but before risk of loss shifts, then risk immediately shifts to buyer (to extent of lack of insurance coverage by seller)

4. **SoL on a breach of a sales K or warranty**
   - Four years after cause of action accrues
     - Generally, cause of action accrues when breach occurs, regardless of whether aggrieved party knows
   - Parties may reduce four-year limitations period to not less than one year, but they may not extend it

FINAL REVIEW OUTLINE: CRIMINAL LAW

I.   **General Principles**

   A.   ***Actus reus***—(i) a voluntary, affirmative act, or (ii) an omission (failure to act), causing a criminally proscribed result

   1.   **Voluntary act**

   - Physical and voluntary

   - Unconscious/asleep/under hypnosis—not voluntary

   2.   **Failure to act when a duty exists**

   - Imposed by statute

   - Contract

   - Special relationship

   - Detrimental undertaking

   - Causation

   B.   ***Mens rea***—a guilty mind or legally proscribed mental state (no *mens rea* for strict liability crimes)

   1.   **Specific intent (SI) crimes**—the defendant (D) has a subjective desire, specific objective, or knowledge to accomplish prohibited result (FIAT):

   - **F**irst-degree murder

   - **I**nchoate offenses

   - **A**ssault with intent to commit battery

   - **T**heft offenses

   2.   **Malice crimes** (CL murder, arson)

   - Reckless disregard of a high risk of harm

   - Requires only a criminal act without excuse, justification, or mitigation

   - Intent can be inferred from the accomplishment of the act

   3.   **General intent crimes** (e.g., battery, rape, kidnapping, and false imprisonment)

   - Require the intent to perform an unlawful act

   - **Intent**—purposely, knowingly, recklessly, or negligently

   - **Transferred intent**

     o   When D acts with intent to cause harm to one person or object and that act directly results in harm to another person or object

     o   Applies only to "bad aim" cases (not mistaken identity)

     o   Usually confined to homicide, battery, and arson

     o   Not for attempted crimes (only completed crimes)

- o MPC—transferred intent not specifically recognized, but liability is recognized when purposely, knowingly, recklessly, or negligently causing a particular result is an element of an offense

4. **Model Penal Code**

- **Purposely**—D's conscious objective is to engage in the conduct or to cause a certain result

- **Knowingly/willfully**—D is aware or knows that the result is practically certain to occur based on his conduct

- **Recklessly**—D acts with a conscious disregard of a substantial and unjustifiable risk

- **Negligently**—D should be aware of a substantial and unjustifiable risk that a material element of a crime exists or will result from his conduct (i.e., a gross deviation from the standard of care)

5. **Strict-liability crimes** (e.g., statutory rape, bigamy, regulation of food and drugs)

- No *mens rea*; proof of the *actus reus* is sufficient for conviction

- Generally disfavored; there must be clear legislative intent to dispense with the *mens rea*

6. **Vicarious liability**

- No *actus reus* by D; imposes criminal liability on D for the *actus reus* of a third party

- Generally limited to regulatory crimes; punishment generally limited to fines

- **Corporations**—may be vicariously liable when the act is performed by a high-ranking corporate agent who likely represents corporate policy

7. **Causation**—D's *mens rea* (if required) must cause the *actus reus*, and the act must cause the particular result made unlawful by statute

8. **Mistake as a defense**

- **Mistake of fact**

  - o May negate criminal intent (if an "honest mistake")

  - o A defense to specific-intent crimes, even if unreasonable

  - o A defense to general-intent or malice crimes, only if reasonable

- **Mistake of law**—only valid if:

  - o D relied on court decision/administrative order or official interpretation,

  - o Statutory definition of *malum prohibitum* crime not available before conduct, or

  - o An honestly held mistake of law negates required intent or mental state

C. **Parties to crime**

1. **Principal**—the person whose acts or omissions are the *actus reus* of the crime; must be actually or constructively present at the scene of the crime

2. **Accomplice liability**

- **Accomplice**—a person who, with the requisite *mens rea*, aids or abets a principal prior to or during the commission of the crime

- **Principal in the second degree**—an accomplice who is physically or constructively present during the commission of the crime

- **Accessory before the fact**—an accomplice who is neither physically nor constructively present during the commission of the crime, but who possesses the requisite intent
- Responsible for the crime and all other crimes that are the natural and probable consequences of the accomplice's conduct
- To withdraw, an accomplice must:
  - Repudiate prior aid,
  - Do all that is possible to countermand prior assistance, and
  - Do so before the chain of events is in motion and unstoppable

3. **Accessory after the fact**
- Aids or assists a felon to avoid apprehension or conviction after commission of the felony
- Must know that a felony was committed
- Only liable for a separate crime (e.g., "obstruction of justice" or "harboring a fugitive")

D. **Responsibility**
1. **Insanity**
- *M'Naghten*—D did not know either (i) the nature and quality of the act, or (ii) the wrongfulness of the act, because of a defect of reason due to mental disease ("right from wrong" test)
- **Irresistible impulse**—D lacked capacity for self-control and free choice due to mental disease or defect (inability to conform conduct to the law)
- *Durham*—the unlawful act was the product of D's mental disease or defect ("but for" test)
- **MPC** (combines *M'Naghten* and irresistible impulse)—at the time of the conduct, D lacked substantial capacity to appreciate the wrongfulness of the act or to conform his conduct to law, as a result of mental disease or defect

2. **Intoxication**
- **Voluntary**
  - Intentional taking of a substance known to be intoxicating
  - Need not intend actual intoxication
  - A defense to SI crimes if it prevents the formation of the required intent
  - MPC—a defense to crimes with a mental state that is "purposely" or "knowingly" and the intoxication prevents the formation of that mental state
- **Involuntary**
  - Taken without knowledge of the intoxicating nature, or under duress
  - A defense when intoxication negates an element of a general intent, specific intent, or malice crime

II. **Homicide**—the killing of a living human being by another

    A. **Murder**—the unlawful killing of another living human being with malice aforethought

        1. **Malice**—can be shown by any one of the following:

- **Intent to kill**—conduct that is the legal cause of death + intent to kill

- **Intent to do serious bodily injury**—intent to do serious bodily injury + unintentional killing

- **Reckless indifference to human life**—results from reckless indifference to an unjustifiably high risk to human life + unintentional killing ("depraved heart")

- **Intent to commit a felony**—proximately caused by and during the commission or attempted commission of an inherently dangerous felony + unintentional killing (felony murder)

        2. **Felony murder rule (FMR)**

- Unintended and foreseeable killing proximately caused by and during the commission or attempted commission of an inherently dangerous felony (most common: BARRK— **b**urglary, **a**rson, **r**obbery, **r**ape, and **k**idnapping)

- The prosecution must establish the underlying felony and that D committed that felony

- Agency theory (majority position)—D is not liable for a bystander's death caused by a felony victim or police officer

- Proximate cause theory (minority position)—a bystander's death falls under FMR because the death is a direct consequence of the felony

- D is not liable for a co-felon's death by a victim or police officer

- Does not encompass death occurring after flight from the scene of the crime

    B. **Statutory murder**

        1. **First-degree**

- Deliberate and premeditated murder; or

    ○ After forming the intent to kill, D had time for reflection

    ○ Specific-intent crime (specific-intent defenses are available to D)

- Felony murder

        2. **Second-degree** (malice crime)—committed with the necessary malicious intent (common-law murder), or the default category if not first-degree murder

    C. **Voluntary manslaughter**—homicide committed with malice aforethought, but also with mitigating circumstances

        1. **"Heat of passion"**

- Murder committed in response to a situation that could inflame a reasonable person (e.g., serious battery, threat of deadly force, but usually not mere words)

- NOT a defense, but it reduces murder to voluntary manslaughter

- If there was sufficient time between the provocation and the killing for a reasonable person to cool down, then murder is not mitigated to manslaughter

- Transferred provocation applies if D misidentified her provoker or accidentally kills the wrong person

2. **Imperfect defense**
   - Many states reduce murder to voluntary manslaughter if D started the altercation or unreasonably believed in the necessity of using deadly force

D. **Involuntary manslaughter**—an unintentional homicide committed with criminal negligence or during an unlawful act

1. **Criminal negligence**—grossly negligent action (or inaction when there is a duty to act) that puts another person at a significant risk of serious injury or death

2. **Unlawful act—a killing committed during the commission of:**
   - A *malum in se* misdemeanor (e.g., assault, battery), or
   - A felony that is not treated as first-degree felony murder or second-degree murder

III. Other Crimes

A. Crimes against property

1. **Larceny**
   - Trespassory;
   - Taking and;
   - Carrying away;
   - Of the personal property;
   - Of another;
   - With the specific intent to permanently deprive the owner of the property.

2. **Larceny by trick**
   - Larceny;
   - Accomplished by fraud or deceit;
   - That results in the conversion of the property of another.

3. **Forgery**
   - Making;
   - Of a false writing;
   - With apparent legal significance; and
   - With the intent to defraud.

4. **Embezzlement**
   - Fraudulent;
   - Conversion;
   - Of the property;
   - Of another;
   - By a person who is in lawful possession of the property.

5. **False pretenses**
   - Obtaining title to the property;
   - Of another person;

- Through the reliance of that person;
- On a known false representation of a material past or present fact; and
- The representation is made with the intent to defraud.

6. **Robbery**
   - Larceny;
   - From the person or presence of the victim;
   - By force or intimidation.

7. **Extortion**
   - The taking of money or property from another by threat.
   - Making the threat (not obtaining the property) is the essence of the crime (majority view)
   - The threat need not be of immediate harm or of a physical nature
   - The property need not be on the victim or in his presence

8. **Burglary** (common law)
   - Breaking and;
   - Entering;
   - Of the dwelling;
   - Of another;
   - At nighttime;
   - With the specific intent to commit a felony therein.

9. **Arson**
   - Malicious;
   - Burning;
   - Of the dwelling;
   - Of another.
   - Note: The MBE has not always been consistent with regard to this definition.

10. **Possession offenses**
    - D exercises dominion and control over a prohibited object or substance
    - D is not required to be aware that possession of the object is illegal
    - **Duration of possession**—must be for a period long enough to have provided D with an opportunity to cease such dominion and control

11. **Receipt of stolen property**
    - Receiving control of stolen property;
    - Knowledge that the property is stolen; and
    - Intent to permanently deprive the owner of the property.

B. Crimes against the person

1. **Battery**
   - Unlawful;
   - Application of force;
   - To another person;
   - That causes bodily harm to that person or constitutes an offensive touching.

2. **Assault**
   - An attempt to commit a battery; or
   - Intentionally placing another in apprehension of imminent bodily harm.

3. **Mayhem**—a common-law felony battery that causes the dismemberment or permanent disfigurement of a person

4. **Kidnapping**
   - Unlawful;
   - Confinement of a person;
   - Against that person's will;
   - Coupled with either:
     - The movement; or
     - The hiding of that person.

5. **False imprisonment**
   - Unlawful;
   - Confinement of a person;
   - Without consent.

6. **Rape**
   - Unlawful;
   - Sexual intercourse;
   - With a female;
   - Against her will by force or threat of immediate force.
   - (Most modern statutes are gender-neutral and have replaced the force requirement with lack of consent.); the required intent is negated if D reasonably believes that the victim's lack of resistance indicates consent

IV. Inchoate crimes (specific-intent crimes)

A. Merger—D may be tried, but not punished, for (i) solicitation and the completed crime; (ii) attempt and the completed crime; (iii) under the MPC, more than one inchoate offense (but conspiracy and attempt do not merge under the CL)

1. **Solicitation**
   - Enticing, encouraging, requesting, or commanding another person;
   - To commit a crime;

- With the intent that the other person commits the crime.
- **Renunciation** (MPC)—voluntary renunciation may be a defense if D thwarts the commission of the solicited crime

2. Conspiracy

- An agreement;
- Between two or more persons (bilateral conspiracy);
- To accomplish an unlawful purpose;
- With the intent to accomplish that purpose.
- **Unilateral conspiracy**—may be formed when only one party actually agrees (modern trend and MPC; not recognized under common law)
- **Overt act**
  - **Common law**—no overt act required
  - **Majority/federal law/MPC**
    - Require a lawful or unlawful overt act in furtherance of the conspiracy, but
    - MPC does not require an overt act if the conspiratorial crime is a first- or second-degree felony
- **Scope**—a conspirator is liable for conspiracy and the co-conspirators' substantive crimes committed in furtherance of the conspiracy (*Pinkerton* Rule)
- **Withdrawal**
  - **Liability for conspiracy**
    - **Federal/majority rule**—withdrawal is possible after the agreement and before the commission of an overt act, but D must give notice to co-conspirators or give timely notice to police
    - **MPC/minority rule**—subsequent withdrawal is possible only if D acts voluntarily to "thwart the success" of the conspiracy
  - **Liability for substantive crimes**—for this purpose, D may withdraw by giving notice to his co-conspirators or timely advising legal authorities of the existence of the conspiracy even though such an action does not thwart the conspiracy

3. Attempt

- A substantial step toward commission of crime (beyond mere preparation); coupled with
- The specific intent to commit the crime.
- **Factual impossibility**—not a defense (legal impossibility is a defense)
- **Abandonment**—not a defense after a substantial step is taken (CL)
- If the crime is completed, the attempt merges into the completed crime (D may be charged with both, but may be convicted of only one)

V. Defenses

A. Generally

1. Mistake of fact

- A viable defense, if the mistake is a reasonable one

- o Consider D's physical characteristics, experiences, and knowledge
- An unreasonable mistake is only a defense to specific-intent crimes

B. Specific defenses

1. **Self-defense**—one who is not the aggressor is justified in using reasonable force against another person to prevent immediate unlawful harm to himself

   - **Reasonable force**—may be used to prevent immediate unlawful harm

   - **Deadly force**—may be used in self-defense only if reasonably necessary to:
     - o Prevent death or serious injury, or
     - o Prevent the commission of a serious felony involving a risk to human life

   - **Nondeadly force**—may be used to repel nondeadly force

   - **Retreat**
     - o No self-defense duty to retreat before using nondeadly force, deadly force in home, or (majority view) deadly force elsewhere
     - o Minority view—retreat is required if it can be safely accomplished

   - **Imperfect self-defense** (when a killing in self-defense is not justified)—reduces murder to voluntary manslaughter

   - **Aggressor's right to use self-defense**—an initial aggressor may gain the right to act in self-defense if:
     - o The aggressor's nondeadly force was met with deadly force, or
     - o The aggressor, in good faith, withdrew from the altercation and communicated that fact to the victim

2. **Defense of others**—the right to defend others exists under the same circumstances in which self-defense would be acceptable

3. **Defense of property**

   - Reasonable steps, including nondeadly force, may be used to protect property

   - D must reasonably believe that the real property is in immediate danger of unlawful trespass or that personal property is in immediate danger of being carried away

   - Force cannot be unreasonably disproportionate to the perceived harm

   - Generally, deadly force is not OK in defending property—only OK to prevent forcible entry into a dwelling if the occupant reasonably believes that the intruder intends to commit a felony inside

   - Deadly mechanical devices cannot be used to protect property

4. **Arrest**

   - Police can use reasonable force to make a lawful arrest

   - Police can use deadly force only if the suspect is a threat to the officer or third parties

   - **Resisting unlawful arrest**—D may use nondeadly force to resist an unlawful arrest (never deadly force)

5. **Duress**

- A third party's unlawful threat that causes D to reasonably believe that the only way to avoid death or serious bodily injury to himself or another is to violate the law, and that causes D to do so, allows D to claim the duress defense

- Not a defense to intentional murder

6. **Necessity**

- Forces of nature (not human actions) caused D to commit what would otherwise be a crime

- Not a defense if D set the natural forces in motion (e.g., set a fire) or if there is a reasonably apparent noncriminal alternative

7. **Consent**

- Not a defense unless it:
  o Negates a required element of the crime, or
  o Precludes the harm sought to be avoided by the crime

- Consent must be:
  o Voluntarily and freely given;
  o Involve no fraud; and
  o Be given by one who is competent to consent.

8. **Entrapment**

- The crime is induced by a government official or agent; and
- D was not predisposed to commit the crime.

FINAL REVIEW OUTLINE: CRIMINAL PROCEDURE

I. **Fourth Amendment: Application to Arrest, Search and Seizure**
   A. **General principles**
      1. **Standing**—D must have standing to assert claim
      2. **Exclusionary rule**
         - Prevents introduction at a subsequent criminal trial of evidence unlawfully seized
         - **Does not apply** to federal habeas corpus review, grand jury proceedings, preliminary/bail/sentencing hearings, proceedings to revoke parole, evidence used as impeachment evidence against the defendant, or civil proceedings
         - Suppression decisions made by a judge; factual findings are reviewed for clear error while findings of law are reviewed de novo
      3. **Government conduct**—publicly paid police, private person directed by police, or deputized private police
      4. **Reasonable expectation of privacy** (REP)—as to place searched or item seized
   B. **Arrest**—unreasonable seizure of persons
      1. **Seizure**—when police, by means of physical force/show of authority, terminate/restrain freedom of movement and D actually submits
         - Totality of circumstances
            o If police intent to restrain is ambiguous, or
            o If D's submission is only passive acquiescence,
            o Then a seizure occurs if totality of circumstances would lead reasonable innocent person to believe he is not free to leave
      2. **Stop and frisk**—temporary detention that constitutes seizure if the officer, by means of physical force/show of authority, has in some way restrained (physical restraint or an order to stop) the liberty of a citizen
      3. **Warrant**
         - **Arrest**—must be issued by detached/neutral magistrate upon finding of probable cause (PC) and describe with particularity the D and crime; deficient warrant does not invalidate arrest as long as there was PC (no warrant required for proper arrest based on PC)
         - **Search**—issued by detached/neutral magistrate upon finding of PC, supported by oath or affidavit, & must describe with particularity places to be searched and items to be seized (reasonable belief that contraband will be found)
         - **Facts supporting PC**
            o Officer's personal observations
            o Information from reliable, known informant or verified unknown informant
            o Evidence seized during stop and based on reasonable suspicion, discovered in plain view, or during consensual search
         - **Particularity**
            o Must specify place to be searched and objects to be seized
            o Can also refer to contraband as "other fruits, instrumentalities, or evidence of crime at this time unknown" and still be valid
         - **Knock & announce rule**
            o Police must generally announce purpose when executing a warrant (unless state allows exception for exigent circumstances)

o Violation does not trigger exclusionary rule

4. Warrantless arrests

- Arrest warrant not needed in public place or for felony or misdemeanor in arresting party's presence, but invalid arrest alone not a defense to crime charged (but will affect any seizure of evidence)

- In determining whether a crime has been committed, the question is whether an officer could conclude—considering all of the surrounding circumstances—that there was a substantial chance of criminal activity

C. Search and seizure

1. Government conduct—search must be by government employee or agent

2. Reasonable expectation of privacy (REP) or physical intrusion on protected area

- **Home, private room, or office**—home and curtilage, motel rooms, and business premises are protected; use of drug-sniffing dog is a search if physically intrudes onto constitutionally protected property

- **Luggage**—REP for invasive searches but not for canine sniff

- **Automobiles**—need reasonable suspicion of law violation to effectuate a stop, and PC for pre-textual stops when traffic law violated to investigate whether another law has been violated; fact that a person in lawful possession of a rental car is not listed on the rental agreement does not defeat his REP

- **Open areas**—outside curtilage – no reasonable (objective) expectation of privacy

- **Odor from car**—no REP

- **Technological device**
  - o Attaching a tracking device to a person without consent is a search; collecting cell-site location information from a wireless carrier to track a person requires a warrant
  - o Physically intruding on a suspect's property to install a technological device may be a search
  - o Use of sense-enhancing devices not used by general public is a search

3. Exceptions to search warrant requirement

- **Search incident to lawful arrest**—must be reasonable in scope and incident to a lawful arrest
  - o **Wingspan**—includes contemporaneous search of person/immediate surrounding area including pockets/containers (**does not** include cell phone or laptop unless exigent circumstances exist)
  - o **Home**—a "protective sweep" is permissible, even without probable cause or reasonable suspicion; includes places immediately adjoining place of arrest in home from which an attack could be launched and in which a person might be hiding (adjacent rooms, closets, showers); the search area can be broadened if based on reasonable suspicion that confederates are hiding beyond these immediately adjacent areas
  - o **Vehicle**—justified if:
    - Arrestee is within reaching distance of passenger compartment (weapons/evidence) during search, or
    - It is reasonable that evidence of the offense of arrest might be in vehicle
- **Exigent circumstances**
  - o **Totality of circumstances test**
    - Must have PC and exigent circumstances

- - Police may not create the exigency by threats or conduct that violates the Fourth Amendment
    - o **Hot pursuit**—police in pursuit of a suspect can seize "mere" evidence (not fruits/instrumentalities of crime) from a private building if they have PC to believe the suspect committed a felony
    - o **Emergency**—reasonable apprehension that delay in getting warrant would result in immediate danger of evidence destruction, police/public safety or fleeing felon (judged by police officer's objective reasonable belief)
- **Stop and frisk**
  - o **Stop**—(*Terry* stop) reasonable suspicion (totality of circumstances), based on articulable facts that detainees involved in criminal activity, and is a limited/temporary intrusion on D's freedom of movement
  - o **Frisk**
    - An officer without probable cause may pat down a person's outer clothing if the officer has reasonable suspicion that the suspect was/is involved in criminal activity and that the frisk is necessary for safety
    - Under "plain feel" exception, if officer conducting a valid frisk feels an object whose identity is immediately obvious (i.e., PC of contraband) it can be seized
  - o **Passenger compartment**—permitted if police have reasonable belief suspect is dangerous and may get immediate control of weapons, and the search is limited to places where a weapon could be hidden
  - o **Limitations**—least intrusive means reasonably available to frisk for weapons only, but if suspicion becomes PC, then officer can make arrest and conduct a full search
- **Automobile exception**—can search any part of car (compartments, particular containers (including luggage), trunk, etc.) if PC that it contains contraband/evidence of crime; does not permit warrantless entry of home or curtilage in order to search a vehicle therein
- **"Plain-view" doctrine**
  - o **In public view**—no REP
  - o **In private view**—officer on premises for lawful purpose, incriminating nature of item immediately apparent, officer has lawful access to the item
- **Consent**
  - o **Voluntary**—no threats of harm, compulsion, or false assertion of lawful authority (totality of circumstances); but a government agent may pretend to be someone else
  - o **Third party**—can consent to own property search, but D's property only if agency relationship to D or D assumes the risk of search when giving right to third party to consent to search
- **Warrant authorizing wiretapping**
  - o Limited period of time
  - o PC that a specific crime has been or is about to be committed
  - o Identify persons and describe particular conversations to be tapped
  - o When to terminate tapping
  - o Reveal intercepted conversation to court
4. **Standing to object**—D must show a legitimate expectation of privacy with regard to the search

5. **Exclusionary rule**

- **Fruit of the poisonous tree**—applies not only to evidence initially seized as a result of government illegality but also to secondary derivative evidence resulting from primary taint

- **Exceptions**
  - **Inevitable discovery**—in same condition through lawful means
  - **Independent source**—unrelated to tainted evidence
  - **Attenuation**—passage of time and/or intervening events may purge primary taint
  - **Good faith**
    - Applies to police relying in objective GF on either facially valid warrant later found invalid or existing law later held unconstitutional
    - **Does not apply** if no reasonable officer would rely on affidavit underlying warrant, warrant defective on its face, warrant obtained by fraud, magistrate wholly abandons judicial role, or warrant improperly executed
  - **Isolated police negligence**—not enough to trigger the exclusionary rule; must be sufficiently deliberate that exclusion can meaningfully deter it
  - **Knock and announce**—exclusionary rule doesn't apply when police fail to knock and announce their presence
  - **In-court ID**—not fruit of an unlawful detention

- **Harmless error**—court can refuse to order new trial if error harmless beyond reasonable doubt, i.e., illegal evidence did not contribute to result

II. **Fifth Amendment Rights and Privileges**

A. **The privilege against compulsory self-incrimination**

1. **Rule**—no person shall be compelled in criminal case to testify against himself; applies to states through the Fourteenth Amendment

2. **Testimonial evidence only**—nontestimonial physical evidence (blood, urine, breathalyzer, etc.) not protected

3. **Proceedings**—applies to civil/criminal, formal/informal proceedings if answers provide reasonable possibility of incriminating D in future criminal proceeding

4. **Waiving privilege**—D waives by taking the stand and answering prosecution's questions; witness waives it by disclosing self-incriminating information in response to a specific question

B. **The Fifth Amendment in a police interrogation context**—any incriminating statement obtained as result of custodial interrogation may not be used against suspect at subsequent trial unless police inform subject of *Miranda* rights

1. **Custodial interrogation**

- **Custodial**
  - Substantial seizure, i.e., formal arrest or restraint of freedom equivalent to arrest; would reasonable person believe he could leave?
  - Questioning at a police station is not automatically custodial

- **Interrogation**
  - Questioning and also words/actions reasonably likely to elicit incriminating response
  - Voluntary statements not protected
  - Confessions involuntary only if coerced by police (totality of circumstances)

2. **Compliance**
   - **Content/timing**—warning must be given before interrogation begins (or given again if stopped for long time), need not be verbatim, but must inform suspect of right to remain silent, any statement can be used in court, right to an attorney (or one will be appointed)
   - **Right to counsel**—suspect must make a specific, unambiguous statement asserting his desire to have counsel present, and once invoked, all interrogation must stop until counsel is present, unless suspect voluntarily initiates communication with police (including spontaneous statements) or 14-day or more break in custody and fresh *Miranda* warnings given
   - **Right to silence**—suspect must make a specific, unambiguous statement asserting his desire to remain silent (mere silence is not enough); interrogator must scrupulously honor right if invoked, but if suspect indicates desire to speak, subsequent interrogation lawful if suspect not coerced, and *Miranda* warnings must be given again
   - **Exceptions**
     - Public safety
     - Routine booking questions
     - Undercover police
   - **Waiver**—suspect must knowingly, voluntarily, and intelligently waive right (silence insufficient)

C. **Fruits of a tainted confession**
   1. *Miranda* violation doesn't automatically result in suppression of incriminating statements made after second warnings given
   2. But, second confession inadmissible if circumstances make it clear police approach was intentional attempt to circumvent *Miranda*

D. **Fifth Amendment in the trial context**—D can refuse to testify at criminal trial or other proceedings that might incriminate him in future criminal proceedings; witness may also invoke the privilege, but may raise Confrontation Clause issues if partial testimony already given

III. **Sixth Amendment**—right to jury, public trial, confront witnesses against him, cross-examine witnesses, be present at his own trial, and assistance of counsel for his defense

A. **Applicability: right to counsel**
   1. **Types of proceedings**—any case in which actual/suspended incarceration is imposed
   2. **Applicability**—automatically applies at all critical stages of prosecution after formal proceedings begin, and right automatically attaches when formal judicial proceedings have begun (e.g., post-arrest initial appearance before a judicial officer, formal charge, preliminary hearing, indictment, information, or arraignment); no right to counsel at post-conviction proceedings (e.g., parole, probation)
   3. **Waiver**—must be voluntary, knowing, and intelligent; receiving a *Miranda* warning sufficiently apprises a person of his Sixth Amendment rights and the consequences of waiving those rights (even though *Miranda* rights arise from the Fifth Amendment)
      - **Subsequent waivers**
        - If an accused has not actually asserted his right to counsel (e.g., court automatically appoints counsel), there is no presumption that any subsequent waiver of the right to counsel will be involuntary; if an accused actually asserts the right to counsel, then subsequent waivers are presumed involuntary, but only in a custodial setting
        - Even after Sixth Amendment rights attach, police may initiate non-custodial interactions with the accused outside the presence of his lawyer, and there will be

no presumption that any knowing waiver of the right to have counsel present for the interaction is involuntary

- **Right to proceed pro se**—D can refuse counsel and proceed pro se at trial; court should warn D of dangers and disadvantages, and may appoint "standby counsel;" D may be competent to stand trial yet incompetent to represent himself

4. **Withholding information**—police have no obligation to inform D that counsel has been trying to reach him unless Sixth Amendment has attached

B. **Offense-specific**

1. *Blockburger* **test**—two different crimes in one criminal transaction deemed to be same offense unless each offense requires proof of an element that the other does not

2. *Miranda* **comparison**—Unlike *Miranda*, presence of counsel only applies to interrogations about offense charged; like *Miranda*, D may make knowing/voluntary waiver of right

C. **Remedies for denial of counsel**

1. **Effect on conviction**—D's conviction is automatically reversed even without specific showing of unfairness

2. **Effect on guilty plea**—D has right to withdraw it and it can't be used against him as an admission

3. **Nontrial proceeding**—harmless error analysis

4. **Defendant's statements to informants**—post-indictment statement to informant where situation is likely to induce D to incriminate himself without counsel is inadmissible (but police may place an informant in D's cell to listen without questioning D)

5. **Exclusionary rule**

- **Fruit of the poisonous tree**—the doctrine applies to statements and physical evidence obtained as result of violation; such evidence will be inadmissible

- **Impeachment**—incriminating evidence obtained in violation of Sixth Amendment may be used for impeachment

D. **Ineffective assistance of counsel**

1. **Reasonable competence presumed**—to prove ineffective, claimant must show:
   - Counsel's representation fell below objective standard of reasonableness; and
   - Counsel's deficient performance prejudiced D, resulting in the reasonable probability that the outcome would have been different.
     - Mere inexperience, strategy, or failure to produce mitigating evidence insufficient

2. **Conflict of interest**—representation of Ds with conflicting interests may amount to ineffective assistance of counsel; must show actual conflict and an adverse effect on counsel's performance
   - **Actual conflict**—occurs when a court determines that the defense attorney is subject to an obligation/unique personal interest that, if followed, would lead her to adopt a strategy other than that most favorable to the D
   - **Adverse impact**—occurs when a plausible alternative strategy/tactic might have been pursued but was inherently in conflict with, or not undertaken, due to the attorney's other loyalties or interests

IV. **Pre-Trial Procedures**

A. **Eyewitness ID procedures**

1. **Types**
   - **Corporeal**—"in-person" (e.g., lineups)
   - **Non-corporeal**—not in-person (e.g., photo arrays)

2. **Sixth Amendment right to counsel at lineups**
   - Sixth Amendment right to counsel at in-person post-indictment lineup, but not at non-corporeal
   - Inadmissible if violated but witness can ID the D at trial if ID has independent reliability
3. **Impermissibly Suggestive Identification Procedures—Due Process Rights**
   - **Two-prong test**
     o D must prove ID was impermissibly suggestive; and
     o Substantial likelihood of misidentification
     o Prosecution may prove that it was nonetheless reliable (opportunity to view, degree of attention, accuracy of witness's description, level of certainty, length of time)
   - **Remedy**—suppression hearing (usually outside jury's presence) to determine admissibility; finding of impermissibly suggestive procedures will result in suppression

B. **Preliminary proceedings**
   1. **Probable cause to detain**
      - Must be held within 48 hours of arrest to determine PC
      - Fourth Amendment guarantees D right to be released if no PC
      - No remedy if detention is unlawful (other than exclusion of evidence)
   2. **Initial appearance**—judge advises D of the charges and his rights and appoints counsel if the defendant is indigent; judge may also decide conditions of bail and accept a plea

C. **Right to bail**—no constitutional right to bail, but denial of or excessive bail must comply with Due Process Clause

D. **Competency**—D must comprehend nature of proceedings against him and have ability to consult with lawyer with reasonable degree of rational understanding to be competent to stand trial

E. **Grand juries**—D has no right to present/confront witnesses or introduce evidence, and no dismissal due to procedural defect unless substantial impact on decision to indict

F. **State's duty to disclose**
   1. Affirmative duty to disclose any material evidence favorable to D and relevant to prosecution's case-in-chief that would negate guilt or diminish culpability/punishment
   2. Failure is grounds for reversal if D shows:
      - The evidence is favorable to the defendant, and
      - The failure to disclose caused prejudice against the defendant

V. **Trial**

A. **Jury trial**
   1. **Federal**—Sixth Amendment right to jury trial
   2. **State**—Under Fourteenth Amendment, D has a right to jury trial in criminal cases for non-petty offenses
   3. **Presence**—D has a right (with some exceptions) to be present at initial arraignments, every trial stage, and sentencing
   4. **Length**—right attaches for non-petty offenses (authorized sentence of more than six months imprisonment) regardless of actual penalty imposed
   5. **Waiver**—D can waive right to jury trial and opt for trial by judge by obtaining court's approval, and freely/intelligently entering a voluntary waiver

6. **Jury**
   - FRCP requires 12 members unless waived in writing and approved by court, but a verdict by 11 is permitted if the 12th juror is excused for good cause after deliberations begin; in state courts, juries of fewer than six jurors are unconstitutional, juries of six must return unanimous verdicts, and in juries of seven or more jurors, unanimity is not required
   - **Cross-section**—jury pool must be a representative cross-section of the community, but actual jury selected need not be
   - **Standing**—D can challenge selection process without showing of actual bias
   - **Prima facie case**—for absence of representative cross-section:
     o Distinctive group excluded
     o Group not fairly represented in jury pool, and
     o Underrepresentation resulted from systematic exclusion of group
   - **Neutral principles**—in response to claim of intentional racial discrimination in jury selection, state can use neutral/nonracial principles and must prove absence of discriminatory intent
   - **Peremptory challenge**
     o **Discriminatory use**—Fourteenth Amendment prohibits challenges solely based on race/ethnicity/gender
       ▪ Moving party must establish prima facie case of discrimination
       ▪ Party who exercised the peremptory challenge must provide race-neutral explanation
       ▪ Moving party carries burden of proving other party's reason was pretextual
     o **Loss of challenge**—doesn't violate right to impartial jury
     o **Harmless error**—state can choose between harmless-error review or automatic reversal when judge in good faith erroneously denies D's peremptory challenge
   - **Impartiality**
     o Accused entitled to trial by impartial jury, and claims of juror bias/misconduct subject to harmless-error rule
     o **Race**—D may question a potential jury member's views on race only when racial prejudice involved in case or when race is inextricably bound up in the case
     o **Capital punishment**—jurors opposed to death penalty can be removed for cause if opposition substantially impairs duties during sentencing
   - **Sentencing enhancement**—enhancement of sentence by judge absent jury determination of existence of additional facts violates D's right to a jury trial

B. **Guilty pleas**
   1. **Knowing and voluntary**
      - Must be intelligent and voluntary, and made in presence of judge
      - Judge must advise D and determine that plea not due to force or promises other than in plea agreement
      - Judge must determine there is some factual basis for the plea
   2. **Right to counsel**—D has a right to counsel when entering a plea
   3. **Plea bargain**
      - D has no constitutional right to a plea bargain
      - Plea made in response to prosecutor's threat to bring more serious charges does not violate Due Process Clause

- Prosecutor not required to disclose impeachment information or information related to affirmative defense
  - **Enforcement**
    - Plea bargain is enforceable against prosecutor and D, but not the judge (judge can reject plea)
    - If prosecutor violates bargain, judge can decide whether to order specific performance of bargain or whether D can withdraw plea
    - If D violates bargain, prosecutor can have sentence vacated and reinstate original charges
  4. **Effect on D's rights**—D can attack plea for ineffective assistance of counsel, lack of jurisdiction, or violation of due process
C. **Speedy trial**
  1. **Due Process Clause**—protects pre-accusation delay and SoL is primary safeguard
  2. **Sixth Amendment**—protects post-accusation delay and time period starts at time of arrest/formal charge
  3. **Balancing test**—length and reason for delay, D's assertion of right, and prejudice to D
  4. **Remedy**—dismissal of charges with prejudice
D. **Fair trial**
  1. **Impartial judge**—no actual/apparent bias permitted
  2. **Prosecutor**—cannot misstate law/fact, talk to D without counsel present, express opinions about D's guilt/innocence, make improper remarks about D, or comment on D's failure to testify
E. **Right to confrontation**
  1. **Trial**—accused has right to encounter and cross-examine adverse witnesses and be present at any stage of trial
  2. **Face-to-face**—not absolute right and may be prevented for public policy reasons
  3. **Confrontation Clause and the hearsay rule**
     - Out-of-court statements by witnesses that are "testimonial" are barred under the Confrontation Clause, unless (i) the witnesses are unavailable and the defendant had a prior opportunity to cross-examine those witnesses, or (ii) if the witness is unavailable because the defendant acted with a purpose to prevent the witness from testifying
     - Out-of-court testimonial statements are not barred by the Confrontation Clause when they are used for a purpose other than establishing the truth of the matter asserted
     - **Testimonial statements**—the declarant would reasonably expect it to be used in a prosecution
     - **Non-testimonial statements**—statements made for the primary purpose of assisting the police in the investigation of an ongoing emergency are not testimonial
  4. **Admission of confession** (*Bruton* rule)—by non-testifying co-D at joint trial against D violates Sixth Amendment
F. **Due process**
  1. **Permissive presumption**—regarding an element of an offense is not a due-process violation unless it is irrational
  2. **Mandatory presumption**—per se violation
  3. **Reasonable doubt**—prosecution must prove all elements beyond a reasonable doubt; state may place burden of proving an affirmative defense (e.g., insanity, self-defense, entrapment, or duress) on D

G. **Sentencing**
1. Applicable rights include right to counsel, confrontation, and cross-examination
2. Any fact (other than prior conviction) that can be used to increase statutorily prescribed maximum must be charged in indictment, submitted to jury, and established beyond a reasonable doubt

H. **Cruel and unusual punishment (Eighth Amendment)**
1. **Non-death penalty**—prisoner must show prison officials had actual knowledge of substantial risk to prisoners or serious injury, or sentence grossly disproportionate to crime
2. **Capital punishment**—can only be imposed under statute that provides clear/objective standards, specific/detailed guidance, and opportunity for rational review of process

VI. **Post-Trial Considerations**
A. **Double jeopardy (Fifth Amendment)**—protects against second prosecution for same offense after acquittal/conviction and against multiple punishments for the same offense
1. **Same offense**—*Blockburger* test applied if D's conduct can be prosecuted as two or more crimes so it generally bars successive prosecutions for greater/lesser included offenses unless jeopardy attaches to lesser-included offense before event necessary for greater offense
2. **Attachment**—when jury is impaneled/sworn in or when first witness is sworn in for bench trial
3. **Different jurisdictions**—D can be charged/convicted in federal and state court
4. **Civil actions**—not precluded by criminal punishment for same conduct
5. **Guilty plea**—not automatically waived
6. **Collateral estoppel**—applies when earlier decision must have necessarily determined issue on which collateral estoppel is sought by D

B. **Appeal**—right to appeal is not guaranteed by Constitution
1. **First appeal as of right**—D is guaranteed equal protection and right to counsel (but an attorney may withdraw and there is no right to self-representation)
2. **Discretionary appeal**—indigent D does not have right to appointment of counsel unless conviction was based on a guilty or *nolo contendere* plea
3. **Errors**
   - Generally must be timely preserved for consideration on appeal
   - **Harmless error** (an error that does not affect substantial rights)—will not serve as grounds for reversal
   - **Plain error**—D who failed to preserve claim of error is entitled to appellate relief when: (i) the district court committed error under the law in effect at the time the appeal is heard; (ii) the error is obvious under that law; and (iii) the error affected the defendant's substantial rights

C. **Convictions**—D can attack conviction after unsuccessful appeal under writ of habeas corpus (civil action, so standard is preponderance of the evidence)

FINAL REVIEW OUTLINE: EVIDENCE

I. **Presentation of Evidence**

    A. **Applicability of FRE**—FRE do not apply to:

        1. The court's determination of a preliminary question of fact governing admissibility;

        2. Grand jury proceedings; and

        3. Criminal proceedings for: issuance of a search or arrest warrant or a criminal summons; preliminary examination in a criminal case; extradition or rendition; consideration of bail or other release; sentencing; and granting or revoking probation or supervised release.

    B. **Introduction of evidence**

        1. **Role of judge and jury**

            • **Judge**—decides preliminary questions of the competency of evidence

            • **Jury**—determines the weight and credibility of the evidence

        2. **Challenge to evidence ruling**

            • The ruling must affect a substantial right of a party and the party must notify the judge of the error through an:

                o **Objection,** if the evidence is **admitted**

                o **Offer of proof,** if the evidence is **excluded**

            • Need not renew a challenge after a definitive ruling on admissibility has been made

            • **Plain error** (i.e., an error that is obvious to a reviewing court)—if it affects a substantial right, then it is grounds for reversal (even without a challenge)

            • **Limited Admissibility**—evidence may be admissible for one purpose but not for another; court must restrict evidence to its proper scope and instruct jury accordingly

            • **Completeness rule**—for partial introduction of evidence, an adverse party may compel introduction of an omitted portion to help explain the admitted evidence

        3. **Judicial notice**—the court's acceptance of a fact as true without requiring formal proof

            • **Adjudicative facts** (facts of the case at hand typically decided by jury)—subject to judicial notice if the fact is not subject to reasonable dispute because:

                o Generally known within the community, or

                o Can be accurately and readily determined from reliable sources

            • **Instructing the jury**

                o Civil case—the jury must be instructed to accept the noticed fact as **conclusive**

                o Criminal case—the jury must be instructed that it **may or may not accept** any judicially noticed fact as conclusive

    C. **Mode and order of presentation of evidence**

        1. **Trial process**—the judiciary has control over the order of witnesses/presentation of the case to effectively determine truth and avoid wasted time or witness harassment; may also question or call a witness

        2. **Examination of witnesses**

            • Scope of cross-examination is generally limited to the subject matter of direct examination and witness credibility; redirect and recross may be permitted, the scope is within the court's discretion

- **Motions to strike**—if a witness's answer makes testimony improper, move to strike; only the examining counsel may move to strike an unresponsive answer

3. **Form of questions**
   - **Leading questions** suggest the answer within the question
     - Direct—not permitted unless: a hostile witness, needed to develop the witness's testimony, or the witness struggles with communication
     - Cross-examination—generally, no restrictions on using leading questions
   - **Improper questions**
     - Compound—requires answers to multiple questions
     - Assumes facts not in evidence—assumes as true certain facts that have not been established yet
     - Argumentative—intended to provoke an argument, rather than elicit a factual response
     - Calls for conclusion/opinion—requires the witness to draw a conclusion or state an opinion that he is not qualified to make
     - Repetitive—already asked and answered
     - Lack of foundation—failure to establish necessary predicate, such as authentication of tangible evidence

4. **Exclusion of witnesses**—the court must exclude witnesses from the courtroom so that they do not hear the testimony of other witnesses, except for:
   - Natural person parties to the case,
   - Individual designated as a representative of non-natural person parties,
   - Persons essential to a party's presentation of the case, and
   - Persons whose presence is permitted by statute (i.e., victim).

D. **Burdens and presumptions**

1. **Burden of proof**
   - **Production**—must produce legally sufficient evidence for each element of a claim such that a reasonable trier of fact could infer the alleged fact has been proven (prima facie case)
   - **Persuasion**
     - Civil—preponderance of the evidence (or clear and convincing for certain cases)
     - Criminal—beyond a reasonable doubt

2. **Presumptions**
   - **Rebuttable**—shifts the burden of production (not persuasion) to the opposing party
   - **Conclusive**—cannot be challenged by contrary evidence
   - **Destruction of evidence**—generally raises a rebuttable presumption that the evidence would be unfavorable to the destroying party if the other party establishes (i) destruction was intentional, (ii) evidence is relevant, and (iii) alleged victim acted with due diligence as to the destroyed evidence.

II. **Relevance**

A. **General considerations**

1. **Generally, all relevant evidence is admissible** unless excluded by a specific rule, law, or constitutional provision; evidence is relevant if **probative** and **material**

- **Probative**—the evidence has a tendency to make a fact more or less probable than it would be without the evidence
- **Material**—the evidence is of consequence in determining the action

2. **Direct and circumstantial evidence**

- **Direct**—identical to the factual proposition it is offered to prove
- **Circumstantial**—indirect proof of a factual proposition through inference from collateral facts

3. **Exclusion of relevant evidence** (Rule 403 exclusion)—if the probative value is **substantially outweighed** by the danger of unfair prejudice (confusing issues, misleading jury, undue delay, wasting time, needless presentation of cumulative evidence)

4. **Relevance dependent on existence of fact**—proof must be sufficient to support finding that the fact does exist; may be admitted on condition that proof is later introduced

5. **Curative admission of irrelevant evidence**—admitted when necessary to rebut previously admitted inadmissible evidence to remove unfair prejudice

B. **Character evidence** (generalized information about a person's behavior)—typically inadmissible

1. **Civil cases**

- Inadmissible to prove a person acted in accordance with that character (or trait) on a particular occasion
- Admissible when character is an essential element of a claim or defense, instead of a means of proving a person's conduct (usually defamation, negligent hiring or negligent entrustment, and child custody)

2. **Criminal cases**

- **D's character**

   o By prosecution—not permitted to introduce evidence of D's bad character to prove D has a propensity to commit crimes and so is likely to have committed the crime in question

   o By defense—D is permitted to introduce evidence of good character as being inconsistent with type of crime charged, but must be pertinent to crime charged, and must be reputation/opinion testimony

   o D "opens the door"—once D offers evidence of his good character (or victim's bad character), prosecution can rebut D's claims by attacking D's character

- **Victim's character**

   o By defense—D may introduce reputation/opinion evidence of victim's character when relevant to the defense asserted (evidence of victim's sexual conduct very limited)

   o By prosecution—prosecution can offer rebuttal evidence of victim's good character when D has introduced evidence of victim's bad character (and trait for peacefulness in homicide case to rebut evidence homicide victim was first aggressor)

3. **Methods of proving character**—when character evidence is admissible, it may be proven by testimony about a person's reputation or by witness opinion

4. **Impeachment**—character evidence of witness's untruthfulness is admissible/relevant to impeach a witness

C. **Bad acts**—not admissible to show D's criminal propensity to prove he committed the crime in question

1. **MIMIC evidence** (**M**otive, **I**ntent, absence of **M**istake, **I**dentity or **C**ommon plan)
   - Admissible
   - Subject to admissibility restrictions, may be introduced for any other purpose except to prove D committed the charged crime because D had propensity to commit crimes
   - When criminal D requests, prosecution must provide reasonable notice of the general nature of MIMIC evidence the prosecution intends to offer at trial; must give notice before trial unless the court excuses lack of pretrial notice for good cause

2. **Specific acts as character evidence**
   - **Civil**—when character evidence is an essential element of claim/defense, can be proven by specific acts or opinion/reputation testimony
   - **Criminal**—specific acts are not admissible to show D's criminal propensity; when character is essential element of a charged crime, D may offer specific acts inconsistent with the crime
   - **Cross-examination**—a character witness can be asked about specific acts committed by the person about whom the witness is testifying

D. **Habit evidence**

1. **Definition**—a person's particular routine reaction to a specific set of circumstances

2. **Evidence of person's habit** (or organization's routine) is admissible to prove the person acted in accordance with the habit on a particular occasion

3. May be admitted without corroboration and without an eyewitness

III. **Witnesses**

A. **Competence**

1. **Personal knowledge**—a non-expert witness must have personal knowledge of a matter in order to testify about the matter

2. **Oath**—witness must give an oath or affirmation to testify truthfully

3. **Judge**—cannot testify at trial

4. **Juror**—can testify at trial in limited circumstances, but generally may only testify after trial about (i) extraneous prejudicial information brought to jury's attention (ii) improper outside influence, or (iii) mistakes on verdict form

5. **Child**—no specific age requirement; can testify if able to differentiate truth from falsehood and understand the requirement to tell the truth; federal law rebuttably presumes a child who suffered abuse or witnessed a crime is competent to testify

6. **Dead Man's statutes**—protects decedent's estate from parties with financial interest in the estate; predecessors in interest or those directly affected financially may be disqualified
   - **Waiver**—an interested person or protected party can waive the protection by failing to object to a disqualified witness or introducing protected evidence
   - Not applicable in criminal cases

B. **Impeachment**—a challenge to a witness's testimony can be based on character for untruthfulness, bias, ability to perceive or testify accurately, contradictory prior statement, or another witness

1. **Witness's character for truthfulness**
   - **Cannot bolster witness credibility**—evidence of truthful character only admissible after witness's truthful character directly attacked
   - **Opinion/reputation testimony**—admissible to attack witness's character for untruthfulness
   - **Specific instances of conduct**—generally not admissible as indication of character for truthfulness
     o On cross-examination, OK if probative of witness's truthfulness or truthfulness of another witness about whose character the witness has testified
     o When witness denies specific act, extrinsic evidence not admissible to prove specific act (exception exists for criminal convictions)

2. **Criminal conviction** (but not arrest)—can be used to impeach witness's character for truthfulness
   - **Crimes involving dishonesty/false statement** can be used to impeach any witness for any conviction
   - **Conviction NOT involving dishonesty/false statement**—admissible to impeach witness only if crime is punishable by death or imprisonment > 1 year
     o If witness is criminal D—admissible only if its probative value outweighs the prejudicial effect to that D (stricter than usual balancing test)
     o Other witnesses—generally admissible; discretion to exclude if probative value is substantially outweighed by its prejudicial effect
   - **Conviction or release > 10 years ago**—admissible if probative value substantially outweighs prejudicial effect and reasonable written notice of intent to use evidence
   - **Pardon**—conviction not admissible if subject of a pardon, annulment, or other action based on a finding of innocence; pending appeal does not prevent impeachment
   - **Juvenile adjudication**—not admissible to impeach D; may impeach other witness's character for truthfulness in criminal case if an adult conviction for that offense would be admissible and admitting it is necessary to determine guilt or innocence

3. **Prior inconsistent statements**—can be used to impeach if inconsistent with material part of the witness's testimony
   - Extrinsic evidence of prior inconsistent statement admissible only if witness has chance to explain/deny statement and opposing party can examine witness about it (this opportunity not required for hearsay declarants or opposing party statements)

4. **Bias or interest**—can be used to impeach witness because relevant to credibility

5. **Sensory competence**—can be impeached for deficiency in capacities to perceive, recall, or relate information

6. **Impeachment of a hearsay declarant**—credibility of declarant can be attacked by any evidence admissible if declarant had testified as witness; if declarant called as a witness, he can be examined as if under cross-examination

7. **Rehabilitation of a witness**
   - Explain/clarify on redirect examination
   - Offer opinion/reputation evidence of witness's character for truthfulness (only if character was attacked on that ground)

- Offer prior consistent statement to rebut express/implied charge that witness lied due to improper motive/influence

8. **Religious opinions and beliefs**—cannot be used to impeach credibility, but admissible to show bias/interest

9. **Contradictory evidence**—can be used to impeach if it contradicts witness's testimony, including contradictory material extrinsic evidence

10. **Collateral issues**—generally, cannot impeach credibility of witness by introducing extrinsic evidence of a collateral matter

C. **Recollection refreshed**

1. **Present recollection refreshed**—witness may examine any item to refresh witness's present recollection; testimony must be based on refreshed recollection, not item

   - Adverse party may inspect item and enter relevant portions as evidence
   - Item may be redacted by court, and admissible for substantive purposes only if satisfies other restrictions on admissibility

2. **Past recollection recorded**—memo/record about matter witness once had knowledge of but now has insufficient recollection of to testify about may be admissible under recorded recollection hearsay exception; may be read into evidence, but received as an exhibit only if offered by an adverse party

D. **Opinion testimony**

1. **Subject matter of testimony**

   - **Lay witness opinion**—admissible if (i) rationally based on the witness's perception, (ii) helpful to clear understanding of witness's testimony or determination of a fact in issue, and (iii) not based on scientific, technical, or specialized knowledge

   - **Expert witness testimony**

     o Subject matter must be scientific, technical, or some other specialized knowledge (testimony is reliable) that helps trier of fact understand the evidence or determine a fact at issue (testimony is relevant)

     o Some courts hold that expert testimony that goes to the credibility of a witness improperly invades the province of the jury to determine whether the witness is telling the truth

2. **Qualified expert**

   - **Requirements:**

     o Qualified as an expert by knowledge, skill, experience, training, or education

     o Testimony based on sufficient facts/data

     o Testimony product of reliable principles and methods

     o Witness applied principles/methods reliably to facts of case, and

     o Reasonable degree of certainty (i.e., "probably")

   - **Ultimate issue**—expert may not state an opinion about whether criminal D had the requisite mental state

   - **Basis of opinion**—opinion based on inadmissible facts admissible if experts in the particular field would reasonably rely on those kinds of facts and data in forming an opinion on the subject; may disclose underlying facts to the jury if probative value substantially outweighs prejudicial effect; need not ask in form of hypothetical; can challenge the adequacy of the expert's knowledge on cross

E. **Payment of witness**

1. **When prohibited**—a lawyer may not offer to pay a witness any consideration:

- In excess of the reasonable expenses of the witness incurred and the reasonable value of the witness's time spent in providing evidence, except that an expert witness may be offered and paid a noncontingent fee;
- Contingent on the content of the witness's testimony or the outcome of the litigation; or
- Otherwise prohibited by law.

2. **When permitted**—a witness in attendance in federal court or a deposition pursuant to a federal rule or court order is entitled to:

- An appearance fee; and
- A travel allowance.

IV. **Tangible Evidence**

A. **Authentication**—all tangible evidence must be authenticated with sufficient evidence to support a finding that the thing is what its proponent claims it is

1. **Physical objects**—generally authenticated through personal knowledge, distinctive characteristics, or chain of custody (when applicable)

- **Reproductions** (photos, diagrams, maps)—authenticated by testimony of witness with personal knowledge that object accurately depicts what its proponent claims it does
- **X-rays, EKGs**—process used was accurate, machine works, and operator qualified

2. **Documentary evidence**—usually authenticated by stipulation, eyewitness testimony, or handwriting verification

- **Ancient documents**—at least 20 years old, in condition unlikely to create suspicion, and found in a likely place if it were authentic
- **Public records**—recorded/filed in public office
- **Reply letter**—written in response to communication
- **Handwriting verification**—comparison or non-expert with personal knowledge
- **Self-authenticating**—doesn't require extrinsic evidence (e.g., gov't authorized documents, certified public records, or newspapers)

3. **Oral statements**

- **Voice ID**—can be identified by any person who has heard voice at any time
- **Telephone**—party to telephone conversation may authenticate statements made during that conversation if caller recognized the speaker's voice; speaker knew facts that only a particular person would know; caller dialed number believed to be speaker's, and speaker identified himself upon answering; or caller dialed a business and spoke about business regularly conducted over the phone

B. **Best Evidence Rule** (BER)

1. **Original document** (or reliable duplicate)—must be produced to prove contents of writing when contents are at issue or witness is relying on contents when testifying

- Duplicate reliable unless there is a genuine question as to the authenticity of the original; or the circumstances make it unfair to admit the duplicate

  o Handwritten copies of original are not duplicates

- Original not required when originals are lost or destroyed in good faith, party against whom original would be offered failed to produce it, or document not closely related to controlling issue
- Contents of a public record are generally proved by a certified copy
- **Voluminous documents**—contents of voluminous documents may be presented as summary if such contents cannot be conveniently examined in court; proponent must make originals or duplicates available for examination and copying by other parties at a reasonable time and place; court may order proponent to produce the originals or duplicates in court
- May prove contents of original by admission by party against whom it is offered without accounting for original

C. **Parol Evidence Rule** (PER)—operates to exclude evidence that, if introduced, would change the terms of a written agreement

1. **Complete integration**—contains all terms to which the parties agreed; PER in effect and no extrinsic evidence is admissible

2. **Partial integration**—contains some but not all agreed upon terms
   - Extrinsic evidence that adds to writing admissible
   - Evidence that contradicts not admissible

3. **Exceptions**—Extrinsic evidence always admissible to clarify ambiguity, prove course of dealings, show fraud/duress/mistake, or show presence/absence of consideration

4. **Only evidence of prior or contemporaneous negotiations is subject to the rule;** negotiations after contract executed not prohibited by the rule

V. **Privileges and Other Policy Exclusions**

A. **Privileges**

1. **Confidential communications**—necessary for a privilege to apply
   - If overheard, privilege destroyed unless (i) no knowledge of third party's presence; or (ii) third party is necessary to assist in communication (e.g., a translator)
   - Privilege waived if privilege holder (i) fails to timely assert it, (ii) voluntarily discloses communication, or (iii) contractually waives it in advance

2. **Spousal privilege**
   - **Spousal immunity**
     - Married person cannot be compelled to testify against his spouse in any criminal proceeding regardless of who D is
     - Witness spouse holds privilege in federal court and majority of states; party spouse holds privilege in minority of states
     - Applies to testimony about events before/during marriage; privilege expires upon divorce or annulment
   - **Confidential marital communications**
     - Spousal communication during marriage is privileged when made in reliance on sanctity of marriage
     - Majority view (and most federal courts)—both spouses hold the privilege in civil and criminal cases; either spouse may assert the privilege and refuse to testify about the communication or prevent the other spouse from testifying
     - Privilege begins with marriage and continues indefinitely

- Neither spousal privilege applies when one spouse sues another or spouse is charged with a crime against the other or the children of either

3. **Attorney-client privilege**
   - Confidential communication between client (who holds privilege) and attorney for the purpose of seeking legal advice or representation (attorney doesn't need to give advice or agree to representation)
     - Privilege exists until waived by the client (or the client's guardian or successor-in-interest)—can survive termination of the attorney-client relationship and even the client's death
     - Federal law extends privilege to communications by a non-control-group employee (i) about matters within the employee's corporate duties (ii) made for the purpose of securing legal advice for corporation client
   - Exceptions for communications:
     - Made to enable or aid commission of what client knew or should have known was crime/fraud
     - Relevant to dispute between attorney and client (e.g., a malpractice allegation)
     - Relevant to dispute between parties who claim through the same deceased client
     - Between former co-clients who are now adverse to each other
   - **Work product**—not "communication," but protected unless party seeking disclosure (i) demonstrates substantial need, and (ii) cannot obtain the information by any other means without undue hardship

4. **Physician-patient privilege**
   - Statement privileged so long as made for the purpose of obtaining medical treatment
   - Patient holds privilege
   - Privilege does not exist if:
     - Info acquired for reasons other than treatment
     - Patient's physical condition is at issue
     - Statement is part of crime
     - Dispute exists between patient and physician
     - Patient contractually waives privilege
     - Federal question case

5. **Psychotherapist-patient privilege**—patient holds privilege, but doesn't exist if patient's mental condition is at issue, statement was result of state ordered exam or case is commitment proceeding against patient

6. **Self-incrimination**—Fifth Amendment protection allowing witness to refuse to give testimony that may tend to incriminate him
   - Covers only current statements
   - Does not apply to physical characteristics or mannerisms
   - Does not apply to corporations or other organizations

7. **Other privileges**
   - Clergy-penitent
   - Accountant-client
   - **Professional journalist**—no federal privilege regarding source

- **Government privilege**—government privileged against disclosing informant's identity in a criminal case and communication of official information by or to public officials

B. Public policy exclusions

1. Subsequent remedial measures

- Not admissible to prove negligence, culpable conduct, defective product/design, or need for warning/instruction
- Admissible for other purposes such as impeachment, ownership/control, or feasibility of precautionary measures

2. Compromise offers and negotiations

- Not admissible by either party to prove/disprove validity or amount of disputed claim, or for impeachment by prior inconsistent statement or contradiction
- Admissible to prove bias or prejudice of witness, negate claim of undue delay, or prove obstruction of criminal investigation/prosecution
- Admissible in a subsequent criminal case if made during compromise negotiations w/ governmental agency during its regulatory, investigative, or enforcement authority

3. Evidence of payment, offers, or promise to pay medical expenses—not admissible to prove liability for the injury, but statements that accompany the payment, offer, or promise to pay are admissible

4. Plea negotiation—withdrawn guilty pleas, pleas of no contest, and statements made while negotiating plea bargain or during plea proceeding are not admissible

- **Exceptions**—another statement made during the same plea or negotiation has already been admitted and fairness requires that the statement in question also be admitted; also admissible in subsequent perjury prosecution if they were false statements made under oath, on the record, and with counsel present

5. Liability insurance

- Not admissible to prove whether person acted negligently or wrongfully
- Admissible to prove agency, ownership/control, or witness's bias/prejudice

6. Sexual conduct

- **Victim's conduct**
  - Rape shield—evidence of sexual behavior/predisposition generally not admissible in any proceeding involving sexual misconduct
  - Specific acts admissible to prove D not source of physical evidence in criminal case
  - Sexual behavior/predisposition of victim admissible in civil case if probative value substantially outweighs unfair prejudice
  - Reputation admissible only if placed in controversy by victim
- **Defendant's conduct**—evidence of sexual assault in criminal/civil case admissible to prove any relevant matter (not limited to convictions)

VI. Hearsay

A. Definition—out-of-court statement offered to prove the truth of matter asserted

1. **Declarant**—must be a person
2. **Statement**—oral, written, or assertive nonverbal conduct
3. **Offered to prove the truth of the matter asserted**—if offered to prove something other than the truth of the matter asserted (legally operative facts, effect on recipient, state of mind, identification, and impeachment and rehabilitation), not hearsay

4. **Multiple hearsay**—hearsay within hearsay may be admissible as long as each part of combined statement conforms to hearsay exception

B. **Non-hearsay**

1. **Prior statements**—declarant must testify at present trial to be admissible; cannot apply if witness is dead or otherwise unavailable to testify

- Prior inconsistent statements made under penalty of perjury admissible to impeach declarant's credibility and as substantive evidence
- Prior consistent statements admissible to rebut express/implied charge that declarant recently fabricated it or acted with improper motive, but must be made before declarant had reason to fabricate
- Prior statement of identification of a person after perceiving that person is admissible as non-hearsay substantive evidence even if witness has no memory of identification

2. **Opposing party's statement**—made by party to current litigation; admissible without personal knowledge and can be in form of an opinion; need not have been against the party's interest at the time that it was made

- **Judicial admission**—an admission made during pleading, discovery process or proceeding is conclusive evidence
  - Withdrawn guilty plea generally not admissible in subsequent proceedings
- **Adoptive admission**—statement of another person that party expressly/impliedly adopts as his own
  - Silence in response to a statement is considered an adoptive admission if:
    - The person was present and heard and understood the statement;
    - The person had the ability and opportunity to deny the statement; and
    - A reasonable person similarly situated would have denied the statement.
- **Vicarious statements**—statement made by one person imputed to another based upon relationship between them (employee/agent, authorized speaker, co-conspirators)

VII. **Hearsay Exceptions**

A. **Declarant unavailable as witness**

1. **Unavailable declarant** unless unavailable due to procurement/wrongdoing of proponent in order to prevent the declarant from testifying at or attending the trial

2. **Former testimony** given as witness is not hearsay if party against whom testimony is offered had an opportunity and similar motive to develop testimony

3. **Dying declaration**

- Declarant believes her death is imminent and statement pertains to cause/circumstances of her death (need not actually die)
- Applies only in homicide prosecutions and civil cases

4. **Statement against interest**—was against declarant's proprietary/pecuniary interest at time made and reasonable person would not have made statement unless it was true

5. **Statement of personal/family history**—birth, adoption, marriage, divorce or other similar fact of personal or family history

6. **Statement against party that caused declarant's unavailability**—statement offered against party that wrongfully caused declarant's unavailability is not excluded

B. **Declarant's availability as a witness immaterial**

1. **Present sense impression**—statement explaining or describing event/condition made while or immediately after declarant perceived it

2. **Excited utterance**—statement about startling event/condition while declarant is under stress of excitement that it caused

3. **Statement of mental, emotional, or physical condition**—statement of then-existing state of mind (present intent, motive or plan) or emotional, sensory or physical condition

4. **Statement made for medical diagnosis/treatment**—describing medical history or past/present symptoms is not excluded as hearsay if it is made for purpose of medical diagnosis or treatment; can be made to physicians, other medical personnel or even family members; need not necessarily be made by the patient

5. **Recorded recollection** (witness no longer able to testify)—record not excluded if on a matter that witness once knew, made when matter was fresh in witness's memory, accurately reflects witness's knowledge, and witness states that he cannot recall even after consulting record on the stand

6. **Business records** (extends to any organization, including nonprofit)—record must be kept in course of regularly conducted business activity, making of record was regular practice, and record was made at or near the time by someone with knowledge

7. **Public records**—statement of public office/agency that sets out activities of office, observation of person under duty to report (but not police in a criminal case), or factual findings of a legal investigation

8. **Learned treatises**—statement in treatise, periodical or pamphlet not excluded if expert witness relied on statement during direct/cross, and publication is reliable authority

9. **Judgment of previous conviction**
   - Final judgment must be entered after trial or guilty plea
   - Conviction was for crime punishable by death or imprisonment for > 1 year
   - Evidence offered to prove any fact essential to sustain judgment

C. **Residual exception**—"catch-all" exception for a statement that is not otherwise covered by the FRE

VIII. **Constitutional Limitations**

A. **Hearsay evidence restrictions**—two grounds

1. **Sixth Amendment**—Confrontation Clause and hearsay evidence
   - Requires declarant to be unavailable and D had prior opportunity to cross-examine declarant
   - **Testimonial statements**—objective analysis—if primary purpose is emergency assistance, not testimonial
   - **Unavailability of the declarant**—D must have purpose of making declarant unavailable, and fact that D made declarant unavailable does not mean he had purpose if he is on trial for the act that made witness unavailable

2. **Fourteenth Amendment**—Due Process Clause—may prevent application of hearsay rule when rule unduly restricts D's ability to mount defense

B. **Face-to-face confrontation**—Confrontation Clause prefers face-to-face confrontation, but can be denied if important public interest at stake

FINAL REVIEW OUTLINE: REAL PROPERTY

I. **Ownership**

    A. **Present estates**—an estate is a freehold if immobile and for indeterminate duration

        1. **Fee simple absolute (FSA) or fee simple (FS)**—absolute ownership of potentially infinite duration

- "To A" or "to A and his heirs"
- Freely alienable and no accompanying future interest

        2. **Defeasible fee**—potentially infinite duration, subject to termination by the occurrence of an event; alienable, devisable, and descendible

- **FS determinable (FSD)**
  - Limited by specific durational language (e.g., "so long as," "while," "during," "until")
  - Automatically terminates upon happening of a stated event
  - Future interest: Grantor (or his successor in interest) retains possibility of reverter
- **FS subject to condition subsequent (FSSCS)**
  - A present fee simple that is limited by specific conditional language (e.g., "upon condition that," "provided that," "but if," or "if it happens that")
  - Will terminate only if the grantor affirmatively demonstrates intent to terminate
  - Future interest: Grantor reserves right to terminate estate upon happening of a stated event; grantor must specifically retain right to reenter
- **FS subject to executory interest/limitation (FSSEI)**
  - A present fee simple that is limited by specific durational or conditional language
  - Automatically terminates upon happening of the stated event, and title passes to a third party
  - Future interest: Executory interest held by the third party (i.e., someone other than the grantor)

        3. **Life estate (LE)**—present possessory estate fully transferable during measuring life

- If third party: "to A for life," "to B after the life of A," or "to B for the life of C" (*pur autre vie*); "to A for life, but if he drinks, then to B" (*defeasible*)
- If measured by the grantee's life, not devisable/descendible
- Life tenant's (LT) rights/duties:
  - Right to possess
  - Right to collect rents, lease/sell/mortgage (must pay taxes on financial benefit from the land)
  - Duty not to commit waste

        4. **Waste**—limits the rights of a holder of a LE

- **Affirmative**—occurs when overt conduct causes a decrease in property value
  - Holder of a **vested** future interest—may bring suit against LT for **damages**

- o Holder of **any** future interest—may bring suit against LT for an **injunction**
- o Exception: Exploitation of natural resources is not waste if: (i) authorized by the grantor; (ii) in effect when the tenancy began; or (iii) necessary to maintain the property
  - **Permissive**—occurs when LT permits the premises to deteriorate through neglect, failure to preserve, or a failure to reasonably protect the property; LT must make reasonable repairs (up to amount of income produced by property or, if LT is in actual possession, the fair rental value)
  - **Ameliorative**—occurs when a change in use of the property increases its value; LT may alter structures on the property when a substantial and permanent change in the neighborhood makes it necessary in order to continue reasonable use of the property, so long as the property value is not diminished

B. **Future interests (FI)**—an interest in presently existing property or in a gift or trust, which may commence in use, possession, or enjoyment sometime in the future

1. **Reversion**—held by a grantor who transfers a LE or estate for years without conveying the remaining FI to a third party; not subject to RAP; alienable, devisable, and descendible

2. **Possibility of reverter**—a FI retained by a grantor when a FSD is conveyed; alienable, devisable, and descendible

3. **Right of reentry**—(right to terminate; right of entry; power of termination) a FI retained by a grantor after a FSSCS is granted; no *inter vivos* transfer permitted under common law, but permitted in some states; devisable and descendible in most states

4. **Remainder**—a FI that becomes possessory upon the natural expiration of a prior estate that is created in the same conveyance in which the remainder is created

   - **Vested**—not subject to any conditions precedent; ascertainable grantee

     - o **Vested subject to open (class gifts)**

       - **Class gift**—group of unspecified persons whose number, identity, and share of the interest is determined in the future
       - If at least one class member is qualified to take possession at the time of the conveyance (but less than all of them), each class member's share is subject to partial diminution because additional takers not yet ascertained can still vest
       - Once a class closes, any person who might otherwise have become a class member cannot claim an interest in the property as a class member
       - **Rule of convenience**—closes the class when any class member is entitled to immediate possession

     - o **Vested subject to complete divestment**—the occurrence of a condition subsequent will divest the remainder

   - **Contingent**—created in an unascertainable grantee or is subject to an express condition precedent to grantee's taking (because of unknown beneficiary or known beneficiary subject to condition precedent that has not yet occurred)

     - o **Survivorship contingency**: majority—applies at termination of interest that precedes remainder; minority—requires surviving only testator, not life tenant

5. **Executory interests**—a FI in a third party (not a remainder) that cuts the prior estate short upon the occurrence of a specified condition; transferable and subject to RAP

   - **Shifting**—cuts short a prior estate created in the same conveyance, so the estate shifts from one grantee to another grantee upon the happening of a condition

- **Springing**—divests the grantor's interest or fills a gap in possession in which the estate reverts to the grantor

6. **Transferability**—remainders/executory interests are transferable inter vivos and devisable/descendible

7. **Rule Against Perpetuities (RAP)**

   - Specific FIs are valid only if they must vest or fail by the end of a life in being plus 21 years

   - **Affected FIs**—RAP applies to contingent remainders, vested remainders subject to open, executory interests, powers of appointment, rights of first refusal, and options; RAP **does not** apply to FIs that revert to the grantor (reversion, possibility of reverter, right of reentry)

   - **Measuring lives**—must be human; there can be more than one; if not specified, then the measuring life is the life directly related to the FI that is subject to RAP

   - **Creation events**—RAP tests the FI as of the time that it is created

   - **"Vest or fail" requirement**—if there is **any possibility** that it will not be known whether the interest will vest or fail within the applicable period, then RAP has not been satisfied

   - **Effect of violation**—except in rare cases when voiding the FI undermines the grantor's intent, only the offending interest fails

   - **Special rule for class gifts** ("bad as to one, bad as to all")—if RAP voids a transfer to any class member, then the transfer is void as to all class members, even those whose interests have already vested

     o **Rule of convenience**—can operate to prevent application of RAP to a class transfer, but the application of the rule of convenience to a class transfer does not automatically forestall the application of RAP

     o **Exceptions**—transfers of a specific dollar amount to each class member; transfers to a subclass that vests at a specific time

   - **Common violations:**

     o **"Survival beyond age 21" condition**

     o **Fertile octogenarian**

     o **Unborn spouse**

     o **Defeasible fee followed by executory interest**

     o **Conditional passage of interest**

C. **Concurrent estates (co-tenancies)**

   1. **Tenancy in common (TC)** (default co-tenancy)

      - Two or more grantees with unity of possession

      - No right of survivorship (ROS)

      - Each co-tenant holds undivided interest with unrestricted rights to possess whole

      - Interest freely devisable/transferable

   2. **Joint tenancy (JT)**

      - Requires express language creating JT

- Two or more persons own the property with ROS
- Interest is alienable (but not devisable/descendible)
- **Four unities (PITT)**
  - Equal rights to **p**ossess the whole
  - With identical equal **i**nterests
  - Created at the same **t**ime
  - By the same **t**itle
- **Severance**—converts a JT into a TC (but only with respect to the severed share)
  - **Sale**—don't need consent; severs JT as to seller but JT of non-transferors remains intact
  - **Mortgage**—severs JT under title theory, but not under lien theory
  - **Judicial lien**—the lien typically will not sever the JT; severance occurs when the property is levied and sold

3. **Tenancy by entirety (TE)**
- Same unities as JT, plus unity of person (parties must be married to each other when deed is executed or conveyance occurs)
- Neither party can alienate or encumber the property without the consent of the other
- Recognized in about half the states; where recognized, majority presume a conveyance to a married couple creates a TE, and that divorce converts it to a TC

4. **Rights/obligations**
- Each co-T has the right to possess the entire property and is generally not required to pay rent when other co-Ts do not use the property (unless co-T has been ousted)
- Co-T is liable to other co-Ts for third-party rents (after deducting operating expenses and necessary repairs)
- Co-T can collect contribution from other co-Ts for operating expenses (e.g., taxes), but if in sole possession, only if they exceed the rental value of the property
- Co-T can only compel other co-Ts to share expenses for repairs if (i) the repairs are necessary, and (ii) the co-T seeks accounting or partition; may maintain a separate action for contribution in some states if notified other co-Ts of need for the repairs
- Co-T has no right to reimbursement for improvements (except in accounting/partition)
- Co-T owes a duty of fair dealing to other co-Ts, but generally does not owe fiduciary duties to other co-Ts; exception: a co-T buys the property at a tax or foreclosure sale (the other co-Ts can buy back their interests within a reasonable time)
- **Partition**—a TC or JT (but not a TE) generally has the right to unilaterally partition property; a partition in kind, preferred by courts, is a physical division of the property

D. **Special Real Property issues**

1. **Fair housing and discrimination**—federal Fair Housing Act (FHA) prohibits discrimination in renting/selling, terms, refusing financing, etc.

- Owner-occupied buildings with no more than four units (including the owner's unit) and single-family homes sold or rented without a broker are generally not subject to FHA (but are subject to advertising rules)

2. **Conflict of laws**—generally apply law of the situs in RP cases (i.e., state where RP is located)

   - Exceptions: document (instrument, will) specifies applicable law; certain issues involving marriage; mortgage notes; foreclosure-related rights

II. Landlord (L) and Tenant (T)

A. Types of tenancies

1. Tenancy for years

   - Any fixed period of time
   - Automatically terminates at end of term (no notice needed)
   - May be terminated before the end of the term (e.g., breach of lease covenant gives rise to right to terminate)
   - Created by express agreement
   - If term longer than one year, SOF applies: written lease signed by party to be charged must identify parties, premises, lease duration, and rent to be paid

2. Periodic tenancy

   - Repetitive, ongoing estate by set periods of time with no predetermined termination date; term may be fixed by the parties or by their actions
   - Automatically renews at end of each period unless valid termination notice
   - SoF does not apply unless initial term exceeds one year
   - Created by express agreement, implication (no mention of duration), or operation of law (holdover tenant)
   - **Termination notice**—must be given before last period begins; late notice is effective for the next period; generally effective as of the last day of the period; oral notice sufficient under common law, but most states now require some writing

3. Tenancy at will

   - Does not have a specific term; continues as long as L and T want
   - Created by express agreement or by implication
   - May be terminated by either party; at common law, no notice required, but L must give T reasonable time to vacate; most states now require notice; may also be terminated by operation of law

4. Tenancy at sufferance (holdover tenancy)

   - T wrongfully remains in possession after the expiration of a lease
   - T is bound by terms of the lease the existed before expiration, including payment of rent
   - Tenancy lasts until T vacates, L evicts T, or L elects to hold T to periodic tenancy

B. Duties of the tenant

1. **Pay rent**—duty to pay unless premises destroyed (lease terminated and tenant excused), or material breach by landlord

2. Avoid waste

   - **Affirmative waste**—T is prohibited from committing voluntary waste

- **Ameliorative waste**—T may make changes to physical condition of property that increase the property value if reasonably necessary for T to use property in reasonable manner, unless L and T agree otherwise

- **Permissive waste**—unless relieved by lease, statute, or ordinance, T has a duty to repair the premises to keep it in its pre-rental condition; no duty to repair normal wear and tear (unless L and T agree)

3. **Repair**—non-residential leases, T may be contractually liable for all damage to property (unless caused by L)

4. **L's remedies for T's breach**

- **Failure to pay rent**—(majority) L can sue for damages **and** evict **and** terminate lease (could not evict or terminate lease at CL)

  o **Future rent**—no anticipatory repudiation (AR) in most states; where AR applies, damages limited to difference between future rent under lease and either (i) reasonable rental value or (ii) actual rent collected from re-letting

  o **Late rent**—L entitled to damages; whether L can sue to remove depends on if breach is material or L waived right to evict by accepting late rent

- **Abandonment**—treated as offer to surrender rights under the lease

  o **L accepts surrender**—lease terminates and T liability for future rent ends

  o **L rejects surrender**—T remains liable for rent, but under majority rule, L has duty to mitigate damages

- **Holdover T**—L can accept holdover tenant as periodic tenant or tenant at sufferance or sue after notice to vacate

C. Duties of L

1. **Possession**—L must deliver actual physical possession or no obligation for T to pay rent

2. **Repair**—except for T damages, L must repair for residential but not for commercial leases

3. **Warranty of habitability (residential)**—premises must be fit for basic human habitation (health/safety), and if breached:

- T must notify L of defect and give reasonable time to repair, **and**

- Then T can refuse to pay rent, make reasonable repairs and deduct cost from future rent, or remain in possession, pay rent, and seek damages

4. **Covenant of quiet enjoyment (commercial and residential)**

- T has a right to quiet use and enjoyment of the premises without interference from L

- L has duty to control other tenants' nuisance in common areas

- Breach may amount to **eviction**

  o **Actual**—if L excludes T from premises, then lease is terminated and T's obligation to pay rent ends

  o **Partial**—T excused from paying rent for L's partial eviction, but must pay reasonable rental value if partial eviction by third party with superior claim; T not excused from paying rent for partial eviction by adverse possessor/trespasser

  o **Constructive**—substantial interference caused by L's actions or failure to act, T must give notice of problem, L fails to respond, and T **must vacate** premises within reasonable time after L fails to fix problem o **Retaliatory**—L may not evict a residential T for reporting housing code violations or refusing to pay rent when L breaches the warranty of habitability (defense not available to T in arrears)

   5. **Security deposit**

      • Amount and terms (e.g., more for pet) generally set by state statute

      • Usually retained in an escrow account and must be promptly returned at the end of the lease, absent an explanation for retaining it

D. Tort liabilities

   1. **Tenant**—duty of care to invitees/licensees/foreseeable trespassers and may be liable for dangerous conditions/activities

   2. **Landlord**

      • **CL**—liable for injuries in common/public areas, non-common areas under L's control, or from hidden defect/faulty repair by L or L's agent

      • **Modern trend**—general duty of reasonable care; liability for defects existing prior to T's occupancy, failure to make required repairs, and criminal activities of third parties who injure Ts

E. Assignment/sublease

   1. **Assignment**—complete transfer of T's remaining lease term (transfer of a physical portion for remaining lease term is partial assignment)

   2. **Sublease**—any transfer for less than the entire duration of lease

   3. **Parties**

      • **Assignee tenant**

         o Assignee-T liable to L for rent/covenants running with lease because assignee-T is in privity of estate (P/E) with L

         o If assignee-T reassigns lease, his P/E with L ends and the subsequent T is now in P/E with L

      • **Sublease tenant** (sub-T)

         o Not liable for rent/covenants in lease to L because not in P/E or privity of contract (P/C) with L (still liable to original lessee)

         o If sub-T expressly assumes covenants, then personally liable to L

         o Sub-T can enforce all covenants made by original lessee in sublease, but not any made by L

      • **Original tenant**

         o Liable for lease covenants unless **novation** by L because still in P/C with L

         o P/E with L ends upon assignment but not sublease

      • **Landlord assignments**

         o Generally, L may assign lease rights to a third party (e.g., as part of a transfer of ownership) but L remains liable to T for all covenants in the lease

         o T must pay rent to assignee-L and obey lease covenants; assignee-L must perform any burden imposed by lease covenant

- o **Attornment** (T's acknowledgement of a new L)—usually arises automatically upon payment of rent to assignee-L or notice to T but formal acknowledgement of an assignee-L's ownership may be required in commercial leases

  4. Limitations

  - T can still assign/sublet if lease prohibits, but L can terminate for breach and recover damages

  - L can only withhold permission to grant assignment or sublease on **reasonable grounds in relationship to the property being leased** and not on a whim or personal prejudice

III. The Land Sale Contract

A. Formation—subject to general contract requirements

  1. Real-estate broker

  - **Seller's agent**

    - o Listing broker—helps set the asking price and advertises the property

    - o Selling broker—subagent of the listing broker; finds a buyer

    - o Listing broker and selling broker generally share the commission

  - **Buyer's agent**—may also receive a commission

  - **Dual agent**—represents both buyer and seller; prohibited in many jurisdictions

  2. Statute of Frauds (SoF)

  - **Formalities**—land sales K must be in writing, signed by the party to be charged, and contain all of the essential terms (parties, property description, terms of price/payment)

    - o SoF also applies to other property interests such as assignments and options regarding the purchase of real property, leases over one year

    - o A deed need not satisfy the SoF, but must be in writing, signed by the grantor, contain a description of the property, and identify the grantee; the deed must contain words of transfer

  - **Part performance** (SoF exception)—buyer takes possession of land, buyer remits all or part of purchase price, and/or buyer makes substantial improvements (most jurisdictions require at least two acts)

  - **Detrimental reliance**—specific performance (SP) permitted when party seeking enforcement has reasonably relied on K and would suffer hardship

  3. Exceptions to SoF

  - Part performance—consider payment of all or part of purchase price; possession by purchaser; substantial improvement by purchaser

  - Detrimental reliance

  - Admission

B. Performance

  1. Marketable title

  - Title free from defects or unreasonable risk of litigation

- Seller generally not required to deliver marketable title until closing; seller can use sale proceeds to pay off an existing mortgage, eliminating the related title defect

- Buyer can rescind/recover out-of-pocket and earnest money payments, sue for breach, or sue for SP with an abatement of purchase price

2. **Time of the essence**—not enforced unless part of K (express/implied), but party failing to perform on closing date is in breach

3. **Implied warranty of fitness**—only for new homes, warrants use of adequate materials and workmanship; includes latent construction defects

4. **Duty to disclose defects (all homes)**—seller must disclose all known material physical defects not readily observable

5. **Tender of performance**—concurrent conditions, so if one party repudiates then non-repudiating party excused, but B must give S sufficient time to cure title defect

6. **Merger**—land sales K obligations (e.g., duty to deliver marketable title) merge into deed upon delivery unless obligations collateral to/independent of conveyance

C. **Remedies for breach**

1. **Damages**—difference between K price and market value (some jurisdictions: limited to B's out-of-pocket expenses if seller (S) is unable to deliver marketable title but acted in good faith)

   - **Buyer's deposit as liquidated damages**—generally, deposits of no more than 10 percent of the purchase price have been found to be reasonable liquidated damages, but courts may consider factors relating to the transaction or refuse to enforce liquidated damages clauses when the S suffers no actual loss; when the K is silent, courts consider the same factors, and usually allow S to retain the deposit when reasonable

2. **Specific performance** (mutuality of remedies)

D. **Equitable conversion**—S's interest converted by K into interest in proceeds of sale not in RP, once K is signed, B is owner of land subject to the condition he pay the purchase price at closing, but in interim between K and closing, B bears risk of loss if land is destroyed

E. **Options and rights of first refusal**—subject to SoF

IV. **Titles**

A. **Adverse possession (AP)**

1. **Continuous/uninterrupted**

   - Through statutory period (20 years at CL)

   - Seasonal use okay if consistent with type of property (e.g., vacation home)

   - Tacking permitted, but no gaps and via non-hostile connections only (e.g., descent, devise, contract, or deed)

2. **Actual**—actual entry giving exclusive possession that is open/notorious, but if only actually possess portion of property, constructive AP gives title to whole

3. **Hostile**—must possess the land without owner's permission

   - Majority of jurisdictions—ignore subjective intent; instead, must show objective intent to claim land as his own

   - Minority of jurisdictions—consider subjective intent:

- o Good faith—must believe the property is unowned or that he owns it
- o Bad faith—aggressive trespass

4. **Exclusive**—possession cannot be shared with true owner, but two or more people can adversely possess as tenants in common

B. **Delivery and recording of deeds** (legal instrument that transfers ownership)

  1. **Delivery**
     - At time of transfer, grantor must **intend to make present transfer** of property interest to grantee
       - o Typically, intent is shown by delivery of the deed
       - o Execution and recording—creates a rebuttable presumption that the deed is to be presently operative
       - o Parol evidence admissible to establish intent when grantor keeps deed
     - Transfer to grantor's agent is not delivery but transfer to grantee's agent is
     - Transfer to third party with a condition is not delivery if grantor keeps absolute right to recover deed, but if not, treated like future property interest
     - If conditioned upon death, grantor must intend to make a present gift
     - Acceptance presumed for beneficial transfers

  2. **Deed**
     - Many states allow real-estate brokers to prepare real-estate sales K; some states limit this to form Ks and some require attorney review
       - o Non-attorneys may prepare mortgage lending docs
       - o Jurisdictions are split as to requirement of attorney at closing, but non-attorney may not answer legal questions
     - Valid deed requirements
       - o Identified parties
       - o Grantor's signature
       - o Words of transfer
       - o Reasonably definite property description (extrinsic evidence admissible)
     - Agent may execute deed
       - o **Equal dignities rule**—agency authorization for real estate Ks must be in writing

  3. **Recording acts**
     - **Types**
       - o **Notice**
         - BFP (purchaser for value without notice) of **prior interest prevails** over prior grantee who failed to record
         - Must record against subsequent purchaser (e.g., "no conveyance/mortgage of RP good against subsequent BFP unless same be recorded according to law")

- o **Race**
  - **First to record prevails**, regardless of knowledge of prior conflicting interests (e.g., "no conveyance/mortgage of RP good against subsequent purchaser of value unless first recorded by law")
- o **Race-notice**
  - Subsequent BFP protected only if he takes **without notice *and* is first to record** (e.g., "no conveyance/mortgage of RP good against subsequent BFP unless first recorded by law")
- **Notice**—tested as of the time of the conveyance; notice obtained after conveyance does not prevent purchaser from benefitting from recording
  - o **Actual**—a grantee with actual, personal knowledge of prior interest cannot prevail under notice or race-notice statute
  - o **Inquiry**—if reasonable investigation would disclose prior claims, a grantee cannot prevail against them (e.g., someone other than grantor has possession or documents referenced in chain of title)
  - o **Constructive**—properly recorded and appears in chain of title

4. **Types of deeds**
   - **General warranty**
     - o **Present covenants**
       - **Seisin**—grantor owns land as described in deed
       - **Right to convey**—grantor has right to transfer title
       - **Against encumbrances**—no undeclared encumbrances against land
     - o **Future covenants**
       - **Quiet enjoyment**—grantee not disturbed in possession by third party's lawful claim
       - **Warranty**—grantor will defend grantee against third party's claim
       - **Further assurances**—grantor will do whatever future acts reasonably necessary to pass title if later determined title is imperfect
   - **Special warranty**—same covenants of title as general warranty deed, but only warrants against defects arising during the time grantor has title
   - **Quitclaim deed**—no covenants of title

V. **Mortgages and Security Interests**
   A. **Mortgage**—an interest in RP that serves as security for an obligation
      - Must satisfy SoF
      - Lien theory (majority)—debtor/mortgagor has title and right to possession until foreclosure and creditor/mortgagee has lien and right to land if there is default
      - Lien stays on land if mortgage instrument properly recorded
      - Creditor can foreclose by judicial proceedings which terminate junior interests (subordinate interests must be joined or remain on land and B takes subject to senior interests)

B. **Mortgage alternatives**

1. **Deed of trust**—trustee holds title for beneficiary (lender); mortgagee-lender cannot purchase property at a non-judicial foreclosure sale, but a beneficiary-lender can.

2. **Installment land contract**—seller retains title to RP until buyer makes final payment

3. **Absolute deed**—transfers unrestricted title to RP (may actually be a disguised mortgage if an obligation is created contemporaneously with the transfer)

4. **Conditional sale and repurchase**—RP sold and then leased back to the seller; if the lease is for a long time with option to repurchase, may be a disguised mortgage

C. **Transfer**—unless lender agrees to release, borrower remains liable after transfer of RP

1. **Mortgagor's liability**

   • If transferee assumes mortgage, then borrower is secondarily liable (i.e., if borrower makes payments, she can seek reimbursement from transferee)

   • Borrower may be relieved of liability if lender impairs borrower's right of recourse against transferee by: (i) modifying loan terms, or (ii) releasing transferee of liability; or if lender releases or impairs the RP subject to the mortgage

   • Due-on-sale clause—lender can demand immediate payment of full amount due

   • Due-on-encumbrance clause—lender can accelerate mortgage upon second mortgage

2. **Transferee's liability**

   • If transferee assumes mortgage, transferee is personally liable for mortgage obligation

   • If transferee takes RP "subject to" mortgage, then transferee is not personally liable upon default (but RP may be sold at a foreclosure sale)

D. **Pre-foreclosure rights and duties**

1. **Lien theory state**—mortgagee cannot take possession before foreclosure; **title theory state**—mortgagee theoretically entitled to possession at any time (but typically cannot take possession until default by mortgage terms)

2. **Mortgagor has duty not to commit waste**

3. **Equity of redemption**—after default but before foreclosure sale, mortgagor may regain title by paying amount of loan obligation currently owed, plus interest (can be full amount of unpaid loan is there is an acceleration clause)

E. **Foreclosure**—mortgagee takes RP when mortgagor defaults (i.e., no payment)

1. **Methods**—judicially supervised sale, private sale, or strict foreclosure

2. **Priority**—if two+ mortgages, foreclosure terminates jr. interest and has no effect on sr.

   • "First-in-time, first-in-right"

   • Purchase-money mortgage (PMM) exception—mortgage used to purchase RP generally has priority over others

   • Recording-act exception—mortgages subject to general recording act, so a recorded interest may take priority over an unrecorded one

   • Other exceptions—subordination agreements, mortgage modifications and replacements, future-advances, after-acquired property

3. **Effects on parties**

   • Mortgagor—interest eliminated

- Purchaser of RP—takes property free of junior interest, subject to senior
- Senior interests—unaffected
- Junior interests—destroyed

VI. Disputes About the Use of Land

A. Easements

1. Types

- **Express**—affirmatively created by parties in writing that satisfies SoF; by grant or by reservation

- **Implied**

  o **Necessity**

  - Created when property is virtually useless without benefit of easement across adjacent property
  - Dominant/servient estates must be under common ownership and necessity must arise when estate severed
  - Access involving other property does not preclude easement by necessity when the owner of dominant estate does not have a legal right of access through the other property

  o **Implication**—if easement previously used on servient estate by earlier owner, court implies intent for easement to continue if prior use was continuous, apparent, and reasonably necessary to dominant estate's use/enjoyment, the estates were once under common ownership, and a quasi-easement existed at severance

- **Prescription**—continuous, actual, open and hostile for statutory period (20 years at CL)

- **Estoppel**—good faith, reasonable, detrimental reliance on permission by servient estate holder, issued to prevent unjust enrichment

- **Negative**—prevents owner from using land in specific ways, must be expressly created by writing signed by grantor, and usually only recognized for light/air/support/stream water from artificial flow

2. Transfer

- **Easement appurtenant**—benefit transferred automatically with dominant estate

- **Easement in gross**—benefits individual/legal entity, not RP, and usually commercial easements freely transferable to third party

3. Scope—court looks to reasonableness of use and intent of original parties and ambiguities resolved in favor of grantee

4. Termination

- **Release**—by writing that satisfies SoF

- **Merger**—easement merges into title when owner of dominant or servient estate acquires fee title to the other estate

- **Severance**—severed by attempt to convey appurtenant easement separate from land it benefits

- **Abandonment**—owner affirmatively acts to show clear intent to abandon right (statements of intent without conduct and mere non-use insufficient to extinguish easement right)

- Destruction/condemnation, prescription, estoppel

- Express easement not recorded against servient estate against BFP (not "terminated," but may be unenforceable under recording act)

5. **Duty to maintain**—easement owner has right and duty to maintain the easement; may seek contribution from co-owners of the easement after notice and opportunity to participate in repair decisions

6. **Profits**—entitles holder to enter servient land and take from it the soil or some substance of the soil such as mineral, timber, and oil

7. **Licenses**

- Privilege to enter another's land

- Freely revocable unless estoppel (may result in easement by estoppel)

- Does not need to satisfy SoF

- Invalid oral easements may create license

B. **Covenants running with the land**

1. **Real covenants**

- **Writing**—must comply with SoF to be enforced as real covenant

- **Intent**—rights/duties to run with land through explicit language or implied from totality of circumstances

- **Touch/concern**—benefit or burden must affect promisee/promisor as owners of land

  o **Negative covenants**—run with the land if they restrict the owner's use or enjoyment of the land

  o **Affirmative covenants**—run with the land if they require the owner to do something related to the use and enjoyment of the land

- **Notice (burden only)**—must be constructive or actual

- **Privity**

  o **Horizontal privity**—(burden only) when estate and covenant in same instrument

  o **Vertical privity**—(covenant based on mutual/successive interest in land burdened/benefited by covenant)

  o **Modern trend**—no privity required; affirmative covenants run to successors of an estate of the same duration as the estate of the original party; negative covenants are analyzed similarly to easements

2. **Equitable servitudes**

- Must be in writing (except for implied reciprocal servitudes)

- Requires intent for restriction to be enforceable by and against successors

- Must touch/concern (no privity required)

- If the servitude is to be enforced against a purchaser: Notice (actual, record, or inquiry)

3. **Implied reciprocal servitude**

   - Intent to create servitude on all plots (common scheme); no writing required

   - Negative servitude (promise to refrain from doing something)

   - Notice (actual, record, or inquiry) by party against whom enforcement is sought

4. **Defenses to enforcement of covenants and equitable servitudes**—changed circumstances; laches; unclean hands; acquiescence; estoppel

5. **Transfer and termination**—these real property rights and obligations are transferred along with the real property itself. Notice is generally required to enforce them against a BFP. They are terminated upon release, merger, abandonment, estoppel, condemnation

6. **Common-interest ownership communities**—individually owned units are burdened by a covenant to pay an association that provides services and enforces other covenants

   - Types

     o Property owners' association

     o Condos (owners own unit and share of common areas)

     o Cooperatives

   - **Governance**—governed by association, which is overseen by a board of directors. Rules laid out by declaration and other governing documents

   - **Powers of community**—levy assessments (for general upkeep, repairs, improvements); manage, acquire, improve common property; adopt rules governing use of property (must not unreasonably interfere with owners' rights); enforce governing documents and rules. Community has corresponding duties

C. **Fixtures**

1. **Definition**

   - **Fixture**—chattel attached to RP such that it is treated as part of the RP when determining its ownership

   - **Trade fixture**—chattel used in a trade or business that is attached to RP (e.g., restaurant stove)

2. **Structures built on RP and items incorporated into structure**—become part of realty, but can be removed if:

   - Seller reserves right to remove fixture in sale K

   - Leased property can be restored to former condition without damage in reasonable time

D. **Government regulation of land (Zoning)**—local government's authority to regulate land use is usually granted by an enabling act; states have mostly delegated to local; federal regulations are generally authorized by Article IV, Sec. 3 power over federal lands

1. **Void regulations**—lack of authority; irrational or arbitrary (must be rationally related to a legitimate gov. purpose)

2. **Types**—based on use (residential, commercial, industrial); development (setbacks, density regulation); special concerns (environmental protection, historic preservation)

3. **Challenges**—based on Takings Clause, 14th A. Sub. Due Process and Eq. Protection, 1st A. Freedom of Speech, Fed. Fair Housing Act, Federal Religious Land Use and Institutionalized Persons Act, state constitution and statutes

4. **Existing non-conforming property**—may be "grandfathered" in, possibly subj. to amortization period; non-conformity cannot be expanded; can increase frequency or upgrade means of use if does not constitute a substantial change; can be transferred

5. **Post-ordinance non-conforming property**—owner may request special exception permit or administrative variance

   - Party seeking variance must show unique unnecessary hardship, that hardship not self-induced, and that variance would not result in substantial harm

   - May be use or area variances, and they may be subject to conditions

6. **Other types of zoning**—contract (permits in exchange for promises); floating (rules regarding use not linked to a particular area); cluster (consider zoning requirements as a whole, not lot by lot); planned unit development (not focused on plots, but on entirety)

7. **Comprehensive plan**—generally required and development must adhere to plan

8. **Relationship to covenants**—**compliance with a zoning restriction does not protect an owner from a suit for breach of a covenant; compliance with a covenant** does not protect an owner from a zoning violation action

E. **Other property rights (air, water, support)**

   1. **Theories**

      - **Riparian rights**—water belongs to those who own land bordering the watercourse; owners may make any reasonable use of the water; water rights cannot be transferred separate and apart from the adjoining land

      - **Prior appropriation**—water rights are determined by priority of beneficial use; subsequent users must not infringe upon the rights of prior users; water rights may be transferred separately from the adjoining land

   2. **Support rights**—the right to have the land supported in its natural state

      - **Lateral support**

        o **Undeveloped** (i.e., no improvements)—landowner who excavates on his land is strictly liable for damage to undeveloped adjoining land

        o **Improvements**—landowner who excavates on his land is strictly liable only if adjoining land would have collapsed in its undeveloped state

        o **Improvements contribute to collapse**—landowner who excavates on his land is only liable if he is negligent

      - **Subjacent support**—owner of the mineral rights is strictly liable for any failure to support the land and any buildings on the land **at the time the rights were conveyed**

   3. **Air rights**—landowner has limited right to reasonable use and enjoyment of the airspace above his land as long as it does not interfere with another's reasonable use and enjoyment of land

FINAL REVIEW OUTLINE: TORTS

I. **Intentional Torts Involving Personal Injury**

   A. **In general**

      1. **Act**—voluntary

      2. **Intent**—purposeful, or defendant (D) knows the consequence is substantially certain

   B. **Battery**

      1. **Harmful or offensive contact** (objective standard; no actual harm required)

      2. **To person of another** (or anything connected to it)

      3. **Causation** (direct or indirect)

      4. **D's intent**

         • **Single-intent rule (majority rule)**—D may be liable if D (i) intends to bring about the contact; D need not intend (ii) that the contact is harmful or offensive

         • **Double-intent rule**—D must (i) intend to bring about a contact, and (ii) intend that the contact be harmful or offensive

         • Transferred intent applies

   C. **Assault**—act or threat by D intended to cause apprehension of imminent harm or offensive contact

      1. **Conduct or other circumstances** (mere words not enough)

      2. **Plaintiff (P) must have reasonable apprehension and awareness of D's act or threat**

      3. **Imminent threat of harm**

      4. **Intent** (includes transferred intent)

   D. **IIED**

      1. **Intent or recklessness**

         • D must intend to cause severe emotional distress or must act with recklessness as to the risk of causing such distress

         • Transferred intent **does not** apply to IIED when D intended to commit a **different** intentional tort (e.g., battery) against a different victim (but see "Third-party victim," below)

         • Transferred intent **may** apply to IIED if, instead of harming the intended person, D's extreme conduct harms another

      2. **Extreme and outrageous conduct by D** (beyond human decency, outrageous)

      3. **Public figures/concerns** (public figures must show falsity and actual malice; private P cannot recover if issue was of public concern)

      4. **Third-party victim** (distresses member of victim's immediate family—with or without resulting bodily injury—or other bystander resulting in bodily injury)

      5. **Causation** (factual-cause test)

      6. **Damages**—severe emotional distress (beyond reasonable person's endurance or D knows of P's heightened sensitivity)

E. False imprisonment

    1. Intent to **confine or restrain** another within boundaries (no reasonable means of safe escape); **confinement**; victim is **conscious** of confinement or **harmed** by it

    2. Methods of confinement (physical barriers or force, threats, invalid use of legal authority, duress, failure to provide means of escape)

    3. Time—immaterial except as to amount of damages

    4. Intent—purposeful act or knowing confinement is substantially certain to result

    5. Damages—actual damages necessary only if P was unaware of confinement

    6. Shopkeeper's privilege—reasonable detention of suspected shoplifter

II. Defenses to Intentional Torts Involving Personal Injury

A. Consent

    1. Express—invalidated by duress, fraud as to essential matter, and mistakes caused or knowingly utilized by D

    2. Implied—implied by custom/usage, emergency situations, consensual combat/athletics

    3. Invalid—lack of capacity (e.g., youth, intoxication, incompetence) may negate consent

B. Self-defense

    1. Reasonable force—force proportionate to anticipated harm; reasonable mistake does not invalidate defense

    2. Deadly force—ok only if reasonable belief of serious bodily injury/death

    3. No duty to retreat (majority)—before using force, including deadly force, in defense

    4. Initial aggressors—generally not entitled to claim self-defense

    5. Not liable for injuries to bystanders—so long as injuries were accidental and actor was not negligent

C. Defense of others

    1. Reasonable belief that defended party entitled to use force to defend self; reasonable mistake ok

    2. Reasonable force—force proportionate to anticipated harm

D. Defense of property

    1. Reasonable force allowed—if reasonable to prevent tortious harm to property

    2. No deadly force allowed—including deadly traps

    3. Reasonable force to prevent intrusion on one's land—generally ok, unless visitor acting under necessity; generally not permitted to repossess land/realty

    4. Reasonable force to reclaim personal property wrongfully taken—ok

E. Parental discipline

    1. Reasonable force/confinement ok—considering age of child and gravity of behavior

    2. Educator has same privilege—unless parent restricts privilege

F. Privilege of arrest

    1. Felony

- **Private**—ok if crime was actually committed and reasonable to suspect the person arrested committed it (reasonable mistake only defense as to identity of felon)

- **Police**—ok for felonies if reasonable to believe it was committed and to suspect the person arrested (no tort liability for mistake as to commission of felony)

    2. Misdemeanor—only if committed in presence of arresting party; private only if breach of peace

III. Harms to Property Interests

A. Trespass to chattels (tangible personal property)

    1. Intentional **interference with P's right of possession** by either—

- Dispossessing or

- Using or intermeddling with P's chattel

    2. Only intent to do the act is necessary—transferred intent applies

    3. Mistake of law or fact—about legality of actions is not a defense

    4. Damages (actual and loss of use; no loss of use damages without dispossession)

    5. Remedy (compensation for diminished value or cost of repair)

B. Conversion

    1. Intentional act

- Must only intend to commit the act that interferes (intent to damage not necessary);

- Mistake not a defense

- Transferred intent does not apply; must intend to control the particular property

    2. Interference with P's right of possession (exercising dominion or control)

    3. So serious (based on duration/extent, intent to assert a right, D's lack of good faith, extent of harm and P's inconvenience) **that it deprives P of the use of the chattel**

    4. Damages (full value of property or replevin)

C. Trespass to land

    1. Intent to enter land or cause physical invasion, not to trespass; transferred intent applies

    2. Physical invasion of property

    3. Proper P—anyone in actual or constructive possession of land

    4. Necessity as defense

- **Private**—qualified privilege for limited number of people to enter or remain on land to protect own person/property from serious harm; not liable for trespass but responsible for actual damages

- **Public**—unqualified/absolute privilege to avert imminent public disaster; not liable for damage if actions reasonable or reasonable belief that necessity existed, even if initial entry not necessary

D. Nuisance

1. **Private**—substantial and unreasonable interference with another's use or enjoyment of his land

   - **Proper P**—anyone with possessory rights in real property

   - **Interference** must be intentional, negligent, reckless, or result of abnormally dangerous conduct

   - **Substantial**—offensive to average reasonable person in the community (objective)

   - **Unreasonable**—injury caused outweighs usefulness of the action

   - **Defenses** to private nuisance

     o **Regulatory compliance**—incomplete defense; admissible but not determinative

     o **Coming to the nuisance**—does not entitle D to judgment as a matter of law but jury may consider

2. **Public**—unreasonable interference with a right common to the general public; defenses in private nuisance generally applicable

   - **Proper P**—private citizen suffering harm **different in kind** from general public

3. **Remedies**—damages; injunctive relief (balance the equities)

4. **Abatement**

   - **Private**—Reasonable force permitted to abate; must give D notice of the nuisance and D refuses to act

   - **Public**—Absent unique injury, public nuisance may be abated only by public authority

IV. Negligence—Failure to exercise care a reasonable person would exercise; breach of the duty to prevent foreseeable risk of harm to anyone in P's position; breach must be the cause of P's injuries

A. Elements

1. **Duty** (obligation to protect another against unreasonable risk of injury)

2. **Breach** (failure to meet that obligation)

3. **Causation** (close causal connection between action and injury)

4. **Damages** (loss suffered)

B. Duty—owed to all foreseeable persons who may be injured by D's failure to meet reasonable standard of care; foreseeability of harm to another sufficient to create general duty to act with reasonable care

1. **Failure to act**—generally no duty to act

2. **Foreseeability of harm to P**

   - *Cardozo*—D only liable to Ps within the zone of foreseeable harm (*Palsgraf* majority rule)

   - *Andrews*—if D can foresee harm to anyone resulting from his negligence, D owed duty to everyone harmed (foreseeable or not) (minority rule)

3. **Special foreseeable Ps**

   - **Rescuers**—D liable for negligently putting rescuer/rescued party in danger

     o Can apply comparative responsibility if rescuer's efforts are unreasonable

- Emergency professionals barred from recovery if injury results from risk of the job ("firefighter's rule")

- **Fetuses**—duty of care owed to fetuses viable at time of injury

4. **Affirmative duty to act**—exceptions to general rule that there is no duty to act

- Assumption of duty

- Placing another in peril

- By contract

- By authority

- By relationship (e.g., employer-employee, parent-child, common carrier-passenger)

- By statute imposing an obligation to act

C. **The standard of care**

1. **Reasonably prudent person**—objective standard

- Physical (not mental) characteristics are considered in determining reasonableness

- Voluntarily intoxicated person held to same standard as sober person

- Child—reasonable child of similar age, intelligence, and experience

  o But child engaged in high-risk adult activity held to adult standard

  o Children under age of five generally found incapable of negligent conduct

2. **Standards of care for specific classes of Ds**

- **Common carriers (planes, trains, buses)**—highest duty of care consistent with practical operation of the business (majority)

- **Innkeepers**—ordinary negligence (majority); "slight negligence" (common law)

- **Automobile drivers**—absent "guest statute" (minority—refrain from wanton & willful misconduct), ordinary care to guests as well as passengers (majority)

- **Bailor**

  o Gratuitous—duty to warn bailee of known dangerous defects

  o Compensated—duty to warn bailee of defects that are known or should have been known by the bailor had he used reasonable diligence

- **Bailee**

  o Gratuitous—liable only for gross negligence

  o Compensated—must exercise extraordinary care

  o Mutual benefit—must take reasonable care

- **Sellers of real property**—duty to disclose known, concealed, unreasonably dangerous conditions; liability to third parties continues until buyer has a reasonable opportunity to discover and remedy defect

3. **Standard for possessors of land**

- **Trespassers (traditional/majority approach)**—refrain from willful, wanton, reckless or intentional misconduct towards trespassers; no "spring-guns"

  o **Discovered**—warn or protect against concealed, dangerous, artificial conditions

- o **Undiscovered**—generally no duty unless owner should reasonably know that trespassers are entering land, then same duty owed a licensee (majority)
- o **Attractive nuisance**—liable for injuries to trespassing children if artificial condition poses unreasonable risk of serious bodily injury, children cannot appreciate the danger, burden of eliminating danger slight compared to risk of harm, and owner fails to exercise reasonable care to protect children
- **Invitee (traditional approach/majority)**—Invited to enter for purposes for which the land is held open or for business purposes
  - o Reasonable care to inspect, discover dangerous conditions, and protect invitee from them; non-delegable duty
  - o Duty does not extend beyond scope of the invitation
  - o **Recreational land use (some jurisdictions)**—possessor who opens land to public for recreation generally not liable for injuries sustained by recreational land users unless (i) charges a fee or (ii) acts willfully, maliciously, or with gross negligence
- **Licensee (traditional approach/majority)**—enters land of another with permission or privilege (social guest; emergency personnel)
  - o Warn of concealed dangers that are known or should be obvious
  - o Use reasonable care in conducting activities on the land
  - o No duty to inspect
- **Modern and Third Restatement Approach (minority)**
  - o Reasonable care under all circumstances; no invitee/licensee distinction
  - o Fact of trespass considered by jury in determining reasonable care
  - o Duty not to act in intentional, willful, or wanton manner causing physical harm is only duty owed to **flagrant trespasser** (Third Restatement)
- **Landlords and tenants**
  - o Landlord liable for injuries occurring in common areas resulting from hidden dangers about which landlord fails to warn, on premises leased for public use, as a result of a hazard caused by negligent repair, or involving a hazard landlord agreed to repair
  - o Tenant liable for injuries to third parties due to conditions within tenant's control
- **Off-premises victims**
  - o No duty for harm by **natural** condition (except rotting trees in urban areas)
  - o Duty to prevent unreasonable risk of harm caused by **artificial** condition

D. **Breach or violation of duty of care**

1. **Burden of proof** (preponderance of the evidence)
   - Greater probability than not that D failed to meet standard of care (as shown by custom/usage, statutory violation, or res ipsa loquitur)
   - Failure was proximate cause of injury and P suffered damages

2. **Traditional approach**—compare D's conduct with what **reasonably prudent person** would do under the circumstances (objective)

3. **Modern and Restatement approach (cost-benefit analysis)**—consider (i) foreseeable **likelihood** that D's conduct would cause harm, (ii) foreseeable **severity** of resulting harm, and (iii) D's **burden** in avoiding the harm

4. **Custom**
   - Evidence of custom is generally admissible but not conclusive in establishing proper standard of care
   - **Professionals**—expected to show same skill, knowledge, and care as an ordinary practitioner in same community; specialists may be held to higher standard
     - For professionals, deviation or compliance with custom is dispositive of breach
     - An expert must generally establish the standard of care unless negligence is so obvious that it would be apparent to a layperson (e.g., a surgeon amputating the wrong leg)
   - **Physicians**
     - Majority rule—**national** standard (including specialists)
     - Minority (traditional) rule—**"same or similar locale"** standard
     - Failure to comply with **informed consent** requirement is medical negligence (malpractice) unless risk is commonly known, patient is unconscious, patient waives or is incompetent, or disclosure too harmful

5. **Negligence per se**
   - **Elements**
     - Criminal or regulatory statute imposes a specific duty for protection of others
     - D neglects to perform the duty
     - D liable to **anyone in the class** of people intended to be protected by statute
     - For **harms of the type** the statute was intended to protect against
   - **Causation**—once the elements of negligence per se are established, D is liable for injuries that were proximately caused by D's violation
   - **Defenses**
     - Compliance impossible or more dangerous than noncompliance
     - Violation reasonable under the circumstances
     - Statutory vagueness or ambiguity
     - Compliance with federal regulation preempts common-law tort action

6. **Res ipsa loquitur** (circumstantial evidence; doesn't change standard of care; establishes an inference of negligence sufficient to avoid dismissal)
   - P's harm would not have occurred if D used ordinary care (no injury would typically occur in absence of negligence); but P need not conclusively exclude all other possible explanations
   - P not responsible for injury (loosely applied in most comparative fault jurisdictions)
   - P's injury under D's exclusive control
     - Modern trend favors generous interpretation of exclusivity

- o Many courts ignore exclusivity for product liability if manufacturer wrapped the package or it is clear that negligence took place during production
- o If many medical personnel had access to P during surgery in malpractice claim, some jurisdictions presume each D has breached a duty of care unless each D rebuts

E. Causation

1. **Cause in fact/actual cause**—"but for" D's act/omission, injury wouldn't have occurred; most courts require causal link; substantial-factor test for conduct of 2+ Ds or causes; if unclear, burden shifts to multiple Ds to prove each did not cause P's harm

- **Joint and several liability**—may apply if 2+ Ds are each a factual cause of indivisible injury or Ds acted with common plan or design
- **Loss of Chance**—applies in some jurisdictions if P's chance of recovery was <50% before D's conduct; can recover percentage of total damages equal to difference between chance of recovery before and after D's negligence

2. **Proximate cause/scope of liability**

- **Limitation on liability**
  - o Foreseeability—D liable for reasonably foreseeable consequences of a foreseeable type (majority); D liable for all direct consequences (minority/Andrews test)
  - o Ps who can recover—P can recover if P was a foreseeable victim of D's conduct (majority) or P's harm was within scope of liability of D's conduct (minority)
  - o Eggshell skull rule—extent of damages need not be foreseeable

- **Intervening and superseding causes**
  - o Direct cause—uninterrupted chain of events from D's act to P's injury—foreseeability of type of harm does not necessarily preclude liability (majority)
  - o Intervening cause—a cause of P's harm that occurs after D's tortious act
  - o Superseding cause—breaks the chain of proximate causation; D not liable; **unforeseeable** intervening cause is a superseding cause ("Act of God;" criminal act; intentional tort of third party); **negligent** intervening acts are **foreseeable** (medical malpractice) and may lead to joint and several liability

F. Damages

1. **Actual damages**—must prove actual injury (personal injury or property damage), not just economic loss; nominal damages and attorney's fees not permitted in negligence actions

- **Parasitic damage**—if tort caused physical harm, may add emotional distress damages (e.g., NIED claims)

2. **Compensatory damages**—make the victim whole

3. **Duty to mitigate**—not a duty to D, but may reduce P's recovery

4. **Personal injury**—past/future pain and suffering, medical expenses, lost wages/reduced future earnings; "eggshell skull" rule applies (liable for full extent of P's injuries; may be increased because of preexisting condition)

5. **Property damage**—generally, difference between fair market value before injury and immediately after; most courts allow cost of repair as alternative if cost of repair does not exceed value of property, or cost of replacement for household items

6. **Collateral source rule**

   - **Traditional rule**—benefits from outside sources (P's insurance) not credited against D's liability; payment by D's insurer are not from a collateral source and are credited against D's liability

   - **Modern trend**—statutes have eliminated or substantially modified rule

7. **Punitive damages**—clear/convincing evidence, malicious, willful & wanton, or reckless behavior; can include torts that inherently involve this state of mind or behavior; constitutionally limited to amounts within a single-digit ratio to compensatory damages

G. **Special rules of liability**

   1. **NIED**

      - **Zone of danger**

        o P was within "zone of danger" (feared for safety); threat of physical impact caused emotional distress

        o Proof: Majority—emotional distress must be manifested by **physical symptoms** (e.g., nightmares, shock, ulcers); minority—allow recovery without a physical manifestation of harm

      - **Bystander recovery**

        o A P outside the zone of danger can recover if: (i) closely related to person injured by D; (ii) present at the scene; and (iii) personally observed or perceived the injury

        o Proof: Majority—requires **physical symptoms** (see above)

      - **Special relationship**

        o No threat of physical impact or physical symptoms required (e.g., mishandling a corpse)

   2. **Pure economic loss**—only recoverable with related personal injury or property damage

   3. **Wrongful death**—recoverable damages include loss of support, companionship, society, and affection, but not pain/suffering of P; recovery limited to what decedent could recover

   4. **Survival actions**—survival statute may permit representative of decedent's estate to pursue any claims decedent would have had at time of death; may include pain/suffering

      - If survival and wrongful death actions permitted, no double recovery allowed

   5. **Loss arising from injury to family member**—loss of consortium for spouses; loss of services for injured child

   6. **Wrongful life**—minority allows action by child for failure to perform contraceptive procedure or diagnose congenital defect; damage limited to those attributable to disability

   7. **Wrongful birth**—if birth due to failed contraceptive procedure or diagnosis of defect, many states permit parents to recover medical expenses for caring for disabled child; some states allow mother to recover pain/suffering damages and medical expenses for labor

H. **Vicarious liability**

   1. **Liability of employer for employee's torts**

      - Occurs when employer has a **right to control** the means and methods of employee (otherwise, see IC)

- Tort within **scope of employment** (acts employee is employed to do or acts intended to profit or benefit employer); not liable for intentional torts unless force inherent to job (i.e., bouncer), or authorized to act/speak for employer and position provided opportunity for the tort (i.e., fraudulent contract as employer's agent)

- Employer may be liable for **detour** (minor deviation from scope) but not **frolic** (unauthorized and substantial deviation)

- **Direct liability**—negligent hiring, training, supervision, or entrustment of employee is employer's negligence (not vicarious liability)

2. **Independent contractors (IC)**—employers generally not liable for IC's torts, except for:

- Negligent selection of independent contractor (primary negligence, not vicarious)

- Vicarious liability for non-delegable duty, or

- Vicarious liability for IC acting under apparent agency

3. **Business partners; joint enterprise participants**—liable for tortious conduct of each other if committed within scope of business purposes

4. **Car owners**

- **Negligent entrustment** of car or other object with potential for harm (if D knows/should know of driver's or user's negligent propensities)

- **Family-purpose doctrine** (D liable for family members driving with permission) **versus owner liability statutes** (liable for anyone driving with permission)

5. **Parent/child**—vicarious liability only if child acted as parent's agent, state statute applies, or if assumed liability on child's driver's license application for negligent driving

- Primarily negligent if fails to exercise reasonable care to prevent minor child from intentionally or negligently harming third party if parent (i) can control child and (ii) knows or should know the necessity and opportunity for exercising such control

6. **Dram-shop liability**—many states recognize cause of action against seller of intoxicating beverages when a third party is subsequently injured due to buyer's intoxication; most states only allow liability if buyer was minor or intoxicated at time of sale; many states extend to social hosts for injuries to intoxicated guest and/or third parties

I. **Limitation of liability due to D's identity or relationships (immunities)**

1. **Government**

- **Federal**—traditionally immune, but now immunity is limited by FTCA

    o Sovereign immunity not waived for enumerated torts, discretionary functions, gov't contractor product liability (unless failed to warn or conform with gov't specifications), and most traditional gov't activities

    o Immunity waived for intentional torts committed by law-enforcement officers

- **State**—most states have waived sovereign immunity, at least partially, but acts vary

    o **Municipalities/local gov't agencies**—usually governed by state tort claims acts; immunity traditionally attached only to governmental functions

    o **Public-duty rule**—no liability to any one citizen for municipality's failure to fulfill a duty that owed to public at large, unless special relationship creates special duty

2. **Government officials**—immunity applies if is performing **discretionary functions** entrusted by law unless acts with malice or improper purpose; no tort immunity for carrying out **ministerial acts**

   - **Absolute immunity from personal liability**—legislators performing their legislative functions, judges performing their judicial functions, prosecutors

3. **Intra-family**—interspousal immunity extinguished in most states; parent-child immunity generally limited to core parenting activities

4. **Charitable**—eliminated or capped in most states

J. **Sharing liability among multiple Ds**

1. **Joint & several liability**—each D found liable for single indivisible harm liable for the entire harm

2. **Pure several liability**—(majority rule) each D liable only for his proportionate share

3. **Satisfaction & release**—no double recovery

4. **Contribution**—tortfeasor who paid more than fair share of common liability generally can recover excess of fair share from joint tortfeasor; can recover no more than the joint tortfeasor would be liable to P for; not generally available for intentional tortfeasors

5. **Indemnification**—shifting of loss from vicariously liable tortfeasor to primarily responsible party; may be based on agreement, equity, subsequent additional harm, or strict product liability

K. **Defenses to negligence**

1. **Contributory fault**

   - P's fault is complete bar to recovery (common law/traditional rule)

   - Not a defense to an intentional tort, gross negligence, or recklessness

   - **Last clear chance rule**—abolished in most jurisdictions; P may mitigate legal effect of own fault if D had last clear chance to avoid injuring P; D's actual knowledge of P's inattention required for liability to inattentive P; D liable to helpless P if knew or should have known of P's helpless peril

2. **Comparative fault**

   - **Pure**—not a complete bar to recovery; P's damages reduced by proportion that P's fault bears to total harm

   - **Partial**

     o If P is less at fault than Ds combined, P's recovery reduced by percentage of fault

     o If P is more at fault than Ds combined, P recovers nothing

     o If P and D are equally at fault, P recovers 50% of his total damages (in minority jurisdictions P recovers nothing if equally at fault)

   - Comparative fault will not reduce P's recovery for intentional torts

3. **Assumption of the risk (A/R)**

   - **Traditionally**—unreasonably proceeding in face of known, specific risk affects recovery

   - **Contributory negligence jurisdiction**—no recovery

   - **Comparative fault jurisdiction**—merely reduces recovery

- **Exculpatory clauses in contracts**—unenforceable if (i) disclaims liability for reckless or wanton misconduct or gross negligence;(ii) gross disparity of bargaining power (iii) exculpated party offers services of great importance or practical necessity to public; (iv) subject to typical contractual defenses; or (v) against public policy

    o Generally, common carriers, innkeepers, and employers cannot disclaim liability for negligence

V. Strict Liability (S/L)—DAD (Dangerous activities, Animals, and Defective/dangerous products)

A. Elements

1. **Absolute duty to make P's person or property safe**

2. **Actual & proximate causation**

3. **Damages**

B. Abnormally dangerous activities

1. Not commonly engaged in; inherent, foreseeable, and highly significant risk of harm (look to gravity of harm, inappropriateness of place, limited value of activity)

2. S/L limited to harm expected from activity

C. Animals

1. **Wild animals**—not by custom devoted to the service of humankind where it is being kept

    - Owner is S/L for harm done by wild animal despite owner's precautions to prevent harm, as long as harm arises from dangerous propensity characteristic of animal or about which owner has reason to know

    - Owner S/L for reasonably foreseeable damage caused by trespassing animal

    - Owner S/L for injuries caused by P's fearful reaction to unrestrained wild animal

    - Owner not S/L to undiscovered trespasser except for injuries by vicious watchdog

2. **Domestic animals**

    - Owner S/L for injuries if knows or has reason to know of dangerous propensities and harm results

    - Owner S/L for reasonably foreseeable damage caused by trespassing household pets if owner knows or has reason to know that the pet is intruding on another's property in a way that has a tendency to cause substantial harm; general negligence standard applies if pet strays onto a public road and contributes to an accident there

D. Defenses to S/L

1. **Contributory negligence not a defense** in contributory negligence jurisdictions—does not bar recovery

2. **Contributory negligence** may reduce P's recovery in most comparative fault jurisdictions under a S/L claim (Third Restatement approach); courts divided, some do not allow reduction

3. **Assumption of Risk/"Knowing contributory negligence"**—bars recovery

4. **Statutory privilege**—no S/L for D performing essential public services

VI. Products Liability

A. Negligence

1. **Duty**—reasonable care owed to any foreseeable P by commercial manufacturer, distributor, retailer, or seller

2. **Breach**—failure to exercise reasonable care in inspection/sale of product (i.e., defect would have been discovered if D was not negligent)

3. **Causation**—factual & proximate

4. **Damages**—actual injury/property damage, not pure economic loss

5. **Defenses**—contributory/comparative negligence and A/R

B. Strict products liability

1. **Elements**

   - Product was defective (in manufacture, design, or failure to warn)

   - Defect existed when it left D's control

   - Defect caused P's injury when the product was used in a reasonably foreseeable way

2. **Defective product** (res ipsa may apply)

   - **Manufacturing defect**—product does not conform to D's own specifications

   - **Design defect**

     o Consumer expectation test—dangerous beyond expectation of ordinary consumer

     o Risk-utility test—risks > benefits and reasonable alternative design (economically feasible) available; failure to use that design rendered product unreasonably unsafe

   - **Failure-to-warn defect**

     o (i) Foreseeable risk of harm, (ii) not obvious to ordinary user of product, and (iii) risks could have been reduced or avoided with reasonable instructions or warnings

     o **Learned-intermediary rule**—manufacturer of prescription drug typically satisfies duty to warn by warning prescribing physician of problems with the drug, unless (i) manufacturer knows drug will be dispensed without personal intervention or evaluation of a healthcare provider, or (ii) in the case of birth control pills

3. **Plaintiff**—not required to be in privity of contract; anyone foreseeably injured may recover

4. **Defendants**—must be in the business of selling (includes manufacturer, distributor, and retail seller)

   - If D provides both products and services, generally liable if product is consumed, not if product is only used (i.e., hospital not generally liable as a distributor of defective implants)

   - Casual sellers, auctioneers, P's employer, and service providers generally not S/L

5. **Damages**—personal injury or property damage, pure economic loss must be brought under warranty action

6. **Defenses**

   - **Comparative fault**—P's negligence reduces recovery as will A/R (majority)

- **Contributory negligence**—P's negligence not a defense if P misused product in reasonably foreseeable way or negligently failed to discover defect
- **A/R**—complete bar to recovery in contributory-negligence jurisdictions; in most comparative-fault jurisdictions A/R only reduces recovery
- **Unforeseeable** misuse, alteration, or modification by the user precludes (most contributory-negligence states) or reduces (most comparative-fault states) recovery
- **Compliance with governmental safety standards**—not conclusive evidence that product is not defective, but may be considered
- **State-of-the-art standard**—product conforms with level of scientific, technological, safety knowledge existing and reasonably feasible when product was distributed; compliance with state-of-the-art standard will only bar recovery in some states; n/a to manufacturing defect claims
- **Statute of limitations**—begins to run against P with personal injury when P discovers, or should discover with reasonable care, his injury and its connection to the product
- Unforeseeable intervening causes

C. **Warranties** (against seller, manufacturer, and distributor of product)

1. **Implied warranties**
   - **Merchantability**—product is generally acceptable and reasonably fit for ordinary purpose
   - **Fitness**—product fit for particular purpose; seller must know purpose and buyer must rely on seller's skill or judgment in supplying product
   - Privity requirements
     o Alternative A (majority)—allows only purchaser or member of his family/household to recover for personal injury (not property damage or pure economic loss)
     o Alternative B—anyone reasonably expected to use, consume, or be affected by the product may recover for personal injury
     o Alternative C—Alternative B + recovery for property damage and economic loss
   - **Damages**—personal injury; property damage; pure economic loss

2. **Express warranties**
   - Affirmation of fact or a promise about product; part of the basis of bargain
   - Seller liable for any breach of express warranty, regardless of fault

3. **Defenses**
   - **Disclaimers**
     o Consumer goods—limitation of consequential damages for personal injury is unconscionable
     o Express warranties—valid only if consistent with warranty (usually not)
   - **Comparative fault and A/R**—same as in S/L claims
   - **Contributory negligence**—not a bar except when it overlaps A/R

- **Misuse**—prevents recovery under the implied warranty of merchantability when the product is warranted to be fit for ordinary purposes (majority)
- Claim generally fails if P fails to provide seller with notice of breach of warranty within the statutorily required time period or "a reasonable period of time"

VII. Defamation, Invasion of Privacy, and Business Torts

A. Defamation

1. Elements

- **Defamatory language**—diminishing respect, esteem, or goodwill toward P
- **Of or concerning P**—reasonable third party believes language refers to particular P
- **Publication**—intentional or negligent communication to third party who understands defamatory nature; republication identifying original speaker and uncertainty as to accuracy of the statement still may satisfy this element
- **Falsity** (public concern)
  - If statement relates to matter of **public concern** or P is a **public figure**, P must prove defamatory statement is **false**
  - **Private** P suing on a statement that does **not** involve matter of public concern not required to prove falsity; D may prove truth as an affirmative defense
- **Fault**
  - Public figure—actual malice (D knows of falsity/reckless disregard of truth)
  - Private figure/matter of public concern—D acted with fault; either negligence or actual malice
  - Private figure/not matter of public concern—at least negligence

2. Libel/slander distinguished

- **Libel**—written, printed or otherwise recorded in permanent form; general damages that compensate P for harm to reputation (generally includes radio and television)
  - Common law allowed recovery for presumed damages
  - Libel per quod—if defamatory statement requires proof of extrinsic facts to show it is defamatory, P must prove either special damages or a category of slander per se
- **Slander**—spoken word, gesture, or any form other than libel; special damages required; third party heard comments and acted adversely to P; usually, but not always, economic loss
- **Slander per se**—no special damages required if accused of committing a crime, conduct that reflects poorly on P's fitness to conduct trade or profession, loathsome disease, sexual misconduct; general damages then permitted as parasitic damages

3. Constitutional limits on damages

- **Private person/matter of public concern**—actual damages but if actual malice proven, punitive or presumed damages also permitted
- **Private person/not public concern**—general, including presumed, damages without proving actual malice

4. Defenses

- **Truth**—complete defense

- **Consent**—cannot exceed scope

- **Absolute privilege**—for remarks: (i) during judicial/legislative proceedings (generally must be made by participants and related to proceedings); (ii) by legislators or federal/state executive officials in course of official duties; (iii) between spouses; or (iv) in required publications

- **Qualified privilege**—affecting important public interest, in the interest of D or third party; privilege is lost if abused; burden on D to prove privilege exists; burden on P to prove privilege abused and lost

B. **Invasion of privacy—I FLAP** (**I**ntrusion, **F**alse **L**ight, **A**ppropriation, **P**rivate facts)

1. **Applies only to individuals, terminates upon death**

- **Intrusion upon seclusion**—D's act of intrusion into P's private affairs, objectionable to a reasonable person (no publication required)

- **False light**—publication of facts about P or attributing views/actions to P that place him in false light objectionable to a reasonable person under circumstances; truth not always a defense; in matters of public interest, P must show malice

- **Misappropriation**—unauthorized use of P's picture or name for D's advantage; lack of consent; injury (some states allow action to survive death)

- **Public disclosure of private facts**—public disclosure of private facts (even if true) about P that would be highly offensive to a reasonable person and is not of legitimate concern to the public; in tension with First Amendment—disfavored tort

2. **Damages**—proof of emotional/mental distress enough, special damages not required

3. **Defenses**—absolute/qualified privilege for false light/public disclosure; consent applies to all types of privacy torts, but any mistake re: consent negates defense; truth not a defense

C. **Intentional misrepresentation**

1. **False representation of material fact**—generally no duty to disclose

2. **Scienter**—knowledge or reckless disregard of truth

3. **Intent to induce** P to act or refrain in reliance on misrepresentation

4. **Causation**—actual reliance

5. **Justifiable reliance**—not justifiable if statement obviously false or lay opinion

6. **Damages**—actual economic loss/consequential damages; no nominal damages; no damages for emotional distress

D. **Negligent misrepresentation**

1. **D** (accounting firm or other supplier of commercial information)

2. Provides **false information** to P as a result of D's **negligence** in the course of D's business or profession

3. **P justifiably relies** on the information and incurs **pecuniary damages** as a result

- P must be in contractual relationship with D or D knows P is a member of a limited group for whose benefit the information is supplied

- Information must be relied on in a transaction that D intends to influence or knows recipient intends to

4. **Defenses**—standard negligence defenses

5. **Damages**—reliance and consequential

E. **Intentional interference with business relations**

   1. **Intentional interference with contract**

      - D knew of valid contractual relationship between P and third party

      - D intentionally interfered with contract in a way that substantially exceeds fair competition and free expression, resulting in a breach and

      - Breach caused damages to P

      - **Defenses**—justified if motivated by health, safety, or morals; contract is terminable at will; D is business competitor

   2. **Interference with prospective economic advantage** (no contract)

      - More egregious conduct required for liability, should be independently tortious; violates federal or state law; improper conduct per balancing analysis

      - Business competitor will not be liable for encouraging switching business

   3. **Theft of trade secrets**

      - P owns valid trade secret (provides a business advantage)

      - Not generally known

      - Reasonable precautions to protect

      - D took secret by improper means

F. **Injurious Falsehoods**

   1. **Trade libel**—malicious publication of derogatory statement relating to P's title to business property/quality of products, and interference or damage to business relationships; proof of special damages required and mental suffering damages unavailable; truth and fair competition are valid defenses

   2. **Slander of title**—publication of false statement derogatory to P's title to real property; malice; special damages as a result of diminished value in the eyes of third parties

G. **Wrongful use of legal system**

   1. **Malicious prosecution**—intentional & malicious institution of legal proceeding for improper purpose; no probable cause; action dismissed in favor of the person against whom it was brought

      - Damages can include legal expenses, lost work time, loss of reputation, emotional distress

      - Judges and prosecutors have absolute immunity from liability

   2. **Abuse of Process**—use of legal process against P in a wrongful manner to accomplish a purpose other than that for which the process was intended; willful act; proof of damages required